Natural Science through the Seasons

NATURAL SCIENCE THROUGH THE SEASONS

100 Teaching Units

BY

J. A. PARTRIDGE

Hillside Education

Book Design by Mary Jo Loboda
Cover design by Ted Schluenderfritz
New content and images compiled by Margot Davidson

Special thank you to Jennifer Mackintosh for donating the use of her family's nature study photos.
(Cover images, as well as pps 76, 119, 131, 195, 235, 338, 389, 401)

Originally published by Macmillan Canada, 1955

Important note regarding copyright: Every attempt has been made to contact the Partridge family, but we have been unable to find them. We respectfully request that if you have any information about the descendants of James A Partridge that you contact us.

Hillside Education
475 Bidwell Hill Road
Lake Ariel, PA 18436

www.hillsideeducation.com

To

My Daughter Joan

and to

all other girls and boys—and grown-ups —whose lives are being enriched daily by their love of birds and butterflies, of trees and flowers, of clouds and beautiful sunsets—of all the things of nature round about them, this book is dedicated.

Acknowledgement

Acknowledgment is gratefully made:

To Mr. Don Farwell, Instructor in Art, Tweedsmuir Senior Public School, Hamilton, for a large proportion of the drawings appearing in this book.

To the following graduates of my classes in Normal School:

Misses Ruth Fornataro, Ruth Welsh, and Virginia DeLaurier, for valuable assistance in collecting and organizing material, preparing manuscript, and reading proof.

To *The School* Magazine, Toronto, for generous permission to draw freely from the manuscript and the illustrations of many articles by the author in former editions of the magazine, and for permission to reproduce the monthly calendars, and the series of monthly plates entitled "Beautify Your Surroundings" and "Science in Action". For such generosity I am deeply indebted to the Editor of *The School*.

To *Canadian Nature* Magazine, Toronto, for permission to reproduce a large number of full-page plates (including the end papers) and other illustrations, appearing on pp. 46, 48, 59, 156, 176, 182, 195, 206, 232, 243, 252, 259, 262, 268, 273, 283, 288, 335,354,388, 391, 397, 440, 448, 450, 451, 456, 479, 497.

To The Ryerson Press and Miss Helen M. Hubbs, publishers and author, respectively, of *Seasonal Activities for Primary Grades,* for permission to reproduce the enterprises, "Preparing for Winter" and "Who Has Seen the Wind?".

To the following for valuable ideas which have become a part of this book: Mr. E. A. Miller, Normal School, Toronto, for suggestions gained from personal experiences with him, and from his articles in *The School*; Mr. E. L. Palmer, in his nature writings in the *Cornell Rural School Leaflets*; and Dr. W. Vinal, through his book, *Nature Guiding*.

To the following for kind permission to reproduce illustrations on the pages listed:

Sir Isaac Pitman & Sons, Limited, from Miss E. Benton, *Pictorial Paper Cutting*, and from Miss M. Swannell, "Earth and Sky Knowledge", from *The Practical Infant Teacher*—pp. 21, 72, 211, 212, 226, 233, 348, 390; Hugh M. Halliday, for illustrations on pp. 46, 48, 59, 243, 262, 440 (but not left centre or circular one).

- Buffalo Museum of Science, pp. 2, 3, 82, 385, 387, 476.

- National Audubon Society, pp. 29, 30 (fig. 2), 215, 356, 425, 480.

- Wild Flower Preservation Society, pp. 445, 447, 449.

- Brooklyn Botanic Garden, pp. 43, 55, 265, 402, 416.

- American Museum of Natural History, frontispiece.

To various authors, publishers, and other organizations for permission to reproduce their works, literary and art, credit for which has been given throughout the book.

Table of Contents

APRIL

MAY

JUNE

Introduction

"To initiate the children into the romance and wonder of science, and to enhance their natural desire to get to know the world around them and find an explanation of its phenomena"; to so arrange the pupils' environment that they may associate with nature in those ways that make life most worth while now, to the end of developing those tastes, habits, and attitudes that will continue to make life most worth living—these are the problems of the teacher of natural science in the elementary school. To give helpful suggestions in solving these problems, rather than to suggest any specific course of study or any narrow system of methods, this book has been prepared.

The Science Teacher's Objectives

It matters little where we turn for lists of objectives in science teaching; we are always met with the same general principles, perhaps differently stated. Everywhere, in theory at least, we find emphasis upon the encouragement of active, desirable attitudes of observation and inquiry, the development of an appreciation of the beauties of nature, and an understanding of the natural phenomena round about, such as will add zest to life in the present, and inspire a healthy, enjoyable means of spending our constantly increasing leisure time. It is a deeply rooted characteristic of human nature to want to observe natural phenomena and to make deductions from these observations. With every experience in observing there must result a corresponding increase in interest in the various living things about us, And so the circle of new observations and new interests constantly widens.

To accomplish these objectives, the teacher must be prepared to discard the time-worn beliefs that learning must take place within the four walls of a classroom, that book facts have some mystically increased value over first-hand experiences with nature, that there is some uniform body of knowledge of natural phenomena that should become the heritage of all, or that pupils must be taught by question and answer, by blackboard summaries, or even by the teacher. Let us go forth with our pupils "into the child's natural laboratory" where, together, we may find "the birds and insects of the air, the living animals of field and wood, the trees and flowers and shrubs, the water and the earth", the sun and other stars— "things which will attract and hold the child's eye, arouse his wonder, stimulate his inquiries, and give him opportunities for discovery." In these places let nature answer the constant flow of questions that spring up in the minds of curious youth. Let us concede that though we be teachers we must still be learners and can share the joy of discovery with our pupils.

"As far as possible men are taught to become wise, not by books, but by the heavens, the earth, oaks, and beeches, that is, they must learn to know and examine things themselves, and not the testimony and observations of others about the things."[1]

Judging the Suitability of Pupil Activities

Activity for activity's sake is as ineffective as are facts for facts' sake. We must look for deeper values than those of merely doing something or of having the tangible product of some activity. It is not enough to have prepared an attractive collection of waxed, mounted, and labelled leaves. The project can hardly be justified unless its planning and execution have opened new avenues of interest and satisfaction for the pupils; have given them a consciousness of new power; have challenged them to explore new fields of endeavour; have helped them to acquire habits of "accuracy, thoroughness, persistence, good organization and planning, and neatness"; and have strengthened their habits of careful observation and unbiased thinking.

The teacher must subject each proposed activity to several considerations. *It should appeal to the child.* The assignment should preferably have come from the child's own suggestion. It should not be too difficult, nor should it require too long to complete. We must keep in mind that pupils are individuals with widely different interests and capacities. While aquarium work will make a strong appeal to one pupil, an investigation of the local trees which provide food for birds in winter will bring much satisfaction to another. Let us respect this individuality and not endeavour to make pupils into machines without personal feelings or preferences. *Enterprises and other activities should be of two types, individual and group.* The former will doubtless lead to greater personal satisfaction and initiative; the latter will prove worthwhile in training children to live and work in co-operation with their fellows. *An activity must never be a task assigned.* Unless a pupil is really desirous of undertaking it, much of its value will be lost. *To obtain the most educational good, the pupil or pupils must have a large share in actually planning the method of carrying out the project.* The pupil is frequently robbed of much training in creative activity and of much of the joy of accomplishment by the over-zealous teacher. We are not primarily concerned with the facts that grow out of the activity; our chief interest should be in providing an avenue of expression for the pupil, through which his latent powers may function and develop. *The project should be carried forward until real satisfaction results* either through the pupil's joy of personal achievement, or in a more attractive classroom environment.

The activities suggested throughout this book are meant not only to deepen the pupil's interest in, love for, and understanding of his natural surroundings, but also to provide fruitful correlations of natural science with other branches of learning. Ample scope is provided for individual interests and for variety in local conditions and in available facilities. At some time each pupil should have an opportunity to report to the rest of the class his pleasure and his success in connection with his project. Home projects should be encouraged to the same extent as school ones.

Grading Science Teaching to Age Levels

In keeping with the commonly accepted practices in elementary schools and teachers' colleges, the term "Primary" in this book includes Grades I and II (ages 6 to 8). Activities under the heading

---

1   Commenius

"Junior" are for Grades III and IV (ages 8 to 10); those under the heading "Intermediate", for Grades V and VI (ages 10 to 12). Many of the latter are suitable for Grades VII and VIII. The content of science for any specific topic should be graded according to the ages of the pupils. For any topic, primary pupils will be interested in knowing the thing by sight, and where to find it; junior pupils will be more interested in what the thing does, and how it does it, while intermediate pupils can grasp some understanding of the principle of adaptation by structure and habit, and are becoming more interested in life histories.

Pupils of ages 6 to 8 years (primary) show great curiosity concerning the world around them, and keen interest in the behaviour rather than in the appearance of living things. They will love to watch a snake sticking out its tongue, or a bunny nibbling a carrot. Such observations lead to a true enjoyment and appreciation of nature. These children are realists; they like to see things as they are and to express the truth in simple language and in simple drawings. With them we should say that a winter bud contains next year's leaves neatly packed, ready to open in the spring, rather than using a cloak of sentimentalism by saying that "the bud is a sleeping fairy with woollen blankets, and when old Mother Nature touches the wonderful covering with her magic wand, the fairy will jump out and shake her emerald tresses."

These children are not capable of sustained attention unless associated with bodily activity. Lesson periods should therefore be short, informal, and characterized by spontaneity. Free scope should be given for conversation, pupil questions, and expressions of fear and wonder and enjoyment.

Pupils of junior and intermediate grades are so curious and so active physically that a good learning motto in science might be "Whatsoever thy hand findeth to do, do it with all thy might." Great nature events of the year such as the scattering of seeds and the migration of birds, the blooming of wild flowers and the sprouting of seeds, appeal to them strongly. The making of calendars and charts, of leaf prints and of insect cages, gives scope for their desire to be mentally and physically creative. While in the primary stage, it was enough to know that a young deer had pretty spots, the older ones can appreciate the fact that these spots harmonize with the mottled shadow effect under trees, and keep the fawn from being seen by Its enemies. When pupils begin to ask "Why?", greater emphasis should be placed upon the ways in which plants and animals are adapted to live in their natural conditions.

Intermediate pupils are becoming more interested in following the life story of plants from seed to seed, of animals from egg to egg, or birth to birth. They think of an animal in terms of all its needs and activities—home life, feeding, travelling, breathing, reproducing. They begin to appreciate the broad picture of interrelationships of living things—of plants and animals living together. Formal academic teaching of mere facts will defeat its own purpose and kill that inquisitive tendency of pupils which permits science teaching to become a disciplining of the child's power to see and think.

Making Science Teaching Seasonal

Most phenomena of science happen by seasons; science teaching should therefore follow a seasonal sequence. Study snow-flakes with the first fall of snow, evergreens and mistletoe at Christmas time, the habits of winter birds down South when living here would be most dangerous for them, and seed germination when we are ready to sow our seeds. With the march of time through the year new curiosities and ways of satisfying them should come to the pupils with every turn of the seasons.

Although a seasonal sequence has been planned throughout this book, in certain topics some activities have been included which can be performed better at other seasons. It is suggested therefore that teacher and pupils prepare a booklet entitled "Things To Do In————" and leave a page for each month. In this book make a note of the things you wish to do later.

Helping Pupils Develop a Consciousness of the Need for and the Methods of Conserving Our Natural Resources.

Beginning in the primary grades, the basic needs, principles, and practices of conservation should be integrated throughout the programme of science teaching. Many opportunities to do so will come to mind while conducting excursions, teaching about trees and flowers, carrying out activities related to the protection and feeding of birds, and throughout many other Units of the book. All teaching with such objectives as the appreciation of beauty in nature, the cultivation and deepening of right attitudes towards animals of all kinds, and the stimulation of wonder about and interest in the whole world of nature round about us will lend itself well to integration with imparting knowledge and cultivating right attitudes toward the conservation of our natural resources. In addition, Unit 99 (page 421) provides some guidance in making an organized review of the principles and practices of conservation.

NOTES: A monthly calendar and full-page illustrations entitled "Science in Action" and "Beautify Your Surroundings" have been included for each month's units to suggest nature observations and activities. Teachers are cautioned against having pupils copy these—a useless waste of time and material—also against the monotonous habit of making such calendars each month unless this project is distributed among the grades a month at a time. Pupils who have imagination, and who are encouraged by the teacher, will use these pages regularly as a source of ideas.

Directions to teachers for the carrying out of some general types of activities are given in Unit 21 (page 84).

In Unit 46 (on page 196), the method of the enterprise has been suggested, using the topic, "Coal, from Mine to Furnace", as an example. The sequence of enterprise procedures given there applies in general to other enterprises.

References to additional sources of information, some suitable for supplementary reading by pupils, others providing ideas for teachers, are listed at the end of most units. In addition to these, a list of books of value in connection with several units is given on page 473.

Teachers will find the addresses of a number of publishing companies on page 475.

Such Beautiful Things

The world is so full of such beautiful things— Like mountains at sunset or butterfly wings, Or rivers and gardens and trees in the rain, Or thickets of roses and curves in the lane!

Some beautiful things are ever so small You have to look twice to just see them at all, While some are so gorgeous and far-off and grand They give you a feeling you can't understand.

Oh, don't miss a rainbow while looking at mud, Or just see the thorn and not see the bud;

While looking for beauty your heart always sings, For the world is so full of such beautiful things.

ELIZABETH C. WHERRY
Reprinted from *Better Homes and Gardens* Magazine

NATURAL SCIENCE — SEPTEMBER — DAY BY DAY

SUNDAY	MONDAY	TUESDAY	WEDNESDAY	THURSDAY	FRIDAY	SATURDAY
					1 "Come forth into the light of things, Let Nature be your teacher"	**2** Have you seen the red berries of the Jack-in-the-Pulpit?
3 "I think that I shall never see A poem lovely as a tree"	**4** LABOUR DAY	**5** SCHOOL OPENING	**6** Last Quarter. See me in the morning	**7** Explore the school garden	**8** Find the time of sunrise and sunset and the length of day	**9** You may transplant irises
10 Have hydrangea flowers started to turn colour?	**11** Start a group collection showing how seeds travel	**12** Make a bouquet of wild flowers. Name them	**13** New Moon. Can you see me?	**14** What birds are going south now?	**15** Has the King Billy left for the south?	**16** Trim your hedge for the last time
17 Learn to know one new Flower	**18** Start a group chart showing food preservation	**19** A hike around the school grounds to name the trees.	**20** First Quarter. Look for me in the south-west. What time do I rise?	**21** Watch the sunflower face to the sun	**22** Find a spider's egg-case. Save it	**23** Look for winter muskrat homes
24 Find one beautiful thing in Nature new to you	**25** Start a group diary of how plants prepare for winter.	**26** Find me, Queen Cassiopeia. Look north	**27** Record to-day's temperature, brightness, wind direction and strength, humidity.	**28** Full Moon. Where am I at 8 p.m.? 9 p.m.? 10 p.m.?	**29** Pot plants from the garden for indoor enjoyment.	**30** Remove weeds from your lawn at home

J A PARTRIDGE

Drawn by D Farwell

Have your pupils build this calendar day by day on blackboard or chart
Use substitutions if desired

SEPTEMBER

Unit 1—Exploring Nature

To explore can be a satisfying human venture; to explore nature satisfies the human longing to associate with and live in harmony with other living things. The urge to be with nature is particularly strong when pupils must exchange the outdoor freedom of summer for the indoor restraint of the classroom. We as teachers, therefore, must arrange in September a wide variety of pupil activities, directly and indirectly connected with the out-of-school environment. These will keep pupils nature-minded and at the same time increase their enjoyment of nature round about them.

Excursions, as a learning opportunity, come closest to fulfilling the aims of teaching natural science. They bring the pupils and the teacher in such close contact with nature that they gain firsthand impressions of nature's ways—not merely learn facts about nature. Through such outdoor study, pupils come to understand the things of nature in their natural environment, while classroom study of these same things may give a distorted viewpoint.

Excursions provide for pupils the individual, personal observations and direct experiences which are necessary for thoughtful discussion in class and for worthwhile creative expressions in art. Not to be ignored are the social experiences of the outing. Undesirable conduct and lack of business-like attitude on the part of the pupils are due to the newness of the experience, and perhaps to a deeply fixed idea that learning is expected of them only when their faces are solemn and their bodies rigidly erect in the seats. After two or three well-conducted hikes, pupils will realize that here are opportunities to see, do, and learn interesting things.

The teacher must make preparations for the excursion. Having set an objective and located and explored a suitable place to visit, consideration must be given to matters which concern the principal, the parents, and also the health and comfort of the pupils. For an excursion from a rural school, the inspector or superintendent should be notified lest he has planned to visit you that day. In a graded school the principal is consulted. Written permission from parents lessens your responsibility. Pupils should be instructed with respect to suitable clothing. Identification books, collecting facilities, a whistle, etc. must be planned for.

The class must be prepared mentally. They should know the objectives of the trip and be anxious to start out. Some advance teaching may be needed. Groups, conveners, and reporters should be arranged for. All should realize the importance of obedience. Conveners should have special advance instruction, preferably a preview of the area with the teacher. Signals for assembling, after dispersing in groups, should be known by all. A talk about respect for the property of others may be timely. Planning a picnic lunch will add interest and, while being enjoyed, will provide a restful opportunity for talking about objects seen and collected. With experience all these preparations become natural routine.

During the excursion, discipline should be informal but not lacking. Its basis is mutual respect and an understanding that an excursion is a learning experience. Part of the time all pupils observe with the teacher as guide; at other times, groups led by conveners will seek for things suggested or make their own discoveries. Then all will meet again to discuss their finds. Materials collected may be for class use or may be the property of the pupil collector.

Classroom activities after the excursion may include: learning how to press and mount leaves (Unit 11, page 43), arranging materials in the classroom museum (Unit 33, page 131), setting up an aquarium or vivarium (Unit 7, page 24), making scrapbooks, writing diaries or imaginative stories or other records, answering questions asked by pupils, correcting inaccurate observations or conclusions, assigning further observations, or planning new excursions.

Most difficulties peculiar to ungraded schools may be overcome. If the topic interests all pupils, take them all. Senior pupils may go hiking after younger ones have been dismissed. Where a desirable school spirit has been attained, senior pupils may be left with work to be done while the younger ones go.

Graded schools present different difficulties—distance and travel handicaps, size of class, absence of older pupils to act as assistants. The Home and School Club may provide transportation. Half the class may be taken at one time and the remainder at another.

Do you still shy from excursions? If you do so because of lack of self-confidence or of failure to appreciate the value of such outings, try a few, and the experiences will change your mind. A little tact and perseverance, and the pleasure experienced by the pupils, will break down parental objections. The school timetable is surely sufficiently elastic to accommodate excursions without using Saturday or after-school hours. Some suitable places are always at hand—in the country there are fields, woods, roadsides, streams, farms, gardens; in the city we have parks, gardens, green-houses, vacant lots, lawns.

To give pupils firsthand information, directed observations, assigned by the teacher, will provide a few of the advantages mentioned above. They should be used when the teacher cannot be with the pupils or when pupils observe individually. A series of questions or directions, prepared by the teacher and given to the pupils, will bring to their attention many natural phenomena which they might otherwise not notice. The experiences gained in this way also provide a background for class discussions.

Activities

Teacher

- Make a list of nature materials which are available now and which will be needed later in the year for nature lessons—decorations, crafts, drawings, etc. Tell the class what they are, and plan a treasure hunt to find them.
- Teach pupils the good manners of hiking: to leave woods and parks as beautiful as you find them, not to destroy the wild flowers or cut or carve trees, etc.

All Grades

- Take excursions to various types of environment near the school. List your discoveries and report them in class. Take a friend to see your most interesting finds. Tell your family about them.
- During your tour of the school grounds do something to improve their appearance or usefulness—remove a weed, stone, or other objectionable object; tie up some damaged plant, or cut a broken branch from a tree or shrub; destroy an injurious insect; collect a caterpillar or a cocoon.

- Look under rubbish, boards, and stones in the schoolyard, and under fence rails, for beetles, crickets, centipedes, millipedes, wood lice, ants, earthworms, and spiders. Talk about them—both pupils and teacher asking questions. In the classroom, each pupil write a list of what he saw.
- Each pupil begin a notebook called "My Discovery Book." In it keep personal records of nature—of birds and insects, of life in stream and marsh, of plants both wild and cultivated. This book should express the child's personality through his personal sketches and notes and his choice of clippings and pictures. Continue it throughout the year.
- The teacher marks a circle one yard in diameter and each pupil has to find all the living things he can in that space.
- Find spider webs which are circular, some which are like sheets, and some like funnels.
- Find a garden snail. See how it pushes its foot out of its shell and uses it to creep along. Find its feelers and eyes. Touch a feeler.
- Some more things to look for: caterpillars spinning cocoons or eating, a squirrel hiding nuts, nut-shells from which squirrels have taken meat (How?), a squirrel home, little gullies worn away by streams, a garden slug with a slimy path behind it, etc.

Primary Grades

- At intervals of a week or two, take a hike along a marked route in or near the school grounds. Watch for some of these: flowers becoming fruits, seed pods ripening, leaves changing color, leaves falling, squirrels gathering nuts, winter buds already formed, caterpillars on leaves, crickets and grasshoppers on the ground. Pupils may make simple sketches and save them to tell a continuous story about autumn changes.
- Encourage pupils to explore their home surroundings—fruits being picked and stored, potatoes fading dug, pumpkins and other vegetables being harvested, nuts being picked—and tell about them in class.
- During short trips to the school grounds, talk about directions—where the sun rises, where it is at noon, where it sets; name the plants now in flower— shrubs, perennials, annuals; name each tree and collect a leaf from it. Find three kinds of weeds in the lawn or school grounds, and have each pupil remove one of each kind.
- Using toothpicks as a framework, and buds and flowers for heads, hands, skirts, etc., make flower ladies. For men, use vegetables.
- Rule a blackboard space for a flower calendar. As flowers are brought in and talked about, put down the date, a drawing of the flower, and its name. Later, when flowers are present for bouquets, have pupils choose a flower, name it, and match it on the flower calendar.
- Each pupil make a booklet, "My Garden Book" or "My Flower Book." In it, print little stories and riddles, draw outlines, etc.
- Make a sand-table representation of the area explored.
- Have a treasure hunt to find the weed with the longest root, the flower with the tiniest seeds, the largest flower, the prettiest flower, the reddest flower, the largest leaf, etc.
- Play flower games and recognition games.
- Color outline drawings of flowers, vegetables, leaves, etc.
- Make flower cutouts and arrange them as a bouquet in a paper vase.
- Make flower forms by grouping pupils in a circle facing inward, having them raise their

forearms together in the center and bend the wrists outward with the fingers outstretched to form the rays of a flower such as gaillardia.

- An indoor game: MARY: I saw an aster in the garden this morning. I knew it by its purple flower. Have you seen one, John? JOHN: Yes, I have seen one. I saw a _____ in the garden. I knew it by _____. Have you seen one, Sally?

Junior and Intermediate Grades

- Inaugurate a "Learn One New Plant a Day" campaign and continue it until the names of all flowering plants in the garden have been learned. Then plan a scavenger hunt to bring in a leaf, a petal, etc. of each plant studied to date, and of two others.
- Plan a scavenger hunt or a treasure trail to find named insects, tendrils, climbing plants, tree seedlings.
- Each pupil remove all weeds from a given area in the school lawn.
- List plants having sweet perfume, resistant to early frosts, having red flowers, suitable for a border, for a hedge.
- Keep class and individual diaries entitled "Exploring Nature."
- Visit the lawn. Learn to know the common weeds there. Find out how dandelion, plantain, and chickweed plants are adapted to live in lawns (low-growing; leaves flat, spreading, and facing the sun; below level of lawn mower; not injured by tramping; flowers and seeds forming quickly between mowings;, or flower stalks bending before lawn mower). Remove a few (by spudding).
- See, name, and list the weeds of the roadside, the playground, a vegetable garden, and a meadow. Find out who cuts the roadside weeds, and how those in the other places are controlled.
- Take a trip to observe and, if possible, destroy plants injurious to our health—ragweed, poison ivy.
- A nature trail will provide lively interest for any group of children. Trees, shrubs, flowers, types of soil, rocks, birds' nests, animals' homes—all are marked by signs along the nature trail. What child wouldn't enjoy discovering the name of each thing, why it exists, and how it helps or hinders the things about it? Have a nature trail. Make and place such labels as: "This is hemlock, the only evergreen near here with small cones on the ends of the twigs."

Read

Beauchamp et al., *Look and Learn* (Primary): "Outdoors", pp. 53-69. Gage (Scott, Foresman).

Candy. *Nature Notebook*. Allen (Houghton Mifflin).

Dowling et al., *Wonder Why* (Primary); *Seeing Why* (junior), pp. 1-30; and *Learning Why* (grades 3-4). Winston.

Foley, *Garden Flowers in Color*, Macmillan.

Frasier et al., *Through the Year* (grades 2-3): "An Autumn Walk," pp. 13-19, and "Homes for the Animals," pp. 20-23; *Winter Comes and Goes* (grades 3-4) : "Looking for Insects," pp. 5-15, and "An Insect Home," pp. 16-17. Dent (Singer).

Graham & Dersal, *Wildlife for America*. Oxford.

Huntington, *Let's Go Outdoors*. Doubleday.

Parker, *Fall Is Here* (grades 2-3), and *Summer Is Here* (grades 2-3), The Basic Science Education Series. Copp Clark (Row, Peterson).

Partridge, *Everyday Science*, Book One: "The Garden in September," pp. 1-18, and "The Orchard in Autumn," pp. 38-45; *Everyday Science*, Book Two: "We Visit the Lawn," pp. 1-19. Dent.

Smith & Clarke, *Along the Way* (primary). Longmans, Green.

Sterling, *Billy Goes Exploring*. Doubleday.

Stewart, *Straight Wings*: "Meet Mr. Cricket," "Meet Mr. Grasshopper," "Meet Mr. Grasshopper's Cousins." Gage (American Book Co.).

Treat, *City Nature* (Around the World in a City Block or On a Walk Down Main Street), Audubon Nature Bulletin, National Audubon Society.

E. B. Browning's poem, "Out in the Fields with God."

New to this Edition

Comstock, Anna Botsford. *Handbook of Nature Study*, various publishers

Cornell, Joseph Bharat. *Sharing Nature with Children*. Dawns Pbns, 1998.

Dunlap, Julie. *Companions in Wonder: Children and Adults Exploring Nature Together*. The MIT Press, 2012.

Leeuwen, M.V. *The Nature Corner: Celebrating the Year's Cycle with a Seasonal Tableau*. Floris Books, 1990

Leslie, Clare. *The Nature Connection: An Outdoor Workbook for Kids, Families, and Classrooms*. Storey Publishing, 2010.

_____. *Keeping a Nature Journal: Discover a Whole New Way of Seeing the World Around You*. Storey Publishing, 2003.

Ludwig, L.K. *Mixed-Media Nature Journals: New Techniques for Exploring Nature, Life, and Memories*. Quarry Books, 2008.

Potter, Jean. *Nature in a Nutshell for Kids: Over 100 Activities You Can Do in Ten Minutes or Less*. Jossey-Bass, 1995.

Unit 2—Let's Learn to Arrange Flowers

"If I had two loaves of bread,"
Mohammed said,
"I would sell one that I might buy
Sweet hyacinths to satisfy
My hungry soul."

Some people just have a knack of arranging flowers; their bouquets are always lovely. The rest of us may improve our bouquets by learning some of the principles of flower arrangement.

Pupils absorb their environment without much help from the teacher. Vases of beautiful flowers tastefully arranged and placed in the classroom develop in the child a desire for beautiful surroundings; experience in arranging attractive bouquets enables him to fulfill this desire.

The selection of the container and of the flowers depends upon the background for the bouquet; the size and the floral arrangement, upon the place in which we display it. For a large space have a large bouquet; for a dining table, low flowers in a shallow bowl. A mirror beneath or behind increases its beauty.

Four systems of color combinations may be followed in making bouquets. To explain this to children, draw a circle on the blackboard; color and label its circumference in equal spaces in this sequence: yellow, yellow-green, green, blue-green, blue, blue-violet, violet, red-violet, red, red-orange, orange, orange-yellow.

1. *Analogous color combinations*: any three successive colors in the circle.
2. *Complementary colors*: any two directly opposite colors in the circle.
3. *Split complementary colors*: any three consecutive colors, and the complementary color of the middle one.
4. *Mixed colors*: flowers selected in a variety of colors according to the particular tastes of the artist.

Any classroom can have a variety of containers: plain glass jars of various shapes and sizes, jars decorated by painting them or by pasting on them a mosaic of colored papers, shallow bowls, painted cans. For dark flowers, pottery or bronze-colored containers serve well; for light flowers, plain glass receptacles; for peonies, gladioli, or other long-stemmed flowers, use pails or large jars. The color of the container should either harmonize with the color of the flowers or be neutral.

Flowers are best cut in early morning when wet with dew, or in the evening. Select long stems bearing considerable foliage and flowers in various stages of development. Cut them obliquely with sharp scissors or a knife. Remove the leaves below the water level. Charcoal helps to keep the water sweet. Stems are best cut back and the end crushed just before being placed in water, and each day thereafter.

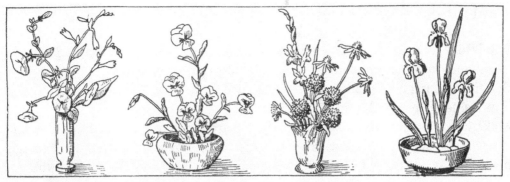

Figure 1—Flowers Tastefully Arranged in Appropriate Vases

A few flowers gracefully and simply arranged, accompanied by sufficient foliage to resemble the growing plant, are preferable to a denser grouping. Too much symmetry or formality should be avoided. A layer of well-washed sand in the container helps to hold the flowers in the desired arrangement.

For permanent bouquets of dried material, several plants are suitable. Seed pods and grasses combine well. Witch-hazel sprays adorn wall pockets. Sumach branches alone, or in groups of two or three, lend dignity. Straw flowers, Japanese lantern, statice, bittersweet, cattail, and honesty may be collected and tastefully arranged. Other material suitable for permanent or winter bouquets are: the irregular clusters of winged seeds on docks, the branches of evening primrose, goldenrod (quickly dried), hydrangea dried hanging downward in autumn, empty milkweed pods, tall spikes of mullein, seed-heads of teasel.

Bouquets are not meant for autumn only. Try branches with berries in November, evergreen sprays and red ribbon tastefully arranged in December, cattail or teasel and other decorative seed pods collected in autumn for January bouquets, pussy willows and twigs of fruit trees in water for February, twigs of Japonica and Forsythia blooming indoors in March.

Activities

All Grades

- Each pupil make one bouquet of wild or garden flowers according to one of the systems mentioned above. Make bouquets of wildflowers of the roadside, wildflowers of the woods, wildflowers of the pasture, vegetable leaves of various colors and shapes, attractive weeds, evergreens and colored autumn leaves, grains and wild grasses, berries of mountain ash, marigolds and blue ageratum, asters with goldenrod or wild carrots, goldenrod with chicory.
- Correlate bouquet-making with art by having pupils gather flowers, press them carefully, and mount them in suitable groupings in paper baskets or vases made by themselves.
- Play games such as "Flash" (Unit 16, page 65), or use other devices, to learn the names of all the flowers which appear in classroom bouquets.

Primary Grades

Use bouquet-making to teach pupils different shades of color. Have them try to imitate these colors with crayons—perhaps while drawing a bouquet in color, using circles for flowers.

Junior and Intermediate Grades

- Pupils take turns keeping the windows or the teacher's desk attractively decorated with bouquets, and caring for these until their usefulness is past.
- Practice making and judging bouquets according to color harmony, relation to container, arrangement, and condition of materials used.
- Make flower portraits as follows: cut the top from a cardboard box and cover it with tissue paper as for a peep-show; remove all of the front except a three-inch margin; place a bouquet just inside the front to represent a picture in a frame. A colored lining in the box will improve the setting. Try making flower portraits with different shapes, sizes, and color effects.

Read

Cutler, Junior *Flower Arranging* (grade 5-up). McLeod (M. Barrows).

New to this Edition

Packer, Jane. *Complete Guide To Flower Arranging* (DK Living), 1999.

Unit 3—Brighten the Schoolroom with Indoor Plants

You and your pupils live in your classroom almost one-half of your waking hours. Then why not make it as cheery and as pleasant as you can? A touch of beauty and color such as we enjoy in our gardens in summer and an entirely different classroom atmosphere in winter will be provided by a few plants. Obtain them by transplanting flowering plants from the garden, making cuttings, or planting bulbs (Unit 15, page 60).

Transplanting Plants from the Garden

The most common plants suitable for transplanting are geraniums, begonias, petunias, marigolds, and foliage plants (coleus). Make your choices—from among these and others—according to the directions in which the windows of your school face.

Figure 1—An Attractive Window Garden

Some houseplants demand a full day's bright sunlight; others are better without any. If your classroom faces the south, you will naturally have to select some of the sun-loving flowering plants such as geranium, Christmas cactus, fuchsia, or some of our common bulbous flowering plants. You may add to this list many of those listed for west and east windows. For west windows, receiving the afternoon sun, the warmest of the day, the following varieties are recommended: geranium, impatiens, primula, sansevieria (snake plant), wandering jew, English ivy. For east windows, receiving only the comparatively weak morning sunlight, try asparagus and sprengeri ferns, sansevieria, wandering jew, flowering begonias, primula, fuchsia, and bulbs. The north windows will produce a splendid showing with common ferns, Rex or other foliage begonias, English ivy, wandering jew, baby's tears, palms, and rubber plant. Sun-loving plants should be kept as close to the glass as temperature and draught conditions will permit, while ferns may be placed some distance from the window.

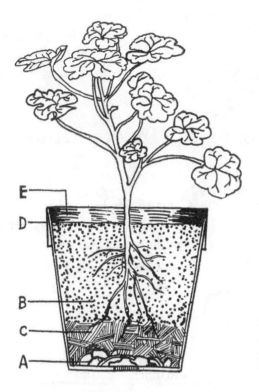

Figure 2—A Geranium Correctly Potted

A, broken pottery over the drainage outlet; B, soil firm; C, peat, moss, or coarse compost; D, soil level; E, ¾" water space.

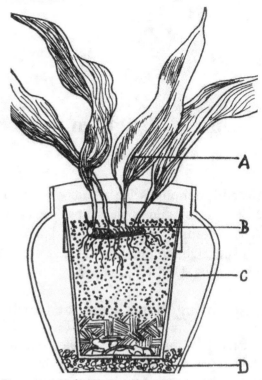

Figure 3—A Jardinière Properly Used

A, newly divided Aspidistra; B, root-stock near surface; C, air space; D, pot raised clear of surplus water.

Containers for house plants must provide: (1) good drainage and aeration, (2) correct soil volume, and (3) cleanliness. Wooden boxes, glazed or unglazed clay pottery, or even tin cans may be used with good results, if provision is made for free escape of surplus water and unhampered entrance of air into the soil (fig. 2). It should be remembered that plants are nourished by the capillary water that adheres to soil particles rather than the "free water" that fills the spaces between these particles. The presence of the latter excludes air, the oxygen of which is so necessary to prevent souring of the soil, to promote proper root development, and to permit bacterial action in liberating mineral plant foods. For the same reason it is essential that pans, saucers, or jardinières containing potted plants should be kept free of surplus water, or that the pots should be elevated a short distance on a layer of pebbles, broken pottery, or wood supports (fig. 3). The size of the container is important. If it is too large, there is likely to be an over-development of foliage at the expense of bloom because of the extra food supply; if it is too small, the plants may suffer from lack of food, water, or sufficient space for root development. Cleanliness of the pots prevents rootlets from adhering to the inner surface.

When the containers are ready, select small, compact plants. Dig them up with plenty of undisturbed soil around the roots and pot them in a suitable soil mixture (Unit 14, page 58) as shown in fig. 2. Be sure that every particle of soil is thoroughly watered. Keep the potted plants in a cool, shaded place until their roots are again established; then cut them back about one-third and leave them in a sunny window. When plants are brought to the classroom before there is artificial heating, they are likely to make more natural growth.

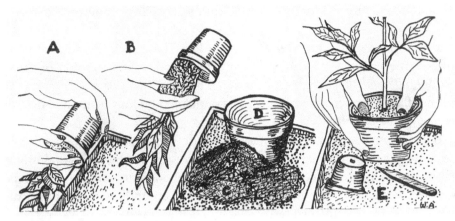

Figure 4—Removing and Repotting a Plant

A, "knocking out" the plant from the pot; B, root-bound soil; C, fresh soil ready; D, new and larger pot; E, pressing the new soil firmly.

Making Cuttings of Flowering Plants

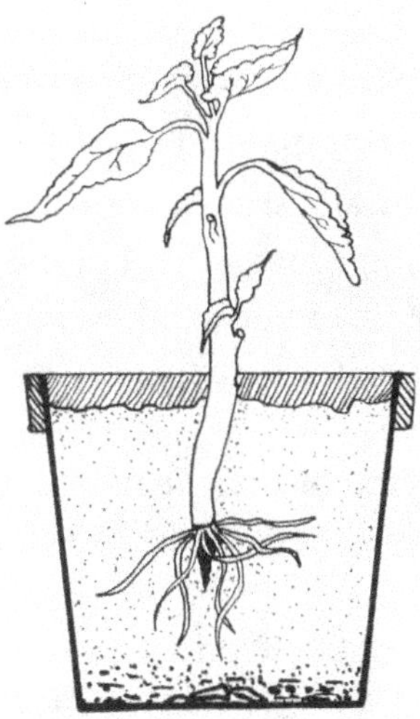

Plants commonly propagated by cuttings are geraniums, begonias, foliage plants (coleus), fuchsia; you might try ageratum and carnation. Select two or three joints of comparatively new growth. Sever cleanly just below a joint with a sharp knife. Remove all flowers and buds and reduce the leaf surface to the equal of one or two normal leaves. Insert the cutting in sand to the second joint and press the sand firmly around it. Keep the sand moist and the cuttings shaded to reduce transpiration. Transplant them to small pots in good potting soil as soon as the leaves have shown new growth (fig. 5).

Caring for Plants in School

For successful growth, plants require sufficient water, good drainage, free entrance of air into the soil through the bottom of the pot, ventilation, sufficient humidity, suitable temperature, freedom from insect pests, and occasional meals of plant foods.

Figure 5—A Cutting Transplanted

Judicious watering is the most important requirement. Water is an essential plant food in itself. It is also the plant's only means of obtaining soluble raw foods from the soil and conveying them to the food-manufacturing leaves. Water plants only when they need it, that is, when the surface soil is dry. But when you do water a plant, water it thoroughly, until water escapes from the hole in the bottom of the pot. Too frequent watering may lead to unnecessary leaching of plant foods from the soil, a scarcity of air in the soil, and a cooling of the soil by evaporation. The need for water is increased by heavy foliage, sandy soil, dry atmosphere, strong sunlight, high temperature, and smallness of pot. The water used should be as warm as or warmer than the room temperature. An occasional shower or sponge bath is advisable to remove from the leaves dust which might otherwise plug the pores used for taking in carbon dioxide, for breathing, and for transpiration.

Good drainage is essential to admit to the soil sufficient air for healthful root development. Ventilation of the surroundings provides fresh air for breathing.

A temperature of from 65° to 68° Fahrenheit seems to be best. Draughts and sudden changes of temperature are injurious. Indoor air, artificially heated, is usually too dry for the healthful growth of plants unless some moisture is added to the air from water pans, a boiling kettle, or some similar source.

The most common insect pests are *aphids* or *plant lice.* These suck the nourishment from leaves, stems, and flowers. They may be controlled by spraying them with a solution of nicotine sulphate. Whitish, dusty-looking *mealy bugs* are common in the axils of leaves of coleus plants. They are easily removed by means of a stiff brush and soapsuds. The same method may be used to destroy *scale insects* on ferns and rubber plants.

The growth of plants may be increased by feeding them from time to time. Manure, but only when well rotted, may be applied in pulverized form as a top-dressing mulch, or in liquid form by watering the plants occasionally with water which has contained about one-tenth of its own volume of fresh manure for a day or two. Bone meal may be worked into the soil around the plant at the rate of about one teaspoonful to a 7-inch pot. Commercial fertilizers, in tablet or powder form, offer a proper balance of necessary plant foods. Refrain from fertilizing resting plants.

Activities

All Grades

- Each pupil make a cutting. Plant it in sand in an individual pot, or, with those of the other pupils, in a larger box. Each care for his own or take turns caring for all. Transplant them into pots bearing the owner's name. Use them for classroom decoration or take them home.
- Pot several plants of geranium. Place some in a south window, some in a west window, and some in a north window. Under which conditions do geraniums grow best? Repeat the experiment with begonias and foliage plants.
- Learn to name the plants in your classroom. Make tracings or drawing of their leaves and flowers, and color them. Make prints of their leaves (Unit 21, page 84). Make Plasticine or salt-and-flour models of the flowers. Color the latter.
- Grow ivy sprays in painted bottles or jars attached by wire to the sides of the window frames.
- Even the youngest pupils may take turns in watering, washing the leaves, removing dead leaves, decorating the pots, etc.
- Place some pebbles, then some leaf mold, in the bottom of a large glass bowl or aquarium. In this, plant moss, hepaticas, violets, tiny trees, and other low woods plants. Nearly cover the container with a glass. Place it where it will receive little direct sunlight. Water the plants when needed. Enjoy this little bit of nature through the winter. You will need it for your Winter Flower Show (Unit 57, page 238).

Junior and Intermediate Grades

- Experiment with potted plants to discover that leaves turn and face outward and upward toward the source of most light.
- Water selected pots of plants from the saucer to show that water rises through soils. (Pupils of these grades should not call this capillary action.)
- Perform experiments to show that mulching the topsoil in flowerpots reduces evaporation from the soil. Keep the topsoil cultivated, or covered with tea leaves, sand, pulverized manure, peat, ground cork, or sawdust.

- Use the school plants for experiments suggested in Unit 4.
- Experiment with various commercial plant fertilizers to determine their relative values.
- Make suitable window boxes, about 8 inches wide at the base, 9 inches wide at the top, and 8 inches deep. The length should suit the windows. To support these, place shelves or brackets a few inches below the window ledge. Here the plants get as much light as if in the window, are less in the way, and remain moist longer.
- *Note:* See also Units 4 (page 14), 15 (page 60), 57 (page 238), and 81 (page 336).

Read

Dowling et al., *I Wonder Why* (Primary). Winston.
Goldsmith, *Picture Primer of Indoor Gardening.* Allen (Houghton Mifflin).
Partridge, *General Science,* Intermediate, Book 1: "Using Plants Indoors," pp. 66-72, and *Everyday Science,* Book One, pp. 47-52. Dent.
Selsam, *Play with Plants* (grades 4-6), pp. 7-22. McLeod (Wm. Morrow).
Smith & Henderson, *Beneath the Skies* (grade 6): "Growing Plants Indoors," pp. 7-30. Longmans, Green.

New to this Edition

Carlson, Laurie. *Green Thumbs: A Kid's Activity Guide to Indoor and Outdoor Gardening (A Kid's Guide series).* Chicago Review Press, 1995. Cutler, *Junior Flower Arranging* (grades 5-up), pp. 110-119. McLeod (M. Barrows).
Krezel, Cindy. *Kids Container Gardening: Year-Round Projects for Inside and Out.* Ball Publishing, 2005. Parker, *Garden Indoors* (grades 4-6), The Basic Science Education Series. Copp Clark (Row, Peterson).
Walker, Lois. *Get Growing!: Exciting Indoor Plant Projects for Kids.* Jossey-Bass, 1991

Unit 4—Understanding Green Plants

Pupils in the elementary school should develop by progressive stages a simple but sympathetic understanding of how a green plant lives. This is not accomplished by teaching them to name and describe its parts, but by leading them to think of it as a valuable, living thing, rooted in the soil, gathering and making food, growing, and producing flowers and seeds.

Primary pupils, from association with living plants, should learn that a seed grows into a plant, that the roots of a plant hold it in the soil and take in water and food for it, that stems and leaves help it to make its food, and that its flowers finally produce for it new seeds.

Junior and intermediate pupils should broaden their knowledge to include such facts as: seeds need warmth and moisture to begin growth (Unit 74, page 310); roots gather other foods from the soil besides water; green leaves prepare the food for the growth of the plant; stems hold up the leaves and flowers and carry water and food; green plants need sunlight to keep healthy and to make food; plants store food for later use; green leaves give off moisture (fig. 1); seeds contain small living plants ready to start growth again (Unit 74, page 310).

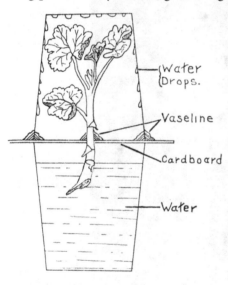

Figure 1—Healthy Living Leaves Give Off Water

Outdoor study of living plants provides the best opportunities for learning about them. Visit a corn (or other) plant in the garden and try to discover how it lives. What keeps it in place? Try to pull it up. See what held it. Notice the number, length, and direction of the roots, and the soil that they brought up with them. What does the plant use to drink? Look at the roots again. See the damp soil sticking to them. Every little root drinks water from the soil even though it looks quite dry to us. There are other things in this soil which the plant likes for food. Thus the discussion proceeds.

Then speak of the leaves as the plant's kitchen: they make the food ready for the growth of the plant. They need light for this—just as we need heat in our kitchens to cook our food. The foods which they make are starch (potato) and sugar (maple). (Pupils below grade 7 cannot understand the absorption or use of carbon dioxide from the air as food.) Carrying the comparison further, the soil becomes the grocery store and the roots and stem the delivery boy who brings the food to the kitchen.

Food prepared in the kitchen is partly eaten at once and partly stored in the pantry. So with the plants: food made in the leaf kitchens is partly used for growth at once and partly stored for later use. Most plant pantries are underground, the roots of carrots and parsnips, and the bulbs of tulips. To illustrate the storage of food for future use, ask the pupils to bring to school a potato, a carrot, a beet, a cabbage, beans, and peas. Past experience shows that these give food to man. Teach that the food was not stored for us but for the plant to begin growth again. Plant each of these and see where growth starts. Show that this food nourishes the plant until new green leaves are formed.

Plants must do more than merely make a living for themselves. They must make new plants to follow them. Even primary pupils can understand that flowers make seeds, and can watch a tomato or pumpkin develop from a flower and become a ripe fruit. Pupils of Grades 5 and 6 might be taught that the seeds or fruit are formed by the middle of the flower. They see the yellow pollen and may learn that it, too, helps to produce the seeds—but they cannot understand how. They see bees visiting flowers and learn that they carry pollen to other flowers where it can help to produce seeds. The colored leaves (petals) help to attract the bees and protect the seed-producing parts within. The green outer leaves (sepals) form still another protection before the flower opens.

Throughout this study, observations and simple experiments will illustrate what plants and their different parts do, but the answers to how and why questions such as the following must be left for later grades: How do roots take in moisture? Why do leaves need light? How does pollen help to produce seed? How do plants breathe?

In studying flowering plants in Grades 4 to 6, it must be remembered that pupils are not interested in, and profit little from, describing botanically the shapes, colors, and size of roots, stems, leaves, and flowers. Include only such information as would be gathered from questions and assignments like the following used in the study of the petunia plant: For what purpose do we plant these in the garden? How can you tell these from other garden plants? (Several answers, including colors and shapes of flowers.) Why was it not necessary to plant the plants closer than 15 inches apart? Why do your hands become sticky when picking petunias for bouquets? Compare a bud with an open flower, and observe the changes from one stage to another. What makes the flower like a tube in shape? Find ripe seed pods, large green seed pods, and small green seed pods. Can you find the part in the flower which produces the seed pod?

Activities

Junior and Intermediate Grades

- Plant beans or other seeds in damp sawdust or soil in a warm place. Observe their growth. (Seeds need warmth, moisture, and air to germinate, but the need for air cannot be understood before about Grade 7.)
- Pull up a growing plant and hang it for a day with its roots in water colored with red ink. How does this show that the roots take in moisture?
- Place the cut end of a branch of a green plant such as corn, carnation, or white phlox in red ink. Leave it for a day. The red color in the leaves and flowers show that stems carry moisture.
- Find how plants place their leaves where they get the best light. Observe: dandelion and plantain leaves lying flat in the lawn, but growing taller in long grass; house plants growing toward the light.
- Cover some grass with a board. After a few days, observe the yellow color of the grass; then uncover it. Pupils will learn that sunlight produces a healthy green color again.
- Place a dry, wide-mouthed bottle over a leafy branch of a growing plant, and pack the mouth of the bottle with cotton batting. Where did the mist or water drops come from? Others may perform the experiment illustrated in fig. 1 in sunlight. The top tumbler is dry to begin with.

- Plant a potato in moist sand. Watch it shrivel as its food is used to produce a new plant.
- Find out what use the stems of plants are to us. (They give lumber, pulpwood, rayon, posts, linen, food, shelter, clothing, etc.)

Read

Beauchamp et al., *All Around Us* (primary), pp. 61-77; *Discovering Our World*, Book 1 (grades 4-5), pp. 197-214; *Discovering Our World*, Book 2 (grade 5): "Where Does All the Food in the World Come From?" pp. 205-219; and *How Do We Know?* (primary and junior): Plants," pp. 53-72. Gage (Scott, Foreiman).

Dickinson, *The First Book of Plants* (grades 5-8). Ambassador (Watts).

Frasier et al., *How and Why Experiments:* "How Plants Get Their Food," pp. 237-251. Dent (Singer).

Hanrey and Lay, *Adventures into Nature*, Book II A: "How Plants Live" and "About Flowers," pp. 20-8. Macmillan.

Miner, *The True Book of Plants We Know* (primary). Book Society (Children's Press).

Parker & Frank, *Plant Factories* (grades 4-6), The Basic Science Education Series. Copp Clark (Row, Peterson).

Partridge, *General Science*, Intermediate, Book 1: "How Green Plants Make a Living," pp. 21-40; "Plants Prepare for the Future," pp. 41-57; "Plants Use and Store Food," pp. 41-47; also *Everyday Science*, Book One: "How a Plant Lives," pp. 19-32, and "Flowering Plants Produce Seeds," pp. 33-34. Dent.

Phillips & Wright, *Plants and Animals* (grades 4-6): "Plants and Their Work," pp. 11-39. Copp Clark (Row, Peterson).

Schneider, *Science for Here and Now* (grade 2), pp. 181-194. Copp Clark (Heath).

Selsam, *Play with Leaves and Flowers* (grades 4-6): "Leaves Move," pp. 7-25, and "Leaves Catch Insects," pp. 26-35; *Play with Plants* (grades 4-6), pp. 7-22 and 43-63; and *Play with Trees* (grades 4-6): "Pipelines in the Tree," pp. 19-23, and "How a Tree Grows," pp. 24-30. McLeod (Wm. Morrow).

Smith & Clarke, *Around the Clock* (grades 3-4), pp. 7-38 and 99-126. Longmans, Green.

Stephenson, *Nature at Work*, Book 3 (grades 5-6). "Plants Give Out Water Vapor," and "Plants Check Their Loss of Water Vapor," pp. 98-104. Macmillan (A. & C. Black).

Webber, *Up Above and Down Below*. Allen (Wm. R. Scott).

Zim, *What's Inside of Plants?* McLeod (Wm. Morrow).

New to this Edition

Jordan, Helene, J. *How A Seed Grows (Let's Read and Find Out Science 1)*. Collins, 1992

Gibbons, Gail. *From Seed to Plant*. Holiday House, 1993.

Helbrough, Emma. *How Flowers Grow* (Usborne Beginners). Usborne, 2007.

Spilsbury, Louise. *Why Do Plants Have Flowers? (World of Plants)*. Heinemann-Raintree, 2005

Stewart, Melissa. *How Do Plants Grow? (Tell Me Why, Tell Me How)*. Marshall Cavendish Children's Books, 2008.

Whitehouse, Patricia. *Roots (Plants)*. Heinemann-Raintree, 2009.

_____. *Seeds (Plants)*. Heinemann-Raintree, 2009.

_____. *Flowers (Plants)*. Heinemann-Raintree, 2009.

Unit 5—Some Birds Go South

How carefully we mortals study road maps, consult information bureaus, and pack our traveling necessities when about to take a journey! We make sure that everything is provided for. How different it is with the thousands of birds now starting southward to more distant places, over routes never traveled before, and with no sky maps or road signs to guide their way!

Pupils of primary grades can observe and understand that some birds go south in fall while others stay; that all seem to have the same number of feathers to keep them warm; that the robins, swallows, and orioles disappear before the ducks and geese; that blackbirds gather in groups before they start to go south; that flocks of geese are in the form of a V with the leader in front.

Pupils of junior and intermediate grades have broader interests. They observe the different speeds of flight, where birds feed and rest, and other similar things. They wonder about why some are never seen going south (night travelers), where the birds are going, how they will find their way, what dangers they will meet.

The study of this topic should give pupils answers to these questions and help them to learn by sight more of our common birds that go south in winter, to learn of their habits and actions at migration time, and to marvel at other wonders of migration.

> Whither, 'midst falling dew,
> While glow the heavens with the last steps of day,
> Far, through their rosy depth, dost thou pursue
> Thy solitary way?

Long ago, people thought that some birds changed into different birds in the winter. During the summer there seemed to be millions of cuckoos flying about, but during the winter there were millions of sparrow hawks. Surely the cuckoos turned into sparrow hawks! Then some people had the idea that birds buried themselves in mud—just the same as frogs and toads do. How these ideas have been changed! Careful observation and the banding of birds to keep a check on their courses of flight have shown us why birds leave, how fast they travel, the routes they take, where they stay.

The reason for going south is commonly misunderstood. It is not the cold, but the lack of suitable food when winter comes which has caused them to form the habit. Those birds which eat worms and insects from the ground (bobolink), insects from the air (swallows), or fruits (robins), seek other winter quarters; those which eat weed seeds, often projecting above the snow (tree sparrows), and insects from the bark of trees (downy woodpecker), can obtain their food here all winter.

Activities

All Grades

- Watch for birds flying south. If you see one you cannot name, compare its size with that of a robin, and notice its color markings; then find the name from pictures at school.
- Watch for swallows and blackbirds gathering in flocks (fig. 1). Count the number in a flock. Are birds more active in autumn? Noisier? Do they sing during flight? Listen for their calls. Are there more birds along streams now? Keep a diary of your observations. Enter them on the class bird calendar.
- Read this story told by a cowbird, and make a mural or frieze to illustrate it.[1]

Figure 1—Make This Poster by Free Paper Cutting

Clouds, white; sky, blue; sun and rays, orange; wires, birds, and pole, black.

". . . September came and passed, and then October with its frosty nights . . . For a time during September the roving flocks of our species, as well as those of the Red-wings, were made up largely of us youngsters, (while) the old birds were finishing the molt of their wings and tails . . .

"Then came great flocks of Blackbirds from farther north with tales of ice and snow; also Crackles, Red-wings, and Rusty Blackbirds as well as Cowbirds, and we began to feel it in our bones that we too must soon be moving . . . Finally I could stand it no longer, and one cloudy day in mid-October . . . I started off on what I knew was to be the longest flight that I had ever made. I had been living well all fall and had become excessively fat; and while my appetite was still good, I realized that, if necessary, I could now go for considerable periods without food, and I no longer feared venturing into a strange country where I would be unfamiliar with the good feeding-places.

"For over a month I had been hearing small birds flying overhead at night calling to one another, especially on cloudy nights when they were flying low to avoid passing through the mists; but I never heard any Blackbirds, for all of us prefer to do our migrating by day. We are accustomed to long flights through the open country and we can find food as we go if necessary. So that morning, when I left my roost in the cattails, 1 knew I would not be coming back for a long time. About two hundred of us started together . . .

"How thrilling it was to climb higher and higher than I had ever flown before, and to know that far away to the south were lands that I had never seen . . . At times clouds shut out all view of the earth below, but again it was clear, and we could see for miles and miles before us. We

---

1   From *American Bird Biographies*, by A. A. Allen.

passed by clouds of smoke that marked the location of cities; . . . villages looked to us like handfuls of confetti scattered on a green lawn . . . As the sun grew low on the horizon . . . we knew that night was approaching. . . . What a coast we had descending from our great height—it certainly was thrilling! . . . (Finally) we were low enough to see the marsh . . . and to choose the section where we might alight with the greatest certainty of meeting friends and being safe for the night . . .

"By the next morning we were hungry . . . and followed some of the local birds to a pasture where there were plenty of grasshoppers and weed seeds. We loafed all that day and part of the next . . . Some days we would fly 300 to 400 miles, and then again we hung around some places for nearly a week at a time. Had our geography been better, we would have recognized the various landmarks as we passed them, but we were traveling entirely by instinct . . . At last we came to Texas with its great open plains. And here were enough cattle to satisfy any Cowbird, only by this time we had lost all interest in cows and the insects about them, and were feeding almost entirely upon weed seeds . . ."

- Read other stories of bird journeys. Then write a report such as you would if you were a reporter travelling with them.
- Draw, color, tut out, and mount on a V-shaped wire a flock of geese going touth. Show the wings in various positions in flight (fig. 2).
- Make up a poem about bird migration.
- Look for birds still with us. Find out what birds stay all winter.

Suggestions for other correlated activities: sketching birds in flight, cutouts of birds in flight, oral talks on such topics as "If I Were a Bird Going South," a month's diary of a bird on its way south, a class booklet, dramatizing a "Farewell to Our Birds."

Figure 2—Wild Geese Flying South

Junior and Intermediate Grades

- Imagine that you are a bird going south. Make a list of difficulties which you would fear, and of sources of help along the way. (Difficulties: changing weather conditions, high winds, tall buildings and lighthouses, flying long distances over open water, attacks by man or birds of prey, how to find food; sources of help: ravines and woodlots, grain fields and meadows, small ponds and streams.)

- Make friezes, murals, booklets, or posters to illustrate birds going south, using such titles as: Dangers along the Way, The Traveling Suits of Birds, Eating-places for Bird Tourists, Routes to Southland. Each pupil should work on the topic in which he is most interested.

Intermediate Grades

- Each pupil in the class chooses for special study a bird passing through the neighborhood. Find out where the bird spends the various seasons, where it rears its young, and the approximate date when it will pass through the community in spring.
- Look for changes in the color of birds in autumn. Try to distinguish young birds by their color. Look for feathers shed by birds when they molted. (The autumn feathers of several birds [e.g., tanagers and bobolinks] are much duller than their summer ones—a protection during migration.)
- On a large piece of wallboard draw a map of North and South America. With colored ribbons and thumbtacks mark on this the summer home, route southward, and winter home of one or more of our common birds.
- Look for flocks of monarch butterflies ready to go south. Read about this migration in *Everyday Science*, Book Two, pp. 516-517.

Read

Andrews, *Advtntures in Science*, Book VI (grades 6-7), pp. 161-172. Moyer.
Boulton, *Travelling with the Birds*. Book Society (Donohue).
Comstock, *Handbook of Nature-Study*, pp. 35-37. Allen (Comstock).
Frasier et al., *The Seasons Past* (grades 4-6): "The Birds Migrate," pp. 34-39; and *How and Why Experiments* (grades 6-8): "Birds Migrate," pp. 30-55. Dent (Singer).
Lincoln, *Bird Migration*. U.S. Fish and Wildlife Service Circular No. 16. Superintendent of Documents, Washington 25, D.C. 35c.
Parker & Park, *Animal Travels*, The Basic Science Education Series. Copp Clark (Row, Peterson).
Partridge, *General Science*, Intermediate, Book 2: "Migration of Birds," pp. 40-43. Dent. Patch & Howe, *Outdoor Visits* (grades 2-3) : "Some Birds Go South," pp. 27-38. Macmillan.

New to this Edition

Elphick and Lovejoy. *Atlas of Bird Migration: Tracing the Great Journeys of the World's Birds*. Firefly Books, 2011.
Gans, Roma. *How Do Birds Find Their Way? (Let's-Read-and-Find-Out Science 2)*. Collins, 1996.
Lerner, Carol. *On the Wing: American Birds in Migration*. HarperCollins, 2001.
Sony Pictures: *Winged Migration* (DVD) directed by Jacques Perrin.

Note: See Unit 50 (page 212), "With Our Bird Friends Down South."

Unit 6—Summer Homes of Animals

As pupils become interested in living animals, they naturally become curious about where they live and the kinds of homes they have.

Some live in the ground—chipmunks, woodchucks, earthworms, some rabbits, ants. Others live on the ground—toads, some snakes, and our common domestic animals. Some live most of the time in the air—birds and most insects.

Some animal homes are mere temporary shelters (ladybird beetles crowded together at the base of a plant, aphids under a leaf, garter snakes grouped together under rocky ledges, and crayfish under stones in a stream). Others build more or less permanent living-quarters (groundhogs, foxes, woodpeckers). Still others may choose to live in manmade homes (bluebirds, honeybees, dogs, rabbits, cats).

Animal homes which pupils may find and investigate in summer may be classified as follows:

In Treetops. Nests of birds, tents of tent caterpillars, squirrels' nests of sticks and leaves (probably a nest deserted by a crow or hawk).

In Hollows or Tunnels in Wood. The entrances to nests of such birds as the flicker, woodpeckers, the chickadee, and the bluebird; tunnels made by carpenter ants in dead wood; large hollows in trees occupied by raccoons; tunnels of wood-boring larvae such as the apple-tree borer; the homes of wild honeybees.

On the Ground. The shallow fur-lined home of a rabbit; the nests of such birds as the killdeer and nighthawk; trout nests (cleared place in the beds of streams).

In the Ground in Caves, Tunnels, or Burrows. The burrows of groundhogs, skunks, chipmunks (among the roots of a tree); the burrows of bank swallows and kingfishers in banks; the caves and tunnels of earthworms and white grubs; the many-tunneled homes of ants; tunnels of muskrats in banks of streams near marshes.

Made of Special Materials. The silken cocoons of moths, and the webs of spiders; the large paper homes of the paper-making wasp; the mud homes of the mud-dauber (a blue-black hornet which builds its home against rafters), of swallows, of robins (partial); the white frothy home of the spittle insect (among grasses and shrubs); the nests of the chimney swifts fastened to the bricks by means of saliva; various shaped galls found on oak leaves and goldenrod stems, each containing a little insect; the skillfully woven homes of orioles and hummingbirds.

Some homes are also storage places for food. Mice, squirrels, beavers, and chipmunks usually have a store of food in the home or buried nearby. Hawks and owls store mice for their young on the edge of the nest. Bees store honey for themselves and their young. Before laying an egg in a brood cell, the mother mud-dauber paralyzes and stores a spider within it as a source of food for the young larva.

Activities

All Grades

- Visit an anthill. Watch the ants running about carrying their eggs and young. See where they enter the home. Spade into the nest to find the network of tunnels.
- Look for little swellings on the leaves of oaks, willows, and elms, and on the stems of goldenrods. These "galls" are the homes of tiny insects. The mother insect lays her eggs on or in the skin of the plant. As the egg hatches, the young larva seems to irritate the plant tissue, causing it to grow into a swelling at this point. The little larva lives in this swelling.
- Find deserted nests of birds. Make a list of materials used in making them.
- Perhaps someone will climb high enough to examine a squirrel's nest. See how the sticks were woven together to form the framework. How did the squirrel build the leafy cover?
- For your classroom museum (Unit 33, page 131) collect: the mud home of a mud-dauber; different kinds of galls on goldenrod, oaks, and other trees; a home of the paper-making wasp, other paper homes; a mouse nest; a sac containing spider eggs.
- Try to find a piece of wood with insect tunnels in it. Bring it to school. Were the tunnels made by carpenter ants or by wood-boring larvae?
- Obtain from the National Museum of Canada, Ottawa, motion picture films describing the homes of beavers and ants.
- Make a survey of the schoolyard to find the entrances of birds in poles or trees. Look for chips on the ground beneath. How did the bird remove the wood?
- Examine the home of the paper wasp to discover of how many layers it is made, the nature of the paper, the cells in which it rears its young. Just think of the patience and skill used by the wasps!
- Examine the shells of snails, turtles, and clams to find how these movable homes protect their owners.
- Dig open a woodchuck's burrow to find the series of living quarters within.
- Make a frieze with sections to illustrate animals that live in trees, animals that live on the ground, animals that live in the water (fig. 1).

Figure 1—Summer Homes of Some Animals. In trees: A, raccoon; B, squirrel; C, bird. In ground: D, groundhog; E, earthworm. In water: F, turtle; G, fish; H, frog.

Primary Grades

- Draw and color pictures of several animals and their summer homes.
- On a large piece of paper sketch a scene containing trees, water, earth, etc. Prepare and paste paper animals on this as they would appear in such a scene—a chipmunk carrying nuts to its home, a woodchuck eating clover in front of its burrow, a robin pulling a worm for her babies, a sparrow salvaging a crust of bread, a little girl playing with her pet rabbit beside its hutch, a snake lying under the edge of a rock.

Junior and Intermediate Grades

- Tear open an old cocoon. Test the strength of the silk. Examine how it is woven.
- Broadcast to your class as if you were visiting the home of an ant family (or that of a woodchuck or squirrel). Tell what is going on about you.
- Paint the inside of a box to make it look like the out-of-doors. Make cardboard cutouts of several animals. Place such animals as toads and frogs near the water, squirrels in trees, raccoons on the ground, etc.

Read

Craig & Bryan, *Science Near You* (primary), pp. 10-23. Ginn.
Frasier et al., *The How and Why Club* (grades 5-6): "How Beavers Live," pp. 28-43. Dent (Singer)

New to this Edition

Aloian, Molly. *Introducing Habitats Series*, Crabtree Publishing, 2006.
Gregoire, Elizabeth. *Whose House Is This?: A Look at Animal Homes - Webs, Nests, and Shells (Whose Is It?)*. Picture Window Books, 2004.
Lock, David. *DK Readers: Animals at Home*. DK Children, 2007.
Press, Judy. *Animal Habitats (Williamson Little Hands Series)*, Williamson, 2005.
Wilkes, Angela. *Kingfisher Young Knowledge: Animal Homes*. Kingfisher, 2003.

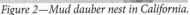
Figure 2—Mud dauber nest in California.

Unit 7—Animal Life in the Classroom

Living things always intrigue pupils. To have them in the classroom under proper conditions provides training opportunities which no teacher of natural science can afford to be without. On field trips, life is seen in its natural environment; in the classroom, a closer view of plants and animals is possible. Only when pupils have both opportunities can their curiosities concerning plants and animals be satisfied.

Terraria (for land plants and animals), aquaria (for water plants and animals), and vivaria (for all these), are a constant source of pleasure, inspiration, and satisfaction for pupil curiosities, information useful for a proper understanding of the activities of plants and animals, and materials for class study.

Terraria and Vivaria

1. *The General-purpose Terrarium or Vivarium* (fig. 1). This is a home for wood plants, frogs, toads, salamanders, and snakes. The best container is an ordinary aquarium tank. An inexpensive homemade one may be constructed in any classroom (fig. 2). Obtain these: an ordinary bake pan; glass for the sides, ends, and top, according to the dimensions of the pan, and wide enough to make the terrarium about 10 inches high; 2 or 3 pounds of plaster of Paris; and a roll of adhesive tape. Assemble as in the diagram, leaving the glass spaced to permit bending of the corners, when applying the tape. Mix the plaster of Paris with enough water to make a thick paste (Unit 21, page 84); pour this into the pan, and shake it level. Insert the glass frame while the paste is still soft. Do not disturb it for a few hours. The completed terrarium will be rigid, conveniently equipped with handles, and sufficiently moisture-resistant.

Frogs, toads, and salamanders like to spend part of their time in water. Use a shallow bowl or tray to provide a pond for them. Sand in this pond will make it more naturalistic. A rock ledge will serve as a diving board.

Figure 1—A Vivarium–An Indoor Home for Animals

To prepare the terrarium for planting, place first a layer of sand or gravel, then one of leaf-mold and loam. Plant some of these: ferns, mosses, violets, hepaticas, wild geranium, wintergreen, wild lily of the valley, or even begonias, wandering jew, etc. Mossy stones, pieces of branches, and hills and dales will add a woodsy atmosphere. Sprinkle the materials until all the soil is moist. Place a glass cover with some air space under it. Keep the vivarium out of direct sunlight. Add to it one or two medium-size frogs, toads, salamanders, and land snails, but keep snakes in a separate home.

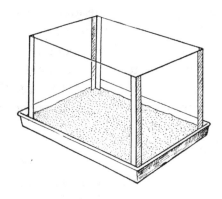

Figure 2—A Vivarium You Can Make

2. *Homes for Spiders, Ants, and Earthworms.* To prepare a spider's home (fig. 3), place a layer of pebbles and sand, then one of ordinary soil, in a battery jar or a two-quart sealer. In this, plant some moss and a taller plant or two, and insert a branchy twig. Moisten the soil. After putting in a spider or two, cover the home with netting. See fig. 4.

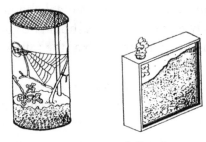

Figure 3—A Spider Home (left) and an Ant Home (right)

An ant home may be made as in fig. 3. A preserving jar may be used for one. When the soil and ant colony have been put in, cover the sides of the home with dark paper and the top with screen. Place a sponge in a space above the soil and keep it moist. Feed the ants a little honey or sugar on the sponge or in the crevices of bark.

A home for earthworms is similar to one for ants. Place rich soil in a glass jar or in a narrow box with a glass front. Then add a few medium-size earthworms. A paper cover will darken the home so that the earthworms will burrow naturally. From time to time remove the paper and observe the earthworms at work, their tunnels, and their castings. Even junior pupils should learn by observation that earthworms live in burrows in damp, rich soil, that they come out at night to feed upon decaying vegetation while holding to their burrow with their tails, and that their shape enables them to burrow easily.

Vivarium animals must be regularly cared for and fed if pupils are to have humane feelings developed. Frogs and toads will eat earthworms, flies, mealworms, bits of beef or liver. Turtles should

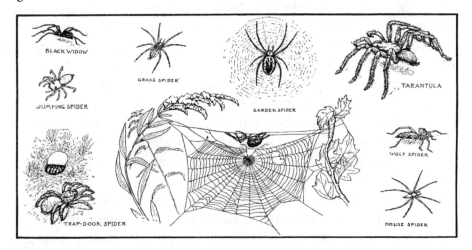

Figure 4—Some Common Spiders and the Home of the Garden Spider (Courtesy General Biological Supply House, Chicago, and the American Museum of Natural History)

be fed prepared turtle food, bits of meat, earthworms, bits of vegetables, or insects—and always under water. Snakes will eat earthworms or insects. When kept cold, all three of these animals may go for long periods without food.

For winter feeding, rear some animal foods in the classroom. Earthworms do well in a large box of damp rich soil in the cellar; feed the worms meat or vegetables. Mealworms, found under boxes or barrels of chop or grain, may be reared in oatmeal.

Aquaria

Animals which live in water not only arouse in our pupils new curiosities, but they also demonstrate ways of life quite different from those of land plants and animals. Naturally the first phase of study should be in a creek or pond where the animals live in a natural way. (Observation here will show how to provide suitable homes indoors for these animals.) If the observations are to be carefully made, the pupils should be guided by the teacher on a hike, or by a series of definite questions and assignments such as the following:

> Approach a stream containing fish. When do the fish first detect you?
> How? Test their sense of sight. Slap the water a little distance sway.
> Can they hear? Where do they hide? Why is it hard to see them when
> looking down on them? Fish for them with different kinds of bait.
> Which do they like best? How do they take it in?

When set up, an aquarium should look like a miniature pond (fig. 5). The containers may be of the usual rectangular type, the traditional fish bowl, or glass jars of various shapes and sizes. Rectangular ones are best since they do not distort the view of the fish. Small ones, preferably of 2-gallon capacity, have these advantages: they are more easily moved, cleaned, and changed; by having more than one, they provide for different animals, more points of interest in the classroom, and increased individual responsibility. To buy them is more satisfactory than to make them. Other things required are a small net for handling the fish or other animals, gravel for the bed, suitable water plants and animals, and food.

A balanced aquarium contains sufficient plant life to supply enough oxygen to the water that the fish and other animals may breathe efficiently. This oxygen is, of course, a byproduct of the food-manufacturing process of the plants. For raw food, the plants take in carbon dioxide which is breathed out by the animals and which would soon accumulate in harmful quantities. For this process a moderate amount of light is essential. We must therefore provide for our aquarium the correct amounts of plant and animal life and the proper exposure to light.

Starting a Balanced Aquarium. (1) Thoroughly dean the aquarium with salt and water. (2) Wash the sand or gravel free from all clay or sediment by placing it in a shallow vessel, such as a dishpan, and forcing water through it with a hose, or stirring it thoroughly. Continue until the water is clear. (3) Arrange about 2 inches of sand irregularly in the bottom of the aquarium. (4) Add about 2 inches of water to float the plants while placing them. (5) Arrange the plants tastefully and naturally in small clumps, leaving a space on the exposed side in which the fish may swim about. Anchor the plants in the sand with stones or by coiling solder wire about the ends of the clumps. Your aquarium should be like a picture. Its front edges are the frame of the picture; your arrangement of the sand and plants, the composition of the picture. But the picture will change as the plants grow.

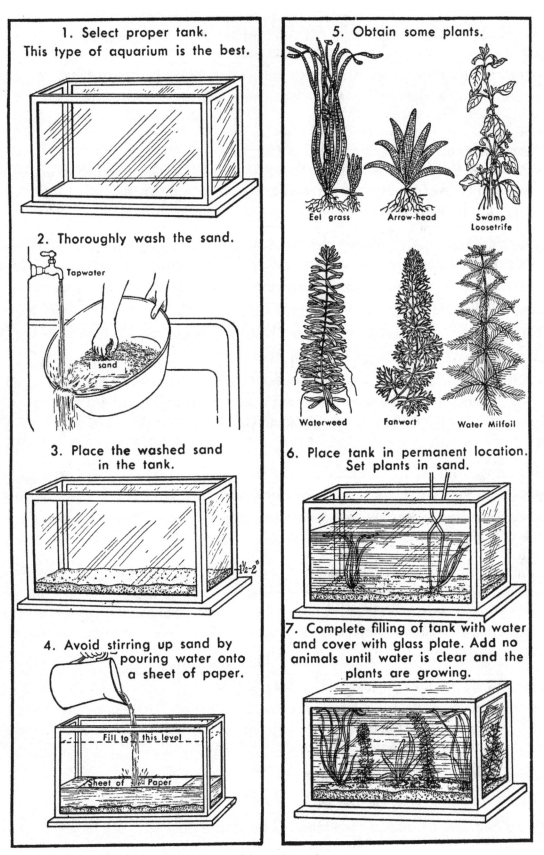

1. Select proper tank. This type of aquarium is the best.

2. Thoroughly wash the sand.

Tapwater

sand

3. Place the washed sand in the tank.

1½-2"

4. Avoid stirring up sand by pouring water onto a sheet of paper.

Fill to this level

Sheet of Paper

5. Obtain some plants.

Eel grass   Arrow-head   Swamp Loosetrife

Waterweed   Fanwort   Water Milfoil

6. Place tank in permanent location. Set plants in sand.

7. Complete filling of tank with water and cover with glass plate. Add no animals until water is clear and the plants are growing.

Figure 5—Some Common Spiders and the Home of the Garden Spider (Courtesy General Biological Supply House, Chicago and the American Museum of Natural History)

(6) Add water to within 2 inches of the top, pouring it on a dish or a floating piece of paper to prevent disturbing the sand or plants. (7) Add the animal life after a day or two, when the plants have become established. See also fig. 5.

Water for the Aquarium. Pond water is best. Tap water should be left exposed to the air for some hours. Add water as it is needed as a result of evaporation. Change it only when foul or unclean-looking. Covering the aquarium with glass helps to keep out dust and to prevent evaporation. When necessary remove the water with a siphon and thus avoid disturbing the plants. Sediment which accumulates on the sand may be removed similarly.

Location of the Aquarium. The aquarium should be in a well-lighted place, but not in direct sunlight, for this will cause an unsightly layer of green algae to grow on the glass.

Plant Life for the Aquarium. Fig. 5 illustrates the most commonly used plants. These and other varieties are available from supply stores. Some may be collected from ponds.

Animal Life in the Aquarium. Fish, snails, tadpoles, and a clam or two are suitable for an aquarium.

Fish should be limited in quantity to one to two inches of length per gallon of water. Small fish are to be preferred. Pond fish such as minnows and sunfish are more natural and quite satisfactory. The fish may be fed commercial foods, small earthworms, or mealworms raised in oatmeal. It is best to feed them only two or three times a week. Avoid feeding more than the fish will clean up at once as surplus food will foul the water.

Snails may be gathered from ponds and will help to keep the aquarium clean by feeding on algae on the glass. A clam will obtain its food from minute particles in the water. Two or three tadpoles per gallon of water will help the snails to keep the bottom and sides of the aquarium clean.

Remove any sick animal from the aquarium at once. Fish should be placed in salt water (one tablespoonful of salt per gallon of water) for 15 to 30 minutes and then removed to fresh water in a separate vessel.

Using the Aquaria. Some common uses of aquaria are: to study the habits of fish, snails, clams, etc., and the life histories of such animals as mosquitoes, frogs, and toads; to observe that plants give off a gas (oxygen) in sunlight and to learn about the interdependence of plants and animals; to develop in pupils a sense of responsibility and habits of observing carefully and concluding thoughtfully.

To guide pupil observations of fish and other water animals in the aquaria, place directions and questions on the blackboard from time to time. Include assignments dealing with what the animals eat, how they take in food, how they swim and float and dive, what organs they use for each method of locomotion, their breathing movements, the keenness of their senses of sight and hearing, how they avoid or escape from danger.

No useful purpose can be served by teaching junior pupils technical names for the fins of fish. By observation they will learn that the tail fin serves as a propeller and a rudder, while the back fins keep the fish erect in the water. The two pairs of fins along the sides of the body (arm and leg fins) help the fish to raise, lower, and balance itself in the water. The tapering shape of the fish makes it easier for it to move through water, while the scales protect it from injury.

Activities

Teacher

Do what this teacher did. "We took a walk to hunt grasshoppers. Their protective coloring was noticed. The children played with them in the schoolroom, watching how far they could jump, and observing the legs used for jumping, the saw-like edge of the back legs, the number of wings, the manner of flying, the production of 'tobacco juice' (as the children called it), the large head and eyes. The grasshoppers were fed grass. The children were interested in the way they bit and chewed their food."[1]

Assign the care of the animal life to individual pupils, each taking charge for a definite period. Be sure that all animal life is humanely cared for, that overcrowding is not permitted, and that water, food, sanitation, and ventilation are provided for. When a project is completed, all animal life should be restored to a suitable natural environment.

Mealworms may be collected from some neighboring feed store or granary, and reared in oatmeal in the classroom; these are acceptable food for fish, frogs, and salamanders.

All Grades

- Take an excursion to collect materials for an aquarium and a vivarium. Take with you baskets, a trowel, a pail, a water net, and several glass containers. From a slow stream gather minnows, tadpoles, clams, snails, water insects, and small pond weeds; from the nearby marsh bring one or two medium-size frogs and garter snakes; from a garden bring in a small toad or two.
- When you return to school, arrange your materials to make attractive homes for both water animals and land animals.
- Collect water plants from a local stream. Transplant them in mud or sand in an aquarium or tub. Find which grow well enough to be used as aquarium plants; then set up a permanent aquarium.
- While on the playground, discover how the color of the grasshoppers protects them; how far grasshoppers can jump and fly; how they bite and chew grass blades; how they spit out their "tobacco juice"; how a cricket runs and how he makes his music.
- Prepare a terrarium without water. For plants, use sod only, and keep it moist. Into this home put some crickets and grasshoppers. Watch them move about. Do the crickets like light? (No—they prefer darkness.) Listen to your Nature orchestra.
- Set up an earthworm home. Once or twice a day remove the dark cover to find the earthworms out of the soil. Do they know when it is light? How do they show it? See their burrows and watch how they make them.
- Find some "woolly bears," put them in a screened jar or cage, and watch how they spin their cocoons, weaving their hair in with the silk. Place the jar in a protected, cool place until spring and watch the moths emerge.
- Find an anthill. Dig some soil with some members of the ant family from it, and place them in a quart jar. Place the jar in a dish of water so that the ants cannot crawl away. Wrap the jar with black paper or cloth. Remove the covering from time to time and observe the ants and their tunnels. Watch the ants carrying their young from place to place, caring for their eggs, cleaning themselves and their young, feeding, and talking to each other. Place a few leaves bearing aphids in the ant home. Watch the ants care for the aphids and collect honey dew for their services.
- Set up a spider home containing a spider or two. Screen the top securely. Watch where and how a spider fastens its web; how it spins the silk and fashions the web—the foundation

---

1   Report of grade 1 activities, Teacher College, Columbia University.

lines, the spokes, the spirals around the spokes; where the spider rests when waiting for prey (a fly put in). How does it know when to come forth again? What does it do with the insects? You may see the spider spinning a small sac-shaped case. In this she stores a few hundred small, round eggs which may hatch if the autumn is warm. If the spiders hatch, see how similar they are to their parents. See how their numbers dwindle as they eat each other.

- Make a drawing of a spider's web and the supports which hold it.
- Arrange a tall, upright object in a basin of water. Place a spider on it—it cannot get away. Watch it spin and throw out a silken thread into the air. When a spider falls, why does it not bump?
- Look around spider webs, under loose bark, among stones and other rubbish for small silken cases of spider eggs. Place them in the spider home. If the eggs do not hatch in a few days, store the cases in a screened, glass vessel away from indoor warmth where they will hatch in spring.
- Observe all the ways you can find in which spiders travel—on water; through the air; down from a high object by weaving a drag line; running or walking (see experiments suggested elsewhere); ballooning (by throwing out webs which carry them); delicately walking over their web.
- Study the delicate beads of dew on spider webs in early morning.

Primary Grades

- Keep a frog and toad in the classroom in a comfortable little home containing soil covered with moist moss, and a swimming pool. See how they talk (fig. 6, A), how they eat worms and flies (fig. 6, B), how they jump and crawl about, how they make their homes in the soil, how they swim. Touch the toad on the back. How do you know it gets sulky? You may see the toad change its suit when it gets too tight. He will roll up the old suit and swallow it.
- Bring pretty caterpillars to school and some of the plants on which they feed. Put them in a screened box. Keep them supplied with fresh food. Watch them eat, and see what the plant looks like when the caterpillars have eaten. Watch them grow. You may see an old skin that one has shed. How do they spin their cocoons?

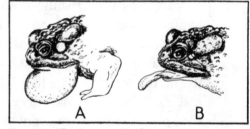

Figure 6—*The Common Toad* (Courtesy *The American Humane Association*)

A. *Hopper's throat swells up like a bubble when he trills.*
B. *Hopper's tongue is attached to the front of his mouth*

- Make an insect tourist camp for the classroom. Tourist cabins (in which you may keep insects for one day for observation) may be made of small cardboard boxes with a cellophane window and a screened one, or by making cylinders of screen with card or wood ends.
- Keep grasshoppers and crickets for several days in a screened box containing moist sod. Feed the crickets apple cores. Watch how they crawl, jump, fly, lay their eggs, hold their food while they eat, chew. Listen to the music of crickets and grasshoppers. Watch the movements of their bodies and wings. (They rub their wings together.)
- Put a goldfish in a big bowl at school or at home. Watch how it swims forward, sideways, upward, downward. Feed it some flakes of oatmeal and see how it eats. Can it see you? Bring a cat near it. See how the cat watches it.

- Put some snails from a pond into the aquarium. Watch them toboggan on the glass—up, down, sideways—turning as they wish.
- Put a tadpole in the aquarium. See how he uses his tail to swim. Watch his legs begin to grow. Which ones grow first? How does he swim when he has all four legs? Perhaps you will see him eating from the bottom of the aquarium or from the glass.
- Make a picture book of animals that live in the water—fish, snails, clams, crayfish, water beetles.

Intermediate Grades

- Have pupils make observations to determine in which part of the classroom the aquarium should be placed in order to receive a correct light exposure for plant growth without being exposed to direct sunlight for more than an hour or so a day.
- Plan, calculate the cost of, and construct a suitable shelf for the aquarium.

Read

Alexander and Cormack, Bruce and Martin, Woodsmen: "Spider Hunt,," pp. 62-83. Gage (American Book Co.). Firefly Books, 2007.

Blough and Campbell, *Making and Using Classroom Science Materials,* pp. 39-88. (Dryden).

Blough and Huggett, *Methods and Activities in Elementary-School Science,* pp. 156-159. Ryerson (Dryden).

Blough and Parker, *An Aquarium* (grades 4-6), The Basic Science Education Series. Copp Clark (Row, Peterson).

Dowling et al., *Explaining Why* (grades 4-5), pp. 56-65, and *Seeing Why* (junior), pp. 98-106. Winston.

Evans, *Aquariums.* Allen (Muller).

Miss Frances, *My Goldfish.* Allen (Rand McNally).

Frasier et al., *Through the Year* (grades 2-3): "Homes for Animals," pp. 10-11, 20-23; *Winter Comes and Goes* (grades 3-4): "Jane Plans an Aquarium," pp. 29-35; *The Seasons Pass* (grades 4-5): pp. 46-63; *The How and Why Club* (grades 5-6): "A Spider's Bridge" and "More About Spiders," pp. 57-71 and 81-87. Dent (Singer).

Gall and Crew, *Little Black Ant* (grades 4-6). Oxford.

Hussey & Pessino, *Collecting Cocoons* (grades 4-7). Ambassador (Crowell).

Hylander, *Out of Doors in Winter* (grades 6-7) : "An Aquarium and Its Inhabitants," pp. 126-139, and "The Semi-aquatic Terrarium," pp. 139-143. Macmillan.

Morgan, *An Aquarium Book for Boys and Girls.* Allen (Scribner).

Parker, *Fishes and Spiders,* The Basic Science Education Series. Copp Clark (Row, Peterson).

Partridge, *Everyday Science,* Book Two: "Ants and Their Ways" and "Nature's Plowmen," pp. 1-11; "How Plants and Animals Live in Water," pp. 594-605; "Pond Life Indoors," pp. 89-99; also *General Science,* Intermediate, Book 1: "An Aquarium," pp. 416-418. Dent.

Phillips & Wright, *Some Animal Neighbors* (grades 4-6): "Life in an Insect City," pp. 4-37, and "The Earthworm," pp. 122-132; *Plants and Animals* (grades 4-6): "Getting Acquainted with the Fishers," pp. 186-213. Copp Clark (Row, Peterson).

Smith & Henderson, *Across the Land* (grades 4-5): "Making an Aquarium," pp. 55-78. Longmans, Green.

Stephenson, *Nature at Work,* Book 2 (grades 4-5): "A Home for Pond Animals," pp. 51-55; "Pond Animals in Their New Home," pp. 56-60; and "Caterpillars," pp. 97-102. Macmillan (A. & C. Black).

Stewart, *Straight Wings:* "Meet Mr. Cricket," "Meet Mr. Grasshopper," and "Meet Mr. Grasshopper's Cousins." Gage (American Book Co.).

Wells, *Tropical Aquariums, Plants, and Fishes;* also *Aquariums and Fish Ponds.* Allen (Warne).

New to this Edition

Alderton, David. *Firefly Encyclopedia of the Vivarium: Keeping Amphibians, Reptiles, and Insects, Spiders and other Invertebrates in Terraria, Aquaterraria, and Aquaria.*

Bearce, Stephanie. *A Kid's Guide to Making a Terrarium (Gardening for Kids).* Mitchell Lane Publishers, 2009.

Case, Russ. *Beginning Vivarium Systems: Lizards, Beginning Vivarium Systems: Turtles and Tortoises,* and *Beginning Vivarium Systems: Snakes.*

Hiscock, Peter. *Creating a Natural Aquarium (Interpret Handbooks).* Howell Book House, 2000.

Hosoume, Kimi. *Terrarium Habitats.* Gems, 2000.

Tullock, John H. *Freshwater Aquarium Models: Recipes for Creating Beautiful Aquariums That Thrive.* Howell Book House, 2006.

Unit 8—Let's Have a Nature Club

What a different satisfaction comes from doing something initiated by oneself rather than something suggested by someone else! Yet how seldom we extend to our pupils this pleasure which we covet for ourselves. Adults have their lodges, clubs, and study groups; children out of school have their Brownie groups, their Guides, Scouts, and Tuxis organizations. Why not give children in school similar opportunities through a school Nature Club?

Clubs make social beings out of individualists. They train children in giving and taking, in making suggestions and in listening to and considering the suggestions of others, in cooperating with their fellows in carrying out joint projects democratically agreed upon.

Clubs bring adventure to children. They are free to think up a plan and to try it out for themselves. If it works, the satisfaction is theirs; if it does not, they have learned something from their experience, perhaps to take advice from others.

Of course the Nature Club in a school must have supervision—broadminded, sympathetic supervision. The counselor is a constructive critic and adviser—one to whom the club executive and members are glad to come with their problems, and one from whom advice is likely to be accepted.

A club needs an executive, perhaps consisting of president, vice-president, secretary, and treasurer. But the members will decide this. They may also wish to have a larger group of conveners for special activities such as bird study, programs, hikes, etc. Then comes the election during which the members gain practical experience in civics problems. Nominations are held in the correct manner, policies are advanced, and speeches made. Then all, showing good sportsmanship, agree to abide by the will of the majority and to support the elected candidates. What a training in everyday living!

It will be the teacher's responsibility to instruct the pupils concerning their duties: the president—to conduct meetings, make announcements, and, with the assistance of the others, plan all programs; the vice-president—to help the president at all times and take charge if the president is ill; the secretary—to keep the minutes (a record of the program) and read those of the previous meeting, to notify the class of meetings; the treasurer—to keep a record of expenses and dues and report when asked.

Now for the business of the club. What kinds of programs shall we have? How often? How shall we plan hikes? Where? How often? Will money be needed? How much? How shall we get it? Here are opportunities to train all pupils in thinking out real situations, in expressing their thoughts for the benefits of others, in listening to and weighing the ideas expressed by their fellows, all with one objective—the betterment of the club as a whole, and therefore of themselves as individuals.

But our club should not be a self-centered one. There are other similar clubs, so why not make it an Audubon Junior Club and thus become a part of the larger group sponsored by the National Audubon Society! This organization then helps in planning nature adventures, field trips, and meetings. It supplies the club with a club paper and a special leaflet, "Things To Do." To each member it gives a membership button, bird leaflets with color plates, and outline drawings. Of course there is a small club fee of 10¢ per member to assist in covering the cost of these. (Note: Write to the National Audubon Society, 1006 Fifth Ave., New York, or to the Audubon Society of Canada, Toronto, for particulars and registration forms.)

The Nature Club not only seeks to further the nature interests and education of its own members; it seeks to spread its influence to others, too. Among activities which the members may plan are: setting up aquaria and vivaria, conducting hikes and excursions, sponsoring motion-picture shows, performing science experiments and demonstrations, publishing a club paper, preparing a science exhibit, contributing to the school science museum, planning and carrying out a "Feed the Birds" project, etc.

A special period should be set aside in the school timetable for the Nature Club as is frequently done for the Red Cross Club. See that the children are fully convinced that the period is theirs and that they are responsible for planning worthwhile learning activities. Thus, certain standards of what is acceptable socially gradually become the guiding principles of each member. They learn to do the right sort of thing just because it is the right sort of thing, not because the teacher says so.

The planning and teaching in other subjects may be timed to coincide with the activities of the Nature Club.

Some correlations of other subjects with the Nature Club's activities follow. *Arithmetic:* problems when the club is planning a garden, measurement problems when making bird houses. *Art and Crafts:* study of composition when arranging displays; color harmony when making bouquets; posters when discussing wildflower conservation; constructing feeding devices while the club studies winter birds. *Social Studies:* civics topics when organizing the club and electing the officers; bulb-growing in Holland while planting bulbs. *English:* nature essays for club competition; debating as a club activity; verse-making after club hikes; a growing seasonal list of nature words.

Activities

All Grades

- Invite members of the community to talk about some such topic as "Making Gardens Beautiful," "Protecting Our Birds," etc.
- Have a "Nature News" scrapbook in which to paste seasonal clippings concerning nature.
- Plan monthly programs.

September—"September, the Month of Flowers": Organization meeting, a junior committee to keep the classroom decorated with flowers, an intermediate committee to plan and carry out the beautification of a small part of the school grounds.

October—"October, the Month of Color": Juniors, collecting, pressing, and arranging colored leaves as classroom decorations, delivering bouquets to shut-ins; intermediates, planning to beautify the classroom with winter plants—transplanting from the garden, from cuttings, grown from bulbs; holding a flower and vegetable show.

November—"Getting Ready for Winter": Cleaning up the garden, protecting delicate plants, discovering what birds are still with us and the hardships they will face, planning a bird-feeding campaign.

December—"Getting Ready for Christmas": Finding out about holly, mistletoe, etc.; a hike to identify evergreens; making Christmas wreaths, sprays, and other evergreen decorations.

January—"The Month of Snows": An experiment meeting, making frost, ice, etc.; a hike to investigate snowbanks; a table representation of a winter scene.

February—"An Indoor Garden": Bulbs in bloom, twigs of shrubs and fruit trees placed in water to force blossoms, dish gardens of grass and clover in a sponge, and carrot and beet tops in a soup plate.

March—"Goodbye to Winter": Observing the sun getting higher day by day and recording increases in temperature; studying the wind—directions, speed, relation to weather.

April—"Enjoying the Wildflowers": An illustrated lecture on wildflowers; transplanting hepaticas and violets to the classroom and observing the buds formed in autumn as they open; a treasure hunt for wildflowers (pick sparingly) in the woods; planting a wildflower garden at school.

May—"Garden Month": A talk on making school grounds prettier; an excursion through the school grounds to identify flowering bulbs and other plants.

June—"Looking Skyward": An evening meeting to identify stars; learning to tell time by the sun (a sundial) ; getting to know clouds and their stories.

Primary Grades

- Elect officers and name them after common flowers. We might call the president, Jack-in-the-pulpit, the important person, and the vice-president, "Sonflower," if a boy, or "Prim Rose," if a girl. The secretary writes, so we might call him "John Quil," or her "Joan Quil." Perhaps the treasurer should be called "Honesty" or "Forget-me-not"; then we'll be sure to pay our dues to him.
- Take a walk to the garden or woods as a little group. See how snapdragons open and shut their mouths. Watch squirrels playing and gathering nuts, etc. Plan other excursions.
- Make pretty things for a club show. Cover glass jars with a patchwork of colored paper, or paint them. In them, place little bouquets. Make little dolls or baskets by using burdock fruits.
- Have an art show. Draw, color, cut out, mount, and display flowers, birds, trees.
- Plan a spring hike to find wildflowers and birds. Have a picnic lunch. Plant a small wildflower garden at school.
- Make bouquets and send them to members of the club who are ill.

Read

Frasier et al., *The How and Why Club*: "The Science Club," "The First Science Trip," and "The First Experiments," pp. 5-27. Dent (Singer).

New to this Edition

Gunther, Alice. *Haystack Full of Needles: A Catholic Home Educators Guide to Socialization.* Hillside Education, 2009

Unit 9—The Ways of Moths and Butterflies

In the sunny days of autumn, monarch, sulphur, and cabbage butterflies flit about from flower to flower with grace and beauty unsurpassed. Their presence all about in field and garden makes this the logical time to interest pupils in their ways of life. The life habits of the less colorful insect aviators, the moths, which gather around lamps, streetlights, and lighted windows, are none the less interesting.

Butterflies and moths differ from each other chiefly in their habits, body shape, and feelers. Butterflies are active by day, and hold their wings vertically over their bodies when at rest; their bodies are slender, and their antennae knobbed at the tip. Most moths are active only at night, and spread their wings out wide when at rest; their bodies are stout, and their feelers may be either feather-like or thread-like. Butterflies and moths alike feed by sucking up liquids, commonly the nectar of plants, through long, sucking tubes which they coil up under the chin when not in use.

One of our most common butterflies is the monarch (King Billy). It lives about milkweed plants on which it lays its eggs. These hatch into greenish caterpillars marked with black and yellow bands. When full grown, after several molts, the caterpillar suspends itself with a silken thread from the underside of a leaf. Then comes the magic change to a smooth green chrysalid, the green house with the golden nails. From this the adult emerges, dries its wings, and is ready for its long journey to the South. Somewhat similar to the monarch, though smaller, is the viceroy butterfly.

The black swallowtail butterfly serves as a good example from which to study the life story of a butterfly (fig. 1). The female lays her eggs on the under surface of leaves of carrot, parsley, celery, and parsnip. In a little more than a week spiny, black caterpillars, with a white patch in the middle of the back, hatch and begin feeding. Each grows rapidly and soon its skin is too tight for it. Then this splits down the back, and out crawls a smooth, green caterpillar banded with black. Its skin is so soft and elastic that, while new, it stretches readily. Close observation shows that it walks on three pairs of small clawed feet near the head, and four pairs of short, fat "prolegs" (prop-legs) farther back. Continuing to devour the soft foliage, the caterpillar grows until it is about 2 inches long.

The mature caterpillar finds a sheltered place, frequently under a fence rail. There it attaches its last prolegs with a patch of silk and, reaching out, spins a silk thread attached to the rail and around its body like a sling. Thus suspended, it sheds its last skin, and appears as an angular, brownish chrysalis well protected by its color. There it remains until spring, when the beautiful, black swallowtail butterfly breaks out and expands its damp, crumpled wings.

The common yellow butterflies (clouded sulphur) are common in fields and gardens and around mud puddles, from which they sip water. The larvae feed on clover. Mourning cloak butterflies are recognized by their blackish wings with yellowish borders and a row of blue spots just inside the border. The caterpillars hatch from eggs laid on twigs of elms and willows. The adults come out of

Figure 1—Life Story of the Black Swallowtail Butterfly

the chrysalids in autumn, seek protection in the woods, and are seen on warm days in early spring flitting about the leafless woods.

Observation of the tomato worm is a fitting approach to the study of moths (figs. 2 and 3). These large, velvety-green caterpillars, so like the tomato leaves, may be observed feeding and growing from day to day. When full grown, they dig into the ground and gradually become pupae by becoming brownish in color, shorter, more pointed and cigar-like in shape. If dug from the ground and examined from day to day, gradual changes may be seen. The pupa, when held in the hand, swings gently around, showing that it is alive, not inactive, as commonly thought. In spring the sphinx moth, commonly mistaken for a hummingbird as it flits about flowers, emerges from this chrysalid. See also fig. 4.

Primary pupils should know what caterpillars are, that they eat leaves and crawl about; that some spin cocoons, and later become pretty moths; while others go to sleep for a while without a silken cover, and later become butterflies.

Junior and intermediate pupils should, by observation, add to this knowledge a more detailed understanding of how caterpillars eat and molt and grow, of the changes in structure from one stage to another, of the time elements in their life history, of how the adults feed and lay their eggs, and of the economic importance of some of them to man.

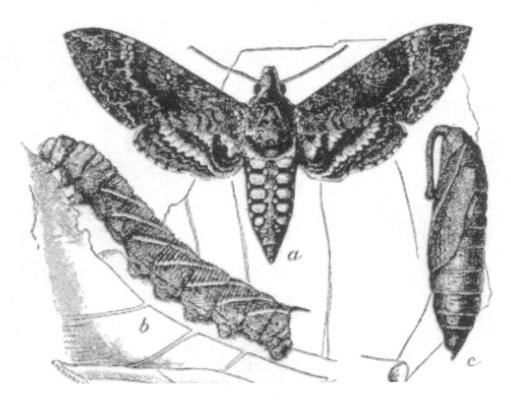

Figure 2—The Tomato Worm (Courtesy Ontario Department of Agriculture)

Figure 3—Larva of Tomato Worm Bearing Cocoons of a Parasitic Fly

The adult fly lays its eggs in the caterpillar's back. The tiny larvae from these eggs feed within the body of the caterpllar. When full grown, they eat their way out of its back. Then they spin their white cocoons. These are carried around on the back of the sickly caterpillar until the flies emerge.

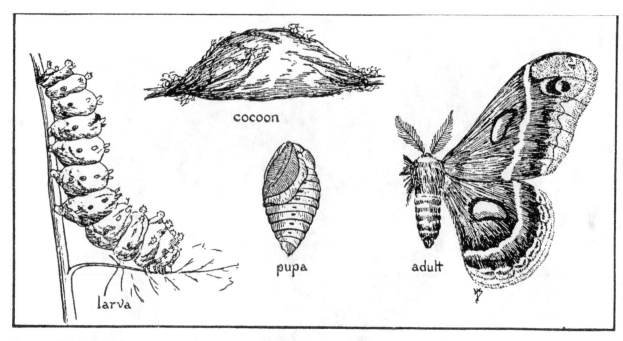

Figure 4—Life Story of the Cecropia Moth (Courtesy General Biological Supply House, Chicago)

Activities

All Grades

- Take an excursion to find caterpillars and butterflies. Look on milkweeds for green caterpillars with black and yellow bands (monarch butterfly), on tomato vines for stout green caterpillars with a spine at the back (sphinx moth), on carrot leaves for the banded caterpillars of swallowtail butterflies, on cabbage leaves for the velvety-green caterpillars of the cabbage butterfly.
- Catch a butterfly. Rub its wing slightly. The tiny scales which you removed give the wing color and strength. Use a lens to see how they overlap. Now look at the butterfly's two large eyes. These are called compound because each of the little, bead-like parts which you see is a small eye capable of seeing straight ahead of it. Find and unwind the long, coiled sucking tube under its head.
- Observe how butterflies differ in flight—slowly drifting, darting, gracefully approaching a flower.
- Observe the habits of caterpillars. Into a breeding cage (figs. 5 and 6) place a tomato worm and tomato foliage. Observe: how the worm eats, the appearance of the eaten plant, the growth of the caterpillar, its disappearance into the ground. Dig up the pupa (fig. 2) from day to day and note its changes in color, shape, size, and activity. Leave it in the soil in the pot over winter in a cool, damp place. The moth should emerge in June.
- Collect black swallowtail caterpillars (fig. 1—striped around the body) from the leaves of celery, parsley, carrot, or parsnip. Place them in a caterpillar home with foliage of the food plant. Do not keep too many in one box. Observe their habits as above. Note particularly how they hang themselves on the host plant by means of a silken girdle and change to motionless chrysalids. The black swallowtail butterflies emerge about May and lay their eggs. Store the dead

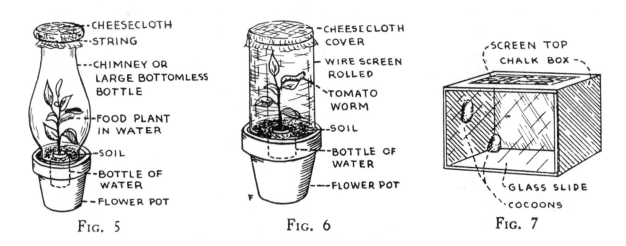

FIG. 5

FIG. 6

FIG. 7

Indoor Homes for Insect

plant remains and chrysalids in a box in a cool place—the school woodshed, porch, or even on an outer window-ledge. There they will not dry out as they will in a warm, dry classroom.

- Collect woolly-bear caterpillars (caterpillars of the Isabelle tiger moth). Store them in a chalk box with a screen top and glass slide front (fig. 7). Watch how they spin their cocoons. How long do they take? Which part do they spin first, the outer or the inner? How does the caterpillar weave the hair from its body into the cocoon? How does it fasten the cocoon to the box? What changes take place in the worm as it completes the spinning?
- Collect as many kinds of cocoons as you can find. Store them in a cool, protected place, but not in a warm, dry classroom. Figs. 3-6, Unit 77 (page 324), will help you to identify both the cocoons and the moths which will come out.

Primary Grades

- Go for a walk to find some crawling caterpillars. See how they walk, climb, look about, hold on, eat. Each pupil find a woolly-bear. Start them all at the same point and have a race. Visit a carrot patch and find some striped caterpillars feeding there. Bring one or two of each kind of caterpillar back to the room.
- Put the caterpillars in separate, ventilated boxes or jars, each with its own kind of food. Feed them well. Watch how they crawl and eat. Find the holes they leave in the leaves.
- Give some pupils in the class outlines of moths and butterflies and others outlines of plants bearing flowers. Color them all and mount them on an attractive mural.

Junior and Intermediate Grades

- Prepare several homes for caterpillars so that you may watch them feed, grow, and change (figs. 5, 6, 7). Pails or jars may be used in place of flowerpots. The water in the bottle will keep the food plant fresh. By lifting the chimney or screen, fresh plants or insects may be put into the home. The soil serves to hold the bottle in place, and provides a burrowing place for mature tomato worms. The screened chalk box is for full-grown caterpillars to spin their cocoons.

- Find larvae of codling moths in their cocoons under the bark of apple trees. Bring some to the classroom. Compare these larvae with the apple worms to see that they have not yet changed to pupae. Keep some in the warm classroom to see when they do become pupae.
- Think what a caterpillar, a pupa, and a butterfly look like. Then list all the changes that must take place in the quiet-looking pupa stage.

Read

Beauchamp et al, *Discovering Our World,* Book 1 (grades 4-5): "How Do Insects Grow?" pp. 186-191. Gage (Scott, Foreman).

Blough, *The Insect Parade,* The Basic Science Education Series. Copp Clark (Row, Peterson).

Candy, *Nature Notebook,* pp. 65-71. Allen (Houghton Mifflin).

Frasier et al., *Sunshine and Rain* (grades 1-2), pp. 26-29; *Through the Year* (grades 2-3): "Caterpillars,"pp. 5-11, "The Butterfly," pp. 24-26, and "Moths," pp. 122-127; *Winter Comes and Goes* (grades 3-4): "Three Butterflies," pp. 18-24, "The Butterfly," pp. 160-162, and "The Moth," pp. 163-169; *The Seasons Pass* (grades 4-5): "The Life of a Butterfly," pp. 32-33, and "A Box Full of Silkworms," pp. 242-259. Dent (Singer).

Friskey, *Johnny and the Monarch* (primary). Book Society (Children's Press).

Gall *& *Crew, *Here and There and Everywhere,* pp. 1-8. Oxford.

Hunt & Andrews, *Butterflies and Moths.* Moyer.

Hussey & Pessino, *Collecting Cocoons* (grades 4-7). Ambassador (Crowell).

Hylander, *Out of Doors in Spring* (grades 6-8): "Some Butterflies and Their Caterpillars," pp. 109-112, and "Some Common Moths and Their Caterpillars," pp. 112-16. Macmillan.

Klots, *A Field Guide to the Butterflies.* Allen (Houghton Mifflin).

Marcher, *The Monarch Butterfly.* Allen (Holiday).

Nicol et al., *The Nature Hour,* Sixth Year—Autumn and Winter: "The Butterfly," pp. 21-43. Gage (Silver, Burdett).

Parker, *Six-legged Neighbors* (grades 2-3), The Basic Science Education Series. Copp Clark (Row, Peterson).

Partridge, *General Science,* Intermediate, Book 2: "The Monarch Butterfly," pp. 12-15, and "The Silkworm," pp. 85-6. Dent.

Peterson, *Wildlife in Color.* Allen (Houghton Mifflin).

Podendorf, *The True Book of Insects* (primary). Book Society (Childrens Press).

Rutley, *Nature's Year,* Book III (grades 5-6): "Butterflies on a Summer's Day" and "More Lovely Butterflies," pp. 69-78. Macmillan.

Sherman, *The Real Book About Bugs, Insects and Such:* "The Caterpillar Circle," pp. 105-14. Blue Ribbon Books (Garden City).

Stephenson, *Nature at Work,* Book 2 (grades 4-6): "The Pupa and the Butterfly," pp. 105-11. Macmillan (A. *&* C. Black).

Sterling, *Insects and the Homes They Build:* "They Build with Silk," pp. 17-37. Doubleday.

Westell and Harvey, *Butterflies and Moths,* Book V of "Look and Find Out" series. Macmillan

New to this Edition

Beadle and Leckie, *Peterson Guide to Moths of Northeastern America* (Peterson)

Burris and Richards, *The Life Cycles of Butterflies: From Egg to Maturity, a Visual Guide to 23 Common Butterflies* (Storey Publishing, LLC)

Carter, Smithsonian *Handbooks: Butterflies and Moths* (DK Adult)

Cox, *Butterflies and Moths* (Usborne First Nature) (Usborne)

DK Eyewitness Books: *Butterfly and Mother* (DK Publishing)

Heiligman, *From Caterpillar to Butterfly* (Let's-Read-and-Find-Out Science, Stage 1), (Collins)

Knudsen, *From Egg to Butterfly* (Start to Finish: Nature's Cycles), (Lerner Pub Group)

Opler, Peterson, and Wright, *Peterson First Guide to Butterflies and Moths* (Houghton Mifflin Harcourt)

Pyle, Hughes, Peterson, *Butterflies (Peterson Field Guide Color-In Books),* (Houghton Mifflin Harcourt, 1998)

Soffer, *Exotic Butterflies and Moths Coloring Book* (Dover)

Unit 10—Some Growing Nature Calendars

Growing calendars are records of a sequence of observations concerning a given topic, expressed in some organized form. The making of such calendars, both class and individual, have several educational values. For the information required in them, pupils must observe carefully. This develops the habit of being observant, desirable not only for its scientific value, but as a distinguishing characteristic of a wide-awake citizen. This habit broadens one's interests in nature, and the more interests we have, the more we see—and so the circle enlarges.

Seeing leads to reasoning. The more a pupil sees, the more he thinks, and the more logical conclusions he arrives at. Thus, he develops scientific attitudes.

Of lesser importance are the facts the pupil learns, but no one will deny that the more he sees for himself, the better he will retain the knowledge gained. The observant pupil, therefore, contributes more, both to his own education and to class discussion.

The making of systematic records develops skill in organizing ideas. The wealth of ideas gained by his observations is a constant asset in expressing himself in oral and written English.

Thus, a growing calendar motivates a pupil to see and to think, to organize his ideas, and then to express himself, and also to broaden his knowledge of nature.

Growing calendars call for a sequence of observations. These lead to an appreciation of how wonderfully nature changes from day to day. The observant pupil, seeing this progress in natural events, may be influenced to pattern his thinking along more progressive lines.

Activities

All Grades

Complete the following leaf-fall calendar in preparation for Unit 31.

Trees that shed their leaves suddenly	Trees that shed their leaves gradually	Trees that hold some of all of their leaves during winter
horse-chestnut	maple	some oaks

- Make a calendar to show when frost kills plants in autumn. At the left write the date of each frost; in the second column, the names of flowers not yet killed; in the third column, the names of the flowers killed by that frost. Which flowers can withstand frost best? What annual flowers should be planted in the home or school garden to give the most bloom in late autumn?
- Make a large, four-page class book entitled "The Seasons." Decorate one page for autumn and, at later dates, other pages for winter, spring, and summer.
- For a class record of essential information about animals, use a large card or paper to make a growing chart entitled "Animal Acquaintances." Use such headings as: name of animal,

where found, how recognized, habits, food, life history, enemies, protection, seasonal changes, and relation to nature and man (Unit 48, page 202). When information has been obtained about a certain animal, including insects, fish, birds, mammals, etc., from observations, readings, interviews, and class discussions, add it to this table.

- For a calendar entitled "Trees Are Changing Colors," rule three columns and insert the headings: Tree, Date, Color—leaving several lines for each tree. Watch for all conspicuous changes in color from the time the leaves are all green until they fall.
- Make a mural or frieze depicting "The Seasons Come and Go." Begin it in September and carry it through the year. Give plenty of scope for pupil initiative in planning it and for free expression in executing it. By the end of the year, yon will have a panorama showing nature's changes as the seasons pass.
- Make a motion picture, "Month by Month with Nature," adding a new scene each month. Primary children may use cutouts and pictures freely; older pupils should include only original work.

Primary Grades

- On mural paper, rule a calendar form for a month, leaving a space about 6 inches by 8 inches for each day. Write in the dates. Each individual pupil or group of two chooses something interesting in nature on the day assigned and draws and colors it.
- Make a calendar of flower colors, using the common colors as headings. Fill in beneath these the names of flowers having these colors.

Junior and Intermediate Grades

- In your notebook, make a calendar of annual flowers, heading the columns from the left as follows: Name, Where growing, How I know its leaf, How I know its flower, What I like about it, A drawing. Make a similar table for perennials in the garden.
- Rule a section on the blackboard for a diary of garden activities in autumn. Place the date of each entry at the left. Beginning with the mowing of the lawn when school opens in September, include such entries as: Made a survey of the grounds, Repaired the gate, Painted the arbor, Removed weeds from the lawn, Planted some shrubs, Spaded and fertilized flower beds for next year.
- Make a calendar as shown in fig. 1. Rule a chart to have a column at the left for dates, and 30 other columns, each a quarter-inch wide. Color yellow the correct number of spaces from the left to represent the number of hours of daylight, and the rest black to represent the hours of darkness.
- Make a chart of two columns. In one record the work of man, and in the other the work of nature. Carry this out for each season of the year.

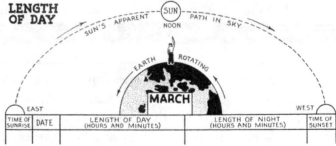

Figure 1—The Sun Determines the Length of Day

Twice a week, from September 21 to December 22, and from March 1 until June 29, fill in the information asked for. Get the times of sunrise and of sunset from the daily paper to check with pupil observations. From time to time discuss the changes in the lengths of day and night.

Unit 11—Getting to Know the Trees—A Hike

We all like to know the trees which beautify our surroundings—to call them by name, to enjoy their shade, to understand how they live. This applies to children as well as to adults. Our task is to give children the opportunity to appreciate the trees, and some help in doing so. Trees are most interesting in autumn, when they form their fruits, display their bright colors, and finally get ready for winter. And of course, the only way to really get to know the trees is to visit them—preferably as a class.

Figure 1—Leaves and Fruits of Common Street Trees

1. Norway maple; 2. red maple; 3. silver maple; 4. sycamore tree; 5. sycamore or plane; 6. gingko; 7. American elm; 8. basswood or linden; 9. pin oak; 10. Carolina poplar.

The teacher need not know all the trees by name to act as guide; it is good for pupils to know that we are all learning together. If you have a copy of *The Forest Trees* of Ontario by J. A. White, or Native Trees of Canada by B. R. Morton, take it (or them) with you. Their keys and illustrations will help you greatly. Better still, make hectograph outlines of leaves of the common trees of the locality so that each pupil may have one. The books or outlines should always be present on the nature table or on the bulletin board of the classroom. If necessary, pupils should be warned not to damage trees by breaking branches, carving initials, etc.

The characteristics of a tree should be observed from a distance, and then from close up. If pupils make sketches of them, they will be likely to observe them more carefully. Lengthy descriptions are more harmful than beneficial, because they fail to keep the pupil conscious of the essentials. Such facts as these are about all that are needed:

Elm: round top; branches high and drooping; umbrella-like; leaves simple, not lobed, doubly toothed, and having one-sided bases.

Sugar maple: characteristic branching (draw it); rough gray bark; leaves five-lobed with rounded notches and a few large teeth; winged fruits.

Oak: characteristic branching (draw it); gnarled branches; very rough bark; leaves lobed (white oak—rounded lobes; red and black oak—sharp lobes ending in a bristle); fruit an acorn.

White pine: characteristic irregular shape (draw it); sloping branches; needles five in a cluster (Jack pine—2 short needles in a cluster; red pine—2 needles, 5 or 6 inches long in a cluster); cones with thick scales.

Spruce: cone-shaped; needles single, rolling between the thumb and finger; cones with thin scales.

White cedar: cone-shaped; bark scaly and easily stripped; leaves like tiny scales; cones very small.

Making individual leaf collections should be an important part of the tree hike. Since pride of ownership is such a vital factor in children's lives, it may be capitalized to lead to intimate contacts with nature, closer observation, manual skill in preparing and arranging specimens, and a deepened appreciation of nature's wonders. The chief value of collections, of course, lies in the making, rather than in the having. The joys experienced and the strengthened mental impressions formed while collecting, coupled with the satisfaction of owning, displaying, and explaining the collection to others, make such undertakings well worthwhile. By respecting individual preferences the teacher can easily obtain a wealth of experiences for class enjoyment, and materials for class display and study.

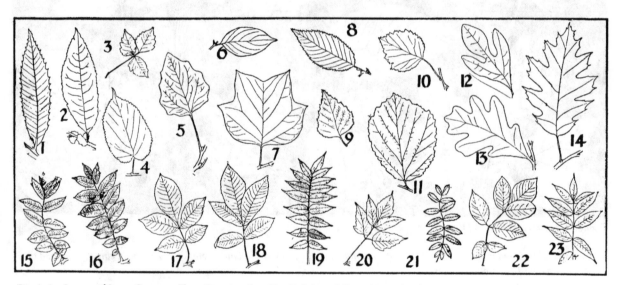

Figure 2—Leaves of Some Common Trees (Drawings from New York State College of Agriculture)

1. chestnut; 2. pussy willow; 3. poison ivy (also a shrub); 4. basswood; 5. white poplar; 6. dogwood; 7. tulip tree; 8. ironwood; 9. white birch; 10. hawthorne; 11. witch hazel; 12. sassafras; 13. white oak; 14. red oak; 15. black walnut; 16. butternut; 17. bitternut; 18. shagbark hickory; 19. staghorn sumac; 20. box elder; 21. mountain ash; 22. white ash; 23. black ash.

Activities

All Grades

Where to Go and What to See	Pupil Activities
Trees in the schoolyard or park or on the street (fig. 1). Their beauty when viewed from a distance; their characteristic sizes and shapes; how to recognize their leaves and fruits; the length of shadow at different times of the day; their effect upon flowers, grass, or weeds growing beneath or near them; how their roots keep soil from being washed away; nests of squirrels and birds; how decayed cavities are repaired by filling.	Remove dead or injured branches. Select one tree and sketch it. Collect, mount, and label leaves and seeds. Decide what trees should be removed and where trees should be planted to improve the school ground. Rake up fallen leaves and place them in the compost. Inquire what trees are native and what ones are imported. Write for government pamphlets dealing with forests and trees.
Trees in the woods (fig. 2). The kinds of trees present; evidences of injury to trees by insects, disease, grazing animals, lightning, and fire; all the kinds of things that make up the forest floor; kinds of plants in the undergrowth; the stages of decay from leaves to humus.	Collect, mount, and label leaves of forest trees. Make blueprints of ferns or leaf sprays (Unit 21, page 91). Make exhibits of nuts and other tree fruits. Discover whether squirrels gnaw or crack nuts. Gather leaf-mold, dry it, then discover how much water it will absorb. Discover what the government does to protect and replace forests. Find the location of Canada's national parks.
Along the nature trail. Plants which are labeled and plants which should be labeled; interesting patches of wildflowers; young trees beginning growth; haunts and nests of birds.	Get the owner's permission to establish a nature trail to interesting places. Make and place labels on trees and shrubs. Make and place signs to encourage conservation. Make a map of the trail for the school. Try to interest local citizens in your undertaking.

- Collect fruits and seeds of oak, beech, elm, maple, ash, and other trees (fig. 3). Plant the seeds in soil; watch the little trees start to grow.
- Observe and list ways in which nuts and other seeds may be carried far from their mother tree.
- After class or individual excursions, make leaf collections (both individual and class) under the headings: Trees in Our Schoolyard, Trees in . . . Park, Trees in Mr. . . . .'s Wood, Common Maples, etc.
- Use leaves to make figures—Miss Maple, Sir Poplar, etc.

Primary Grades

- For a tree game, imitate the shapes of trees; for example, for the poplar tree, stand up tall and touch your hands above your head.
- Watch squirrels gnawing (not cracking) nuts; going up trees, going down trees, hiding nuts, jumping from tree to tree.
- Label a large cardboard "Leaves Around Our School." As leaves are brought in, identify and press them. Later plan the arrangement and mount them.
- Trace the outlines of leaves of common trees such as maple, oak, beech, and elm. Cut them out and color them green. Draw twigs on paper and place these leaves in proper position.
- Play this squirrel-and-nut game. "The children remain in their seats, bowing their heads in one arm as though sleeping. The right hand is stretched out on the desk so as to form a cup in which the nut may be dropped. One player, who is chosen to be the squirrel, runs lightly up and down the aisles and drops the nut into one of the hands. The child who receives the nut jumps up at once and chases the squirrel, trying to tag him before he can run around the room and reach his seat. If the squirrel is tagged, he must be the squirrel the second time; but if he reaches his seat in safety, the player who received the nut is the squirrel for the next game. (Children wake up to watch the chase.)"[1]

---

1   Bancroft's *Book of Plays and Games*

Figure 3—Fruits of Some Common Trees

Top: left, shagbark hickory; right, black walnut. Center: left, beaked hazelnut; right white oak. Bottom: left, bur oak; right, butternut.

An Autumn Sand-table Scene. After a hike to a wood to see trees and wildflowers, hills and streams, birds and other animals, have pupils set up a sand-table showing what they saw. Include twigs for trees, nuts and dead leaves, branches of fresh wildflowers, cutouts of birds and animals.

Some More Expression Work to Follow Tree Hikes. Use acorns, chestnuts, and leaves in number stories; rhythmic exercises to imitate falling, dancing, and whirling leaves, and swaying trees; modeling buds, twigs, bark, fruits, and leaves in Plasticine; reading poems and stories about trees.

Junior and Intermediate Grades

- Measure the height of a tree as follows: Measure the length of the tree's shadow. Measure the length of a yardstick's shadow. The tree's shadow is how many times the length of the shadow of the yardstick? The tree's height is this number of yards.

- Make some of the following leaf collections: four kinds of maple, two kinds of birch, three kinds of oak, three kinds of shrubs that bloom in autumn, four kinds of fruit trees, four kinds of evergreens, trees of the schoolyard, trees on the street (fig. 1). Be sure to name the leaves while at the tree rather than after they are pressed. Press and dry them between layers of paper for about two weeks. Wax the thoroughly dry leaves by dipping them in melted paraffin, or by enclosing them in folded waxed paper and passing a hot iron lightly over a sheet of paper on top of the waxed paper. Mount them on heavy paper and print labels.

Read

Cormack, *The First Book of Trees* (grades 4-6). Copp Clark (Heath & A Co.).

Frasier et al., *Winter Comes and Goes* (grades 3-4): "Leaves in Autumn" and "Trees," pp. 36-41; *The Seasons Pass* (grades 4-5): "A Trip to the Park," pp. 13-31. Dent (Singer).

Kieran, *An Introduction to Trees.* Blue Ribbon (Hanover Home).

King, *Telling Trees* (grades 5 and up): leaves and fruits illustrated by size. McLeod (Wm. Sloane).

Mathews, *Field Book of American Trees and Shrubs.* Allen (Putnam's Sons).

Parker, *Leaves* (grades 2-3), and *Trees* (grades 4-6), The Basic Science Education Series. Copp Clark (Row, Peterson).

Partridge, *General Science,* Intermediate, Book 1, pp. 254-258, and *Everyday Science,* Book One: "A Hike in the Autumn Woods," pp. 58-71. Dent.

Peterson, *Wildlife in Color.* Allen (Houghton Mifflin).

Podendorf, *True Book of Trees.* Book Society (Children's Press).

Potzger, *What Tree Is That?* Book I and Book II: paper-covered text-activity books. Mover (Kenworthy).

Selsam, *Play with Trees* (grades 4-6): "How Trees Are Different from Each Other," pp. 31-55. McLeod (Wm. Morrow).

Stephenson, *Nature at Work,* Book 3 (grades 5-6): "Tree Leaves and How To Know Them," pp. 93-97. Macmillan (A. & C. Black).

Sterling, *Trees and Their Story.* Doubleday.

Swenson, *A Child's Book of Trees.* Ryerson (Maxton).

Van Camp and Shaw, *Fifty Trees of Canada.* Book Society.

New to this Edition

Arbor Day Foundation. *What Tree Is That?: A Guide to the More Common Trees Found in North America.* Arbor Day Foundation, 2009. (Illustrated by Karina Helm)

Aronson, Steven. *Fandex Family Field Guides; Trees.* Workman Publishing Company, 1998.

Brockman, C. Frank. *Trees of North America: A Guide to Field Identification, Revised and Updated* (Golden Field Guides). Golden Guides from St. Martin Press, 2001.

Burns, Diane. *Tree, Leaves & Bark (Take Along Guides).* Cooper Square Publishing, 1995.

Coombes, Allen. *The Book of Leaves: A Leaf-by-Leaf Guide to Six Hundred of the World's Great Trees.* University of Chicago Press, 2010.

Gibbons, Gail. *Tell me, Tree: All About Trees for Kids.* Little Brown Books For Young Readers, 2002.

Ingoglia, Gina. *The Tree Book for Kids and Their Grown Ups.* Brooklyn Botanical Garden, 2008.

Watts, Mary Theilgaard. *Tree Finder: A Manual for Identification of Trees by their Leaves* (Eastern US) (Nature Study Guides). Nature Study Guild Publishers, 1991.

Unit 12—Diaries of Trees in Autumn

Diaries are personal things which cannot be dictated by others. They tell the interesting things that happened yesterday and today. To make diaries of interesting things in the life of a tree, pupils must visit the tree frequently. They must think of it as a living thing—eating, drinking, growing, making seeds for new trees, becoming homes for friendly squirrels and birds as well as unfriendly insects, giving welcome shade—even food for man, and, at the end of its life, providing man with many useful things.

Pupils of different ages will look upon trees in different ways and will want to write different things about them.

Primary children's interests in trees will be chiefly aesthetic; those of older pupils, utilitarian.

Short visits to the trees, to see them and talk about them, are essential in giving pupils sufficient material for their diaries. Following these experiences, the diaries become interesting, individual expressions.

This unit is placed this early in the season (early October) to give pupils an early start, but the diary should continue throughout the year, becoming a record of the tree's experiences from month to month.

Writing diaries provides motivated English exercises. Even the pupil who dislikes writing his thoughts should find some little pleasure in writing about something in which he is keenly interested.

Activities

Primary Grades

Visit an oak tree. Find acorns on it and under it. Talk about these as cups and saucers. Fit some saucers on cups. Cut an acorn open and see the little plant within. Plant the acorn and see how the young oak tree begins its life. As the events happen, make simple blackboard diaries of them, illustrated by drawings. Make Plasticine models of different stages.

Junior and Intermediate Grades

Begin a diary of some particular tree. Keep a record throughout the year of all the changes you can see in it. Watch for the color of the leaves in summer, the kind of fruit in fall, how the seeds are scattered, autumn color changes, when leaves begin to fall, when the last has fallen, buds in autumn before the leaves fall, these same buds in winter and in spring, insects or their eggs, diseases, any damage caused by weather or animals in the winter, opening of buds in spring, spring flowers, growth of leaves and increasing shade from day to day. Include in your diary pressed leaves, flowers, and fruits; sketches of the tree in summer and winter, pictures; leaf prints of various kinds; a chart showing the use of the tree to man.

Make a dated calendar to show the changes in colors and the progress of leaf fall for each of several trees. Use headings such as: Date, Name of Tree, Progress of Leaf Fall, Colors, or: Kind of Tree, Date Leaves Begin Falling, Date Tree Becomes Bare.

Read

Frasier et al., *Winter Comes and Goes* (grades 3-4) : "Trees," pp. 38-41. Dent (Singer).
Partridge, *Everyday Science,* Book One: "An Oak Tree Tells Its Story," pp. 72-82. Dent.

New to this Edition

Gibbons, Gail. *The Seasons of Arnold's Apply Tree* (Sandpiper, 1998).
Morrison, Gordon. *Oak Tree* (Houghton Mifflin Books for Children, 2000).

BEAUTIFY YOUR SURROUNDINGS ~ SEPTEMBER

"A THING OF BEAUTY IS A JOY FOREVER"

CLEAN UP GROUNDS:

TRIM OUT DEAD PERENNIALS

TRIM EDGES OF GRASS PLOT

MOW THE GRASS

REMOVE WEEDS FROM LAWN AND FLOWER BEDS

MAKE BOUQUETS:

PLASTICENE

TRY A BRANCH OF SUMAC

ALWAYS AVOID OVER-CROWDING

SEND 10¢ TO COCA-COLA CO., TORONTO, FOR BOOKLET "FLOWER ARRANGING."

BRING PLANTS INDOORS:

TRANSPLANT GARDEN PLANTS TO POTS AND BOXES FOR THE CLASSROOM

MAKE CUTTINGS -

NEW CUTTINGS IN BOX OF SAND

ROOTED CUTTING IN POT

WATER SPACE - 3/4"

FIRM SOIL

MOSS OR COARSE COMPOST

BROKEN POTTERY OVER DRAINAGE HOLE

DECORATE BULLETIN BOARD:

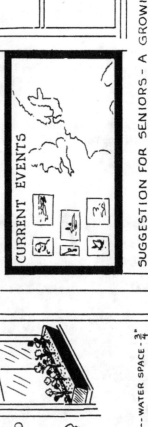

BULLETIN BOARD CAN BE MADE OF SUITABLE WALL-BOARD OR CORRUGATED CARD-BOARD.

CURRENT EVENTS

SUGGESTION FOR SENIORS - A GROWING MAP OF CURRENT EVENTS

FOR JUNIORS - HOW TO KEEP HEALTHY

(SPACES OTHERWISE UNUSED, SUCH AS THOSE BETWEEN WINDOWS AND CORNERS, CAN BE MADE INTO SATISFACTORY BULLETIN BOARDS.)

TEACHERS SHOULD SELECT SUCH BEAUTIFYING ACTIVITIES SUGGESTED ABOVE AS ARE FEASIBLE, AND AT THE TIME BEST SUITED TO THE LOCAL CONDITIONS

D. FARWELL

SCIENCE IN ACTION ~ SEPTEMBER

THE STARCH TEST:

A DROP OF IODINE IN A MIXTURE OF STARCH AND WATER WILL PRODUCE A DEEP BLUE COLOUR.

ON A FRESHLY-CUT PIECE OF GARDEN VEGETABLE, PUT A DROP OF IODINE. A BLUE COLOUR PROVES THE PRESENCE OF STARCH. TEST SEVERAL VEGETABLES.

OF WHAT VALUE IS STARCH IN THE DIET?

FROM FLOWER TO SEED:

THE LONG-FLOWERING PETUNIA PLANT WILL PROBABLY SHOW SEVERAL STAGES IN THIS DEVELOPMENT. CAREFULLY TAKE A FLOWER APART. A DISSECTING NEEDLE WILL HELP.

(LOOK UP THE NAMES AND LEARN THE USES OF THE VARIOUS PARTS)

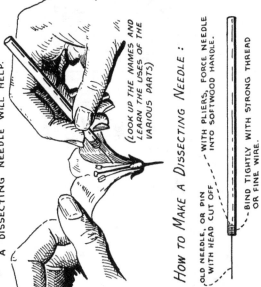

How to Make a Dissecting Needle:

OLD NEEDLE, OR PIN WITH HEAD CUT OFF — WITH PLIERS, FORCE NEEDLE INTO SOFTWOOD HANDLE.

BIND TIGHTLY WITH STRONG THREAD OR FINE WIRE.

AN OUTDOOR ACTIVITY:

COLLECT SEEDS OF MANY KINDS. CLASSIFY, AS TO THEIR WAY OF SPREADING, UNDER THE HEADINGS:

1. BY WIND
2. BY ANIMALS OR MAN
3. BY EXPLOSION
4. BY WATER

HERE ARE A FEW EXAMPLES:

BURDOCK (ANIMALS)

MILKWEED (WIND)

RAGWEED (WATER)

DANDELION (WIND)

WITCH HAZEL (EXPLOSION)

HOW IS EACH SEED FITTED FOR ITS PARTICULAR METHOD OF DISPERSAL?

FOR INSECT STUDY:

COLLECT CATERPILLARS AND PIECES OF THEIR FOOD PLANT. PUT THEM IN INSECT CAGES. WATCH THEM SPIN COCOONS OR FORM THEIR CHRYSALIDS.

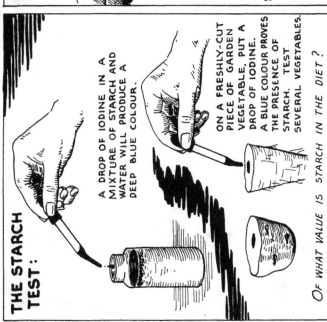

CHEESECLOTH OR NETTING
RUBBER BAND
LARGE BOTTLE WITH BOTTOM BROKEN OUT (OR LAMP CHIMNEY)
FOOD PLANT
SMALL BOTTLE OF WATER, SUNK IN SOIL
FLOWER POT

LARVA — CABBAGE BUTTERFLY — PUPA

LARVA — BLACK SWALLOWTAIL BUTTERFLY — PUPA

FRUIT PRESERVING:

USING SMALL JARS OR MAYONNAISE BOTTLES, TRY THE FOLLOWING EXPERIMENTS:

① RAW FRUIT IN SEALED JAR
② COOKED FRUIT IN SEALED JAR
③ COOKED FRUIT INCAPPED BUT UN-SEALED JAR
④ COOKED FRUIT IN OPEN JAR
⑤ COOKED FRUIT IN SEALED JAR, KEPT IN LIGHT AND WARMTH

PUT IN COOL, DARK PLACE

FOR THE PURPOSE OF THESE EXPERIMENTS, SEALING MAY BE DONE BY DIPPING THE TOP OF THE FILLED, CAPPED JAR IN MELTED PARAFFIN SEVERAL TIMES.

IN WHICH JAR DOES THE FRUIT KEEP BEST? WHY?

D. FARWELL

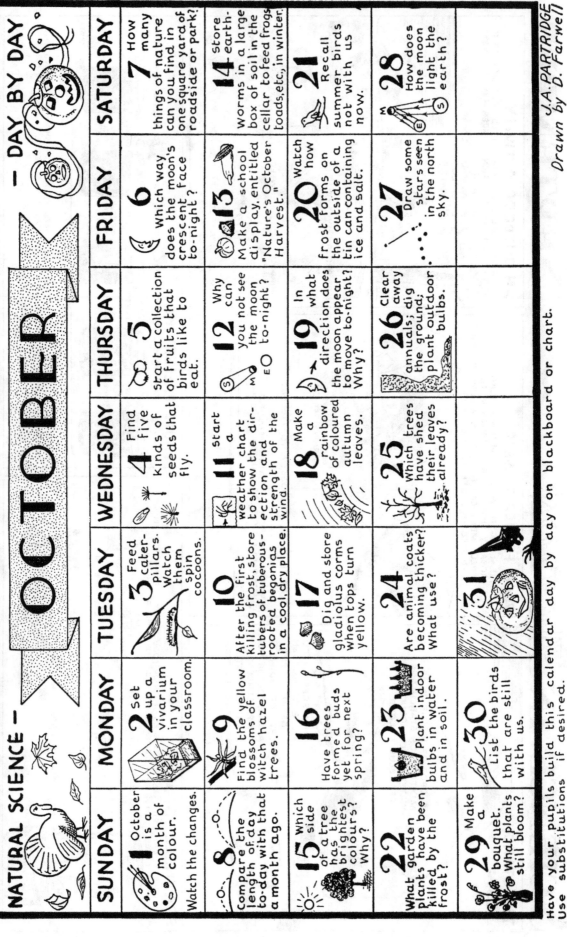

NATURAL SCIENCE — OCTOBER — DAY BY DAY

SUNDAY	MONDAY	TUESDAY	WEDNESDAY	THURSDAY	FRIDAY	SATURDAY
1 October is a month of colour. Watch the changes.	2 Set up a vivarium in your classroom.	3 Feed caterpillars. Watch them spin cocoons.	4 Find five kinds of seeds that fly.	5 Start a collection of fruits that birds like to eat.	6 Which way does the moon's crescent face to-night?	7 How many things of nature can you find in one square yard of roadside or park?
8 Compare the length of day to-day with that a month ago.	9 Find the yellow blossoms of witch hazel trees.	10 After the first killing frost, store tubers of tuberous-rooted begonias in a cool, dry place.	11 Start a weather chart to show the direction and strength of the wind.	12 Why can you not see the moon to-night?	13 Make a school display, entitled "Nature's October Harvest."	14 Store earthworms in a large box of soil in the cellar to feed frogs, toads, etc., in winter.
15 Which side of a tree has the brightest colours? Why?	16 Have trees formed buds yet for next spring?	17 Dig and store gladiolus corms when tops turn yellow.	18 Make a rainbow of coloured autumn leaves.	19 In what direction does the moon appear to move to-night? Why?	20 Watch how frost forms on the outside of a tin can containing ice and salt.	21 Recall summer birds not with us now.
22 What garden plants have been killed by the frost?	23 Plant indoor bulbs in water and in soil.	24 Are animal coats becoming thicker? What use?	25 Which trees have shed their leaves already?	26 Clear away annuals; dig the ground; plant outdoor bulbs.	27 Draw some stars seen in the north sky.	28 How does the moon light the earth?
29 Make a bouquet. What plants still bloom?	30 List the birds that are still with us.	31				

J.A. PARTRIDGE
Drawn by D. Farwell

Have your pupils build this calendar day by day on blackboard or chart.
Use substitutions if desired.

OCTOBER

Unit 13—Preparing to Beautify the School Grounds

"Oh, I should never want to go home if I went to this school!"

"Doesn't the smooth, green lawn in front of the school look pretty? And how interesting the frame of shrubbery looks around it!"

"I couldn't go to this school with dirty hands or face and without my lessons up, could you?"

Are the grounds around your school so beautiful that your pupils speak this way to each other?

"The human soul absorbs its environment." There is no time in our lives when this is more true than during the impressionable ages of our elementary school days. Since our boys and girls spend approximately one-third of their daylight hours at school, it is very important that all of us

Figure 1

who are directly concerned think carefully and act resolutely in determining the environment into which we invite or send them. Cary[1] says: "Children delight in the beautiful; they are educated by the beautiful and appropriate. The sense of the beautiful develops under favorable conditions and affects for good the whole attitude toward life. The love for the beautiful is necessary to the whole man." Surely, then, we should surround these citizens of tomorrow with the best environment possible, not only in the already beauty-conscious community, but even more especially in the more remote parts of Canada, where the lives of the parents, too, can be thus enriched. The task is one for all of us.

The effect of well-planted and attractive grounds, characterized by beauty, care, and order, upon the plastic minds of children will be evident throughout their lifetime. He who has spent his child-

hood days in beautiful surroundings will not later turn aside from campaigns for the beautification of parks and other public grounds. At the same time, beautiful school grounds awaken in students a deeper interest in nature in general. The benefits stand out all the more when the pupil himself has helped to plan, plants, and care for the grounds.

Figure 2

The two primary objects in planning to improve the school grounds should be: (a) instruction and (b) beauty and utility. The grounds should serve as an object lesson for the rest of the community, both in general ideas of planning and in details of plants used. Considerations of beauty and utility should dictate the arrangement of walks, drives, shrubbery, flowerbeds, and playing areas. Study figs., 1, and 2.

The key to success is the individual teacher. It will be through her influence upon the pupils, the parents, and the trustees that results of a lasting nature will be accomplished. Upon the interest, enthusiasm, and initiative of the teacher will depend the enthusiasm of the pupils. Pupil enthusiasm becomes parent enthusiasm, a nucleus for general community interest. This interest will deepen and broaden in proportion to the amount of community participation involved in the teacher's plan of procedure.

The strongest and most enduring factor in the whole plan is a community pride in the school's

---

[1] C. P. Cary, in *The School Beautiful*, State Department of Public Instruction, Madison, Wisconsin.

appearance, based upon a consciousness of the influence of beautiful school surroundings in molding the pupil's appreciation of, and desire for, beauty in all his surroundings. This pride may be increased by a campaign involving local or provincial competition, with awards as incentives toward worthwhile local improvements. Any movement based upon competition, however, must be accompanied by enough genuine interest to provide for adequate care and attention after the initial planning and planting. Failure in this respect will give the whole movement a serious setback and will hinder any future undertakings.

Plans for school-ground improvement must be made in the fall if the most returns for labor are to be obtained. Planning is easier in the fall because we can see then what shrubs and perennial and annual flowering plants look like when in full leaf, and know best where to use them on our grounds. Time is not so precious in the fall at school or at home as it is in the spring. It is easier, therefore, to get the necessary physical work done by pupils and by ratepayers.

Thorough preparation of the soil is absolutely essential for the best results, whether we plan to grow shrubs, perennial flowering plants, or annuals. This work is done not for one season, but for several. The digging should be done to a depth of 2 feet or more to provide the depth of good prepared soil for the roots of plants, and to reduce the need for later continuous watering. If the soil is clay, the addition of sandy loam will improve it; if it is sandy loam, clayey loam should be added. The addition of humus-providing materials such as well-decayed manure or decomposing leaves is advisable. If the soil of borders or beds is enriched and cultivated in the fall, frost action leaves it in a better condition for spring planting. Many shrubs and other perennial plants make earlier growth in the spring if they are transplanted to their permanent place in autumn.

In planning school-ground improvement, several factors must be taken into consideration. The extent of the project will be determined by the amount of money available, the number of pupils present to do the work, and the provision that can be made for upkeep thereafter. If some previous plan has been carried out, unnecessary changes should be avoided. Every school should have a lawn in front, but not too large for the pupils to keep it mowed. To join the lawn or playground with the building, a foundation planting of shrubs should be planned. Flowerbeds, both perennial and annual, should be provided for in sunny places. A hedge may be found advisable to separate the lawn from the playground. The plan should be drawn up in fall.

Some Ontario sources of help in making school-ground plans are: Superintendent of Horticultural Societies Branch, Parliament Buildings, Toronto; Department of Horticulture, Ontario Agricultural College, Guelph; the local County Agricultural Representative; Ontario Forestry Branch, Parliament Buildings, Toronto. Other provinces and states have similar institutions. Local units of Women's Institutes, Home and School and Parent-Teacher Associations, and Horticultural Societies may also help to plan and finance school-ground beautification.

Activities

The Teacher

1. Make up your mind that you are going to enter upon a definite plan of beautification.
2. Organize a "Clean-up" campaign. Clear away all loose stones, sticks, papers, dead plants, weeds, and other unsightly or undesirable objects.
3. Visit a home or school which has been attractively landscaped. Ask parents to assist in transportation, thereby creating in them an interest in your project.

4. With the pupils make a survey of present conditions of the grounds of the school and of possible improvements. Are there shrubs that have grown too close together and require separating? Do you enter the school between or alongside tastefully arranged flower beds? Are the foundation walls and the corners of the buildings pleasingly joined to the surrounding grounds by means of well-chosen shrubs? Are there unsightly fences or outbuildings which might well be screened by climbers or shrubs?

5. Write to a nursery or other source of help asking for a suggested plan, including names, placement, and prices of suitable shrubs for the front and sides of the school. Enclose a sketch of the school and grounds, showing to scale, through measurements made with the pupils, the dimensions and cardinal directions of the grounds; positions and dimensions of buildings, porches, pump, walks, and gates; the position and height of windows (to enable selection of shrubs of proper height); position and kinds of present trees and shrubs. Mention the nature of the soil. Ask for the usual discount.

6. Approach your trustees with a plan for the project; describe the grants which will finance the project.

7. Discuss with them plans for holding a community "bee" to prepare the grounds for spring planting.

8. Have the pupils write and deliver personal invitations to all ratepayers to join the "bee" on a given afternoon. The pupils will bring back a reply.

9. Ask a trustee to plan for the bringing of the necessary implements, such as plows, scraper, wagons, pickaxes, and shovels, and to direct activities at the "bee" in accordance with the plan.

The "Bee." It is important that all useless soil, cinders, gravel, stones, twitch grass, and other undesirable materials be entirely removed from the place to be planted. Refill the space with carefully selected, fertile loam, leaving a depth of at least 10 inches of well-cultivated soil. Allow for later settling. Be sure that the border around the school follows the plan accurately and to a liberal width. A load of well-rotted manure mixed in will help. Leave the area in a rough condition for beneficial frost action in winter. A row of edging stones, large enough to project a few inches above the ground when settled into place, will help to retain the proper curves as planned and to protect the planted area from tramping. Have prospective flower beds and lawn areas fertilized and either plowed or spaded this autumn. This should complete the autumn work, since it is probably wise to leave all planting until spring. See Units 73 (page 304), 82 (page 339), and 83 (page 342).

Junior and Intermediate Grades

- Measure the garden, grounds, flowerbeds, paths, etc., of your schoolyard; draw them to scale and color them. Then draw plans of what you would like the grounds to look like. In a class period, discuss these plans, select the best ones, and from them make one final plan.

- Do not prune shrubs or roses or cultivate around them or perennials this late. New growth, thus encouraged, will be too tender to survive the winter.

- Plant bulbs among shrubs or in formal rows or beds.

- After the ground has frozen, cover tender perennials with brush, evergreen boughs, straw, manure, or leaves to keep the ground from alternate freezing and thawing in early spring.

- Rake up leaves and other plant remains from the ground; bury or burn them (fig 5).

- Transplant seedling perennials from seedbeds to growing areas early enough for the roots to be well established before freezing.

Figure 5—Use Paper Cutting to Make a Mural Like This

Grass, green; flame (torn) and leaves, orange, red, and yellow; figures, bright-colored.

- Move peonies now. Prepare the soil well. Divide the roots so that each part has three or four buds. Plant with 3 inches of soil above them. Do not let manure touch the roots. Mulch for winter with leaves or straw.
- Divide and move iris and other perennial plants. Cover them very shallowly and avoid manure entirely.
- Survey the lawn for thin places or new areas to be seeded. Seed as early in September as possible. Be sure that all weeds are removed and the soil thoroughly loosened in the thin places. Use only a good quality of lawn mixture. Do not prune shrubs or roses or cultivate them or perennials this late. New growth, thus encouraged, will be too tender to survive the winter.
- Plant bulbs among shrubs or in formal rows or beds.
- After the ground has frozen, cover tender perennials with brush, evergreen boughs, straw, manure, or leaves to keep the ground from alternate freezing and thawing in early spring.

Read

Biles, *The Modern Family Garden Book* (Teacher). Longmans, Green (Ferguson & Associates).
Comstock, *Handbook of Nature Study,* pp. 546-554. Allen (Comstock).
Goldsmith, *Picture Primer of Dooryard Gardening.* Allen (Houghton Mifflin).
Gould, *Very First Garden* (grades 5 and up). Oxford.
Partridge, *General Science,* Intermediate, Book 1: "Planning Attractive Grounds," pp. 58-66, and "Planning Attractive Gardens," pp. 399-406. Dent.

New to this Edition

Dannenmaier, Molly. *A Child's Garden: 60 Ideas to Make Any Garden Come Alive for Children* (Timber Books, 2008).
Moore, Robin. *Plants for Play: A Plant Selection Guide for Children's Outdoor Environments* (Mig Communications, 1993).
Nagro, Anne. *Our Generous Garden* (Dancing Rhinoceros Press, 2008).
Tai, Hague, McLellan, and Knight. *Designing Outdoor Environments for Children: Landscaping School Yards, Gardens and Playgrounds* (McGraw Hill, 2006).

Unit 14—Making a Suitable Soil Mixture

A suitable mixture of soil for bulbs and for plants in pots or window boxes should be available at any school where plants are grown to beautify the surroundings. Usually the soil of the garden has not sufficient humus or fertility, and is too clayey or sandy. Much discouragement comes both to teachers and pupils when they attempt to grow beautiful plants in poor soil.

Potting soils must hold the plant in place, absorb and retain sufficient moisture for it, provide it with nourishing plant foods, and admit air freely. To anchor the plant, the soil must be firm; to take in water freely, it must have enough sand and humus to be porous on the top; to retain sufficient moisture, it must have the right proportion of fine particles (clay) and a goodly supply of humus; for fertility, it requires humus, manure, or other fertilizers; to admit air freely, it must let water out freely: sand helps in this respect.

Soil with these characteristics can be made from good garden loam by adding to it one-quarter to one-third as much well-rotted and well-pulverized manure, and about one-eighth as much sharp sand. The loam may be improved with the addition of leaf-mold from under trees, or of well-decayed sods. All parts should be thoroughly mixed, and the lumps crushed. The mixture may be sifted with a coarse screen (not finer than one-quarter-inch mesh) to remove trash and stones. Finer screens take out decayed vegetable matter and fiber, but they may be used to prepare fine soil for seed flats. The fertility of the soil may be later increased by judicious use of fertilizers.

The soil requirement for some plants may differ somewhat. For begonias and ferns, a larger proportion of leaf-mold and sand is advisable; some peat moss also improves it. For geraniums, a heavier, firmer soil, containing a larger proportion of clay, and little or no sand, is best. Soil for indoor bulbs is discussed in Unit 15 (page 60).

An excellent soil mixture ready for use in a year or two may be made by preparing a *compost heap* in an out-of-the-way corner of the schoolyard. It consists of leaves, sods, garden refuse, manure mixed with garden loam and left to decay. Pile the leaves, garden refuse, and soil compactly in layers alternating with layers of manure. Sods from rich, mellow loam may be piled, face down, alternating with the manure. To induce decay, and thus liberate plant foods, the pile should be kept moist. Water is retained best if the top of the pile is flat, or if it slopes inward. Mix the materials thoroughly once a month or so to ensure good aeration, bacterial action, and therefore decay. When well rotted, this soil mixture will be useful for potting plants or top-dressing lawns, flower-beds, or shrubs.

A compost without sod may provide potting soil ready for use in a few months. For this, strip off a thin layer of sod and use the next 3 inches of fibrous loam; pile 6-inch layers of this soil alternately with 3-inch layers of cow manure, leaving the top of the pile flat. Punch holes down through the pile so that water may enter freely. Chop and mix the pile thoroughly after a month or two.

Activities

All Grades

- Visit a wood and observe how leaves over a period of years become more and more decayed until they form leaf-mold. Notice how moist and loose the mixture is. Bring a basketful to your classroom to be used in vivaria and in preparing potting soil.
- Fill one flowerpot with garden loam and another with half garden loam and half leaf-mold. Pour a pint of water into each; catch what goes through, decide which mixture absorbs water better, which mixture holds more water, and which mixture remains moist longer.
- Fill one pot with garden loam packed firmly and another one with garden loam into which one-quarter as much sand has been mixed, also packed firmly. Add water as above to discover how sand affects the entrance and passage of water through soil.
- Fill one pot with clay soil, a similar one with sandy soil, and another with garden soil and leaf-mold. Pack and water the soil in each. Which soil becomes hardest on the surface? Which soaks in water most easily when watered the next time?
- Grow young plants in soils prepared as described in this unit, and in other soils taken from the garden. Draw your own conclusions.

Read

New to this Edition

Bial, Ramond. *A Handful of Dirt* (Walker Childrens, 2000).
Rosinsky, Boyd, and Sheree. *Dirt: The Scoop on Soil* (Amazing Science), (Picture Window Books, 2006),

Figure 1—Compost heap.

Unit 15—Planting Bulbs Indoors and Out

The present trend in the teaching of natural science is toward school experiences that are of immediate interest to the pupils and that will fit them for the everyday problems of later life. All activities connected with planting and caring for flowering bulbs are both interesting and instructive to pupils. The observation of their growth naturally raises many problems, the solution of which will be of real educational value. The knowledge gained will, of course, serve a useful purpose in the pupils' homes. But probably the greatest benefit comes from the development of desirable pupil attitudes toward, and appreciation of, beauty in all plant life.

Growing Bulbs Indoors

General Principles of Bulb Culture. Buy only the best grades of bulbs obtainable from reliable firms. Quality is determined by size, firmness, and freedom from disease. To obtain the best bloom from even the best bulbs, the culture demands a correct soil mixture, a cool place without light for a period of at least six weeks, and a gradual change to warmer and lighter conditions.

Planting of Bulbs

1. *Time.* From September until Christmas gives good results for most bulbs.
2. *Vessels.* Thoroughly washed flowerpots, preferably unglazed; window boxes; deep pans with drainage holes. A 4- or 5-inch pot will hold one large or three small hyacinths, three to four tulips, six to eight crocuses, or about three narcissi, daffodils, or jonquils. A 6- or 7-inch pot will hold five or six tulips, or four or five narcissi or daffodils.
3. *Drainage.* This is essential to keep the soil sweet. In addition to the holes in the container, there should be a bottom layer of broken pottery, cinders, charcoal, broken brick, or stones.
4. *Soil.* For general use, mix two parts of good garden loam with about one part of thoroughly decayed manure or compost, and add enough sharp sand to make the mixture loose and porous. Bone meal may be substituted for the manure in the proportion of one pound to one bushel of soil.
5. *Planting Steps.* Place the layer of drainage materials in the container. Fill it with soil, loosely shaken down, leaving a space equal to the height of the bulbs. Do not press the soil as there must be adequate air space for root development. Place the bulbs as desired, without pushing them down. Cover with soil until the tips of the bulbs are just visible when the soil is gently pressed around them. There should be about three-fourths of an inch of watering space left above the soil. Soak the soil thoroughly; let the pots drain and place them in storage (figs. 1 and 3).

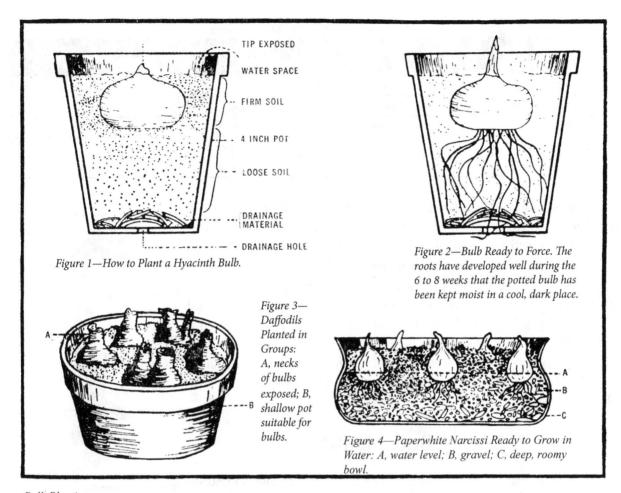

Figure 1—*How to Plant a Hyacinth Bulb.*

TIP EXPOSED
WATER SPACE
FIRM SOIL
4 INCH POT
LOOSE SOIL
DRAINAGE MATERIAL
DRAINAGE HOLE

Figure 2—*Bulb Ready to Force. The roots have developed well during the 6 to 8 weeks that the potted bulb has been kept moist in a cool, dark place.*

Figure 3—*Daffodils Planted in Groups: A, necks of bulbs exposed; B, shallow pot suitable for bulbs.*

Figure 4—*Paperwhite Narcissi Ready to Grow in Water: A, water level; B, gravel; C, deep, roomy bowl.*

Bulb Planting

Care During the Period of Root Development. (1) *Indoor Method.* The essential conditions are moderate moisture, coolness (preferably about 40° Fahrenheit), and sufficient ventilation to prevent mold. Select a cool spot in the cellar. Exclude light by covering the windows or pots. Keep the soil merely moist. Leave until the roots are visible through the bottom of the pots, and as long thereafter as your requirements for bloom demand (fig. 2). (b) *Outdoor Method.* Dig a trench in the garden about one foot deep. Place the pots in this trench on a layer of coal or ashes. Invert an empty pot or box over them to protect the young shoots. Leave for 8 to 12 weeks, or until spring. Transfer the pots, as required, to partial darkness in a cool place in the school.

Forcing. Gradually transfer the pots from the trench or cellar to lighter and warmer places for the growth of leaves and bloom. A temperature of 60° to 70° Fahrenheit is best for good flower development. Keep the flowers well watered. To prolong the period of bloom, place the opened flowers in a cooler room or cellar overnight.

Growing Bulbs in Water (fig. 4). Paperwhite narcissus and Chinese sacred lily are most satisfactory for this method. Fill a shallow dish about half full of stones or pebbles. Arrange the bulbs as desired, and anchor them well with pebbles. Put in enough water so that the lower third of each bulb is immersed. Leave in a cool, dark place for good root development, or to delay bloom.

Planning Table for Indoor Bulb Growing			
Name	Time in Cool, Dark Place	Time Required to "Force to Bloom	Duration of Bloom
Chinese Sacred Lily	8-15 weeks	5 weeks	3 weeks
Paperwhite Narcissus	2 weeks	6 weeks	3 weeks
Daffodils, Narcissus	0-6 weeks	4-6 weeks	2 weeks
Dutch and Roman Hyacinths	7-15 weeks	5-6 weeks	2 weeks
Lily of the Valley	0-2 weeks	2-5 weeks	2 weeks

Special Suggestions. Keep *hyacinth* bulb tips well above the soil level to avoid decay. Plant *amaryllis* bulbs in as small a pot as convenient; use rich soil; embed only about one-third of the bulb; keep merely moist in the classroom until growth starts; then water freely.

Try growing some *lily of the valley* indoors. The *pips* must be frozen about one week or they will not bloom. Purchased ones are treated before being sold. Start them in a very warm room in the dark and bring them to light when they have developed a few inches of top. Water them very freely. *Freesias* and *paperwhite narcissi* should not be frozen. The leaves and flowers of the former should be supported by stakes and strings.

Figure 5—Amaryllis

Growing Bulbs Outdoors

Bulbs for spring bloom in the school garden or border should be planted in October. A summary of necessary information follows:

1. Suggested *kinds* of bulbs: tulips, daffodils, hyacinths, and crocuses. The cost may limit you to the first two.
2. *Soil.* Dig deeply and fertilize with well-rotted manure or bone meal. Raise the level of the bed above the surroundings to provide drainage. Sandy loam is best. Place a layer of sand around bulbs planted in clay soil.
3. *Arrangements.* Clumps of four to six bulbs give pleasing showings. Plant throughout the perennial border with the taller varieties at the back. Early and late varieties, properly distributed, will lengthen the period of bloom.
4. *Depths and distances.* Consult bulb catalogues for particulars. Tulips, daffodils, and narcissi may remain in the ground from year to year. If this is planned, they should be planted to a depth of 7 or 8 inches so that cultivation may take place above them. They should be lifted every 3 or 4 years and separated.
5. *Protection.* Cover the planted area with coarse straw, manure, leaves, or plant remains, after the ground has frozen. This covering should be removed gradually in spring.
6. *Lawns.* Lift bits of sod here and there and insert crocus, scilla, or snowdrop bulbs singly. Replace the sod again. Leave these undisturbed from year to year.
7. *Maturing.* Remove the seed pods that form after the flowers. Do not cut away the foliage until it starts to die. It must be given time to produce plant food to be stored in the bulb for the growth of the following spring.

Bulb-growing activities should be graded so that pupils do not repeat the same experiences year after year. Primary grades might well plant and care for paperwhite narcissi in water, and tulips singly in soil. This provides for pride in individual ownership. They can learn to recognize these when in bloom. Primary pupils cannot appreciate the extra beauty of groups of bulbs, or the differences in the bulbs themselves, or adaptations for growth. Junior pupils may add to these activities group planting in soil and some outdoor planting. They can use other kinds of bulbs. Activities for intermediate pupils should extend their experiences to include other bulbs, group planting in pots and window boxes, formal and informal outdoor planting, recognition of common bulbs by shape and size, and some understanding of how bulbs are fitted to bloom (Unit 56, page 236).

The purchase of bulbs may be financed by Agriculture funds, school or class funds, or by selling bulbs when in bloom to pay the original cost.

Activities

Teacher

- Store a few paperwhite narcissi bulbs in a cool place to be used for later study of the adaptation of bulbs for rapid growth and early blooming (Unit 56, page 236).
- Time the forcing of bulbs to have them ready for the winter flower show (Unit 57, page 238).
- Assign to individual pupils or groups the responsibility for watering, forcing, and displaying bulbs planted as a class project.

All Grades

- Read stories about bulb-growing in Holland.
- Visit greenhouses where bulbs are grown for the sale of the flowers.
- Observe the changes of the color of the foliage of bulbs after they have been brought from darkness to light.
- Plant paperwhite narcissi about November 1 to have them in bloom for Christmas.

Primary Grades

- In a little notebook, make a drawing of your bulb from time to time as it grows.
- Draw a pot or bowl; then make and paste on it (as if growing there) paper cutouts of tulips in bloom.

Junior and Intermediate Grades

Check out gradening catalogs and online sources to select the kinds and numbers that your finances will permit and place your order for the bulbs.

Manure, spade, and level an outdoor plot, and plant tulips in a formal design. Plant daffodils in groups of four or five, the bulbs 3 or 4 inches apart, at a depth of about 6 or 8 inches in open spaces among perennials or shrubs. When the ground has frozen, cover these with garden refuse or manure.

With watercolors, paint on a vertical rectangle about an inch wide a color scale— yellow at the top, gradually changing to green at the bottom. In the morning place a potted bulb with yellow foliage in the sunlight, and at each hour of the day find the part on the scale that is the same color as the leaves, and write the time there. This scale will later show you how rapidly light developed the green color in the leaves.

Read

Comstock, *Handbook of Nature-Study*, pp. 547-555. Allen (Comstock).

Frasier et al., *Through the Year* (grades 2-3): "The Story of a Bulb," pp. 54-57; *Winter Comes and Goes* (grades 3-4): "Susan's Bulbs," pp. 136-138. Dent (Singer). Partridge, *General Science*, Intermediate, Book 1: "Planting Bulbs," pp. 64-70. Dent.

New to this Edition

McGowan, Brian and Alice. *Bulbs in the Basement, Geraniums on the Windowsill: How to Grow and Overwinter 165 Tender Plants* (Storey Publishing, LLC, 2008).

Phillips, Roger. *The Random House Book of Bulbs* (Random House, 1989).

Peterson, Deborah. *Don't Throw It, Grow It!: 68 windowsill plants from kitchen scraps.* (Storey Publishing LLC, 2008).

http://www.kidsgardening.org/node/12167

http://www.canadiangardening.com/how-to/gardening-with-kids/kids-and-bulbs/a/1381

Figure 6—Amaryllis bulbs in a window sill.

Unit 16—Let's Play Nature Games

Everyone loves a game, for to play is instinctive. Nature games deepen the interests of the pupils in the things they play with. It remains, therefore, to choose a nature game which is appropriate to the nature knowledge at hand. Then it should not only deepen the pupils' nature impressions, but should lead them to make new contacts with nature. Nature games must not be allowed to become an end in themselves; they are a means to an end. Nature games are not a substitute for nature study; they are a part of it.

For nature games as for all others, the directions must be clearly understood by the players. They must not be too difficult for the nature knowledge of the group; otherwise the difficulty in learning or applying the rules of the game will take the pupils' attention from the nature experiences which it is planned to make more impressive. Games should not only grow out of and make use of nature experiences; they should lead to new nature ventures.

Nature games bring the teacher and pupils in closer association with each other. The cooperative spirit developed as the teacher enters wholeheartedly into the game leads to a better spirit of cooperation of pupils and teacher in the next nature investigations.

Thus, the tests of the value of a nature game are: Does it teach nature? Does it develop the pupil mentally, socially, morally, and physically? Do the pupils enjoy it enough to call for it again?

Figure 1—A Nature Quiz-Test (Drawings by Ellsworth Jaeger)

1. Is the skunk a member of the weasel family, the cat family, or the rodent family? 2. What animal makes mud pies? 3. Are there animals found in the United States that can exist without drinking? 4. What bird is a ventriloquist? 5. Can mice climb trees? 6. Is there an American reptile that shoots blood from its eyes? 7. What bird makes a Christmas stocking nest? 8. Do snakes have scent? 9. Do ants make scent trails? 10. Are owl eggs round or egg-shaped?

Answers

1. The weasel family. 2. Beavers make mud patties and place beaver scent upon them for matrimonial advertising. 3. Yes, the desert pocket mouse. 4. The barred owl. 5. Yes, the common deer mouse is a tree-climber. 6. Yes, the horned toad. 7. The Baltimore oriole. 8. Yes, they use scent to discourage enemies and in courtship. 9. Yes, they give off formic acid as they travel about. 10. Egg-shaped.

65

Activities

Primary and Junior Grades[1]

Nature Stunts
1. Throw a leaf as far as possible without breaking it.
2. Imitate the call of any bird or animal.
3. Make poems after being given the words which rhyme, e.g., rabbit, habit, white, flight.
4. Hop like a grasshopper. Other characteristic movements will be thought of, either by the pupils or by the teacher.
5. Make impromptu speeches on nature subjects.

Nature Relay. Each child gathers a leaf which he will name and show to his fellow pupils. When each pupil has seen and named all the leaves gathered, the leader divides the class into groups, arranges the pupils in each group behind each other, and places the leaves in piles in front of each line. At a signal the first player in each group runs forward, picks up a leaf, names it, goes back to his place, and starts the leaf "over and under" down the row. The last player runs with the leaf to the front, places it in a discard box, takes a new leaf, names it, takes his place in front of the row, and starts the new leaf on its "over and under" journey. This game may also be played with flowers, weeds, nuts, fruits, etc.

Tree Jerusalem. On a tree hike the leader shouts the name of a tree. The players run to find this tree and stand beside it, only one player to a tree. Those finding the tree in the allotted time get a grain of corn. Count the grains at the end of the hike.

Nature Sounds. This is a quiet game for a hike to the woods. Give the group 5 minutes to make a list of all the things heard in the woods during that time. It may be a raindrop, a crow, the rustling of leaves, the tapping of a woodpecker, or the sound of the brook. Who has the longest list of sounds?

I Am Thinking. A child chooses the name of a fruit and says to the group, "I am thinking of a fruit." Members of the group say, "Is it _____?" until the right answer is given. (Animals and vegetables may be substituted for fruits, or the game may be varied by having the beginning sound of the word given.)

Saw. Tell me one thing you saw on the farm.

Tell me three things your mother saw in the garden.

Tell me two things I saw at the market.

Tell me four things your father saw in the vegetable store.

Tell me five things you saw in the schoolyard.

(Always stress the giving of answers in complete sentences.)

If I Were. Question: Tell me what you would do if you were a farmer.

Answer: If I were a farmer, I would _____.

Question: Tell me what you would do if you were a cow.

Answer: If I were a cow, I would _____.

Flash. Pictures of nature objects—birds, trees, insects, etc. —are mounted on large cards. The teacher shows these pictures one at a time for a short while. Names of the objects in the pictures are written down by the pupils. Pupils are given points for the number of correct answers. The row totaling the most wins.

Who Am I? Cards may be made by the pupils of the class with the aid of the teacher. For example, a card may read:

---

1 *Classroom Teacher,* Vol. 5

1. My home is made in a pond.
2. The members of my family are known as carpenters and engineers.
3. My fur is very valuable.
4. I swim very well.
5. People know I am always very busy. (The Beaver).

These cards may be used individually or by the class as a whole. Cards may be made for insects, birds, animals, trees, flowers.

Flower, Fruit, or Vegetable Game. This game is played very much like "spin the platter." All the pupils sit on the floor in a circle, with the leader in the center. The leader starts the game by pointing to someone in the ring, and saying quickly, "Flower! 1, 2, 3, 4, 5, 6, 7, 8, 9, 10." If the boy or girl who was pointed to names a flower before the leader finishes counting to ten, then he takes the leader's place in the center. The leader may call for a flower, for a fruit, or for a vegetable, but no player can use the flower, fruit, or vegetable that has already been named. Something new must be mentioned each time.

It Is I. A child is blindfolded and seated in the front of the room. Another child slips up behind him and gives the sound some animal makes on the farm, such as, "Moo-moo." He says, "Who is speaking?" The answer is, "It is I." The one who is guessing stays in the chair as long as he guesses correctly. When he makes a mistake, the one who spoke to him takes his place.

Squirrels in Trees. "The players stand in groups of three. Two players join hands, holding them high to form a tree, while the third player, representing a squirrel, stands or squats inside the tree. An odd squirrel stands near the center of them all. The leader gives a signal for all the squirrels to change places. The odd squirrel tries to get a tree, and the one who is left out is the odd squirrel for the next time. Frequently a part of the players who are trees should change with the squirrels so that all get a chance to be squirrels."

Junior and Intermediate Grades

I Want and I Spy. The group starts out with a leader. When an appropriate place is reached, he calls out, "I want shagbark hickory" (or some other tree, flower, bird, etc.).

Some member of the group must then call out, "I spy," pointing to the tree believed to be a shagbark hickory. If he is correct, points are awarded; otherwise a debit is marked. No second credit to anyone else is given. The winner of that tree is given further credit if the reason for identification is given; otherwise, some other member of the group has this opportunity.

This game may be played in one place for quite a time. Errors help to intensify the interest.

Hide and I Seek. This is a game which may be played while out on a hike. When at an appropriate place the leader calls, "Hide," every member of the group goes to a tree or a flower, as the case may be, and stands beside it. The leader goes to each member saying, "I seek." The answer given must be the name of the tree or other object which the pupil is standing beside. If the answer is correct, credit is given. If there is an error, a debit is given. Additional points are given for the basis of identification. A different nature object must be chosen each time.

Spelling Bees (adaptation). Divide the class into groups. Use flowers, insects, or other objects of nature. Hold up a flower. The first in line must name it and give an interesting fact about it. If he fails, he drops out of the line. Start with the most common flowers or other objects.

Pinecone Baseball. Use a pinecone instead of a baseball. The pitcher throws the cone at the batter. If the cone hits the batter, a "strike" is made. If not, it is a "ball." Count strikes and balls as in baseball. The batter may hit the cone. If it is a fair hit he becomes a base runner. Runners may be put out between bases by being hit with the cone in play. Players cannot run with cones. The batter may catch the cone and throw it into the field.

Nature Sayings Contest. Fill in the blanks with the missing words. This in an indoor game.

As _____ as a bee (busy)

As _____ as an owl (wise)

As _____ as a bat (blind)

As _____ as a loon (crazy)

As _____ as a peacock (proud)

As _____ as a mouse (quiet)

As _____ as a crow (black)

As _____ as a hornet (mad)

Violet. Each space below may be filled with a word formed from the letters in the word "Violet."

_____ me now narrate to you the story of a _____ so true,

A youth named _____ once did dwell; his daily _____ he did full well,

No _____ ways had he, forsooth, he was indeed a model youth.

To win a maiden he did try, with others eagerly did _____

Alas the light of hope grew dim, the tender _____ was not for him.

He lost the maid he loved so well, and this is how that _____ befell,

Quoth she: "Look you with favoring mind upon the _____ for womenkind?"

"No," he replied, "I tell you flat I never fail to _____ that."

So ended the romance brief; instead of joy he found but grief.

Adapted from Better Homes and Gardens Magazine

Answers to "Violet." 1. let; 2. love; 3. Levi; 4. toil; 5. evil; 6. vie; 7. tie; 8. it; 9. vote; 10. veto.

Memory Race. This is a good game for a rest period during a hike. Line up two sides sitting on either side of the road. The leader says, "This afternoon I saw a red oak leaf." The player for a given side says, "This afternoon I saw a red oak leaf and an American elm leaf." A player in the second group selected by the leader says, "This afternoon I saw a red oak leaf, and an American elm leaf, and a Baltimore Oriole." Each time a player succeeds in renaming correctly all the things mentioned, he gets a point for his side. The leader should start with the poorest players because the game grows in difficulty.

Nature Alphabet. The entire group decides upon the class of nature things to be used—such as trees, birds, flowers, animals, etc. The leader then names a letter of the alphabet, e.g., *h.* Each player or each group, as the case may be, then names a member of the nature class decided upon (flowers), beginning with that letter (hollyhock). Anyone failing to do so in 5 seconds is out, or the first group to name an object belonging to that class wins a point. The group having the greatest number of points at the end of a given time is the winner.

Read

New to this Edition

Leslie, Clare. *The Nature Connection: An Outdoor Workbook for Kids, Families, and Classrooms* (Storey Publishing LLC, 2010).
http://www.outdoor-nature-child.com
http://wilderdom.com/games/EnvironmentalActivities.html

Unit 17—Enjoying Autumn Colors

October is a month of color. Leaves and shrubs are turning from green to brilliant shades of orange and red. In sunny places, autumn wildflowers array themselves in yellow, blue, and white. The fleshy fruits of trees and shrubs, of wildflowers, even of garden vegetables, add to the colorful scene. The greens of shaded spots, of sun-bathed trees, of grasses waving in the breeze, provide a fitting background for this pageant of color. Most of us, both teachers and pupils, could, if we would, enjoy more fully this canvas of nature stretched over hill and vale. To do so, all we require is knowledge of what to look for, where to look, and how to look, and then some practice in looking. Let us, then, with our pupils, go forth with observant eyes and colored pencils and enjoy the year's best color display.

All around us, in grassy fields, in open woods, and by the roadside, wildflowers greet us. The asters vie with the goldenrods for first place. They range in colors from the dark purple of the tall, stout New England aster of moist places to the lovely violet-blue of the smooth aster of dry, open places, and the many kinds of white-flowered asters. The goldenrods display their gold from July until the frost kills them. Elsewhere we find the lacy foliage and yellow flowers of butter-and-eggs, and white patches of bouncing bet. In damp woods the witch hazel shrub displays its bright yellow flowers in autumn. In swampy places the purple bonset (Joe-pye weed, named after the Indian chief, Joe Pye, who used it for medicine) displays its showy flat-topped clusters of tiny, rose-purple flowers. In quiet lakes or ponds the white water lilies still float at anchor.

Trees and shrubs reach their peak of glory in October. Probably no phase of nature attracts our attention so frequently in October, and in few places is there such a wealth of autumn tints as in Ontario. In primary and junior grades work will be limited to observational studies and varied records. Intermediate grades may well become interested in learning the conditions which bring about various autumn colors.

To make green color, leaves require light, warmth, and certain minerals. Present with the green is always yellow color, invisible because it is overshadowed by the green. But leaf green is temporary and is constantly being lost from leaves. When grass is covered by a board, there is no new green color made to replace what is being lost. In autumn when the days are shorter, cooler, and more hazy, not enough leaf green is made in most leaves to replace what is lost. Therefore they appear yellow.

Red color is commonly formed on the south side of maple trees, for there the sun is brightest. Because only certain trees become red, we believe that the kind of sap in them must help to form the red color, while the sap in other leaves, such as those of bramble bushes and pear trees, causes them to become purple in autumn. When yellow and red colors are both present in the same place, the leaf or a part of it appears orange. When the leaf dies, it sometimes becomes brown (oaks).

Activities

Teacher

Display pictures of the following wildflowers: asters, goldenrod, thistles, milkweeds, butter-and-eggs, cone flower, yarrow, tansy, bergamot, evening primrose, chicory, wild carrot, buttercups. Then have the children find and bring some blossoms of them to school. Place some of each kind in separate bottles of water and label them. When pupils have learned them by sight, play identification games such as: (1) replacing the labels after they have been removed, (2) giving an oral description of a flower while others name it.

All Grades

- Have an aster show. Make and display bouquets showing as many kinds of wild asters as you can find. They may be picked freely, and will keep well in water.
- In a swampy place find dogwoods and willows which have red and yellow branches. Notice their beauty where they grow. Then place some in water in the classroom. Will their buds open?
- Find two kinds of goldenrod—one with the flowers clustered mostly on top of the stem, and another with smaller clusters of yellow flowers where each leaf joins the stem.
- On the bulletin board mount leaves so that they spell out "Autumn Colors." Begin with green, add new colors as they develop, and end with yellows, reds, and browns.
- Make such charts of mounted colored leaves as: varieties of maples, yellow leaves, mottled leaves, the stages through which oaks change from green to brown. Label the name on each leaf.
- Make collections of leaves showing chiefly yellow colors, chiefly red colors, shades of violet colors, chiefly brown colors. Try to name each kind collected.
- Rule a page in six columns headed: Green, Yellow, Red, Purple, Orange, Brown. As autumn passes, list in each the names of trees or shrubs which remain or change to that color at least in part.

Primary Grades

- Make a blackboard display entitled "A Maple Tree's New Dresses." While a tree near the school window is still green, have pupils trace and cut out maple leaves from green paper, and place them on a drawing made on a large card to form the shape of the tree. Look at the tree each day. When it appears in a differently colored dress, pupils will trace and cut out more leaves from paper of the correct color, add crayon where necessary, and paste these on a new drawing bearing a new date. Repeat this from day to day until the tree is bare. Note: The colored leaves themselves may be pressed, waxed, and mounted for this purpose.
- Each pupil bring to school the prettiest leaf he can find, the reddest, the yellowest, the brightest. Mount them on large drawings of trees to make red trees and yellow trees.
- Gather maple leaves showing all the colors possible—starting with green.
- Collect and press colored leaves, then use them to make decorative designs. Trace them, then color the outlines with crayons.

- Display autumn fruits of various colors in the classroom. Model some with Plasticine or clay—then paint them.
- Make a sand-table reproduction of a rural scene showing a beautiful display of autumn colors.

Junior and Intermediate Grades

- Compare the colors of leaves on the shady and on the sunny side of a maple tree. Compare the colors of two leaves on the same tree, one leaf of which overlaps and shades the other. Try to discover what effect, if any, bright sunlight has on autumn colors.
- Make a border design of pressed, colored leaves on the top of the blackboard.
- Make individual booklets with such titles as "My Book of Autumn Colors." Decorate the covers appropriately. For a month or so, place in it clippings, autumn pictures, drawings, little stories, and records of personal observations.

Read

Frasier et al., *Winter Comes and Goes* (grades 3-4): "Leaves in Autumn," pp. 36-37. Dent (Singer).
Hunt & Andrews, *Summer and Fall Wild Flowers.* Moyer.
Kieran, *An Introduction to Wild Flowers.* Blue Ribbon (Hanover House).
Peterson, *Wildlife in Color.* Allen (Houghton Mifflin).

New to this Edition

Elhert, Lois. *Red Leaf, Yellow Leaf* (Harcourt Children's Books, 1991).
Fowler, Allan. *H.D.Y.K. It's Fall? Pbk (Rookie Read-About Science)*, (Children's Press, 1992).
Maestro, Betsy. *Why Do Leaves Change Color? (Let's-Read-and-Find-Out Science, Stage 2)*, (Collins, 1994).
Sohl, Morteza. *Look What I Did with a Leaf!* (Walker Children's, 1995).

Unit 18—Seeds, Fruits, and Vegetables in Autumn

Autumn brings seedtime for plants, and harvest-time for man. To the plants, their seeds and fruits are for reproduction; to man and other animals, they are frequently a source of food. It is true that for domestic plants man has cultivated the soil, planted and cared for the plants, protected them from their enemies, and has therefore earned their harvest. This he takes as food for his stock and for himself, and as protection and clothing. Even then it is the sun and the soil that deserve most of the credit.

With man, "seeds" are things to be planted later. In the meantime, the tiny plants within must be kept alive but not growing. When pupils are led to store seeds of garden flowers and vegetables in dry, well-ventilated places, this concept is impressed upon them.

Primary and junior pupils should come to realize that seeds of garden plants are formed from flowers. Not until their experiences broaden, in later grades, by association with tree flowers and tree fruits, including those of evergreens, will they grasp the idea that all seeds are formed by flowers. The idea that fruits are sweet, juicy things borne on the branches of plants and good to eat, and that vegetables are the parts of plants eaten with the meat course, is good enough for these grades.

Intermediate pupils are more analytic in their way of thinking. They begin, of their own accord, to classify seeds according to the way they occur on the plant. Some seeds, like those of peas and beans, are held in pods. Others, such as those of apples, plums, and tomatoes, are hidden more deeply in fleshy fruits. Still others are covered by hard shells and are called nuts. Then there are some seeds covered only by a thin skin—wheat, oats, rice, and many other grains.

Grains. Intermediate pupils, both rural and urban, should learn to recognize the heads and kernels of common grains which are used as daily food and talked about in their social studies. From specimens placed before them, and with the help of questions to guide their observations, pupils should discover for themselves the knowledge shown in the table below.

Kernels and Heads of Grains		
Name	**Kernel**	**Head**
Wheat	shortest, yellow or cream, grooved, no hull, rounded.	kernels in groups of four, two rows of groups.
Rye	darkest, long, slender, no hull.	kernels in four rows, rough beard.
Oats	almost white, hulled, longest.	head spreading, kernels in pairs.
Barley	creamy color, plump, hulled, shorter than oats.	stout head like wheat, six rows, rough and long.

As an application, pupils should be able to pick from an assortment of heads and kernels the grain with the darkest kernel, and call it rye; the head which is most spreading, and call it oats. Then they may take home a head and kernel of each and name it for their parents.

Harvesting and Storing Vegetables and Fruits. Fresh vegetables and fruits in storage provide better and less expensive winter food than do those which have been canned. Successful storage demands careful selection of the provisions to be stored, and proper storage conditions. Selection

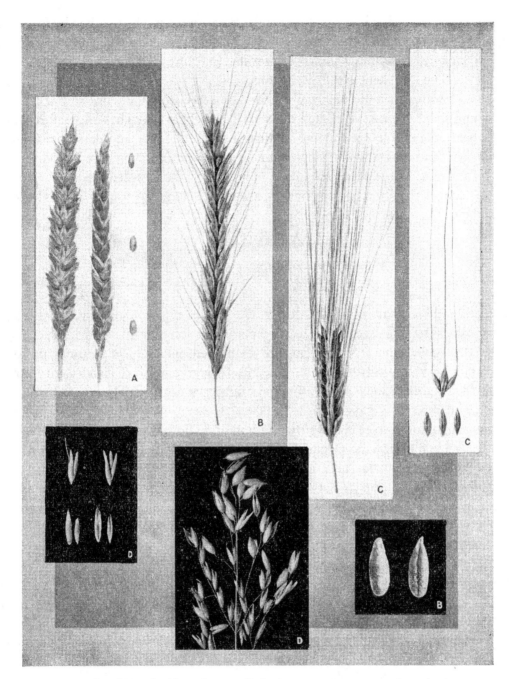

Figure 1—Heads and Kernels of Some Common Grains (Courtesy U. S. Department of Agriculture)

A, Marquis wheat; B, rye; C, six-row barley; D, Victory oats.

is based upon the right condition of ripeness, freedom from disease and insects, absence of woody tissue in vegetables, and favorable size. Safe storage conditions must include the right temperature and moisture, and good ventilation.

Vegetable crops must be harvested at the right time and by correct methods. Pumpkins and squash should be ripe before taking them in. Beets, carrots, and turnips may be pulled and topped as soon as they become a satisfactory size, but before they become woody. Onions should be well ripened and, after being pulled, they should be left lying on the ground until quite dry. The tops of potatoes should be dead before they are dug, but the tubers must not be touched by frost. Cabbages and turnips can stand light frosts. Parsnips not dug in the fall may be taken from the ground and used in early spring. All vegetables should be harvested in sunny weather; then less soil will cling to them, and they will be less likely to rot when stored dry.

Vegetables to be stored should be clean and dry, and free from cuts, bruises, or disease spots. The storage room should be well ventilated and should be kept at the right temperature and humidity. Cool and moist conditions are suitable for turnips, carrots, beets, and parsnips. These are best buried in boxes of sand moistened once in a while. A cool and moderately moist cellar is right for potatoes and cabbages. The potatoes are stored in bins; the cabbages, stripped of the outer leaves, are hung up. A cool, dry place is best for onions; a warm, dry one, for squash and pumpkins.

Activities

All Grades

Collect seeds and seed pods of garden flowers (sunflower, marigold, petunia, snapdragon, nasturtium), vegetables (tomato, pepper, corn), vine plants (melon, pumpkin, squash), grains. If necessary, spread them on a paper to dry; then store them in envelopes, bags, capsules, or bottles with loose tops. Collect seeds from trees and shrubs, too—evergreens (store cones to dry), other trees (maple, elm), shrubs (lilac, mock orange, sumac, coralberry). Most seeds, except those of trees and shrubs, need a rest before being planted.

Make envelopes of uniform size, and store in them dried flower and vegetable seeds. Each pupil might be responsible for one kind of plant. Make larger envelopes for class collections. On them print such titles as: "Seeds from Our Garden," "Seeds from Trees," and "Seeds from Flowers." In spring, plant these seeds in pots or flats (Unit 75, page 316); then transplant the small seedlings individually in small pots or paper cups, from which they may be planted outside at home.

For winter decoration, various seeds and fruits are useful. Cut enough of the fruit-bearing twigs from the plants that they may be arranged tastefully for winter bouquets. For white, cut snowberry; for red, barberry, rose, and bittersweet; for filling in, milkweed and goldenrod.

Visit the market. Go about in groups of four or five. Ask about the names of different fruits and vegetables. See how they are packed for sale. For each vegetable you see, find out what part we eat—root, stem, leaves, or flower.

List all the plant foods that you eat and, after each, name the plant and the part eaten (seed, fruit, flower, root, stem, leaf).

Primary Grades

- Collect and dry seeds of garden flowers. Press and mount a leaf and flower with each. Paste the leaf, flower, and seed side by side on a card. Mount the cards or use them for a recognition game.
- Have pupils collect and bring in several kinds of dried fruits and seeds. In class periods, they may lay them out to form various patterns. Some seeds, when soaked overnight, may be threaded to form a necklace, repeating shapes, colors, and seeds to form definite designs. Pleasing shapes and colors are provided by beans, peas, corn, acorns, beechnuts, and seeds of sunflower, pumpkin, squash.

- Make reproductions of flowers by gluing seeds of melons or pumpkins (for petals) on paper.
- Make a chart of mounted pictures to show that we eat roots, leaves, stems, flowers, fruits, and seeds.

Junior and Intermediate Grades

- In October, it is time to take up the underground part of gladioli and dahlias. Leave short stems on them, and store them in a cool, but not too dry cellar.
- Cut an apple across. Let its surface dry for a few hours; then find the tiny pinpoints standing out on the apple flesh. These are the ends of the food tubes which carry the plant food from the stem to all parts of the apple.

Figure 2 (Courtesy Better Homes and Gardens Magazine)

- Select a long, smooth potato. Find the eyes (buds), stick a pin in each, and then wind a thread around the potato from pin to pin. You will see the pattern nature has followed in placing the eyes on a potato.
- Use sawdust and paste to model a bowl and some fruit. When dry, color all naturally. Other members of the class use papier-mâché (Unit 21, page 84).
- Investigate the origin of some of our common vegetables. Here is an example. It is thought that corn originated in Peru and was developed by the Incas from a wild grass. The North American Indians brought it north and began cultivating it. They discovered new ways of preparing it for food. Even today, corn is used only as fodder in the British Isles.

Read

Dowling et al., *Seeing Why* (Junior), pp. 41-52 and 60-66. Winston.

Parker, *Floaters, Fruits, Seeds,* The Basic Science Education Series. Copp Clark (Row, Peterson).

Partridge, *Everyday Science,* Book One: "Fruits for Winter," pp. 45-46; "Vegetables for Winter," pp. 15-18. Dent.

Phillips, *Construction and Operation of a Home Storage for Fruits and Vegetables.* Publication 743. Department of Agriculture, Ottawa, Canada.

Stephenson, *Nature at Work,* Book 1 (grages 4-6): "The Storehouses of Plants," pp. 38-40; Book 2 (grades 4-6): "The Fruits of the Earth," pp. 17-25. Macmillan (A. & C. Black).

Westell, *Nature's Homes and Habits,* Naturecraft Readers, Book IV (grades 4-6): "Wild Fruits," pp. 26-36. Clarke, Irwin (McDougall).

New to this Edition

Bell and Lindsey. *Fall Color and Woodland Harvests: A Guide to the More Colorful Fall Leaves and Fruits of the Eastern Forests* (University of North Carolina Press, 2007).

Gibbons, Gail. *Apples* (Holiday House, 2000).

_____. *The Pumpkin Book* (Holiday House, 2000).

Hall, Doug. "A Fall Vegetable Garden for children-planting activites that can be done in August." Resource Library: The CBS Interactive Business Network, 2004 (http://findarticles.com/p/articles/mi_m1082/is_n4_v38/ai_15684388/).

Rockwell, Anne. *Apples and Pumpkins* (Aladdin, 2011).

Ruppenthal, R.J. *Fall and Winter Gardening: 25 Organic Vegetables to Plant and Grow for Late Season Food* (Amazon Digital Services).

Sheakoski, Megan. "How Pumpkins Grow Lesson Plan: Teach Elementary Students About the Life Cycle of Fall Vegetables." Primary School @suite 101(http://suite101.com/article/how-apples-and-pumpkins-grow-lesson-plan-a134811).

Unit 19—An Autumn Nature Display

As pupils plan and work with others in preparing displays illustrating "Autumn" (or Winter, Spring, etc.), they develop in knowledge of science facts, in skill and taste in arrangement, and in cooperativeness. The project may be made the responsibility of the Nature Club. It may be timed to have a Thanksgiving significance. Parents may be invited to enjoy it with the pupils.

The display may consist of one large unit or of several smaller ones. For a large unit, ample table space with a bulletin-board background is best. A display here may consist of a sheaf of corn at each end surrounded by a few plants of several kinds of grain. Designs or lettering with colored leaves make a fitting background. In the center may be pumpkins or other large materials. Elsewhere, tastefully arranged, pupils may include common vegetables, fruits, twigs, or vines bearing fruit suitable for bird food. If small displays are planned, the class may be divided into groups, each preparing exhibits of such things as indoor plants, animal homes, woodland plants (a tray with moss and ferns and some wildflowers transplanted to show their readiness for spring).

A carefully planned and supervised nature display has many educational values for pupils. While they collect materials, they have many nature experiences, both new and reviewed. While planning the arrangement, they become originators of ideas and cooperating members of a group. Correct placing of the materials—position, spacing, numbers, heights, balance—gives training in orderliness and tidiness. The planning and printing of a large sign visible across the room, and of small labels, are exercises in conciseness in English, and in art; deciding correct proportions and measurements are correlations with art and arithmetic. When the display has served its purpose, the final disposal of the materials—sending some to needy neighbors, experimenting with others, saving grains, etc., for later study, storing suitable materials for the classroom museum, and tidying up—are exercises in practical citizenship.

Activities

All Grades

In vases of water, display autumn wildflowers such as goldenrod and various kinds of wild asters.

Make sand-table scenes to represent: beaver-land in autumn, animal life in November, a garden ready for winter, a bulb garden as we'd like to see it in spring (use paper models). Make mounted displays of seed journeys, birds going south, etc.

Make a classroom rock garden. The materials required are:
1. a shallow box or table about 18" × 24";
2. good, rich earth;
3. cinders or large clinkers and pebbles;
4. a piece of glass about 9" × 12";
5. rock-garden plants;
6. birdseed;
7. small figures, houses, etc.

Any time of the year is suitable, but it is better to start it in the fall so that the bright, cheery rock garden is there for the duller autumn months. Fill the table with earth to a depth of 2 inches. Arrange clinkers at back to give mountain effect. Drip melted wax over clinkers to give the appearance of a waterfall, leading down to the lake below. Place glass in the foreground to represent a lake. Make little roads and paths in the earth with sand, tiny pebbles, or small stones. Arrange plants suitably around the rocks and along the roads. Little Plasticine men and women and some buildings would add greatly to the attractiveness.

Primary Grades

- After a trip to the market, set up a market scene in the classroom.
- On a large sheet of paper or wallboard, draw an apple tree growing in a grassy place. Paste paper apples on the tree and place modeled vegetables in piles on the grass under the tree.
- Make a sand-table scene to illustrate autumn. Include such things as trees and shrubs with autumn tints, fruits and nuts, corn and pumpkins (Plasticine), decorative grasses and seed pods, perhaps a beaver or muskrat scene (Plasticine).

Junior and Intermediate Grades

- Make sketches of bird nests. Model, or draw and cut out, the birds that live in these particular nests. Place the nests in natural-looking locations on a large tree branch.
- Individuals or small groups may make attractive displays of fruits and vegetables. Some will arrange fruits; some, vegetables; some, a combination of both. Pay attention to color harmony and shape.
- With your autumn display, have a conservation flower show. Make a large map of your county, and on it mount pictures of wildflowers, birds, etc. that should be protected.

Unit 20—Preparing for Winter

(An enterprise for primary grades, to be begun in October, reprinted from Seasonal Activities for Primary Grades, by kind permission of the author, Helen M. Hubbs, and the publishers, Ryerson Press.)

Aims. To quicken the child's interest in the problems of birds and animals; to give him a feeling of comradeship with all outdoor life. To develop the child's power of making careful observations and of drawing right inferences. To give the child the opportunity of expressing his observations through the media of conversation, drawing, modeling, and dramatization.

Approach. Take the class on an excursion to the woods. October has one keynote. The hush of its mellow, smoky days brings a sense of expectancy, a premonition of change. It is in the whisper of falling leaves and the sighing of autumn winds. Children are sensitive to all the moods of nature. In the noisy conventions of crows and blackbirds and the excited chatter of busy squirrels, the country child recognizes a note of urgency, of anxious preparation. In the town or city some children will have recently returned from summer cottages; others may be moving into new homes or preparing to go south with their parents for the winter. All these home activities suggest the problem of preparing for a season of intense cold. In the country, the farmer's preparation for winter is so evident that it will become a topic for discussion without suggestion from the teacher.

Problem 1

How the Family Prepares for the Winter. Father works at harvesting and storing the crop in the barn and cellar for winter use. The money earned buys: warm clothing; fruit and vegetables to store in the cellar; coal, wood, and oil for fuel; outside windows and doors. Mother works in the home: sewing warm clothing for the children; knitting sweaters, caps, and scarves; canning and drying vegetables and fruit. Men build cozy homes to resist winter's cold. Stories of the long ago tell of the preparations for winter in the early days: laying in supplies for the winter (preserves, smoked meats, dried apples and other fruits, maple sugar, nuts, salted fish), grinding the wheat and corn, cutting wood; the visit of the traveling shoemaker; preparation of hides, etc.; warm woollen clothing; the sheep-shearing, the spinning-wheel and loom; furs, stories about trappers; how the early houses were built and made snug for the winter (logs, moss, thatching, fireplace, chimney, etc.).

Things to Do

Watch a house being built: the work of masons, carpenters, painters. Make posters of fruits and vegetables stored for winter. Cut and color winter dresses, coats, and caps for paper dolls. Conversation about snug homes the children have seen and liked. Have the children read "Our Cellar":

Our cellar is a snug and jolly place;
When Mother lets me go with her downstairs
I count the rows of fruit jars one by one,
The crates of rosy apples, golden pears.

Out in the furnace room a giant sleeps
With mountain ranges black on either side;
I hear him snore in drowsy undertone,
His face is red, his mouth is open wide.

But when the storms of winter shake our house
The giant wakes, and roars, and shouts for food;
Then with my dad I hurry down the stairs
To feed him lumps of coal and sticks of wood.

H. M. Hubbs

- Have the children tell stories heard from their grandparents of how early houses were built and preparations made for winter.
- Make a "log" house from two large cartons of heavy corrugated cardboard. Cover it with sheets of bark from a lumberyard. Thatch it. Add doors and windows. It should be large enough for the children to enter.
- Make a mural showing a log house being built in the forest.
- Read "The Story of Jim Coon," given at the end of this Unit.

Problem 2

How Trees and Other Plants Prepare for Winter. The little green "workmen" in the leaves stop their work of making food for the tree. The leaves turn yellow, orange, and red. Ripe fruits and nuts fall; the seeds seek new homes. The leaves fall, forming a winter blanket for seeds. Winter buds form little cradles with baby leaves for the next year inside, protected by tough, varnished scales. Other plants make and scatter their seeds, store food, and die down to the ground.

Things to Do

- Recognize leaves of common trees of the locality. Notice which leaves fall first. Report to the class.
- Make a leaf book. Trace in it outlines of leaves of maple, oak, elm, beech, etc., and color them.
- Wax colored leaves of maple and oak.
- Model in Plasticine or clay small twigs with winter buds.
- Collect sprays of autumn seed pods for indoor bouquets: teasel, milkweed, cattail, etc.
- Find some seeds that fly—dandelion, thistle, milkweed, maple, cattail, etc. Find some seeds that "hitchhike"—burdock, pitchfork burr. Find seeds that swim—milkweed with its "life-preserver."
- Tell the story of a seed that went on a journey.
- The pupils read *Nature Activity Readers,* I: "The Two Trees," "Falling Leaves," and *Nature Activity Readers,* II: "The Warm Sun."
- Learn to sing: in *New Canadian Song Serifs,* II: "Autumn Leaves," "Wood Fairies"; in *Songs of*

Happiness: "Red and Yellow Leaves"; in *Holiday Songs:* "The Sleepy Leaves."
- Read to the pupils, "How the Leaves Came Down," in *Nature Activity Readers,* III.

Problem 3

How the Birds Prepare for Winter. Some birds have new suits of feathers—sometimes the same color as the old, sometimes different. Some birds put on a thick suit of "underwear" under their traveling suit of feathers. They hold farewell parties and conventions to talk over the long excursion. Some birds remain with us: e.g., nuthatch, blue jay, chickadee, English sparrow, starling.

Things to Do

- Watch conventions of crows, blackbirds, etc.; find out why they are excited, what they are discussing, why they are "drilling." Pupils report daily on observations.
- Make a colored frieze of different birds flying southward.
- Sketch wild geese flying south.
- Watch the birds that remain with us. Find out what food they like. Feed them.
- The pupils read *Science Stories,* II, "The Tree That Bloomed in Winter"—a story of winter birds.
- Learn to sing, "Where Do They Go?" in *New Canadian Song Series,* II.

Problem 4

How Other Animals Prepare for Winter. Their coats get longer and thicker. The coats of some animals change color to match the snow—varying hare, weasel. Some gather food and store it up in "cupboards"—squirrel, chipmunk. Some store up food in their bodies—woodchuck, bear, skunk, raccoon. Some sleep through the winter—woodchuck, chipmunk, skunk, bear, raccoon. They prepare warm homes for the winter: woodchuck— a burrow in the earth, tunnel, warmly lined nest; squirrel—in a hollow tree; chipmunk—a burrow in a dry hillside; raccoon—in a hollow tree, several inhabiting the same nest.

Things to Do

- Find chipmunks' and squirrels' "cupboards"—caches of nuts in the ground, hollow rails, fence corners, etc.
- Watch animals storing food for the winter. Notice the chipmunk's bulging cheeks.
- Read the class the stories: "Johnny Chuck Prepares for the Winter," and "Happy Jack Squirrel" in *The Adventures of Peter Cottontail.* The children love to dramatize these stories.
- Read the poem, "Big Words," in *Nature Activity Readers,* III. Then make a mural to illustrate it.

In wintertime my feathered friends—
Except a few—
Forsake my outdoor feeding station,
And all the older people say:
"The birds have left for warmer lands
On their migration."

In little words
I simply say:
"My friends, the birds
Have gone away."

In winter-time my other friends—
Or some of them—
The members of the furry nation,
Are sound asleep in holes and caves.
Wise people call this winter sleep
Their *hibernation.*

But when the drifts
Of snow are deep,
I only know
They've gone to sleep.

The children read the story of "Jerky Tail":

Jerky Tail is a gay little red squirrel. He comes to Mary's window for nuts. This morning Mary is asleep. Jerky Tail finds no nuts. He jerks his tail. He scolds Mary. But she cannot hear him. Now he jumps down in Mary's room. Her stockings are on the floor.

"Just what I need for my winter nest," says Jerky Tail, "the very thing!" Away he goes with the stocking. He tucks it in his nest up in the tree.

"So warm and soft," says Jerky Tail. Now he runs back for the other. He jumps from the window to the tree. But the stocking is caught on a sharp branch. Jerky Tail pulls and pulls.

"Oh dear!" he scolds, "Wake up, Mary, quick!"

Mary wakes up and runs to the window. She sees Jerky Tail tugging at her stocking. He scolds and scolds. He jerks his tail up and down. He tells Mary all about it. Mary laughs and laughs.

"You funny Jerky Tail," calls Mary. "Do you need warm stockings for winter just like me?"

—H. M. Hubbs

- The children read "Fuzzy Caterpillar" in *Along the Way;* "Run, Squirrel, Run," in *Nature Activity Readers,* I; "Whisky Frisky," in *My Bookhouse,* 1; "Getting Ready for Winter," in *Science Stories,* I; "Furry Bear," by A. A. Milne, in *Now We Are Six;* "Putting the World to Bed," in *A Treasury of Verse for Little Children.*

- Make posters (from cut-down pictures) entitled "We sleep all winter," "We store up food," and "We go south." Old picture books of birds and animals may be used.
- Tell the class the story of "The Sleepy Animals" in *Tell-Me-Why Stories about Animals*.

Culmination

Dramatize the story of "The Sleepy Animals," given in *Seasonal Activities for Primary Grades*, pp. 20-23, as a play adapted for grade 2.

The Story of Jim Coon

This "stirring" tale, which children in grade 2 enjoy reading, is based upon fact, the raccoon having been the pet of a lad whose parents were pioneers in the early days of a United Empire Loyalist settlement. The story will stimulate much class discussion.

Ben lived in a tiny log house in the deep woods long, long ago. There were big trees at the back and big trees on each side of the wee log house. One day Father cut a hollow tree. "That will keep us warm this winter," he said.

All at once Ben saw something in the hollow tree. It was a little raccoon—a furry ball with a queer frown on its funny little face. Ben took it home for a pet. He called it Jim Coon. Jim was very wise; always and always he washed his food before eating it, and always he washed his paws after meals. Mother said she once knew a boy who could not remember to do that.

One day Father said, "It is getting cold. Mother and I must go to town before winter comes. We must get sugar and rice, salt and oatmeal, ginger and flour. We must be ready for winter when it comes."

"I will stay home, Father," said Ben. "I will pick up nuts and grind corn and cut some wood. Jim Coon and I will keep house."

Father and Mother were gone all day. They rode in a wagon drawn by two fat oxen, and it was a long, long way. They came home at night very tired. Ben was happy; there were many fat parcels in the wagon—jolly paper bags with strings tied around their necks. Now there would be cookies and gingerbread and Christmas pudding.

"May I take the things in, Mother?" asked Ben.

"Yes," said Mother; "put them all on the table, and I shall take off my coat."

Ben brought in the bags. He stirred up the logs in the fireplace. Then he went out to help Father.

In the corner, under the spinning-wheel, was a round, soft ball. It was not a skein of yarn; it was little Jim Coon having a nap. All at once he jumped up.

"What a nice smell!" thought Jim Coon.

Sniff, sniff. Up on the table he jumped. He saw all the fat bags.

"I must find out about this," he said. So he scratched a little hole in the first bag with his sharp claws. Out came a stream of rice. Then he tried the next bag; out poured the tea.

"What a jolly game," thought little Jim; "a white hill and a black hill; I can make more hills."

Then Jim Coon had an idea. "Why not mix the little hills—make brown and white hills, black and yellow hills? This is fun." Mix, mix, mix, tea and rice and sugar, oatmeal and ginger and salt; stir, stir, stir.

Suddenly Mother opened the door. She saw little Jim Coon stirring up all the hills into one big pudding. In the firelight she saw the busy little paws and the funny little face of Jim Coon with the queer frown between the eyes.

"Oh, oh, oh!" cried Mother. "My nice brown sugar and oatmeal, my tea and salt and ginger! Oh dear, oh dear!"

Then she picked up little Jim Coon. She lighted a candle and put it in the window. She went out into the deep woods. Little Jim squirmed and squirmed. At last she put him down.

"Scat, scat!" said Mother crossly. "Run away, bad Jim Coon, and don't come back!"

Jim Coon was afraid. He ran up a tree. He had no home now.

Old Mr. Moon peeped out from behind a cloud. He winked at little Jim.

"Don't be afraid, little chap," said Mr. Moon. You will find a nice snug home in that hollow tree—the best house in the world for little coons. Just go right in and take a long, long nap until spring."

—H. M. Hubbs

Read

New to this Edition

Smith, Gail Saunders. *Animals in the Fall* (Preparing for Winter) (Capstone Press, 1998).

Unit 21—Nature Crafts

This unit is meant to serve two purposes: to give instructions for the carrying out of certain manual activities useful in the teaching of science, and to suggest a number of activities which will make some worthwhile facts of science more impressive and more meaningful to pupils.

Expression work of this kind develops pupils in many ways: it trains them in coordination of eye and hand; it cultivates a taste for things that are beautiful; it trains them in careful adherence to directions as well as in showing initiative in their activities. At the same time, it teaches pupils to be orderly, to return all supplies and equipment to the proper place, and to leave everything neat and tidy when a project is finished.

Perhaps of greater value than these is the satisfaction of accomplishment gained by the pupils. To be the designer and the maker of something interesting and useful creates such a deep pride that the knowledge connected with it will be both more lasting and more useful to the child.

Making Prints. This activity is commonly applied to the making of leaf prints. For this reason, leaves are referred to in many of the activities below. Many other types of printing will suggest themselves to teachers.

Leaf Printing with Printer's Ink (fig. 1). Place a few drops of printer's ink (from the local print shop) on a smooth slate or glass or pan about 10" × 12". With a photographic print roller or the straight-edge of card, spread the ink evenly and rather thinly, as decided by experience, over the surface. On this, place the selected leaf, underside down, and press it well into the ink by means of the roller or a paper. Remove the leaf and place it carefully between two sheets of paper. Press *once* with a roller, avoiding blurring by slipping of the leaf; or place the leaf and papers carefully in a book and press. Prints of one or both sides of the leaf may be arranged for. Size, shape, margins, and veining should be well represented.

Lamp-black, Stamp-pad, and Carbon-paper Printing. Rub a teaspoonful of lard well into about the same quantity of lamp-black and, using a piece of absorbent cotton, spread the mixture evenly over a sheet of paper about 8" × 10". Or, grease the paper thoroughly with lard, using the fingers, and either sift lamp-black evenly over the greased paper or hold the paper, greased side down and in constant motion, over a burning candle until it is well blackened. Place the paper, prepared side up, on a desk or on a folded pad of cloth. Place the selected leaf, underside down, on the treated paper. Cover it with a sheet of clean paper and rub the latter thoroughly over the leaf. Remove the paper, then the leaf carefully by the stem, and place its blackened surface on a sheet of paper resting on the desk or another folded cloth pad. Again cover the leaf with a sheet of clean paper and, carefully avoiding any slipping, rub the paper with the fingers to ensure contact of all parts of the leaf with the lower paper. Remove the top paper, then the leaf very carefully, and put the print away to dry. With experience all detail will show clearly. A stamp-pad may be used in place of the treated paper.

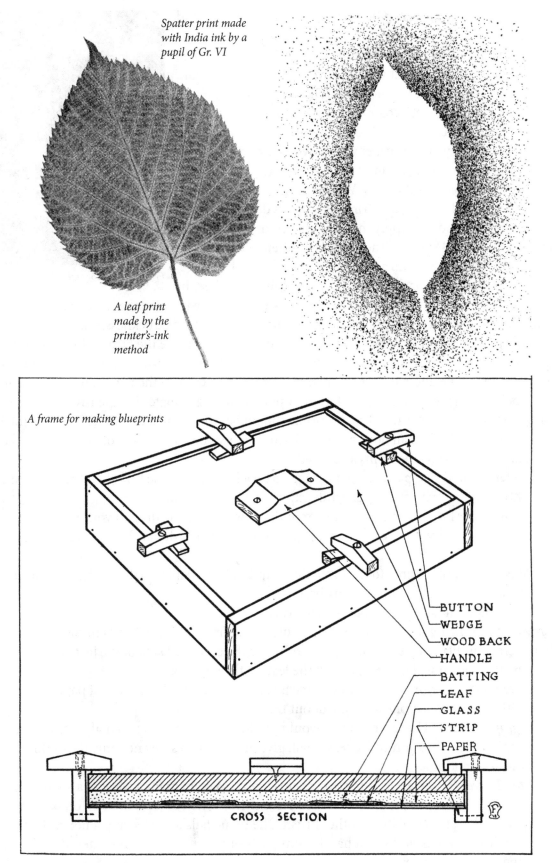

Spatter print made with India ink by a pupil of Gr. VI

A leaf print made by the printer's-ink method

A frame for making blueprints

BUTTON
WEDGE
WOOD BACK
HANDLE
BATTING
LEAF
GLASS
STRIP
PAPER

CROSS SECTION

Figure 1—Making Leaf Prints

Spatter Prints (fig. 1). Fasten the paper on a board or desk, and place the leaf or leaves on the paper to give the desired composition. Pressing the leaves in a heavy book for a few hours in advance to permit wilting and lying flat will improve the detail of the print. Pin the leaf, if necessary, near the edges. Dip a tooth brush into a little diluted india ink, watercolor, or tempera solution. Shake off the surplus liquid. Run the brush over a screen or the edge of a knife so that the spray hits the paper vertically around the leaf margin. Both the amount of liquid in the brush and the pressure on it will determine the size of the dots. When the solution has dried, remove the pins and the leaf, and trim the print as desired.

A speedier method is to apply the ink, watercolor, or dissolved tempera from a small sprayer. The results are often better, too.

Figure 2—Photographic Print of Leaf

Blueprinting (fig. 1). Obtain a printing frame of the desired size, as in fig. 1. Place the leaf or the spray of leaves against the glass. In *subdued light* cut the blueprint paper to the right size, and place it facing the leaves. Cover this with a layer of felt or absorbent cotton to allow for the varying leaf and twig thicknesses and to hold all parts tight to the glass. Button the back of the frame into place and expose the face to direct sunlight with the glass perpendicular to the sun's rays until the paper has been observed to change from the original greenish white to blue and has again turned back to cream. Remove the paper and immerse it for 5 minutes or more in a bright orange solution of potassium bichromate (inexpensive), about a tablespoonful to two gallons of water. The leaf prints should be whitish on a deep blue background. Wash them in clear water for half an hour or more. Then dry them between layers of newspapers, changed as needed. Trim and label the prints as desired.

A simpler method is to place the paper face up on a board, then the leaf, then the glass, and hold them tightly together with the hands while exposing them to light.

Blueprint paper loses its sensitivity in a month or two. Buy according to your immediate needs. It can be obtained from any dealer in art supplies at about one dollar for a 10-yd. roll, 24 inches wide.

- Make sets of blueprints to illustrate different kinds of maples, oaks, evergreens, ferns, trees in the schoolyard, fruit trees, shrubs, etc.
- Make blueprints of photographic negatives.

Crayon Prints. Bring in leaves with showy autumn colors. Color the leaves in their natural color with wax crayons. Place a piece of paper or cloth over the crayoned side of the leaf and press it with a hot iron. The crayon will make a print of the leaf on the paper or cloth.

Another kind of crayon print may be made by placing a leaf under a sheet of paper and rubbing green or other colored crayons over it. Cut out the print.

Photographic Prints. Use leaves as you would photographic negatives to make contact prints on photographic paper. Thin or mottled leaves will give prints which show not only the outline but also the veining and mottling.

Skeleton Leaves. Select leaves with strong veins (oak). Soak them for a week in a solution of caustic soda (keep the hands out!); then wash and press them. When dry, place them on blotting-paper or on a pad, and beat them with a clothes brush. The tissue falls away leaving a network of veins.

Look for leaves of oak and witch hazel, from parts of which insects have eaten the green material, leaving a skeleton of veins.

Potato Prints. Raw potatoes (turnips, apples, or carrots) are used to make all-over patterns for such things as book covers and wrapping-paper. The design, which must be simple, is first sketched on paper, then painted on the flat cut surface of the potato. The background is then removed with a knife. The color is put on the potato with a brush before printing. The first prints may be blurred because of moisture in the potato. This will later be absorbed.

Cork Prints. Draw on paper a circle the size of the cork. In this circle draw a very simple design. Draw, or transfer with carbon paper, your design on the top of the cork. With a sharp knife, cut out spaces around the design to a slight depth. Stamp your cork on an ink pad, and print the design on paper.

Modeling. *Sawdust and paste* may be used for modeling. The following are directions for modeling a bowl of fruit: Mix equal parts of sawdust and paste until of a plastic consistency. Shape the mixture with the fingers to form the desired model; then rub a coat of paste over the entire surface to prevent cracking. Allow the model to dry thoroughly. Color it with tempera, watercolor, or enamel paint. If tempera color is used, a coat of clear varnish or white shellac may be applied, but this is not essential. To model the bowl, use the above mixture, but mold it over an inverted bowl which has been covered with tissue paper well greased on both surfaces. Finish as above.

Papier-mâché provides another useful medium for modeling. Tear newsprint or other soft paper into shreds. Soak these in warm water for at least 2 or 3 days. To work the soaked paper into a pulpy mass, hold pieces of paper flat in one hand and rub the surface with the fingers of the other hand until it is worn away in fine curls of fibers. Soak this again until it is required for modeling. It will keep thus for a month or more. When ready to use it, drain off the water and squeeze the pulp until very dry. Into this, work enough cooked flour paste to produce the required modeling consistency. Shape the models as desired. Smooth the surfaces with the damp fingertips. Place the models near heat so that they will dry quickly. When dry, they may be smoothed with sandpaper. Paint them the desired colors with tempera or poster paint. The painted surface may later be given a smoother finish by applying wax, varnish, or white shellac. Note: One tablespoonful of alum and a few drops of oil of cloves stirred into a quart of flour paste will preserve it for a considerable time.

Asbestos powder is an inexpensive and easily prepared medium for comparatively large models. Mix it with enough water to make most of it barely damp. With this, mix enough cooked flour paste to give the desired modeling consistency. Shape the objects (an igloo, over a bowl, etc.), then place them over heat so that they will dry very quickly. When thoroughly dry, paint them with tempera or poster colors.

Note: *Papier-mâché* and asbestos powder are frequently used to model scenes. It should be remembered, however, that large, high mountains cannot be built of wet modeling substances, as the mass rarely dries out before molding. Most of the height should be built up by means of rags, crumpled paper, excelsior, inverted boxes, etc., and then a fairly thin layer of modeling substance applied over the surface. This can be painted when it becomes dry and hard.

For starch and salt models, mix two parts of salt with one of cornstarch and moisten with enough water to make a batter. Heat this slowly, stirring it constantly, until it thickens into a stiff dough. Remove this from the heat and work it like putty. Mold it into the desired shape—a pear, orange, banana, etc. When dry and very hard, paint the models the appropriate color.

A *salt and flour* mixture is useful in modeling over the top of articles such as an inverted bowl or cup, or modeling on cardboard.

Plasticine is most convenient for modeling twigs, fruits, birds or other animals, bird houses, etc.

Modeling clay has many uses.

Plaster Casts and Plaques. For practice, make a plaster-of-Paris plaque in a fruit dish. Remove it, and color it. Do it this way: Have the dish clean and ready. Smear the surface with liquid soap or a colorless grease, such as face cream. Into a tumbler pour about the same volume of water as you will need of the mixture. Into this, *without stirring,* carefully sift the plaster of Paris, a little at a time, until the plaster is even with the top surface of the water. When mixed, it should be of the consistency of very thick cream, smooth, and free from lumps. Pour it into the dish at once. (It must not be stirred or poured after it begins to set.) It will harden in a few hours. Then invert the dish, and, while holding down on it firmly with one hand, lift one edge with the other hand, and let it go. The plaster cast falls out. Paint or decorate it as you wish.

To prepare a hanger for the plaque, embed a bent piece of wire in the part which you wish to be the top. It must be put in as soon as you pour in the plaster mixture, and the loop must project so as to take a string or ribbon. All containers used for plaques must have sloping sides.

To make a plaque bearing on its surface a cutout of a colored flower, cut out the picture, wet its face, lay it face down in the mold (fruit dish) with all edges pressed flat on the dish, pour the plaster mixture over this. When removed from the mold, the plaque will have the picture embedded in the front.

Make a plaque of acorns lying on their sides or on end. Roll out a thick layer of Plasticine. On its surface, mark off the shape of the plaque. Oil one or more acorns and embed them not quite to the widest part. Level and smooth the surface of the Plasticine, then carefully remove the acorns. Rub softened soap carefully over the imprints and the flat surface. Place a frame about the shape that you desire. Carefully add the plaster mixture a little at a time, blowing to remove air bubbles. Fill the frame to the desired thickness. Immediately insert a hanger. When the plaque is thoroughly dry, remove the frame and Plasticine, and paint the plaque as desired.

Useful and Ornamental Objects. *Acorn Snakes.* Bore holes lengthwise through about twenty acorns of graded sizes. On the largest acorn carve a mouth and eyes. Smooth off the tips of all others with sandpaper. Thread them on a string. Daub them with colored paint or enamel to make them more lifelike.

Cone Critters. These require cones of evergreen trees, acorns, chestnuts, beechnuts, orange pips, seed cases, winged seeds, twigs, feathers, bark, and moss. Tools and supplies needed are: a sharp penknife and a small awl, cutting-pliers and scissors, liquid glue, colored beads, pins, sandpaper, watercolors, corks of various sizes, pieces of flat wood for a cutting-block. For birds, cones will form the bodies; seed keys will form heads and beaks. For eyes use soft seeds on pins, and for the tail use feathers.

Other Nature Creations. For mushrooms or toadstools invert acorn cups on small twigs held erect by Plasticine. Butterflies and dragonflies will materialize from the wings of the maple fruit if they are trimmed, fastened to twig bodies, and colored.

- Make window transparencies as shown in fig. 3.
- Make attractive necklaces or bracelets in these ways: String large seeds such as those of pump-

Figure 3—A Window Transparency (Courtesy Better Homes and Gardens Magazine)

Cut the frame and the pictured objects from the same or from different colored papers. Paste the tissue paper on the frame, then the objects on the tissue paper. Hang the picture in the window.

kins on waxed linen thread; hang them up to dry; when dry, color them. Shellac and string acorns, colored if you wish.

- Make lapel ornaments by combining acorns with tiny cones.
- Make birch-bark baskets and canoes by first soaking the bark stripped from a fallen log, and then shaping it.
- Make salt and pepper shakers of nuts by scraping out the inside, cutting corks to fit the openings, and using a hot nail or a sharp tool to punch the holes.

Salvaged materials become interesting scenes. Use up old window shades in this way: Trace leaves or birds on discarded window shades; color them with colored chalk; blend by rubbing with cotton batting; spray with a fixative (half white shellac with half wood alcohol [methyl hydrate]) applied with a fly sprayer; then fasten them on a branch with unraveled picture wire. Broken glass is useful, too. Cut the broken panes into suitable sizes. Lay the glass over a sketched scene; with black enamel, trace all the outlines, filling in any desired parts, such as tree trunks, etc. Remnants of linoleum, preferably plain, make mounts for nature pictures. Cut them into ovals, circles, rectangles, etc.; on these, paste pictures of nature scenes; varnish over the whole surface, and hang them.

Finger Painting. Interesting posters and folders may be designed by finger painting with a colored paste. A simple method is to use powder paint and water. Two better methods follow. In each case see that desks are protected with paper, and that each pupil is supplied with a cloth.

Mix thick, cooked paste with tempera colors. Wet a piece of cardboard or heavy paper, then cover it with this prepared paste. With the index finger make ovals over the entire surface, or only where the design is desired. If unsatisfactory, merely rub the hand over the card and begin anew. Various colors may be worked into a design. Fine details may be put in with the thumb nail. A simpler method is to paint a page with the cooked laundry starch by means of a large brush, then work in the desired tempera colors while the page is still damp.

"Mix one-half box of laundry starch (one and one-half cups) with just enough cold water to make a paste. Add one quart of boiling water. Cook until clear, or glassy-looking. Stir continually so lumps will not form. Add one-half of a cup of talc, if available. Let the mixture cool a little. Add one and one-half cups of soap flakes, stirring until evenly distributed. This mixture may now be poured into eight half-pint jars with tops. To each jar of the mixture add one-half of a tablespoon of coloring (poster paints are good). Be sure the paint is thick and not watery. Stir thoroughly."[1]

Sand-table Scenes. The sand-table is valuable only if used correctly; this means chiefly by the children, rather than by the teacher. An elaborate and almost perfect sand-table model is mute evidence not only that the teacher did most of the work, but that the aim was to have something beautiful to look at, rather than to develop pupils through genuinely educative personal activities. The children themselves should plan the set-up with the teacher's help, then make and place the devices. Such materials as sand, glass, white paper, blue paper, scrap cardboard, paste, glue, cotton batting, twigs, small stones, and small jars and boxes should always be at hand. A worthwhile sand-table project grows gradually, involving many correlated learning activities.

Materials Useful in Crafts. Alcohol for thinning shellac, for spraying murals and for cleaning shellac brushes; blueprint paper, orange crates, and other empty boxes; inexpensive brushes in various sizes from ½" to 1 ½"; cardboard of different colors and thicknesses; cellophane; cheesecloth; modeling clay; construction paper; cotton batting; wax crayons; crepe paper; flour; pieces of glass; glass cutter; glue; colored inks; lacquer for a quick-drying finish; mirror glass; nails in various sizes; paste; paints; plaster of Paris (vinegar to slow setting); Plasticine; plastic wood; poster colors or

---

1   From *Nature Is Recreation*, by M. Ickis.

tempera paint; potassium bichromate for blueprinting; sandpaper; screw eyes; shellac—white and orange; soap for carving; tacks (carpet and thumb); turpentine for thinning paints and varnish and for cleaning brushes; wallboard; watercolors; wire of various sizes.

The following hand tools are suggested: hacksaw, coping saw, hand drill and small drills for same, ½" wood chisel, nail set, pliers, file, screwdriver, yardstick.

Read

Gaudette, *Things to Do in Nature* (nature crafts), Audubon Nature Bulletin, National Audubon Society.
Newkirk, *Integrated Handwork for Elementary Schools* (a teacher's guide in use and techniques), and *You Can Make It*. Gage (Silver, Burdett). Selsam, *Play with Trees* (grades 4-6): leaf and twig collections and leaf prints: pp. 43-55. McLeod (Wm. Morrow).
Arts and Crafts with Inexpensive Materials. Girl Scouts Inc., National Equipment Service, 243 West 17th St., New York City.

New to this Edition

Bethmann, Laura Donnelly. *Nature Printing: 30 Projects for Creating Beautiful Prints, Wearables, and Home Furnishings* (Storey Publishing LLC, 2001).
Diehn, Gwen. *Nature Crafts for Kids: 50 Fantastic Things to Make with Mother Nature's Help* (Sterling Publishing, 1997).
Kohl and Gainer. *Good Earth Art: Environmental Art for Kids (Bright Ideas for Learning)*, (Bright Ring Publishing, 1991).
Martin, Laura. *Nature's Art Box: From t-shirts to twig baskets, 65 cool projects for crafty kids to make with natural materials you can find anywhere* (Storey Publishing LLC, 2003).

Unit 22—Seed Travelers

Little children enjoy and profit much from blowing the white hair from old dandelions and telling the time by them, from setting maple seeds a-sailing in the wind, from watching burdocks cling to things, and from floating seed boats down the stream—all these long before their experiences or mentality makes possible any adequate teaching of why seeds should be dispersed, or how they are adapted for dispersal. These latter phases of the study should be reserved for intermediate grades.

Personal observations by pupils in the garden, field, or wood, or beside roadside or local stream are essential. For these, there should be an excursion or definite directions by the teacher. Pupils will discover interesting facts about the number of seeds produced by plants, how they occur on the plants, by what agencies they are carried away, and how they are fitted to be carried in this way. They will learn that many seeds fall into water, on barren soil, in places too warm or too cold, that others are eaten by birds, mice, and man. It is well, therefore, that most plants produce a great many more seeds than would be necessary if they all grew.

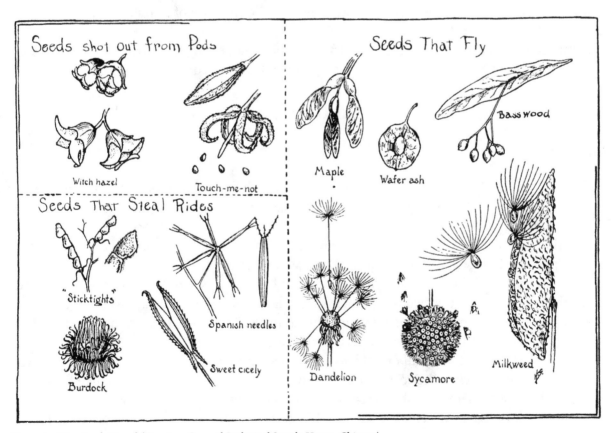

Figure 1—How Seeds Travel (Courtesy General Biological Supply House, Chicago)

In all grades, pupils should be kept conscious of the welfare of the plant whose seeds are being scattered. Picture what would happen if all the seeds from a maple fell directly under it and grew there the next year. They would be very much crowded, would not have enough water or other raw food, would shade each other so much that they could not make enough plant food to grow well. What sickly and stunted plants they would turn out to be! But nature does not work this way. We see that the seeds are carried long distances by the wind. Then when we pick up a maple seed, we find that it has large, flat, light wings which make it possible for the wind to carry it easily. Throughout this study, the sequence of questioning and of observing should follow the pupil's natural sequence of discovery—how the seed is carried, how it is fitted to be carried in this way. The table to follow illustrates this natural order of presentation.

How Seeds Are Scattered		
Plants Observed	**How Seeds or Fruits Are Carried**	**Adaptations for This Means**
maple, elm, ash, pine, spruce	wind	wings—light, of large area, easily caught by the wind
burrs, burdock	animals	hooks (observe with lens). Which way do the spines point?

(In each case the fruits or seeds should be allowed to flutter down in view of pupils.)

Follow a similar plan for: cherries, apple, etc.—flesh attracts squirrels and birds, which discard uneaten or indigestible seeds; ragweed, marsh-marigold—carried by water, due to lightness, boat-like shape, etc.; witch hazel, squirting cucumber, violet, balsam—pods spring open and throw seeds; weeds and other small seeds—carried in packing and on machinery; thistle and milkweed—carried by wind on tufts of hairs; tumbling mustard, Russian thistle, and tumble-weed—rolled by the wind along the ground; poppy—pods swayed by wind until the seeds are thrown out; nuts—hidden by squirrels and forgotten about; seeds of marsh weeds—carried by birds in mud on their feet.

Some applications are: classifying other fruits as above; collecting some fruits or seeds to illustrate each means of dispersal; making a poster to illustrate how seeds travel (fig. 1).

Activities

All Grades

- Look for: tumbleweeds blowing along the ground or lying in fence corners (roll one on paper and find the seeds) ; poppy pods swaying back and forth in the wind (find the little holes near the top).
- Along streams look for the orange-yellow flowers of the jewel-weed, or wild balsam. Squeeze a pod and feel it twist as it throws its seeds. Jar a plant and feel the shower. Also look for the tall witch-hazel shrubs; bring some branches bearing flowers and seed pods to school. When the seed pods dry, they will shoot their shiny black seeds all the way across the room.
- Collect seeds from the fur of dogs and other animals. Pick weed seeds from seed grain. Find nuts hidden by squirrels. Gather seeds from trees such as oak, elm, basswood, ash, maple. Mix them. Drop a handful of all these 2 or 3 feet onto a coat. Which flutter down slowly? Why? Which stick to the coat? How? Roll them from the coat into water. Which float?
- Visit a forest where several different kinds of trees grow. Collect seeds of pine, spruce, and hemlock (in cones which open as they dry in the classroom and free the seeds); birch (in

catkins); locust; sycamore; hickory; butternut; beech; oaks; elm. Either sow the seeds at once out of doors or indoors in a box of soil covered with glass, or store them in a box of moist sand covered with a foot or more of soil and leaves. Sow the latter in spring. Use well-drained soil, cover them lightly, press them firm, and keep them moist and partly shaded.

- Make such drawings as: a dandelion parachute; a partly eaten apple being dropped by a squirrel; a pitchfork burr or burdock fruit cluster riding on an animal's fur or on your clothing; a squirrel carrying a nut; a maple key traveling in the wind.
- Use some white fluff from milkweed seeds as a background for pressed flowers.

Primary Grades

- Find seeds that travel like airships or parachutes (thistle, goldenrod, dandelion, aster); seeds rolled by the wind (tumbleweed, Russian thistle), seeds that fly on wings (maple, elm, ash, and basswood); seeds that hitchhike on clothing or on animals (burdocks, stick-tights, pitchfork burrs); seeds which go sailing (ragweed); seeds that are shot (balsam, witch hazel, jewel-weed); seeds lost by the wayside (apple cores, cherry pits, nuts).
- Make these: baskets, wagons, etc., by using burdocks; the word "pumpkin" with pumpkin seeds; an outline of maple seeds by drawing them on cardboard, pricking holes, and sewing.
- Imagine you are a maple seed. Draw your picture on the board, tell who you are, where you grew, and how you travel about.

Junior and Intermediate Grades

- Collect seeds of as many kinds of trees as you can. Sew or glue them to a cardboard mount. Label each with three words: the seed's name, what distributes it, and what part of it helped it to get the ride.
- Try to find the approximate number of seeds on one plant of red-root pigweed. Shake the seeds onto white paper marked into ten squares. Spread them evenly and count the number in one square. How does the information gathered show the importance of destroying weeds before they go to seed?
- Make a class booklet of ten or twelve pages. Label it "Seed Travelers." Each pupil become responsible for one page dealing with one topic. The title may be "Autumn Winds Play Football with Tumble Weeds"; the top half, a drawing to illustrate the title, and the bottom half, a description of how seeds are thrown far and wide during "scrimmages" on the playing field, and a touch-down is made when the ball (plant) lands in the fence. Ideas for other pages are: "Autumn Hitchhikers," "Plants Play Slingshots."
- Examine some burrs with a lens and find how they hang on to cloth or fur.
- Write a story of a dandelion seed from the time it first lifted its parachute from the flower stalk until it landed in a neighboring lawn and became a pesky weed.
- List several ways in which man helps nature to spread her seeds to better growing places.
- Tell the story of a coconut that swam across the ocean and grew on a new island.

Read

Alexander and Cormack, *Bruce and Marcia, Woodsmen*: "Moving Time in Seedland," pp. 18-39. Gage (American Book Co.).
Dickinson, *The First Book of Plants* (grades 5-8). Ambassador (Watts).

Dowling et al., *Seeing Why* (Junior), pp. 35-39. Winston.

Frasier et al., *Winter Comes and Goes* (grades 3-4) : "How Seeds Are Scattered," pp. 42-46. Dent (Singer).

Harvey and Lay, *Adventures into Nature*, Book III A: "Seed Scattering," pp. 7-11 and 16-20. Macmillan.

Hethershaw & Baker, *Wonders to See:* "Seeds and How They Travel," pp. 41-74. Gage (World Book).

Hylander, *Out of Doors in Autumn* (grades 6-8): "Plants Begin Their Travels," pp. 58-73. Macmillan.

Miner, *The True Book of Plants We Know* (primary), pp. 28-34. Book Society (Children's Press).

Parker, *Seeds and Seed Travels,* The Basic Science Education Series. Copp Clark (Row, Peterson).

Partridge, *General Science,* Intermediate, Book 1: "Seeds Must Be Scattered," pp. 50-52, and *Everyday Science,* Book One: "The Seeds Are Scattered," pp. 34-7. Dent.

Patch & Howe, *Outdoor Visits* (grades 2-3) : "Flyaway Seeds," pp. 21-26. Macmillan.

Phillips & Wright, *Plants and Animals:* "How Seeds Get to Their New Homes," pp. 40-48. Copp Clark (Row, Peterson).

Selsam, *Play with Leaves and Flowers* (grades 4-5), pp. 52-59. McLeod (Wm. Morrow).

Stephenson, *Nature at Work,* Book 1 (grades 4-5): "Seeds That Ride on the Wind," pp. 7-10; *Nature at Work,* Book 3 (grades 5-6): "Seeds That Go for a Ride on Animals" and "Plants That Scatter Their Own Seeds," pp. 7-14. Macmillan (A. & C. Black).

Webber, *Travelers All.* Allen (Wm. R. Scott).

New to this Edition

Aston and Long. *A Seed is Sleepy* (Chronicle Books, 2007).

Carle, Eric. *The Tiny Seed* (Little Simon, 2009).

Pascoe, Elaine. *How and Why Seeds Travel (How and Why Series)*, (Creative Teaching Press, 2000).

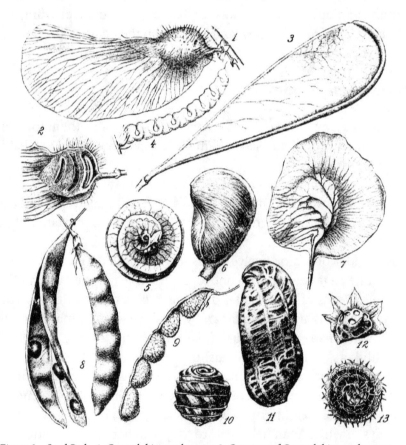

Figure 2—Seed Pods: 1. Centrolobium robustum 2. Cutaway of Centrolobium robustum 3. Brazilian Fire-Tree (Schizolobium excelsum) 4. Hippocrepis unisiliquosa 5. Button Clover (Medicao obicularis - top view) 6. Purpleheart (Peltogyne paniculata) 7. New Guinea Rosewood (Pterocarpus indicus) 8. Golden Rain (Laburnum anagyroides) 9. Canadian Trick-trefoil (Desmodium canadense) 10. Button Clover (Medicago obicularis – side view) 11. Peanut, or groundnut (Arachis hypogaea) 12. Sainfoins (Onobrychis aequidentata

Unit 23—Plants with Climbing Ways

The leaves of all green plants must have sunlight if they are to make food for the plant's growth. The stems of most plants are strong enough to stand erect and thus hold out the leaves so that all receive enough light. But the stems of some plants cannot stand up alone and must depend upon trees, walls, wires, or other objects to support their weight and help them to hold their leaves where the sun may shine on them. These are the climbing plants. When these plants find no support and grow in shady places, they soon die.

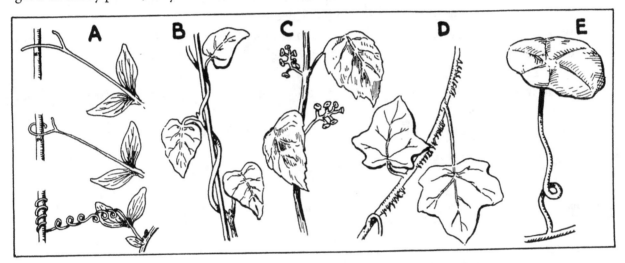

Figure 1—How Plants Climb

A. pea tendrils, reaching, grasping, lifting; B. twining stem of morning glory; C. suckers of Virginia creeper; D. aerial roots of ivy; E. twining leaf stalk of nasturtium.

Climbing plants obtain support in several ways. Some (morning glory, scarlet runner bean, wild buckwheat, bittersweet, honeysuckle) twine their slender stems to wrap themselves about such supports as tree trunks, wires, and posts. These are called *twining plants*. Others (grape, wild cucumber, clematis, and peas) have peculiar leaves or stems which act like fingers. These so-called tendrils grow outward, touch an object, curl around it, become shorter by twisting into a coil, and lift the plant just as we lift ourselves each time we reach to the rung of a ladder, grip it with the fingers, and pull ourselves up by bending the elbow. Boston ivy clings to walls and trees by means of little roots which grow from the stems into little niches or chinks, and there attach little sucker-like discs to the object. Some other climbing plants such as bramble berries are content to scramble over any bush, fence, or rock pile nearby.

Activities

Junior and Intermediate Grades

- Find a young tendril just beginning to grow from a grape or other vine near a wire or other support. In the next day or two, look at it often to discover what it does when it touches the support, how it gets a grip on the support, how it becomes shorter and lifts the plant toward the support. Compare what you have seen with the way in which you use your hand when climbing a ladder.
- Head a table "Plants with Climbing Ways," and use columns headed: Name of Plant, How It Climbs, Color and Time of Blossom, Color of Leaves in Autumn. Fill it out for as many climbing plants as you can locate. From pupils' tables, make one large class table.
- Make a mounted and labeled collection of the leaves, climbing parts, and flowers or fruits of some climbing plants.
- Find some place in the schoolyard which would be improved if covered with vines. From catalogues decide what kind of annual or perennial vine is best for that place.
- Find a bittersweet or other plant which has killed the tree around which it grew.
- Inquire if neighbors have any of these garden climbers: Boston ivy, Engelman ivy, clematis, or honeysuckle. Ask to see them. See how they climb. Collect a leaf from each. Tell about them in class.
- Stand well back from poison ivy and draw its leaf. Get a leaf from a Virginia creeper vine and compare it with your drawing.
- Make a chart or poster entitled "How Plants Get Up in the World."

Read

Harvey and Lay, *Adventures into Nature,* Book IV A : "Climbing Plants," pp. 64-70. Macmillan.

Knight, *The Golden Nature Readers,* Book Three (grades 4-6): "The Pea and Other Climbers," pp. 139-148. Clarke, Irwin (University of London Press).

Nicol et al., *The Nature Hour,* Sixth Year—Autumn and Winter: "Vines," pp. 68-74. Gage (Silver, Burdett).

Stephenson, *Nature at Work,* Book 2 (grades 4-6): "Plants That Climb," pp. 112-119. Macmillan (A. & C. Black).

New to this Edition

Cobb, Lowe and Farnsworth. Peterson Field Guide to Ferns: Northeastern and Central North America, 2nd edition (Houghton Mifflin Harcourt, 2005).

Marsh and Bovey. Mosses Lichens & Ferns of Northwest North America (Lone Pine Publishing, 1988).

Unit 24—Plants That Don't Have Seeds

Most of our common plants bear flowers and, by them, produce seeds. This is as true of trees and grasses as of garden flowering plants. Though ferns and mosses are green and resemble flowering plants in some ways, they have no flowers and cannot produce seeds. Their green color does, however, enable them to make their own plant food. There is another group of living things —known to be living because they grow and multiply—which includes mold on fruit, bread, or cheese; mushrooms and bracket fungi in the woods; mildew on lilac leaves or damp clothing; scabs on apples and potatoes; rusts and smuts of grain plants. These have no green color and therefore make no food; they have no flowers and therefore produce no seeds. (For the study of germs, see Unit 61, page 254.)

Primary and junior children are familiar with ferns in home and wood. They can appreciate their lacy foliage and their graceful droop, and look for flowers in vain. They have sat on mossy stones and liked this green woodland carpet; they can use it to make pretty dish gardens. Puffballs, toadstools, and bracket fungi have been to them things to wonder at, toys to play with; they can learn that they are real plants by watching them spring up, and soon die (fig. 1). But primary and even junior pupils don't care how any of these plants make a living or produce new plants.

Intermediate pupils should come to understand a little about how these special plants live, grow, and reproduce. Knowing that green leaves make food in sunlight, they can understand that ferns and mosses need water and soil and light. Missing flowers, they should wonder how such plants can make new ones. Then they should be shown the little brown patches on the underside of fern leaves (fig. 1), and the little cases swaying on moss plants; they should be told that both of these contain tiny seed-like things which blow to moist places and make new ferns or mosses. By com-

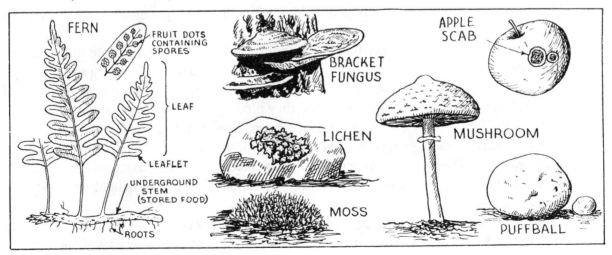

Figure 1—Some Common Plants which Don't Have Seeds

97

paring the puffballs, mushrooms, bracket fungi, molds, and rusts with people who cannot work and cannot make their own living, we can lead them to see that the absence of green leaves prevents these plants from making their own food; therefore they need no sunlight. They must therefore get their food ready-made from other plants or their decaying remains. How they do this is beyond the pupils' understanding. Neither can the pupils profit from knowledge of the structure of such plants. By placing a full-grown mushroom with its stem removed, on white paper, they can see the tiny, dark, dust-like spores, and learn that these can make new plants. Experiments with bread mold help to clarify their ideas of how molds grow, use food, and reproduce.

Activities

All Grades

- Collect and press very carefully as many different kinds of ferns as you can find so that you can make blueprints of these later (Unit 21, page 84).
- Collect different kinds of mosses and transplant them into a vivarium. Select an interesting kind and plant it in a small bowl for the dining-room table.
- Let some moss dry up, and then see how much water it will soak up, and how quickly it turns green again.
- Examine leaves of fern plants for small raised spots, usually brownish, on the under surface. From these come many tiny spores, each of which can produce a new fern plant.

Junior and Intermediate Grades

- Make a chart of plants without flowers. Mount and label pictures of various kinds.
- Visit a florist's shop and find out the names of several kinds of ferns.
- Collect specimens of mushrooms, puffballs, toadstools, etc.
- Find mushrooms growing in a fairy ring. Write an imaginative story about them.
- Decay of fruits and vegetables is caused by invisible plants growing in them. Then why should storage places be thoroughly cleaned before filling them with vegetables or fruits?
- Make a chart showing the good and harm done by plants without seeds.
- When you find flowers on a fern, you will know that it is an asparagus fern and not a real "fern."
- Find some mushrooms or toadstools (poisonous mushrooms) of which the umbrella-like cap is opened widely. Cut off the stalk of the mushroom and leave the cap on a sheet of white paper for a few hours. Then remove the mushroom. The black lines on the paper consist of spores. When these fall in damp rich earth, they produce new mushroom plants.
- Grow a mold garden. In five tumblers, place respectively some jam, preserved fruit, bread, and two other foods of your own choice. Expose them to air for a day. Cover them with a glass sealer top. Observe the way mold grows, the colors, the little black knobs which come on it and contain spores. The spores will start new mold plants if they alight on moist food in a warm place.
- Look on weathered rocks, fences, logs for flat, gray, papery patches of plant life. These are lichens. They can withstand long drought. As they grow, they wear away part of the rock and make a little bit of soil.

Read

Comstock, *Handbook of Nature-Study,* pp. 693-731. Allen (Comstock).

Dickinson, *The First Back of Plants* (grades 5-8). Ambassador (Watts).

Frasier et al., *The How and Why Club* (grades 5-6): "Why Does Food Spoil?" pp. 148-167; *How and Why Experiments* (grades 6-8): "Some Plants Do Not Grow from Seeds," pp. 15-29. Dent (Singer).

Hylander, *Out of Doors in Spring* (grades 6-8): "Mosses and Ferns," pp. 84-101. Macmillan. Nicol et al., *The Nature Hour,* Sixth Year—Autumn and Winter: "Ferns," pp. 55-67. Gage (Silver, Burdett).

Partridge, *Everyday Science,* Book One: "Plants without Flowers," pp. 268-270. Dent.

New to this Edition

Leahy, Peterson, and White. *Peterson First Guide to Insects of North America* (Houghton Mifflin Harcourt, 1998).

Llewellyn, Claire. *The Best Book of Bugs* (Kingfisher, 2005).

Winner, Cherie. *Everything Bug: What Kids Really Want to Know about Bugs (Kids' FAQs),* (NorthWord Press, 2004).

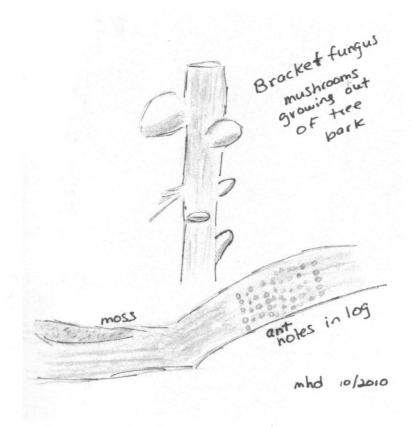

Beautify Your Surroundings – October – 1

BULBS:

FOR INDOORS

FOR OUTDOORS

FOR THANKSGIVING, A DISPLAY OF FLOWERS AND VEGETABLES GROWN IN YOUR SCHOOL GARDEN.

PLAN NEXT YEAR'S LANDSCAPING ACTIVITIES ON THE SAND-TABLE.

A **VIVARIUM** AND AN **AQUARIUM**, PROPERLY KEPT, WILL BE NEVER-FAILING SOURCES OF BEAUTY AND INTEREST

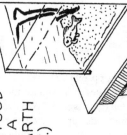

(EARTHWORMS FOR FOOD CAN BE STORED IN A LARGE BOX OF EARTH IN THE BASEMENT.)

BLACKBOARD STENCILS ARE EASY TO MAKE:

① DRAW THE OUTLINE ON HEAVY WRAPPING PAPER.

② PUNCH AROUND THE OUTLINE WITH A LARGE DARNING NEEDLE.

③ HOLD STENCIL AGAINST BLACKBOARD, TAP WITH DUST-FILLED BRUSH. DOTTED OUTLINE FOR COLOURING IS FORMED ON BLACKBOARD.

TEACHERS SHOULD SELECT SUCH ACTIVITIES SUGGESTED ABOVE AS ARE FEASIBLE, AND AT THE TIME BEST SUITED TO LOCAL CONDITIONS.

D. Farwell

Science in Action ~ October

CUTTINGS:

Choose good healthy stalks. Remove all but one or two leaves. Plant in moist sand. In about two weeks, when new growth has started, transplant into pots.

Put a fresh cutting in water that has been coloured by the addition of a little red ink. Discuss the results.

FIND A BRACKET FUNGUS:

With a stick, draw a picture on the white underside

(Why does the pressure of the stick leave brown marks?)

Gather some galls from the goldenrod. Cut them open and see if you can find the tiny grub inside

And, of course, such activities as:

LEAF COLLECTIONS	WEED COLLECTIONS
SPATTER PRINTS	BLUE-PRINTS
	VARIETIES OF TREE BARK

A LONG-TERM EXPERIMENT:

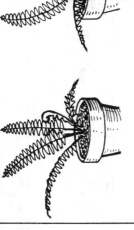

Choose two ferns as nearly alike as possible. Care for each similarly, but use fertilizer tablets for one fern. Note what changes occur over a period of several months.

"CONVECTION" CURRENTS:

PAPER CHIMNEYS

SMOKING STRING

HOLES IN TOP OF BOX

CHALK BOX WITH GLASS SLIDE IN PLACE OF LID

SMOKE

CANDLE

GLASS BOWL OR JAR

WELL-SOAKED SAWDUST IN WATER

SUPPORT

ALCOHOL LAMP

Use these simple experiments to show how stoves or furnaces provide warmth for cold rooms.

D. Farwell

NATURAL SCIENCE — NOVEMBER — DAY BY DAY

SUNDAY	MONDAY	TUESDAY	WEDNESDAY	THURSDAY	FRIDAY	SATURDAY
			1 Start a school display of fruit or vegetables.	2 Find out how best to store potatoes, cabbages and apples	3 Find and list animals that store food in winter.	4 Find and name fruits suitable for bird food now.
5 Start a collection of poetry suitable for November.	6 Why do I face to your right now? (S) (M) (E)	7 Why does smoke go up the chimney?	8 How is the length of day changed since a month ago? Why?	9 Learn to recognize five kinds of house plants by sight.	10 Why are wool clothes warmer than cotton ones?	11 What wild animals are still active in your neighbourhood?
12 How many days since the last new moon? Why?	13 Bring a pet to school for a week and care for it.	14 At the first opportunity watch ice crystals form on water.	15 Search the garden for flowers still in bloom.	16 Have tree buds changed since a month ago?	17 Cut a wormy apple. Draw the worm's tunnel.	18 Look for codling moth larvae in cocoons under tree bark.
19 With D window as sun, two pupils place themselves as earth and moon.	20 Start a picture story of coal or other fuel.	21 What birds are still here? Feed them.	22 Sketch the height of the sun at noon.	23 Sketch your bulbs planted a month ago.	24 Search for tent caterpillar egg on twigs of trees and shrubs.	25 Sketch a November landscape with green and leafless trees.
26 A walk in the woods will be interesting.	27 Make a temperature chart for a week.	28 Repeat what you did on November 19. (E) (M)	29 Where are frogs, toads, and snakes now?	30 Cover your perennials with straw manure or garden refuse.		

J.A. PARTRIDGE
Drawn by D. Farwell

Have your pupils build this calendar day by day on blackboard or chart.
Use substitutions if desired.

NOVEMBER

Unit 25—Insect Friends and Foes in Autumn

Insects in general are probably man's greatest enemy. They outnumber all other forms of animal life and all flowering plants. There are some fitted to live in nearly every kind of condition, wet or dry, cold or warm, on plants or on animals. Their rapid multiplication makes them an immediate threat when even one pair appears.

Many devour plant life to such an extent that, if uncontrolled, they would soon destroy the food of man's stock and even of man himself. When field insects have taken their toll, others continue to destroy stored crops or products. Still others attack man's domestic animals, his clothing, and even his stored meat. When man succeeds in conserving the necessities of life, other insects carry disease to him, or at least prove to be a constant nuisance.

But we should not forget that we have insect friends as well as enemies. The bees supply us with honey, and the silkworms make our silk. Ladybird beetles and dragonflies destroy many harmful insects, and other tiny parasitic insects lay their eggs in the bodies of harmful caterpillars, finally causing their death.

Insects should, for these reasons, be important objects for firsthand observation and both scientific and economic study by all of our children before they leave the elementary school. Such study should, as largely as possible, consist of personal observations of the insect, either in its natural environment or in cages in the classroom.

If the pupil can recognize some of our most common insects, realize the harm they do, and witness the change from egg to adult, he will be better able to understand the measures of control to be taken against the harmful varieties, and will know when those measures should be applied.

Insects Injurious To Garden Plants

Cabbage Butterfly. *Recognition:* on cabbage and cauliflower plants; caterpillar about 1 ¼" long, green, faint golden line down back; butterfly white. *Habits:* adults emerge in May and lay yellowish eggs singly on underside of leaves: eggs hatch in about 5 days; caterpillars feed upon leaves and heads of plants maturing in 2 or 3 weeks and changing to pupae on leaves or stems; adults emerge in about 9 days; usually two more generations, with pupae wintering on plants or other shelter. *Harm:* reduce leaf surface, cause unsightly heads, lower market value. *Control:* spraying, arsenate of lead, 2 lbs. to 40 gals. water. *Seasonal activities:* May, watch for new adults; June-Sept., observe eggs, larvae, and eaten cabbages.

Tomato Worm. *Recognition:* brown, cigar-shaped pupae dug up from garden soil in May; gray moths in June; fat green caterpillars on mature plants. *Habits:* pupa winters in soil; adult emerges in June, active at night, and feeds on nectar from flowers; yellowish-green eggs laid singly on underside of leaves and hatch in about a week; caterpillars feast on tomato leaves, maturing in about a month, then burrow into ground and pupate. *Harm:* caterpillars eat leaves, preventing food-making and reducing yield. *Control:* hand-picking. *Seasonal Activities:* May, collect pupae from ground; June, watch moths emerge, look for eggs on plants; July-Sept., observe feeding by larvae, protective coloration, and partially eaten leaves; Sept., collect caterpillars, feed in chimney vivarium over soil, observe burrowing and pupation.

Insects Injurious to Fruit Trees

Codling Moth. *Recognition:* white or pinkish worm in apples; small grayish-brown moth in May. *Habits:* worms, escaped from apples in autumn, live over winter in cocoons under loose bark; pupate, and moths emerge in May; eggs laid on blossoms; worms enter apples soon after petals fall

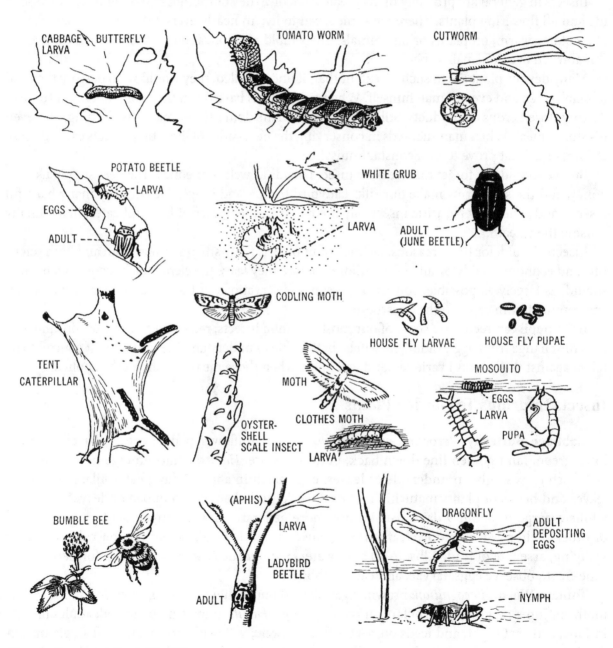

Figure 1—Some Insects Pupils Should Know

and feed until July or August; usually two broods a year; cocoons spun in autumn. *Harm:* wormy apples fall early; marketed apples worth less; decay frequent at worm-holes during storage. *Control:* spray immediately after petals fall, with 2 lbs. arsenate of lead in 40 gals. dilute lime-sulphur. *Activities:* May, find tiny worms ready to enter newly formed apples, practice controls; September, observe worm and its burrow in apples; November, search for cocoons under tree bark.

Insects Injurious Or Annoying To Man

Clothes Moth. *Recognition:* moths small, white, or cream-colored; larvae slender, white, ½"; among woollens, furs, feathers, hair, etc. *Habits:* adults active in April, May, June, nocturnal and do no direct harm; eggs laid in dark parts of woollens, furs, etc.; larvae eat holes in these materials, chiefly from May to November, then pupate in cases made of cloth and silk. *Harm:* destruction of clothing, upholstered furniture, bedding, etc. *Control:* moth balls or dichloricide crystals. *Activities:* May, kill every moth you find; clean textiles well before storing for summer; study larvae, if unfortunate enough to find any.

Insect Friends

Bumblebee. *Recognition:* adult thick, yellow, and black, about fields. *Habits:* queen only lives over winter in protected place; in May queen seeks deserted mouse nest in grassy place, collects pollen and nectar, and lays her eggs on this; young larvae hatch in 4 to 5 days and feed on the stored food, then pupate in tough cocoons in the nest; young worker bees gather pollen and nectar and make more bee-bread for the increasing family, while queen continues to lay eggs: honey is stored in deserted cavities formerly occupied by larvae. *Benefit to Man:* pollination, especially red clover. *Activities:* name flowers visited by bumblebees; watch bees gather pollen and pack it in pollen baskets to be carried away; search for bumblebee nests—cautiously.

Ladybird Beetle. *Recognition:* adults small, hard-backed, black and red; larvae with yellow and orange spots. *Habits:* winter as adults in sheltered spot: eat aphids and scale insects; eggs laid in spring on plants; larvae active, shed skin; pupate on plant, hanging by tail; adults emerge in few days. *Benefit to Man:* rid house and garden plants of aphids and scale insects. *Activities:* May, observe adults on plants infected with aphids or scale insects; notice larvae feeding; find pupae on plants later.

Activities

Teacher

To guide pupils in collecting materials for incidental observation, study, and discussion, and, if suitable, for display or storage in the museum (Unit 33, page 131), write the following list on the board: *specimens showing insect damage*—cloth damaged by clothes moths, stems or ears of corn damaged by corn-borers or earworm, roots and potato tubers partially eaten by white grubs, leaves curled by plant lice (aphids), leaves damaged by leaf miners (leaving the veins only), maple and oak leaves bearing galls, grain or meal containing mealworms, wood showing tunnels made by ants or wood-boring beetles; *specimens showing insect values*—beeswax and honey, silk, clover seed (result of pollination by bumblebee).

All Grades

- Examine cabbage leaves closely for green cabbage worms and tiny eggs. Place some caterpillars in a screened cage and keep them supplied with fresh leaves. Observe how they eat, grow, and become chrysalids.
- Look for the following insects about the garden—squash bugs, grasshoppers, plant lice, crickets, tomato worms—and find out why each is hard to see.
- Collect as many kinds of insects as you can find, in the air, on plants, on land, under boards, in water. Pack in a small box or bottle the ones which you cannot name and mail them to the Zoology Department, Ontario Agricultural College, Guelph, for identification.
- Place a few crystals of sugar and bits of jam and fresh fruit in a bottle with a housefly. Close the bottle with cloth; watch how the fly dissolves solids and sucks up juices. A lens will help.
- Follow a plow in sod and look for white grubs, the larvae of May beetles. Look for their burrows.
- Look in stalks of corn for corn-borers. How do they make their tunnels?
- For your museum (Unit 33, page 131) collect things which show the work of insects—nests, cocoons, galls, honey, comb, carvings in wood, worm-eaten apple, etc.
- Collect and destroy the egg clusters of tent caterpillars.

Junior and Intermediate Grades

- Make an insect cage. Obtain two lids of coffee tins. Roll a screen to form a cylinder which will fit between the lids. Tie it. Mix plaster of Paris (Unit 21, page 84) to fill one lid, and fit one end of the screen cylinder into this. Leave this to harden. The other lid will be the cover. See Unit 7 (page 24) for other ideas. Use these for the indoor study of insects.
- Each pupil survey a garden for insects and damage done by them. Collect materials to use in giving an oral report to the class.
- Each group of two or three pupils select one common insect. Find out all you can about its life habits, the harm it does, and how to control it. Then plan and make a chart illustrating this information. Display the charts in groups under the headings "Insect Foes and "Insect Friends."
- For a class record, prepare an insect calendar recording what you have found out about common local insects under the main heading "Insects We Know" and subheadings: Name, Activities in Autumn, How It Winters, Activities in Spring and Summer, Control.
- Make a puppet stage from a cardboard carton. Build up a garden scene as a background. Use cardboard insects for puppet heroes and villains. Have an insect orchestra. Study the life of each insect and make your play true to nature.

Read

Adrian, *Honeybee.* Allen (Holiday).

Karlowe, *A Child's Book of Insects.* Ryerson (Maxton).

Blough, *Animals That Live Together* (grades 2-3), The Basic Science Education Series. Copp Clark (Row, Peterson).

Blough & Parker, *The Insect Parade* (grades 4-6), The Basic Science Education Series. Copp Clark (Row, Peterson).

Donne, *A Book of Nature,* pp. 30-31 and 76-77. Oxford.

Frasier et al., *How and Why Experiments* (grades 5-7): "Some Insects Are Harmful," pp. 102-115, and "Some Insects Are Helpful," pp. 102-115. Dent (Singer).

Hunt & Andrews, *Insect Parade.* Moyer.

Hussey & Pessino, *Collecting Cocoons* (grades 4-7). Ambassador (Crowell).

Johnstone, *Science in the School Garden* (grade 7): "The Honey Bee," pp. 23-35. Macmillan.

Mason, *Animal Sounds:* "Insect Music," pp. 48-53. McLeod (Wm. Morrow).

Parker, *Insects and Their Ways* (grades 4-6), The Basic Science Education Series. Copp Clark (Row, Peterson).

Parker & Gregg, *Insect Friends and Enemies,* Tl.e Basic Science Education Series. Copp Clark (Row, Peterson).

Partridge, *General Science,* Intermediate, Book 2: "Insect Friends and Foes," pp. 83-106; "The Grasshopper," pp. 1-6; and "The Honeybee," pp. 6-11. Also *Everyday Science,* Book One: "Insect Enemies in the Garden," pp. 6-12, and "Codling Moth," pp. 40-42; *Everyday Science,* Book Two: "Ants and Their Ways," pp. 1-6; "Insect Enemies," pp. 47-56; and "Bee Ways," pp. 72-88. Dent.

Phillips & Wright, *Some Animal Neighbors* (grades 4-6): "Ladybirds," pp. 64-67. Copp Clark (Row, Peterson).

Podendorf, *The True Book of Insects* (primary). Book Society (Children's Press).

Sherman, *The Real Book About Bugs, Insects and Such.* Blue Ribbon Books (Garden City).

Shuttlesworth, *Exploring Nature with Your Child:* "The Wonderful Ways of Insects and Spiders," pp. 232-288. Nelson (Greystone).

Smith & Clarke, *Around the Clock* (grades 3-4), pp. 39-62. Longmans, Green.

Stewart, *Straight Wings:* "Meet Mr. Cricket," "Meet Mr. Grasshopper," and "Meet Mr. Grasshopper's Cousins." Gage (American Book Co.).

Tibbets, *The First Book of Bees* (grades 4-6). Ambassador (Watts).

Williamson, *The First Book of Bugs* (grades 4-6). Ambassador (Watts).

New to this Edition

Locker, Thomas, Water Dance (Sandpiper, 2002).

Malnor, Bruce. *A Teacher's Guide to Drop Around the World: Lesson Plans for the Book a Drop Around the World* (Dawn Publications, Tch Edition, 1997).

McKinney, Barbara. *A Drop Around the World* (Publications, 1998).

Olien, Rebecca. *The Water Cycle (First Facts: Water All Around),* (Capstone Press, 2006).

Relf, Pat. *The Magic School Bus Wet All Over: A Book About The Water Cycle* (Scholastic, 1996).

Van Cleave, Janice. *Janice VanCleave's Earth Science for Every Kid: 101 Easy Experiments that Really Work* (Wiley, 1991).

Wick, Walter. *A Drop of Water: A Book of Science and Wonder* (Scholastic, 1997).

Figure 2—(Photo courtesy of Sergei Loboda)

Unit 26—The Story of a Raindrop

FUNNY WATER

The teakettle's dry! The teakettle's dry!
The water has boiled off in vapor.
Where has it gone? Oh where has it gone?
It's cutting a runaway caper.

The vapor has vanished! It's floated away!
1 cannot think where it can be—
Oh, here on the windowpane gathered in drops
The vapor has settled, I see.

Water, oh water, how funny you are!
The heat makes you vanish in steam,
The cold brings you back into millions of drops
For teakettle, ocean, and stream.
Reprinted from *Better Homes and Gardens* Magazine

Water has been called a great tourist. Visibly it falls as rain or snow from the clouds, collects in streams, and fills the lakes and oceans; when evaporated from there, it once again forms rain and ice and snow. Water is also a transport. Having fallen on the soil, it dissolves minerals, and carries these along with sediment to lower levels. There it may enter a plant, and invisibly carry its load of dissolved minerals through the roots and stems to the highest leaves. Leaving its load behind, it evaporates into the air and again becomes a cloud.

While carrying on its work, water takes three different states—vapor, liquid, and solid. Of these states, children and even adults frequently have many inaccurate ideas. Water vapor is always invisible and is always present to some extent in the air. Steam is merely water vapor near the boiling point; therefore we never see steam. What we see a little way from the kettle spout is a small cloud condensed from the steam and present as minute drops of water.

The presence of water vapor in air can be proved either by showing that liquid water disappears (evaporates), and must therefore be in the air, or by changing water vapor in the air to the liquid state by causing it to condense on a cold object, as when a cold plate is held near the spout of a teakettle containing boiling water. This water vapor in the air comes from the surface of rivers, lakes, ponds, and oceans, from pavements and the earth, from wet clothes, from plants, and even from us. The warmer the air is, the more water vapor there can be in it, and the more rapid is evaporation of water into it. The cooler the air is, the less water vapor there can be in it; hence, when warm, moist air is cooled by coming close to a cold object—a window in winter, a pitcher of cold water in summer—some of the water vapor in the air condenses to drops of water on the object. In a similar manner, dew forms on grass or other objects which are cold in the night, then disappears as vapor again when the sun warms the air and the objects.

Clouds, like dew, are made up of water. When warm, moist air rises and is cooled, some of the water vapor in it changes to tiny drops of water. A large number of these make up a cloud. When they grow larger or combine, they form larger drops of water, which fall as rain.

When rain reaches the ground, it may either evaporate, sink into the ground, or run off and form a pool. If it evaporates, it again becomes a part of a cloud. If it soaks into the soil, it may find its way underground to a spring, and thence to a surface stream from which it evaporates; or it may enter the roots of a plant, pass through its stems and leaves, and again enter the air.

Everyone has watched raindrops run down a windowpane, one sliding into the other and slipping to the bottom. Raindrops do the very same thing on ground where they do not soak in. Small drops join others, these join still others until there is so much water running down the hill that we call it a creek or a river. From the river it may become a part of a lake or an ocean. But finally it again climbs back into the air as vapor, then joins its fellows in a cloud.

Throughout all the ins and outs of drops of water man both gains and loses. From them we obtain the rain for our crops, for our streams and lakes, for our cisterns, springs, and wells. But, uncontrolled, the same water stops our work and play, soils our clothes, washes away our soils and plants, floods our valleys and streets. To learn about its ways and to know how to control it for our benefit are worthwhile to all of us.

A JOURNEY TO CLOUDLAND AND BACK

Some little drops of water
Whose home was in the sea,
To go upon a journey
Once happened to agree.
They had a cloud for carriage,
And drove a playful breeze,
And over town and country
They rode along at ease.
But, oh, there were so many
That soon the carriage broke,
And to the ground came tumbling
The frightened little folk.
Then through the moss and grasses
They were compelled to roam
Until a brooklet found them,
And carried them all home.
SELECTED

The study of a raindrop might well begin on a rainy day. The age of the pupils will determine their interests, and therefore the subject matter. Primary and junior grades will be interested in such topics as where the rain comes from, how it forms little streams and pools, how the sun and wind dry up the puddles, how it makes the flowers and grass grow, how it cleans the sidewalk and street and carries little sticks and straws, how it paints the rainbow, how it gives drink to animals and to us. In addition to such observational studies, intermediate pupils should learn to understand the nature of water vapor and steam, the conditions favorable for evaporation (wind, warmth, and dry air), the need for a low temperature for condensation, something of the formation of dew and clouds and rain, what becomes of rain after it falls—its experiences before it returns to a cloud.

I am the daughter of Earth and Water,
And the nursling of the Sky;
I pass through the pores of the ocean and shores;
I change, but I cannot die.
SHELLEY

Activities

All Grades

- Place a dish of dust or flour where rain is falling. What shape are the raindrops which fall on it? Compare them in size.
- Make a finger-painting of a rainstorm. Paint a rain scene during a sudden shower. Include a pupil holding an umbrella or some other article used on a rainy day.
- Make a picture of a rainy day. Show umbrellas, raincoats, rubbers, and other articles to indicate rain.

Primary Grades

- Make a drawing of: "Out in the Rain," "The Rain Is Falling All Around," or "Rain, Rain, Go Away."
- Learn to distinguish 1 inch, 2 inches, ½ inch while measuring the rain which fell in a dishpan.
- Make rainbows by blowing soap bubbles.
- Watch birds and other animals take baths in little pools after a rain. How do they dry themselves?

Primary and Junior Grades

- Boil some water in a kettle or a tin cup. Notice that the water gradually disappears. Where does the water go? What comes from the kettle? Hold a dry dish in this steam. Now we see the water again. Where must the water go when there isn't any dish there? See the little cloud at the mouth of the kettle. This is made up of water.
- Place a tablespoonful of water in each of three saucers. Put one in a sunny window, another in a shaded window, and another under the radiator. Which dries first? Hang a wet cloth in a sunny window, another wet cloth in the shaded window, and another near the radiator. Which

dries first? What helps to dry up water? On what kind of day will mother's clothes dry best?

- Make up little stories of the things you have seen and learned. Your teacher will write them on the board, where you may all read them. Draw a clothesline filled with clothes on a sunny day.

Junior and Intermediate Grades

- Why does it rain? Soak a sponge with water. Squeeze it gently. What happened? A cloud may be compared to the sponge, holding water. When the cloud gets colder it cannot hold so much moisture. Some of the water drops from the cloud as it did from the sponge when you squeezed it.
- Notice water on the inside of windows and on people's glasses when they come inside on a cold day. This water came from the air. Discuss why water doesn't form on walls and doors; feel that they are not as cold as the glass. Watch the mist on the glass form into drops heavy enough to run down.
- Write a story beginning: "Just as the party broke up, it started to rain."

Intermediate Grades

- Learn more about evaporation. Place equal quantities of water in six saucers and place them respectively where it is cold, warm; calm, windy; shady, sunny. What happens to the water in each dish? Could you see the water leave? Where did the water go? Invisible water is water vapor. Water changes to water vapor by evaporation. How can evaporation be speeded up?
- In what three ways may water disappear after a shower (run off, soak in, evaporate)? List examples of evaporation which you have seen. Where does dew go? Frost? Perspiration? The water in wet hay or clothing?
- Cover a vivarium or an aquarium with glass. Observe drops of water forming on this. Where did the water come from? Why do we not see it in the air? What causes it to gather on the glass? (The water vapor in the air, evaporated from the water, soil, or leaves, condenses on the cool glass. Later it returns to the soil and waters the plants.)
- Observe your breath on a cold day. What you see is a small cloud. Why did the water vapor breathed out form this cloud? What became of the cloud later?
- Read stories of the difficulties in obtaining fresh water aboard sailing ships in early days. Investigate the methods of obtaining a supply of fresh water on modern liners. Boil some sweetened water in a teakettle. Hold a plate in the escaping steam. Catch drops of water falling from it. Taste them. They are not sweet because the water vapor did not contain any of the sugar.

Illustrate this in your notebook:
- *The sun*—evaporates water from
- *The lake*—which forms
- *A cloud*—which produces
- *Rain*—which makes
- *A river*—which forms
- *A waterfall*—over which water falls, making
- *Power*—from which
- *Electricity*—is produced.

You will learn more about clouds and rain in Unit 70 (page 291).

Read

Blough & Parker, *Water Appears and Disappears* (grades 4-6), The Basic Science Education Series. Copp Clark (Row, Peterson).
Frasier et al., *Winter Comes and Goes* (grades 2-3): "Water in the Air," pp. 122-125. Dent (Singer).
Parker, *Clouds, Rain, and Snow.* Copp Clark (Row, Peterson). Partridge, *General Science,* Intermediate, Book 1, pp. 88-92 and 99-101; and *General Science,* Intermediate, Book 2: "Weather and Moisture," pp. 347-355. Dent.
Zim, *The Sun:* "The Cycle of Water." McLeod (Wm. Morrow).

New to this Edition

Breen and Friestad. *The Kids' Book of Weather Forecasting (Williamson Kids Can! Series),* (Ideals, 2008).
DK Publishing. *Eye Wonder: Weather* (DK Children, 2004).

Figure 1—Niagara Falls, water source for Niagara-Mohawk hydroelectric system.

Unit 27—Let's Keep a Weather Calendar

The study of weather in school may be justified in many ways. It is useful as well as interesting and educative. It helps to make more vivid the study of our own or other lands. Understanding of rainfall is more real when a pupil has actually measured it. Such study helps to remove the more or less common popular dependence upon superstitions and replaces it with a scientific dependence upon more careful observations, unbiased thinking, and reliable conclusions.

Weather means much to the daily activities of the average pupil. It influences his games, his clothing, his travel, his food. When conscious of these things, pupils may be easily motivated to make weather observations and to record these in class or individual charts and calendars.

The making of weather calendars must not degenerate into a mere routine for pupils. It should make pupils so weather-conscious that they will notice weather phenomena and use them to forecast future weather conditions as a help in planning their daily activities. As they advance through the elementary school their experience should broaden from isolated observations of wind and calm, sun and rain, heat and cold, to an understanding of the relationships among them. Weather diet, like food, must be in keeping with the children's capacity to digest it.

Success in weather study and weather recording demands: firsthand weather study by every pupil; teacher guidance by directing such observations by grade groups; brief oral discussions in class; individuality and variety in the way in which pupils express weather ideas in their calendars or charts; integration of this work with crafts, art, and English; a later comparison of pupils' records (particularly above primary grades) to form a basis for weather forecasting.

Knowledge of what the weather will be interests all of us. It helps children to plan their hikes, picnics, and sporting activities; it helps adults to plan farming operations, business trips, boat sailings, and shipments of perishable goods.

After considerable observing and recording of weather conditions, pupils should draw such conclusions as these: NW. winds bring fair, cool weather; N. winds bring still colder but fair weather; NE. winds bring cold and snow in winter and chilly rains in summer; E. winds bring rain, and SE. ones still more-rain; S. winds bring warmth and showers, and SW. ones rapidly melt the snow. A clear sky at sunset is usually followed by a clear day, while a ring around the moon or sun indicates a coming storm. They should also be able, from the records in their calendars, to understand the truth or fallacy of such weather sayings as these: "Rainbow at night is the shepherd's delight (true)." "Red sky at morning is a sailor"s sure warning (true)." "The higher the clouds, the finer the weather (true)."

Observations and records made by many others have led to the following summary of weather signs. *Continued fair weather is promised by:* a gentle wind from W., NW., or SW.; sunsets in a cloudless sky, reddish, glowing, or like a ball of fire; starry skies, or moon rising clear; rainbow at night; blue sky between clouds.

Storms or rain may come after: the W. wind drops suddenly or shifts to S. or NE.; the sky looks

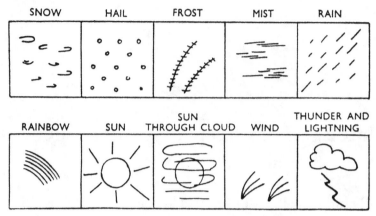

Figure 1—Symbols for Weather Charts (Courtesy A. & C. Black Ltd.)

like fish scales (mackerel sky), or a ring shows around the moon or sun; a morning rainbow or a red sunrise; smoke falls; the sun "draws water" (rays between clouds). *Clearing weather is suggested by:* wind changing from E. to W.; rapidly falling temperature; clouds breaking with blue patches between.

Activities

Teacher

Primary and junior pupils develop very simple concepts about the weather. Through their everyday experiences they learn that the wind blows things about, pushes against them while they walk, and pulls on umbrellas. A little later they realize that the wind may help them to school in the morning, but hinder them on the way home, i.e., that wind has direction. Similarly they learn about the sun and the rain and temperature. These, then, are suitable topics to be included in their calendars.

The weather records of primary and junior pupils must have a high degree of interest for them. They may be introduced by using cut-outs of children dressed for different weathers. These may be named Sally Sunshine, Carl Cloud, Rufus Rain. The appropriate cut-out will be put before the class each day. A little later, a class chart of a week's weather may be made on the blackboard by using such symbols as a yellow circle for a sunny day, a closed umbrella for clouds, an open umbrella for rain, and a kite for wind.

Some weeks later, make another class weather chart for a month. On the blackboard, from a common centre, draw four circles, the outer one as high as the blackboard. From the inner circle to the outer circle, draw radii to make spaces for each day of the month. In the inner circle, place the name of the month; in the next, the date; in the third, weather symbols; in the outer one, drawings of nature observations for that day.

The next stage may consist of individual weather records written as simple stories and drawn on calendars. These should be required for only short periods at a time.

Here is a correlation of weather records with composition and blackboard reading. After talking about the weather, have pupils make a blackboard picture to illustrate it for the day. Beneath this compose, write, and read such little stories as: "Today is bright and sunny", "The clouds are big and woolly", "The wind blows the clouds and trees", "We can have our picnic".

Pupils of intermediate grades have experiences and mental capacity which warrant an extension of their weather observations to include definite readings of temperature, measurement of the direction and the speed of the wind, a more analytical report of sky conditions (sun, cloud, and rain), and perhaps an introduction to the measurement of air-pressure.

The following weather symbols may be used for pictorial representation of weather in any grades. *Sunny:* yellow color, cutouts of yellow circles, sun with rays. *Cloudy:* cutouts of child carrying an umbrella, a circle half-shaded or half-gray. *Fog:* F in a circle. *Hail:* a shaded triangle. *Sleet:* an unshaded triangle. *Rain:* cutouts of an umbrella held up or of a person with a raincoat, shading in two directions, circle shaded or gray. *Snow:* chalk blotches on the blackboard, white crayon or paint, circle in white or enclosing S, stars falling, sleighing. *Ice:* skating, icicle cutouts. *Wind:* kite cutouts; blowing paper, hat, snow or dust, clothes; wind vane or direction arrows; words. *Temperature:* cold shown by winter coat, blue circle, mittens; warm shown by red circle; readings. Others are given in fig. 1.

Activities

All Grades

- Make a large class weather book with one page for each day. Several pupils contribute drawings, cutouts, or pictures to illustrate the weather of each day—wind blowing, sun shining, rain falling, play suitable to the day, etc. Each pupil take his turn at placing these.
- Each pupil make a weather booklet with a page for each day. Include pictures, drawings, and little stories.
- Draw free expression pictures to represent: N. wind, S. wind, rainy day, bright day, etc.

Primary and Junior Grades

- Find the direction of the wind by watching smoke.
- Once a day make a drawing to show whether the sky is clear, cloudy, or very cloudy.
- Cut a card 16 inches wide and 12 inches high. In a rectangle 4 inches wide across the top, print "Today's Weather Is." Divide the rest of the card into two rows of 4 squares each. On the four inner squares, draw pictures to illustrate sunny, rainy, cloudy, and windy weather. The two squares on each side should be cut so that they can close as doors over the pictures. Use paper clips as door handles. On each day, note the weather and open the right doors.
- Make a Peter Rabbit written calendar. Rule black mural paper as a monthly calendar, with spaces about 8 inches square. Date each space in one corner. Trace and cut out a paper rabbit for each day and a number of red coats and blue hats to fit the rabbit, and also a number of small umbrellas and yellow suns. Each day a pupil will paste a rabbit in place. On cold days, place a red coat and a high, blue hat on the rabbit; on windy days, place the hat as if blown off his head; on rainy days, place an umbrella in bunny's paw and show falling raindrops by means of colored chalk; show sunny days by a yellow sun; on very warm days, have the rabbit without a hat or coat. Combine the different symbols as needed. See also fig. 2.
- When winter comes, make another calendar. Rule squares on a large card for a month's weather chart. In the upper left corner of each square, print the date. To represent weather conditions, attach colored cutouts made by pupils to include rain (umbrella), wind (kite), cold weather (mittens), snow (sled), frost (icicles), sunny weather (sun).

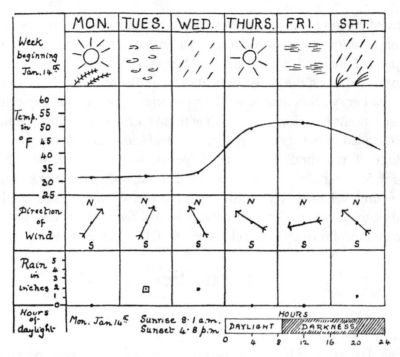

Figure 2—A Week's Weather Record

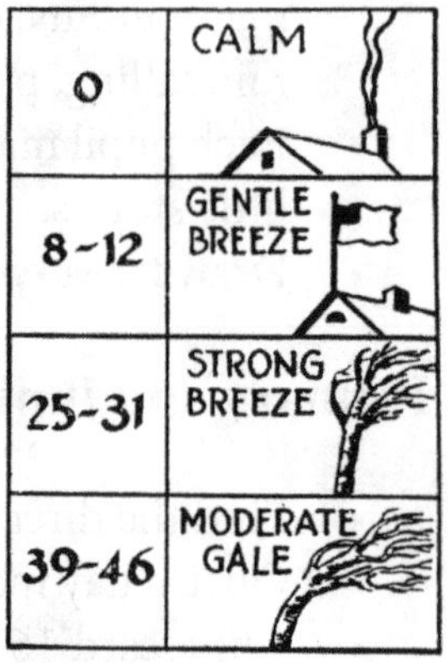

Junior and Intermediate Grades

- Keep a dated scrapbook with published weather forecasts in one column and actual weather conditions for the same day in a second column.
- Make a weather clock. Cut a card 2 feet square. Draw its diagonals. Then draw circles with radii 12 inches, 8 inches, and 3 inches respectively. Label: the inner circle—N, NE, E, SE, S, SW, W, and NW; the sections of the second circle—calm, gentle breeze, strong breeze, and moderate gale; and the sections of the outer circle—sunny, slightly cloudy, very cloudy, and rainy. Attach three clock hands labeled wind direction, wind strength, and sky. Have pupils take turns in placing the hands where they belong each day.
- In a weather booklet, mount pictures, poems, and other clippings concerning weather.
- Make blackboard and individual weather calendars like the one below.

Figure 3—A Simple Beaufort Scale to Measure Wind Speed.

The figures at the left indicate the speed of the wind in miles per hour.

| Date | Sky Appearance | Rain or Snow | Wind | | Temp. | Remarks |
			Direction	Speed		

Indicate observations as follows: sky appearance—bright, cloudy, dark; rain or snow—none, light, heavy, or by measurement; wind speed—use the terms in the scale below or in fig. 3; temperature—junior grades: cool, warm, or hot; intermediate grades: actual reading.

A Modified Beaufort Wind Scale			
Key Number	Terms Used in Weather Forecasting	How Detected	Speed in Miles per Hour
0	Calm	Smoke rises vertically	0
1	Light	Smoke and wind vane move; wind felt in face	1-7
2	Gentle	Light flag extended	8-12
3	Moderate	Dust and small branches move	13-18
4	Fresh	Small, leafy trees sway	19-24
5	Strong	Hard to walk or to hold an umbrella	25-38
6	Gale	Tree limbs broken off	39-54

Intermediate Grades

- Each day, during a discussion, make a weather forecast for the next day. Then check the accuracy of your forecast.
- Find an almanac in which the weather is forecast throughout the year. Check it with the actual weather conditions from day to day.

Read

Beauchamp et al., *Look and Learn* (primary): "Days and Days," pp. 39-52. Gage (Scott, Foresman).

Craig & Hill, *Adventuring in Science* (grades 6-7): "The Weather Today and Tomorrow," pp. 44-63. Ginn.

Dowling et al, / *Wonder Why* (Primary). Winston. Frasier et al, *Through the Year* (grades I-II): "A Record of the Weather," pp. 106-7. Dent (Singer).

Partridge, *General Science*, Intermediate, Book 2: "Making Weather Records," pp. 341-343 and 345-346; and *Everyday Science,* Book Two: "Keep Weather Records," pp. 459-460. Dent.

Stephenson, *Nature at Work*, Book 3 (grades 5-6): "Recording the Daylight and Weather," pp. 33-37. Macmillan (A. & C. Black).

Tannehill, *All About the Weather* (grades 7-8). Random House.

Westell, *Among Nature's Children,* Naturecraft Readers, Book I (grades 3-5): "The Weather," pp. 15-30. Clarke, Irwin (McDougall).

Unit 28—Why Not Make a Weather Station?

Mark Twain once said, "Everybody talks about the weather, but no one ever does anything about it." To a certain extent, this is true in our schools. We talk about the weather, and sometimes record it, but seldom do we go to the trouble of having pupils actually measure the wind, the rain, and other elements of which it is composed. But these are necessary to complete our weather calendars just begun. So let's begin now by establishing a simple weather station (fig. 1).

As the weather becomes colder, and frost kills our vegetables and flowers, children become conscious of lowering temperatures. This is the time to begin to study the measurement of temperature and, incidentally, to establish the weather station. To get a true idea of the temperature of the air, the thermometer must be placed on the north side of a post and shaded from the morning and evening sun.

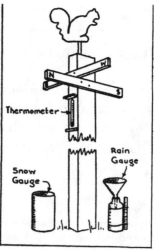

Figure 1—A Weather Station Pupils Can Make

But temperature depends in part upon the direction of the wind; hence the need for a wind vane. When the wind blows harder, we feel the cold more. This leads to a discussion of wind speed and methods of measuring it. (See the Beaufort scale, Unit 27).

Frequently, pupils lack a vivid idea of the meaning of so many inches of rainfall. This is perhaps due to abstract methods of presentation and the lack of personal experiences. To actually measure the amount of rain during a moderate or heavy rainfall would strengthen the understanding that one inch of rain means that the rain that fell would measure one inch in depth if it had been spread over a level surface. The rain gauge is easily arranged, as shown in fig. 1. Into a tall, straight-sided glass bottle, about 2 inches in diameter, insert a funnel about 6 inches across, sealing around the bottle neck with Vaseline. Rainwater will be collected in the bottle and its depth there measured by means of the ruler, correctly attached, as shown, to read from the inside bottom of the bottle. If the funnel has a diameter three times that of the bottle, its area will be nine times as great (the square), and the depth of rainfall in inches will be one-ninth that of the depth of water in the bottle.

When snow melts, it serves the same purpose as rain. Therefore, to get a clear picture of the number of inches of water (rain and melted snow) falling annually in any place, we must measure the depth of snow, too (Unit 41, page 167).

To support the thermometer and wind vane, we need a high post far enough from buildings that air currents will not be interfered with. This post may also be used as a shadow stick.

Responsibilities for the making and care of the weather station and for making readings and records should be divided among pupils of all ages, according to their abilities. One may read the temperature each day at 9:00 a.m. and at 4:00 p.m.; another, the length of the shadow at noon; and another, the direction and speed of the wind. Or one pupil may serve as weatherman for the day. Observations should be made at the same time each day.

The weather station will make possible more accurate observations, and more complete records in weather calendars. These then become more scientific and more useful in weather forecasting.

Activities

Junior and Intermediate Grades

- For a simple rain gauge, place a coffee can in an open, level place. After a rain, measure the depth of the water in inches.
- Make a wind vane. Find and study pictures and plans. Use light wood such as pine, basswood, or cedar. Shape it to have an arrow head on one end. The other end must be flat, broader, and resting on edge so that it will catch enough air to keep it turned in the direction toward which the wind blows; the arrow will then point to the direction of the wind. Drill a hole through the wind vane so that it will balance on the post. Through this, insert a nail small enough to let the wind vane turn easily. Nail two direction sticks to the post, one pointing N.—S., the other, E.—W.
- Attach a pinwheel to the wide end of the wind vane so that its turned-down points face the wind. Its speed will vary with the speed of the wind.
- Hang up a piece of seaweed. It will be damp when the air is moist and rain is likely, and dry in fine weather.
- Measure the depth of snow in a pan during a calm snowstorm. Measure the depth of water when this snow has melted. How many inches of snow make one inch of water?

Read

Beauchamp et al., *Discovering Our World,* Book 3 (grades 5-7): "What Does the Weatherman Do?," pp. 50-59. Gage (Scott, Foresman).

Frasier et al., *Winter Comes and Goes,* (grades 3-4): "The Weather Vane," pp. 131-132 and *How and Why Experiments* (grades 5-8): "What Makes the Weather?" pp 174-191 Dent (Singer).

Parker, *Ask the Weatherman* (grades 6-8) and *The Ways of the Weather* (grades 6-8) Copp Clark (Row, Peterson).

Partridge, *General Science,* Intermediate, Book 2: "A School Weather Station," pp 340-343; also *Everyday Science* Book Two: "Your Weather Station," p. 461, and "Weather for Tomorrow," pp. 470-478. Dent.

Patch & Howe, *The Work of Scientists* (grades 5-6): "What the Weather Man Does," pp. 29-40. Macmillan.

Smith & Henderson, *Beneath the Skies* (grade 6), pp. 79-98. Longmans, Green

Tannehill, *All About the Weather* (grades 7-8). Random House.

New to this Edition

Gibbons, Gail. *Weather Words and What They Mean* (Holiday House, 1992).

http://www.ambientweather.com/weather-stations-for-kids.html
http://www.weathershack.com/education/school-weather-stations.html

Unit 29—Goodbye, Autumn

This unit is inserted about the middle of November, a time when pupils begin to think that autumn is passing away and winter is at hand. It is meant to form a sort of connecting link by reviewing some autumn phenomena and introducing preparations for winter.

"Current events" in school work have been by tradition largely connected with social-studies topics. Although man's world moves fast, nature's world moves faster. Through daily observation of its changes, pupils gradually become aware that people live in a world of change and must constantly adapt themselves to it in food and clothing, in work and play, and in their social relationships. "Current events" should therefore include references to seasonal changes such as flowers killed by frosts, leafless trees showing deserted birds' nests, some birds flying south and others remaining behind, the insect chorus of sunny October somewhat silenced, man and wild animals preparing for winter, etc. The reports may supply a close correlation with art as well as language if pupils are encouraged to illustrate their observations with free, though perhaps crude, sketches. With such a beginning, the teacher may plan a rather broad program of class activities calculated to provide really worthwhile learning situations, traditionally classified under subject names.

Activities

All Grades

- Find out how to know when plants have been killed through freezing. List the plants in the garden which are already dead and list some plants which frost does not kill. Find green leaves which frost does not harm.
- Different pupils represent various trees, flowering plants, animals, etc., and tell in the first person how they say farewell to autumn.
- Make a sand-table scene of autumn. Include trees with colored leaves, green and brown grass, named weeds bearing seeds, autumn wildflowers, models or cutouts of birds still present, twigs to represent evergreen trees, winter homes of various animals.
- List children's work and play activities: first, common in summer; second, in autumn, but impossible in winter. This should show how seasonal changes affect children.
- Plan to feed birds that remain for winter.

Primary Grades

- Dramatize a conversation between a plant whose leaves have been killed and one whose leaves have not been harmed.

- Plan a mural entitled "Goodbye, Autumn." Have some pupils draw in a background; others may color and cut out outlines of birds going south and animals gathering food or preparing winter homes; still other pupils may prepare colored outlines of autumn fruits, etc. Let each pupil place his work in the proper place on the background.
- Collect picture clippings from magazines and mount them in a scrapbook entitled "Goodbye, Autumn."

Primary and Junior Grades

Make a chart to illustrate autumn. Plan and begin a corresponding chart to illustrate "Winter Is Coming."

Junior and Intermediate Grades

- Make a blackboard frieze to show a typical autumn landscape with the dead remains of autumn wildflowers, the bare trees silhouetted against a hazy November sky and enlivened by a few contrasting evergreens, a local stream labeled "But I go on forever," a flock of birds southward bound, a few winter bird friends such as the downy woodpecker and the chickadee. In building up this record of autumn's passing, pupils would naturally be expected to read appropriate prose and poetry, and to tell the class of their findings. Such reports would include valuable natural science information concerning bird migration, autumn fruits of the garden, field, and forest, as well as weather studies, etc. Class periods in the arts could be profitably devoted to the preparation of material that would also contribute to the frieze.
- Write a story of "My Discoveries About Autumn."
- Correspond with children farther north and south than you to find out about their changing seasons.

Read

New to this Edition

Albert, Toni. *A Kid's Fall Ecojournal* (Trickle Creek Books, 1997).
Leslie, Clare Walker. *Keeping a Nature Journal: Discover a Whole New Way of Seeing the World Around You* (Storey Publishing LLC, 2003)

Unit 30—How People Prepare For Winter

In Unit 20, the whole topic of preparation for winter was dealt with through the enterprise method, but only for primary children. Here the topic is presented briefly from the standpoint of junior and intermediate pupils as an introduction to their more advanced study of how plants and animals prepare for winter (Unit 31 on page 124 and Unit 32 on page 127).

Through this study, pupils should gain a deeper consciousness of the need for people to adapt themselves to seasonal changes. Thus, this science study of adaptation contributes to the everyday life of pupils in showing that we must constantly adapt ourselves to changes both in our physical environment and in our relationships with other people. The topic may be analyzed on the basis of the five essential requirements of people, including the children themselves—namely, food, clothing, shelter, work, and recreation.

Food for winter is largely prepared for in autumn. The farmer and the owner of a garden must harvest, prepare for market, and either store or sell his crop of apples and other fruits, potatoes and other vegetables (Unit 18, page 72). People without gardens must either lay in their winter supply under proper storage conditions or depend upon retail stores to keep them supplied. The retailer can obtain his supplies only if the wholesale and storage businesses have laid in their supplies. Throughout the harvest season, fruits and vegetables are canned at home and in the canning factories.

Anticipation of winter not only causes us to buy or take from storage warmer clothing; it determines the kind of stock laid in by retailers and wholesalers. Months before autumn is actually here the manufacturers of all sorts of clothing have made their supplies of winter goods.

For winter, our homes must be heated and kept warm. To heat them, furnaces must be cleaned, stoves put up, and supplies of coal, coke, and wood must be brought from the mine or woods—where they were being prepared months in advance. To retain heat in our houses, storm windows and doors are put up, doors and windows are weather-stripped, and, for some homes, the foundations are banked or insulation placed where it is needed.

If man's work is to continue without interruption in winter, he must prepare to meet winter weather conditions. The farmer provides winter food and extra shelter for his animals. For travel, he exchanges the wagon for the sleigh. To make highway traffic possible, snow fences are put up, snow plows arc prepared for action, and defrosters attached to automobile windshields.

Some changes are necessary to adapt the ways we use our leisure time and obtain recreation from summer to winter conditions. Instead of continuing to care for our roses and lawns, we turn off the water from fountains and pools, and prepare plants and bulbs for winter bloom. Mindful that spring is coming, we cover many outdoor plants to protect them for the next growing season. Fishing lines and bathing suits are exchanged for sleighs and snowsuits.

Activities

Junior and Intermediate Grades

- Find what each of the following are doing to get ready for winter: your parents, a farmer you know, a storekeeper, a market gardener. List what you are doing about it. Make a large drawing illustrating what each person named is doing.
- We always like to be comfortable. Display pictures to show (1) how we obtain comfort in summer (light clothing, electric fan, shade tree, cooling drinks), (2) what we do in autumn so as to be comfortable in winter (stove, mitts, coal, storm windows).
- Dramatize: father ordering coal, mother asking Dad to put on storm windows, mother buying apples and vegetables.
- Make a frieze consisting of five sections, dealing with how people prepare for winter in relation to food, clothing, shelter, work, and recreation. Junior pupils collect and mount pictures; intermediate pupils use their own drawings.

Read

Copeland, *The True Book of Little Eskimos.* Book Society (Children's Press).
Schneider, *Science for Here and Now* (grade 2): "We Store Food," pp. 89-100. Copp Clark (Heath).

Unit 31—How Plants Prepare for Winter

The leaves and stems of most plants are too tender to withstand frost. The roots of some plants die along with the leaves and stems. The only way these plants can produce new growth in spring is to form new seeds in autumn. Such plants are called *annuals*.

When the leaves and stems of carrots or beets are killed in autumn, the roots remain alive. Each root has invisible buds on the top ready to produce new leaves, even stems and flowers, when warmth and moisture are supplied in the following spring. Food stored within the root makes this possible. The plant dies at the end of the second year after having produced seeds. Plants that live in this way are called *biennials*.

Many other green plants die down to the ground each autumn, but their roots live over winter for several years. Among these are peonies and rhubarb. Their spring growth begins from buds formed in autumn and fed in spring by stored food. Such plants are called *perennials*. Trees and shrubs are also perennials. Most of them form buds in late summer, store food in their stems and roots, shed their leaves in autumn, and produce a new crop of leaves from their buds in spring. Some trees and shrubs—the evergreens—retain their leaves all winter without harm to tree or leaf. But these plants have other special structures which enable them to meet winter conditions.

To give pupils a satisfactory explanation of leaf fall is impossible; we do not understand the causes ourselves. Certainly frost is not a necessary cause, as is shown by the fact that many leaves fall before the occurrence of frosts. To state that leaves are shed to avoid being frozen is indeed illogical. The theory that branches would be injured by the weight of snow held by retained leaves is disproven when we observe that an oak tree that has not shed its leaves is free of snow in winter while neighboring evergreen trees are laden down. Leaf fall seems to be an annual habit of trees, the cause of which is not fully understood.

All living green leaves constantly give off moisture. Plants absorb moisture more slowly from cold soil than from warm soil. If a tree should keep its leaves in autumn, it would probably lose more moisture through its leaves than it could gain through its roots. This would injure the tree by causing it to dry out. Therefore, instead of trying to tell why leaves fall, we should be content to show that it is a good thing for the tree that they do fall—and this to pupils of intermediate and senior grades only. Primary and junior pupils cannot be expected to go beyond an observational study of leaf fall.

Before trees and shrubs shed their leaves, they produce buds. These serve two purposes. As winter buds, they protect the tender, growing points of branches. As spring buds, they produce stems and leaves in spring, both enlarging the tree and giving it a new collection of food-making factories. Pupils should observe these buds in autumn to learn that they are a preparation for winter; in winter, to see that they are resting, merely protecting the tender parts within; in spring, to follow their enlargement and the development of the tiny stems, leaves, and perhaps flowers, within. Observe the buds of several kinds of trees so that pupils will not conclude that all buds have varnish or a woolly layer within. When varnish is present, it helps to keep sap in and water out, and to seal the scales together. The overlapping scales help to protect the inner parts from injury by rain, insects, and drying winds. The soft layer (if present) within insulates the inner growing parts from sudden changes of temperature. The little stem and leaves tightly packed within the bud are a preparation for spring's awakening rather than for winter.

For future growth, food is stored by most plants in seeds; by some, in roots (carrot); by some, in leaves (cabbage); by some, in underground stems (potato); by some, in stems above ground (maple).

The stored foods may be sugar (detected by sweetness), starch (shown to be present when a drop of iodine produces a blue color), oil or fat (shown when it produces a grease spot on paper), and also proteins.

Sugar-beet roots and maple stems contain a great deal of sugar; parsnip roots, potatoes, and wheat kernels contain much starch. Many nuts contain fat. This food enables new growth to begin from buds or embryo plants when suitable growing conditions return, as in spring.

Activities

Teacher

Discuss the pupils' reports which are given in their calendars as suggested in Unit 10 (page 41), Unit 12 (page 48), and Unit 17 (page 69).

Junior and Intermediate Grades

- Draw a plant such as peony before it dies down to the ground and after.
- Draw and color a tree before the leaves fall and after.
- Find whether it is easier to take leaves from a tree which has begun to shed its leaves, or from a geranium or petunia plant. On which stem are the leaf scars the smoother and drier? This shows that trees actually get their leaves ready to be shed. What effect have wind and rain on the number that fall? It is the weight of the rain and the pressure of the wind that causes leaves to fall a little earlier than they would otherwise.
- Examine a twig for leaf scars. Draw a few. Feel their surfaces. This corky layer keeps the sap from being lost when the leaf falls.
- Dip a twig with its varnish-covered buds in water. How can you tell that they are waterproof?
- Crush fallen leaves and green leaves. Which contain more sap?
- Examine trees and shrubs for buds. These will open in spring. Find the overlapping scales which cover them; see how closely they fit. Rain and insects cannot enter between them. Find some horse-chestnut buds. Their varnish-like cover forms an extra raincoat. Dig into one. The white woolly substance serves as a sweater keeping the delicate growing-point inside from too sudden changes in temperature, but not preventing it from freezing. Now find tiny green leaves wrapped together in the center. These are well protected until spring, when warming days will make them throw off their covers and become next year's leaves and stems. Open some large buds of horse-chestnut, lilac, or fruit trees. What do you find that makes you think there is a little flower already formed?

Intermediate Grades

- Place a begonia or foliage plant in a refrigerator for a few days. What happens to the leaves? Why does the plant wilt? Though there was water in the soil, the plant could not drink it because it was too cold. Most trees in fall do not get enough water to drink because the soil is cold. At about that time they drop their leaves.

- Burn some fallen leaves. The ash shows what they return to the soil—namely, mineral foods. Pile some leaves, mixed with soil, to decay. The soil which they make will be rich in minerals needed by plants.

- Saving for a rainy day! Most plants, like thrifty people, save for the future. The food which they do not need now, they store to use when they start work the following spring. Bring to school some underground parts of quack grass, ferns, iris, potatoes, parsnip, sweet potato, gladiolus. Notice how thick and fleshy they are. Do they contain plant food?

- Shake some starch with water (milky color); add a drop of iodine (brown color); observe the blue color of the mixture. No other substance is known to produce a blue color in the presence of iodine. Add a drop of iodine to a slice of each of the above-mentioned plant parts. What food does each of these contain? What purpose is served by this food in spring?

- Transplant in flowerpots some harvested carrots, beets, turnips, or parsnips. Keep the soil moist and the plants in a warm place. Observe the new growth of leaves and the shrinkage of the root. Why do the roots shrink?

- Remove a nut from a shell and crush it. Rub it against white paper. The greasy appearance shows that there is oil or fat in the nut.

- Do plants store food in their seeds? Soak some beans, corn, wheat, and rice for a day to soften them. Break or cut them open, then add a drop of iodine to the surface. Is there starch in them? Chew some wheat until it become sweet. Your saliva changes the starch to sugar.

- What kind of food is stored by maple trees? Where?

Read

Blough, *Plants Round the Year* (grades 2-3), The Basic Science Education Scries. Copp Clark (Row, Peterson).
Hylander, *Out of Doors in Autumn* (grades 6-8): "Plant Life Prepares for Winter," pp. 95-113. Macmillan.
Stephenson, *Nature at Work,* Book 3 (grades 5-6): "The Trees Prepare for Winter," pp. 25-32. Macmillan (A. & C. Black).
Webber, *Anywhere in the World.* Allen (Wm. R. Scott).
Williams & Campbell, *Easy Lessons in Nature Study,* Book IV (grades 4-6): "The Fall of the Leaves," pp. 94-99. Oxford.

New to this Edition

Kalman, Bobbie. *The Life Cycle of a Tree* (Crabtree Publishing Co, 2002).
Wyatt, Valerie. *Wacky Plant Cycles* (Mondo Publishing, 2000).

http://www.uvm.edu/pss/ppp/articles/prepare.html

Unit 32—How Animals Prepare for Winter

Winter is the trying time of the year for many forms of life. But most plants and animals have some particular way of meeting the problems brought on by that season. Neither do they await its coming. They prepare in advance, mostly by instinct, and are ready when the unfavorable conditions arrive.

Probably the most pressing problem of animals in winter is to obtain enough of a suitable kind of food when the ground is frozen and frequently snow-covered. The insect- and plant-eating animals are the first to suffer. Those feeding upon flesh find less difficulty in getting food.

We seldom think of the disappearance of the animals until autumn stillness has set in. Then we suddenly miss them. Where are they? What are they doing? A pupil search of hollow trees and logs, burrows in the ground, and the mud beneath the streams, and even of the nooks and crannies of the garden or house will show them some of the secret hiding places.

Warm-blooded Animals. Animals of this class have a fairly constant body temperature. Ours, like that of most animals, should be about 98.6° Fahrenheit. Birds may have a temperature of 104° to 110° Fahrenheit. The body heat of warm-blooded animals must be maintained by the oxidation of either a fresh or stored food supply, through the breathing process.

Animals That Remain Active Throughout Winter. The red squirrel and the black squirrel store up their food when it is easily obtained in autumn. In addition to hiding nuts carelessly in the ground or storing them in hollow trees, the red squirrels, with more forethought or a more beneficial instinct, dry mushrooms on tree twigs as a future substitute for fresh vegetation. With a plentiful food supply always available, such animals can remain active much of the winter, taking to their hollow-tree nests only in severe weather. Rabbits and field mice, though dependent upon vegetable food, can remain active all winter by substituting twigs and bark of trees, frequently of our orchards, for herbaceous vegetation. Carnivorous animals such as the fox, the weasel, and the mink continue to catch birds, rabbits, mice, squirrels, and even poultry for their winter food.

Searching for food on snow-covered ground exposes animals to winter enemies. The weasel and the varying hare obtain protection by getting a new coat resembling the white surroundings. The cottontail rabbit does not so change for winter.

Some other animals that remain active over winter find it necessary to modify their ways of living in keeping with the winter conditions. Beavers start early in autumn to build their elaborate dams to make ponds. These must be deep enough to provide them with a storage place for tree branches and logs for food, and an entrance to their homes from under the ice. Muskrats continue to remain active under the ice or in open streams, especially at night. Their homes consist of tunnels in high banks or dome-shaped houses projecting above the ice, but well protected from the winter storms.

Most mammals, both domesticated and wild, which remain active in winter, and therefore exposed to severe weather—cats, dogs, horses, cattle, sheep, squirrels, beavers, muskrats, minks, weasels, etc.—grow a warmer coat of hair, fur, or wool for the cold season. The shorter, thicker hairs close to the body imprison so much air that they form an efficient insulating layer. The longer hairs help to shed snow and rain. Birds, too, that remain for winter usually have a heat-retaining layer of down feathers next the body.

Animals That Hibernate. Most common animals such as "The Seven Famous Sleepers," including the bear, the woodchuck, the skunk, the raccoon, the chipmunk, the bat, and the jumping mouse (fig. 1) do not store food for winter and do not remain sufficiently active to eat it if they did. But even these animals must continue to use food to keep the body warm. This food is stored throughout the autumn as heavy layers of fat. Many such animals also develop a deeper and thicker coat of fur or hair to insulate the body.

Figure 1—The Seven Winter Sleepers (Courtesy W. J. Gage & Co., Ltd.). Bear, woodchuck, skunk, raccoon, chipmunk, bat, jumping mouse.

THE RACCOON PUTS ON ENOUGH FAT IN FALL TO LAST IT THROUGH THE WINTER. USUALLY SEVERAL CURL UP TOGETHER IN THE SAME NEST FOR THEIR WINTER SLEEP.

Figure 2

Hibernating animals differ widely in the soundness and length of their sleep. A bat remains in complete stupor until the warmth of spring awakens it. The bear may shift to another part of his den to find more comfortable quarters, even in midwinter. The woodchuck or groundhog may venture forth in early spring and then return for another nap. The raccoon will peer out of the entrance of his hollow tree or log (fig. 2) in mild spells or in early spring before most sleepers awake. The chipmunk stores a variety of foods, chiefly grain and nuts, in an underground system of tunnels and dug-outs. This provides ready food, not only for autumn days, during which he still sallies forth, but also during winter. Huddled in his underground home, with the doorway securely plugged, the chipmunk eats between sleeps and comes out in spring much fatter than his neighbors.

Animals That Migrate. Animals which cannot find food in winter or store sufficient nourishment in the form of body fat to enable them to hibernate in sheltered quarters for the winter must travel to a more favorable climate. Most of our birds must prepare for winter in this way. In the north, the reindeer seek food and protection by migrating from the barren coastal regions far inland to the northern forests, where they get moss for food. Even man, when he can afford it, may migrate to the more comfortable climates of California or Florida.

Cold-blooded Animals. Insects, fish, frogs, toads, salamanders, snakes, turtles, crayfish, and earthworms do not have a constant body temperature: they remain at about the temperature of their surroundings. A warm coat of hair, fur, or feathers or a layer of fat would be of no value to them. To prepare for winter, they select a place where they may continue to breathe in their own way and where the least changes of temperature are likely to occur.

Land animals such as snakes, toads, and salamanders, seek out protected places under rocks, leaves, or logs, and sometimes in caves. Frogs burrow into the mud in the bed of a stream, empty their lungs, and continue to breathe slowly through their skins, obtaining enough oxygen from the water in the mud. Even the slow use of flesh as food for breathing makes them rather thin by spring.

Insects prepare for winter in a variety of ways. Only the queens of the bumblebee and white-faced hornet colonies live over winter. Honeybees continue to feed upon stored honey and produce some warmth in their hollow tree or manmade hive by exercising. The monarch butterfly avoids winter by flying south.

Some insects, such as the tent caterpillar, grasshoppers, and aphids, lay their eggs in autumn and die; others, such as the codling moth and the European corn-borer, remain inactive in the larva stage under a protecting cover of bark, plants, stalks, and other garden refuse. Most moths spend their winter protected by a silken cocoon.

Water animals may either remain active, travel to new quarters, or become inactive. Most fish do not change their ways of living to any extent. They must remain beneath the ice with a diet limited to smaller fish and other water animals. The eel travels from fresh waters down to sea in autumn, ready to lay its eggs in the South Atlantic in spring, and then die. Clams, snails, and crayfish remain in the bottom of the

Figure 3

stream, and are less active because of the coldness of the water. Water insects accustomed to coming to the surface in summer dive into the mud for winter.

Activities

All Grades

- Look for these and tell in class about what you find: flocks of monarch butterflies ready to go south; dogs, horses, and cattle with long, shaggy hair; insects hiding in crevices about buildings; earthworms deep in the ground; animals under piles of rubbish; egg sacs of spiders.

- Make such drawings as: a muskrat beside its new home, a cocoon, eggs of tent caterpillar on a twig, grasshopper eggs in the ground, a beaver cutting a log for its dam, a squirrel carrying a nut, a fat groundhog entering its burrow, a frog in the mud at the bottom of a stream. Use these to make a frieze, mural, or booklet.

- Make a poster to illustrate how animals prepare for winter. Show a group of animals approaching a place where roads cross. Draw a signpost bearing such signs as: "Insects will find warm beds underground," "Birds—this way (south)," "A good place for a beaver pond," etc.

- Each group of three pupils make a three-section frieze illustrating one of these: animals that build winter homes (beaver, muskrat, mouse); animals that store food for winter (red squirrel, black squirrel, chipmunk); animals that go to sleep; animals that change color (varying hare, weasel, snowshoe rabbit); animals that go below the frost line in the ground (earthworm, potato beetle, frog).

Primary Grades

- Look for animals storing food, making winter homes, leaving for the South, spinning cocoons, growing different-colored or thicker coats (dog, cat, horse, cow).

- Make a blackboard chart entitled "How Animals Get Ready for Winter." Each good observation made by a member of the class will be entered on the chart. Use column headings like these: Name of Animal, How It Was Getting Ready for Winter, What It Looked Like (a drawing), Observer's Name.
- Read stories of animals which hibernate, and tell them to the others in your class.
- Make a little booklet, "My Animal Friend Gets Ready for Winter." On the cover draw a picture of the animal, and inside write a story about him. Draw pictures inside the book, too.
- Collect pictures of animals in their summer clothes and in their winter wraps. Then use them in a mural or frieze.
- Make a mural or frieze showing how animals prepare for winter. Show squirrels storing nuts, a bear going into a cave, a fox entering his burrow, a raccoon looking out of a hollow tree, birds and butterflies going south.
- Collect pictures of animals which store food for winter, which go to sleep in protected places, which travel to warmer countries for winter, and those which remain active and must find food in winter. Mount them in groups on the bulletin board.

Junior and Intermediate Grades

- Make a list of many animals such as: spiders, earthworms, flies, ants, house mouse, beaver, robin, chickadee, turtle, etc. Each member of the class should find out how some one of these prepares for winter, and report to the class.
- Make a blackboard or wall frieze entitled, "How Animals Prepare for Winter." Assign sections such as "Store Food," "Become Fat," and "Change Color" to groups of pupils for illustration.

Read

Alexander & Cormack, *Bruce and Marcia, Woodsmen*: "Winter Cradles," pp. 110-122; "Bear Swamp," pp. 123-134; and "Where Muskrats Dwell," pp. 153-170. Gage (American Book Co.).

Blough, *Animals Round the Year*, pp. 2-19, The Basic Science Education Series. Copp Clark (Row, Peterson).

Craig & Hurley, *Discovering with Science* (grades 5-6): "Animals and the Seasons," pp. 20-33. Ginn.

Frasier et al., *Through the Year* (grades 1-2): "Winter Is Coming," pp. 36-41; *The Seasons Pass* (grades 3-4): "The Birds Migrate," "Where Are the Frogs?," and "No Earthworms," pp. 34-51; *How and Why Experiments* (grades 5-7): "Some Mammals Migrate" and "Some Animals Hibernate," pp. 61-75. Dent (Singer).

Gall & Crew, *All the Year Round*, pp. 25-36. Oxford.

Hamilton, *Winter Sleep—Animals That Hibernate*. Audubon Nature Bulletin. National Audubon Society.

Hethershaw & Baker, *Wonders To See*: "How Animals Spend the Winter," pp. 75-114. Gage (World Book).

Hylander, *Out of Doors in Autumn* (grades 6-8): "Animal Life Prepares for Winter," pp. 114-131. Macmillan.

Smith & Henderson, *Through the Seasons* (grades 5-6), pp. 7-27. Longmans, Green. Stephenson, *Nature at Work*, Book 1 (grades 4-5): "The Winter Sleep," pp. 21-29. Macmillan (A. & C. Black).

Webb, *Song of the Seasons* (grades 4-6) : Autumn, pp. 71-94. McLeod (Wm. Morrow).

Webber, *Anywhere in the World*. Alien (Wm. R. Scott).

Willers, *Adventures in Science*, Book III (grades 3-4), pp. 46-51.

Moyer. *Hibernation—The Winter Sleep of Animals*. Royal Ontario Museum of Zoology, Toronto.

New to this Edition

Berger, Melvin. *What Do Animals Do in Winter?: How Animals Survive the Cold* (Ideals Publications, 1995).

Pascoe, Elaine. *How and Why Animals Prepare for Winter (How and Why Series)*, (Creative Teaching Press).

Shields, Amy. *National Geographic Little Kids First Big Book of Why* (National Geographic Children's Books, 2001).

Unit 33—Have a Nature Museum

For vital science teaching, there must be a place indoors where personal observations and practical activities are possible. Adequate space for group work, good lighting, and facilities for rearing living things and storing others are essential. A nature room in an urban school, a nature corner in a single classroom—a sort of museum of living and non-living things of nature—serves these purposes well. The classroom museum is not a place for "canned goods," or curios, or things marked "Don't touch!" It is a place where pupils may be active, interested, and learning—where living pupils and nature come together indoors (fig. 1).

In the background of the nature museum should be a bulletin board for the display of nature pictures, mounted collections, clippings, bird migration maps, calendars, charts, etc. Shelves will serve to display mounted birds, bird nests, small preserved specimens such as insects and galls, living animals in small cages, rocks and minerals, books and magazines. Aquaria and vivaria may be placed on a well-lighted table. A larger table, with or without sand, is convenient for exhibits of

Figure 1—Investigating and discovery in the classroom nature museum. (Photo courtesy of Jen Mackintosh)

beaver life, and the woods in winter, and for daily practical work. In the nearest window may be living plants and experiments to illustrate their functions. A bench or seats should be at hand to accommodate two or three pupils at a time.

The science museum is of value only insofar as motivation and opportunities are afforded pupils to use it. Probably most profitable will be incidental use of it by pupils in groups of two or three when they, of their own volition, visit it to observe and study nature firsthand, or read about it, when they have completed assignments. Free conversation about the exhibits, subject to personal restraint in fairness to other pupils, contributes to interest and learning. To sustain interest and keep up the habit of going to see what's new, the materials on display should be changed frequently, in keeping with class work or seasonal changes.

Most materials for the museum will be brought in by pupils. Every member can contribute something—an interesting leaf or shell or insect. Some will lend rarer specimens from their homes. A seasonal exhibit day, or a public exhibit once a year, will stimulate contributions.

Success of the museum will depend upon the arrangement of materials. Little expense is required. Sturdy cardboard can be covered tightly with old white cloth to serve as mounts. Specimens can be attached anywhere by means of strips of white cloth pasted down with flour paste; where this will not hold, a needle and thread can be used. Seeds may be stored in small bottles or pill boxes, each labeled and placed in a larger box. Trays for rocks, minerals, and shells may be made by pupils. Orange crates on end provide bookcases and display shelves.

Since order is nature's first law, orderliness and tidiness are of first importance in the museum. Dust, broken materials, and refuse mar the attractiveness of the museum and kill interest in it. The care necessary for its upkeep may be assigned to a curator, with or without helpers, whose duties consist of labeling (with name, source, and contributor) and arranging supplies, and maintaining cleanliness and tidiness. The office should be one of honor given to pupils meriting it.

Activities

Teacher

Advance planning will make the classroom museum more valuable. By checking the Program of Studies, the teacher can list many kinds of specimens which will be useful in later teaching. Knowing what the list contains, pupils can collect many of the things required, and place them in the classroom museum. Here are some general needs: collections of leaves, woods, grains (heads and kernels), seeds (of garden flowers, vegetables, etc.), weeds, fruits suitable for bird food, rocks, and minerals.

- Take time in the morning to discuss any additions to the museum.
- Have a "What Is This?" shelf in a conspicuous place. Pupils bring objects to be placed there. Place reference books nearby for pupils to use in finding answers. Name each object the next day. Change such objects frequently. Nearby have a mystery box where pupils may place questions or mysteries to be solved. Give credit to pupils providing solutions.

All Grades

- Make an exhibit like the one reported here: "The pupils gathered two empty orange crates, a can of paint, cotton batting, and cellophane. The boys painted the orange crates and stood them side by side. The girls covered the shelves with cotton batting and made cellophane curtains for the fronts. All pupils brought materials such as nuts, other seeds, leaves, shells, puffballs, a bowl of gold fish, and a pet canary; then they all helped to arrange the exhibit."
- Arrange three sides of a large cardboard carton in the form of a stage with a background and two wings bent outward. From time to time make a new display consisting of background scenes painted on paper and attached in place, and foreground scenes consisting of real or modeled objects resting on the stage.
- Make a collection of minerals, rocks, and shells of your locality. To each, attach a piece of paper or adhesive tape bearing a number. On a card nearby list the numbers and, after each, the name of the object bearing that number.
- Make a nature den—a secret place in which you and your fellows keep nature curios. Select a secluded corner in the schoolyard or woodshed, an attic room at home, etc. Store there the things that interest you in nature.
- Arrange a corner of your museum as a school zoo. In it keep, for a day or two at a time, a pet animal. Find out more about how this pet sleeps and eats, its likes and its dislikes.

Unit 34—Insects in Winter

Each kind of insect has its own way of tiding over the winter. Most species become inactive, some in the egg stage, some as larvae or pupae, some as adults. A few, chiefly those living in places kept warm by man, remain active all winter.

The eggs of grasshoppers and crickets are the only living stage of these insects during the winter. They are laid in the ground in autumn and covered. The warmth of the spring sun causes them to hatch. Neither the eggs nor the young have any parental care— all the young are orphans destined to lay their eggs and die when autumn comes. Plant lice (aphids) face winter in a still different manner. Throughout the summer many new generations, consisting entirely of females, are produced by the direct birth of living young. The last generation, consisting of males and females, produces fertile eggs which will endure winter conditions and hatch when trees and shrubs are leafing in spring.

The codling-moth larvae found in apples in autumn crawl out, seek shelter under bark scales of trees, spin cocoons, and spend the winter as larvae in these protecting covers. They do not change to pupae until spring. Then follow the moths, which lay the eggs on the blossoms.

The pupae of many insects carry the race through from one year to the next. In protected places near cabbage patches, the unprotected chrysalids of the second or third generation of cabbage butterflies winter over, ready to give up gauzy-winged adults in spring. Safe in the ground, the cigar-shaped chrysalids of the tomato worm lie inactive from fall to spring. Within is wrapped the fully matured sphinx moth, ready to crawl out and dry its wings at the call of spring. Many other pupae are protected from the storms of winter by tightly woven silken cocoons. In these we find the winter stage of such moths as Cecropia, Luna, Promethea, and Polyphemus (illustrated in Unit 77, page 324). Some of these have the extra protection of a leaf wrapped about the cocoon. Still other pupae neither are chrysalids nor have cocoons. Those of the potato beetle, resembling a sleeping adult, remain deep in the soil from freezing time until thawing time.

The adults of several kinds of insects live over winter. The common housefly makes no change for this season. Any sort of crevice large enough to hide it will make good enough sleeping quarters. When the bumblebee family has finished the year's work in autumn, all except the queen die. She seeks some well-protected grassy patch for her winter's sleep, and in spring lays eggs for the new generation. In autumn, too, the honeybee drones are cast out by the workers in an effort to conserve enough honey for winter food. The queen and workers live through the winter in the natural protection of a hollow tree or in their modern hive. There they continue to eat even though they remain quite inactive.

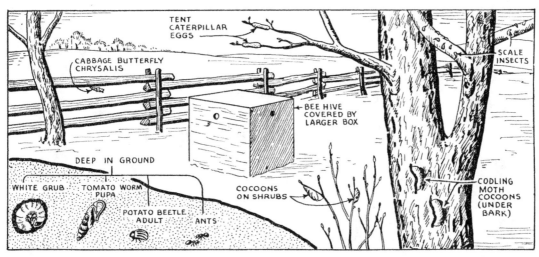

Figure 1—Insect Homes in Winter

Activities

Junior and Intermediate Grades

- Place apples containing codling-moth larvae in a glass jar; with them put several pieces of cardboard. After the larvae emerge and spin their cocoons on the cardboard, place the jar in a cold place for several weeks. Then bring it back to the classroom. Watch for emerging moths.
- Collect various kinds of cocoons from shrubs. Leave them in a cool, protected place until spring.
- With scissors open a large cocoon such as that of Cecropia. Examine the pupa within, then remove it. Open the pupa case to discover how far the moth has developed.
- Find out whether the cocoon is waterproof. Examine a piece to see how the silk is woven in it.
- Test the strength of a piece by pulling on it without twisting.
- Look for apple worms (larvae of codling moths) in their cocoons under bark scales of apple trees. Bring some to school.
- Make a mural showing a rural scene in which there might occur the winter stages of several of the insects mentioned in this chapter, or make a frieze illustrating in each section the winter quarters of one insect.

Read

Barlowe, *A Child's Book of Insects.* Ryerson (Maxton).

New to this Edition

Glaser, Linda. *Not a Buzz to Be Found: Insects in Winter* (Millbrook Press, 2011).
Hansen, Amy S. *Bugs and Bugsicles: Insects in the Winter* (Boyds Mill Press, 2010).

Unit 35—A Month with the Moon

The long, comfortable evenings of autumn are ideal for pupils to observe the moon and stars. The full moon seems to be a logical starting-point in many respects. Junior pupils are naturally attracted more by this than by other phases. The moon rises in the eastern sky at a convenient time for observation by junior pupils—namely, just as the sun sets. Its motion westward may be followed through the evening. With intermediate grades, it is easier to show the cause of moonlight by reference to a full moon than by observation of earlier phases. It is true that the early phases show growth, but explanations are then more difficult, especially since the new moon itself is invisible. After this preliminary study, organized observations should be made for a full month, beginning at the time of new moon.

To carry through this month's observations, and to interpret them to the pupils day by day, the teacher must be sure that she, *but not the pupils,* understands the following facts about the moon.

1. The moon travels from west to east around the earth about once a month.
2. The moon does not move from east to west each night as it appears to do; it is constantly moving eastward, but because we on the earth are moving eastward faster than it is, it seems to come from the East, meet us, and later set in the West.

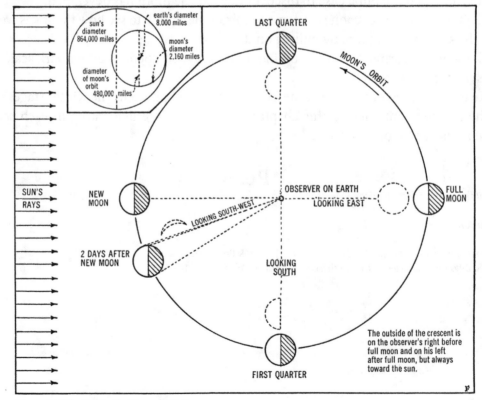

Figure 1—Why We See the Moon as We Do

136

3. Because the moon continually travels eastward, we are about 50 minutes later coming in sight of it each night, and so we say it rises later.
4. At new moon, the moon is between the sun and us; its lighted half is therefore invisible to us.
5. At full moon, the moon is on the side of the earth farthest from the sun. We see the whole-lighted half of it as a complete circle.
6. At first quarter, we see one-half of the lighted half of the moon (one-quarter) with the sun lighting it from our right and causing that side of it to appear curved.
7. At last quarter (third quarter) the sun shines from our left toward the moon, making the moon appear a half circle with the curve at the left.

Knowledge of these generalizations will naturally grow very gradually with the pupils as the month passes, or in a review following the month's observations. Generally speaking, such knowledge is gained through three stages: first, motivation and assignments by the teacher; second, observations and personal records or sketches by the pupils; third, a class period in which the observations are discussed, and expression work carried out to impress the new learning. Long-range planning is essential in such teaching.

The study of the moon must be carefully graded all through the elementary school. Primary children should gain some definite, though elementary, knowledge of it. Even to pre-school children, the moon is the only big, bright light after sunset. From their own observations, they learn that the moon has different shapes at different times. Sometimes it is round, sometimes half-round, sometimes still narrower. To understand how the moon changes in shape, pupils must make careful daily observations. Assign these at the time of new moon. Tell them where to look for it and when. Have them sketch it as they see it, perhaps with a tree or two between them and it. About three nights later, have them make another observation and sketch. Conclude that it is growing. Give the names "new moon" for the first stages, "growing moon" for the next ones. Later it may be called "half moon"; then, when two weeks old, "full moon." There is little opportunity for primary pupils to see later stages. Of course they cannot conceive of the moon's distance, size, surface, reflected light, and motion around the earth.

In junior and intermediate grades, pupils have greater power of sustained interest, and are up later in the evening. They therefore have an opportunity to make observations over longer periods each night, and to include observations after full moon. They can grasp the facts of the earth's rotation (explaining why the moon appears to move toward the west and set each night). But it is very doubtful if a pupil below twelve years mental age can actually visualize the relative positions of the sun, earth, and moon, or the relation between the earth's revolution and rotation and the moon's monthly journey around the earth.

By a month's observations, they should gain the following knowledge: *new moon*—visible in the

Figure 2—Growing and waning moon. Before full moon the curved side is to the right; after full moon it is to the left.

West in early evening, horns point eastward, sets early; *first quarter*—visible in the South, shape of half a circle, appears to move toward and set in the West; *full moon*—a full circle, rises in the East, shines all night; *last quarter*—rises in the East late at night, half a circle, horns point to the West. They should understand the changes of shape between the four phases mentioned, and that the moon receives all of its light from the sun and reflects it to the earth.

Activities

Teacher

See illustrations in *Everyday Science,* Book Two, pp. 154-157.

Primary Grades

- Make silver or yellow cutouts of a full moon, a half moon, and a young moon.
- Make sketches of the moon twice a week for 2 weeks. Bring the sketches to school.
- Make a blackboard drawing of a night scene. Include green trees, brown ground, fences, etc. Show the moon in its place far in the West by pasting on silver paper. Show its shape and position half a week later at the same time of night.
- Look for the moon on a cloudy night. Why can you not see it?

Junior and Intermediate Grades

- Make a drawing of the moon each night for 2 weeks after new moon. Compare its shapes from day to day. Label "new moon," "growing moon," "half moon," and "full moon."
- While the moon is still young, look for it just after sunset in the western sky. Draw, color, and date it; then make a cutout. Put this near the lower right corner of a picture of a country scene. Make and place cutouts daily at the same time.
- Look at the moon through a telescope or through field glasses.
- Stand a pupil in the middle of the room to represent the earth. Have another pupil walk around him, always facing him, to represent the moon. Sing this song (Tune: Farmer in the Dell) while he goes:

> The moon goes round the earth; the moon goes round the earth;
> High over Jericho, the moon goes round the earth.
> The moon goes round the earth, it takes a month to go,
> High over Jericho, it takes a month to go.

Model the moon, half with gray Plasticine, and half with yellow (or insert a knitting needle through an orange painted half black, half white). Hold the yellow side toward you for full moon, and the gray side toward you for new moon. Now turn it so that you see only a small yellow crescent at the right to illustrate the young moon; next turn it so that you see a small yellow crescent to the left to illustrate the old moon.

The moon is like the earth; it does not give out any light. Why then can we see it? To find out, hold up a piece of white paper in a partly darkened room or corner. It can hardly be seen. Now hold a flashlight so that the light shines on the card; we can see the card clearly; in fact, it lights the surroundings by means of the light reflected from it. The card represents the moon; the flashlight, the sun. The light from the moon lights our surroundings just as the light from the card lights its surroundings.

Hold a mirror in a perfectly dark room. Can you see any light from it? Bring the mirror into bright sunlight and catch some of the sun's rays. You will be able to shoot a beam of light in any direction as long as you can catch light from the sun on the mirror. The mirror is like the moon in that it has no light of its own, but it reflects light.

Consult the calendar and make a table as illustrated below to show the date of each phase of the moon for the 12 months of the year. Use it to show the average length of time between the moon's phases.

Month	Full Moon	Last Quarter	New Moon	First Quarter
May _____	3	11	18	25
June _____	1	9	17	23
July _____	1	9	16	23

Observe the faintly illuminated surface of the whole moon just after new moon. It is lighted by the sun's light reflected from the earth to the moon. Make individual or class booklets with appropriate titles. Write the story of an imaginary trip to the moon.

Intermediate Grades

Rule rectangles and draw half circles as in fig. 3. At 8:00 p.m., 3 days after new moon, at first quarter, and at full moon, draw the moon in proper position and shape. On the evening of full moon, observe the position of the moon at three successive hours; then draw it in its proper place on the half circle. One or two mornings after last quarter, look for the moon and draw it with correct shape and position in the rectangle labeled "last quarter."

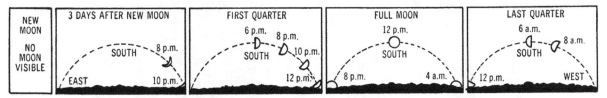

Figure 3—*A Chart of the Shape and the Position of the Moon at Different Times of the Month and at Different Times of the Night.*

Is the moon as large as the sun? Stand at one end of the schoolyard and have a chum hold an orange a few feet from you. Then have another person hold a basketball at the far end of the schoolyard. Do the two objects look to be the same size? The differences in distance away from you made them appear equal in size. The moon is much smaller than the sun, but it is so much closer that it appears to be about the same size.

Each pupil be responsible for one day on the monthly calendar. Label east at the left, south at the top, and west at the right of each date space. At 8:00 p.m. each evening observe the moon; prepare a cutout of it; then mount this in its correct position on the rectangle bearing the date. When the month has passed, review from this calendar the daily shape and position of the moon at 8:00 p.m.

Why do we see a man in the moon? Telescopes show us that there are very high mountains and huge holes on its surface. The sun's light shines on these in such a way that they appear to form the shape of a man's face. In fact, no life is possible on the moon because there is neither air nor water.

139

Read

Beauchamp et al., *Discovering Our World,* Book 1 (grades 4-5), pp. 124-129. Gage (Scott, Foresman).

Comstock, *Handbook of Nature-Study,* pp. 855-859. Allen (Comstock).

Frasier et al., *The Seasons Pass* (grades 3-4) : "The Moon," pp. 161-165. Dent (Singer).

Freeman, *Fun with Astronomy* (grades 6-8), pp. 16-22. Random House.

Hethershaw & Baker, *Wonders to See:* "The Moon," pp. 176-181. Gage (World Book).

Partridge, *General Science,* Intermediate, Book 2: "The Moon," pp. 321-327; and *Everyday Science,* Book Two: "The Moon," pp. 153-160. Dent.

Patch & Howe, *The Work of Scientists* (grades 5-6): "Moon," pp. 109-117. Macmillan.

Smith & Henderson, *Across the Land* (grades 4-5): "Looking at the Moon," pp. 99-118. Longmans, Green.

New to this Edition

Branley, Franklyn M. *The Moon Seems to Change (Let's Read and Find Our Science 2),* (Collins, 1987)

Crelin, Bob. *Faces of the Moon* (Charlesbridge Publishing, 2009).

Fowler, Allan. So *That's How the Moon Changes Shape* (Rookie Read-About Science Series), (Childrens Press, 1991).

Gibbons, Gail. *The Moon Book* (Holiday House, 1998).

Olson, Gillia M. *Phases of the Moon* (Patterns in Nature Series), (Capstone Press, 2008).

http://airandspace.si.edu/events/apollo30th/moontheater/phases.html

Nature Journal Excerpts

Merritt Pond
Beaver Sign

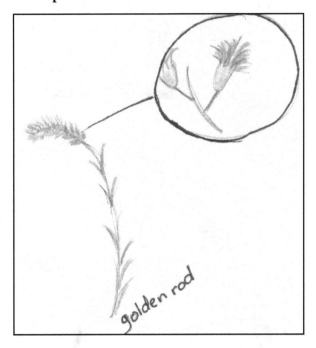

golden rod

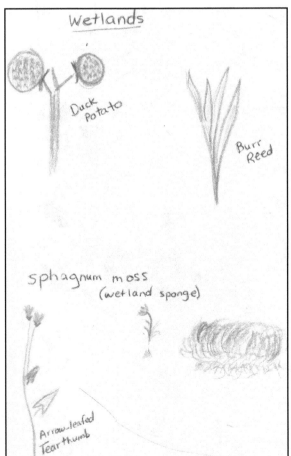

Wetlands

Duck
Potato

Burr
Reed

sphagnum moss
(wetland sponge)

Arrow-leafed
Tearthumb

Clockwise from top left: beaver sign; goldenrod; plants of the wetlands; decomposers in late fall, early winter..

BEAUTIFY YOUR SURROUNDINGS — NOVEMBER

"To you, from failing hands, we throw the torch —"

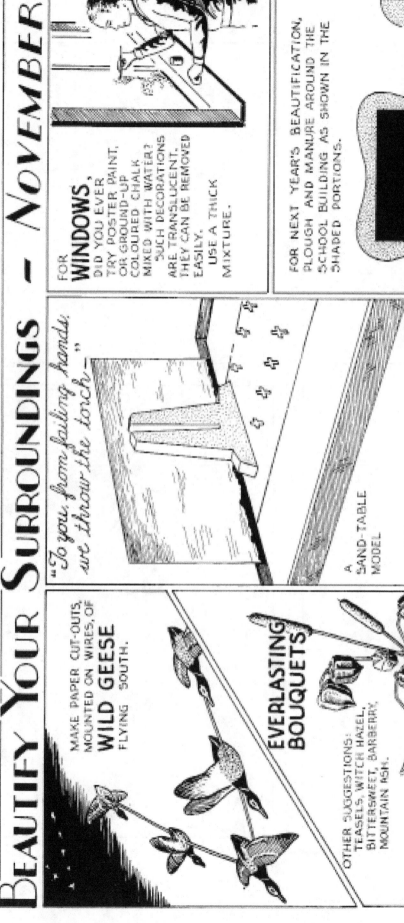

FOR
WINDOWS,
DID YOU EVER
TRY POSTER PAINT,
OR GROUND-UP
COLOURED CHALK
MIXED WITH WATER?
SUCH DECORATIONS
ARE TRANSLUCENT.
THEY CAN BE REMOVED
EASILY.
USE A THICK
MIXTURE.

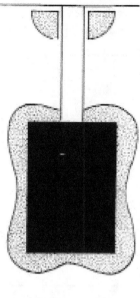

FOR NEXT YEAR'S BEAUTIFICATION,
PLOUGH AND MANURE AROUND THE
SCHOOL BUILDING AS SHOWN IN THE
SHADED PORTIONS.

A
SAND-TABLE
MODEL

MAKE TWO CUT STRIPS FOR
SIDES, CENTRE AND TOP.
FASTEN WITH GUMMED
PAPER FROM INSIDE, AS
INDICATED AT RIGHT.
USE SUNSET CARD
FOR BACKGROUND.

MAKE PAPER CUT-OUTS,
MOUNTED ON WIRES, OF
WILD GEESE
FLYING SOUTH.

EVERLASTING
BOUQUETS

OTHER SUGGESTIONS:
TEASELS, WITCH HAZEL,
BITTERSWEET, BARBERRY,
MOUNTAIN ASH.

MAKE CONTAINERS
OF REED, RAFFIA, OR
OTHER MATERIAL. THIS ONE
IS A JAM JAR, ENAMELLED BLACK,
DAUBED WITH A SPONGE DIPPED IN
GOLD PAINT.

HERE ARE TWO BLACKBOARD BORDER DESIGNS FOR NOVEMBER: MAKE STENCILS AS SUGGESTED LAST MONTH.

D. FARWELL.

SCIENCE IN ACTION — NOVEMBER

INSULATION:

PLACE AN ICE CUBE IN AN EMPTY CHALK BOX. BURY A SECOND ICE CUBE IN SAWDUST IN ANOTHER CHALK BOX. COVER EACH BOX. WHICH CUBE OF ICE MELTS FIRST? WHY?

HOW IS THIS PRINCIPLE APPLIED IN THE INSULATION OF HOUSES?

AND INSULATORS:

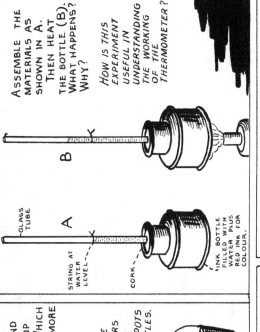

HOLD A SPOON AND A PENCIL IN A CUP OF HOT WATER. WHICH BECOMES WARM MORE QUICKLY?

FIND THE INSULATORS ON YOUR KITCHEN POTS AND KETTLES.

HOW A THERMOMETER WORKS:

ASSEMBLE THE MATERIALS AS SHOWN IN A. THEN HEAT THE BOTTLE (B). WHAT HAPPENS? WHY?

HOW IS THIS EXPERIMENT USEFUL IN UNDERSTANDING THE WORKING OF THE THERMOMETER?

GLASS TUBE

B

A

STRING AT WATER LEVEL

CORK

INK BOTTLE FILLED WITH WATER PLUS RED INK FOR COLOUR.

AQUARIUM WEEDS:

ANACHARIS

CABOMBA

INSTEAD OF PLANTING SUCH WEEDS AS ANACHARIS AND CABOMBA, TRY LETTING THEM FLOAT FREELY ON THE SURFACE. ANY ADVANTAGES? DISADVANTAGES? *D.FARWELL*

BLOTTERS:

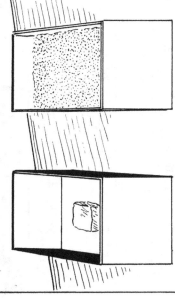

GLASS TUBES WITH BORES OF VARIOUS SIZES

TWO PIECES OF GLASS

USE EITHER THE TUBES, OR THE GLASS, OR BOTH COLOUR THE WATER WITH RED INK. THE WATER RISES BECAUSE OF "CAPILLARY ACTION".

CAN YOU UNDERSTAND BETTER HOW A BLOTTER HELPS TO DRY THE INK?

SOMETHING TO MAKE !

A MODEL OF EGNATIO DANTI'S FIRST ANEMOMETER FOR MEASURING THE FORCE OF THE WIND:

HEAVY WIRE LOOPED LOOSELY OVER NAIL

NAIL

CARDBOARD OR METAL SCALE

HEAVY CARD OR LIGHT METAL

SIZE - ACCORDING TO CHOICE. THE FOLLOWING TABLE WILL HELP YOU IN MARKING THE SCALE :

SMOKE RISES STRAIGHT UP - 0 m.p.h.
SMOKE MOVES, FACE FEELS WIND - 1-7 m.p.h.
HANDKERCHIEF EXTENDED - 8-12 m.p.h.
SMALL BRANCHES MOVE 13-18 m.p.h.
SMALL TREES SWAY - 19-24 m.p.h.
HARD TO WALK - 25-38 m.p.h.
TREE LIMBS BROKEN - 39 m.p.h. and up.
m.p.h. = miles per hour.

NATURAL SCIENCE — DECEMBER — DAY BY DAY

SUNDAY	MONDAY	TUESDAY	WEDNESDAY	THURSDAY	FRIDAY	SATURDAY
					1 Start the month right. Plan to feed the birds every day.	**2** What birds and other animals are still active?
3 When does the moon rise to-night?	**4** Explain how your breath forms on a cold day	**5** How do birds keep warm now?	**6** Compare the height of the sun to-day at noon with its height two weeks ago.	**7** Bring bulbs planted six weeks ago to light and warmth.	**8** Draw four shapes of snow-flakes the first day it snows.	**9** Draw and name two kinds of winter buds.
10 New moon. Show which side of the moon is lighted now.	**11** What season is it in Australia? Why?	**12** Where are our summer birds? What doing?	**13** Learn to know the Christmas cactus and the poinsettia.	**14** Record the length of day and night to-day.	**15** Plan a sand-table Christmas scene.	**16** Look for materials for your sand-table scene.
17 Read about the Star of Bethlehem	**18** Why is moonlight really sunlight?	**19** Spruce needles will roll between the thumb and finger.	**20** Hemlock needles are single, flat, each with a tiny stalk.	**21** Balsam needles are single, flat, with no stalk; branches have circular scars.	**22** Compare the length of day and night with those December 14.	**23** Draw holly and mistletoe.
24 How old is your Christmas tree?	**25** "I want to know Nature better in 1940." MERRY CHRISTMAS!	**26** Draw trees and their shadows as seen from your window at night	**27** Birds eat weed seeds from above the snow.	**28** Use your old Christmas tree for a bird shelter in your backyard.	**29** Pour melted suet on its branches for bird food.	**30** Draw tracks of a cat and dog in snow.
31						

By drawing which side of the moon is lighted now.

Sun Rises? Sun Sets?

J. A. PARTRIDGE
Drawn by D. Farwell

Have your pupils build this calendar day by day on blackboard or chart.
Use substitutions if desired.

DECEMBER

Unit 36—The Stars In December

The stars are always visible—winter and summer, day and night—for our sun is a star. All the equipment we need to study these is interest and willing eyes; for the sun, a cloudless day; for the other stars, a clear, moonless night.

The sun star, the closest to us, makes the earth so bright throughout the day that we cannot see the other stars. But in December it shines upon us for the shortest daily period and, on account of its low position in the sky, gives us the least heat. Though the sun will be studied in more detail in Unit 67 (page 278), Unit 68 (page 281), and Unit 69 (page 283), pupils should now observe when and where it rises and sets and its low position in the southern sky, and should connect these with shortening days and cooling weather.

In December, too, the Christmas season, people are likely to be looking skyward as they think of the stars guiding the Wise Men. At this time of year, too, observation is easy because the evenings are longer and the sky is clear. "To know night's goodly company of stars" is the right of every child before he leaves school. Indeed, to lead pupils to see and know some of "those bright lords that deck the firmament" is as much the duty of the teacher as to teach about the phases of the moon, day and night, and the seasons. This does not mean the making of blackboard and notebook diagrams and notes; it means actual, awe-inspiring star-gazing at night.

Through the study of this topic, pupils should become more observant of, and interested in, the heavens. Constellations and "shooting-stars" should take on added meaning. A scientific attitude should be developed in pupils as they learn of the careful study of the heavenly bodies by scientists, and of their annual discoveries of new information.

Star study must follow two principles. First, there must be graded progress through the grades from very simple observations (the Big Dipper and Queen Cassiopeia) in primary grades, to some understanding of some sky myths, the recognition of more constellations, the rising and setting of stars, and their variations in size and brightness and distance, in intermediate grades. Second, there must be the three stages of study—classroom motivation and assignments (e.g., Big Dipper: to the north, 7 stars, shape of dipper), pupil observation and sketching at night, class discussion and expression work (yellow or silver circles properly arranged on black paper).

A few stars are seen in early evening. These are the brightest ones. As the night grows darker, dimmer stars become visible. A small telescope or field glasses will help.

The great distance of stars makes them appear stationary points of light scattered through space. But they are huge balls of fire, some many, many times the size of the sun and many times as far away. Like the sun, they appear to rise in the east and set in the west each night—this because we on the earth travel from west to east. Because the earth revolves around the sun once a year, the stars rise and set 4 minutes earlier each evening, and different stars and constellations become visible at different times of the year. For this reason Orion is visible by night only from November until May.

Stars twinkle. Thus we distinguish them from planets. Perhaps their twinkling began the senseless tradition of drawing stars with five points. But since they *are* round, they should be drawn or cut out by pupils in that shape. A jagged edge will illustrate the twinkling.

Constellations (stars together) are particularly interesting because of the legends which shepherds made up in early times. These will give motivation if read before observing the stars. The term Big Dipper, however, has more meaning to pupils than Great Bear.

Star study usually begins with the Big Dipper. In line with the end of the bowl, we find the North Star, the beginning of the handle of the Little Dip-

Figure 1

per. Close by are Cassiopeia, Cepheus, and Draco (fig. 1). Another easily found constellation is Orion, recognized by the three bright stars in the belt. The accompanying star map (fig. 2), hectographed to show the desired constellations, will assist pupils. While on a stargazing hike, use a focusing flashlight to point out stars or constellations.

Activities

Teacher

Make a blackboard drawing of the Big Dipper and the North Star. Direct pupils to find them. Next day have pupils paste yellow circles in their books to form the Dipper. Then add the Little Dipper to the blackboard drawing. Continue in this way from one constellation to another.

All Grades

Make a picture story of "The Man in the Moon."

> The Man in the Moon, as he sails the sky,
> Is a very remarkable skipper;
> But he made a mistake when he tried to take
> A drink of milk from the Dipper.
> He dipped it into the Milky Way,
> And slowly and carefully filled it;
> The Big Bear growled, and the Little Bear howled,
> And scared him so that he spilled it!
> From *A Garden of Stories*

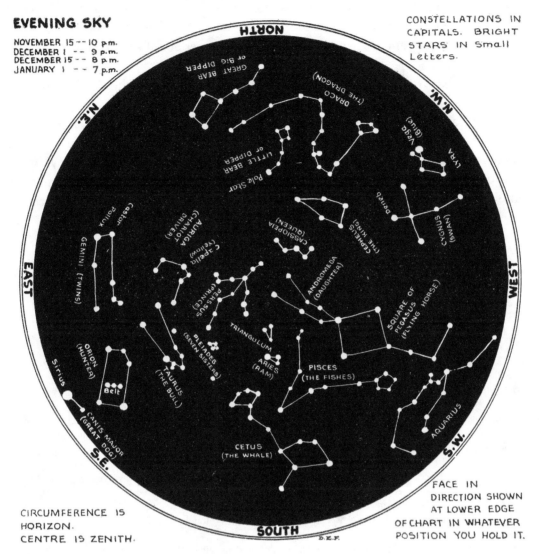

Figure 2—A Star Map for December

In large, blue cardboard cut holes to represent the positions of stars in some constellation. Use Christmas tree lights for stars.

Primary Grades

On a piece of blue paper, mount circular pieces of yellow or silver paper to show the shape and position of the Big Dipper, the Little Dipper, and Cassiopeia.

Junior and Intermediate Grades

- Throughout December, make a blackboard calendar with columns headed: Date, Time of Sunrise, Time of Sunset, Length of Day. Obtain the information from the daily paper. By later study of this calendar, you will discover how the days change in length at this time of year, and when we have the shortest day.

- Use the star map to find the following stars: Sirius, brightest of all stars, in the Great Dog; Vega, in Lyra; Castor and Pollox in the Twins; Deneb in Cygnus, the Swan.
- Look in the library and elsewhere for myths and stories about constellations. Read some to your class.
- Find the Milky Way—an uneven band of light stretching across the sky. This is made up of many thousands of very distant stars.
- Draw four equal circles on a piece of paper. Label the center of each "North Star" and the top "North." Observe and sketch the dipper on these at four successive hours. If you could keep on for each of the 24 hours, you would find that the dipper would move around the circle. Which way?
- Find out how scientists study the stars. Look up the location of several observatories.
- Find out how stars were used by sailors and other travelers before compasses were invented.

Read

Andrews, *Adventures in Science,* Book V, pp. 58-70. Moyer.

Barlowe, *A Child's Book of Stars.* Ryerson (Maxton).

Beauchamp et al., *Discovering Our World,* Book 1 (grades 4-5), pp. 112-123. Gage (Scott, Foresman).

Comstock, *Handbook of Nature-Study,* pp. 815-833. Allen (Comstock).

Frasier et al., *The How and Why Club:* "Pictures in the Winter Sky," pp. 176-191. Dent (Singer).

Freeman, *Fun with Astronomy* (grades 6-8), pp. 50-57. Random Home.

Frost, *Let's Look at the Stars.* Allen (Houghton Mifflin).

Hethershaw & Baker, *Wonders to See,* pp. 161-175. Gage (World Book).

Hood, *Observing the Heavens* (senior grades). Oxford.

Hunt & Andrews, *Sky Studies.* Moyer.

Lewellen, *You and Space Neighbors* (grades 6 and up). Book Society (Children's Press).

Nicol et al., *The Nature Hour,* Sixth Year—Autumn and Winter: "The Parade of the Stars," pp. 103-111. Gage (Silver, Burdett).
    Olcott, *Field Book of the Stars.* Allen (Putnam's Sons).

Parker, *The Sky Above Us,* The Basic Science Education Series. Copp Clark (Row, Peterson).

Partridge, General Science, Intermediate, Book 2: "Discovering New Worlds," pp. 317-336; also Everyday Science, Book Two: "The Starry Firmament," pp. 163-77. Dent.

Proctor, Wonders of the Sky. Allen (Warne)

Rey, Find the Constellations and The Stars—A New Way to See Them. Allen (Houghton Mifflin).

Schneider, *You Among the Stars.* Allen (Wm. R. Scott).

Shuttlesworth, *Exploring Nature with Your Child:* "Recognizing the Stars," pp. 405-423. Nelson (Greystone).

Treat, *A Guide to the Stars:* small pocket guide. Cleveland Museum of Natural History, Cleveland, Ohio.

Williams, *A Dipper Full of Stars* (grades 5-8). Ambassador (Follett).

Wylie, *Our Starland.* Ryerson (Lyons & Carnahan).

Zim, *The Sun.* McLeod (Wm. Morrow).

Zim & Baker, *Stars*—A Guide to the Constellations, Sun, Moon, Planets, and Other Features of the Heavens. Musson (Simon & Schuster).

Signpost to the Stars. Muyer (Philip & Son).

Stars at a Glance. Muyer (Philip & Son).

New to this Edition

Celestron Sky Maps

Graun, Ken. *Guide to the Stars* (Ken Press, 2010)

Rey, H. A. *Find the Constellations* (HMH Books, 2008).

_____. *The Stars* (HMH Books, 2008)

Sky Publishing: Night Sky Star Wheel.

VanCleave, Janice. *Janice VanCleave's Constellations for Every Kid: Easy Activities that Make Learning Science Fun (Science for Every Kid Series),* (Wiley, 1997).

http://www.polaris.iastate.edu/NorthStar/Unit9/unit9_sub6.htm

science-teachers.com/space/winter_constellations.doc

Unit 37—Knowing, Enjoying, and Sheltering Our Winter Bird Friends

By now, most of the birds with which pupils were familiar in summer are far to the south. Had they remained, they would have starved before this time because the frozen ground, the snow, and the ice would have prevented them from finding worms, insects, or fruit to eat. Whether we think of their appeal to our aesthetic tendencies, their economic value, or their daily struggles for food and warmth, we must conclude that our winter birds are among our best friends and deserve our conscious appreciation and protection.

Personal pupil activities, especially out of the classroom in the natural environment of the birds, will make the main contribution to the development in our pupils of a love for our bird friends, an appreciation of their life problems and how they solve them, and a real desire to render some assistance to them as a partial reward for their aesthetic and economic values to us. The main responsibility of the teacher lies in providing the necessary information for the identification of the common birds of the locality, in kindling a desire to understand our bird friends a little better, and in supplying the necessary guidance and facilities for direct pupil experiences with them.

All of us like to call people, plants, and animals by name. So do our pupils. The first concern, then, is to recognize our bird friends by sight. To recognize our common black-capped chickadee by sight requires only a mental image of "a gray and white bird, smaller than a sparrow, with a *black cap* and a *black bib*" (fig. 1). All other descriptive words are not only superfluous but actually a hindrance to quick recognition. The essential identification features may profitably be committed to memory, preferably through frequent association with the bird itself.

Birds which are with us in winter belong to two groups: those which are here all year, *permanent residents,* and those which come from farther north each autumn to spend the winter with us, *winter residents.* Occasionally, individual birds of a species usually classified as winter residents remain

Chick a   dee dee dee dee.   Fe bee

Figure 1—(From Trafton, "Nature Study and Science," Macmillan)

farther south in summer; for example, the brown creeper. In the accompanying tables, our birds of these two classes are listed, and their identification characteristics given. See also fig. 2.

Permanent Resident Birds

(Comparative sizes in parentheses; special characteristics in italics)

Black-capped chickadee—(sparrow–), about homes and woods; gray and white with a *black cap and a black bib.*

White-breasted nuthatch—(sparrow), in trees; *white breast,* blue-gray back and *black cap;* frequently *upside down* on tree trunk.

Downy woodpecker—(sparrow), in trees almost anywhere; *white back;* spotted and checkered with *black and white;* males with *red patch* on back of head, females without.

Hairy woodpecker—(robin–), like downy, but larger, especially the bill.

Blue jay—(robin+), *blue above and whitish below; crested.*

Starling—(robin–), everywhere; a *short-tailed* "blackbird"; winter plumage much *speckled;* bill dark, turning yellow in spring.

Cardinal—(robin–), gardens and open woods; male our only *crested red bird;* female yellowish brown with red bill and crest.

Pheasant—(hen), borders of fields; long, pointed tail; male highly colored.

Ruffed grouse—(hen), deep woods; red-brown; hen-like, fan tail.

Cedar waxwing—(sparrow+), orchards; *brown bird with crest;* tip of tail *yellow.*

Goldfinch—(sparrow–), woods, roadsides; *yellow with black cap, tail, and wings.* (Yellow warbler is all yellow.)

Screech owl—(robin+), orchards; small owl with "horns."

Purple finch—(sparrow), woods; raspberry or *rosy head and back.* (Pine Grosbeak is much larger.)

Golden-crowned kinglet—(tiny), woods; *orange or yellow crown, bordered by black;* white stripe over eye; chips.

Herring gull—(crow+), around dumps or flying over; *white and gray, wings* long, pointed, *with black tips.*

Winter resident birds

(Comparative sizes in parentheses; special characteristics in italics)

Brown creeper—(small), always climbing up tree trunks; *creeping;* slim and *brown;* stiff tail used as prop.

Slate-colored junco—(sparrow–), wood edges; slaty gray; *white-edged tail;* white underparts sharply defined from dark breast.

Tree sparrow—(sparrow), woody places; *reddish cap* and *black breast spot;* two white wing-bars.

Snow bunting—(sparrow), open fields; large, *white wing patches* show in flight; white below; flocks.

American merganser—(crow+), open water; male *white, with black head and back;* female gray with reddish head and crest, and large white wing patch.

Golden-eye duck—(crow), open water; white with black head and back; white wing patch seen in flight; *white spot between eye and bill.*

Birds continue their valuable services to man in winter somewhat as in summer. Then their usefulness is particularly noticeable in orchards and fields. There the hairy and downy woodpeckers destroy scale insects on the bark, the larvae of codling moth beneath the bark, and other in-

Figure 2—Five Winter Bird Friends

sects which live in the burrows in the wood. Their strong, chisel-like bills, their pointed tongues, their strong, sharply clawed toes—two pointing backward—and their stiff, propping tail feathers fit them well for this work. The black-capped chickadees search for the eggs, larvae, and adults of tiny insects under the edges of the bark. The white-breasted nuthatch, while clinging to the tree, often upside down, tears away the loose bark to find the insects beneath. The brown creeper, quite frequently wintering with us from the north, probes for insects in every nook and crevice while he creeps spirally up and down the trunks of orchard and shade trees. At the same time the tree sparrows, juncos, and snow buntings continue to destroy weed seeds on plants that are tall enough to project above the snow.

> Shrewd little haunter of woods all gray,
> Whom I met on my walk of a winter day—
> You're busy inspecting each cranny and hole
> In the ragged bark of yon hickory bole;
>
> Head upward, head downward, all one to you,
> Zenith and nadir the same in your view.
>
> *Describing the acrobatics of a nuthatch,*
> *by Edith M. Thomas*

Figure 3

Winter presents many difficulties to the birds that are with us. Snow prevents ground feeders such as tree sparrows and snow buntings from getting seeds unless the weeds are above the snow level. Layers of ice on trees keep insect eaters (woodpeckers and brown creepers) from gathering their food from beneath bark. Yet it is when the temperature is low and the wind biting that birds need most food to keep their bodies warm.

We must do something to tide birds over these difficult times if we want them to remain nearby so that they may continue even in winter to rid our fields of weed seeds and our orchards of such insect pests as the apple worm hidden in its cocoon beneath the bark. Evergreen trees, even bird houses (fig. 3), will shelter them from storm and cold and provide feeding places free from snow. Here we may give them daily meals of crumbs, scraps, grain, sunflower seeds, and suet. See also Unit 38 (page 156) and Unit 39 (page 159).

Activities

Teacher

Try these selections in choral reading.

MR. DOWNY'S BREAKFAST

Girl: Why are you tapping up there in that tree,
         Mr. Downy? Answer me, please.

Downy: To look for my breakfast, my dear little girl;
         'Tis a long time since supper, you see.

Girl: What will you find for your breakfast up there?
         I'm sure it won't taste very good.

Downy: Just wait, little girl, I'll find insects inside—
         And they make me very fine food.

Girl: But the wood is so hard, and the insects so deep,
         How can you get them at all?

Downy: My beak is so strong, and so sharp and so long
         I can chisel a nice little hole.

Girl: Then how will you get the spry little worm?
         You've no fingers to catch it, you know.

Class: Just then a fat grub came right into view,
         And Downy wasn't so slow!
         He put out his tongue—a long, sticky tongue—
         And he got that little grub, too.

Downy: Yum! Yum!

Class: said the Downy.

Girl: Good work!

Class: cried the girl.

Girl: But I don't think I'll breakfast with you!

              ADAPTED

          Although I'm a bird, I give you my word
          That seldom you'll know me to fly;
          For I have a notion about locomotion,
          The little Brown Creeper am I,
          Dear little Brown Creeper am I.
          Beginning below, I search as I go
          The trunk and the limbs of a tree,
          For a fly or a slug, a beetle or bug;
          They're better than candy for me,
          Far better than candy for me,
          Far better than candy for me.
                    Author Unknown

All Grades

- After studying pictures on the bulletin board, try to find the little chickadee with a black cap and black bib, the white-breasted nuthatch frequently upside down on a tree trunk, the black and white downy woodpecker, the snow bunting with white on the wing patches and below, and other winter birds. Then draw a winter scene on a large sheet of paper or on the blackboard, and place the pictures where they belong on this scene.
- Make a table display of winter birds in their natural environment. Provide for deciduous and evergreen trees, a lake (glass over blue paper), artificial snow, and models of bird houses, birds, and feeding-stations.
- Make a drawing to illustrate this poem:

> N is for Nuthatch,
> That stands on his head,
> And lives on our trees,
> But likes to be fed.

- Write other four-lined poems about winter birds, and have fellow pupils illustrate them.

Primary Grades

Arrange a sand-table scene illustrating "Making Friends of Winter Birds." Pupils will likely suggest such furnishings as a snow covering of cotton, a school or home with a yard and shrubbery, a hillside with trees bearing Plasticine fruits, some evergreens to shelter the birds, weeds above the snow, paper or Plasticine birds feeding or perching, a simple feeding-station, and many other features. The scene should grow from day to day. Print neat labels.

Junior and Intermediate Grades

- To find out what birds remain with us in winter, put out suet, grains, and table scraps in a protected place away from people. Observe which birds come to feed. Identify them by examining pictures of the winter birds listed in this chapter.
- Find out whether there are bird sanctuaries nearby; if so, where?
- With the coping saw, make a woodpecker feeding on a tree, a chickadee perched on a branch, a junco eating from a feeding-shelf. These should be drawn, cut out, sandpapered, and painted.
- Make a class scrapbook entitled "Our Winter Bird Friends." Elect an editing committee to receive and insert suitable poems, magazine or newspaper clippings, pictures, and original drawings.
- Each pupil choose a winter bird and investigate its recognition characteristics, its food and feeding habits, its winter protection, and methods of attracting and feeding it. Bring pictures and books to the nature reading table. Report your discoveries to the whole class.
- Make a class book entitled "Winter Birds." Assign a page for each bird On this page, draw its portrait, and insert stories or poems about it.
- Try to list the birds nesting in your locality by taking a census of the birds' nests to be found. Remember that these nests may be used by the birds again in spring, and that they must, therefore, not be molested in any way. The absence of foliage makes winter an ideal time for

154

the study of birds' nests. Identify them by noting their position, the materials used in building them, and their size.

- Make salt-and-flour bird pictures. Trace outlines of branches, birds, etc. on boards about 12 inches by 9 inches. Make salt-and-flour modeling mixture; fill in the outlines (showing by depth both smooth and ruffled feathers). When thoroughly dry, color the pictures with watercolors or poster paint. Provide suitable background and frame using paint alone, or salt and flour, and then paint.

- Write and act a play with the following characters: Fluff, the chickadee, wearing a black cap and bib; Chip, the downy woodpecker; Slender, the brown creeper; Bluff, the nuthatch; and a little boy and girl. The scene should be a garden in the morning when the little boy and girl discover the birds feeding. Each bird should tell the children how valuable he is, and the children should decide to do something helpful in return.

Read

Alexander & Cormack, *Bruce and Marcia, Woodsmen:* "An Ice Storm," pp. 171-185. Gage (American Book Co.).

Allen, *Everyday Birds* (Primary). Allen (Houghton Mifflin).

Blough, *The Birds in the Big Woods* (grades 2-3), The Basic Science Education Series. Copp Clark (Row, Peterson).

Comstock, *Handbook of Nature-Study.* Alien (Coimstock).

Gates & McClenaghan, *Animals Work, Too* (grade 2): "Winter Birds," pp. 10-14. Macmillan.

Harvey & Lay, *Adventures into Nature,* Book III A: "The Needs of Birds in Winter," pp. 63-67. Macmillan.

Hausman, *Beginner's Guide to Attracting Birds,* pp. 16-63 and 75-77. Allen (Putnam's Sons).

Henry, *Birds at Home.* Book Society (Donohue).

Hunt & Andrews, *Winter Birds.* Moyer.

Hylander, *Out of Doors in Winter* (grades 6-8): "Winter Bird Life," pp. 68-104. Macmillan.

Kieran, *An Introduction to Birds.* Blue Ribbon (Garden City).

Nicol et al., *The Nature Hour,* Fifth Year—Autumn and Winter: "The Junco, a Winter Visitor" and "The Acrobat Chickadee," pp. 45-49. Gage (Silver, Burdett).

Parker, *Birds in Your Back Yard* (grades 2-3), The Basic Science Education Series. Copp Clark (Row, Peterson).

Partridge, *Everyday Science,* Book Two: "Bird Stay-at-homes" and "Winter Residents," pp. 499-503. Dent.

Peterson, *Wildlife in Color.* Allen (Houghton Mifflin).

Pettit, *Birds in Your Backyard.* Musson (Harper).

Williamson, *The First Book of Birds* (grades 4-6). Copp Clark (Heath).

New to this Edition

Alderfer, Jonathan. *National Geographic Backyard Guide to the Birds of North America* (National Geographic, 2011).

Burton, Robert. *The Audubon Backyard Birdwatcher: Birdfeeders and Bird Gardens* (Thunder Bay Press, 2012).

Lerner, Carol. *Backyard Birds of Winter* (HarperCollins, 1994).

Unit 38—Nature's Eating-Places for Hungry Birds

Scarcity of food is probably the greatest hazard faced by winter birds. But they are adaptable creatures, and usually manage to eke out an existence by making use of anything that is edible. The main natural vegetable foods available to land birds in winter are the seeds of weeds and evergreens, fruits and berries which remain on plants over winter, and, to some extent, the foliage of plants which remain green. Insects in various stages under the bark of trees provide food for other birds.

Most weed seeds are buried under snow, especially in midwinter. As the snow deepens, the supply of seeds diminishes by being covered. Some taller weeds such as ragweed and wild carrot still project through the snow. Birds profit when farmers leave weeds uncut in pastures and fence corners (fig. 1). Among the more common seed eaters are the juncos, the sparrows, and the goldfinches. The seeds in cones of evergreens are always available, but can be removed only by those birds with thick, strong beaks, among them the finches, sparrows, and American cross-bill. See also fig. 3, Unit 51 (page 214.

Among other vegetable foods available in winter are the buds of alder, birch, and poplar, and the green foliage of chickweed, white clover, and wintergreen—ready food for grouse. The nuts of oak, beech, hazel, and hickory are eagerly sought by the showy blue jay. Some of these he eats, and some, when weather permits, he tucks away under leaves or earth where, forgotten, they grow. The fruits of juniper, sumac, and Virginia creeper, available so long as the supply lasts, are tasty morsels for some winter birds.

Figure 1—(Drawing from New York State College of Agriculture)

Insect life composes the main diet of the downy woodpecker, the white-breasted nuthatch, and the brown creeper. The downy, the smallest and most useful of our woodpeckers, likes our orchards. There he makes a fairly good living by digging out the eggs, larvae, and pupae of insects hidden in bark crevices. Perhaps his main service is in ridding our orchards of codling-moth larvae. The white-breasted nuthatch also combs the bark for whatever insect life he can find. The brown creeper helps to rid orchard and shade trees of enemies missed by their regular summer boarders while he was up north. As he makes his way spirally up a tree trunk, his long, slender, curved bill probes every crevice. Meanwhile the black-capped chickadee searches beneath the bark for tiny eggs, larvae, and adult insects.

Activities

Teacher

Read this autobiography of a chickadee to the class.

> We wander about a good deal in the late summer, and especially during the fall, looking for good feeding-places for the winter. We are then in family groups, or sometimes different families come together, and we are joined by others from elsewhere and by numbers of Nuthatches and Woodpeckers and Brown Creepers until we form a merry band trooping through the woods and gardens. Sometimes we find a tree that is covered with scale insects or with the eggs of the cankerworm moth; sometimes it is a beech tree with its delicious nuts not too difficult for a Chickadee to open; again it is a patch of giant ragweed with rich, nutty seeds; or an apple tree in the garden infested with codling moths. Best of all, we like to find a feeding-shelf at a window or a piece of beef suet fastened in a tree to which we know we can come back when other food is scarce or difficult to get on account of ice and snow. . . .
>
> From *American Bird Biographies,* by A. A. Allen

Study this poem as a correlation with Literature.

THE DOWNY WOODPECKER

The Downy is a drummer-boy, his drum a hollow limb;
  If people listen or do not, it's all the same to him.

He plays a Chinese melody, and plays it with a will,
  Without another drumstick but just his little bill;

And he isn't playing all for fun, nor just to have a lark,
  He's after every kind of bug or worm within the bark;

Or, if there is a codling moth, he'll get him without fail,
While holding firmly to the tree with all his toes and tail.

He is fond of every insect, and every insect egg;
He works for everything he gets, and never has to beg.

From weather either cold or hot he never runs away;
So, when you find him present, you may hope that he will stay.

SELECTED

All Grades

- Search for winter feeding-places for birds. Visit meadows, fence corners, and roadsides. List the kinds of weeds, wild fruit trees, and shrubs which contain food for birds in winter. Collect, mount, and label some of them. What birds do you find feeding on these plants?
- Discover the value of stout bills to seed-eating birds.
- Encourage farmers to leave long grass, wild fruit trees, and shrubbery in fence corners as a means of protection and a source of food for birds in winter.
- List the main hazards of winter birds and after each state how nature or man helps to overcome it.

Read

Blough, *The Big Birds in the Big Woods* (grades 2-3), The Basic Science Education Series Copp Clark (Row, Peterson).
Comstock, *Handbook of Nature-Study.* Allen (Comstock).
Hausman, *Beginner's Guide to Attracting Birds,* pp. 82-87. Allen (Putnam's Sons).
Mason, *Picture Primer of Attracting Birds.* Allen (Houghton Mifflin).

New to this Edition

Lawrence, Gale. *A Field Guide to the Familiar: Learning to Observe the Natural World* (UPNE, 1998).
Leslie, Clare. *The Nature Connection: An Outdoor Workbook for Kids, Families, and Classrooms* (Storey Publishing, 2010.

Unit 39—Setting Up a Bird Cafeteria

Figure 1—Don't stop with looking at this picture–make some of the devices shown. (Courtesy Flower Grower Magazine)

We never really know our winter bird friends until we bring them near enough to be seen and heard. Aside from our enjoyment of them, we must consider the value to us of winter birds, and their special need for food at this time of year.

Feeding birds is an activity for urban schools as much as for rural ones. Both the need and the returns apply in both places. The birds are as anxious to eat, and the pupils are as anxious to see them in one type of school as in another.

Bird feeding is not an activity for older pupils any more than for primary. In fact it is easier while the children are young to arouse the necessary attitudes of good will toward the birds and instill the habit of expressing these feelings in a tangible manner by feeding the birds. Primary pupils can provide all that the birds need—namely, a protecting cover under which a supply of food is always present: they can place grain, lunch remains, and suet under an inverted cardboard box with one side removed.

To plan a bird-feeding project, we need to know what foods our winter birds prefer. Suet is the first choice of the brown creeper and downy woodpecker. Chickadees and nuthatches are partial to nuts and sunflower seeds, but they also like crumbs and suet. Juncos and sparrows seem to prefer crumbs to other foods. Although the blue jay likes nuts, seeds, and suet best, he will also take bread. The game birds, pheasants and quail, prefer grain. By leaving out shocks or ears of corn or sheaves of grain, or by placing grain under protecting shelters, the continued reduction in number of these birds may be checked.

Feeding birds is so easy that no teacher need ever shrink from it. Suet may be nailed to a post or tree trunk, or tied there with string or poultry wire. Crumbs and grain may be placed where the ground is free from snow, under evergreens or boxes with one side removed. Other devices are described in the activities.

Feeding birds should be begun in late October, before the birds go elsewhere because of scarcity of food. Even then, unless there is always a supply of food present, birds may change their minds and go to live with someone else. Otherwise the birds may perish, since they have become accustomed to their human provider and have not sought any feeding-place other than the local trees or weed patches. We must not fail them in their times of greatest need.

Knowledge of what to feed birds and how to do it is of little value to pupils unless actual practice gives them an opportunity to feel the birds' appreciation of this help. This experience develops deep-seated attitudes which will motivate the pupils to continue protecting and feeding birds out of school. At the same time actual participation develops in the pupils sympathetic feelings toward all nature and the habit of careful observation and unbiased reasoning.

Definite questions or assignments by the teacher are necessary if pupils are to make the most of their observations. Some suggestions follow: Which birds are particular in choosing food? Which eat several kinds? Are the visits of the birds to the feeding-counter any more frequent after the ground is frozen? Which kinds of birds show the least fear of children? Which the most? In what kinds of weather do birds come to the feeding-station most often? Which stay to eat? Which take food away? How early in the morning do birds come for food? How late in the afternoon? What attitude do most birds take toward the English sparrows?

Activities

All Grades

- Provide grains, poultry scratch feeds, chaff, weed seeds, crumbs, corncobs, etc., for seed-eating birds such as the cardinals, blue jays, bobwhites, pheasants, and tree sparrows. Clear away all snow from under protective shelters such as evergreen trees of native or ornamental types, or the discarded Christmas tree if available. Keep the cleared space plentifully supplied with food so that the birds may depend upon this feeding-place at all times.
- A recommended mixture for these birds in winter consists of 50 percent sunflower seed, 25 percent canary seed, 10 percent millet, 15 percent poultry scratch feed.
- Feed waterfowl cobs of corn on the ice when water is frozen.
- Provide suet in coarse mesh bags, nailed to or suspended from any support where birds visit and where pupils may observe them from the classroom. The suet may be tied with several winds of cord to tree trunks or to the undersides of larger branches of trees. Wire soap-dishes or bags made of chicken wire may be used; they have the advantage of being squirrel-proof, but the disadvantage of possibly injuring birds' eyes when the wire is frosty. The fat furnishes the heat-producing substances needed in cold weather. It is readily eaten by seed-eating as well as insect-eating birds; its cost is low; it keeps well and does not freeze hard. The more clumsy, ground-feeding house sparrows are unable to balance on a swaying, suet-filled bag.

Outside the Window

- Make a small lean-to of evergreen boughs and place under it grain, crumbs, and other scraps of food.
- Game birds such as pheasants and quail will not come near you. Place shelters and grain where they stay, even though it is out of your way.
- Keep a record of birds which feed at your feeding-station—and the kind of food each takes.
- You can feed birds in the same manner as some other pupils did. They made hanging baskets from the skins of halves of oranges and grapefruit, filled them with food, and hung them on trees. They tied little balls of suet and meat, also small nuts to trees at home and in the

schoolyard. They brought boards for a shelf outside the window and arranged to have the janitor put the shelf up. Then they placed scraps from their lunches on it each day and watched the birds eat. They stuffed cones of evergreen trees with melted suet and tied them to trees. Nor did they forget to place warm water out for their bird friends every day.

Primary Grades

Remove one side from a large cardboard box. Invert it and place it in a sheltered spot in the school grounds and weight it down with wood or stones. Feed the birds crumbs, dinner refuse, grains, etc. each day in this box. Keep it turned with the opening away from the wind.

Junior and Intermediate Grades

- Make a school collection of bulletins and other literature telling how to feed winter birds.
- Find pictures of bird shelters, feeding-trays, and baths. Look for real ones. Learn how to make some.
- Invite someone who attracts and feeds birds to tell your class how they do it.
- The girls may crochet small suet bags to be hung in trees.
- Make a class display of fruits, seeds, and insects used by birds as food in autumn. (Fruits: chokecherry, mountain ash, wild grapes and apples, barberry, elderberry, etc.; insects: flies, caterpillars, moths and butterflies, crickets, grasshoppers, aphids; seeds: sunflower, millet, grain.)
- Place the discarded Christmas tree in view of the classroom window. On this, place apples, bread, strung popcorn, orange halves hollowed out and filled with suet which has been melted and poured into the hollow, and then sprinkled with grain or nuts.
- Make decorated menu cards for bird guests.
- Around the school flagpole or a tree, about 4 feet from the ground, make a bird lunch counter about 8 inches wide, edged with a barrel-hoop or other thin wood to keep food from being blown off. Make some pupil *bird steward* for the week. It will be his or her duty to keep the counter free from snow and to

Figure 2—A Bird Lunch Counter Outside the Window

Attach the shelf A to the window sill. B. Use evergreen twigs to screen the window and the interior from the birds' view. C. Keep the hopper filled with crumbs, oatmeal, grains, nut meats, sunflower seeds, pumpkin seeds, etc. D. Place suet in a loosely-woven mesh bag. Place a dish of warm water on the counter frequently.

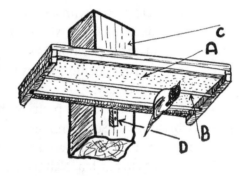

Figure 3— A Saunders' Inverted "Birdstone" Feeding Tray

A, tray; B, perches; C, post or tree to which the tray is attached; D, bracket on the back of the tray by means of which to attach it.

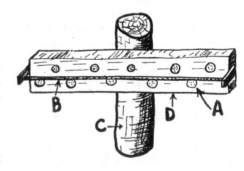

Figure 4— A "Birdstone" Lunch Counter

Pour melted "birdstone," A, into holes bored in a round or square piece of wood, D, to which a perch, B, has been attached. Fasten the lunch counter to a post or tree, C.

collect all dinner scraps and place them on it for the bird neighbors. Extras may be brought purposely for the birds. Do not overlook nuts, eggshell, apple cores, meat, and fresh water. Keep the lunch counter clean. Learn to know the birds that visit it, and what kind of food each likes best. See also figs. 2, 3, 4, and 5.

Figure 5—A Downey Woodpecker Eating Suet

- Construct a Saunders inverted "bird-stone" feeding-tray as shown in fig. 3. It should be about 15 inches long, 1 inch deep, and 6 inches wide, with narrow perches upon which the woodpeckers, nuthatches, and chickadees may rest upside down while feeding. Drive some tacks or small nails into the bottom of the tray to retain the food. Melt some suet or other kitchen fats, and into it stir a liberal supply of various kinds of seeds, breadcrumbs, nuts, meat scraps, etc. with a small portion of sand for the grinding of the other food in the birds' gizzards. Pour the mixture into the prepared tray and permit it to harden. Support the tray in an inverted position as shown in fig. 3. A tree or verandah post makes a suitable support. The inverted position keeps the food free from snow and ice. Replenish the supply of food when necessary.

- Make a "food tree" by pouring "birdstone," prepared as above, over the branches of a discarded Christmas tree or evergreen branches collected for the purpose. The "birdstone" board, shown in fig. 4, may be prepared by boring holes into a piece of board and pouring "birdstone" into the holes to harden. Nail the board to the side of a post or other suitable support.

Read

Frasier et al., *Through the Year* (grades 1-2): "The Lunch Counter," pp. 58-61; *Winter Comes and Goes* (grades 2-3): "Winter Birds," pp. 98-101; *The Seasons Pass* (grades 3-4): "The Winter Lunch Counter," pp. 140-145, and "How to Make Feeding Shelves," pp. 151-155. Dent (Singer).

Hausman, *Beginner's Guide to Attracting Birds*, pp. 16-60 and 88-90. Allen (Putnam's Sons).

Mason, *Picture Primer of Attracting Birds*. Allen (Houghton Mifflin).

Nicol et al., *The Nature Hour*, Fifth Year—Autumn and Winter: "Winter Feeding of Birds," pp. 50-52. Gage (Silver, Burdett).

Partridge, *Everyday Science*, Book Two, pp. 521-527. Dent.

Patch & Howe, *Outdoor Visits* (grades 2-3): "A New Year's Party," pp. 69-79. Macmillan.

Pettit, *Birds in Your Backyard*. Musson (Harper).

New to this Edition

Campbell, Scott. *Easy-to-Make Bird Feeders for Woodworkers* (Dover Publications, 1989).

Meisel, Paul. *Bird-Friendly Nest Boxes and Feeders: 12 Easy-To-Build Designs that Attract Birds to Your Yard* (Fox Chapel Publishing, 2012).

Roth, Sally. *The Backyard Bird Feeder's Bible: The A-to-Z Guide To Feeders, Seed Mixes, Projects, And Treats* (Rodale Books, 2003).

http://buildyourownbirdhouseplans.com/

http://www.osweb.com/kidzkorner/feeder.htm

http://www.artistshelpingchildren.org/birdfeedershousesperchescraftsmakingartscraftsideaskids.html (turn on your pop-up blocker for this site)

Nature Journal Excerpt

The Birdfeeder
In the back of our house, situated conveniently outside our living room window, is a large weathered bird feeder perched atop a sturdy, if slightly lop-sided, wooden pole. Dad built this maybe five years ago as a present for mom. Really it is only the frame of a house, set on a wide base. Fiberglass walls close in the sides, with slots at the bottom to release bird seed (which is added to the feeder through the detachable roof). Racks on either side hold seed cake and suet for the birds to eat. This feeder attracts an incredible variety of birds, from nuthatches, sparrows, and chickadees to the doves, starlings, and grackles to cardinals, blue jays, and titmouses. All through the winter when food is scarce, we fill the feeder and birds simply flock to partake of the easy food. Probably our most numerous species are starling, grackles, chickadees, and sparrows. It is not uncommon to see ten or more chickadees or sparrows at the feeder at a time. Starlings and grackles are the bully-boys; they will chase away other birds, so it is also not an uncommon sight to see ten or more of them with the feeder all to themselves.

Unlike the starling or the grackle, the timid dove prefers to feed on the abundance of seed fallen to the ground around the feeder rather then from the actual feeder.

Our most honored and rare visitors, however, are the blue jays and cardinals. The blue jay is another bully-boy, bigger and with less strength in numbers. The cardinal is shy and timid and comes less often.

Bird feeders are an excellent way of studying birds and their habits. I love our feeder and can't imagine our yard with it.
                                                    —C.C.M.D, Grade 8, 2011

Unit 40—What's The Temperature?

Even the youngest pupils feel changes in temperature in the room, out of doors, and in wash water. But the feelings of all of us are unreliable in this respect. The metal on a desk often feels colder than the wood, but it is not; a room feels cold to one, but warm to another. These and similar illustrations show even primary pupils the need of measuring how hot a thing is. Thus, the study of temperature and the thermometer should begin in primary grades and continue with increasingly difficult concepts throughout the grades.

Primary and junior pupils should be taught more definite meanings for the words *hot, warm, cool,* and *cold,* as applied to food and drink and to indoor and outdoor conditions. Then they learn to know a thermometer by sight, and that it can tell us more accurately how warm or cold a place is. They should know that when the "red line" is high, the surroundings are warm, and that when the "red line" goes lower, the surroundings are becoming cooler. Figure values on the thermometer can have no meaning for them, but they should be able to interpret such thermometer labels as "warm enough indoors for work or play," "cold enough outdoors to need mittens," "cold enough for water to freeze."

Intermediate pupils should be able to read readily the temperature in degrees on a Fahrenheit thermometer. They should also be able to use and write correctly the degree sign.

Activities

Teacher

To help pupils to interpret the meanings of various readings, draw a large thermometer on the blackboard. Graduate and label it somewhat as follows: 212° F.—Water is boiling; 130° F.—Mother's tea is cool enough to drink; 90 °F.—Let's go into the shade; 80° F.—It's nice to play out in the sun; 68° F.—Our room is comfortable; 50° F.—It is cool enough to wear a coat; 32° F.—Water on the street is freezing; 20° F.—Dress very warmly to go out to play; 0° F.—Wear fur or woollen earmuffs.

Practice in reading a thermometer may be given by making an adjustable model of a thermometer. Make a half-inch slit crosswise near each end of a long piece of card. Cut a red ribbon the length of the space between the slits. Tie a string to each end of the ribbon so that the ribbon and string form a belt around the part of the card between the slits. Graduate the card between the slits as a thermometer with readings from -20° F. to 212° F. The red ribbon, indicating the liquid, can be moved up and down to various readings while pupils give the reading and tell something of what that temperature means.

Pupils can practice reading the thermometer by finding and recording the temperature: at the north and south sides of a building, in the sun and in the shade, in snow and above snow, in water and in air, under a black cloth in sunlight and under a light cloth in sunlight.

All Grades

Place one hand in quite warm water and the other in quite cold water. Then place both hands in lukewarm water. How does it feel to the hand which was in cold water? To the hand which was in hot water? Why is it necessary to have a thermometer to tell us just how warm or cold anything is?

Primary Grades

Hold the bulb of a thermometer under the cold-water tap, under the hot-water tap, in your hand, in snow. When does the liquid in the thermometer rise? When does it fall?

Junior Grades

- Put the thermometer outdoors and watch the line go down. Notice that it stops at number 32 when the weather is just cold enough to freeze water. Where does the red line end indoors when it is just comfortable?
- Make a drawing of a thermometer showing: 90° F.—child in sun-suit; 80° F.—light dress; 68° F.—sitting at desk in school; 50° F.—with coat on outdoors; 32° F.—a dish with water freezing—child in snow-suit looking on; 0° F.—child in snow-suit with hood over head, wearing thick mitts, and holding one hand over his nose.

Junior and Intermediate Grades

- Read the temperature of water when the first film of ice begins to form.
- On the monthly calendar record the temperature each day at noon.
- Take the temperature inside the closed hand of a person who says he feels hot and a person who says he feels cold. What difference is there?
- Make a large drawing of a thermometer on the blackboard or on heavy paper. Mark the numbers on it from 20° below zero F. to 212°F. Color the liquid line red. Collect and mount pictures to illustrate such temperatures as 20° below zero, zero, freezing point, and those of a living-room, a healthy person's body, a cup of hot tea, and steam.
- For what things are high temperatures useful? Low temperatures?

Intermediate Grades

- Observe and record the temperature out of doors at each hour of the day. How does the height of the sun affect the warmth of the air?
- Guess the temperature of each of these, then measure it with a thermometer: the classroom, the inside of a refrigerator, a glass of drinking water, hot wash water, water with ice in it, the soil in a flower pot, the middle of your closed hand. How nearly right were you?
- List as many purposes as you can for which a thermometer is used.

Read

Carpenter & Neurath, *Icebergs and Jungles:* "Hot, Cold and In-Between," pp. 4-5; "Riddle of the Seasons," pp. 13-15; "The Hot Places," pp. 15-16; "The Cold Places," pp. 17-19; "The In-Between Places," pp. 22-24. Blue Ribbon (Hanover House).

Frasier et al., *Through the Year* (grades 1-2): "A Surprise," pp. 79-81; *Winter Comes and Goes* (grades 2-3): "Colder Weather," pp. 73-75; *The Seasons Pass* (grades 3-5): "Reading Thermometers," p. 119; and *How and Why Experiments* (grades 5-8) : "How Temperature Is Measured," p. 151. Dent (Singer).

Parker, *Thermometers, Heat, and Cold* (grades 4-6), The Basic Science Education Series. Copp Clark (Row, Peterson).

Schneider, *Science for Here and Now* (grade 2): "A Thermometer," pp. 113-122. Copp Clark (Heath).

New to this Edition

Cosgrove, Brian. *DK Eyewitness Books: Weather* (DK Children, 2007).

Crabtree. *What is Temperature? (Weather Close-Up)*, (Crabtree, 2012).

Rodgers, Alan. *Temperature (Measuring the Weather)*, (Heinemann-Raintree, 2007).

VanCleave, Janice. *Janice VanCleave's Weather: Mind-Boggling Experiments You Can Turn Into Science Fair Projects* (Wiley, 1995).

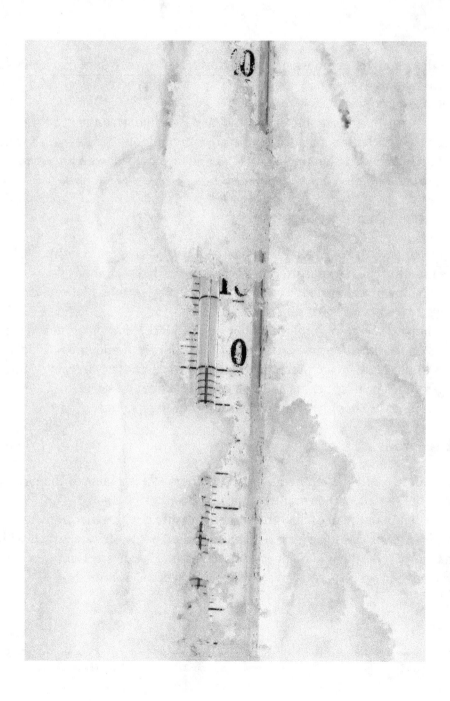

Unit 41—Frost, Snow, and Ice

What beauty there is in the symmetrical form of a snowflake, in the exquisite tracings on a frosted windowpane! Appreciation of these has been felt by poet, nature lover, and scientist, by old and young alike. Observation of them is almost always possible at this season, both outdoors and indoors, at school and home and office. These are a part of our very life from day to day. Our ways of living are constantly affected by the benefits or the inconveniences of frost and snow and ice. These three play a large part in determining the nature of our homes, our clothes, our methods of travel, our health and recreation, our businesses. What greater claims can be offered by any phenomena of nature for school study from the kindergarten to the high school?

Frost

> Little Jack Frost comes as still as a mouse;
> He paints all the windows of everyone's house;
> He pinches your nose, and he pinches your toes,
> But he gives us the ice and the white, sparkling snows;
> And without him much pleasure would surely be lost.
> Hurrah for the coming of little Jack Frost!
>
> BERTHA E. BUSH

Frost is not frozen dew, but, like dew, it forms directly from water vapor in the air. Its crystals grow on the surface of grass, roofs, fences, and windows when the temperature of these objects is below freezing point. The feathery or fern-like shapes and other patterns and designs formed by the frost make its study most interesting to pupils. A "killing frost" of fall or spring indicates low enough temperature to kill some kinds of plants.

Snow

> Softly from the sky is falling
> Snowflakes white as lilies fair;
> Gently to each other calling
> As they float down through the air.
>
> Softly, softly, oh so softly,

167

Figure 1—Some Common Forms of Snowflakes

> Do they come from dizzy heights;
> Gently, gently, oh so gently,
> Do they lay a blanket white.
>
> Over all the many housetops,
> Over shrubs and tall, tall trees,
> Over hills and fields and meadows,
> Hiding stones and restless leaves.

EMMA LOUISE CLAPP

Snow is formed when water vapor in midair changes to the solid state and the tiny crystals collect in symmetrical patterns called snowflakes. These usually grow larger as they fall through the cool air and collect more of the water vapor, changed to crystals. Snowflakes are always alike in being six-sided, symmetrical, and made up of tiny crystals. But they differ widely in size and in design, some being feathery, some star-shaped, others quite plain. Probably no two snowflakes are ever exactly alike. Fig. 1 shows a number of such patterns, over one thousand of which have been photographed.

Primary and junior pupils should, by directed observations, discover these characteristics of snowflakes; lightweight, slow downward drift, six-pointed shape, variety in sizes and patterns; made of frozen moisture, melt when warm, resemble window frost. Follow-up activities may include drawings, oral discussions, paper-cutting, and writing simple stories.

Ice

> The icicle hung on a red brick wall,
> And it said to the sun, "I don't like you at all."
> Drip, drip, drip.
>
> But the sun said, "Dear, you've a saucy tongue;
> Remember, I'm old and you are young."
> Drip, drip, drip.
>
> But the icicle only cried the more,
> Tho' the good sun shined on it just as before,

Until at the end of the warm spring day
It had cried its poor little self away.
Drip, drip, drip.

SELECTED

When the temperature of water falls below the freezing point (32° Fahrenheit), the liquid usually changes to ice. Ice, therefore, differs from frost and snow in that it is formed from liquid water, not from water vapor.

Ponds, ice rinks, and slides provide interesting learning opportunities for pupils. Here they see that the surface layers of water, exposed to the cooling atmosphere, are the first to change to ice, and that the water in swiftly running streams doesn't freeze until later. This causes intermediate pupils to wonder why. As soon as the water at the surface has cooled to 39° F. it sinks. Finally all the water is this cool. Then the water at the surface continues to cool until it reaches 32° Fahrenheit, at which temperature it begins to change to ice. Gradually the ice thickens, but the water at the bottom of the stream remains at about 39° Fahrenheit, a temperature quite satisfactory for fish, frogs, or turtles.

Some facts which primary and junior pupils should learn are: that ice is frozen water; that it forms when the weather becomes very cold, and melts again when warmed; that ice floats on water; that icicles grow longer because water runs down them and freezes; and that fish are safe in the water beneath ice.

The Value of Snow and Ice to Plants and Animals. Snow is of great value to plants in winter. Frequently we have observed that a fresh fall of snow delays the freezing of the soft earth which it covers, while the ground freezes rapidly in places from which we have shoveled the snow. In the same way a layer of snow keeps frozen ground from thawing during a mild spell. Thus the snow is valuable to plants by reducing the frequency and the suddenness of changes in temperature where they are, and by keeping the snow-covered plants in a frozen state during temporary thaws and until later in spring. Often have we noticed in spring how much healthier are areas of clover and fall wheat where snowbanks along fences have covered the ground until much of the freezing and thawing of spring has passed. Snow also helps plants by supplying the soil with water for spring and summer.

Let us avoid giving pupils in junior grades inaccurate ideas which must be corrected later. The statement that leaves and snow fall *to keep the tender plants warm* is not only unscientific, but quite untrue. Care should be taken to see that pupils do not gain a false idea that winter covering of garden plants by means of garden rubbish and snow prevents plants in the ground from freezing. Such covers only make the changes in temperature of the soil less frequent and more gradual both at times of freezing and at times of thawing.

The relation of snow and ice to birds and other animals may be investigated and discussed under such headings as: the increased need for body warmth in winter; the insulating value of air imprisoned in layers of hair, fur, wool, and feathers; the difficulties in obtaining winter food when snow and ice cover weed seeds, tree fruits, and dormant insects; the insulating value of loose snow over the homes of groundhogs and skunks in their burrows, and of earthworms in the ground; and the protecting value of ice to fish in streams and to frogs in the mud of streambeds.

The importance of snow and ice to man will be brought out by considering such topics as: the source of water for summer crops, rivers, water power, and irrigation systems; snow and ice as means of traffic in the country, in woods, and over bodies of water; snow and ice as one basis of the lumber industry; snow as a protective home for man (igloos); the value of ice in preserving foods; winter sports; the suffering and damage resulting from floods caused by the rapid melting of snow in spring or during winter thaws; the interruption of traffic on highways, railway lines, and city streets, and the financial cost of removing snow and of replacing broken wires and poles; the freezing of pipes and radiators containing water; the dangers of icebergs and of mountain slides.

Activities

Teacher

Boil water in a small kettle, as shown in fig. 2 and have students learn: that water changes to steam (A), which is invisible at the mouth of the spout; that this steam takes a visible form as a small cloud of minute droplets of water (B); and that this cloud in turn becomes invisible water vapor (C), distributed through the room.

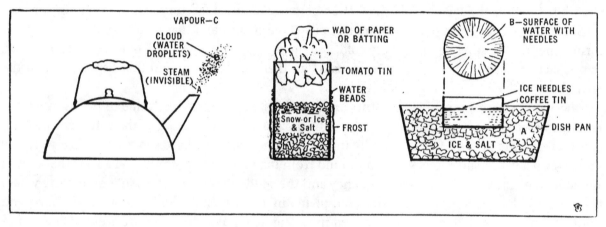

Figure 2—Experiments to Show the Formation of Water Vapor, Frost, and Ice

Crack or crush some ice and mix this with half as much salt in a tin can, as in fig. 2. Plug the mouth of the can with cotton or crumpled newspaper. In a few minutes, frost will form on the tin and gradually thicken. Above this will be an area covered with drops of water, some frozen to ice. Careful breathing on the tin will increase the amount observed. Use this experiment to explain the formation of frost on cold windowpanes and of snowflakes in cold air. Have pupils observe the formation of very small particles of frost, and how they grow with interlacing arms to form a variety of star-like crystals. Notice how the frost designs spread over windows until leaves and trees seem to be pictured.

Partly fill a dishpan or wooden pail with a mixture of snow or ice and salt. In this mixture, embed a coffee tin containing cold water, as in fig. 2. Leave this for some minutes, preferably covered with a sheet of glass. The surface of the water will soon show how ice starts to form as needle-like crystals. Observe how the crystals grow larger, come together, and interlace, until a layer of ice results (fig. 3). This experiment may be modified by punching a hole in the bottom of the coffee tin and observing the crystals left projecting from the sides of the tin as the water slowly lowers. Arrange to have pupils discover that ice floats on water, that you can see light through thin layers of it, and that ice, when warmed, melts and forms water.

Figure 3—Types of Snowflakes (Courtesy of Kenneth G. Libbrecht, California Institute of Technology)

171

Figure 3— Snowflake Photographs (Photo courtesy of Kenneth G. Libbrecht, California Institute of Technology)

All Grades

Observe and appreciate the many designs formed by frost on windowpanes. Watch them grow. Find the little crystals in them.

Catch snowflakes on a cold, black cloth or paper, or stand before a partly opened window as the flakes fall upon the dark, cold sill. With the naked eye or with a hand lens observe the shapes of a variety of forms. Try to draw several while looking at them and notice that all are six-pointed. Observe that the large flakes, which fall when "the old woman is picking her geese," often consist of many flakes grouped together. Pack some snow lightly and notice how the flakes are broken up.

Take a trip around the schoolyard some morning when the frost remains white until school is open. Look to see if it is on sidewalks, on automobiles, on fences, on bare ground, on grass in shade, on grass in the open, on trees.

> Sing a song of snowflakes
> Dancing through the air!
> See them whirling, playing,
> Falling everywhere.

> ADELLE J. GRAY

Make up some other verses to come after this one.

Here are some more things to make:

1. A January scrapbook containing pictures of snow scenes, winter sports, dog-teams in North-lands, methods of winter travel in other countries, snow-covered tree scenes, traffic difficulties caused by snow and ice, interrupted telephone services; poetry; original observations and drawings; snapshots.

2. A snowflake booklet with drawings, paper cutouts and constructions, stories, poems, original observations, etc.

3. A sand-table scene with cotton batting for snow, snow-covered trees made by dipping branches in hot starch and sprinkling them with artificial snow, icicles of white crepe paper covered with artificial snow, etc.

4. Blackboard designs of snowflakes.

Learn this for choral reading:

> Pretty little snowflakes,
> Shining like a star,
> Did you come to find us
> From some world afar?
> Nay, my home was nearer,
> Dear, than you suppose;
> From the kitchen kettle
> Through the air I rose.
> I longed in chilly cloudland
> To see you once again;
> And so I flew, a snowflake,
> To your windowpane.

> AUTHOR NOT KNOWN

Primary and Junior Grades

- Draw an imaginary picture of Jack Frost working in the garden.
- Watch the first snowstorm and think of all the ways in which it differs from a rainstorm. Then draw it on blue paper with white chalk.
- Give all the reasons that you can why you like snow, and why you don't like it. Make some pictures to help tell your stories.

Junior and Intermediate Grades

- Watch icicles forming. Why do they grow bigger?
- Take a trip to a body of water when freezing is just beginning. Take the temperature of the water and the air. Where does the ice begin to form, and what shape are the crystals? Notice if spring water freezes before or after surface water.

Intermediate Grades

- Fill a bottle with water, cork it tightly, and leave it on a window-ledge on a very cold day. What happens? Water expands when it freezes to ice. As it does so, it may break radiators or water pipes.
- During a very cold spell, soak some pieces of brick or of porous stone in water for several hours. Then place them in saucers on the outside window-ledge. What evidence have you that frost breaks rocks (fig. 4)? In the same way, the water in lumps of soil freezes in winter and breaks them into finer particles, leaving the soil loose and mellow.

Figure 4

- Find the depth of water which is formed when the snow of a storm melts. Measure the depth of snow where it is not blown; then consider that 10 inches of snow equals one inch of water (average ratio), and calculate the equivalent depth of water. Or the snow may be caught in a straight-sided snow gauge (fig. 1, Unit 28 on page 118), melted, poured into the rain gauge, and measured in terms of rain. The snow gauge may be inverted into level, freshly fallen snow, the surrounding snow scraped away, then the contained snow melted and measured as rain.

Read

Comstock, *Handbook of Nature-Study,* pp. 808-14. Allen (Comstock).
Fenton & Fenton, *Our Changing Weather,* pp. 68-76. Doubleday.
Frasier et al., *Through the Year* (grades 1-2): "Snow" and "Ice," pp. 72-78. Dent (Singer).
Parker, *Clouds, Rain and Snow,* The Basic Science Education Series. Copp Clark (Row, Peterson).
Partridge, General Science, Intermediate, Book 1: "Water as a Solid in Nature," pp. 93-97; and Everyday Science, Book Two: "Snow," pp. 467-469. Dent.

New to this Edition

Bentley, W.A. *Snowflakes in Photographs* (Dover Publications, 2000). [This is the Bentley featured in the picture book listed below: Snowflake Bentley.)
Cassino, Mark. *The Story of Snow: The Science of Winter's Wonder* (Chronicle Books, 2009).
Frost, Helen. *Water as a Solid.* (Capstone Press, 1999).
Martin, Jacqueline Briggs. *Snowflake Bentley* (Sandpiper, 2009).
Thompson, Jean M. *Water Wonders Every Child Should Know: Little Studies of Dew, Frost, Snow, Ice and Rain* (Kessinger, 2005) [This is a reprint of a book from 1909, 220 pages.]

(Courtesy US Department of Agriculture)

Unit 42—Christmas Things

Deck the halls with boughs of holly. . . .
'Tis the season to be jolly. . . .
Don we now our gay apparel. . . .
Fa, la, la, la, la, la, la, la, la.

A Christmas enterprise finds a ready response with all pupils of all ages and all environments. There are no limits to its possibilities. The teacher will be able to drop very much into the background while the pupils' natural interests provide sufficient motivation for the success of the project.

Planning the Enterprise

An introductory discussion period will raise many problems for study, such as are listed below. Each pupil will have his or her own particular field of interest. A small group may wish to investigate Christmas foods; a larger group may wish to find the origin of a number of our Christmas stories and carols; other groups may desire to learn more about Christmas in other lands, Christmas for the birds, and such topics. It is well to have each pupil follow up a topic of his own choice and largely in his own way. Encourage pupils to ask questions whenever necessary. But the best kind of help is to show them how to find the information for themselves. Suggest that they make full use of the home, school, and public libraries. Arrange so that each group reports its findings to all other groups through oral, written, and graphic or manual expression. Keep the search for understanding in the foreground and the visible results will follow naturally. Plan the school timetable so that pupils may work together at the enterprise for at least an hour a day. Give groups freedom to meet, discuss, plan, and work out their activities together. Arrange to have each group contribute whenever possible to the work of other groups.

Subtopics and Activities

Christmas in Song and Story. Pupils may find out about some of these topics, according to their grades: how Christmas came to be celebrated; the birth of Christ; the origin of the idea of

Christmas gifts, Christmas cards, the story of St. Nicholas, legends of Christmas long ago, the first Christmas carols.

All Grades

Make Christmas cards for friends. Learn carols and sing them. Read and tell Christmas stories.
Christmas Decorations (fig. 1). Find out all you can about these things: the kinds of decorations commonly used, countries that specialize in making them, how to connect up electric lighting, how to discover which bulb is burnt out, safety rules about electricity and fire.

All Grades

Don't spend money on Christmas tree decorations—make your own. Here are some suggestions. Take an expedition outside to collect pine and spruce cones, chestnut burrs, large acorns, seed pods of ordinary weeds, and cockle burrs. Use a piece of adhesive tape to attach a loop of cord to each cone or pod. All should be coated with glue. Then they may be sprinkled with colored powder or artificial snow, or they may be left to dry before being brightly painted. Acorns may be painted and then decorated with gilt. These will look very effective on a tree when strung together on a cord. Spools painted with thick, bright paint, or covered with tinfoil or bright colored paper make lovely tree decorations. They may also be painted with glue and sprinkled with artificial snow. String them together or hang them up singly. Pleasing effects are obtained by hanging tinfoil-covered spools in the center of an evergreen wreath in the window or by draping a long string of spools over a doorway or from a mantle.

Figure 1—Making Christmas Decorations

- Strings of cranberries or of popcorn, natural or painted, look beautiful when arranged tastefully about a room.
- Aluminum paints have no limit to their use. Paint spools, acorns, and pressed ivy leaves with aluminum paint. Decorate painted acorns and cones with it. Brush it over the ends of evergreen branches.
- Make a holly design for a Christmas card.
- Identify the Christmas cactus and poinsettia.

Primary Grades

- Make potted Christmas trees in this way: From green construction paper, cut two Christmas trees of the same size. Cut one half-way up from the bottom; cut the other half-way down from the top. Fit the two together. Then fit the base into the center of a spool. Cover the spool with bright paper.
- Drinking-straws, cut into pieces and strung with alternating squares of bright paper, make pretty garlands. The straws may be colored; in place of squares, tinfoil may be crushed to form flowers.

Junior and Intermediate Grades

- A beautiful Christmas bouquet can be made in this way: Make a starch of flour and water, and boil it until it is the thickness of gravy. Obtain branches of evergreen cut to fit a vase, dip them in the cold mixture, and allow them to drip for several minutes. Put artificial snow in a large paper bag, insert the treated evergreen branches, and shake well until the snow sticks to the branches. Place them in the vase and, when dry, the branches will be covered with sparkling snow.
- To make a Christmas border for the blackboard, cut strips of rough icicles from heavy white drawing-paper; paint these with glue, and sprinkle artificial snow over them; then put them up and at intervals insert gay bells, clusters of holly, or colored cones. See also figure at Unit heading.
- Find out about the habits of growth of holly (originally called holy berry), and the value of the prickles in keeping animals away. The creamy holly blossoms are followed by the berries, first green, then yellow, and finally red. Investigate how the mistletoe lives on oak trees and from them absorbs ready-made food, how it was revered by the Druid priests in Early Britain before the Romans came.
- Make a candle by melting and pouring paraffin into a paper cylinder through which a coarse string is held to serve as a wick. When the paraffin is hard, remove the paper, sharpen the candle, and light it.
- Make evergreen wreaths by fastening two ends of a number-9 wire together to form a circle and wrapping about it balsam twigs intermingled with evergreen cones.

Christmas Scenes. To express the theme of Christmas, children may build up Christmas scenes, large or small, according to the number of pupils, space, and other facilities available.

Figure 2—Paper Cutting For Primary and Junior Pupils

Sky, purple; moon, orange; snow, white; trees, green, with brown trunks; children, rope and log, black.

Figure 3— A Screen Made by Paper Cutting.

Use bright colors for all except the elves (black) and the snow.

All Grades

A manger scene made by the children will stir their artistic imagery and increase their reverence. Obtain a large cardboard box. To give it a rustic appearance, paint it in streaks with brown and black poster paint both inside and out. Scatter hay on the stable floor. For the crib use a corner of a wooden chalk box. Model the animals and other figures of Plasticine, clay, or asbestos powder. If modeled in the latter two, the creatures and figures may be painted when the models are dry.

Junior and Intermediate Grades

Is there a corner in your room where you could make this? Place sand on the floor to form a realistic desert scene. Make a fairly large stone stable by mixing pebbles and clay together, and modeling it to the right shape. Place models of palm trees outside the door of the stable. A crib can be easily built, and cows and woolly sheep modeled. Pipe cleaners make excellent figures which can be dressed in brightly colored pieces of cloth. Clay camels with models of the Wise Men as mounts may be placed on the sand. It will make the display realistic if these are placed as though coming from an Arab tent made of gaily striped paper. In one corner an oasis can be built with a small mirror for water, and grass and palm trees placed around it. The background could be made by painting a large piece of paper a dark blue with silvery stars above, and one particularly bright star over the stable. Palm trees and low, gray houses with orange windows and doors, may be placed on the background.

179

In another corner, or on a table, you might try this: Cover the surface with cotton. Make cardboard houses painted or colored with crayon. For windows cut out sections and paste red tissue paper or red cellophane over these on the inside. Draw, color, and cut out small wreaths and paste them on windows and doors. To make evergreen trees, cut small branches from trees, set them in blocks of wood, Plasticine, or clay, and place them artistically on the landscape. People may be fashioned from soap or clay, and dressed in bits of fur. The background will be very effective if drawn with chalk and blended to form mountains, trees, and houses in the distance. To make the whole scene more beautiful, sprinkle artificial snow over everything.

Christmas Foods. Mm—Mm. Doesn't Christmas dinner smell good! The table groans under its weight of good things. Where did they all come from?

Junior and Intermediate Grades

Trace the stories of such Christmas foods as fowl, dressing, cranberries, nuts, and Christmas pudding from their beginnings until they are served. Read about the "Christmas Pudding," in Ch. XXIII of *Geography Through a Shop Window*, by Finch (Dent). Visit a grocery store and get information about Christmas foods by asking the grocer or by reading wrappers. Make a chart to show what goes into a Christmas pudding. Trace the story of suet from the sun to grass, to the cow, to the pudding. Find the countries from which the various foods come. Make maps and mounts of articles and pictures.

Christmas Games. Christmas is such a happy time that we seem charged with excess energy—especially the children. So let's take time to play games with them.

All Grades

Santa's Whiskers. Santa stands in the center looking bewildered, for he has lost his whiskers (a whisk broom). The players, with hands behind their backs, form a shoulder-to-shoulder circle. They pass the whiskers around behind their backs. Whenever possible, the players try to tickle Santa with his whiskers without being caught. Santa tries to find who has his whiskers. If he is successful, the one caught becomes Santa.

Weaving the Holly Wreath. Place three red beads on a green cord long enough to reach round a circle of players surrounding "it" in the center. All the players shuttle their hands back and forth, passing the holly berries (beads) along the string. When "it" catches a player with the berries in his hand, that player becomes "it."

Christmas in Other Lands. We would never want to part with the Christmas season. How do people in other lands celebrate their Christmas?

Junior and Intermediate Grades

Find out how Christmas is spent in other lands. Arrange for several pupil reports such as follows: In Sweden lighted candles are placed in windows early Christmas morning to light the way of people going to church. In Holland children clean their wooden shoes and fill them with hay and oats for St. Nicholas's white horse. In France Santa Claus is called Father Christmas. He brings presents, but his companion brings switches for bad children. In Norway all domestic animals are given a special Christmas menu.

Write to a grade-8 girl, in care of the Superintendent of Education, Canberra, Australia, or to pupils in other lands, to discover how they spent Christmas. Tell how it is spent here. Write a composition entitled "Christmas in Summer."

Christmas Gifts. Let us try to bring the truly beautiful spirit of Christmas gifts into the classroom. Children will feel proud and happy to give gifts they themselves have made.

All Grades

Bags of colored mosquito netting when filled with mixed pine, spruce, or fir cones, and allowed to dry will make welcome gifts for people who have a fireplace. The cones will burn brightly with a delightful smell. Make hemlock wreaths for friends. Color the cones red, gold, and silver.

Junior and Intermediate Grades

Make trays by cutting thin wood to the right size and fastening gilded cones around the edge.

Christmas for the Birds. While pupils are actuated by the Christmas spirit, their feelings of generosity may be directed toward their bird friends. Although they have been feeding them regularly for some weeks, a special Christmas treat may be prepared. In Norway it is customary to save a sheaf of grain from the harvest to place on a pole for the birds at Christmas time.

All Grades

Plan to give the birds about home or school a special feed on Christmas Day. Place the discarded Christmas tree in the backyard as a shelter under which to feed birds. Pour melted suet over the branches to harden for bird food. Tie strings of popcorn to tree branches for birds. Fasten pieces of suet to tree trunks. Make and place feeding-shelters.

Christmas Trees. (See Unit 43 on page 182.) Be safe with Christmas trees and Christmas decorations. Keep the tree away from a grate fire; do not light candles on a tree. Check electric wiring carefully.

Read

Partridge, *Everyday Science,* Book One: "The Science of Christmas Things," pp. 120-130. Dent.
Patch & Howe, *Outdoor Visits* (grades 2-3): "Holly Trees and Holly Bushes," pp. 128-130. Macmillan.
Stephenson, *Nature at Work,* Book 3 (grades 5-6): "The Holly and the Ivy," pp. 43-47. Macmillan (A. & C. Black).

New to this Edition

Ashcroft and Cox. *Natural Ideas for Christmas* (New Line Books, 2006).
Bradford, June. *Christmas Crafts from around the World (Kids Can Do It),* (Kids Can Press, 2003).
Collins, Ace. *Stories Behind the Great Traditions of Christmas* (Zondervan, 2003).
Cusick, Dawn. *Nature Crafts for Christmas: A Step-By-Step Guide to Making Wreaths, Ornaments & Decorations* (Rodale Press, 1994).
Nelson, Gertrud Mueller. *Build Your Own Bethlehem: A Nativity Scene and Activity Book for Christmastime* (Liturgy Training Publications, 2007).
Gibson, Cay. *Christmas Mosaic: An Illustrated-Book Study.* Hillside Education, 2009).
Woram, Catherine. *Christmas Crafting With Kids: 35 Projects for the Festive Season* (Ryland, Peters & Small, 2008).

Unit 43—Evergreens at Christmas Time

Can you imagine a "Merry Christmas" without Christmas trees? Since the early days of Queen Victoria's reign, following her marriage to the German Prince Albert, the Christmas tree custom has added enjoyment to the Yuletide season for young and old alike throughout English-speaking countries. The Germans had inherited the idea from the Roman Empire. It is fitting that at this season we should become more familiar with the ways of our native evergreens.

The study of structure in plant life has little value for pupils, except when it is necessary to identify unknown plants, or when it helps them to understand the functions or ways of life of the plant. Many of the observable facts concerning our evergreens have little place in classroom teaching. But there is a somewhat universal satisfaction in being able to correctly name them and to understand how they live.

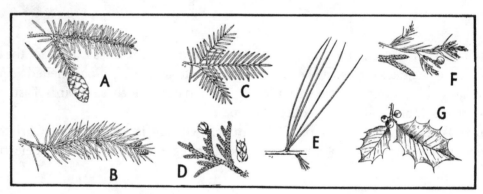

Figure 1—Evergreens We All Should Know

A, hemlock; B, white spruce; C, balsam; D, white cedar; E, white pine; F, red cedar; G, holly.

The term *evergreen* is applied to all plants that retain their green foliage the year round. Two classes of plants are included: first, those that bear broad leaves similar to those of our common deciduous trees, and secondly, those that bear narrow needle-like or scale-like leaves, usually rather stiff and thick. To the first class belong trees that live in the tropical rain forests and remain active all year, as well as such plants as holly and our native winter-green. To the second class belong all of our cone-bearing trees with the exception of tamarack.

Adaptations of Our Evergreens for Winter Conditions. How are our evergreens fitted to survive our Canadian winters, characterized by cold and drought, while they still bear their canopies of leaves? Most of our trees have already shed their leaves. Thus they avoid continued transpiration at a season when absorption from the roots is hindered, or at least seriously reduced, by cold soil con-

182

ditions. But our evergreens live in similar soil conditions; therefore we must look to their leaves for some specific winter adaptations. Here we find transpiration reduced below the danger line by their small surface exposure. This characteristic of the needle-like leaves may be illustrated to pupils thus. Cut two equal-size pieces of cloth. Thoroughly wet each one, wring out all the water possible, then leave one tightly rolled up, and the other spread out beside it to dry. Note the rapid drying out of the unrolled piece in comparison with the rolled one. Consider the results to explain the rapid evaporation from the broad leaves of deciduous trees as compared with that from evergreen, needle-like leaves. A cross-section of an evergreen leaf will show its extremely heavy covering, which materially reduces transpiration. Probably the resinous deposits within the leaf also help considerably in reducing loss of moisture.

Evergreen trees have two definite advantages over deciduous ones: their leaves are always ready to start making food when even temporarily favorable weather conditions occur; they do not have to produce a complete new crop of leaves each spring.

Evergreens Do Shed Their Leaves. The popular belief that evergreens never shed their leaves is quite false. Careful observation of any pine or spruce tree will show these facts: the surrounding ground is carpeted with fallen needles; twigs more than 2 or 3 years old usually have no needles; the green canopy covering the tree is all on the outside parts and is made up of needles on the youngest parts of twigs.

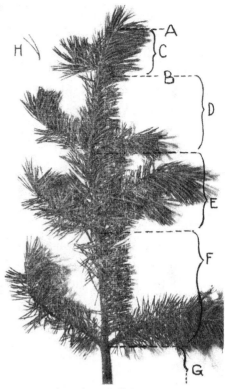

Figure 4— The jack pine tells its own story. A, terminal buds, well developed, ready for winter rest and spring growth into new main stem and side branches; B, cone produced during the preceding summer; C, growth in length during the past summer; D, E, growth made during the preceding 2 years; F, wood from which some needles, now about 3 ½ years old, have been shed; G, wood, now about 4 ½ years old, from which all needles have been shed; H, needles, two in a cluster on jack pine.

Identifying Our Evergreens. To be able to name our Christmas trees is satisfying to all of us. Few facts need be known to serve this purpose. Primary and junior pupils will learn these facts best by comparing specimens with pictures while the teacher helps. Older pupils will profit more and gain more personal satisfaction if they find the names of specimens by the use of a key.

A simple form suitable for pupils of grade 5 and upwards is given below.

A Simple Key to Our Common Evergreens	
1. Leaves long and needle-like.	
(a) Needles in clusters of 5 each:	White Pine
(b) Needles in clusters of 2 each, 4" to 6" long, shining:	Red Pine
(c) Needles in clusters of 2 each, not over 2" long:	Jack Pine
(d) Needles all separate from each other, easily rolled between the thumb and finger:	Spruce
(e) Needles separate, flat, each on a little stalk:	Hemlock
(f) Needles separate, flat, not having any stalks, but leaving round scars on twigs:	Balsam
2. Leaves like little scales completely covering the twig, twig flat and yellowish green:	White Cedar

All specimens to be identified are placed on the pupils' desks and the key written on the blackboard. The teacher should assist in naming the first sample picked up. The procedure consists of reading heading 1 and comparing the facts stated with those observed when examining the specimen. If the facts apply to the specimen, he knows it belongs in Group 1 and continues to read until he finds all facts which apply to it. The pupil is learning to discover names for himself—the task that will be his later, when he has no teacher.

When selecting a Christmas tree, the balsam should be our first choice. Its shape is attractive, its fragrance pleasing, and its needles stay on well. Norway spruce, or any other kind of spruce, is next best. Its shape is desirable, and its branches stiff enough to hold decorations and parcels, but its needles are likely to fall after a week or so. Cedars, pines, and hemlocks are less desirable in color and shape. Their branches bend too easily when loaded.

Some broad-leafed plants hold their green leaves all winter. Among these are our low-growing wintergreen plant, common in some woods, and holly plants, small trees whose leaves have spiny teeth and wavy margins. The latter grow in the eastern United States. The leaves of such plants are protected in winter by their tough, leathery texture, and their waxy coverings.

Activities

Teacher

One evergreen tree might be given some detailed study. While approaching it, observe its general shape, the main stem straight up through the center, the many branches quite close to each other, the shade of green. Pupils will sketch it while observing it. A close-up study will reveal its bare center and green outer canopy, and the parts of the branches and twigs from which needles have been shed. Listen to the wind blowing through the tree. Notice how the needles are arranged—singly or in clusters, with stalks or without stalks. Look for cones; pry open the scales of one and see the seeds inside.

All Grades

- Decorate living Christmas trees out of doors. Name some evergreens around the school and at home.
- Make a winter window box by inserting the ends of evergreen twigs in the soil and decorating them as suggested in Unit 42 (page 176).
- Use evergreen boughs and cones for classroom decorations.
- Bring some cones to the classroom. Watch them open and set their seeds free as they dry. Let some seeds flutter downward or drift in the wind. Put the stem of an open cone in a tumbler of water. Watch it close. Then let it dry, and watch it open again.

Primary Grades

- Play an action game to imitate an evergreen tree. Stand tall and straight like its trunk. Put your hands together over your head to show its shape. With your arms show how the branches of a pine and of a spruce grow out from the trunk.
- Draw the outline of an evergreen tree on stiff paper. Model the tree with green Plasticine.
- Read, enjoy, and illustrate this poem.

If Mother Nature patches the leaves of trees and vines,
I'm sure she does her darning with the needles of the pines;
They are so long and slender, and somewhere in full view,
She has her threads of cobwebs and a thimble made of dew.

WM. H. HAYNE

Set up a winter scene on your sand-table. Make cardboard cutouts of evergreen trees and color them.

Junior and Intermediate Grades

Figure 4—A Christmas Poster Made of Evergreen Materials

- Visit a group of young evergreens which were planted 5 to 10 years ago. What would be the advantage to those left with respect to light, space, and water if some of these were removed for Christmas trees?
- Notice that white pine trees in autumn look brownish and ragged because many needles have become brown and ready to fall. Examine the thick layer of needles of previous years under the tree.
- Find the name of your Christmas tree, of those of neighbors, of those displayed for sale.
- Set up a display in the classroom showing the values of evergreens to nature and man. Beneath a tree, place a carpet of fallen needles, models of birds seeking protection, food given to the birds, etc.
- Find out where we get holly and mistletoe, and tell the class.
- Make a display of cones of different kinds of evergreens.
- Investigate the number of Christmas trees used on the American continent each year; there are enough to form 40 rows around the earth, if the trees were spaced 1/10 of a mile apart.

Make a class poster by writing the words "Merry Christmas" by means of leafy twigs of hemlock or balsam (fig. 3).

For the words, cut hemlock twigs into short lengths and fasten them with mucilage to outlines of the letters about 8" high. Press them under a heavy book for an hour or more. Attach other decorative materials as pupils wish.

Read these poems: Lowell, "To a Pine Tree" and "Growth of the Legend"; Bryant, "Forest Hymn"; Longfellow, "My Cathedral" and the parts of "Hiawatha" which tell of the pine forests.

Read

Cormack, *The First Book of Trees* (grades 4-6): "The Evergreen Trees," pp. 42-65. Copp Clark (Heath).
Frasier et al., *Winter Comes and Goes* (grades 3-4) : "Evergreen Trees," pp. 81-83. Dent (Singer).
Hunt & Andrews, *Trees*, pp. 3-10. Moyer.
Hylander, *Out of Doors in Winter* (grades 6-8): "The Evergreen Trees," pp. 9-35. Macmillan.
Kieran, *An Introduction to Trees.* Blue Ribbon (Hanover House).
King, *Telling Trees* (grades 5 and up): leaves and fruits illustrated by size. McLeod (Wm. Sloane).
Patch & Howe, *Outdoor Visits* (grades 2-3): "Some Trees with Cones," pp. 80-90. Macmillan.
Peterson, *Wildlife in Color.* Allen (Houghton Mifflin).
Stephenson, *Nature at Work*, Book 1 (grades 4-5): "Evergreens," pp. 30-32. Macmillan (A. & C. Black).

New to this Edition

Blomgren, Jennifer. *Where Would I Be in an Evergreen Tree?* (Sasquatch Books, 2011).
Prevost, John F. *Evergreen Trees* (Abdo and Daughters, 1998).

Beautify Your Surroundings ~ December ~

THE CRANBERRY GROWS IN LOW MARSHY LAND.

POINSETTIA THE RED "PETALS" ARE REALLY LEAVES.

HOLLY - A COMMON ENGLISH HEDGE-PLANT.

THE MISTLETOE GROWS ON SOME VARIETIES OF TREES.

THE CHRISTMAS CACTUS BLOOMS ONCE A YEAR.

PREPARE A FRIEZE SHOWING SOME INTERESTING FACTS ABOUT SUCH CHRISTMAS PLANTS AS THOSE SUGGESTED ABOVE.

TWINKLING STARS

COVER CARDBOARD CUT-OUTS WITH TINFOIL. HANG THEM ON LONG STRINGS FROM LIGHTS OR WIRES.

CHRISTMAS TREE,

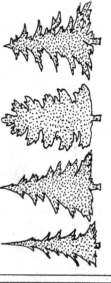

FOR THE CHRISTMAS TREE, MAKE COLOURED CANDY-BOXES.

MAKE GREEN CUT-OUTS OF COMMON EVERGREEN TREES.

WINDOWS:

A SANTA ASSEMBLED FROM RED AND WHITE TISSUE PAPER AND OPAQUE BLACK PAPER IS EFFECTIVE FROM WITHIN AND WITHOUT.

CORNERS FASTENED INSIDE WITH GUMMED PAPER.

MAKE THIS REINDEER-AND-SLEIGH ORNAMENT OF HEAVY CARD. FILL THE SLEIGH WITH EVERGREEN TWIGS AND CONES.

A SAND-TABLE

CHRISTMAS SCENE:

A CHRISTMAS TREE FOR THE BIRDS:

MELTED SUET, POURED ON THE BRANCHES, WILL HELP ATTRACT OUR FEATHERED FRIENDS.

BORDER SUGGESTIONS

D. FARWELL

MAKE STENCILS - SEE OCTOBER PAGE.

Science in Action --- December

An experiment in glass blowing will teach you much about the qualities of glass:

Seal the end of a glass tube by rotating it slowly in a hot flame until the edges of the tube's end soften and run together.

Then blow into the other end of the tube as you continue to rotate it. Be careful not to touch the hot part of the tube. What do you learn from this experiment?

ALCOHOL LAMP (OR BUNSEN BURNER)

A "TELEPHONE" EXPERIMENT

RUBBER BANDS
PAPER
THREAD
BUTTON TIED INSIDE TO END OF THREAD

Cut both ends from two tin cans. Over one end of each stretch tightly a piece of tough paper and fasten it in place with rubber bands. Join the two paper diaphragms with a conveniently long, waxed thread as shown. Pull taut. Talk. Why won't it work when the thread is loose? When the thread is touching something?

Put a tray of water, and one containing a solution of salt, in an electric refrigerator. Which freezes first? Why? Then how is salt of use when it is scattered on icy sidewalks?

A little tasty science in the kitchen:

Toffee Recipe:

1 cup brown sugar
1 can condensed milk (NOT EVAPORATED MILK)
½ cup butter
½ cup corn syrup

Boil, stirring CONSTANTLY, till brittle in water. (Takes 25 minutes or more.) Pour into buttered pan.

To help prevent the needles of your Christmas tree from dropping, set the base of the tree in a container of moist sand. Keep the sand moist.

Use your tree lights safely: bind them to twigs in such a way that the hot bulbs can touch neither needles nor decorations.

With a simple pendulum like this, experiment to find out how long the string must be so that the pendulum will swing at the rate of sixty times a minute. Add more weight to the string's end. What change, if any, do you notice in the rate of swinging?

Why doesn't the pendulum of a clock come to a stop as quickly?

NAIL OVER DOORWAY
STRING
WEIGHT

Did you know that a single drop of water, placed on top of a tiny hole in a piece of metal, can be used as a microscope? Such an object as a hair, if placed close under the hole, is magnified many times.

D. FARWELL

NATURAL SCIENCE — JANUARY — DAY BY DAY

SUNDAY	MONDAY	TUESDAY	WEDNESDAY	THURSDAY	FRIDAY	SATURDAY
	1 The sun is rising in a NEW YEAR.	**2** Draw the Big Dipper as you see it at 8 p.m. to-day.	**3** Find and draw Queen Cassiopeia's chair in the north sky.	**4** Measure the length of your shadow at noon.	**5** Draw a line like this pointing to the sun at noon.	**6** The gray squirrel searches under snow for food.
7 He comes out to enjoy his pine cone dinner.	**8** The red squirrel stays in his hollow tree shelter.	**9** The chipmunk enjoys his stored food underground	**10** Mice play about on the snow and girdle trees.	**11** How has the length of your shadow changed?	**12** Do you what did on January 5.	**13** Find the tiny "seed-birds" fluttering from birch catkins.
14 The friendly chickadee has a black cap and a black bib.	**15** The Downy Woodpecker likes the insects under bark.	**16** Downy will stay if you feed him suet	**17** The snowbird comes from the north to winter with us.	**18** Compare your shadow to-day noon with that a week ago.	**19** Is the sun getting higher or lower at noon during these three weeks?	**20** Watch frost form on the window.
21 The frost came from water vapour in the air.	**22** Do this and you will see how frost forms.	**23** You should sleep with your window open. Do you?	**24** Learn to read the thermometer.	**25** Read the temperature of your room to-day.	**26** Read the outdoor temperature each hour from 9-4 o'clock	**27** Read the thermometer of your oven during baking
28 Keep your living-room at 68° for good health	**29** Place branches of fruit trees or flowering shrubs in water in the classroom.	**30** Which way do leaves of window plants face?	**31** Turn a potted plant around and observe 2 days later.			

Have your pupils build this calendar day by day on blackboard or chart. Use substitutions if desired.

J.A. PARTRIDGE
Drawn by D. Farwell

JANUARY

Unit 44—Learning While We Play

Effective learning requires interest and personal experiences. Nothing is closer to the heart of a child, or closer to his experiences, than play. What unbounded opportunities come to teachers to help in the education of pupils (in the real sense) through informal conversations and discussions with pupils about their games, their play, and their holiday activities. We will have these opportunities only if we associate with the children in their games and recreation and thus become familiar with their interests and their past experiences.

This unit is suggested for immediately after the Christmas vacation, a time when pupils' interests in Christmas toys and in holiday play are at the peak. All will be anxious to talk about their experiences, and to bring their new toys to school to show how they work. The mechanisms of toys and the methods of using them are applications of the principles of science. While the toys are used, these principles of science are introduced, and at least partly understood.

Toys that travel must have something to provide the power. Those that wind up have a spring which can do nearly as much work in moving the toy as we did in winding it up. The same principle applies to most clocks and watches. The rubber-band motor of a toy airplane turns the propeller as it untwists. The chain of a bicycle transfers the pressure on the foot pedal from the large to the small sprocket wheels, thus turning the rear wheel. Gliders and darts make use of the buoyancy of air. The smooth runners of sleighs illustrate the value of reducing friction. The sound produced by blowing a whistle leads to experimenting with different lengths of air columns. The force of a sprung bow shows the tendency of some substances to spring back to their original position after they have been bent. The floating of boats on water illustrates the buoyant force of water.

It is not expected that activities such as these and the ones below will result in the use of formal terms or accurately worded statements of principles of science. The learning of scientific generalizations is somewhat like being cured by taking medicine; it is not the first dose, but the

Figure 1— A Scene to Be Made by Free Cutting from Showy Colored Paper

189

cumulative effect of a series of doses that brings about the desired results. Over a period of time, the child gradually learns the principle.

All Grades

Experiment: A child using a coping saw found the blade uncomfortably hot.
Discovery: When things rub together, they produce heat.
Experiment: A new sleigh is found to run better after being used a while.
Discovery: Smooth runners slip more easily.
Experiment: Roller skates shoot out from under you.
Discovery: Weights are moved easily on wheels.

Figure 2—Foucault's Pendulum at Thomas Aquinas College, Santa Paula, California

Primary and Junior Grades

Experiment: A paper windmill turns when held in front of a fan or when blown upon.
Discovery: Air in motion presses on things.
Experiment: Jimmy floated his toy boat in the wash basin. When he blew on the sail, it moved.
Discoveries: Water holds things up; moving air pushes things.
Experiment: A primary class made a sand-table scene of an ice rink.
Discoveries: They learned how to measure, make hockey nets, skates, hockey sticks, etc.

Intermediate Grades

Experiment: Willie showed how his celluloid pinwheel turned when held under falling water.
Discovery: When water falls, it presses on things. Falling water may be made to turn wheels and produce electricity.
Experiment: Tommy's sleigh with rusty runners couldn't go as fast as Sally's sleigh with shiny runners.

Discovery: Smooth surfaces rub past each other more easily than rough ones—there is less friction. Gravity pulled both sleighs downhill.

Experiment: Two boys experimented with a weight tied on the end of a string (a pendulum).

Discovery: So long as the pendulum is the same length, it will swing the same number of times a minute; the shorter the pendulum, the more swings per minute.

Experiment: Jimmy made a paper dart and folded the back edge of the paper upward; then he shot it. The dart curved upward.

Discovery: When a bird in flight wants to go up, it tips its tail up.

Experiment: As many coppers as possible were dropped into a tumbler full of water to find when the water would overflow.

Discovery: The water heaped up. Water seems to have a membrane over its surface. Some insects can walk on this.

Experiment: Sunlight was reflected from a mirror to the blackboard.

Discovery: When light strikes a mirror at less than a right angle, it is reflected away at the same angle, in the same way as a ball is reflected from a wall when tossed at it at an angle of less than ninety degrees.

Experiment: Ted used a glass triangle and produced a spectrum of seven colors. Then Helen brought a top painted seven colors in seven bands. When spun, it looked white.

Discovery: White light is made up of the seven colors of the spectrum.

Experiment: Ruth found that she had to sit further back from the center of the teeter board than her heavier brother, Jim.

Discovery: A light weight a long way from the balancing point of scales will hold up a heavier weight close to this point.

Read

Bcauchamp et al., *Science Problems I* (grades 7-8): "How Do Magnets Work?" pp. 224-259 Gage (Scott, Foresman).

Craig & Bryan, *Science Near You* (primary), pp. 24-41. Ginn.

Craig & Daniel, *Science Around You* (junior), pp. 110-121. Ginn.

Craig & Lembach, *Science Everywhere* (grades 4-5), pp. 64-85. Ginn.

Frasier et al., *Winter Comes and Goes* (grades 2-3): "Christmas Toys," pp. 86-91, and "In the Park," pp. 212-215; *The Seasons Pass* (grades 3-4): "Why Susan's Balloon burst" pp. 131-135. Dent (Singer).

Freeman, *Fun with Science* (grades 6-8). Random House.

Gray et al., *The New Fun with Dick and Jane* (primary), pp. 65-82. Gage (Scott, Foresman).

Hethershaw & Baker, *Wonders To See:* "Magnets and How They Work," pp 115-142 Gage (World Book).

Lewellen, *The True Book of Toys at Work.* Book Society (Children's Press).

Parker, *Magnets,* The Basic Science Education Series. Copp Clark (Row, Peterson).

Podendorf, *The True Book of Science Experiments* (Primary). Book Society (Children's Press)

Schneider, *Let's Find Out.* Allen (Wm. R. Scott).

Schneider, *Science for Here and Now* (grade 2), pp. 149-163. Copp Clark (Heath).

Schneider, *Science Far and Near* (grade 3): "Machines," pp. 243-263. Copp Clark (Heath)

Smith & Henderson, *Beneath the Skies* (grade 6), pp. 31-52. Longmans, Green.

Wyler, *The First Book of Science Experiments* (grades 4-8). Ambassador (Watts).

New to this Edition

Macaulay, David. *The Way Things Work.* (Houghton Mifflin.Walter Lorraine Books, 1988).

Potter, Jean. *Science in Seconds with Toys: Over 100 Experiments You Can Do in Ten Minutes or Less* (Jossey-Bass, 1998).

Taylor, Poth, and Portman. *Teaching Physics with Toys: Activities for Grades K-9* (McGraw-Hill, 1995) [You'll have to find a used copy of this one.]

Taylor, Portman, Gertz, and Sarguis. *Teaching Physics With Toys: Hands-on Investigations for Grades 3-9* (Terrific Science Press, 2006).

Taylor, Beverly. *Exploring Energy with TOYS: Complete Lessons for Grade 4-8* (Terrific Science Press, 1998).

Unit 45—Correlations?—Yes!

Reasons for Correlations

The schoolroom should be a place in which pupils live natural, enjoyable lives. Learning conditions there should be as similar as possible to out-of-school living conditions. The more nearly this ideal condition is secured, the greater is the likelihood that the child will make use of his school experiences to meet his everyday out-of-school problems. In everyday life we learn by experiences, by activities engaged in, not by "subjects." Most of such experiences involve the content of several so-called "subjects," closely interwoven or integrated. Therefore, if integration is the natural and usual procedure in ordinary life, it should be considered an essential characteristic of most of our teaching. Integration, in this sense, must be distinguished from a rather too common practice of teaching a "sequence" of lessons which are classified as natural science, literature, reproduction story, reading, art, etc., on one topic such as "The Spider and the Fly." In a true integration the worthwhile natural science subject matter, as well as language and art, may well be taught through an unbroken chain of class activities.

Suppose we make a winter nature booklet. We search for a topic ("Our Winter Bird Friends"— natural science); we go out to observe the birds (more science plus health); we measure for the size of the booklet (arithmetic); we illustrate the cover and contents (art); we write reports and poems (composition, spelling, writing); we read some reports aloud (oral reading)— and so on. No, our project was not the addition of separate subjects—natural science, health, arithmetic, art, etc.—it was an integrated activity—mental, physical, and social—a bit of real life to the pupils. As such we must not value the project in the light of the visible, finished product, but rather by its success in leading pupils, through their experiences, to appreciate nature more, and to express better their feelings and thoughts related to nature.

Another time, the experience might begin with the reading of a poem, leading into choral reading. This leads to a literary study of it. But the facts in it are based upon natural science. Then we decide to dramatize it, to make a mural or frieze to illustrate it. Thus the topic grows. It should be carried on as long as the pupils are interested, and the educational values justify its continuance.

Probably no subject in the elementary school program of studies offers such a wealth of material to vitalize other fields of study as does science. For health, social studies, English, the arts and crafts, and even for arithmetic and music, much of value and interest will be found in the current science. But the contributions are not one-sided; learning situations provided by the other subjects may be made to assist greatly in fulfilling the special objectives of the science program.

English, natural science, and art are frequent partners since pupils profit in all three directions through the same experience. Practice in reading, both silent and oral, comes while pupils seek for

Figure 1—A Suggested Cover for a Christmas Booklet

new information, for facts not observable, for verification of observed phenomena, and, while they engage in supplementary reading for mere enjoyment. By reporting to class concerning assigned readings, they learn to express their feelings and ideas orally.

Facility in written composition is increased when pupils write science records in good English, when they use science topics of special, personal interest for compositions, and when they compose verse. No field of study requires more careful choice of words and accuracy of statement than does science.

Plants, animals, and other natural objects provide interesting subjects for art as applied to title pages, calendars, posters (fig. 2), booklet covers, designing in pupils' books and on the black board, and for modeling in clay, soap, and any other media. Even when we view art from the point of view of the child's standards, not the teacher's, such expression in art requires careful observation in science. Picture study is made more interesting through nature pictures, and in turn brings out new ideas and attitudes traditionally taught through science.

Individual Nature Observation Booklets

The course of studies in natural science consists chiefly of personal experiences in nature; it recognizes the individual interests, capacities, and opportunities of pupils. Formal les-

Figure 2—A Window Transparency

Pupils will like to make this with bright colors

sons, aiming at having all pupils see the same things, perform the same acts, learn the same facts, and express their ideas through the same media, can accomplish only a small part of the objectives of the course. We, as adults, are not equally appreciative of a pot of narcissi, a beautiful sunset, the desirability of knowing by name the common planets and constellations, the singing of bird neighbors, the croaking of the frogs in an indoor vivarium; nor do we wish to be. And we express our feelings toward nature in various ways, some by selecting appropriate poetry, some by lifelike artwork, some by simple though accurate description. Let us give our pupils the same freedom of choice of what is of most interest in nature, as well as of the method of expressing thoughts which arise from these interests.

Probably no part of our planning serves these purposes better than our encouragement of a constant alertness for new nature experiences, day by day, in class and out. Two tested and proven devices are: provide a brief space on the timetable each day during which pupils report orally anything of interest in their daily contacts with nature; develop a system of individual pupil nature records or observation booklets.

A valuable art experience in constructive work may be had while planning and making a suitable cover for the pupil's records. Free choice of color is consistent with present-day art principles as well as pupil satisfaction. Needless to say, uniformity has no particular merit. "Cellophane" outer covers will keep the others clean and attractive. Grade level will largely determine how the cover is decorated. Fig. 2 illustrates a cover design with some worthwhile correlations of English, art, and nature that are fitted to the Christmas time. There is ample opportunity for individuality of choice of heading, poem, and other decorative features. Not so with uniformly constructed covers patterned by hectograph outlines, which entirely deprive the pupil of personal choice of design or creative expression in carrying out his design. It is not the product itself, but the personal satisfaction of having produced it that counts. Teacher supervision may be provided for by having the pupils sketch their designs in rough before drawing them on the covers. Some discussion of the general principles of designing such covers will of course have its place before beginning the first booklet.

Ideas for cover titles are legion. Each month has its own significance: December, the Month of Evergreens; January, the Gateway to the New Year; May, the Month of Flowers, etc. Much could be said for wide variety. A pupil derives satisfaction from having a booklet which deals with a phase of nature different from his neighbor's. Opportunity might be given for two or three pupils to cooperate in making one booklet over a period of a month, a sort of loose-leaf frieze on a small scale. At the very same time, the following titles may be found in the same classroom: Our Winter Bird Friends, Christmas Plants and Animals, Animal Life in Winter, The Friendly Snow, Milk for Health, My Aquarium Book, My Pets, Trees in Winter, Our Evergreen Trees, Our Sky Friends.

Pupils should be encouraged to be original in their method of expressing their observations. Individuality suffers by the insertion of hectographed outlines which pupils may color. Such do not represent individual interests, creative expression in art, or even a real observation in nature for several pupils of a class. It is not the appearance, but rather the evidence of pupil experiences of an educational nature that makes the booklet of value. On the other hand, any of the following methods of expressing a personally observed incident in nature may be useful: picture cutouts, a suitable poem or prose quotation, a pressed specimen, simply written description, pencil or pen sketches, crayon or watercolor painting, or a combination of several. Such a booklet should not under any circumstances become merely a notebook of facts and illustrations growing out of class lessons; individuality is its best claim to existence.

A few ideas follow for pupil investigations and records for a booklet entitled "Trees in Winter," for grade 5 or 6: (1) sketches or mounted pictures of named tree outlines, of landscapes with bare

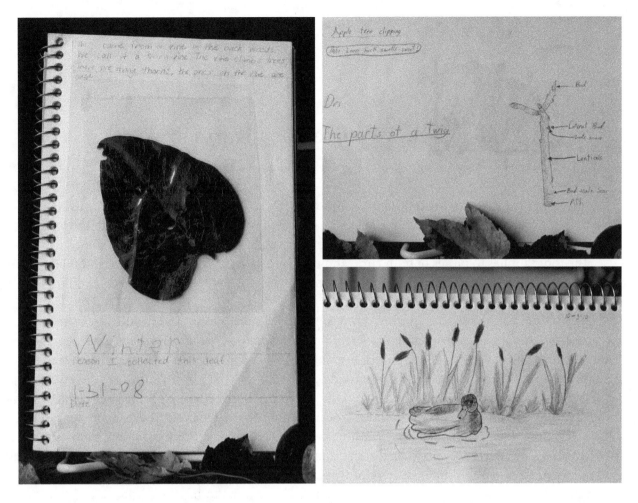

Figure 3—Children can record their observations in a nature sketchbook or journal.

and evergreen trees on a snowy background, of winter birds feeding beneath protecting shrubbery, of winter buds ready for spring, of old nests of summer birds, of kinds of evergreens, of hedges serving as protecting windbreaks, of trees as the homes of wild animals and insects; (2) written reports to accompany the above and to describe incidental observations; (3) information with respect to the measurement of tree heights by their shadows, the amount of wood or lumber in a standing tree, the uses of trees to man; (4) poems suited to the topic.

Unit 46—How People Keep Warm in Winter

Midwinter is an appropriate time to study this topic. By January the pupils will have had a rich background of experiences upon which the teacher can draw in discussion, and enough of the winter remains to give the pupils an opportunity to apply, in actual experience, new knowledge gained in class.

The topic applies to pupils of both rural and urban schools, to pupils of all ages, and therefore to all grades. In rural schools it may well become one phase of an enterprise entitled "Keeping Warm in Winter."

In addition to the sun, our clothes, homes, fuel of various kinds, and food all help to keep us warm in winter. Each individual teacher will know best what type of pupil activities are suited to the interests and capacities of her pupils. Pupils of all grades might deal with the subject under the subheadings: clothing, homes, fuels, and foods.

With primary and junior pupils, discuss the difference between our summer and winter clothing. Teach the importance of wool and fur clothing, and of wool blankets. Include the story of wool from the time it kept the sheep warm until it kept the child warm. Pupil experiences may be used to bring out the differences between our summer cottages and our winter homes. As social studies correlation, discuss the simple shelters of tropical people as compared with the thick snow walls of igloos. Even these young children know what fuels we burn to heat our homes, and that ashes are left when the fuel burns. They can appreciate a simple story of wood from tree to the stove, and of coal from the coal yard to the cellar. In health studies, they may be expected to learn that some kinds of food are better than others for keeping us healthy and warm in cold weather.

Pupils of intermediate grades will realize the important part that warm clothing has played with explorers, pioneers, and airmen. From daily experiences they may be taught that loosely knit woolen mittens are warmer than leather ones on a calm, cold day, and that a woolen sweater keeps them warmer in winter than a closely woven raincoat. While studying homes as a protection against cold, draw on social-studies knowledge connected with the homes of Indians, present-day primitive people, and of explorers in winter. When studying fuels, a collection of different kinds and sizes of coal and coke may be made and correctly labeled by pupils. Discuss the sources of our coal and a little about how coke is made. In these grades take the story of coal from the mine to the furnace or stove, but do not expect the pupils to understand how coal is formed from prehistoric forests. Pupils of intermediate grades should learn that breathing uses food to make body warmth. Thus they may be taught the importance of eating in winter such heat-producing foods as fat meat, butter, cream, and bread.

An Enterprise—Coal, From Mine to Furnace

The enterprise may naturally arise from a discussion, from remarks of pupils showing appreciation of classroom warmth on some particularly cold morning, or *motivation* may be provided when fuel is seen being delivered to the school or elsewhere. The *teacher's pre-planning* should include a survey of the Program of Studies to discover related topics in various subjects; a plan of the particular knowledge, skills, and attitudes which should be developed through the enterprise; some definite purpose toward which the pupils should aim (a demonstration for parents' night, etc.); and a list of activities suitable to the grade or grades. In the third step in the enterprise, *the class discussion to organize the undertaking,* the teacher will tactfully lead pupils to suggest many of the things which she has planned. The topic may be sub-divided into such units as: the early coal forest, the coal before man found it, the mine, preparation of coal for market, transportation of coal to the local coal yard, delivery to the coal bin, use in the home. Pupils will arrange themselves in groups.

The fourth step consists of the *planning and working in the groups.* Each group must be free to hold group conferences. They must be shown that research and investigation are the most important part of their work; that reading, examining pictures, visiting coal yards, holding interviews, etc. are essential. Within the group, all must share their information with the others. Then follows the planning for the group's expression work—preparing a display of kinds of coal, a model of a coal mine, a play, a mural or frieze (fig. 1), a sand-table scene.

In the fifth stage, *each group makes known its findings to the whole class.* Thus all pupils profit from the planning and labor of all groups. This is an essential step to avoid one-sided points of view by pupils. The culmination may take the form of a school program. A public presentation has value chiefly in the motivation of the pupils to better work. A good display, naturally of the pupils' work

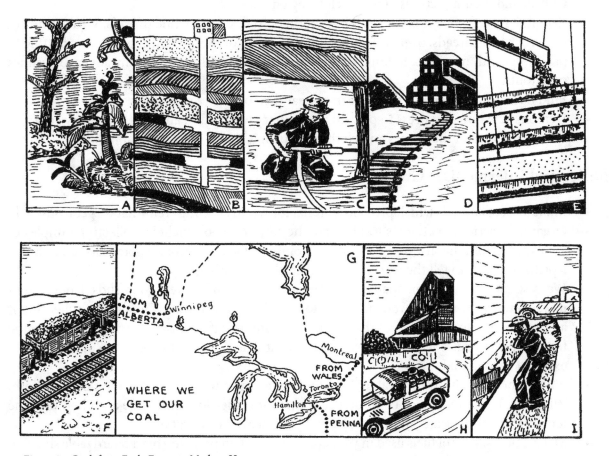

Figure 1—Coal, from Early Forest to Modern Home

only, gives them that feeling of satisfaction which comes from having cooperated with others to produce it.

The last step, an important one, is the *evaluation by the teacher and by the pupils*. Was the time devoted to the enterprise profitably spent, judged on the basis of usable knowledge gained, worthwhile skills improved, acceptable personal and social attitudes developed—changes which will appear in the pupils' daily behavior?

No attempt is made here to organize such an enterprise. It just grows—differently in each school. These activities might, however, find a place in it: a chart or blackboard diagram of coal in the earth; a model of a coal mine, including working levels, and models of coal carts, miners, etc.; a map showing the location of the mine, the routes of transportation, and marketplaces; a display of coal samples showing kinds, sizes, and prices; a bulletin-board display of pictures; oral and written reports about things read or otherwise discovered, or an autobiography of a piece of coal written by a group; a class book and individual books entitled "Coal"; a frieze entitled "Coal, from Early Forest to a Modern Home." In rural schools, all pupils may take part according to their abilities. Perhaps two weeks may be profitably spent on this work.

Activities

Primary Grades

- Collect and mount pictures of warm clothing and covers.
- Examine wool from a sheep. Comb it smooth; twist fibers into little threads. Weave some of these, or other threads, over and under. Study pictures of sheep; then attach cotton batting to paper, wet with mucilage, to build up outlines of sheep, without using any advance outlines or cutouts.
- Find out what mother and father burn to heat the home.
- Demonstrate how you dress to play on an ordinary winter day, and when it is very cold.
- Collect pictures of the homes and clothing of people living in warm countries.

Junior and Intermediate Grades

- Make a list of animals which provide material for warm clothing. Tell what we get from each.
- Organize a series of activities to illustrate the story of wool. Include: collecting samples of wool direct from the sheep, of washed and combed wool, of various woolen fabrics. Arrange a picture display to tell the story of wool from sheep to sweater.
- Wash some woolen garment at school. Use a mild soap to make a good suds. Cool it until it is lukewarm. Leave the woolen article to soak for a few minutes. Wash it by squeezing it and working it up and down in the water. Use more suds if necessary. Use water at the same temperature to rinse it. After squeezing it, dry it where it is not exposed to sunlight or to extreme heat or cold.
- Fill two bottles with warm water. Take the temperature to see that it is the same for both. Wrap one bottle in a piece of wool. Leave them together for some time and then take the temperature of the water in each. What purpose did the wool serve?
- Make a class survey of fuels used in your community. Then prepare a blackboard table showing the general uses of these fuels: wood, hard coal, soft coal, charcoal, coke, peat, oil, natural gas.

- Feel an eider-down quilt. Compare its weight and warmth with others. In the far north (Iceland and Norway) the mother eider duck covers her eggs with down taken from her own breast. Because the people take this down and the eggs, she continues to lay eggs throughout the season. Finally the people permit her last eggs to hatch and collect the down when the young have left for the South.
- Bring samples of insulating materials to school. Notice how they provide many fine air spaces which help them to hold heat. Obtain pictures to show that snow does not melt on the roof of an insulated house.
- Examine pieces of coal to find evidences of old plant remains.
- Collect and mount pictures of foods which keep us warm in winter.

Read

Frasier et al., *How and Why Experiments* (grades 5-8): "How Our Bodies Keep Warm," pp 207-212. Dent (Singer).
Partridge, *Everyday Science,* Book Two: "Buried Sunshine," pp. 120-136, and "How Our Homes Are Heated," pp. 198-226. Dent.
Schneider, *Science Far and Near* (grade 3), pp. 211-229. Copp Clark (Heath).

New to this Edition

Langley, Andrew. *Everyday Materials: Wool* (Crabtree Publishing Company).
Raum, Elizabeth. *Fossil Fuels and Biofuels* (Heinemann Library, 2008).
_____. *Solar Energy* (Heinemann-Raintree, 2008).
_____. *Nuclear Energy* (Heinemann-Raintree, 2008).
_____. *Water and Geothermal Energy* (Heinemann-Raintree, 2008).

http://geology.com/rocks/coal.shtml
http://www.coaleducation.org/q&a/how_coal_formed.htm

Figure 2—Wool fleece ready to be processed.

Unit 47—How Animals Keep Warm in Winter

Keeping warm is an important problem for both people and other animals in winter. Cold-blooded animals such as fish, frogs, toads, and snakes, always remain at about the same temperature as their surroundings. They solve the winter problem—that of not being frozen—by seeking shelter in autumn out of reach of frost. Warm-blooded animals keep their temperature high enough throughout the winter to keep them from freezing. This is done by living in sheltered places and by having body coverings which keep too much heat from escaping to the cold surroundings.

Winter shelters of animals may be either permanent homes or temporary covers. The winter homes of animals are described in Unit 49 (page 208). Among animals seeking temporary shelter in winter are rabbits, grouse, mice. Rabbits take advantage of bushes, brush piles, or piles of rocks, until the temperature is near zero; then they establish more permanent quarters such as an abandoned burrow of a woodchuck or skunk. Grouse frequent densely wooded places, especially among evergreens. For extra protection from cold winds and low temperatures, they may bury themselves in snow drifts. Often a coating of ice imprisons the birds. Although mice have permanent homes beneath snow-banks, they seek temporary shelter in snow tunnels, or under stocks of corn.

The covering of warm-blooded animals usually consists of a coat of hair, fur, or wool. Each of these layers is made up of numerous fine hairs lying close enough together to hold in layers of air. It is this air which prevents heat from escaping. The feather coats on the birds' bodies serve the same purpose as hair. Air is enclosed by the many tiny barbs of the feathers and prevents heat from passing out freely. The cave man covered his body with the skin and the fur of animals. Wool and fur make warm clothing for us because of the air imprisoned between the fibres or hairs.

All body heat is produced by the process of breathing. The oxygen of the air breathed in by animals is distributed by the blood throughout the body. When it combines with digested food, also carried in the blood stream, heat is produced in much the same way as it is when oxygen in the draught entering a furnace causes the fuel in it to produce heat. In winter all animals must secure enough food to keep them warm by the process of breathing. See Unit 32 (page 127), Unit 49 (page 208), and Unit 63 (page 263).

Birds that remain here over winter must obtain a liberal supply of heat-producing food. Seed-eating birds, such as the grouse and the sparrows, continue to get their food from weed tops above the snow level. The downy and hairy Woodpeckers and the chickadees stay wherever they can obtain enough insect eggs or larvae on or under the bark of trees. Feeding them suet will help to keep them and will not make them less efficient in ridding our orchards of insect pests.

Hibernating animals have the advantage of a protecting cover at all times. Although they become cold and stiff, they breathe enough to keep their bodies from freezing. The fact that they emerge from the burrows in spring without having become very thin shows that the demand for this kind

Figure 1—Some Warmth Problems (Drawing from New York State College of Agriculture)

of fuel is not very great with most of them (fig. 1). Raccoons winter together in hollow trees. Thus they help to keep each other warm, sleeping in severe weather, and venturing out on warmer days.

Activities

All Grades

- Each two pupils plan and make a drawing to show how one animal keeps warm in winter.
- List some ways in which we use the coverings of animals to keep ourselves warm.

Junior and Intermediate Grades

- Watch the cottontail rabbits in your neighborhood, following their tracks if necessary, to find out where they find shelter and at what temperature they decide to find permanent homes. In some localities, they stay out until the temperature is 10° Fahrenheit, in others, -10° Fahrenheit.
- Find out: why hibernating animals become thinner during the winter, how Arctic explorers take care of their dog teams in winter, why suet and fat meat is better bird food in winter than bread and seeds.
- How does the fluffing out of their feathers help to keep sparrows warm on a cold day? Examine the small, downy feathers close to the body of a pigeon or hen. What purpose do these serve? Why do our winter birds need more food in cold weather?
- Make a table to compare the methods by which birds keep warm in winter with those by which people keep warm in winter. Use as the headings of three columns: Methods, People, Birds. Use as side headings: Shelter, Covering, Food, Exercise.

Read

Hethershaw & Baker, *Wonders To See:* "How Animals Spend the Winter," pp. 75-114. Gage (World Book).
Morgan, *Field Book of Animals in Winter.* Alen (Putnam's Sons). *Hibernation—The Winter Sleep of Animals,* a leaflet obtainable from the Royal Ontario Museum of Zoology, Toronto.

New to this Edition

Burns, Diane. *Frogs, Toads & Turtles: Take Along Guide* (Cooper Square Publishing, 1997).
Crossingham and Kalman. *What is Hibernation?* (Crabtree Publishing, 2001).
Pascoe, Elaine. *How and Why Animals Prepare for Winter* (Creative Teaching Press, 2000).

http://beyondpenguins.ehe.osu.edu/issue/keeping-warm/lessons-and-activities-about-heat-and-insulation (NOTE: Scroll down the page to the section called "Keeping Warm" for the information about animals keeping warm.)

Unit 48—Some Of Our Common Wild Mammals

Since they played with furry toy animals in the nursery, children have been intensely interested in animals of all kinds. Reading has further interested them in animals of the farm and circus, animals of the woods and forest. Interest and enthusiasm aroused in this way should be taken advantage of and turned into worthwhile learning experiences. The study for older pupils may grow out of the fur-trading topic in social studies. Whatever the motivation, let's not make this a dry oration of facts, but rather a co-operative search for fresh and interesting but accurate material pertaining to the animal in question. The activities suggested later may help you to carry out a worthwhile and interesting enterprise or project on "Our Common Mammals."

As in all study of wildlife, the subject of conservation should not be overlooked. Out of this grows the eternal question—"Why?" Wild mammals should be protected because of both their aesthetic value and their usefulness to man. The latter takes many forms. Most mammals of the woods and forest are valuable because of their pelts; the flesh of some (rabbit, deer) is used as food. Each animal helps by its choice of food to keep the balance in nature, sometimes assisting man in his war on one of its harmful predacious relatives.

Most children, urban or rural, are familiar with the more common domestic mammals. Younger children especially are also interested in their animal friends of the circus, and could with profit and

Figure 1—Young rabbits.

interest carry out a project on either "Circus Animals" or "Animals of the Farm." For the steps of an enterprise see Unit 46 (page 196).

Beaver. *Habitat:* originally all Canada where trees and water were. *Recognition:* dark brown back and sides; chunky; broad, flat tail. *Habits:* cuts trees; digs canals; floats logs; builds dams of sticks, stones, and sod. *Food:* strictly vegetable; leaves, bark, twigs, berries. *Life History:* young born in May; live with parents 2 yrs. *Enemies:* lynx, man. *Protection:* home in water. *Relation to Nature and Man:* dams help in flood control; fur.

Red Squirrel. *Habitat:* woods, parks, and orchards; in same tree year after year. *Recognition:* red to rusty; underparts grayish white; tail bushy. *Habits:* active mostly in daytime; stores seeds and acorns; mischievous. *Food:* seeds and nuts; mushrooms, berries; birds, and their eggs. *Life History:* 5-6 young born in May. *Enemies:* man, cats, dogs. *Protection:* nests in hollow tree; and stumps, in branches; escape. *Relation to Nature and Man:* destroys birds, seeds of trees; food for flesh-eaters.

Gray Squirrel. *Habitat:* woods and parks; in hollow trees and nests of leaves. *Recognition:* grayish above and lighter beneath; long tail. *Habits:* peaceable and friendly; active; stores nuts in ground and trees. *Food:* nuts, grain, other seeds, apples, buds, roots. *Life History:* two broods of 4-6 each. *Enemies:* hunters, hawks, red squirrels, owls, dogs, parasites. *Protection:* hiding in holes and behind branches. *Seasonal Changes:* inactive in very cold weather.

Chipmunk. *Habitat:* woods, roadsides, piles of stone and wood, burrows with hidden openings. *Recognition:* smaller than squirrels; brown with stripes along; sides of back; undersides lighter. *Habits:* active by day; sociable and inquisitive. *Food:* nuts and other seed; berries; insects, mice, and birds. *Life History:* two broods a year. *Enemies:* hawks, weasels, snakes, cats, dogs. *Protection:* burrows closed; escape. *Seasonal Changes:* hibernates. *Relation to Nature and Man:* helps to control insects and weeds.

Woodchuck (Groundhog). *Habitat:* hillsides, fields, or wooded areas; dens with elaborate passageways. *Recognition:* grayish or reddish brown, lighter beneath; fur coarse. *Habits:* cautious, solitary; about by day or night. *Food:* vegetation. *Life History:* one brood in early spring. *Enemies:* man, dogs, hawks. *Protection:* fighting; escape; closing burrow. *Seasonal Changes:* hibernates. *Relation to Nature and Man:* destroys crops; holes trip horses.

Red Fox. *Habitat:* most of Canada; woods and wastelands; in burrow. *Recognition:* 3 ½ ft. long; reddish above and lighter beneath; tail bushy, with white tip; pointed nose and ears. *Habits:* active by day or night; intelligent, but sly and crafty. *Food:* rabbits; mice; birds and poultry. *Life History:* 4-9 young in spring. *Enemies:* man. *Protection:* escape by running, or to burrows; cunning. *Relation to Nature and Man:* destructive to mice, rabbits, and poultry; fur valuable.

Cottontail Rabbit. *Habitat:* woods; roadsides; fields. *Recognition:* brown mixed with gray; underparts white. *Habits:* active by day and night; timid. *Food:* vegetation. *Life History:* 2-6 young several times a year. *Enemies:* man; flesh-eaters. *Protection:* hiding; running; a hollow in the ground. *Relation to Nature and Man:* injury to crops and orchard trees; sport and food; food for flesh-eaters.

Varying Hare. *Habitat:* wooded areas; in brush. *Recognition:* brown in summer; white in winter; large; snowshoe-like feet. *Habits:* active mostly by night; does not store food. *Food:* vegetation in summer; buds, bark, and evergreen foliage in winter; no drink. *Life History:* young born in May in a hair-lined, grassy nest; shift for selves in 2 weeks. *Enemies:* foxes, hawks, man. *Protection:* running with 8-10 ft. bounds; color change in winter. *Seasonal Changes:* white in winter. *Relation to Nature and Man:* injures buds and bark of trees; food.

Muskrat. *Habitat:* most of America; ponds; lakes; along rivers and marshes. *Recognition:* nearly

2 ft. long; compressed; fur dark brown, lighter beneath. *Habits:* active chiefly at night; washes food before eating; shy. *Food:* roots, fish, clams, crayfish, insects, plants. *Life History:* 4-9 in each of three broods. *Enemies:* hawks, owls, foxes, man. *Protection:* escape to water; a good fighter. *Relation to Nature and Man:* valuable fur; food for flesh-eaters; a scavenger.

Raccoon. *Habitat:* most of America, to S. Canada; wooded areas near streams and cornfields. *Recognition:* grayish brown; black band across face and eyes; black rings on long bushy tail. *Habits:* nocturnal; inquisitive; sociable: washes food before eating; places hind feet in tracks of front feet when walking. *Food:* corn, vegetables, honey; frogs, fish, and insects. *Life History:* 3-6 young born in April or May. *Enemies:* man. *Protection:* hollow trees or logs; fighting. *Seasonal Change:* hibernates. *Relation to Nature and Man:* excellent fur; sport: destroys mice and insects; takes some poultry and crops.

Figure 2—*"Is It Spring Yet?" Asks the Racoon. (Canadian National Parks Commission)*

Skunk. *Habitat:* all America; woods, fields, towns. *Recognition:* black with a conspicuous white stripe down back and tail. *Habits:* active at night; inquisitive; gentle and sociable. *Food:* insects (especially grasshoppers, fig. 3); garbage; frogs, mice, snakes, birds, and chickens. *Life History:* one brood of 4-10 in spring. *Enemies:* man, dogs. *Protection:* disagreeable odor. *Seasonal Changes:* hibernates. *Relation to Nature and Man:* fur valuable; destroys insects and mice.

Mink. *Habitat:* under logs and roots near ponds and streams. *Recognition:* like a small slender cat; dark brown with white under chin. *Habits:* runs by leaps; quiet and sly; sleeps between meals. *Food:* rabbits, fish, birds, mice, muskrats, insects, some poultry. *Life History:* one litter of 4-12 in April or May; young remain with mother throughout summer. *Enemies:* man, owls, large flesh-eaters. *Protection:* a powerful fighter; escape; unpleasant odor. *Relation to Nature and Man:* excellent fur; can be reared in captivity; destroys many mice and some poultry.

Weasel. *Habitat:* chiefly woods, some open fields. Recognition: shiny brown outer hair and softer underfur; whitish beneath; tip of tail black. *Habits:* strong desire to kill; chiefly nocturnal; burrows underground. *Food:* any animal it can overcome (fig. 3). *Life History:* a litter of 4-8 in spring. Enemies: man, owls, other weasels. *Protection:* fighting; escape. *Seasonal Changes:* all except tip of tail turns white in winter. *Relation to Nature and Man:* helps to control mice and rats; takes some poultry.

Little Brown Bat. *Habitat:* empty buildings, caves, hollow trees. *Recognition:* membranous, leathery "wing." *Habits:* active at dusk and dawn; lives in colonies. *Food:* insects. *Life History:* one brood in summer. *Enemies:* parasites, man. *Protection:* hiding; flight. *Seasonal Changes:* hibernate or migrate southward. *Relation to Nature and Man:* control many night-flying insects.

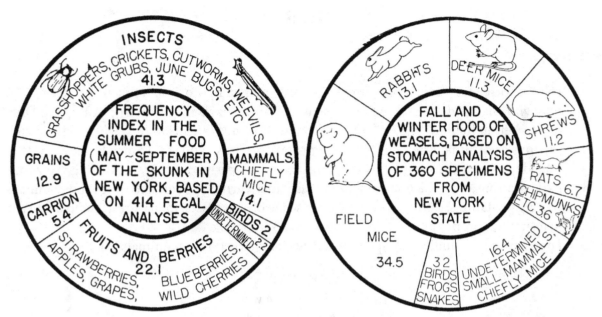

Figure 3—Left: Summer Food of Skunks; Right: Fall and Winter Food of Weasels. (Drawings from New York State College of Agriculture)

Bear. *Habitat:* forests remote from man. *Recognition:* glistening black or brown coat; about 5 ft. long. *Habits:* roam; solitary; take to caves; climb trees. *Food:* berries, leaves, shoots, nuts; ants, grasshoppers; fish; honey. *Life History:* young born in early spring; remain with mother more than year. *Enemies:* man. *Protection:* strength; caves; climbing trees. *Seasonal Changes.* hibernate. *Relation to Nature and Man:* destroy many ants and grasshoppers.

White-tailed Deer. *Habitat:* forests. *Recognition:* grayish brown; tail white; males with antlers. *Habits:* keen sight; runs by bounds. *Food:* leaves, other vegetation. *Life History:* spotted fawns born in May or June; stay with mother until September; coat changes color. *Enemies:* man and dogs. *Protection:* coloring; speed; protected valleys in winter.

Meadow Mouse. *Habitat:* meadows and grain fields. *Recognition:* brown to gray; underparts lighter; short, thick hair. *Habits:* active day and night; follows trails to feeding grounds; shy. *Food:* seeds, vegetation, roots; some insects. *Life History:* 4-6 litters of 4-8 young in each; born in nest lined with silk of milkweed or cattail. *Enemies:* hawks and owls, snakes, skunks, foxes, weasels. *Protection:* hiding; running. *Relation to Nature and Man:* girdles raspberry canes and young fruit trees; destroys grain and clover; food for flesh-eaters.

White-footed Deer Mouse. *Habitat:* woods and waste places. *Recognition:* fawn colored; feet and underparts white. *Habits:* most active at night; timid; stores seeds and grasses. *Food:* seeds, insects. *Life History:* up to four broods of 3-7 in each litter. *Enemies:* hawks and owls, cats, weasels, minks. *Protection:* nocturnal habits; hides in homes in vegetable matter, hollow logs, or crevices. *Relation to Nature and Man:* destroys insects, also seeds; food for flesh-eaters.

Coyote. *Habitat:* W. Canada, near farms and ranches. *Recognition* like small wolves; buffy gray above, lighter beneath; tail tipped with black. *Habits:* hunt in family parties in summer; cunning at eluding enemies. *Food:* mice, rabbits, ground squirrels; wild fruits; poultry. *Life History:* 5-9 young in spring. *Enemies:* man. *Protection:* burrows, dens among rocks; protective color; cunning. *Relation to Nature and Man:* help to control rodents; take some fowl.

Activities

Teacher

- Have a correlated project on animals. Arouse interest by stories and pictures. Read from: *Fun with Dick and Jane,* "The Pony," p. 50; "A Family in the Barn," p. 61 ; "A Big, Big Dog," p. 65 ; "Little Rabbit," p. 87 ; "What Sally Saw," p. 140; *Friends and Neighbors,* from such sections as "Animal Friends," "New Story Book Friends," and "Old Story Book Friends."
- Include some of these activities in planning and preparing a program: visiting the zoo or park; drawing and modeling animals in Plasticine; learning poems and songs about animals; writing invitations; setting up a sand-table scene of a circus, farm, or forest, and placing animals in their proper places; making an animal scrapbook.
- For each animal studied, compose sentences for chart stories of animals, e.g.,

THE BEAR
The bear lives in the woods.
He is brown or black.
He likes honey.

These may be printed on stiff cardboard and mounted with a picture of the animal on the bulletin board.
- Make up a play with animals as the characters. Make up riddles about the animals you know.
- Take a trip to animal land with an animal as a guide.
- Make an animal parade of all the animals you study.

Junior and Intermediate Grades

- Make a class list of mammals seen at some time of the year in your locality. Each pupil select one of these and find out about its home, its food and feeding habits, how it gets about, and its seasonal activities. Report your findings to the class.
- Each pupil bring to school one good animal story to be left in the classroom library for others to read.
- See for yourself how rabbits injure fruit trees by gnawing away the bark.
- In a scrapbook of mammals, place pictures, clippings, and original stories, using a class composite poem for an introduction.
- Study those animals valuable for their fur, and make a frieze or mural entitled "Fur-bearing Animals."
- Discuss the value of bats and shrews and make an exhibit of pictures and models showing them in their natural surroundings.
- Study for art appreciation: "Deer Family," by Landseer; "The Fox," by Eberhardt; and "The Lone Wolf," by Bonheur.
- Make a frieze of stuffed crepe-paper animals.
- Make a table display of a Beaver Village. Model beavers of clay or Plasticine, use blue paper for the water, and build the home and dam of twigs and small sticks. Cut holes in the paper to show the home in the water and some beavers swimming.

- Have a newspaper for your Beaver Village. Call it "Beaver News." Plan the paper in your English class. Include such articles as: "Repairing the Dam," "Election in Beaver Town," "The Mayor's Warning," "Beaver Social News," etc.
- Animal peep-shows are easily made from shoe boxes and moving picture shows from larger cartons. Use one of your murals for the "film."

Read

Allen, *Tammy Chipmunk and His Friends* (primary) Allen (Houghton Mifflin).

Bauer, *Animal Babies:*. Book Society (Donohue),

Beauchamp et al., *All Around Us* (primary): "Animals," pp. 3-28; *Look and Learn* (primary): "Animals," pp. 3-24; and *How Do We Know?* (primary and junior): "Round the Year," pp. 3-31. Gage (Scott, Foresman).

Blough, *Animals That Live Together* (grades 2-3), The Basic Science Education Series. Copp Clark (Row, Peterson).

Blough & Parker, *Animals Round the Year,* The Basic Science Education Series. Copp Clark (Row, Peterson).

Burt & Grossenheider, *A Field Guide to the Mammals*. Allen (Houghton Mifflin).

Cahalane, *Meeting the Animals* (grades 5 and up): habitats, descriptions, and life histories of 66 mammals; beautiful line drawings. Macmillan.

Candy, *Nature Notebook,* pp. 17-26, 78-83, 92-97, and 104-114. Allen (Houghton Mifflin).

D'Aulaire, *Animals Everywhere* (primary). Doubleday.

Duane. *A Book of Nature,* pp. 28-29 and 72-75. Oxford.

Dowling et al., *I Wonder Why* (primary). Winston.

Earle, *Paws, Hoofs, and Flippers* (grades 7-8). Excellent presentation of mammal classification. McLeod (Wm. Morrow).

Erickson, *Cattail House* (grades 3-5), and *The True Book of Animals of Small Pond*. Book Society (Children's Press).

Eschmeyer, *Charley Cottontail, Freddy Fox Squirrel,* and *Willie Whitetail*. Book Society (Fisherman Press).

Frasier et al., *The Seasons Pass* (grades 3-5): "High in the Mountains" and "The Woodchuck," pp. 100-110; also *The How and Why Club* (grades 5-8): "How Beavers Live" and "Other Gnawing Animals." Dent (Singer).

Gray et al., *The New Streets and Roads* (primary and junior) (squirrel, chipmunk, deer, bear, raccoon, and beaver), pp. 193-248; and *The New More Streets and Roads* (primary and junior): "Along Animal Trails" (bear, prairie dog, otter, porcupine, opossum, fox, and squirrel), pp. 155-206. Gage (Scott, Foresman).

Halliday, *Wildlife Friends*. Allen.

Hawkini, *Zooparade*. Allen (Rand McNally).

Hunt & Andrews, *Animals of Woods and Plains*: descriptions of Canadian mammals; paper-covered. Moyer.

Mason, *Animal Sounds*: "Singing Mice," pp. 59-60, "Warning Signals," pp. 64-67, 71, "Coyotes," pp. 72-75, "The Moose," pp. 76-81, and "Frightening Noises," pp. 83-91; *Animal Tracks* (excellent drawings of mammals and their tracks) ; and *Animal Weapons,* pp. 7-47, 66-70, and 76-79. McLeod (Wm. Morrow).

Palmer, *The Mammal Guide*. Doubleday.

Parker, *Animals We Know* (grades 4-6), The Basic Science Education Series. Copp Clark (Row, Peterson).

Partridge, *General Science,* Intermediate, Book 2, pp. 26-31, and "How Wildlife Helps Us," pp. 372-82. Dent.

Peterson, *Wildlife in Color*. Allen (Houghton Mifflin).

Schmidt, *Homes and Habits of Wild Animals*. Book Society (Donohue).

Semrad, *The Zoo*. Allen (Rand McNally).

Seton, *Wild Animals I Have Known*. Allen (Scribner).

Shuttlesworth, *Exploring Nature with Your Child*: "Animals in the Wild," pp. 83-136. Nelson (Greystone).

Smith & Clarke, *Under the Sun* (primary), pp. 7-36. Longmans, Green.

Webb, *Song of the Seasons* (grades 4-6). McLeod (Wm. Morrow).

New to this Edition

Cuddy, Robbin. *Learn to Draw Forest Animals & Wildlife: Step-by-step instructions for 25 different woodland animals* (Foster, Walter Publishing, October, 2012).

Ganeri and Oxlande. *DK Pockets: Mammals* (DK Children, 1998).

Kays and Wilson. *Mammals of North America* (Princeton Field Guides). (Princeton University Press, 2009).

Unit 49—Winter Habits of Some Wild Mammals

In Unit 32 we learned some ways in which animals prepare for winter conditions. Some birds, unable to get their accustomed food, go south; others remain here and feed upon exposed seeds or insects, or upon buds of trees. Frogs, toads, and snakes find some protected quarters and remain inactive until the warmth of spring returns. Insects may spend the winter in the egg, larva, pupa, or adult stage, but are seldom active in cold weather. Some mammals sleep away the cold season (hibernate); others sleep for most of the time in cold weather, but waken occasionally; still others remain active during all but the most severe weather.

Figure 1—Wild Life Has Various Ways of Spending the Winter (Drawings from New York State College of Agriculture)

The purpose of this unit is to show briefly how some of our more common wild mammals are adapted by habit and structure to obtain adequate shelter and food during this unforgivable season of the year.

Weasel. *Protection habits:* does not seek shelter in winter; all but the end of the tail becomes white, in harmony with the snow. *Food habits:* continues its quest for food; is predacious.

Cottontail Rabbit. *Protection habits:* heavy new coat of fur; seeks protection under brush and bushes; sometimes occupies the deserted burrow of a woodchuck or skunk. *Food habits:* feeds upon buds, bark, and twigs all winter.

Varying Hare. *Protection Habits:* does not seek shelter; all except the tips of its ears becomes white. *Food Habits:* eats buds, bark, and evergreen foliage.

Raccoon. *Protection Habits:* sleeps in early winter, then comes out occasionally; outer coat of long hairs sheds snow and rain; fur underneath keeps it warm; retreats to a home in a hollow tree, *Food Habits:* does not store food, but eats until it becomes fat before hibernating; wakens in early spring (March or April) when food is scarce, then becomes thin and weak.

Skunk. *Protection Habits:* dens up in a burrow in a dry hill; sleeps on a bed of grass; young born in April or May. *Food Habits:* lives on food stored as body fat.

Mink. *Protection Habits:* gets a heavy coat of new fur; remains active throughout winter near open water. *Food Habits:* must continue to seek food, mostly animals.

THE **GREY SQUIRREL**
SEARCHES FOR FOOD
UNDER THE SNOW —

AND COMES OUT TO ENJOY
HIS PINE-CONE DINNER.

Figure 2

Gray Squirrel. *Protection Habits:* nest in hollow tree or fork of tree; commonly has two homes or nests for use in winter; in cold weather spends days at a time in his hollow-tree home, but in mild weather uses his outside nest. *Food Habits:* feeds on nuts or seeds stored in hollow trees.

Red Squirrel. *Protection Habits:* nests in hollow trees or stumps or in branches; is active all winter. *Food Habits:* eats buried cones, nuts, or mushrooms placed in forked branches.

Muskrat. *Protection Habits:* in marshes builds a rounded house 1 or 2 ft. above the water surface; a breathing-hole left in the top; nest made of rushes, reeds, sedges, and grasses; two or more entrances under water; home lined with grass; along swiftly flowing streams its home is a burrow in the bank; spends much of the winter sleeping, but does not hibernate; comes out often beneath the ice houses built in water deep enough not to freeze to the bottom. *Food Habits:* eats water plants and roots and the flesh of clams, fish, and crayfish.

Meadow Mouse. *Protection Habits:* tunnels beneath the snow; comes to the surface at night; does not hibernate. *Food Habits:* gnaws bark from trees; eats some grass beneath the snow.

Red Fox. *Protection Habits:* lives in a den under rocks or in a burrow in the ground; coat brighter in winter. *Food Habits:* hunts chickens, rabbits, and mice as in summer.

Chipmunk. *Protection Habits:* digs a burrow in the ground, commonly among the roots of trees, below frost. *Food Habits:* feeds upon nuts and other food stored in autumn.

Woodchuck (Groundhog). *Protection Habits:* hibernates in a burrow in underbrush, in an open field, or under stones or fences, especially on hillsides. *Food Habits:* lives on food stored in the body as fat in autumn.

Beaver. *Protection Habits:* lives in lodges made of branches woven together and plastered with mud; entrance to home under water; living-room above the water level. *Food Habits:* feeds on twigs and logs stored under water in autumn.

Black Bear. *Protection Habits:* hibernates in caves lined with moss; moves about to other quarters as spring approaches. *Food Habits:* uses stored fat.

Activities

Teacher

For grades 1 and 2 prepare hectographed outlines of the winter homes of several mammals known to your pupils. Have the pupils color these. On mural paper or the blackboard prepare a background, such as a hillside beside a marsh, where the animals' homes might be found in winter. Have the pupils attach the colored pictures to complete the scene to their satisfaction.

For pupils of grade 3 and higher grades all artwork should be original.

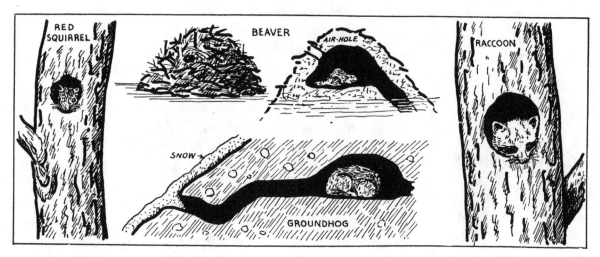

Figure 3—Winter Homes of Four Common Mammals

All Grades

- Make a booklet, chart, or blackboard design entitled "Homes of Animals in Winter." Include collected pictures, personal drawings, clippings, observations, and discoveries made while reading or discussing with others.
- Visit the marsh. Find the winter homes of muskrats. Of what are they made? Find the breathing-hole in the top.

See also Unit 4 (page 14), Unit 5 (page 17), Unit 6 (page 21), Unit 7 (page 24), Unit 8 (page 32), Unit 51 (page 214), and Unit 53 (page 221).

Primary Grades

- Look for animals playing in the woods, on the street or roadside. What is each doing? How does it get its food? Try to follow some to their homes.
- Make drawings of squirrels climbing trees or carrying nuts, a rabbit running through bushes on the snow, etc. Make a class picture gallery of these original drawings.

Junior and Intermediate Grades

- Rule a blackboard border into several squares. Assign one square to each pupil. He will find out all he can about the winter habits and the home of one assigned animal, then draw this in the square with colored chalk. When finished, he should describe to the class what the animal does in winter, its home, where the home is usually found, and how it is fitted to keep the animal comfortable in winter.
- As a mural, prepare a winter scene showing several animals of the forest. Include a background of bare trees (black paper strips or cutouts, or crayon sketches) and evergreens (cutouts or colored drawings).

Read

Beauchamp et al., *How Do We Knout* (primary and junior): "Round the Year," pp. 30-36. Gage (Scott, Foresman).

Blough, *Animals Round the Year,* The Basic Science Education Series, pp 20-25. Copp Clark (Row, Peterson).

Craig & Daniel, *Science Around You* (Junior), pp. 64-69. Ginn.

Hethershaw & Baker, *Wonders to See:* "How Animals Spend the Winter," pp. 75-114. Gage (World Book).

Hylander, *Out of Doors in Winter* (grades 6-8) : "Winter Mammals and Their Tracks," pp. 105-123. Macmillan.

Morgan, *Field Book of Animals in Winter.* Allen (Putnam'sl Sons).

Schneider, *Science for Here and Now* (grade 2): "Animals in Winter," pp. 101-112. Copp Clark (Heath).

Webb, *Sent of the Seasons* (grades 4-6), pp. 110-126. McLeod (Wm. Morrow).

New to this Edition

Bancroft, Henrietta. *Animals in Winter (Let's-Read-and-Find-Out Science 1),* (Collins, 1996).

Hall, Margaret. *Hibernation (Patterns in Nature Series),* (Capstone Press, 2008).

Rustad, Martha. *Animals in Winter* (Capstone Press, 2008).

Gans, Roma. *How Do Birds Find Their Way? (Let's-Read-And-Find-Out Science),* (Perfection Learning, 1996).

BBC Video: The Life of Birds (DVD), narrated by David Attenborough.

Sony Pictures: *Winged Migration* (DVD) directed by Jacques Perrin.

See also reading reference for Unit 48 (page 202).

Figure 4—Young Blonde bear coming out of hibernation in New Mexico.

Unit 50—With Our Bird Friends Down South

Bird study is intensely interesting, but too often we limit it to the lives of the birds while here with us. We forget completely that our bird friends have an interesting life in their southern homes too.

If in the fall you and your pupils traveled with the birds to the south, you will now be prepared to spend a short time with these birds in their winter quarters. Primary pupils will want to call on the robin in Georgia, and the wren in Florida, while older children will want to circle South America to find the kingfisher in Northern Brazil, the bobolink in Southern Brazil and Paraguay, and the scarlet tanager in Peru. This personal interest will lead to valuable investigations of the social studies of the countries visited.

The habits of birds change considerably when they go to their winter resorts. Bobolinks change their diet from insects to rice when they pass through Louisiana. As a result, they are called rice-birds, and are frequently shot because of their thefts. Robins band together in flocks in Georgia, and show more fear of harmful hawks than they do here. Bluebirds would appear strange to us, searching for food in a cotton field in South Carolina. Orioles do not sing as lustily in Central America as they do here. Neither do birds in the South build nests or rear young. How different we would find our familiar bird friends down South!

NEWS ITEMS FROM BIRD REPORTERS[1]
(for children of all ages)

Jenny Wren wrote in her diary: "October 15. So this is Florida! ... It it as flat as a pancake and not a stone big enough to throw at a cat. Plenty of flowers and plenty of insects, though, so perhaps I can be happy until March, when it will be time to start north again. I never did see so many snakes, though; I will be lucky to get out of here alive. First place I struck had a feeding-log for birds in the garden, and some of my northern friends, the chipping sparrows, were mingling with the cardinals and mockingbirds and ground doves. So I have decided to stay right here for a while and hunt Florida spiders around these lantanas and orange trees."

The Oriole has this to say: "You would be interested in the strange people that we see on our travels, and if you are fond of bananas you would enjoy every minute of the winter, for we are scarcely ever out of sight of a plantation once we arrive in Central America. Of course, there are miles and miles of tropical forests, especially in the mountains, where very few people live, but every year sees more and more

---

1   From Allen, *American Bird Biographies*

of the coast taken up with bananas, and the sides of the mountains with coffee, and with cacao, from which chocolate and cocoa are made. Then, too, you would be interested in our bird's-eye view of the Panama Canal and the great ships passing from ocean to ocean through the enormous locks."

Cock Robin tells of his winter in Georgia: "You know the people down there do not feel quite the same about us as you do up North. We robins don't sing for them and we don't play about their dooryards. We all band together in flocks before we leave here in the fall, and we stay more or less together all winter wherever we can find hackberries and mistletoe. Some . . . people down there haven't heard yet that we are protected by law and they still think that we are legitimate game for their potpies. We forget all about having to dodge guns up North, and it makes it rather exciting when they begin banging at us down here. Then, too, there were many of those sharp-shinned and Cooper's hawks wintering in the same country with us, and we had to be on the jump every instant."

Activities

All Grades

Make a large map of North and South America on the blackboard or on a movable board. On this, mark an imaginary airplane journey in winter through the eastern states of the United States, around South America, and back to Canada through Central America, Mexico, and the Mississippi Valley. Imagine, too, that you could stop where you liked to visit your bird friends spending the winter there. The map shows a number of your stopping-points. Each of you

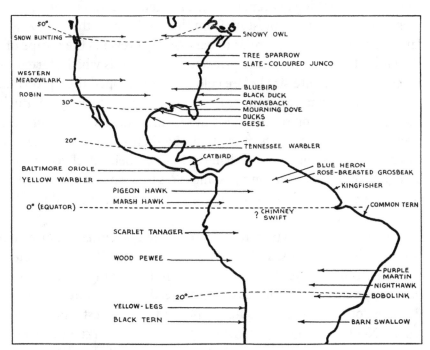

Figure 1—Winter Resorts of Some Common Birds

find out what one particular bird friend might show you when you arrived. Then on the map attach pictures collected or drawn to illustrate scenery in that land. Include plants and animals which the birds see there, and activities of the birds themselves. Read and tell your class about what people do at this time of year in these lands. For each bird make a class booklet of pictures, poems, and clippings, describing its winter home and its actions in the South.

Unit 51—Fields And Woods in Winter

Both teachers-in-training and experienced teachers have often asked what there is to be seen in nature in winter and what practical work pupils can do during that season to bring them into closer contact with nature. It is true that a white mantle of snow covers most evidences of life, and that inactivity and monotony seem to be the order of the day. Animal life is largely out of sight; most plants are in a resting, inconspicuous state; cold weather seems even to take away from interest in weather. But it is really only the rest before the race of nature in spring, the period of waiting, of readiness both to survive the winter's chill and to waken into new activity again. Probably our trees and shrubs illustrate this state of readiness as well as does any other phase of nature.

Of all plants, trees and shrubs are most exposed to winter's drying winds, sleet, and cold. But they are also best prepared. Their cork-like bark is tough enough to withstand freezing sleet and the frequent rubbing of branch against branch; it is waterproof enough to prevent the drying winds from taking too much moisture from the tree. Where the leaves have separated from the branch, a layer of corky material, similar to bark, safely prevents the escape of sap. The tenderest parts of all, the ends of the tiny twigs, are protected by the buds which started to form late in the summer and reached their mature size before cold weather stopped their growth.

These same buds are primarily an adaptation for spring. Within them are the leaves, and perhaps the flowers, compactly folded in readiness for the return of warm weather. These, too, are well protected. The outer scales of the buds, by their toughness, protect the delicate organs within from insects, freezing rain, and mechanical injury. Their effectiveness is increased by their overlapping, shingle-like arrangement, and in some cases by a varnish-like, waterproof covering. With some buds, harm from sudden changes of temperature is prevented or reduced by an insulating, cotton-like layer inside the scales.

Leaves of evergreen trees remain unharmed in winter because of their extremely tough covering, their resinous contents, and their needle-like form. These characteristics of the leaves also protect the tree from a wasteful loss of moisture in the drying winds of winter. Such leaves, too, are ready at the approach of any periods of warm weather to commence food-making operations for the tree.

Many of these facts are naturally beyond the interest and comprehension of primary and junior pupils. Neither can they appreciate heights of trees, markings of bark, and details of branching and arrangement of buds. They gradually become acquainted with trees by repeated association with them, and by such activities as: demonstrating the position of buds by modeling them, sketching the shapes and branchings of trees out of doors; and using named specimens to produce sand-table scenes.

Outdoor observations are essential for identification of trees. These should impress upon primary and junior pupils such simple recognition characters as: *elm*—shaped like a vase or an umbrella, with its branches as the ribs of the umbrella; *spruce*—shaped like an inverted ice cream cone, with the trunk going right to the top, and needles that will roll between the thumb and finger; *birch*—

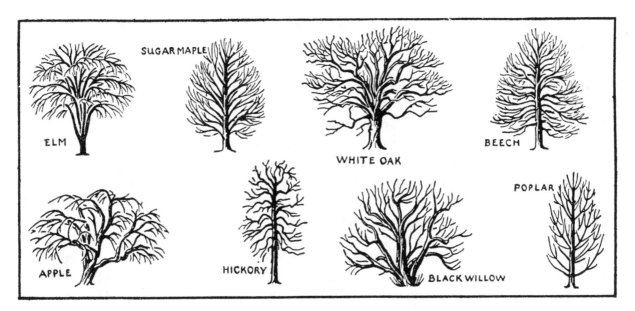

Figure 1—Winter Silhouettes of Some of Common Deciduous Trees

bark smooth, white, and easily peeled; many slender, drooping branches. Older pupils should be shown more accurate methods of identifying trees.

In summer we identify the trees by observing, among other things, whether the leaves are placed singly (alternate) or in pairs (opposite). But all buds are formed where the leaves join the stem. In winter, then, the leafless trees have leaf scars and buds where the leaves were in summer. We therefore study the arrangement, shape, and size of the leaf scars or buds, or of both, to identify the trees in the leafless condition. On the surface of the leaf scars of horse-chestnut trees and others there are small, projecting marks called bundle or vein scars.

When we discover a tree having conspicuous leaf scars in opposite pairs, each bearing numerous bundle scars in a curved line, we know that it is an ash tree. But when we find a tree having leaf scars in opposite pairs and three bundle scars on each, and end buds not more than one-half inch in length, we are quite certain that it is a maple tree. Another tree having leaf scars singly placed, but in vertical rows, and the buds smooth, long, and sharp-pointed is sure to be beech. These facts show the ease with which pupils may learn to identify deciduous trees in winter. The characteristics of evergreen trees were described in Unit 43 on page 182).

Attractive colors in trees and shrubs are not limited to summer and autumn. In winter the evergreens, with their various shades of green, add their bit of beauty among the leafless trees silhouetted against a snowy background. The red-brown bark of some wild cherry trees, the yellow-tinted branches and twigs of willows and of poplars, the snowy white of birches, and the bright red stems of dogwood shrubs are all worth discovering. And what could form a more fitting background for all of these than the pictures in black and white where sunlight and shadows play over the snow?

Animal life in the woods is also a suitable winter study. The feeding and other activities of winter birds may be learned. The nests of all birds show to advantage in the leafless trees. Varying hares, jackrabbits, and squirrels are active in all fine weather. The tracks of birds and of four-footed animals present interesting stories to be read (Unit 53, page 221). The winter forms of insects may be sought—under logs, the furry cocoons of woolly-bear caterpillars; on the trunks of trees, the cocoons of the tussock moth; in bushy thickets, the larger cocoons of Cecropia and Promethea moths (Unit 77, page 324); in the forks of branches of wild cherry trees, the remains of last year's tent-caterpillar nests and, nearby, the egg clusters. A treasure hunt will motivate pupils to find many of these.

Fields are no less interesting for winter study than are woods. Fence rows, with their weed patches and shrubbery, provide shelter for winter birds and small burrowing animals. In uncultivated fields and waste places, and on roadsides, grouse, pheasants, varying hares, mice, and even deer may be seen. Here we learn firsthand of their winter habits.

Weed tops above the snow are worth investigating. Around some of them, especially those of ragweed, lamb's quarters, and red-root pigweed, we will find the tracks of many birds which have gathered there to feed. The stems of others, e.g., the milkweed and dogbane, contain tough fibers which are useful to man. The heads of the mullein, teasel, and St. John's-wort provide natural winter bouquets, while the frost-covered tops of wild carrots lend beauty to the landscape. Some weed tops tell us about the land in which they grow. When we find the seed-bearing tops of burdock, mullein, teasel, and evening-primrose plants, we can be quite certain that the land was not cultivated the previous summer—for these are biennials. Even the farmer who disdains these weeds in his meadow benefits from them when, by holding snow in winter, they prevent winter killing of clover, caused by alternate freezing and thawing in spring.

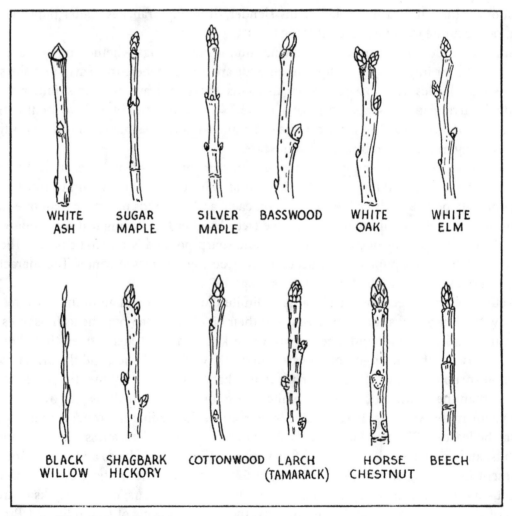

Figure 2—Winter Buds of a Few Trees

Figure 3—Weeds Above the Snow—the Finches' Dinner Table

Activities

All Grades

- While out of doors, or while looking through the classroom window, sketch the shape and branching of an elm and a maple tree.
- Find seed pods of mullein plants like little rattles swaying in the wind. Are the seeds still in them, or have they been scattered or eaten by birds? Break a head of a cattail plant and watch the seeds fly away. Find heads of teasel and feel the roughness of the seed head. Shake out some seeds. What shape are they? Shake a head of wild carrot against your coat. Notice how the spiny seeds cling to the cloth.
- Find what animals are playing about in the woods. What is each doing? How does it get its food? Where is its home? What are its tracks like?
- Notice that oaks sometimes fail to shed their leaves, and that snow does not cling to them.

Primary and Junior Grades

- Make baskets, trays, and little toys of clusters of burdock fruit.
- Find milkweed pods above the snow.
- Each pupil bring in something found in the woods or fields—a cocoon, feather, cone, seed pod, weed head, or twig and buds of some common tree or shrub. Model it in Plasticine, and

make a class display.

- Make a sand-table scene to represent "Fields and Woods in Winter." Build hills with paper over inverted boxes. For snow use cotton batting; for trees, twigs mounted in Plasticine anchors; for rail fences, criss-crossed twigs. Include glass for ice, paper sleighs and skis, Plasticine birds and other animals. Sprinkle artificial snow over the scene. While glancing out of the window occasionally, make a Plasticine model of a maple or elm tree.

Intermediate Grades

- Snowbanks have their secrets to be discovered. In which of these places do they form: in open fields, near fences, among trees, beside buildings, in low roads? Do they form before or after the wind blows through a fence or past some other obstruction? Observation shows it is after the wind has been slowed down by such obstacles that it drops some of its snow. Find honeycombed places on snowbanks. On which side of the bank are they? Notice the icy covers over the spaces. When the sun is shining, hold a thermometer in one of these. Compare the temperature there with that outside. What makes such cavities so dirty? Because the south side of a snowbank faces toward the sun, it receives more heat than snow in other places. Therefore it begins to melt. In the cavities formed, the snow is protected from cold wind, and melts faster. Dirt in the snow remains on the surface, making the snow appear dirty.
- Dig a tunnel into a bank. Where is the snow firmest—near the top or bottom? Why? On a cold day read the temperature of the snow near the bottom of the bank. How does the information gained explain the value of snowbanks to wild animals' Look for burrows of mice or hiding-places of other animals.
- Remove 1 cubic foot of snow from within a snowbank. Melt it and measure the resulting water. Estimate how much water the bank contains. This water helps next year's crops to grow.

Read

Alexander & Cormack, *Bruce and Marcia, Woodsmen:* "Sealed Up for the Winter," pp. 186-200 Gage (American Book Co.).
Hunt & Andrews, *Trees:* "Trees in Winter," pp. 15-26. Moyer.

New to this Edition

Albert, Toni. *A Kid's Winter EcoJournal: With Nature Activities for Exploring the Season* (Triple Creek Books, 1998).
Archer, Cheryl. *Snow Watch: Experiments, Activities and Things to Do with Snow* (Kids Can Press, 1994)
Frost, Robert. (Jeffers, Susan, illustrator). *Stopping by Woods on a Snowy Evening* (Dutton Juvenile, 2001).
Miller, Dorcas S. *Winter Weed Finder: A Guide to Dry Plants in Winter* (Nature Study Guild Publishers, 1989).
Watts, May T. *Winter Tree Finder: A Manual for Identifying Deciduous Trees in Winter (Eastern US),* (Nature Study Guild Publishers, 1970).

Unit 52—Winter Hikes through Streets and Parks

Nature displays her scenes of beauty over city and country alike. True, the rural scene shows more variety; but the city parks and streets have many natural features of interest.

At first thought, winter presents the fewest opportunities to observe nature, but even then trees and shrubs, birds and other animals, clouds and snow, rinks and slides, present much of interest to children and of value in interpreting nature.

The bare trees and shrubs silhouetted against snow and sky show their general shape and branching. Then, too, we see on the ends of the branches the delicate lacework of fine twigs which in summer will support the tree's canopy of leaves. Closer observation of the twigs of trees and shrubs show the multitude of buds, their shape and arrangement. These, well prepared in autumn, are protecting the delicate ends of the twigs and are ready to produce the new crop of leaves in spring. When encrusted with ice or sparkling with frost, even greater beauty awaits our appreciation.

Many evidences of animal life may be found in winter, too. The birds which stay with us throughout the cold weather may be observed seeking their food or fluffing out their feathers to keep themselves warm. Accurate knowledge of bird population in summer may be estimated now by counting the number of bird nests. The winter habits of squirrels may be studied at firsthand. Tracks of all animals may be identified and the stories told by them interpreted. See Unit 53 on page 221.

Most insects are in resting stages. But even some of these may be discovered. Among thickets of shrubs will hang the cocoons of the Cecropia and other large moths (Unit 77, page 324). Beneath the bark of trees may be the smaller silken cases of the tussock moth. Even the eggs of tent caterpillars encircling the ends of small twigs may be found.

Looking skyward would be worthwhile. Over chimneys and factories the rising smoke will show the speed and direction of the wind; and escaping steam, the formation of tiny clouds. Spreading or drifting across the sky may be seen the feathery cirrus

Figure 1—Buds in the winter

219

clouds, the streaky layers of stratus clouds, or the heaps of wool-pack or cumulus clouds. To these may be added for observation and appreciation the blue sky and sunset colors.

Round about us lies the glistening snow dappled by the shadows of trees. Here are opportunities for the study of snow crystals and the changing height of the sun. On another day we may see how the snow blows and piles in drifts where buildings or other obstructions have slowed down the wind. You will see hollows in the snow around the bases of trees. Here the wind, blowing around the tree, carried away some snow, and the sun, by warming the tree and by shining into the protected cavity, caused some snow to melt.

Activities

All Grades

- While on the roadside or in the park, make sketches of leafless trees to show their shape and branching.
- Make up a set of rules for safety on the street in winter.
- Make posters to illustrate such topics as "Fun in the Park," "Safety on the Street," "Trees in Winter."
- Prepare individual booklets with various titles, all dealing with nature on the street or in the park. Include a labeled map, newspaper and magazine clippings of winter scenes, original drawings, etc.
- Make and place signs to encourage safety at the slides and on the pond.
- Each pupil make up a four-lined poem about fun in the park.

Junior and Intermediate Grades

- Take a census of the birds' nests in all the trees in the neighborhood. Then estimate the number of bird families living there the summer before.
- Write a letter to the parks superintendent inviting him to tell you how the park is managed. When he has spoken, have a question-and-answer period.
- Notice how snow around foot-tracks melts more slowly than snow that has not been pressed down. Which melts more quickly, ice or snow?
- Prepare a sand-table scene of the park in winter. Elect a parks superintendent to be the class leader, an engineer to oversee the planning and measuring on the sand-table, a forester to superintend the planting of trees and shrubs, a recreation leader to have charge of the rink and slides.

Read

Hylander, *Out of Doors in Winter* (grades 6-8): "The Deciduous Trees," pp. 36-67. Macmillan.
Parker, *Winter Is Here* (grades 2-3), The Basic Science Education Series. Copp Clark (Row, Peterson).
Patch & Howe, *Outdoor Visits* (grades 2-3): "Eggs on a Branch" and "A Winter Butterfly," pp. 56-67. Macmillan.

New to this Edition

60 Hikes Within 60 Miles Series (Menasha Ridge Press).

Unit 53—Animal Trails and Tracking

Many animals write their diaries with their feet. We can read those diaries and tell who wrote them. In order to protect themselves and obtain their food, Indians had to rely upon their ability to read the stories told by footprints.

To study pictures of tracks serves no useful purpose unless this activity is associated with actual observation of real tracks of animals. Pupils will be interested in reading the stories told by such tracks: what made them, in what direction the animal was going, whether the animal was running or walking, why it stopped or turned, how it got over a log or through a fence, what blood spots indicate, the home the tracks lead to or from. Having observed tracks, pupil expression work may include sketches, imaginary stories, editing newspaper reports dealing with them, making plaster casts, compiling a class scrapbook.

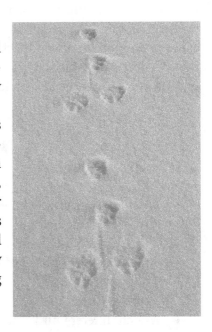

Some Animal Tracks

Rabbit. The rabbit places his long hind feet leap-frog fashion in front of his forefeet at every short hop or long bound. Be careful not to misinterpret the direction when looking at his tracks.

Cat. Observe that the cat walks on the tips of its toes without using its thumb or unsheathing its claws. The hind feet step in the tracks of the forefeet, leaving round tracks about an inch apart.

Dog. Hind feet seldom step in the tracks of the forefeet. Claws leave marks.

Squirrels. Tracks of front feet side by side and shorter than those of hind feet. Tracks of hind feet of gray squirrel about 3 ½ inches from outside to outside, and those of red squirrel about 3 inches.

Chipmunk. Tracks of front feet one slightly behind the other.

Raccoon. Tracks about 2 ½ inches long resemble the imprints of a child's hand and foot. Hind feet toe inward slightly.

Skunk. Lumbers along putting down the whole foot, leaving a track showing all five toes and claws.

Figure 1—Here Is the Way a Rabbit Puts His Best Foot Forward (Drawings from New York State College of Agriculture)

Deermouse. In the woods, tiny tracks found on logs, trees, etc., always showing a tail mark.

"The snow of open fields is commonly marked by the tracks of birds of many kinds. Some, such as the pheasants and quail, show no hind-toe mark. The starlings, sparrows, and crows show the presence of this toe so necessary to their safety on a perch. Many of these birds live largely on the seeds of weeds whose heads rise above the snow. Most of the sparrows hop from one weed top to another, leaving paired tracks. Others, including the pheasant, quail, crows, starlings, and the long-hind-toed horned larks, walk."[1]

Tracks and clues by means of which we can interpret animal stories are left in many ways other than by the feet. Fruit trees stripped of bark near the ground show that rabbits or mice have been feeding. Hair and the height of the mark indicate which animal. Chips of wood at the foot of a tree cause us to look for a woodpecker hole above. By observing the shape, structure, and position of nests we learn what birds lived there. Pellets of fur and bones show both the presence and the food of owls. A single feather may tell us that it was a grouse that visited the corn patch.

Activities

All Grades

- Visit a playground where boys and girls have walked about. Follow one person's tracks to discover where he came from, whether he walked or ran, and where he went.
- Find tracks of horses. Can you tell whether they were walking idly or pulling a load?
- Make sketches of tracks found around the yard. Identify them as cat, dog, bird, mouse.
- Follow the tracks of a mouse to its burrow, those of a squirrel to hidden nuts, those of a hen across a yard.
- Watch different birds walk across the yard. Then sketch their tracks and compare them.
- Make an "Animal Autograph Book" containing the picture of an animal on one page, and of its tracks on the opposite page.

Primary Grades

- Look at your hands. Think what kind of marks they would make in the snow, in the mud, in the sand. Think which would make bigger marks, your hands or your feet. Suppose you walked, jumped, ran; suppose your finger nails were as long as claws; suppose you had a very long tail—what kind of marks would you leave?
- Look in snow for tracks of people. Were they made by men, women, or children?
- Let your cat or dog walk in snow; then draw the foot prints.
- Find tracks of birds and mice in the snow in the yard.

Junior and Intermediate Grades

- Visit a patch of weeds. Look for bird tracks about the weeds. They will usually show three forward toes. If the tracks are in pairs, it is likely they were sparrows or juncos, for they hop along. If the tracks are one after the other as ours are, the bird was walking. Look for remains of seeds left in the snow beside the plants.

---

1   From Cornell Rural School Leaflet, *Fields in Winter.*

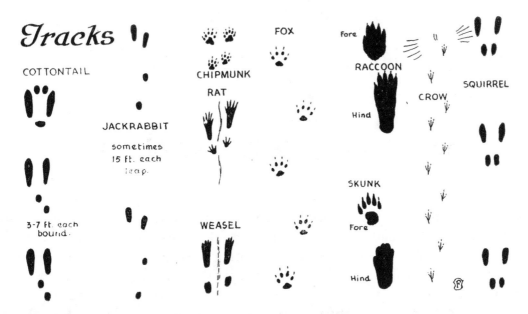

Figure 2

- Play a detective game. Each pupil, by himself or with another, follow some animal's tracks. Interpret the stories the tracks tell. Read the stories in class and see who was the best detective.
- On a thick card make a salt-and-flour mixture, or a plaster-of-Paris mixture with a little vinegar to slow down its hardening. When just about ready to set, let a cat, mouse, dog, or pigeon walk over it. Then let the paste set.

Read

Alexander & Cormack, *Bruce and Marcia, Woodsmen*: "Tracks in the Snow," pp. 201-217. Gage (American Book Co.).

Benton, *Children of the Green Earth*, Book One: "Tracks in Winter," Chapter IV. Pitman.

Erickson, *Cattail Home* (grades 3-5), end papers. Book Society (Children's Press).

Frasier et al., *Winter Comes and Goes* (grades 2-3): "A Story in the Snow," pp, 110-111; and *The How and Why Club* (grades 5-8): "Winter's Picture Book," pp. 169-175. Dent (Singer).

Jarger, *Tracks and Trailcraft* (grades 4-8): by a well-known writer and illustrator; nearly 400 pages of track and trailcraft lore; profusely illustrated. Macmillan.

Mason, *Animal Tracks*: excellent drawings of mammals and their tracks. McLeod (Wm. Morrow).

Murie, *A Field Guide to Animal Tracks*. Allen (Houghton Mifflin).

Palmer, *The Mammal Guide*: Skunk, p. 119; fox, p. 125; squirrel, p. 194; cottontail, p. 278; and many others. Doubleday.

Patch & Howe, *Outdoor Visits* (grades 2-3) : "Tracks on the Snow," pp. 91-98. Macmillan.

Treat, *Track Stories in Mud, Sand, and Snow*. Audubon Nature Bulletin, National Audubon Society.

New to this Edition

Barrett-George, Lindsay. *In the Snow: Who's Been Here?* (Greenwillow Books, 1999).

Dendy, Lisa. *Tracks, Scats and Signs* (Cooper Square Publishing, 1996).

Hero Arts Ink and Stamp Set, Animal Prints

Johnson, Jinny. *Animal Tracks and Signs: Track Over 400 Animals From Big Cats to Backyard Birds* (National Geographic Children's Books, 2008).

Murie and Peterson. *A Field Guide to Animal Tracks* (Houghton Mifflin Harcourt, 1998).

Nail, James. *Whose Tracks Are These? A Clue Book of Familiar Forest Animals* (Roberts Rinehart, 1996).

Selsam, Millicent. *Big Tracks, Little Tracks: Following Animal Prints* (Let's-Read-and-Find-Out Science, Stage 1), (Collins, 1998).

Young Scientist Club. Animal Tracks

Unit 54—Reading the Stories Told by Trees

Trees, like animals, write stories of their past where we may read them. More than that, some of them tell us by their actions and by their structures what they are going to do in the future.

Not long ago a school trustee was telling me of cutting down a slippery elm tree with 175 rings of growth at the base of the first log. What interest the pupils of the neighboring school would take in looking at the center of such a stump, and thinking of that tree as starting to grow at about the time Wolfe and Montcalm were fighting their memorable battle on the Plains of Abraham! Only the Indians knew this part of Ontario at that time. The tree was already large when the first settlers entered this locality, and it might well have been used for timber in the school built seventy years ago. New interest would be given if historical events were timed by putting the date on a slab of an old tree such as this. Some idea of growth conditions, amount of rainfall, and possibly hardship through scarcity of water could be gained by comparing the thickness of the rings of wood year after year.

Leaf scars, bud-scale scars, and fruit scars tell us about the recent past of trees, when each part grew, and something of the conditions under which it grew. The story of the growth of evergreens is recorded by their branching, the distance between two whorls marking one year's growth. The inside of winter buds contain the stems, leaves, and flowers of the next season, well enough developed to show in advance what the tree will produce in spring.

Activities

Teacher

While each pupil in intermediate grades observes a twig on which the buds and leaf scars are well marked, read the twig's story as written in leaf scars, bundle scars, and fruit scars. Leaf scars show where leaves were in past years, and therefore their arrangement. Their shape identifies the tree. The bundle scars or vein scars on the leaf scars show where food traveled from the stem into the leaf. Fruit scars show where fruits, and therefore blossoms, have been.

When buds open in spring, the covering scales either develop into leaves or drop off. When bud scales fall they leave a ring of scars which mark the beginning of that year's growth. By picking the scales from a horse-chestnut bud, the pupils can easily see what the ring looks like. Have them look farther down the twig for a similar ring of scars left by the bud scales which fell last spring. Similar portions of the branch show the growth of other years. With this knowledge, children can find the age of a twig, compare the amount of growth in particular years, and estimate whether rain and other growing conditions were favorable or unfavorable during that year.

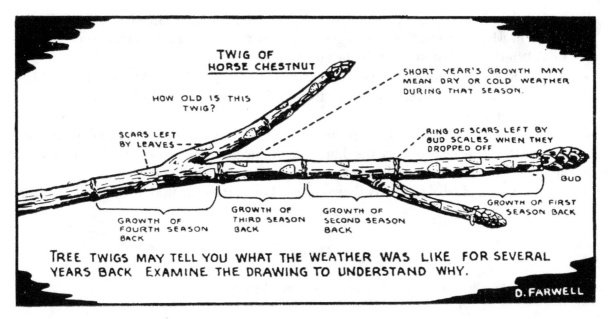

Figure 1

Saw a 2-inch slab from the end of a large log, plane it smooth, leave it several days in a warm room to dry, shellac the planed surface, and keep it in the classroom for observation and study of rings of growth.

Use a small evergreen tree or a twig of one to show how to tell the age of evergreens. At the end, find the buds ready to open in spring. The first whorl of branches shows where last year's buds were. The next whorl is 2 years old. Find the age of the oldest needles not yet shed.

Open a large horse-chestnut bud and show that there is a little stem and some leaves packed in the center and ready to grow in the spring. Careful dissection will enable you to show the number of leaflets on each leaf, also veins. Show pupils that the terminal buds will elongate the twigs, and the lateral buds will produce new branches.

All Grades

For a number of kinds of trees, sketch or model in Plasticine the following: 6 inches at the end of a twig showing the shape of the buds and the way they are arranged, the scars left by leaves which have fallen, a ring of scars around the twig showing where last year's end buds were.

Junior and Intermediate Grades

Some trees living today were growing a thousand years before Christ. How do we know? Look at the end of timber or a block of wood. Find the rings of light and dark wood circling round it. Each pair, a ring of dark wood and a ring of light wood, make up a year of growth. Find the age of each of several logs or blocks of wood.

Intermediate Grades

- Read the story of a twig's life as told by the twig itself. Find where last year's end bud was. Tie a labeled tag in each year's growth. On this, report these findings: In what year did that part grow? In what year was the growth greatest? Least? In what year was there probably most rain? Which grew fastest, a side branch or the main stem?

- Make a motion picture of the life of a tree, with drawings to show (a) the nut from which it started, (b) a seedling tree, (c) a mature tree, (d) a twig with markings to tell its story, (e) the stump with its rings of growth.
- Visit a sawmill and observe the sap coming out of freshly cut logs on warm days, the rings of growth on the ends of logs, the difference in the grain of different kinds of lumber, the amount of brown heart wood and of white sap wood at the end of the log.
- Draw a twig and label the parts shown in fig. 1, also the growth of each of the past three years.

Read

Partridge, *Everyday Science*, Book One: "An Oak Tree Tells Its Story," pp. 72-80, Dent.
Sterling, *Trees and Their Story*, pp. 22-31. Blue Ribbon (Hanover House).

New to this Edition

Burns and Garrow. *Trees, Leaves and Bark* (Cooper Square Publishing, 1995).
Gibbons, Gail. *Tell Me, Tree: All About Trees for Kids* (Little Brown Books for Young Readers, 2002)

http://www.bigsiteofamazingfacts.com/how-can-you-tell-how-old-a-tree-is
http://www.open.edu/openlearn/nature-environment/natural-history/how-does-nature-tell-the-time

Figure 2—Cross section of a tree showing rings.

Nature Journal Excerpt

Sunset in Winter
Across the fields, free of snow for the first time in months, across the swaying, bare-boughed
trees, above the blue and black hills silhouetted against the sky, the sun sets, leaving brilliant
rays of orange and red to light the lonely trees. The grass of the field, flattened and crushed by
the snow, is a hopeful olive green, reminiscent of spring. The trees look sad and almost skeletal,
and emit a mournful humming as the wind whips through them. In contrast the evergreens stand
out with a warm and vibrant green that often passes unnoticed in summer. The hills behind are
a deep blue-black, making a sharp background against the approach of twilight. Yet, even as the
chill wind shrieks mercilessly up the hillside, the smell of spring hangs lightly in the air and gives,
if but briefly, a ray of hope in the bleakest part of the winter.
—C.C.M.D, Grade 8, 2011

Beautify Your Surroundings – January

A **MURAL** SHOWING THE ACTIVITIES OF WINTER ANIMALS AND BIRDS WILL BE INSTRUCTIVE.

PHEASANT

RABBIT

RUFFED GROUSE

SQUIRREL

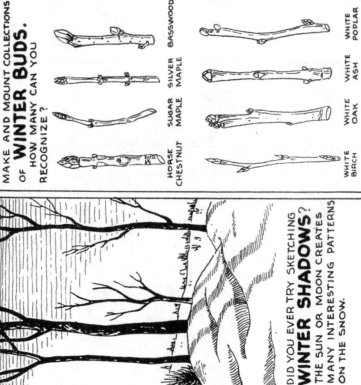

MAKE AND MOUNT COLLECTIONS OF **WINTER BUDS.** HOW MANY CAN YOU RECOGNIZE?

HORSE CHESTNUT

SUGAR MAPLE

SILVER MAPLE

BASSWOOD

WHITE BIRCH

WHITE OAK

WHITE ASH

WHITE POPLAR

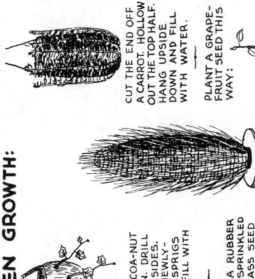

DID YOU EVER TRY SKETCHING **WINTER SHADOWS?** THE SUN OR MOON CREATES MANY INTERESTING PATTERNS ON THE SNOW.

GREEN GROWTH:

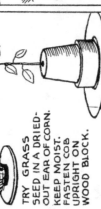

CUT A COCOA-NUT AS SHOWN. DRILL HOLES IN SIDES. INSERT NEWLY-ROOTED SPRIGS OF IVY. FILL WITH SOIL.

CUT THE END OFF A CARROT. HOLLOW OUT THE TOP HALF. HANG UPSIDE DOWN AND FILL WITH WATER.

PLANT A GRAPE-FRUIT SEED THIS WAY:

TRY GRASS SEED IN A DRIED-OUT EAR OF CORN. KEEP MOIST. FASTEN COB UPRIGHT ON WOOD BLOCK.

BELOW, A RUBBER SPONGE, SPRINKLED WITH GRASS SEED AND KEPT MOIST.

AS A SUGGESTION FOR **PICTURE STUDY** WHY NOT USE WINTER SCENES BY OUR OWN CANADIAN ARTISTS? WRITE TO THE ART GALLERY OF TORONTO, DUNDAS ST. W., FOR LISTS. COLOURED PRINTS ARE REASONABLY PRICED.

D. FARWELL.

BORDER SUGGESTIONS

SCIENCE IN ACTION

SOME EXPERIMENTS WITH AIR PRESSURE — JANUARY

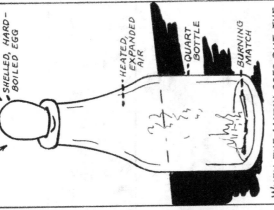

AIR PRESSURE
SHELLED, HARD-BOILED EGG
HEATED, EXPANDED AIR
QUART BOTTLE
BURNING MATCH

WHEN THE MATCH GOES OUT, THE AIR IN THE BOTTLE COOLS AND CONTRACTS. THE GREATER AIR PRESSURE OUTSIDE THE BOTTLE THUS PUSHES THE EGG INSIDE.

PIECE OF TOY BALLOON TIED OVER TOP OF BOTTLE

INVERTED VIAL, WITH JUST ENOUGH AIR IN IT TO MAKE IT FLOAT

PRESSURE UPON THE RUBBER MEMBRANE PASSES THROUGH THE AIR IN THE BOTTLE, THROUGH THE WATER, AND FORCES MORE WATER INTO THE VIAL. THUS THE VIAL SINKS.

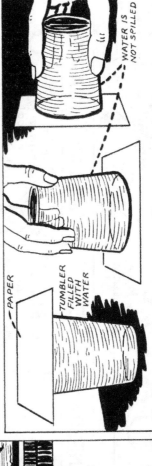

WATER IS NOT SPILLED

PAPER

TUMBLER FILLED WITH WATER

WHEN THE TUMBLER IS INVERTED, OR TURNED SIDEWAYS, THE WATER INSIDE PUSHES AGAINST THE PAPER — BUT THE AIR OUTSIDE THE TUMBLER PUSHES HARDER AGAINST THE PAPER.

D. FARWELL

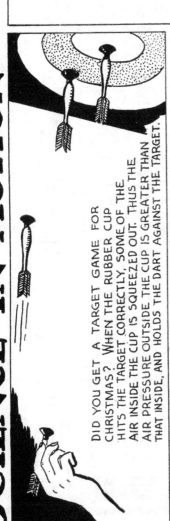

DID YOU GET A TARGET GAME FOR CHRISTMAS? WHEN THE RUBBER CUP HITS THE TARGET CORRECTLY, SOME OF THE AIR INSIDE THE CUP IS SQUEEZED OUT. THUS THE AIR PRESSURE OUTSIDE THE CUP IS GREATER THAN THAT INSIDE, AND HOLDS THE DART AGAINST THE TARGET.

CAN YOU EXPLAIN WHY THE BOY ON THE LEFT CANNOT GET THE WATER TO RISE IN THE STRAW, WHILE THE BOY ON THE RIGHT MANAGES IT EASILY?

A SIPHON:
WHEN THE TUBE, FILLED WITH WATER, IS PLACED IN THE POSITION SHOWN, WATER FALLS DOWN THE LONG PART (A). THE AIR ABOVE THE SURFACE (B) FORCES MORE WATER FROM THE AQUARIUM INTO THE TUBE. THUS THE FLOW CONTINUES.

WHY WON'T THE WATER FLOW INTO THE FLASK UNTIL THE FINGER IS REMOVED FROM THE TUBE?

NATURAL SCIENCE — FEBRUARY — DAY BY DAY

SUNDAY	MONDAY	TUESDAY	WEDNESDAY	THURSDAY	FRIDAY	SATURDAY
				1 How does the heat get from the stove or furnace to your desk?	**2** Don't believe that the woodchuck comes out to see his shadow to-day.	**3** Find and name two kinds of animal tracks in snow. mouse rabbit
4 Water house plants thoroughly and not again until the top soil looks dry.	**5** How long is to-day? Sun rises—? Sun sets—?	**6** Search for cocoons for your classroom.	**7** The snow protects the ruffed grouse and the weeds supply him with seed.	**8** Why is a frosty window a sign of healthy air in the room?	**9** The more snow, the more need to feed birds. bag of suet.	**10** Get pussy willow twigs and place them in water in the house.
11 The blue jay still enjoys acorns for a winter meal.	**12** Compare the length of to-day with a week ago.	**13** Why does the sun not shine as far into a south room to-day as a month ago at noon?	**14** The English sparrow, always present, is called a permanent resident.	**15** Only the father sparrows wear a black necktie.	**16** In what direction does the sun rise to-day? Set?	**17** Examine your ferns for brown, oval, humped scales.
18 Find green growth on the north side of trees.	**19** Again compare the length of day with that a week ago. Sun rises—? Sun sets—?	**20** On which side of a snow fence do snowbanks form? Why? wind drift fence	**21** Does the top of a drift lean toward or away from the wind?	**22** Compare the tracks of a dog and of a cat.	**23** The white-breasted nut-hatch usually walks head downward on trees.	**24** House plants need an occasional washing to remove dust and insects.
25 Learn to know one new star or star group to-night. Orion	**26** On which side of a roof does snow melt first? Why?	**27** Read the weather forecast to-day. Test it to-morrow.	**28** Who will see the first robin?	**29** Why is there a February 29 this year? 1 YEAR 365 d. 5 hr. 48 min.		

Have your pupils build this calendar day by day on blackboard or chart.
Use substitutions if desired.

J.A. PARTRIDGE
Drawn by D. Farwell

FEBRUARY

Unit 55—Using and Protecting Our Trees

"God has lent the earth for our life. It is a great entail.
It belongs as much to those who are to come after us as to us, and we
have no right, by anything we do or neglect to do, to involve them in
any unnecessary penalties, or to deprive them of the benefit
which was in our power to bequeath."

RUSKIN

One has only to learn how much more rapidly our forests are being destroyed than they are growing, and how greatly some of our long-cultivated lands are suffering from erosion by wind and water, scarcity of streams and well-water in summer, and floods in spring, to realize the need for more knowledge about our forests, their values and enemies, and how to protect and conserve them. Knowledge alone will not suffice. We must train our pupils through activities to apply their knowledge through practical projects.

The Value of Forests

Forest Products. The result of a pupil survey of the ways in which we use products which come directly or indirectly from the forest will amaze both pupils and teachers. The list will include Christmas trees, timber, railway ties, poles and posts, lumber of various kinds, furniture, fuel, leather, charcoal, wood alcohol, sawdust, paper, rayon, turpentine and its paint and varnish products, maple sugar, veneer, and many others.

Healthful Recreation. Our forests are important for winter and summer recreation, and for autumn hunting. We enjoy their restful shade in summer, their pleasant aroma in autumn, their welcome protection from wind and storm in winter, and their awakening buds and wildflowers in spring.

Protection for Birds and Other Animals. What a large number of animal friends would be missing without forests! In the woods are the homes of some of our most interesting and valuable birds: ovenbird, phoebe, brown thrasher, scarlet tanager, warblers, kinglets, and many others. Forests give protection for such wild animals as our deer, moose, foxes, beavers, and raccoons, all valuable to man. When we cut the forests, we drive away the owls and beneficial hawks which protect our orchard trees from being girdled by mice and rabbits.

Conservation of Streams and Prevention of Floods. Rains fall gently through the myriads of forest leaves and seep into the spongy layer of mosses, dead leaves, and humus of the forest floor. This constant supply of water furnishes food and drink for the trees and keeps the air moist and healthful. As a result, rains are more likely to be evenly distributed throughout the summer. The

231

winter snow, in an even layer, serves for sleigh transportation where other means would be impossible. In spring the snow melts slowly in a forest and soaks into the ground instead of rushing off in torrents, as frequently happens in the absence of forests, causing damaging floods. Summer streams are kept supplied with water from this forest reservoir.

Preventing Soil from Being Washed or Blown Away. By preventing water from rushing off in torrents, the entangling roots of trees and the layer of leaves and decaying branches prevent the fertile top soil from being carried away. Likewise they hold sandy soil which the wind would easily blow. When forests are cleared from such places, only a barren waste remains until the new forests are started.

Conservation of Forests

Enemies. The three natural enemies of forests—fire, fungi, and insects—combined with man's wasteful methods of cutting, have contributed to our present national forest problem. Careless campers and smokers, railway engines, lightning, and thoughtless burning of brush in dry seasons have led to fires which consumed more timber than we have used. Fungus diseases such as white pine blister rust, chestnut blight, and bracket fungi on tree trunks cause the death of many trees before they are suitable for timber. Woodborers, tussock moths, and tent caterpillars take their toll.

Protection. Forest fires can be reduced greatly by putting out all campfires with water or a covering of soil so that no live coals remain, by breaking all matches before throwing them away, and by safely disposing of cigarette stubs. A fire can be controlled by taking quick action to notify fire rangers; then they limit the fire by cutting a strip across which it cannot jump and by trenching to prevent its spread along the ground. Damage from insects and disease can be reduced by preventing their spread. Trees which are injured by either should be promptly removed. Fallen trees and dead branches should be kept cleared away so that they cannot harbor these enemies. Healthy forests should be made permanent by wise cutting of such trees as have reached maturity, and by protection of younger trees by keeping all grazing animals from the woods. A crop of new trees will then constantly replace those which are cut.

Planting New Forests. Government forests have been planted on otherwise waste land in Northumberland, Durham, Simcoe, and other counties of Ontario. Many private and school woodlots have been started. Similar reforestation projects have been carried out in many parts of Canada and the United States. But there is still a need for thousands of acres of forests throughout Ontario and elsewhere to provide wood products for the future, to conserve suitable climatic conditions, to keep our water supply adequate in summer, to prevent floods and wind erosion, to protect our fast-disappearing wildlife, and to preserve for posterity the recreational advantages of forests.

Activities

All Grades

- Visit a woodlot and ask the owner to explain what trees he ruts, how they are replaced, and why he does not pasture in the woods.
- Make individual booklets on "Trees" appropriate to the grade. In these, insert reports on their uses, clippings and original poems, sketches, rayon and other specimens of products made from trees.
- Make a bulletin-board display to illustrate the following rules to encourage forest conservation: put out your campfire, be sure matches are out, do not burn brush where woods may

be set afire, obey all signs in public parks and forests, observe the game laws, do not injure trees, obey the golden rule.

Primary Grades

- Make a bulletin board display of pictures, poems, and stories about trees or forests.
- Write a story about "Why We Need Forests."
- Plant nuts in flowerpots in the classroom. Watch the little seedlings start growth. Keep them watered.
- Find out which of our foods come from forests.
- Make a large drawing or mural of a forest and mount in place cutouts of birds, wild animals, people, a camp, etc.

Junior and Intermediate Grades

- Take a tramp through the woods and find as many signs as you can of injury to trees—by insects, by disease, by fire, by cattle grazing, and by man's carelessness. Look also for trees bearing fruits suitable for bird food, and hollow trees or logs which may serve as homes for birds or other animals.
- Visit a forest lookout tower, or write for pictures and information about them—their purpose, location, height, equipment, and management.
- Visit a sawmill and lumberyard and see: kinds of logs stored, how they are arranged, markings which identify them to their owners, how the logs are taken into the mill, how they are sawn into lumber, how the lumber is piled for drying, what becomes of the sawdust and other waste. Find out how the lumber is shipped, where it is finished ready for construction, the uses of each kind of lumber. Obtain samples of different kinds of lumber, mount and label them.
- Ask the Parks Department of your city why they spray trees in parks and streets, and what spray they use. Watch how they spray them.
- Make a tree map of the school grounds, park, or wooded area. Number the trees, and place the correct names beside corresponding numbers in the corner of the map. This exercise involves drawing to scale, estimating distances, and knowing tree names.
- Make a class tree book with separate sections for these topics: how to know our common trees (pictures to show summer appearance, winter appearance, leaves and a twig); how trees help man (pictures, clippings, sample specimens to illustrate various subtopics); some enemies of the forest—fire, fungi, insects, pasturing, careless cutting (illustrate in as many ways as possible); friends of the forest—birds controlling insects, forest rangers protecting it from fire, man carrying out tree surgery and reforestation, campers putting out their fires.
- Obtain pamphlets and bulletins from the National Forest Service (or from your state forestry department).
- Make posters with such titles as: "Prevent Forest Fires," "Put Out Your Campfire," "Forests for Tomorrow," "From Tree Seed to Chair."
- Make a mural or a class mount to show how forests are useful to man and to wild animals and birds.

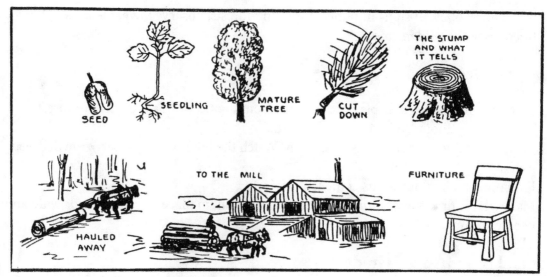

Figure 1—The Story of a Tree, from Seed to Furniture

- Collect specimens to show how insects and diseases have injured wood.
- Make a large drawing of a tree on a card or on the blackboard. On it show in some way the products of each part of trees.
- Finish this story:

    "A beautiful forest was frequently visited by people of the neighboring town. They came to enjoy its shade and flowers, its birds and little wild creatures, and to wade in its cooling streams.

    "Then came a careless smoker. . . ."

- Draw a tree, and on this make drawings to illustrate what trees give us. Make a list of some of the furniture in your home and find out what kind of wood each article is made of.
- Learn the words and music of *Trees,* by Joyce Kilmer.
- Make a frieze of four sections, each showing tree scenes suitable to one season of the year.
- Read these poems: Landers, "When We Plant a Tree," and Stetson, "I Wonder if They Like It—Being Trees?" both in *Everyday Science,* Book One, pp. 292 and 78: Abbey, "What Do We Plant," *Nature Activity Readers,* Book IV.

Intermediate Grades

- Start a school nursery for tree seedlings. Set aside an area measuring about 12 by 40 feet, well protected from school games and grazing animals, either in the schoolyard or in a neighboring field of a pupil's father. Have it well cultivated. Carefully plant several varieties of evergreen and deciduous seedling trees, obtainable free by writing to the Forestry Department, Parliament Buildings, Toronto, for application forms. See that the area is kept free from grass and other weeds. When the trees are about 4 feet tall transplant them to the school grounds for ornament, shade, class identification studies, and observation of tree habits of growth.
- Find out and report to class: how logs are brought by rivers from a distant wood to the mill; what foods we get from forests; what kinds of trees are used for telephone poles, for railway ties, for floors, for furniture, for pencils, for paper; about life in a lumber camp; how we get

rubber from trees; how turpentine is made; what trees Captain Cook found in Australia; how a forest ranger spends his time. Write a letter to "Dominion Forester, Department of Mines and Resources, Ottawa" for booklets about forest products in Canada, for your school library.

Read

Curtis, *Stories in Trees.* Ryerson (Lyons & Carnahan).
Dahlberg, *Conservation of Reusable Resources.* Clarke, Irwin (C. C. Nelson).
Graham & Dersal, *Wildlife for America,* pp. 99-105. Oxford.
Partridge, *General Science,* Intermediate, Book 1: "Using and Enjoying Our Forests," pp. 249-268, and "We Must Protect and Use Our
    Forests Wisely," pp. 269-284; *Everyday Science,* Book One: "The Friendly Forest," pp. 282-293, and "One Good Turn Deserves
    Another," pp. 294-304; and *Everyday Science,* Book Two: "The Gifts of Wood Pulp," pp. 227-245. Dent.
Wall, *Gifts from the Forest.* Allen (Scribner).
Webber, *Thanks to Trees.* Allen (Wm. R. Scott).
Longfellow, "The Village Blacksmith."
Morris, "Woodman, Spare that Tree."
Van Dyke, "The Friendly Trees."

New to this Edition

Brooks, Felicity. *Protecting Trees and Forests* (Usborne, 1994).
Butterfield, Moira. *Protecting Temperate Forests* (Gareth Stevens Publishing, 2005).
Drake and Love. *America at Work: Forestry* (Kids Can Press, 1996).
Lauber, Patricia. *Be a Friend to Trees (Let's-Read-and-Find-Out, Stage 2),* (Collins, 1994).
Synder, Inez. *Trees to Paper* (Children's Press, 2003).
Wallace, Marianne. *America's Forests: Guide to Plants and Animals* (Fulcrum Publishing, 2009).

Figure 2—Oak tree.

Unit 56—Bulbs Unfold Their Secrets

(a topic for intermediate grades)
A BULB
I placed it in the earth—this bulb of mine—
And from its narrow prison house at night
It struggled forth to reach the air and light;
And as it rose and blossomed to the sight,
Its absolute perfection seemed divine!
J. C. ASCHER

In winter, when pupils observe their paper-white narcissi in bloom 6-7 weeks after planting them, this topic will have a natural setting. Show the pupils that the cuttings which they started in autumn have not yet bloomed and that seeds of garden flowers do not produce mature plants for a much longer period of time. Why, then, do narcissi plants mature so soon? How is the bulb fitted to produce the leaves and flowers in so short a time?

When pupils have failed to answer this, their own question, recall the rapid opening of maple buds in spring, and show that they were ready to open because they had leaves and flowers within, and the tree had food in the form of sugar, ready to feed them.

Is it possible that a narcissus bulb has leaves and flowers, and food, all ready for growth? Cut a narcissus bulb, saved from autumn for this purpose, lengthwise through the middle. Pupil observation, guided by the teacher, will show: green leaves ready to elongate, and a flower bud with conspicuous yellow stamens and white petals.

But is there food present? Tasting fails to show the presence of sugar. Try for starch. In Unit 31 (activities for intermediate grades) it was shown that starch—and starch only—produces a blue color in the presence of iodine. Add some iodine to a freshly cut surface of the bulb. Yes, there must be starch, for blue color formed.

Our bulb has told us its secrets. When purchased, it had leaves, flowers, and food. When warmth and moisture were supplied, the leaves and flowers within had only to unfold.

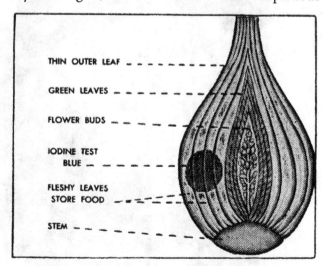

Figure 1—Paper White Narcissus Ready to Unfold

236

Activities

Intermediate Grades

- In a large flowerpot, plant a few onion bulbs and a few onion seeds (very shallowly). Keep the soil moist, and the pot in a sunny window. Which plant grows fastest? Why? Now open an onion and observe the young plant ready to grow, and the food supply ready to feed it. Now you should understand why flowering bulbs develop so rapidly and why some bulbs will grow without soil. When the onion bulbs have grown for some time, pull one out and see how much lighter and softer it has become as it lost food.

- Make a series of sketches to show: the changes which take place as a bud of tulip, daffodil, or other bulb enlarges and opens out to a mature blossom; the falling of petals and wilting of stamens; the production of fruit.

- Make conventional art designs, using tulip, grape hyacinth, daffodil, or narcissus flowers as the unit.

- Dig up tulips to discover tiny bulbels forming beside the old bulb.

- Watch the formation of seed pods on tulips. Remove these so that they will not use food which should be stored in the bulb for next year.

Unit 57—Arranging for a Winter Flower Show

We appreciate flowering plants in winter because of their scarcity during that season. Realizing this, we made preparations to have plants in our classroom by transplanting plants from the garden, making cuttings, and planting bulbs. To motivate pupils to learn and practice other ways of having plants for indoor beautification, a winter flower show to be ready for a day meeting of the Home and School Club, or for a similar occasion, may be planned for midwinter. Preparations for the occasion will provide many opportunities for pupils to learn useful science, to organize and prepare an exhibit, and to take responsibility as individuals and groups for carrying out parts of the project.

The teacher's part will be to inspire pupils to want to make a success of the affair, to instruct them as to how to prepare plants and flowers for the occasion, and to consult with the committee in charge when they express a desire for help with respect to arranging the display. (See suggestions in Unit 19 on page 76.)

Suggestions for preparation of the materials are given in the activities listed below. Class discussions will seek to explain some general principles relative to arranging a display: each plant, dish garden, etc. should be placed so as to show its individual beauty; the tallest displays should form the background; principles of color harmony should be applied; labels showing names and, where needed, directions for preparing the article should be neatly printed and placed so as not to detract from the beauty of the whole. These provide worthwhile learning activities of many kinds. Benefit will come from a visit to a florist shop to study suitable arrangements.

Twigs of fruit trees and flowering shrubs may be brought into bloom indoors in a few weeks. If brought in late in the winter, they bloom in a shorter period of time than when brought in earlier. Of the shrubs, forsythia and Japanese quince make beautiful winter displays. Twigs bearing strong buds should be selected and should be cut nearly 2 feet in length. Care should be taken to select twigs whose removal does not disfigure the shrub. They should be placed in deep vessels of water. Twice a week, the ends of the stems should be cut off, and the water changed. The warmer the room is, the sooner the twigs will bloom.

Activities

All Grades

- In your flower show include the following, prepared earlier in the year: a bouquet consisting of dried cattails, bittersweet, mullein, teasel, etc.; the indoor garden of mosses and other woods plants which you planted in autumn (Unit 3, page 9); the rockery which you made for your autumn display (Unit 19, page 76).
- Cut sprays of English ivy, about a foot long, from the ends of stems. Remove the leaves below

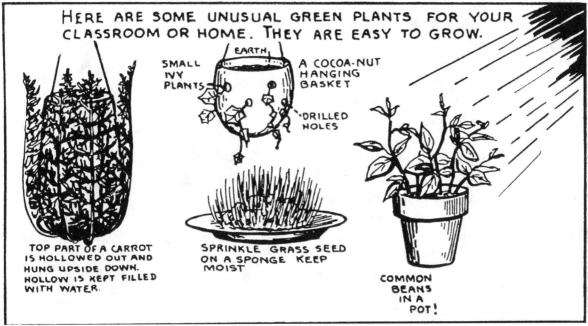

Figure 1

the water level. Two or three sprays are enough for one vase. Plant them in suitably decorated glass bottles hung by wires at the sides of windows. Keep them watered.

- Cut long twigs from various maples. Place them in bottles of water in sunny windows. Observe the opening of flowers and leaves.
- Ask your mother if she will lend you a plant which can be taken to school safely for your flower show. Be sure that you wrap it well in newspaper.
- Plants seeds of lemon, orange, and grapefruit, and see which will grow.

Primary Grades

- You, too, can make little gardens for the winter show. Save some egg shells with just the top taken off. Fill them nearly full with soil and plant vegetable or flower seeds in them. When the plants come up, keep your little gardens in a sunny window.
- Tie some acorns on thread and hang them half an inch above the water in a glass in a warm place for a week. Tiny roots will grow toward the water and stems rise upward.
- Put a sponge in a saucer of water. Sprinkle seeds of grass, clover, beets, and radish on it. Watch the little green mountain grow.
- Make some spool flowerpots. Cover empty spools with green crepe paper. Make paper flowers to fit them, for example, a paper daffodil. Use them to adorn the classroom.

Junior and Intermediate Grades

Your teacher will show you how to prepare indoor shrub gardens in deep vases, and how to care for them. Watch which open first, leaf buds or flower buds. Do the leaves and flowers come from different or from the same buds? What becomes of the scales which wrap the buds?

Try to grow a hanging "carrot vase." Use the top three-quarters of a large carrot. Carefully hollow it out about 2 inches deep from the cut surface. Hang it upside down by means of strings tied through holes. Keep it filled with water. You will enjoy watching the carrot leaves grow outward and upward.

Support a sweet potato in the top of a large bottle or jar kept filled with water. Place it in a sunny window and watch the vines grow.

For a centerpiece on a dining-room table, place cuttings of beets or carrots, together or separately, in a soup plate. Use the top third of beets, and about an inch of the top of carrots. Place the cut surfaces down. Keep the water half an inch deep. Shoots grow from the tops fed by the food stored in the pieces of root.

Arrange to have a bubble bowl. Secure a large glass jar or bowl. Arrange a bouquet somewhat shorter than the bowl is high, and embed the ends of the stems in Plasticine. Fill the bowl with water and drop in the bouquet.

Figure 2—A Dish Garden (Courtesy Better Homes and Gardens Magazine)

Place a soup plate upside-down over the bowl, then invert the whole quickly. The Plasticine should turn the bouquet upright. Leave the bowl in a sunny place.

Read

New to this Edition

http://onions-usa.org/all-about-onions/lesson-plan-on-food-and-nutrition
http://carrotmuseum.co.uk/experiment.html
http://www.hunkinsexperiments.com/pages/carrots.htm (This website shows a picture of what the carrot looks like when you try the experiment in the Junior and Intermediate Grades section.)

Figure 3—Growing avocado seeds.

Unit 58—Learning from Our Pets

Teach us the strength that cannot seek
By deed or thought to hurt the weak.
                    KIPLING

Little children, never give
Pain to things that feel and live.
                    SELECTED

Perhaps no other subject is so dear to the heart of a child as that of his pet. Obtaining and preparing homes for pets and caring for them in the classroom cannot fail to foster more desirable pupil attitudes toward and appreciation of such animals. Informal association while tending them leaves more lasting benefits than formal lessons.

The children should care for the pets, but the teacher must organize and supervise that care. Guidance by the teacher is essential to obtain the most educational values from having pets. Only those pets should be kept for which ample provision can be made. Improper or careless treatment of pets destroys the possible constructive values of having them in the classroom.

First considerations are for the comfort and feelings of the animals. Cleanliness should be insisted upon, and the temperature, dryness, and ventilation regulated according to the animals' requirements. Pets such as guineas pigs, mice, and birds should be fed frequently, as they may starve to death within twenty-four hours. Fish, snakes, frogs, and toads may be unharmed if left without feeding in a natural environment for several days.

Care in handling animals is important. They should be touched or stroked sparingly and gently until they become accustomed to human touch. Most pupils must be taught not to squeeze the body, but to support it comfortably on one hand while the other hand gently rests above. Pets should never be made conscious of excitement, hurry, or restraint. Most pets like to be talked to. Much healthy interest and valuable pupil education may be fostered by arranging to have one or more of such pets as the pigeon, canary, rabbit, squirrel, cat, white rat, and guinea pig in the classroom for a few days at a time. While suitable homes are being made, pupils are receiving training in crafts. When dinner scraps are used as food, children are trained in thrift. When the proper food is studied and supplied, pupils are given useful knowledge and are trained in thoughtfulness. When eggs are laid or hatched, or when young are born, pupils obtain wholesome, natural understanding of the wonder of life. Many opportunities are thus provided for the cultivation of desirable attitudes and for instruction in humane methods of caring for pets.

Figure 1—Giving the Dog Freedom, though Tied (Toronto Humane Society)

Name	Housing	Care	General Suggestions
Rabbit	A large hutch or a suitable box opening in front or above for convenience; sleeping-quarters partitioned off.	Clean, dry hay or fine straw for bedding; feed morning and evening; beets, carrots, lettuce, clover, grass, grain (dry bread or bread and milk for nursing mothers); do not over-feed, and remove all uneaten food; place a teaspoonful of salt in grain weekly; keep supplied with fresh water; leave young with mother for 2 months.	Easily tamed, and takes petting well; to lift, place the hand under the hind quarters and grasp the skin over the shoulders (never lift by the ears); catarrh and cold (sniffles) due to improper ventilation or damp quarters.
Cat	Provide a cushioned box or basket in a partly concealed place for sleeping; change the bedding frequently; leave a shallow box of earth near by; keep the cat inside at night; do not shut it in close quarters.	Feed reguarly, adult cats twice a day, under 5 months oftener; give milk, plus prepared cat food or cooked meat mixed with vegetables; no meat until 6 weeks old; fresh water; give mother cats pelenty of milk; leave kittens with mother from 5 to 7 weeks.	Watch mother feed, wash, and care for kittens; with properly trained children, cat may be allowed to wander around classroom; likes playing, and appreciates good care; scratching or biting due to playfulness or mistreatment.
Dog	Comfortable sleeping—quarters should be provided. Its box should be padded with clean straw or excelsior. In cold weather provide a sheltered place, not too warm.	Feed twice a day; will eat variety of food; should have cooked meat several times a week; dish of fresh water should always be available; the dog should be bathed once a week during warm weather; suds kill germs; dry thoroughly. See fig. 1.	Easily trained; faithful to master. Notice dog's teeth--what are they fitted for? How does a dog show its feelings? Notice tracks of dog on snow. Which of dog's senses are keenest?

Name	Housing	Care	General Suggestions
Guinea Pigs, White Rats, and Mice	Small wire cages or wooden boxes with wire mesh; keep in a warm, dry place; supply dry bedding; perches for rats and mice; provide sleeping-compartment with soft cloth for bed. See fig. 2.	Use sawdust or excelsior on the floor, changed often; feed bread crusts, dry rolled oats, fresh vegetables, grain; add grass, hay, and milk for guinea pigs; keep supplied with clean, fresh water.	All make docile, affectionate pets; guinea pigs produce very little odor, mice more; children delight in playing with them, developing kindly feeling toward animals in general; handle by supporting from underneath with hand over shoulders; protect from cats and dogs.
Squirrels	Use a large box, preferably wired, with a hollow log for seclusion.	Avoid frightening; feed hard-shelled nuts, apples or other fruit, corn, and sunflower seeds; provide climbing facilities; give fresh water in a clean dish.	Pupils like to name their pets; squirrels less easily tamed than other animals.
Birds (canaries)	Cage large enough for exercise; in a quiet place; clean daily; keep supplied with sand or grit; hang in light place by day and cover it at night; avoid drafts. Use large cage or box for pigeons or wild birds; keep wild birds only if injured.	Feed bird food or mixture of grass and millet seeds, plus green lettuce or grass daily, and pieces of apple, potato, carrot, cabbage, hard boiled egg weekly; keep water and food cups cleaned and filled; provide bathing-dish; frequent feeding and scrupulous cleanliness are essential with all birds.	Provide larger cage and nesting material at egg-laying time; eggs hatch in about 2 weeks; observe parents feed and care for young; avoid startling birds by sudden movements; keep their toe-nails cut. Use live pigeon or chicken to observe habits of feeding and drinking, and adaptations for flight.

Activities

Teacher

Organize a "Be Kind to Animals" week. Have slogan, poster, and essay contests. Set up a Junior Humane Society. Have a program at which efforts of pupils throughout the week are recognized. Perhaps an animal picture could be purchased for the classroom and hung that day.

All Grades

- In your classroom, arrange a shelf and an adjoining bulletin board for things pertaining to pets and their care. Include clippings, pictures, "lost and found" and other notices, magazines, and scrapbooks.
- Learn the Humane Pledge, "I promise to be kind to all living creatures and to try to protect them from cruel treatment."
- Visit a pet store, a chick hatchery, or a pupil's home where there are pets, and learn of their housing, feeding, and care.
- Bring wooden boxes with screened side and top, old bird cages, or specially constructed metal cages, well ventilated with screen, or construct them in manual training classes. Then have a pupil bring his pet for a few days. A cat or dog or other pets may be kept for only a day, or brought back day after day. Others such as white mice, guinea pigs, rabbits, chickens, fish, etc. may be given homes in the classroom for longer periods.

- Write to the Canadian Junior Humane Society, Toronto, and to American Society for the Prevention of Cruelty to Animals, 50 Madison Ave., New York City, for posters, pictures, etc.
- Organize a pet club in your classroom and reserve a section of the bulletin board for the club. Entitle the section "Be Kind to Animals." Certain members of the executive become responsible for the display of pictures, leaflets, poems (collected or written), and clippings dealing with the humane treatment of animals.
- Read Edgar Guest's poem "A Dog."
- Interpret pictures such as "Playful Kittens," "The Boy and the Rabbit," "Sheep in Pasture," etc.
- Compose original stories or poems about pets. Sing songs about them.
- Make individual, group, and class booklets, "My Pets," or "Our Pet Book," consisting of interesting pictures, free illustrations drawn by the owner, original poems and stories. Encourage neatness of printing and beauty of arrangement.
- Present the play, "Kindness Pays" (from Nicol et al., *The Nature Hour*, Fifth Year, Autumn and Winter, pp. 111-116).

Primary Grades

- Feed the gray squirrels and black squirrels around your school. Watch them play. See how they run, climb, and eat. Make pets of them.

Figure 2—Feeding the guinea pigs.

- Have a pet show. Each pupil bring the pet he wishes.
- Make a scrapbook of pets which visit the classroom or of those which belong to members of the class.
- Bring your kitten to school. Listen to it purr. Feel its soft fur. Watch how it plays with a ball or a string. Talk about how it shows you that it likes you; how it shows when it is unhappy; the kind of place to give it to sleep; how to feed and care for it. Watch how it drinks, eats, washes its face, curls up to sleep, walks noiselessly, climbs up clothing, jumps to the floor, seizes a ball, takes meat from a bone, closes its eyes.
- Pretend you are: a cat creeping up on a mouse; a dog lapping up some milk; a rabbit eating a carrot; a chicken drinking water.
- Discuss proper treatment of each kind of pet guest brought to school.
- Keep a blackboard chart or a guest book, "Our Pet Guests." Enter their names and the names of the owners.
- Visit a rabbit hutch. Have the owner tell about how he feeds and cares for the rabbits.
- Construct sand-table scenes such as "Tabby and Bowser are Happy" or "A Dog Family at Home."
- Make models and drawings of pets and their homes.

Some Kindness Rules
- Always arrange with someone to care for your pets when you are away.
- Be sure that young animals are left with their mother until they can get food for themselves.
- Sick or injured pets need proper treatment. See that someone who is able gives help.

Read

Aistrop, *Every Child's Book of Pets.* Alien (Dobson).

Bianco, *All About Pets* (Teacher). Macmillan.

Blough, *The Pet Show* (Grs. II-III), The Basic Science Education Series. Copp Clark (Row, Peterson).

Frasier, et al, *Sunshine and Rain* (grades MI), pp. 58-64-; *The Season; Past* (Grl. III-V): "Jimmy's Puppy," "My Cat," and "Dick's Cow," pp. 178-95. Dent (Singer).

Gray et al, *The New Friends and Neighbors*: "Animal Friends," pp. 77-108; *The New Fun with Dick and Jane*: "Fun with Pets and Toys," pp. 45-64 and 83-110; *The New More, Friends and Neighhors*: "Animal Friends," pp. 57-102; and *The New Our New Friends'* New and Old Animal Friends," pp. 79-113. Gage (Scott, Foresman)

Masters, *The Pet Club.* Copp Clark (Heath).

Morgan, *Pet Book for Boys and Girls.* Alien (Scribner)

Myers, *Pets and Friend:* (grades III-IV). Copp Clark (Heath)

Park, *Pel: Are fun.* Alien (Houghton Mifflin).

Taber, *The First Book of Dogs* (grades IV-VIII). Ambassador (Watts).

From the Ontario Society for Prevention of Cruelty to Animals, R.R. 2, Oakvillc Ont these pamphlets: *Care of Goldfish, Care of Rabbits, Care of Your Dog, Children and Their Pet, in the Home,* and *The Classroom Turtle.*

From American Humane Association, Denver, Colorado: *How To Take Care of Cat: How To Take Care of Dog, Hew To Take Care of Fish, How To Take Care of Birds', How To lake Care of Small Animal,, Some First Grade Experience, in Humane Education.*

New to this Edition

Animal Planet Pet Care Library (Cats, Puppies, etc.) (TFH Publishers Inc, 2008)

Damerow, Gail. *Your Chickens: A kid's Guide to Raising and Showing* (Storey Publishing, 1993).

Levy, Barbara Soloff. *How to Draw Pets* (Dover, 2006).

Searle, Nancy. *Your Rabbit: A Kid's Guide to Raising and Showing* (Storey Publishing, 1992).

Soffer, Ruth. *The Cat Lovers Coloring Book (and other pet coloring books)* (Dover, 2007).

Unit 59—Doing Things with Water

This topic may seem novel, but the unit deals with phenomena which lie within the everyday experiences of pupils, and with facts which they can apply in everyday life. Water is one of the most useful substances known. It does much to make possible all life; it is the means of much transportation; it is both a barrier and a connecting link between nations. To children, it provides opportunities for fun and sport in both winter and summer, and is a medium for much useful experimentation individually, in class, or in the Nature Club.

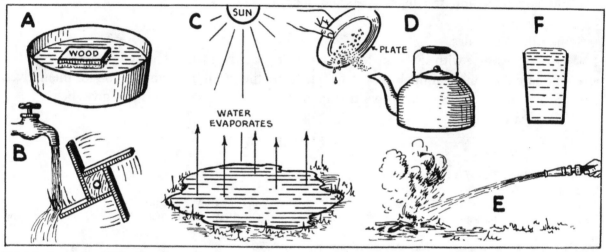

Figure 1—Learn about Water Experimentally

A, holding things up; B, turning water wheels; C, evaporated by the sun; D, changing from steam to cloud to drops; E, putting out fire; F, being heaped up

This topic might well become the subject of an enterprise. As such, its study will not attempt to embrace all the facts about water, but rather to be an investigation by pupils of the importance of water as a part of their environment. Class discussion may lead to a division of the topic into such phases as: water in relation to plants and animals (a home, food and drink, washing, breathing, a medium for travel); water in the home (cooking, drink, cleanliness of clothes and person); water as a source of power (evaporation from streams, rain, waterfalls; steam); water as a medium for commerce and travel (floats logs, carries boats; canals).

246

Activities

Primary Grades

- Perform little experiments to show that water runs downhill; that it holds up boards or boats; that it forms round drops when splashed about; that it makes dry soil stick together (mud pies); that it will roll along stones or sand; that it will soak into a sponge or chalk; that it makes sugar and salt disappear; that it is drink for animals; that it makes plants grow; that it dries up in the sun and wind; that it soaks into some things (cloth), but not into others (rubber); that it becomes ice when it freezes; that it falls as snow; that it boils when it gets hot.
- Breathe on a cold window. Where did the water come from? What became of it when the window dried? Put one saucer of water in the sun and another in the shade. Which dries first?
- What things will water hold up? Try these: a piece of wood, a toy boat, a stone, an egg, a pencil.

Junior and Intermediate Grades

- Make a pinwheel of waxed paper. Hold it on edge and pour water over it. Because water makes big wheels turn, we can have electricity.
- Pour some muddy water through one thickness of cloth, through three thicknesses of cloth, through sand in a tin can with holes in the bottom. These are examples of filtering, a method of removing solid particles from water.
- Breathe into your hands several times. Where did the moisture come from? We always breathe out water vapor.
- Place a mixture of salt and ice in a tin can in the classroom. Where did the water on the outside of the can come from? The mixture inside the can is cold enough to change some water vapor in the air to liquid.
- Whittle a piece of dry wood until it just fits into a metal ring. While it is in the ring, soak it in water for half a day. Then try to remove the wood from the ring. What did the water do to the wood? Why does soaking a hammer in water tighten the handle?

Intermediate Grades

- Catch a tumbler full of water from a tap. Watch bubbles rise through it. These contain air. Leave the water in a warm place. Notice that more bubbles rise. They also contain air which was dissolved in the water like sugar in coffee. But warm water cannot hold as much dissolved air as cold water. Fish breathe the air dissolved in water.
- What causes rain? Place a sheet of metal over a beaker containing about an inch of water. Heat the beaker and watch the formation of drops of water on the cover. Heat changes water to water vapor. The water vapor, cooled by the cooler lid, condenses to drops of water. These join up and grow until they are big enough to fall—as drops of rain do. Perform the experiment illustrated in fig. 1, D.
- The sun evaporates water from pools, plants, etc. The water vapor then rises. If cooled enough, some of it forms a cloud consisting of tiny drops of water. When the drops are heavy enough, they fall as rain.

- Make a frieze showing how water provides sport—fishing, skating, boating, swimming, etc. Draw up a list of rules for safety as applied to these sports. Illustrate the rules, showing the right and wrong ways to paddle a canoe, to rescue a drowning person, to rescue someone who has fallen through thin ice.
- Pour 2 inches of water into each of five tumblers. Add to these respectively one-half teaspoonful each of: sugar, salt, flour, baking soda, sand. Which substances disappear rapidly? Slowly? Which do not disappear? When particles are no longer visible in water, we say the substance has *dissolved*. Such a substance is said to be soluble.
- Fill a tumbler with hot water, and another with cold water. Into these two keep stirring equal numbers of teaspoonfuls of soap flakes as long as any will dissolve. Which dissolves more, hot or cold water?
- When soup cools, you see the grease in it harden. One reason why hot water is better than cold for washing is that it softens the grease. The hot water also lets more soap get at the grease and do its work. The cold water hardens the grease on your hands instead of softening it.
- Dissolve some sugar in water. Taste the solution. Boil the solution and hold a cold dish in the steam. Taste the water on the dish. Repeat the experiment, using muddy water. Is the condensed water dirty? When water evaporates, it leaves particles and dissolved substances behind. When the vapor condenses, the water is pure.
- Wash your hands in well water and in rain water, using the same amount of soap each time. Which water shows more scum? Which water produces the more suds? Which feels the harder on the hands? Look for a gray deposit inside a teakettle in which well water or tap water is used. Well water is usually called *hard water* because it contains chemicals not present in rain water. These substances prevent it from producing suds unless we use a softener such as washing-soda, which helps to remove the chemicals. Soap which forms the scum in hard water is wasted soap.
- Make water heap up by dropping coins or pebbles into a tumbler filled with water.
- Make some water run uphill. Half-fill a pitcher with water. Lay a towel over the edge with one end in the water. How does the rest of the towel get wet? The water traveled through the fine spaces between the threads and fibers as it does in blotting-paper. (When older, pupils will learn that this is called capillarity.)
- Can you get water from fire? Light a short candle and invert a dry tumbler over it. Notice the mist on the glass. Repeat the experiment without lighting the candle. Is there mist? The water must have come from the flame.
- In one beaker or tin cup place pure water, and in a similar one, a solution of salt or sugar. Heat them and take the temperature of each when they begin to boil. Which boils at a higher temperature, pure water or a solution?
- Fill a medicine bottle with water. Cork it tightly and put it on a window-ledge on a cold night. What was the effect of freezing? When water freezes, it needs more space. For the same reason, pipes and radiators burst when the water in them freezes.
- Put some water in a pail or tumbler. Tip the container from side to side. The water still stays on the level. Fill a teakettle with water. Look into the spout and top. How do the levels compare? Lower a straw or a glass tube into a tumbler of water. Compare the levels of the liquid in the tumbler and in the tube. Blow into the tube. What change in levels takes place? Stop blowing. What does the water do? Suck on the tube. How does the water level within

change? Stop sucking. What does the water do? When two bodies of water touch, they come to the same level.

- How can frozen clothes become dry without becoming wet? Give two examples of water vapor changing to solid water.

Read

Dowling et al., *Explaining Why* (grades 4-5), pp. 26-41. Winston.

Frasier et al., *Through the Year* (grades 1-2): "Rain," pp. 48-53; *Winter Comes and Goes* (grades 2-3): "Where Did the Water Go?" pp. 69-72, and "Jimmy Learns Something New," pp. 76-80; and *How and Why Experiments* (grades 5-7): "What Makes Rain?" p. 186. Dent (Singer).

Freeman, *Fun with Science* (grades 6-8). Random House.

Hethershaw & Baker, *Wonders to See:* "Water Dissolves Many Things," pp. 28-31. Gage (World Book).

Partridge, *General Science,* Intermediate, Book 1: "The Ins and Outs of Water," pp. 88-108. Dent.

Podendorf, *The True Book of Science Experiments* (primary), pp. 36-39. Book Society (Children's Press).

Smith & Clarke, *Under the Sun* (primary), pp. 37-64. Longmans, Green.

New to this Edition

Chalufour, Ingrid. *Exploring Water with Young Children* (Redleaf Press, 2005).

Tocci, Salvarore. *Experiments with Water* (Children's Press, 2002).

Young Scientist Series, Set 5: Water (kit 13), Capillary Action (Kit 14) and Air (Kit 15)

http://www.homeschooling-ideas.com/water-experiments.html

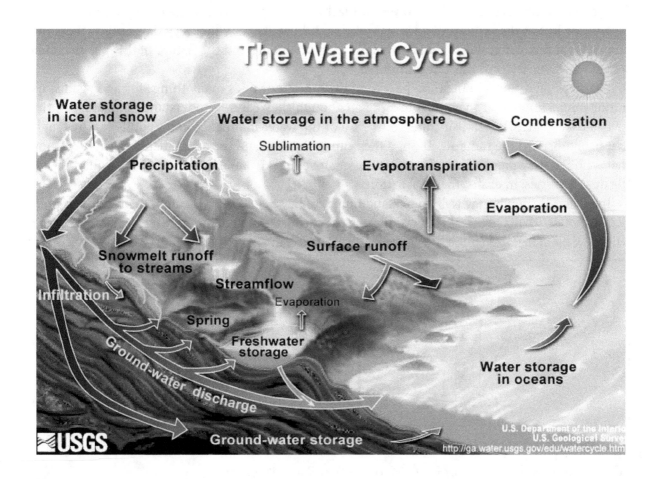

Unit 60—Finding out about Air

Air, like water, is required by all life. Its oxygen is used by all living things, both plants and animals, for breathing; its carbon dioxide makes up a large part of the food used by green plants; its nitrogen dilutes the oxygen of the air enough for animals to breathe it; its water vapor not only makes it healthful for breathing, but makes possible all clouds, rain, and snow; even its dust helps to form raindrops and sky colors.

Air is everywhere. It fills "empty" jars; it moves among soil particles; it is dissolved in the water of all streams. Air helps us in many phases of everyday life. Its oxygen makes fires burn and cans rust; its moisture, in some localities, materially assists in the textile industry (Lancashire cotton mills); its force turns windmills and provides power for machinery; its pressure enables us to pump water.

Yes, we live at the bottom of an ocean of air, and use its benefits every day. Surely, then, our pupils, from the first grades, should gradually learn to understand the nature of this peculiar substance which we feel and use, but cannot see.

Even primary pupils know that the wind (air in motion) does many things for and against us. Junior pupils know that they must breathe air though they cannot understand the nature of this invisible substance. When fish come to the top of the water in an aquarium, pupils can be taught that fish, too, need the same air. Though they cannot understand the constituents of air, they know that we open the draught door of the furnace or stove to let in more air. In beams of light, they see the dust it carries; in drafts, they feel its force.

Intermediate pupils may well understand much of the science of air if taught them through practical activities. They see that it turns windmills, drives boats, and scatters seeds. Simple experiments will show them that this air is a substance requiring space, that it presses on things, that it is necessary

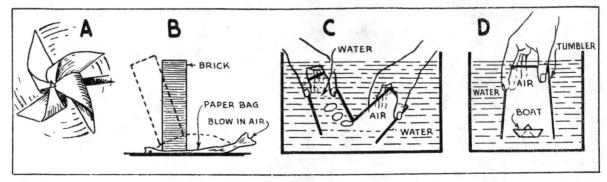

Figure 1—Learn about Air Experimentally

A, turning pin-wheels; B, its pressure tipping a brick over; C, being poured; D, filling space.

for burning. They can be shown that there is water (vapor and sometimes liquid) in it; that it expands, and therefore becomes lighter (per unit of volume) when heated. They can be shown that it permits them to drink through a straw and to play wind instruments; that air is necessary for candles or other fires to burn; that, in water, it enables fish and other water animals to breathe.

Activities

Junior and Intermediate Grades

- Take a deep breath. Hold it as long as you can. You soon decide you must breathe again. All living things need air for this purpose.
- Is there air in soil? Drop a lump of soil into water and watch the bubbles rise. What fills the bubbles?
- Can you push a cork down to the bottom of a vessel of water without touching it? Invert a tumbler over the floating cork and push downward. Why did the cork go down? The air in the tumbler pushed the water down, and the cork went with it.
- Hold the mouth of a small bottle upside down in a pan of water. Why doesn't the water enter the bottle?
- Tie ribbons to a stick. Open the window at the top and bottom. Hold the stick in front of each opening and notice which way the air is blowing there.
- To show that the air around us presses on things: put a tube into the mouth of a paper bag; blow the bag up; now suck the air from the bag. What makes the bag cave in?
- Stand a brick on its side and try to blow it over. Can you do it? Now place the closed end of a paper bag under the side of the brick lying on edge, and blow into the open end. The air blown into the bag pries up the brick and topples it over. Air exerts pressure.
- From a window or the top of a post, drop a large stone and a small stone at the same time. Do they fall equally fast? Now drop a stone, a feather, and an empty cardboard box—all at the same time. Which reaches the ground first? Which did the air hinder the most while falling?
- Why do we put air into tires? Blow up an inner tube or balloon. Squeeze it to see how easily the balloon loses and regains its shape and how spongy it feels when you press on it. Air in tires permits the tire to roll over a stone or other object without bumping the car upward. This makes riding in a car more comfortable. Why does a ball bounce?
- While holding the finger over the end of the tube, work the handle of a bicycle pump up and down several times. How does the temperature of the pump change while you are doing this? How does it change when you pump up a tire? When air is pressed into a smaller space, it becomes warmer.
- List some impurities that you have seen, smelled, or felt in the air. Why is it more healthful to play in the park than in the street?

Intermediate Grades

- To show that there is air everywhere, insert the stem of a funnel through a cork fitted tightly into a bottle or jar. Fill the funnel with water. Why does the water not run freely into the jar? What is in the bubbles which come out?
- Keep the water in a teakettle boiling on the stove. How does it improve the air for us?

- Put some wet soil on a plate, and invert a dry tumbler over it. Leave this in the sunlight. What do you see? Put it in the shade. What happens? Find out why. Air takes up water as vapor from the soil; some of this condenses as little droplets on the glass.
- Try to pour some air from one tumbler into another in this way: invert an "empty" tumbler in a deep basin of water; fill another tumbler with water, and invert it beside the first; tip both so that you pour air bubbles into the second.
- Invert a tumbler filled with water in a basin of water. Put a rubber tube up into the tumbler. What happens when you blow into the tube? When you suck on the tube? Why?
- Fill a bottle with water. Hold a piece of paper firmly over the top and turn the bottle upside down. Take the paper away. Does water run out? What enters the bottle as water leaves?
- How does heat affect air? Partly inflate a balloon, tie it, and push it down into hot water. What happens?
- Would you like to be a magician? Try to push a shelled, hard-boiled egg into a milk bottle. It can't be done, can it? But you can make the egg pop into the bottle—and out again! Place a piece of burning paper in the bottle; then put the hard-boiled egg on the mouth of the bottle, with the pointed end down. Look and listen. (Some of the warmed, expanded air in the bottle pushed out around the egg. When the rest of the air within cooled, it contracted. The air outside, in trying to get into the bottle, pushed the egg in.)
- Light a short candle. Invert a tumbler over it. How does the flame change? Why does it go out? Everything, to burn, must have oxygen. Air contains this. When the oxygen in the air was used up, the candle could burn no longer.
- Using a straw, breathe through some limewater several times. When limewater becomes milky it shows that carbon dioxide is entering it. What must you have breathed out? Carbon dioxide in air is poisonous. Why then must we ventilate the classroom?
- Why do fish die when placed in boiled water or in a sealed jar?
- Make a list of places from which air gets dust.
- Ask your father to show you what increased draft does to the burning of the fire in a furnace.

Read

Beauchamp et al., *Discovering Our World,* Book 1 (grades 4-5): "Why Do All Living Things Need Air and Water?" pp. 47-65. Gage (Scott, Foresman).

Blough & Huggett, *Methods and Activities in Elementary-School Science,* pp. 124-129. Ryerson (Dryden).

Bowers & Bissonnette, *General Science,* Intermediate, Book 3: "The Air We Breathe" pp. 36-69. Dent.

Craig & Bryan, *Science Near You* (primary), pp. 42-49. Ginn.

Craig & Hurley, *Discovering with Science* (grades 5-6): "The Air We Live In," pp. 86-105. Ginn.

Craig & Lembach, *Science Everywhere.* (grades 4-5), pp. 86-97. Ginn.

Dowling et al., *Seeing Why* (junior), pp. 113-123; *Explaining Why* (grades 4-5), pp. 249-263; and *Investigating Why* (grades 7-8), pp. 37-72. Winston.

Frasier et al., *Winter Comes and Goes* (grades 2-3): "Round About Us," pp. 92-97; *The Seasons Pass* (grades 3-4): "Experiments," pp. 122-135; *The How and Why Club* (grades 6-8): "Randy's Experiment," pp. 226-271; and *How and Why Experiments* (grades 6-8): "How Air Works for Us," pp. 164-173. Dent (Singer).

Friskey, *The Air Around Us.* Book Society (Children's Press).

Hethershaw & Baker, *Wonders to See:* "Air We Breathe," "Air and Fire," "How Air Pushes," and "Air Is Real," pp. 5-21. Gage (World Book).

Hood, *The Atmosphere:* teacher reference on atmosphere and weather. Oxford.

Parker, *The Air About Us* and *Our Ocean of Air,* The Basic Science Education Series Copp Clark (Row, Peterson).

Partridge, *General Science,* Intermediate, Book 2: "Air in Man's Service," pp. 147-190; and *Everyday Science,* Book Two: "Weather and Air," pp. 451-461. Dent.

Podendorf, *The True Book of Science Experiments* (primary), pp. 6-22. Book Society (Children's Press).

New to this Edition

Branley, Franklyn. *Air is All Around You (Let's-Read-and-Find-Out Science 1)*, (Collins, 2006).
Tocci, Salvatore. *Experiments with Air* (Children's Press, 2003).
Young Scientist Series, Set 5: Water (kit 13), Capillary Action (Kit 14) and Air (Kit 15)

Figure 2—Wind farm in Washington State.

Unit 61—Little Things We Seldom See—Germs

What a thrill to the Dutch janitor Leeuwenhoek when, with lenses ground by himself, he saw "wee beasties—a thousand times smaller than a louse's eye" in a drop of water! What he saw were the first bacteria seen by human eyes. These tiny, living things eat and grow, travel and multiply, and live lives as real as those of any other plants or animals. They live in almost every sort of place: in water, in soil, in air, on dust, in milk and other food, in and on our bodies; we cannot escape them. This we have discovered by the work they do, and by observing them through powerful microscopes.

Germs, like other plants, require warmth, moisture, air, and food. Some get nourishment from dead material such as plant and animal remains and soil; others, from living plants or animals. As the latter take food from living things, they prevent them from growing normally. In animals they frequently cause fever and death. Bacteria have a very simple way of eating: they merely absorb the food into any part of their bodies.

Most of the known kinds of germs are beneficial. Many of them bring about the decay of sewage and of vegetable remains. The latter not only keep the world from being cluttered with refuse, but they make possible our crops by setting free in the soil many useful plant foods. Others help us in the making of butter and cheese, linen and leather, and even our bread.

The harmful germs that we are most concerned with cause disease in the human body. Some of these enter wounds in the skin and grow and multiply in the blood. As they do so, they produce poisons which may travel throughout the body and bring about death. The germs of tuberculosis, common cold, whooping cough, and other diseases enter our bodies with the air we breathe. Those of diphtheria and typhoid fever may enter with food or drink. Others find a landing-place on the delicate tissues of the nostrils, eyes, and throat. Having once entered the body, some germs multiply very rapidly in the presence of warmth, moisture, and suitable food. Fortunately most of these germs have little chance of living or multiplying if the person is in good health.

Germs spread from person to person in many ways. In the spray of a cough or a sneeze, germs are scattered about. When sputum, spit on the street, dries, germs are blown away. Some germs travel with a kiss. Through careless disposal of wastes, typhoid fever may enter drinking water. Carriers of diphtheria and typhoid fever, not ill themselves, may carelessly infect other people. Germs are also spread by houseflies, rats, the use of common drinking utensils, towels, and handkerchiefs, and the use of unpasteurized milk.

Safety from germs is ensured by avoiding them, controlling or killing them, and resisting them. We avoid them by keeping away from diseased people, breathing as pure air as can be found, and using only pasteurized milk and other safe foods and drink. We may kill germs by letting direct sunlight enter our rooms, by boiling water or food and sometimes by freezing it, by using germicides and soap. We can control their multiplication by keeping food at a low temperature. If

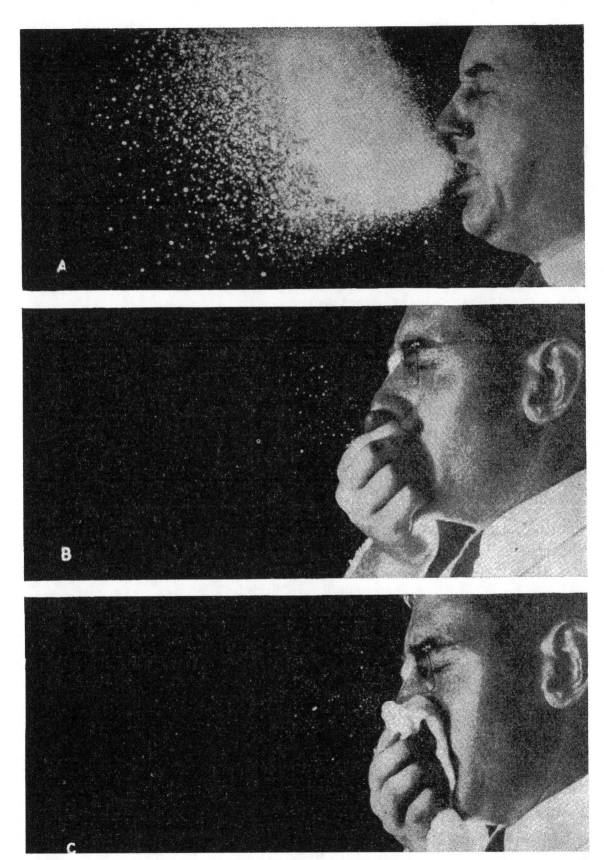

Figure 1—Sneezes Scatter Germs (From Charters et al, "Healthful Ways," Macmillan)

attacked by germs we are better assured of protection if good general health has been maintained through proper food, recreation, rest, and sleep. (NOTE: See Unit 62 for pasteurization of milk.)

Activities

All Grades

Germs hitchhike on drops of saliva, the breath, handkerchiefs, pencils, etc. Make a mural entitled "Little Hitchhikers."

Primary and Junior Grades

Make a frieze to illustrate the following poem.

> Germs that float upon the air
> Are sure to settle everywhere;
> They'll be on pencil and on pen,
> And even on our fingers ten.
> To write our lessons it is true
> We use our hand and pencils too;
> Let's keep them from our lips and tongues,
> So germs won't get into our lungs.
> Of all the doctors in this town,
> Not one can reach such high renown
> As Doctors Sunlight, Rest, Good Food;
> And Doctor Fresh Air, too, is good.
> No medicine these doctors give,
> But they will teach you how to live
> So you will never sickly be,
> But live quite long and happily.
> From *Public Health Rhymes,* Walter S. Groom

Junior and Intermediate Grades

- Place two cups in boiling water for a few minutes; then fill one with raw milk, and the other with pasteurized milk. Cover and leave both in a warm place for a few days. Which milk sours first?
- Place some raw milk in each of two clean bottles. Plug the openings with absorbent cotton. Place one in a warm place, the other in a cold place. Which one sours first? Cold keeps germs from multiplying.
- Read the poem, "Mushroom Song," by Hilda Conkling, from *Nature Activity Readers,* Book IV.

Read

Beauchamp et al., *Discovering Our World,* Book 3 (grades 6-7): "How Do Germs Make You Sick?" pp. 95-119. Gage (Scott, Foresman).

Charters et al., *Habits Healthful and Safe,* Revised (grades 6-7): "Millions of Tiny Enemies," pp. 23-78; and *Healthful Ways,* revised (grades 4-5): "How To Have Fewer Colds," pp. 1-14, and "Safe Milk," pp. 147-149. Macmillan.

Comstock, *Handbook of Nature Study,* pp. 729-731. Allen (Comstock).

Frasier et al., *The How and Why Club* (grades 5-8) : "Why Does Food Spoil?" and "Pasteurized Milk," pp. 148-167. Dent (Singer).

Partridge, *Everyday Science,* Book Two: "Some Ills of Mankind," pp. 338-364. Dent.

Selsam, *Microbes at Work* (grades 7-8): good illustrations and practical experiments. McLeod (Wm. Morrow).

New to this Edition

Berger, Melvin. *Germs Make Me Sick (Let's-Read-and-Find-Out Science 2)* (Collins, 1995).

_____. *Why I Sneeze, Shiver, Hiccup, & Yawn* (Let's-Read-and-Find-Out Science 2) (Collins, 2000).

Manley, Dr. Heather. *Battle with the Bugs: An Imaginative Journey Through the Immune System* (CreateSpace, 2011).

Romanek, Trudee. *Achoo: The Most Interesting Book You'll Ever Read About Germs* (Kids Can Press, 2003)

http://www.hometrainingtools.com/germ-science-projects-for-elementary/a/1467/
http://www.sciencecompany.com/-W155.aspx

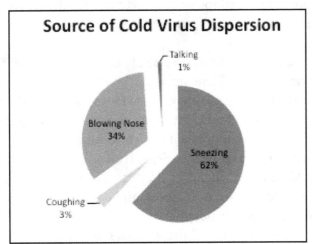

Ref. Buckland, et al 1964

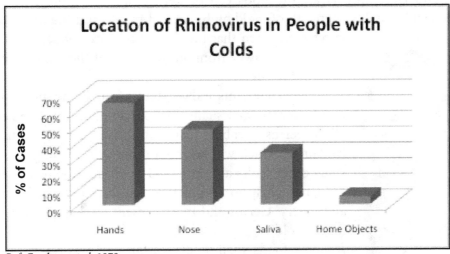

Ref. Gwaltney et al, 1978

Unit 62—What Shall We Eat and Drink?

Pupils of grades 1 to 6 will profit little from formal generalizations or the usual adult classification of foods according to their use. Vitamins can mean little to them. They know that to make a good cake Mother always uses just the right kinds of raw materials in the right quantities. From this it is easy for children to grasp the idea that, to grow, their bodies must have the right foods in the right quantities. Some of these foods are especially good for keeping our bodies warm and active; still other foods play an important part in keeping them in good general health.

Healthful Foods. Foods are needed for body growth and for the repair of worn parts. Children's bodies need large quantities of building foods. These "grow foods" are found in milk, eggs, cheese, leafy vegetables, lean meat.

To be able to enjoy our playtime, we must have plenty of pep and energy. The proper foods will help us to keep up with the other children. Here are some "go" foods: milk, cream, bread, potatoes, peas, beans, meat, fish, eggs, butter, cheese, jam, honey. These foods also help to keep our bodies warm. Fats, however, are best for this. Eskimos, therefore, eat a great deal of the blubber (fat) from seals.

In several foods nature has provided us with a "good-health charm." If we eat these foods, we are more likely to keep in good general health. Fresh fruit and vegetables, foods which provide this good-health charm, should be eaten whenever they can be obtained; otherwise, use canned ones. Other foods useful in the same way are milk, meat, and eggs. To give these foods a fair chance we should play in the sunshine as much as possible.

If our food is to be of full value to us, all three kinds must be present in the right proportion at each meal.

Keeping Food Healthful. Healthful foods can be kept healthful by preventing them from spoiling. Recall with pupils the growth of mold on bread and pastry, and the rotting of fruits and vegetables; teach that molds and rots are robber plants which take nourishment away from our food and at the same time make it less healthful for us.

To keep our fruits and vegetables from being spoiled in these ways we preserve them. Usually this consists of heating them enough to kill all the germs or robber plants on them, then storing them in sealed containers which will keep out other spores and germs. Apples and some other fruits are preserved by drying them. Waxed paper and cellophane help to keep germs and the spores of mold from bread and pastry. Germs and mold present are kept from growing when food is cold.

Some foods spoil by drying out. For this reason we store beets, carrots, and potatoes in a damp cellar.

Notice that milk is in each group of foods mentioned. Milk is our most important food. Therefore the cleanliness or purity of the milk supply of a community must be carefully guarded. Pure milk is one of the best foods; impure milk, one of the worst. How can we be sure it is pure? Use only pasteurized milk. Pasteurizing does not change the food value or the taste of the milk to any extent.

Pasteurization consists of heating milk to a temperature (145 degrees Fahrenheit) high enough to destroy harmful germs, and holding it at that temperature for about half an hour. Then the milk is quickly cooled and bottled. Great care is taken to make sure that the empty bottles are clean and germ-free, and that the full bottles are kept cold and sealed.

Healthful Drinks. Drinks made of fruit juices and drinks made with milk, such as cocoa, eggnogs, and malted milkshakes not only have the materials needed by your body for growth and health, but also have a delicious taste.

Water is essential to the body. It is a food; it dissolves and helps in the digestion of other foods; it makes up a large part of the blood; it carries away body wastes. For these reasons the water supply of a community must be carefully provided for.

Safe Water in Cities. Millions of gallons of water are used in a city each day. This water must be pure and clear. Different cities use different methods of making it safe, i.e., free from harmful germs. Here are some of the ways: treating it with chlorine; filtering it through sand and gravel; storing it in a reservoir. In some cities objectionable odors and tastes are removed from the water by aeration. The water is sprayed into the air where it is exposed to oxygen. Some cities treat the water to make it soft, i.e., to remove minerals.

Safe Water in the Country. The water supply in the country is mainly from wells, springs, and cisterns. The well should be on high ground above buildings and away from animals so that filth and germs cannot run into it. The cover should be tight-fitting.

To purify water coming from a source which is not known to be safe it may be boiled, filtered through charcoal, or distilled (changed to vapor; then back to water).

The School Lunch. Education of the parents concerning school lunches may take place through the children. Observation of the lunches carried to school by your pupils will show you what must be taught about healthful school lunches. In each lunchbox there should be something substantial (sandwiches); something juicy or crisp (orange, tomato, celery, radishes, apple, banana, salad); something sweet (cooked fruit, cookies, candy); something hot (soup, cocoa). The latter may be either carried from home in a thermos or, as is done in some schools, prepared by the home-economics class, supervised by the teacher. The school lunch period should be a happy time of enjoyment and relaxation when the pupils are incidentally and unobtrusively guided in good social behavior as well as in the choice of healthful food and drink.

Activities

All Grades

- Make a survey of the source from which each home in the community obtains its water for drinking and cooking—wells, springs, lakes. Discover what the possibilities are for impurities to enter these sources of water (surface drainage or seepage from manure, sewage, etc.). Is it purified? If so, how? Boil some water to purify it.
- Shake some soil with water and let it settle. The clear water is not necessarily pure. Pour some muddy water through a 2-inch layer of sand supported by a cloth in a strainer. The sand filters out dirt particles, but not all germs.
- Visit a local dairy to watch pasteurization. Write a report, or tell about it in class.
- Make a Mr. Healthy with a milk bottle for a body, a potato for a head, bananas for the arms, carrots for the legs, etc.
- Cover some vegetables with moist sand and leave others of the same kind uncovered, all in a warm classroom for a week. Which ones wilt first? Why?
- Make a poster entitled "It's well to be clean, so be clean to be well."
- List the articles of food and drink which a grocer should have for the children of his locality. Use empty boxes to prepare a model store in your classroom. Use it as a means of learning how to : make change, display foods attractively, prepare posters advertising foods of special value.
- Write a restaurant order for a wholesome breakfast, dinner, and supper.

Junior Grades

- Many of the fresh fruits we eat in winter come from other lands. Which ones are sold in local stores? Why do we need to eat them? Ask the grocer from which country each comes. Find out: what kind of climate is needed by each; how it is grown, harvested, and shipped; the best way to keep it fresh.
- Make up a rhyme such as "An apple a day keeps the doctor away."
- Make a real fruit man with an orange for his head, bananas for his legs, etc.
- Make a picture display of fruits from other lands.
- Write a playlet with fruits as the characters.

Junior and Intermediate Grades

Send a sample of water from your well to the Provincial Department of Health. Ask if it is safe and, if not, how it can be purified.

TEN GOLDEN RULES OF FOOD AND DRINK

1. Eat in moderation and only when hungry.
2. Never take snacks between meals, or your digestion will not have time to do its all-important work.
3. Do not eat and drink at the same time, but make a practice of sipping water freely apart from meals and especially on rising and retiring.
4. Make sure that you have enough body-building and tissue-repairing material. This is contained in meat, fish, poultry, cheese, milk, eggs, beans, peas, and nuts.
5. Remember that fat makes for fitness, not for fatness.
6. Starch may be left to take care of itself. You are certain to get enough and probably too much in bread, potatoes, rice, and other puddings, pastry, cakes, buns, biscuits, sandwiches.
7. Always choose fresh rather than tinned food.
8. Let no day pass without eating some uncooked vegetable or ripe fruit.
9. Honey, dried and raw ripe fruit, should be valued more than sugar, sweets, chocolate, jam, marmalade, or stewed fruit.
10. Children should not have any tea or coffee, but should drink plenty of milk drinks and fruit juices.

ADAPTED FROM THE FOOD EDUCATION SOCIETY, LONDON, ENGLAND.

Read

Beauchamp et al., *Discovering Our World,* Book 1 (grades 4-5), pp. 166-168; *Discovering Our World,* Book 2 (grades 5-6): "Why Do You Need Food?" pp. 177-203; and *Science Problems 1* (grades 7-8): "Why Do You Eat Different Kinds of Food?" pp. 288-325. Gage (Scott, Foresman).

Bibby, *Healthy and Happy* (grades 4-6), pp. 55-79; and *Healthy People* (grades 5-7), pp. 9-13 and "Pure Food," pp. 179-208. Macmillan.

Brownell & Williams, *Hale and Hearty:* "The Foods You Need," pp. 91-128; and *Safe and Sound:* "Know the Food. You Need," pp. 84-138. Gage (American Book Co.).

Charters et al., *All Through the Day* (primary): "Lunch Time," pp. 52-74, 124-128, "Supper Time," pp. 136-151, and "A Good Breakfast," pp. 171-172; *Health and Fun* (workbook; grade 1): units dealing with a healthful breakfast and lunch, and good foods to eat: *Health Through the Year,* revised (grades 2-3): several short stories organized seasonally, presenting basic primary information on food; well illustrated; *Health Secrets,* revised (grades 3-4): "Food and Growth," pp. 73-116; *Healthful Ways,* revised (grades 4-5), "Food Problems," pp. 135-158; and *Let's Be Healthy,* revised (grades 5-6): "Let's Eat," pp. 41-56, "What Foods Are Needed Every Day," pp. 57-86, and "Let's Plan Our Meals," pp 87-104. Macmillan.

Dowling et al., *Explaining Why* (grades 4-5), pp. 132-160; and *Understanding Why* (grades 6-8), pp. 63-68. Winston.

Fisher, *The Wonderful World—the Adventure of the Earth We Live On;* "Man Must Eat," pp. 38-39. Blue Ribbon (Hanover House).

Frasier et al., *Winter Comes and Goes* (grades 3-4): "How To Eat," p. 211; and *The How and Why Club* (grades 5-6): "Foods the Body Needs," pp. 100-113, "Pasteurized Milk," pp. 160-167, and "Three Kinds of Sugar," pp. 222-236 Dent (Singer).

Gruenberg and Adelson, *Your Breakfast and the People Who Made It.* Doubleday.

Haynes, *The True Book of Health* (primary), pp. 16-24. Book Society (Children's Press).

Miner. *The True Book of Plants We Know* (primary): "Plants We Eat," pp. 37-41. Book Society (Children's Press).

Partridge, *General Science,* Intermediate, Book 1: "What Shall We Eat?" pp. 147-165; *General Science,* Intermediate. Book 2: "Milk, the Most Nearly Complete Food," pp. 260-284; *Elementary Science,* Book One: "Our Daily Bread," pp. 137-152; and *Everyday Science,* Book Two: "Milk, the Ideal Food," pp. 402-425. Dent.

Schloat, *Milk for You.* Allen (Scribner).

Scott, *The Milk That Jack Drank* (primary). Allen (Wm. R. Scott).

Food for the Family and *What Foods Do You Choose?,* available from Metropolitan Life Insurance Company.

New to this Edition

Gardner, Robert. *Ace Your Exercise and Nutrition Science Project: Great Science Fair Ideas* (Enslow, 2009).

Rockwell, Lizzy. *Good Enough to Eat: A Kid's Guide to Food and Nutrition* (Collins, 2009).

Scientific Explorer. *Scientific Explorer's Disgusting Science - A Kit for Studying the Science of Revolting Things.*

Van Cleave, Janice. *Janice VanCleave's Food and Nutrition for Every Kid: Easy Activities That Make Learning Science Fun* (Wiley, 1999).

http://www.natureskills.com/survival/water-purification-process/
http://www.sciencemadesimple.com/nutrition_projects.html

Unit 63—How the Body Uses Food

Pupils younger than 11 or 12 years, mental age, have little interest in and no capacity to understand the physiology of digestion, circulation, and breathing. The formal study of these should, therefore, be left until the pupils are older. They can be interested in a simple study of how the food they eat becomes useful to them by being dissolved, absorbed into the bloodstream, distributed throughout the body, and "burned" to produce heat and energy. Study of the structure of the digestive organs, heart, arteries and veins, and lungs should be omitted at this stage.

Getting the Food Ready to Be Distributed to All Parts of the Body. Biting and chewing cuts and grinds the food into small particles and at the same time mixes it with saliva, which dissolves some of the food. To do their work well, the teeth must be sound and must fit together well. To keep them this way, they must be kept clean and free from cavities.

After being swallowed, more of the food is dissolved in the stomach by special digesting liquids. On its long journey through the intestines—more than 20 feet—still more foods is dissolved, and all of the dissolved foods useful to the body are absorbed into the blood, while useless materials pass on to be gotten rid of.

Digestion is helped by regular meal times, fruits and vegetables in the diet, plenty of water, exercise, cheerfulness, and regular elimination.

Distributing Food to All Parts of the Body. The blood is like a stream in which the dissolved food, absorbed from the intestines, moves along. This stream flows through blood tubes to all parts of the body. The muscular heart through which it flows keeps pumping the blood forward; that is why we feel the pulse.

Breathing Makes the Food in the Blood Useful to Us. The food carried by the blood to all parts of the body is something like coal brought to the house. The coal gives us heat when oxygen causes it to burn. The food in the blood must also be "burned" before it can give us any warmth. To burn, it must have oxygen. Breathing supplies the necessary oxygen. While the air breathed in is held in our lungs, some of the oxygen in it passes through the walls of the lungs into blood tubes touching these walls. The blood then carries the oxygen with the food to all parts of the body.

In the bloodstream the food is "burned" by the oxygen, producing body heat and the power to move about. The chief waste product formed, corresponding to ashes and smoke, is carbon dioxide. This the blood carries back to the lungs, which get rid of it when we breathe out.

Activities

Junior and Intermediate Grades

With a knife, scrape several times across the cut surface of a potato, apple, or turnip. The scraping sets the juice free. Chew a piece of apple twenty times. Notice how much liquid forms in your mouth. Part of it is saliva produced to start the digestion of the apple. What formed the rest? Why is thorough chewing important?

Chew some kernels of wheat or some soda biscuit many times. Notice that they become sweeter as you chew. While you chew, the saliva helps to change starch in these foods to sugar—a first step in digestion.

Read

Beauchamp et al., *Science Problem 2* (grades 7-8): "How Is Food Prepared for Use in Your Body?" pp. 303-310. Cage (Scott, Foresman).

Bibby, *Healthy and Happy* (grades 4-6): "What Happens to Our Food," pp. 58-61; and *Healthy People* (grades 5-7), pp. 2-9. Macmillan.

Brownell & Williams, *Hale and Hearty.* "How the Body Uses Its Food," pp. 131-148. Gage (American Book Co.).

Charters et al., *Habits Healthful and Safe,* revised (grades 6-7): "Digesting Our Food," pp. 111-150; and *Let's Be Healthy,* revised (grades 5-6): "What Happens to the Fund We Eat," pp. 105-122. Macmillan.

Frasier et al., *The How and Why Club* (grades 5-6): "How Foods Are Used in the Body," pp. 114-123. Dent (Singer).

Partridge, *General Science,* Intemediate, Book 1 : "What Becomes of Our Food," pp. 171-177. Dent.

New to this Edition

Alton, Steve, *Blood and Goo and Boogers Too: A Heart-pounding Pop-up Guide to the Circulatory & Respiratory Systems* (Dial Pop-up Edition, 2009)

Manley, Dr. Heather. *A Heart Pumping Adventure: An Imaginative Journey Through the Circulatory System* (CreateSpace, 2011).

_____. *The Lucky Escape: An Imaginative Journey Through the Digestive System* (CreateSpace, 2011)

Taylor-Butler, Christine. *The Circulatory System* (Children's Press, 2008)

_____. *The Digestive System* (Children's Press, 2008).

Unit 64—Making Our Environment Healthful

The health of the pupils should be the first concern of the teacher. The healthful state of school surroundings, indoors and out, makes a greater contribution than formal lessons toward maintaining pupil health. Adequate attention to the healthfulness of the pupils' environment at the school motivates them to want a similarly healthful home environment.

Health factors directly under the control of the teach and, through her, of the pupils are chiefly connected with cleanliness and comfort. Cleanliness in every way possible is the first evidence of healthful school surroundings. Clean floors are made possible when pupils use a scraper, mat, and broom at the door, and when all scraps of paper or lunch are carefully kept from falling to the floor. Clean wash basins and plenty of clean water, soap, and paper or individual towels motivate personal cleanliness. Clean toilets, disinfected as needed, are a test of attention to cleanliness. Cleans windows and blackboards, cupboards and desks, and clean clothing contribute to health in the classroom.

The comfort of the pupils rests largely with the teacher. If the answer to each of these questions is yes for your room, the comfort of your pupils is being well provided for. Do the pupils enter a warm, well-ventilated, tidy cloakroom in the morning, and then go to seats of the correct size for their comfort? Are the blinds immediately raised to the top and kept there, except when direct sunlight must be excluded? Are the blinds transluscent, litting in light even when drawn? Are the lights always turned on when there is danger of eye-strain? Are pupils with poor eyesight seated advantageously? Do groups always work in light places? Is the room ventilated by an adequate ventilation system or by opening windows from both top and bottom without causing drafts where pupils sit? Is the room aired at recesses, noon, and during physical activities? Is the air in the room kept at a uniform temperature of about 68 degrees Fahrenheit and moistened in winter by evaporation from pans or kettles on stoves, radiators, or registers?

Freedom from colds and other communicable diseases is more to be desired than favorable attendance records for individual pupils. It is better that pupils with colds should be at home, where they can go to bed, stay there until the cold is better, keep away from others, and drink a great deal of water, than that they should be at school feeling miserable and endangering the health of others. Pupils and parents should be so instructed. Such safeguards of the health of pupils will in the end ensure better attendance.

The teacher can control largely the contributions of the board toward pupil health. She can encourage them to keep the walls clean, and painted in light enough colors to create a cheery atmosphere and to conserve eyesight. Such equipment as basins, towels, indoor toilets, scrapers and mats, adequate lights and blinds, and screens are likely to be provided if the teacher shows definite concern for the health of the pupils. Adequate caretaking services, resulting in a clean room, uniform heating, and well-cared-for grounds tend to follow standards set by the teacher. The ambitious, efficient teacher gets most of what she asks for.

Healthy personalities are as important as healthy bodies. The mental health of the teacher, whether she be depressing or cheerful, dull or with a sense of humor, suspicious or trusting, determines the pupils' mental health. What a privilege to a pupil to attend a school, the atmosphere of which generates brightness and cheerfulness—a school with the teacher tastefully groomed, with the walls and windows made interesting by means of appropriate pictures (some frequently changed) and pleasing plants, and with grounds kept attractive by suitable plantings of lawns, shrubbery, and flowers.

Activities

Teacher

- Use the pupils' consciousness of clean surroundings to motivate personal cleanliness.
- Appoint monitors whose duties will be: caring for the washroom corner—emptying dirty water and supplying clean water, keeping the table tidy, seeing that soap and towels are always supplied, etc.; raising blinds to the top each morning and turning the lights on or off as needed; attending to temperature and ventilation; helping younger children to remove outer clothing and boots and to place these where they will dry; seeing that desks, bulletin boards, etc. are kept tidy; arranging tasteful window decorations.

- See that everyone washes before eating lunch at noon.
- See that pupils engage in wholesome outdoor sports in fine weather, and cheery indoor games in dull weather.
- Plan and tactfully carry out a daily health inspection—hair, hands, nails, teeth, handkerchief, etc.

All Grades

- Search for health stories and bring them to the class for others to read. Make up health limericks.
- Keep toothpicks on hand to clean the fingernails.
- March to music past a mirror labeled "Mirror, mirror on the wall, do you see any dirt at all?" Then answer for the mirror, and act accordingly.

Primary Grades

- Collect pictures of healthy children at play, at work, asleep.
- On a large table, set up a doll's home. Keep it as healthful as possible.

Junior and Intermediate Grades

- Collect pictures to illustrate a poster entitled "Healthful Surroundings."
- Equip an old table or large box with a mirror, and dress it up attractively for a girls' vanity table at school.
- Set up a health camp on a table. Model a cement-covered well, playground equipment, and walks. Construct tents of brown paper, flowerbeds, etc. Place other items to represent cleanliness, sunlight, exercise, healthful foods, pure water.
- Find out what the Medical Officer of Health does to keep the school environment healthful.

Read

Bibby, *A Healthy Day* (grades 2-4): brief conversational readings; *Healthy and Happy* (grades 4-6): short chapters dealing with growing up, keeping clean, food, clothes, happiness, and safety; *Healthy People* (grades 5-7): chapters dealing with a healthy child, a healthy home, a healthy school, and a healthy community. Macmillan.

Bowman & Boston, *Living Safely* (workbook; grades 5-8): presents safety information and exercises in relation to the home, the school building, the farm, fire, playing, and motor vehicles. Macmillan.

Chaters et al., *All through the Day* (primary): "Off to School," "At School," "Lunch Time," "Afternoon in School," "Fun After School," "Supper Time," "Ready for Bed," "Early to Rise," etc.; *Habits Healthful and Safe*, revised (grades 6-7): "A Healthful Home," pp. 81-95, and "Insects That Carry Disease," pp. 95-110; *Health through the Year*, revised (grades 2-3): several short stories organized seasonally to encourage the maintenance of healthful environments; well illustrated; *Health Secrets*, revised (grades 3-4): "A Healthy Day," pp. 1-6; "How to Keep Clean," pp. 17-44; and "Safe and Sane," pp. 175-202; *Let's be Healthy*, revised (grades 5-6): "Keeping Clean," pp. 123-150; "Living Together," pp. 211-232; and "A Happy Worthwhile Vacation," pp. 233-282. Macmillan.

Frasier et al., *Through the Year* (grades 1-2): "Nancy Goes Home," pp. 62-63. Dent (Singer).

Smith & Henderson, *Beneath the Skies* (grade 6): "Living in a Healthful Community," pp. 53-78. Longmans, Green.

New to this Edition

O'Brien-Palmer, Michelle. *Healthy Me: Fun Ways to Develop Good Health* (Chicago Review Press, 1999).

Gale, Karen Buhler. *The Kids' Guide to First Aid: All about Bruises, Burns, Stings, Sprains & Other Ouches* (Williamson Publishing Company, 2001).

BEAUTIFY YOUR SURROUNDINGS ~ FEBRUARY

GROUNDHOG section

NOW IS A GOOD TIME TO PREPARE A CHART OR A MURAL SHOWING SOME OF THE HABITS OF THE **GROUNDHOG.**

WHAT HARM MIGHT HE DO IN THE FIELDS?

THE GROUNDHOG IS A WINTER SLEEPER AND IS NOT LIKELY TO APPEAR ON FEBRUARY 2.

THE DIP IN HIS TUNNEL KEEPS HIS BEDROOM DRY.

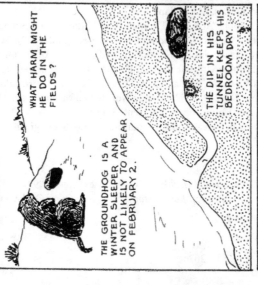

IN A NEAT BOOKLET, MAKE A COLLECTION OF WINTER POEMS.

WINTER POEMS COLLECTED

Birds section

HERRING GULL

GOLDFINCH

BLUEJAY

MAKE A COLLECTION OF PICTURES OF SOME OF OUR MORE COMMON WINTER BIRDS.

SOAP CARVING

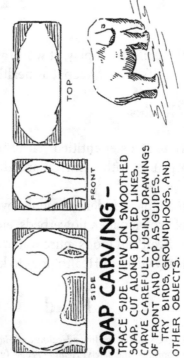

TOP

FRONT

SIDE

SOAP CARVING –

TRACE SIDE VIEW ON SMOOTHED SOAP. CUT ALONG DOTTED LINES. CARVE CAREFULLY, USING DRAWINGS OF FRONT AND TOP AS GUIDES. TRY BIRDS, GROUNDHOGS, AND OTHER OBJECTS.

IN MAKING SLENDER PLASTICINE MODELS, USE "FORMERS" OF FIRM BUT FLEXIBLE WIRE.

TREES section

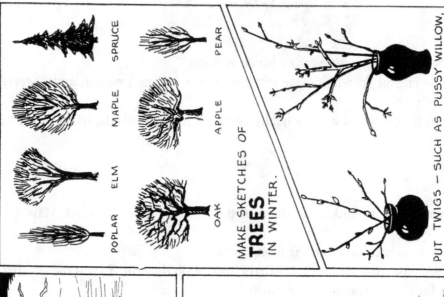

SPRUCE

PEAR

MAPLE

APPLE

POPLAR

ELM

OAK

MAKE SKETCHES OF **TREES** IN WINTER.

PUT TWIGS – SUCH AS PUSSY WILLOW, CHESTNUT, AND MAPLE – IN WATER. WATCH FOR THE TINY LEAVES.

BORDER SUGGESTIONS

D. FARWELL.

BORDER SUGGESTIONS

Science in Action — February

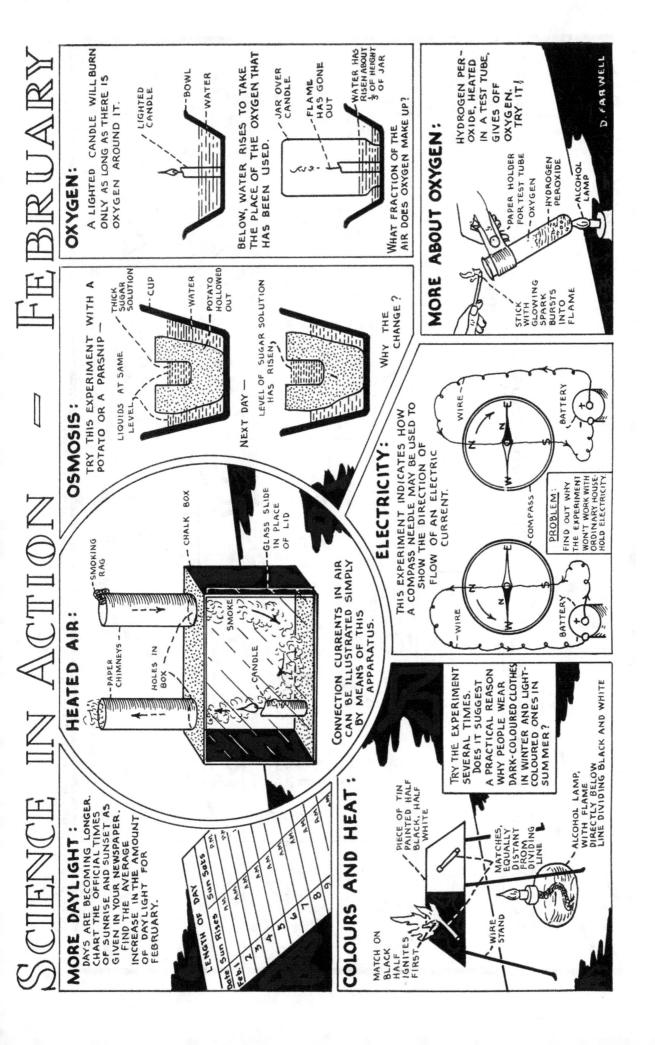

OXYGEN:

A LIGHTED CANDLE WILL BURN ONLY AS LONG AS THERE IS OXYGEN AROUND IT.

LIGHTED CANDLE
BOWL
WATER

BELOW, WATER RISES TO TAKE THE PLACE OF THE OXYGEN THAT HAS BEEN USED.

JAR OVER CANDLE
FLAME HAS GONE OUT
WATER HAS RISEN ABOUT ⅕ OF HEIGHT OF JAR

WHAT FRACTION OF THE AIR DOES OXYGEN MAKE UP?

MORE ABOUT OXYGEN:

HYDROGEN PEROXIDE, HEATED IN A TEST TUBE, GIVES OFF OXYGEN. TRY IT!

PAPER HOLDER FOR TEST TUBE
OXYGEN
HYDROGEN PEROXIDE
ALCOHOL LAMP

STICK WITH GLOWING SPARK BURSTS INTO FLAME

D. FARWELL

OSMOSIS:

TRY THIS EXPERIMENT WITH A POTATO OR A PARSNIP —

THICK SUGAR SOLUTION
CUP
WATER
POTATO HOLLOWED OUT

LIQUIDS AT SAME LEVEL

NEXT DAY —

LEVEL OF SUGAR SOLUTION HAS RISEN.

WHY THE CHANGE?

HEATED AIR:

SMOKING RAG
CHALK BOX
GLASS SLIDE IN PLACE OF LID
PAPER CHIMNEYS
HOLES IN BOX
SMOKE
CANDLE

CONVECTION CURRENTS IN AIR CAN BE ILLUSTRATED SIMPLY BY MEANS OF THIS APPARATUS.

ELECTRICITY:

THIS EXPERIMENT INDICATES HOW A COMPASS NEEDLE MAY BE USED TO SHOW THE DIRECTION OF FLOW OF AN ELECTRIC CURRENT.

WIRE
BATTERY
COMPASS
WIRE
BATTERY

PROBLEM: FIND OUT WHY THE EXPERIMENT WON'T WORK WITH ORDINARY HOUSEHOLD ELECTRICITY.

MORE DAYLIGHT:

DAYS ARE BECOMING LONGER. CHART THE OFFICIAL TIMES OF SUNRISE AND SUNSET AS GIVEN IN YOUR NEWSPAPER. FIND THE AVERAGE INCREASE IN THE AMOUNT OF DAYLIGHT FOR FEBRUARY.

LENGTH OF DAY

Date	Sun Rises	Sun Sets
Feb. 1		P.M.
2		P.M.
3	A.M.	P.M.
4	A.M.	P.M.
5	A.M.	P.M.
6	A.M.	P.M.
7	A.M.	P.M.
8	A.M.	P.M.
9	A.M.	P.M.

COLOURS AND HEAT:

MATCH ON BLACK HALF IGNITES FIRST

PIECE OF TIN PAINTED HALF BLACK, HALF WHITE

MATCHES, EQUALLY DISTANT FROM DIVIDING LINE

WIRE STAND

ALCOHOL LAMP, WITH FLAME DIRECTLY BELOW LINE DIVIDING BLACK AND WHITE

TRY THE EXPERIMENT SEVERAL TIMES. DOES IT SUGGEST A PRACTICAL REASON WHY PEOPLE WEAR DARK-COLOURED CLOTHES IN WINTER AND LIGHT-COLOURED ONES IN SUMMER?

NATURAL SCIENCE — MARCH — DAY BY DAY

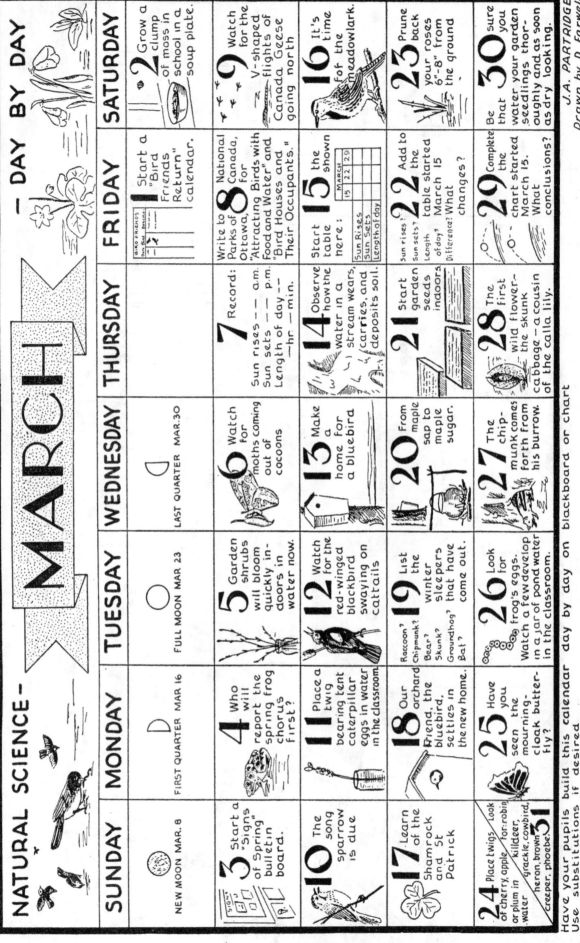

SUNDAY	MONDAY	TUESDAY	WEDNESDAY	THURSDAY	FRIDAY	SATURDAY
NEW MOON MAR. 8	FIRST QUARTER MAR. 16	FULL MOON MAR 23	LAST QUARTER MAR. 30		**1** Start a "Bird Friends Return" calendar.	**2** Grow a clump of moss in school in a soup plate.
3 Start a "Signs" of Spring bulletin board.	**4** Who will report the spring frog chorus first?	**5** Garden shrubs will bloom quickly indoors in water now.	**6** Watch for moths coming out of cocoons	**7** Record: Sun rises — a.m. Sun sets — p.m. Length of day — hr. — min.	**8** Write to National Parks of Ottawa, Canada, for "Attracting Birds with Food and Water" and "Bird Houses and Their Occupants."	**9** Watch for the V-shaped flights of Canada Geese going north
10 The song sparrow is due	**11** Place a twig bearing tent caterpillar eggs in water in the classroom.	**12** Watch for the red-winged blackbird swaying on cattails	**13** Make a home for a bluebird	**14** Observe how the water in a stream wears, carries, and deposits soil.	**15** Start the shown table here: MARCH 15 22 29 / Sun Rises / Sun Sets / Length of day	**16** It's time for the meadowlark.
17 Learn of the Shamrock and St Patrick	**18** Our orchard friend, the bluebird, settles in the new home.	**19** List the winter sleepers that have come out. Raccoon? Chipmunk? Bear? Skunk? Groundhog? Bat?	**20** From maple sap to maple sugar.	**21** Start garden seeds indoors	**22** Add to the table started March 15 What changes? Sun rises? Sun sets? Length of day? Difference?	**23** Prune back your roses 6"-8" from the ground
24 Place twigs of cherry, apple or plum in water	**25** Have you seen the mourning-cloak butterfly?	**26** Look for frog's eggs. Watch a few develop in a jar of pond water in the classroom.	**27** The chipmunk comes forth from his burrow.	**28** The first wild flower— the skunk cabbage — a cousin of the calla lily.	**29** Complete the chart started March 15. What conclusions?	**30** Be sure that you water your garden seedlings thoroughly and as soon as dry looking.
31 Look for: robin, killdeer, grackle, cowbird, heron, brown creeper, phoebe.						

Have your pupils build this calendar day by day on blackboard or chart
Use substitutions if desired

J.A. PARTRIDGE
Drawn by D Farwell

MARCH

Unit 65—Finding Out Why Some Things Change

We live in a world of change—change of shape, change of state, change of position, change of temperature. All about them, children see these changes and ask, "Why?" Opportunities to teach worthwhile principles of science are constantly coming to teachers when pupils experience such phenomena as are mentioned below and are curious enough to seek an explanation. Many satisfactory explanations will come to them through their own experimentation rather than through verbal answering of questions or oral teaching of lessons.

Here are some typical everyday incidents, and their explanations: Ice cubes left in a bowl on the kitchen table could not be found an hour later (ice melts when heated); at 7:00 p.m. the moon was in one position, at 8:00 p.m., in another (the earth rotates); a glass of water tipped over, spilling the water (water runs downhill due to gravity); milk was found heaped up above the bottle one cold morning (liquids expand as they freeze); when an electric iron is disconnected, it becomes cooler (hot objects radiate heat).

The activities in this unit should serve four purposes. They should enable pupils to discover some interesting facts about the forces of nature. They should satisfy many of the pupils' curiosities. They should train them in accurate experimentation. They should motivate them to think up and try new experiments for themselves. To accomplish these objectives, teachers should have a wealth of materials always convenient for pupils to use.

Activities

Primary Grades

- Rub your hands together. They become warm. Rub one hand on the desk. Did it get warm? With the other hand feel if the desk became warm.
- Put a board, a stone, an egg, a piece of coal, a piece of iron, etc. on water. What happens to each? Water pushes upward with enough force to hold up some, but not others. Water holds us up when we swim.
- With a magnet, pick up some pins, tacks, and nails. What can a magnet do that an ordinary piece of iron cannot? Mix some pins with some sand or sawdust. Pull them out with a magnet. Will the magnet lift paper or wood?
- Light a candle; blow on it. What makes the flame move? Blow harder. What happens to the flame? Light two candles. Put a small glass jar over one and a large glass jar over the other. Just as we need air to breathe, a candle needs air to burn. Why did the candle in the little jar go out first?

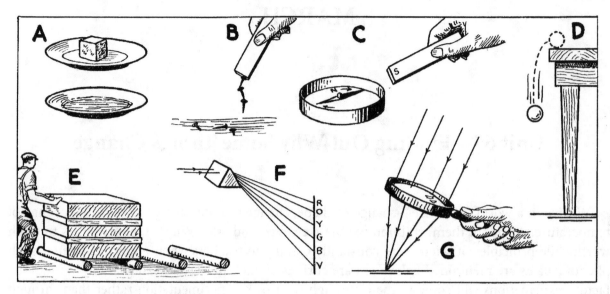

Figure 1—Watching Things Change

A, heat melting ice; B, magnet lifting tacks; C, magnet turning compass needle; D, gravity pulling object; E, rollers moving weight; F, prism changing white light to spectrum colors; G, lens drawing light rays to a point.

- Slide a heavy box on the floor. Then put a pencil under the box and roll it along. Wheels or rollers make things move more easily than when they are dragged.
- Spin a top or a wheel. Hold your finger against it to make it stop. This is like putting the brakes on a car.

Junior and Intermediate Grades

- What makes a windmill turn? An automobile run? A book fall? Nothing moves unless pulled or pushed by a force. Gravity is the force that makes the book fall. Wind and gasoline produce force. Give other illustrations of things being moved by force.
- Move a mirror back and forth in sunlight. Watch the reflection on the wall. How does the light get there? What makes it move?
- Lay a magnet on a table. Cover it with paper, and sprinkle some iron filings on the paper. Examine the pattern caused by the magnet.
- Bring a compass to school. Find out which direction is north from the school. Bring one end of a magnet near the compass. What happens? Try the other end. The compass needle points north and south because the earth is like a big magnet with one end near the North Pole.
- Magnetize the blade of a knife or a needle by stroking it in the same direction several times with the same end of a magnet. How do you know the knife becomes a magnet?
- Why do things fall when left unsupported—a ball, a leaf, a book? Why does a sleigh or a car gain speed going downhill? The earth pulls everything toward it. This pull is called gravity. This makes apples or raindrops fall, iron sink in water. Were it not for gravity, everything would stay where we put it. We could stand on air and place books wherever we liked beside us.
- Why do some things, but not others, float on water? Gravity pulls everything downward; but water lifts everything in it upward. Which will win: the downward pull of gravity or the

upward push of water? It will depend upon how heavy the substance is.

- Drop several objects into a vessel of cold water. Which ones sink? Which ones float? Which of the floating objects have the larger proportion above water? Why?

Intermediate Grades

- Comb your hair several times. Bring the comb near your hair again. It is electricity which makes the hair rise.
- Rub the leather sole of your shoe several times on a rug. Then touch another person with your finger. The spark is electricity, less than in a flash of lightning, but somewhat like it.
- Hold a prism or a piece of glass with a beveled edge in sunlight. Catch the rainbow colors on a piece of paper. The glass changed white light into the seven colors.
- Hold a reading glass in sunlight a little way away from your hand. The glass, thicker at the center than at the edge, made the rays of light and of heat bend and come to one point, causing that place to become hot.
- Hold a stick, a straw, and a piece of wire in hot water. What change can you feel? When heat travels through an object, we say it is conducted, and we call the object a conductor of heat. Which substance was the best conductor of heat? Nearly fill a test-tube with water. While holding it with your hand at the bottom, heat the top part in a flame until it boils. Does water conduct heat?
- Why do we slip on ice? When you step on it, the pressure melts a little of the ice. The water between your shoe and the ice makes you slip just as you slip in a wet bathtub. Then the water freezes behind you.
- Try to find an answer to these questions: Why do your hands become hot when you slide down a rope? What change in temperature takes place when you hammer a coin? Why do sidewalks heave in winter? Why does water put out a fire? Why can you water a plant from a saucer? What makes a candle melt? What becomes of the water when clothes dry?

Read

Beauchamp et al., *Discovering Our World,* Book 1 (grades 4-5) : "What Can Magnets Do?" pp. 139-155; *Discovering Our World,* Book 2 (grades 5-6): "What Makes Things Move?" pp. 45-69; "How Is Our Work Made Easier?" pp. 71-101; and "How Do Heating and Cooling Change Materials?" pp. 103-13; *Science Problems 1* (grades 7-8): "How Do Heating and Cooling Change Materials?" pp. 104-141. Gage (Scott, Foresman).

Craig & Lembach, *Science Everywhere* (grades 4-5), pp. 46-63. Ginn.

Frasier et al., *Through the Year* (grades 1-2): "A New Toy," pp. 96-98; *Winter Comes and Goes* (grades 2-3): "Christmas Toys," pp. 86-91; *The How and Why Club* (grades 5-8): "The Compass" and "How Electricity Works," pp. 272-293; *How and Why Experiment,* (grades V5-8): "Why Some Things Burn," pp. 192-212. Dent (Singer).

Knight, *The Golden Nature Readers,* Book Two (grades 4-6): "Finding Things That Have Disappeared," pp. 91-97. Clarke, Irwin (University of London Press).

Parker, *Gravity,* The Basic Science Education Series. Copp Clark (Row, Peterson).

Schneider, *Let's Find Out, Now Try This,* and *More Power to You.* Allen (Wm. R. Scott).

Smith & Clarke, *Under the Sun* (primary): "Tom and Sue Have Fun with Magnets," pp 116-130. Longmans, Green.

Smith & Henderson, *Across the Land* (grades 4-5): "Experimenting with Electricity," pp. 79-98; and *Through the Seasons* (grades 5-6): "Doing Some Chemistry Experiments," pp. 35-62. Longmans, Green.

New to this Edition

Bradley, Kimberly Brubaker. *Energy Makes Things Happen (Let's-Read-and-Find-Out Science 2)* (Collins, 2002).
_____. *Forces Make Things Move (Let's-Read-and-Find-Out Science 2)* (Collins, 2005.
Branley, Franklyn M. *What Makes a Magnet? (Let's-Read-and-Find-Out Science 2)* (Collins, 1996).

Graham, John. *Forces and Motion (Hands-On Science)* (Kingfisher, 2001).

Kamkwamba, William. *The Boy Who Harnessed the Wind: Young Reader's Edition* (Dial, 2012). (There is an adult book with this same topic as well, perhaps for high school readers.)

Lafferty, Peter. *Forces and Motion (Eyewitness Series)* (DK Children, 1992).

Livingston, James D. *Driving Force: The Natural Magic of Magnets* (Harvard University Press, 1997).

Van Cleave, Janice. *Janice VanCleave's Energy for Every Kid: Easy Activities That Make Learning Science Fun* (Wiley, 2005).

http://topscience.org/ (Lots of different activity/experiment books on motion)

*Figure 2—"**Riding the Plasma Wave:** A cloud forms as this F/A-18 Hornet aircraft speeds up to supersonic speed. Aircraft flying this fast push air up to the very limits of its speed, forming what's called a bow shock in front of them.*

This material that pervades the universe, making up the stars and our sun, and also — far less densely, of course — the vast interstellar spaces in between, is called plasma. Plasmas are similar to gases, and indeed are made of familiar stuff such as hydrogen, helium, and even heavier elements like iron, but each particle carries electrical charge and the particles tend to move together as they do in a fluid. Understanding the way the plasma moves under the combined laws of motion we know on Earth and the less intuitive (to most Earthlings, at least) electromagnetic forces, lies at the heart of understanding the events that spur giant explosions on the sun as well as changes in Earth's own magnetic environment — the magnetosphere."

Source: Nasa Goddard Space Center http://www.flickr.com/photos/gsfc/7597788246/

Unit 66—Living Things Work Together

Orderliness is the first law of nature. All living and nonliving things seem to have their place on the earth and work together for the general good. Soil, water, and air make green plants possible. Green plants alone can use these substances to make the food of all plants and animals. Other plants without green color, and all animals, feed upon the green plants or what they make.

All animals depend upon plants both for food and oxygen. Cows, sheep, and horses eat the green parts of many plants; bees take the nectar and pollen of flowers; many other insects take plant foliage and juices. Dogs, foxes, and wolves eat animal food—and we eat the meat of animals. But the groundhogs eaten by dogs, the birds eaten by foxes, and the sheep eaten by us feed upon grass, clover, and other plant foods. Though large fish eat smaller ones or other water animals, these in turn eat plants in the water. All living animals, too, breathe in the oxygen given off by green plants.

Animals, in turn, contribute much to plant life. Bees, by carrying pollen, help flowers to produce their fruits and seeds; then other animals distribute the seeds where they may grow better. Birds, bats, and skunks help to protect trees and other plants from the ravages of injurious insects. The animals in an aquarium or pond breathe out the carbon dioxide which the plants there must have as food. Earthworms and other ground animals cultivate, aerate, and enrich the soil, making it more useful to plants. Some tiny animals even become the food of special plants such as the pitcher plant.

Man, too, works with plants and other animals. He cuts forests and drains swamps to grow grain and other useful plants. In so doing, he causes floods in spring and dried-up wells and springs in summer, and robs the friendly birds of protection and nesting-places. His new crops attract the injurious grasshoppers, apple worms, and potato beetles, which do not live in forests. Later he finds that he must not only plant new forests, but he must also attract the birds by means of homes, food, and protection so that they may rid his fields of insects. By over-cropping, man robs the soil of its fertility, then finds that he must replace it by adding chemicals to it.

Man has worked with nature largely to make it serve his interests. He uses plants for food, shelter, clothing; and animals as servants, and as sources of food and clothing. Both add to his enjoyment. To make them more valuable, he has domesticated wild plants and animals, given them cultivation and protection, and improved them so that they fulfill his needs better. He has tried to control or eradicate the animals and harmful plants (weeds and poisonous plants), the fungi and insects which attack his crops, and the microscopic forms which cause disease.

Food for Thought

Pussy willows and bees work together. The bees use the nectar and pollen from the willow catkins to make honey and "bee bread." At the same time, they pollinate the willow flowers. In this fair exchange there is no robbery.

Cats eat the birds which eat the worms which eat the leaves which make their food from soil, water, and air.

Tommy is wearing a coat which is made of the wool—(complete this).

Birds and trees are partners. In what ways?

Activities

Primary Grades

- Visit a grocery store (or market) and list the foods which come from plants. Make a list of roots, stems, and leaves which we eat. Talk about the things eaten by your pets, and tell whether these things come from plants or animals.
- Collect pictures of animals that give us food, animals that give us clothing, and animals that work for us.

Junior and Intermediate Grades

- Help all nature around about you by planting trees, vines, and shrubs in gullies and along fence rows; they will prevent soil from being washed away, and will provide homes for birds and other useful animals.
- In what respect is it true that you are eating grass when you drink milk, wheat when you eat eggs, and other grains when you eat pork?
- Make a chart of pieces of cloth or fur, showing from what plant or animal each is obtained or made. Collect and mount pieces of wool in all stages from the time it was cut from the sheep until it became a woolen sweater.
- Collect pictures, make diagrams, and write stories to make up a booklet entitled "Wheat—from a Western Farm to an Eastern Breakfast."
- In a vertical column, make a list of plants and animals which help man, and after each state how. Make a similar list of plants and animals which hinder man.

Read

Andrews, *Adventures in Science,* Book VI (grades 6-7), pp. 7-21. Moyer.

Beauchamp et al., *Discovering Our World,* Book 2 (grades 5-6): "How Do Living Things Help and Harm Each Other?" pp. 11-43; also *Science Problems 1* (grades 7-8): "How Do Living Things Depend on Each Other?" pp. 326-367. Gage (Scott, Foresman).

Blough, *Useful Plants and Animals* (grades 2-3), The Basic Science Education Series. Copp Clark (Row, Peterson).

Craig & Hill, *Adventuring in Science* (grades 6-7): "We Live and Work Together," pp. 254-276. Ginn.

Cunningham, *Man's Use of Plants and Animals* (grades 4-6), The Basic Science Education Series. Copp Clark (Row, Peterson).

Frasier et al., *The How and Why Club* (grades 5-8): "Plants Depend Upon Animals," "Animals Depend Upon Plants," and "The Balance of Nature," pp. 73-91. Dent (Singer).

Huntington, *Let's Go to the Desert.* Doubleday.

Melrose & Kambly, *Plants and Animals Live Together* (grades 5-7): one of a set of four conservation booklets listed in Unit 99. National Wildlife Federation.

Parker, *Plant and Animal Partnership* (grades 4-6) and *Balance in Nature,* The Basic Science Education Series. Copp Clark (Row, Peterson).

Partridge, *General Science,* Intermediate, Book 2: "The Web of Life," pp. 131-146. Dent

Webb, *Song of the Seasons* (grades 4-6). McLeod (Wm. Morrow).

New to this Edition

Collards, Sneed. *Many Biomes, One Earth* (Charlesbridge, 2009).

Kalman, Bobbie. *What Are Food Chains and Webs?* (Crabtree Publishing Company, 1998).

_____. *What Is a Biome?* (Crabtree Publishing Company, 1997).

Latham, Donna. *Amazing Biome Projects You Can Build Yourself* (Nomad, 2009).

Lauber, Patricia. *Who Eats What? Food Chains and Food Webs (Let's-Read-and-Find-Out Science, Stage 2)* (Collins, 1994).

Slade, Suzanne Buckingham. *What if There Were No Bees?: A Book about the Grassland Ecosystem* (Picture Window Books, 2010).

http://www.proteacher.org/c/491_Food_Chain.html

http://www.superteacherideas.com/science6-foodchains.html

Unit 67—The Days Are Getting Longer

This unit deals with the causes of day and night, the changing position of sunrise and sunset from season to season, the changes in the length of day and night (but not the cause), and the course of the sun through the heavens during the day.

Primary pupils know that the sun shines by day and not by night, that it rises and sets, but they do not ask why. They know that they have to go to bed at a set time by the clock, that at one season this is before dark, and at another season, after dark. Even if they are conscious that days are longer in summer than in winter, they do not question "why." These pupils will profit from informal conversations concerning what we do by day and by night. As pupils pass through the junior and intermediate grades, new experiences and increasing mental capacity cause them to ask why the days grow longer as spring approaches. The answer to this question must vary with their development. Junior pupils can understand to some extent that the earth rotates and causes day and night—a simple demonstration will help. Intermediate pupils can observe that the sun rises and sets farther toward the north in summer than in winter. It is easy for them to be shown that as a result the sun travels farther around on a summer day than on a winter day, and takes longer to do it. But it would be futile to attempt to show that the earth's revolution or the direction of its axis are connected with this. What cannot yet be conceived must not yet be taught.

Activities

Junior and Intermediate Grades

Insert a knitting-needle through an orange. In a darkened corner or room, direct light from a flashlight to the side of the orange. How much of the orange is lighted at once? Similarly the sun can light only half the earth at once, giving that half day. Attach a Plasticine man to the side of the orange. Turn the orange. During what part of the man's journey once around does he receive light from the flashlight? The earth, like the orange, turns round, but on an imaginary axis extending from the North Pole to the South Pole. It takes the earth a day to do it. The half toward the sun has day, while the half away from it has night. You will learn in a later grade *why* day and night are not always equal.

Sunrise, Sunset, and Length of Day. The time of sunrise and sunset determines the length of day. When day and night are equal (March 21 and September 21), the sun rises in the east and sets in the west. When the days are longer than the nights (March 21 to September 21),

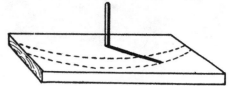

Figure 1—A Modified Shadow Stick

the sun rises to the north of east and sets to the north of west. When the days are shorter than the nights (September 21 to March 21), the sun rises to the south of east and sets to the south of west. The distance the sun has to travel on its apparent path is directly related to the length of day.

Activities

All Grades

In the schoolyard make a 15-yard circle. In the center mark off a home circle large enough to hold all pupils. On the E., SE., S., SW., and W. parts of the large circle make other smaller circles. Divide the class into two groups. Place all in the center. The leader calls "sunset," "sun highest," "sun hottest," "3:00 p.m.," etc. All run to the proper circle. The last to arrive is out. The team first having five out loses.

Primary and Junior Grades

To demonstrate the motion of the sun from morning until night, have the pupils stand, face south, point with the left hand to the position of the rising sun, slowly lift the left arm as if pointing to the sun as it moves southward and westward, halt at the noon position, then change to the right arm, move it onward and downward to the position of sunset.

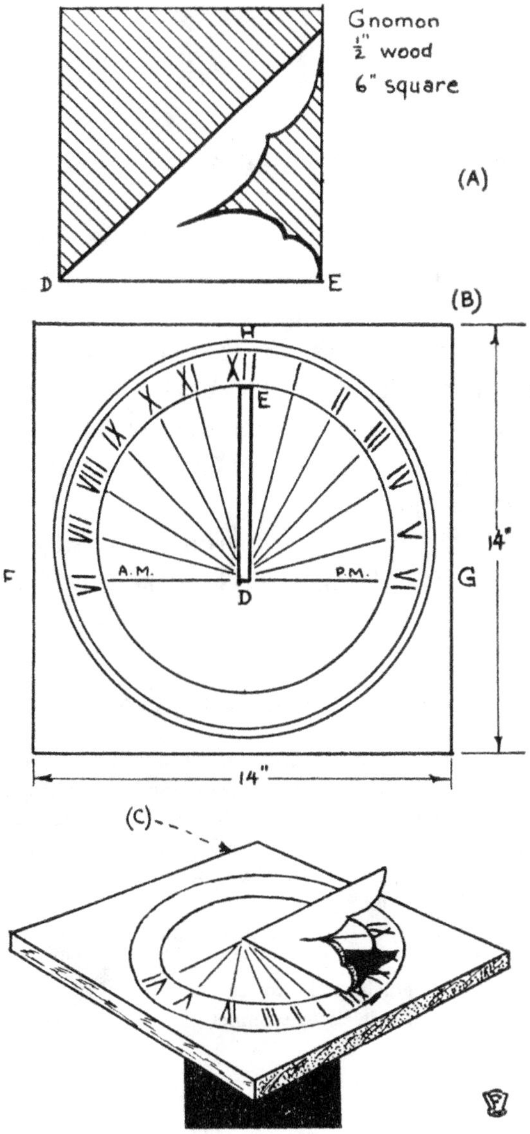

Junior and Intermediate Grades

In September (Unit 10, page 41) you began a calendar which showed you that the days were getting shorter until December 21. If you continued the chart, you discovered that they became longer after that date. How are they changing now?

Figure 2—How to Make a Sundial

Prepare the gnomon (A) with the angle D the same as the local latitude. The dial B may be made of ½" lumber with circles as shown. Set the gnomon DE inside the inner circle with D beyond the center. Label 6 a.m. and 6 p.m. due west and due east from D. Mount the dial as in (C) with the gnomon pointing due north. Paint all parts, the figures in black. (see also Comstock, Handbook of Nature Study).

On a large circle on the floor or a table draw an east-west diameter in the correct direction. Once a week mark on this circle the position of sunrise and of sunset. Show that the farther north the sun rises and sets, the longer the day.

Telling Time by the Sun. From ancient times, the sun has been used to tell time. It is always noon when it is directly south, 6:00 a.m. when it is directly east, and 6:00 p.m. when it is directly west.

Activities

Junior and Intermediate Grades

Make a modified form of a shadow stick as in fig. 1. Cut the board about 18 inches by 14 inches. Erect a 4-inch stick in the center of one side. Cover the board with paper for records. Place the board in a south window with the long edge east-west, and the stick toward the south. At each hour of the day make a dot at the end of the shadow, and record the time there. At night draw a curved line to join the points. Discuss the shortening of the shadow from morning to noon, and its lengthening from noon to night. Review the apparent path of the sun across the sky by using a flashlight as described in fig. 3, Unit 68). Repeat all of the above monthly to obtain different curves as the sun reaches higher angles.

Modify the above experiment by using a stake in the school ground.

Some pupils may wish to make a sundial as described in fig. 2.

Read

Beauchamp et al., *Discovering Our World*, Book 1 (grades 4-5): "Why Do We Have Days and Nights?" pp. 91-111. Gage (Scott, Foreiman).

Dowling et al., *I Wonder Why* (primary). Winston.

Frasier et al., *The Seasons Pass* (grades 3-5): "Day and Night," pp. 156-160. Dent (Singer).

Partridge, *General Science*, Intermediate, Book 2: "The Sun Causes the Seasons and the Changing Lengths of Day," pp. 303-314; also *Everyday Science*, Book Two, pp. 429-435. Dent.

New to this Edition

Anno, Mitsumasa. *Anno's Sundial* (Philomel, Pop Edition, 1987). (Out of print, but well worth the find.)

http://www.sundials.co.uk/projects.htm

http://www.skyandtelescope.com/letsgo/familyfun/Make_Your_Own_Sundial.html

Unit 68—The Sun Is Higher; the Snow Is Melting

The melting of the snow in spring is one of the most obvious evidences that we are receiving more warmth from the sun. A number of observations may be made by pupils as a result of definite assignments to lead up to the fact that it is the gradual increase in the elevation of the sun at noon that causes it to melt the snow and hasten the coming of spring.

Some directing assignments for this purpose follow: On which side of a roof, the north or south, does the snow melt first? Which side faces the sun more directly? On which kind of hill on the highway does the snow melt first, one sloping toward the south, or one sloping toward the north? Which hill faces into the sun? Observe the snowbanks on each side of an east-west road. Which becomes honeycombed first by the melting of the snow? When snow appears very dirty, it is often because much of the snow has melted and the dirt from it has been left. On which side of the road, north or south, does the snow appear the dirtier? Which snowbank faces the sun more directly? Place two books on the window ledge of a south window, one lying flat, the other sloping to face the sun. Which becomes the warmer?

At noon have pupils stand, face south, and point with outstretched arm to the sun. Have them notice how sloping their arms are. Have them from memory point to the position of the sun at noon in January, in July. Discuss at which time we receive the most heat from the sun. It will be evident that it is when the sun is highest in the sky. The following activities will help to demonstrate this fact.

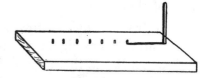

Figure 1—A Shadow Stick

Obtain a smooth board about 4" by 14". In the middle, about 2" from one end, insert a pencil or nail about 3" high.

Activities

Junior and Intermediate Grades

- See how high the sun is in the sky each day at noon. Always stand in the same place and judge its height by its apparent distance above a tree or building. The higher the sun is in the sky, the more heat we receive from it. Why, then, are the days getting warmer at this time of year?

- Make a shadow stick to measure and record the length of midday shadows. Attach this in a south window, the stick next the glass. Mark around the board, so that it can be replaced if moved. Make a line of small holes into which a match peg may be inserted, as shown in the figure, to represent the end of the shadow at any time. Or cover the board with a paper, fastened down with thumbtacks. A foot-rule may be attached from which to read shadow lengths. Mark or measure the end of the shadow at 12 noon weekly, and record the date for each reading. Continue the weekly observations for several months to show the constantly decreasing shadow lengths until June 21, as the sun reaches higher points at noon. These records show that the sun is higher at noon day by day (shown by shorter shadow) as the temperature increases.

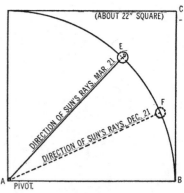

Figure 2—A Method of Recording the Height of the Sun at Noon

- Tack a large card, edgewise, in a north-south direction in a south window. At noon, while looking through colored glass, line up a ruler with the lower, inner corner of the card, and with the sun. Draw a line on the card from the corner along the edge of the ruler. On this line write the date. Repeat this once a week. Notice that the sun is higher in the sky at noon as the days become warmer.

- Mark the end of the shadow of a tree at 9 a.m., 12 noon, and 3 p.m. Compare the lengths of the shadows and account for the differences. Keep a record of the length of the shadow at noon, at weekly intervals, for 6 successive weeks. How does the length of the shadow change? Why?

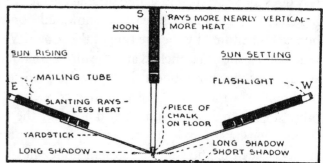

Figure 3—The Higher the Sun, the More Heat We Receive from It.

- Attach a flashlight to the end of a yardstick, pointing toward the center. Rest the other end of the yardstick on the floor beside a vertical piece of chalk (representing a man on the earth). The light represents the sun. Carry the flashlight from the position of sunrise to that of sunset. Observe the changing brightness of the lighted spot and the changing lengths of shadow cast by the chalk man. Discuss how the heating effect of the sun changes from morning until night, showing that more heat comes from the sun when it is more nearly overhead. Leave the explanation for senior grades.

Read

Hethershaw & Baker, *Wonders to See*, pp. 146-160. Gage (World Book).

New to this Edition

Branley, Franklyn. Sunshine Makes the Seasons (reillustrated) (Let's-Read-and-Find-Out Science 2) (Collins, 2005).
Caduto, Michael. Catch the Wind, Harness the Sun: 22 Super-Charged Projects for Kids (Storey, 2011).

http://www.netplaces.com/kids-science-experiments/the-planet-earth/try-this-seasons-in-the-sun.htm

Courtesy Better Homes and Gardens Magazine

Unit 69—The Sun—an Enterprise

The sun affects our lives in so many ways that it forms a natural topic for enterprise study. It is so easily related to the interests of pupils of all ages that the enterprise is suitable for both urban and rural schools. The number and choice of subtopics and activities will vary greatly with the age and number of the pupils, the time taken for the enterprise, and the local facilities. It must be kept in mind that a true enterprise cannot be ready-made or copied; the outline below, therefore, is merely suggestive. The organization of the enterprise should follow, in general, the steps suggested in Unit 46 (page 196).

Through this enterprise, pupils should not only develop the usual skills and social attitudes which come from enterprise work, but will learn much worthwhile information. All pupils should learn that the sun makes our way of living possible. Primary pupils will appreciate better that it gives the heat necessary for plants, other animals, and ourselves; that we receive more heat from it at noon than earlier or later in the day, and more heat in summer than in winter; that trees, buildings, and clouds reduce its heating effect; that its light is good for us and for all other living things.

By the time pupils have left grade 6, they should have discovered how the sun provides its many gifts—that, though it appears small, it is very large and hot; that its light and warmth are needed by plants to make their food; that the sun gives us day and night because of the earth's rotation, not because the sun moves; that the higher the sun is in the sky, the more heat we receive from it, and the longer are our days; that it makes the winds to blow and the rains to fall; that its light even causes the moon to shine.

Figure 1—A Mural

The Sun Is the Source of Most Light, Heat, and Power

> "The sun, sire and center of light, the keystone of the world."
> BAILEY

Most of our light comes from the sun, directly or indirectly. Early man worshiped the sun as the source of heat, light, and power—the gifts of a mighty god. The sun was the god of life, and destruction and chaos would come in that day when the great god, in anger, might turn away his face from the earth.

Our understanding and control of the sun's light and heat, and of its gift of power, goes much further. When the light of the direct rays of the sun fails with night's approach, we still share its softer light as reflected from the moon, and use its light more indirectly in the flame of the candle, or the glow of the oil lamp, gas jet, or electric light bulb. We heat our homes and drive our machinery today with the energy stored up by the sun long ago in oil and gas and coal.

Activities

All Grades

- Observe the colors of the sky and clouds at sunset and at sunrise. Blow soap bubbles in sunlight, and notice the many colors. All light from the sun is white light, but drops of water and other particles in the air break up the colors of white light as did the soap bubbles.
- Hold a lens in bright sunlight. Hold a piece of paper behind it so that there is a small bright spot of light on it. The lens directs the rays to that one spot. The paper chars because the rays bring heat as well as light.

Primary Grades

- Draw and cut out a picture of a cat. Hold it in a sunny window. Why is there a shadow? Make the shadow stand up, then lie down. Make a shadow of your pencil, of yourself. When is your shadow longer, morning or noon?
- Feel the table where the sun is shining on it and where it is not. Which is warmer? What does the sun give the table?
- Have one pupil lead a blindfolded pupil into the sunlight and into the shade. If he knows when he is in the sunlight, he can be leader.
- Make a frieze of an early spring scene. Cut or tear from paper and mount on a brown background a house or school, patches of snow, trees, shrubs, crocuses, patches of green grass, little streams, fleecy clouds (use cotton batting) against a blue background, birds and other animals now present and active, children playing marbles or flying kites or skipping, the sun with yellow rays streaming from it over the landscape.

Junior and Intermediate Grades

- Read the temperature in sun and in shade at the same time. Explain the difference.
- Have pupils keep a record for a week of all the ways in which they observe that the sun gives heat to the earth.
- Use the globe for the earth and a flashlight for the sun. Find out which children of other lands have day when we do, and which have night when we have day.

Intermediate Grades

- Measure the diameter of the sun. While looking through the smoked glass, hold a coin far enough from the eyes to just cover the sun. Measure the distance of the coin from the eye. Then multiply the diameter of the coin by the distance from the sun, and divide by the distance from the eye to the coin.
- Arrange a display of various kinds of fuels. Tell how each has been produced by the sun.

The Sun Determines Weather and Climate

Sire of the seasons! Monarch of the climes,
And those who dwell in them!
BYRON

It is the sun that causes the winds to blow and cool the very place where its rays are spreading warmth. It evaporates the water for the cloud that shuts off its rays from the earth. It dissipates the fog formed by its own power. It melts the snow that fell from the clouds of its own making. It drives man and beast to seek shelter under the tree grown by its own energy. It is the controller of our daily weather and of our seasonal climate.

Activities

All Grades

How does the sun help people to decide what clothes to wear, what work to do, what games to play, whether or not to take a trip? Draw pictures to show your answers.

Junior and Intermediate Grades

Make a weather chart showing the number of hours of sunlight for each day for a month, also the temperature at 9:00 a.m., noon, and 4:00 p.m. Decide from the chart what influence the sun has on temperature during the day.

The Sun Is the Basis of Time and Season

That orbed continent, the fire that severs day from night.
SHAKESPEARE

The simplest unit of time is that which divides our life into days and nights. The earliest scholars developed considerable skill in telling time by the sun. Long ago the shadow stick and the sundial were used to measure time in terms of the length of shadow cast by the sun. Even the tallow candle, an early means of measuring time, was dependent upon the sun for the cotton wick and for the grass that fed the cow which was the source of the tallow. Our larger units of time, the seasons, are caused by the varying angles at which the sun's rays reach the earth from month to month.

THE SUN IS A CLOCK

The sun is a clock with a face made of light,
It doesn't wind up, but it's always just right.

When daylight is gone and there is no sun,
We hop off to bed, for the night has begun.

But when we have sun, we know it is day,
And jump out of bed to work and to play.

When shadows point north, we know it is noon;
When shadows are short, we know it is June.

The sun sets the time for the radio men
And wakens the rooster who crows for the hen.

What would the clocks do if the sun didn't go?
And how would the rooster know when to crow?

Reprinted from *Better Homes and Gardens* Magazine

Activities

Junior Grades

A compass points out north and south. The sun in the south points out noon. How does it point out morning and evening?

Junior and Intermediate Grades

- Make a candle clock by tying black thread around a candle at each inch of length—the length it burns in one hour. Use it to tell time. Make a chart to show that the sun makes possible the grass that feeds the cow that gives the tallow for the candle, and how it also is responsible for the growth of the cotton that forms the candlewick.
- Make a scrapbook to illustrate what people are doing at this season in Eskimo Land, in Florida, in Australia.
- Use the sun and your watch to find directions. Point the hour hand of the watch to the sun; south is halfway between the end of the hour hand and twelve o'clock.

The Sun Is Essential to Life and Health

Sunlight is like the breath of life.
HAWTHORNE

The radiant sun sends from above ten thousand blessings down.
GRANVILLE

"All flesh is grass." It is the sun that makes all green vegetation possible; and green plants directly or indirectly feed all other forms of plant life and, therefore, of animal life. One has only to contemplate how so many plants and animals that have been inactive throughout winter awaken in spring, to realize how living things also depend upon the sun's seasonal changes. To live is not enough; to live healthfully is essential. For this added privilege both plants and animals, those that are tended by man and those that shift for themselves, owe much to the sun.

Activities

All Grades

- Observe how leaves of plants in a window turn toward the light. Find how a plant shows unhealthiness when placed in darkness.
- Make an animated drawing showing sunlight winning a battle over germs.
- Make posters with such topics as: Fun in the Sun; The Sun Says, "Goodbye, Mr. Germ"; Sunny Days Are Healthy Days; Sunshine for Health.

Primary Grades

- Collect and mount pictures illustrating the benefits of the sun to health, to plants, to pets, etc.
- Compare your feelings on a sunny day and on a cloudy day.

Junior Grades

Look at a large ball close by. Now move it far away. Does it look the same size? Why not? The same is true of the sun. Recall how small a bonfire looked when you were far away, and how much larger, brighter, and warmer it seemed as you came closer to it. The sun is so hot that it is good for us that we stay a long way from it.

Junior and Intermediate Grades

- Recall or observe the effect of sunlight upon the color of autumn foliage and of apples, the sturdiness of growth and the blooming of geraniums, the color of the leaves of bulbs when brought to the light from darkness.
- Keep a record of sunny days for 2 months. Using information from the school register at

the end of the time, make a graph of the number of pupils absent by sickness each day. Did the amount of sunlight have any apparent influence upon the amount of time lost by illness?

- Place an aquarium or a prism of glass in direct sunlight. Observe how it breaks up the sunlight into the colors of the rainbow. Look at the violet end. Beyond this are invisible parts of the light which are directly beneficial to health. These ultraviolet rays kill germs.
- Collect or draw, and then arrange, pictures to illustrate the values of the sun to poultry, to indoor plants, to garden and farm crops, to sanatorium patients, to children, to bathers.

Make a large poster on wallboard. Place a figure of the genial Dr. Sun in the middle. Around this mount pictures in groups to illustrate gifts of the sun which contribute to man's health. Some suggestions are: gardens for healthful foods; flowers; grain fields that produce cereals and other crops that are used directly by man, or to feed his stock; direct sunlight with its ultraviolet rays; forests for recreation—and many other gifts. Use strings and thumbtacks to connect related groups.

- Find out how each of the following has depended upon the sun for good health: the early Cave Man, Eskimo people, the American Indians, the farmer, a patient in a sanatorium, a schoolboy or girl.
- How does the amount of sunshine influence the growth of houseplants and of grass on the lawn? The blooming of roses in the garden? The fun children have out of doors? The number of colds people have? How cheerful we feel? The songs of birds? The flight of butterflies and of dragonflies in summer?
- Write a health play entitled "Dr. Sun, the Family Physician," and act it in class.

Sunlight Affects Social Progress

And the thoughts of men are widened with the process of the suns.
TENNYSON

The great social movements of history have taken place in the temperate zone. The social studies program for grades 1 to 8 is limited largely to the study of peoples in these parts of the earth. Just as the sun determines the geographical zones, so it determines the social zones. This study is unlimited in its possibilities and should open a new field of challenging thought to pupils of intermediate and senior grades.

Activities

Junior and Intermediate Grades

Make a list of the nationalities of New Canadians who have settled in Canada in search of new opportunities in the last 2 decades. Which zones seem to produce men with the greater ambition?

Make a large map of the world, preferably on wallboard about 8 feet by 4 feet. Mark on it the zones and the more important countries of the world. Mount pictures showing natural resources, industries, methods of transportation, types of homes, and other evidences of social progress. Consider how the climate of these countries, determined by the sun, affects their ways of living.

General Correlations

Most of the activities will require silent reading for investigation. Several may be supplemented by oral readings to the class. Oral expression will naturally play an important part, both within the groups and in reporting to the class as a whole; written expression will be used freely in records. Social studies correlations will play an important part for all grades. Applications to health and mathematics not listed above will frequently arise. Arts and crafts expression will be exercised freely throughout. Even music may find a natural setting.

Culmination

Write a play to depict a group of pupils informally talking over the experiences of their enterprise work and what they have found out of interest in everyday life. Arrange a display of visible results of the activities, each group being responsible for its own work and the general committee arranging the integration of these different parts. Have each group explain its exhibit, and the class act the play as a program for a Parents' Night or some other special occasion.

Read

Beauchamp et at., *All Around Us* (primary): "Sun, Wind, and Weather," pp. 41-60; also *Discovering Our World,* Book 3 (grades 2-3): "What Is the Universe Like?," pp. 187-313. Gage (Scott, Foresman).

Blough & DePencier, *How the Sun Helps Us* (grades 2-3), The Basic Science Education Series. Copp Clark (Row, Peterson).

Blough & Huggett, *Methods and Activities in Elementary-School Science:* "The Sun and the Planets," pp. 105-117. Ryerson (Dryden).

Carpenter & Neurath, *Icebergs and Jungles.* Blue Ribbon (Hanover House).

Comstock, *Handbook of Nature-Study,* pp. 833-838. Allen (Comstock).

Craig & Lembach, *Science Everywhere* (grades 4-5), pp. 116-133. Ginn.

Frasier et al., *Winter Comes and Goes* (grades 2-3): "The Sun Helps Us," pp. 178-179; and *The How and Why Club* (grades 5-8): "Rainbow Colors," pp. 213-221. Dent (Singer).

Freeman, *Fun with Astronomy* (grades 6-8). Random House.

Hethershaw & Baker, *Wonders to See:* "The Sun," pp. 146-150. Gage (World Book).

Lewellen, *True Book of Moon, Sun and Stars,* also *You and Space Neighbors* (grades 6 and up). Book Society (Children's Press).

Parker, *The Sky Above Us* (grades 4-6); *The Sun and Its Family* (grades 4-6). Copp Clark (Row, Peterson).

Partridge, *General Science,* Intermediate, Book 2: "The Sun in Relation to the Earth," pp. 287-316; and *Everyday Science,* Book Two, pp. 426-450. Dent.

Smith & Clarke, *Around the Clock* (grades 3-4), pp. 75-98. Longmans, Green.

Willers, *Adventures in Science,* Book III (grades 3-4), pp. 36-45. Moyer.

Zim, *The Sun.* McLeod (Wm. Morrow).

New to this Edition

Branley, Franklyn. *What Makes Day and Night (Let's-Read-and-Find-Out Science 2)* (Collins, 1986).

Elenco. Elenco *Solar Deluxe Educational Kit.*

Hillerman, *Done in the Sun: Solar Projects for Children* (Sunstone Press, 2012).

Kaner, etta. *Who Likes the Sun?* (Kids Can Press, 2007).

Poof Slinky. *Solar Energy* (Experiment Kit with 25 experiments).

Simon, Sermour. *The Sun* (HarperCollins, 1989).

Spence, Pam. *Sun Observer's Guide* (Firefly Books, 2004).

Spetgang, Tilly. *The Kids' Solar Energy Book* (Imagine! Publishing, 2009).

Zimmerman, W.Frederick. *Our Splendid Sun: Cool Science Images for Curious Kids #1* (Nimble Books, 2007).

Unit 70—Learning about the Clouds and Rain

> There's rain that's rain
> And rain that's sleet
> And rain that turns to snow;
> There's April showers
> Just in time
> To make the wild flowers grow.
>
> There's rain that's mist
> And rain that's hail
> And one kind that's a fizzle;
> It isn't sleet,
> It isn't snow,
> It's just a silly drizzle.

Reprinted from *Better Homes and Gardens* Magazine

Clouds are such fascinating things, and children can become so interested in them that we cannot afford to ignore them. They form the ceiling of our world just as grass forms the carpet, and shrubs and trees the drapes. Their beauty of shape and color, their motions across the sky (scudding quickly or drifting languidly) make them fit subjects for nature study when interest and appreciation are our main motives. Though their study may not be justified by school traditions or from bread-and-butter points of view, to train pupils to appreciate them should be as much our aim as to train them to enjoy beautiful flowers or thrilling bird songs.

When water vapor changes to the liquid state in midair, it forms a mist, a fog (denser than a mist), or a cloud (higher than a mist or fog). A cloud formation is easily observed near the spout of a teakettle, beyond the steam, or where steam escapes from the whistle of a steam engine. The water particles in a mist, fog, or cloud are formed when the atmosphere is cooled so much that some of the water vapor in it must condense. The water particles first formed are too tiny to fall as rain—so they drift about. When the sun shines or the air is otherwise warmed, the water particles may evaporate again and the mist, fog, or cloud disappear.

> A million little sunbeams came,
> And stole them all away.

If the tiny water particles in the cloud grow or combine until they become large, they become raindrops. These may drift slowly down or fall rapidly, depending upon the size of the drops and the air current through which they fall.

291

Figure 1—Cloud Chariots

A. I want to ride that fluffy cloud that floats up there, but I can't seem to reach it by climbing on my chair.
B. Now if I had a ladder taller than the trees, I'd climb up on that cloud and hitch it to a breeze.
C. I'd steer it with a sunbeam and then I have a notion. If I sailed far enough I'd really see the ocean.

Clouds vary in color and general appearance. Some are large, rounded, and white like cotton batting or soap suds. These cumulus clouds foretell fair weather unless their bases become dark. Other clouds form a thin, whitish, curly or featherlike layer high in the sky. These cirrus clouds, made up of tiny ice crystals, may be the first sign of an approaching storm. There are also layers or sheets of clouds, denser than the cirrus clouds, and resembling layers of fog. These stratus clouds are frequently followed by rain. When we see dark tower-like clouds (thunder clouds) often moving rapidly across the sky, our first concern should be to find shelter from the rain soon to fall. At sunset we frequently see gold- and red-streaked clouds along the western horizon. These sun-colored clouds indicate fair weather, but when seen in early morning before sunrise, they are likely to bring rain.

Primary pupils should, by personal observation, learn that clouds hide the sun, give us rain, blow across the sky, have many colors (gray, black, red, orange, white), at times look like cotton batting and at other times like layers of blankets or of feathers or like piles of coal. The blackest ones bring rain. When clouds disappear, the sun comes out, and we have no more rain.

Intermediate grades should become familiar with the names of common kinds of clouds, and what they foretell. They should see a resemblance among the cloud at the mouth of a teakettle, the cloud formed by our breath on a cold day, fog, mist, and clouds in the sky. They should understand a little of how these are formed.

Activities

Teacher

Develop the primary pupils' vocabulary to include these expressions: light and heavy; sprinkle, shower, and storm; warm and cold; fair, cloudy, and rainy, etc. Such questions as these will help: What shape are raindrops? How do we know when it is likely to rain? What kind of rain do the plants like in spring? Why does the farmer like to have rain? What does rain do to snow? To grass? To sidewalks? To a hot day? To fields?

All Grades

- Put on rubbers and raincoats and take a hike in the rain. Observe: the dark clouds, the direction from which the rain falls, how the wind changes it, the size of the drops, how the raindrops bounce on the pavement, where rain soaks in and where it runs off, little streams carrying things and wearing away tracks, how the streams drop their loads as they slow down, leaves and roof shedding rain, raindrop dimples on water. Imagine what the rain that soaks into the ground does: melts the frost, softens hard ground, gives drink to seeds and roots, wakens the spring flowers. When you return, make a drawing of a rainy day.
- Make drawings of clouds of different shapes, sizes, and colors. Show drops of rain from the dark ones, and the sun beside some light ones.
- Watch for a rainbow. Draw one in class in bright colors over some trees and houses.
- Make a four-page booklet of blue paper. Then illustrate these couplets when you see that kind of cloud.

Figure 2—Four Well-known Kinds of Clouds (Drawn by Florence Farr)

Cirrus clouds look like a feather,
They're made of ice even in warm weather.
Stratus clouds in layers run
Colored by the setting sun.
Cumulus clouds are big and white,
No rain comes down when they are in sight.
Cumulo-nimbus clouds are black,
Now I find an umbrella I lack.

       FROM A PUPIL'S NOTEBOOK

- With paste, attach batting to a blue background to represent different shapes and kinds of clouds.
- Make sketches of clouds. Use cotton batting or white chalk on blue paper (cumulus); gray and black chalk (thunder clouds) on dark paper; red, orange, and yellow chalk on dark blue paper (stratus).

Primary Grades

- Why do we hang wet clothes in the sun? What happens to the water in them? What becomes of the water when sidewalks, lawns, fields, or mud puddles become dry? Now look at the clouds floating in the sky. The water in them went up through the air. It will come down again as rain.
- Why are cloudy days dull and cloudy nights dark?
- Make a drawing of a rainstorm. Include: people with umbrellas, raincoats, and rubbers; streams; windowpanes; and other things. Make a poster like fig. 3
- Read "Two Little Clouds," by R. L. Stevenson. Find other songs, poems, and stories.
- Learn this memory gem:

> Little white cloudlets up in the sky,
> Say, are you snowy ships sailing on high?
> Or are you downy sheep running to find
> Shelter away from the rude blowing wind?

Primary and Junior Grades

Make a frieze entitled "April Showers."

Junior and Intermediate Grades

- Hold a cold object in the steam coming from a teakettle. Watch the mist form, then larger drops of water. When these grow big enough, they run or fall. Clouds are formed somewhat as the mist, and rain is formed somewhat as these drops of water.

Figure 3—Paper Cuting for Primary Grades

Build the scene in bright colors. Cut semi-circles; then add stalks and windows.

- To assist you in observing clouds, make a black mirror by painting one side of a sheet of glass with black enamel. In this you may observe the beauty of clouds, their changes, and their motion more clearly and more easily than by looking skyward.
- Make a list of all the uses of rain to man.
- Have a cloud museum. Collect pictures of various forms of clouds. Mount them on a large background with the horizon near its base. Color the background to indicate prospective clear weather or rain.
- Plan a pantomime of the rising of water vapor, the formation of clouds, the falling of rain, the flowing of streams.
- As new forms of clouds appear in the sky, go outside to sketch them.

READ AND ENJOY

"The Tion (pronounced 'shun') twins are called Evapora and Condensa. Unlike most twins, Evapora Tion and Condensa Tion do not look or act alike. However, they help each other, as one couldn't get along very well without the other. And I am very sure that we couldn't get along without either of them.

"Evapora Tion's job is to turn water into water vapor. He works faster with plenty of heat to help him. You can fairly see him carrying water vapor off the teakettle in great clouds of steam. Sometimes after a rain it is very warm and we say, 'See the garden steam.' That's only Evapora Tion carrying off the water vapor.

"But Evapora Tion works whether there is much heat or not. He even works in freezing weather. He dries off the sidewalks after a rain. He carries off water from the bird bath and takes the moisture out of the washing on the line. Over the ocean he lifts tons and tons of water vapor every minute and he's busy evaporating water over lakes, rivers, gardens, farms, and mud puddles all the time. Oh, he's a busy twin!

"But Condensa Tion is just as busy. He works better when it is cool. You can see him at work when the teakettle vapor finally floats over to the cool windowpane, or when the moisture in your breath touches the inside of the cool car windows on cold days. When the water vapor touches the windowpane Condensa Tion pushes many tiny vapor particles together against the cool pane and turns them into drops of water again.

"On warm days the teakettle vapor floats away out of doors and thins out so much that we can't see it at all. But it is there, and so is the vapor from the bird bath and the lake and your breath. The vapor floats up and up meeting other little particles of vapor, then away above us it becomes a fluffy little cloud all white and dainty with the sun shining through and all around it.

"On goes the little cloud; by and by it meets many other little clouds. When they pile up together there is so much water there that they make one big cloud—so big that the sun can't shine through or around it any more. It looks very dark and gray-blue.

"We say, 'It's going to rain.'

"By and by the little drops get bigger and bigger. When they are too heavy to float anymore, down they come, pell-mell, into the river, the lake, the birdbath, and onto the thirsty garden.

"And we say, 'It is raining.'

"Then Evapora Tion goes after those drops again. And so it goes—Evapora Tion sending water into the air as vapor, Condensa Tion sending it back as raindrops. Such busy, busy twins!

" 'Why bother?' you say? Why not bother? Think how cool and fresh and interesting everything is made all the time just through the activities of the Tion (pronounced 'shun') twins.

Reprinted from *Better Homes and Gardens* Magazine

Read

Andrews, *Adventures in Science.* Book VI (grades 6-7), pp. 41-55. Moyer.
Beauchamp et al., *Discovering Our World,* Book 3 (grades 6-7): "Why Is the Sky Clear or Cloudy?" pp. 43-9. Gage (Scott, Foresman).
Benton, *Children of the Green Earth,* Book Four (grades 3-4): "Sky-signs," pp. 89-95. Pitman.
Carpenter & Neurath, *Icebergs and Jungles,* pp. 9-12 and 24-27. Blue Ribbon (Hanover House).
Craig & Daniel, *Science Around You* (junior), pp. 24-39 and 60-63. Ginn.
Dowling et al., *Investigating Why* (grades 7-8), pp. 73-98. Winston.
Fenton & Fenton, *Our Changing Weather,* pp. 42-67. Doubleday.
Frasier et al., *Sunshine and Rain* (grades 1-2), pp. 48-51; *Winter Comes and Goes* (grades 2-3): "Clouds," pp. 126-128; and *How and Why Experiments* (grades 6-8): "What Makes Clouds?" p. 185. Dent (Singer).
Hood, *The Atmosphere* (teacher reference): "Watching the Clouds," pp. 12-33. Oxford.
Parker, *Clouds, Rain and Snow,* The Basic Science Education Series. Copp Clark (Row, Peterson).
Partridgc, *General Science,* Intermediate, Book 2: "Weather and Moisture," pp. 347-355; and *Everyday Science,* Book Two: "Clouds and Rain," pp. 464-466. Dent.
Patch & Howe, The Work of Scientists (grades 5-6): "Moisture in the Air," pp. 41-51. Macmillan.
Schneider, *Science for Here and Now* (grade 2), pp. 131-142. Copp Clark (Heath).
Cloud Forms (a chart with 12 cloud plates), and *Weather Forecasting,* from the Superintendent of Documents, Washington, D.C

New to this Edition

Branley, Franklyn. *Down Comes the Rain (Let's-Read-and-Find-Out Science 2)* (Collins, 1997).
dePaola, Tomie. *The Cloud Book* (Holiday House, 1985).
Pasachoff, Jay. Peterson *First Guide to Clouds and Weather* (Houghton Mifflin Harcourt, 1998).
Relf, Pat. *The Magic School Bus Wet All Over: A Book About The Water Cycle* (Scholastic, 1996).
Rockwell, Anne. *Clouds (Let's-Read-and-Find-Out Science 1)* (Collins, 2008).
Rubin, Louis D. *The Weather Wizard's Cloud Book: A Unique Way to Predict the Weather Accurately and Easily by Reading the Clouds* (Algonquin Books, 1989).

http://www.stevespanglerscience.com/experiment/cloud-in-a-bottle-experiment
http://www.all-science-fair-projects.com/project282_21.html

Unit 71—Who Has Seen the Wind?

(An enterprise for primary grades, reprinted from *Seasonal Activities for Primary Grades,* by kind permission of the author, Helen M. Hubbs, and the publishers, Ryerson Press.)

Themes. How the wind helps people and how it does harm. The relation between the wind and the weather. The boisterous March wind as a herald of spring.

Approach. With the coming of March there is a hint of change. We recognize it in settling snow-drifts, swelling buds, and rushing streamlets, but most of all in the wild winds which give to March a lion's reputation.

Suggestions for Motivation. Write this riddle on the blackboard on a windy morning for the children to guess:

> Play hide-and-seek; you can't spy me;
> You hear me shout, "Coo-ee, coo-ee";
> Sometimes I call you, loud and clear,
> Sometimes I whisper in your ear.
> I brush your cheek, I pull your hair,
> I'm here, I'm there, I'm everywhere.
> I play with clouds, I toss the trees.
> Now, will you tell me my name, please?
> H. M. HUBBS

Pupils and teachers may go on an excursion to the fields on a windy day. Watch the clouds, trees, waves on the water, etc.

The pupils may read and discuss "Wind on the Hill," by A. A. Milne, which can be found in the volume, *Now We Are Six.*

Class Conference. Discussion about the wind. Some children will insist that they have seen it and may wish to draw it. Discuss where it is going, what it is, how we recognize it. The problems and suggestions for constructive work will be developed from this discussion.

Problem 1

The Wind Is Air Moving. We cannot see it but we see what does. We know it is here because it bends trees, jerks our umbrellas, and moves wind vanes. We feel it on our faces.

THINGS TO DO

- The pupils may make and color "pinwheels." Notice that they turn slightly even when we feel no wind. They may also make fans and produce little winds in the schoolroom.

- Draw a wind vane. Then make wind vanes of thin wood. Mount them on posts and watch the direction of the wind. Learn the points of the compass.
- Learn to sing "The Weather-vane," in *Songs of a Little Child's Day,* and "The Wind," in *Songs of the Child World,* I.
- Pupils read "The Secret," a story of a wind vane in *Science Stories,* II.
- Memorize:

> Who has seen the wind?
> Neither you nor I,
> But when the trees bow down their heads
> The wind is passing by.
> CHRISTINA ROSSETTI

The class may keep a blackboard calendar, marking each windy day with a picture showing children's dresses, kites, sailboats, etc. being blown by the wind.

Problem 2

The Wind Plays Many Tricks and Sometimes Does Us Harm. When it is very strong, it blows down houses, pulls up trees by the roots, makes great waves on the water. It shakes the fruit off the orchard trees and steals our hats and umbrellas.

THINGS TO DO

- Memorize the verse:

> The wind is pushing against the trees,
> It takes off your hat without asking you please.
> ONTARIO PRIMER

- Learn the song, "The Merry Wind," in *Songs of a Little Child's Day.*
- Make a mural showing how the wind has teased you—playing with hats, umbrellas, scarves, kites, etc.
- Read: "The Wind and the Umbrella," in *Science Stories,* I; "An Outdoor Party," in *Science Stories,* II ; "The Wind," by R. L. Stevenson, in *A Child's Garden of Verses.*
- Discuss the way in which winds change the weather. Watch the wind vane from day to day as the weather changes. Discuss the verse:

> 'Tis when the wind is rushing by
> To chase the clouds across the sky
> The waves put on their nice white caps
> To keep from catching cold, perhaps.
> PRIMARY POETRY, BOOK I

Problem 3

The Wind Does Much Useful Work for Us. It brings us fresh air, makes windmills work for us, brings us rainclouds, makes sailing ships move on the water, dries roads and streets for us, etc.

THINGS TO DO

- Discuss the usefulness of the wind. Then tell the class the story of "The Wind's Work," in *Mother Stories.* Learn the song:

> Winds of March, we welcome you,
> There is work for you to do.
> Work and play and blow all day,
> Blow the winter cold away, etc.
> SONGS AND SILHOUETTES

- Discuss the wind as Mother Nature's vacuum cleaner when she begins spring housecleaning in her outdoor home.
- Go on a class excursion to the fields to watch a windmill at work pumping water. Make round windmills for the sand-table.
- Tell the class stories about the wind's work in Holland. Let them make a Dutch windmill of corrugated cardboard large enough for a child to go inside. If it is an octagonal mill, the eight tapering pieces for base and body may be cut and glued together with strips of wrapping paper. The arms should be reinforced with strips of thin wood.
- Learn to sing: "The Windmill," in *Songs of the Child World,* 1, "Old Mother Wind," in *Songs of Happiness;* the singing games, "The Windmill," in *200 Games That Teach,* and "Hanging the Clothes To Dry," in *Songs of the Child World,* 1.
- Make toy sailboats and sail them on a windy day.
- Make a wind frieze showing ships on the sea, windmills, dashing rain, tossing treetops, etc., each child illustrating the feature which interests him most. The children may work in groups on long sheets of wallpaper, or individual pieces may be assembled to form a frieze. Use cutouts, poster paint, or chalk.
- Discuss the importance of fresh air and deep breathing to our health, and how the wind provides us with fresh air.
- Read the poem, "The Busy Wind," in *Songs of a Little Child's Day.*

Culmination

A kite-flying contest.

THINGS TO DO

- The children read the story, "The Kite," in *At Home and Away.* Assemble materials for making the kites—heavy paper, glue, strips of wood, crayons, strong cord, etc.
- Make and decorate kites of varying shapes and sizes.
- Fly the kites on a windy day. The children's parents may be invited to see contest.

Read

Comstock, *Handbook of Nature-Study,* pp. 783-799. Allen (Comstock).

Dowling et al., *Seeing Why* (junior), pp. 131-136. Winston.

Fenton & Fenton, *Our Changing Weather,* pp. 71-102. Doubleday.

Frasier et al., *Sunshine and Rain* (grades 1-2), pp. 12-15; *Through the Year* (grades 1-2): "Wind," pp. 102-103; *Winter Comes and Goes* (grades 2-3) : "The Wind Blows," pp. 129-130, and "The Weather-vane," pp. 131-132. Dent (Singer).

Longfellow, "The Windmill."

Stevenson, "Windy Nights" and "The Wind."

Whittier, "The Wind of March."

New to this Edition

BBC Studios. *Weather* (DVD), 2003. Presented by Donal MacIntyre.

Dorros, Arthur. *Feel the Wind (Let's-Read-and-Find-Out Science)* (Collins, 1990).

Kamkwamba, William. *The Boy Who Harnessed the Wind: Young Reader's Edition* (Dial, 2012). (There is an adult book with this same topic as well, perhaps for high school readers.)

Kjille, Mary Lou Morano. *A Project Guide to Wind, Weather, and the Atmosphere* (Mitchell Lane Publishers, 2010).

Toysmith. Toysmith 4 M Weather Station Kit #4573

http://home.messiah.edu/~kn1193/Page3.html

http://bgsctechclub.wordpress.com/category/wind-speed-meter/

Figure 1—Windmills in Zaandan, The Netherlands.

Unit 72—Preparing Homes for Birds

"When you are putting up another bird-house for Bluebirds, place it in the open garden and not more than five to six feet from the ground. Make the opening about the middle on one side, and not more than 1 ½ inches in diameter. If you leave off the perch below the opening, I will be just as glad, because the Sparrows and Wrens use it more than we do and find it very convenient when annoying us. I don't care whether you make the box of wood or of heavy roofing paper, but if there are any cats or squirrels around, I should prefer that you mount it on top of an iron pipe that they cannot climb. . . ."

Mrs. Bluebird
From *American Bird Biographies,* by A. A. Allen

Yes, now that March is here we should begin to think of the needs of our returning bird friends. The making of birdhouses should be begun a few weeks before the birds return. Interest will be keener, there will be time to complete the houses, and enthusiasm will not be lost before the birds get back.

Pupils of intermediate and senior grades are capable of constructing and erecting birdhouses or shelters. Primary children can later help by putting out string, straw, and other nest materials. The main value is to the birds, but pupils learn to plan, to follow directions, and to use their energies constructively.

Pupils should be encouraged to think of a birdhouse for a certain species of bird and not just for birds. Each bird has its requirements, and these should be studied and kept in mind when constructing a home for it. The bluebird, chickadee, flicker, robin, English sparrow, wren, and martin all use nesting-houses. The woodpeckers and the nuthatch prefer homes in hollow trees. Shelves, shelters, or open boxes are the choice of the robin and the phoebe. The barn and the eave swallow appreciate an opening left in the barn.

Figure 1—Bird Homes Made by Hamilton Manual Training Classes

301

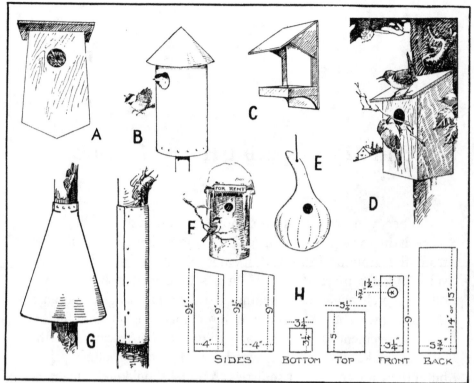

Figure 2—Bird Houses You Can Make

A, for screech owl; B and F, for chickadee; C, for robin; D and E, for house wren; G, cat-guards; H, plans for bluebird's house.

Activities

Primary Grades

- Observe some deserted nests of birds. Talk about different kinds of nests—where they are placed and how they are made (robin— on an open ledge, of dead grass and mud, lined with fine grass).
- On your sand-table set up a garden scene with birdhouses to rent for the spring and summer. How do birds pay their rent?

Junior and Intermediate Grades

- Make a survey of the grounds to see where it is best to erect birdhouses.
- Write to the Ontario Agricultural College, Guelph, and to the National Parks Bureau, Ottawa, for plans for making and erecting birdhouses.
- Organize a campaign to place a birdhouse in each child's yard. Each pupil choose the type of house he wishes. Have a display of finished houses. Judge each house on its fitness for its prospective tenant. This involves correctness of dimensions, correct size of entrance, good ventilation, absence of draughts, freedom from rain, and convenience for cleaning. The following table gives specifications for houses for common birds.

Birdhouse Specifications (after L. D. Wooster)					
Species	**Floor of Cavity Inches**	**Depth of Cavity Inches**	**Entrance above Floor Inches**	**Diameter of Entrance Inches**	**Height above Ground Feet**
Bluebird	5 x 5	8	6	1 ½	8 to 10
Robin	6 x 8	8	open	open	8 to 15
Chickadee	4 x 4	8 to 10	8	1 1/8	8 to 15
House wren	4 x 4	6 to 8	6	1	8 to 10
Martin	6 x 6	6	1	2 ½	10 to 20
Flicker	7 x 7	16 to 18	16	2 ½	10 to 20
Downy woodpecker	4 x 4	8 to 10	8	1 ½	10 to 20

- Follow these directions to make a wren's house. Cut 7/8" lumber as follows: floor, 4" square; sides, 4" × 8"; front and back each 5 ¾" × 8"; roof, 7 ½" square. Assemble all but the roof. Drill a 1"hole in the front, 6" above the floor. Cut the top with ½" slope toward the front. Attach the roof, hinged at the back, and hooked at the front to make cleaning easy. Drill ventilation holes under the edges of the roof. Attach a small perch below the entrance. Erect the house on a post or on the side of a building or tree 8' to 10' above the ground. Attach a tin cat-guard below.
- Make a bluebird house as described in fig. 2.
- Make a wren house out of an old tomato can. Place it where it will be shaded; otherwise the tin will become very hot.
- Make a birdhouse for woodpeckers or for chickadees by cutting about one foot from a small hollow log and nailing a board on the top and bottom. Cut a hole in one side as an entrance. Hang it where these birds are likely to find it.
- Have a poster contest, using such topics as: "One Good Turn Deserves Another," "Build a Birdhouse." You will think of many others.

Read

Candy, *Nature Notebook*, pp. 3-9 and 60. Allen (Houghton Mifflin).

Earle, *Birds and Their Nests*. McLeod (Wm. Morrow).

Gates & McClenaghan, *Animals Work, Too* (grade 2): "Bird Houses," pp. 2-4. Macmillan.

Hausman, *Beginner's Guide to Attracting Birds*, pp. 64-74. Allen (Putnam's Sons).

Kimball & Webb, *Birds in Their Homes*. Blue Ribbon (Garden City).

Mason, *Picture Primer of Attracting Birds*. Allen (Houghton Mifflin).

Partridge, *Everyday Science*, Book Two: "Providing Homes and Nesting Materials," pp. 527-529; and *General Science*, Intermediate, Book 2, pp. 122-125. Dent.

Sawyer, *Bird Houses*. Cranbrook Institute of Science. Bloomfield Hills, Michigan.

Bird Houses and Their Occupants. National Parks Bureau, Ottawa.

New to this Edition

Barlowe, Sy. *Beginning Birdwatcher's Book: With 48 Stickers* (Dover, 2000).

Bird Watcher's Digest. *Bird Watching for Kids* (2010)

Boring, Mel. *Birds, Nests & Eggs* (Cooper Square Publishing, 1998).

Brandt, Deanna. *Bird Log Kids: A Kid's Journal to Record Their Birding Experiences* (Adventure Publishing, 1998).

Henry, Marguerite. *Birds at Home* (Checkerboard Press, Revised Edition 1972) [This is a beauty, out of print, but well worth the find.]

Sill, Cathryn. *About Birds: A Guide for Children* (Peachtree Publishers Ltd, 1997)

http://www.birdwatching-bliss.com/bluebird-house-plans.html
http://www.nabluebirdsociety.org/nestboxplans.htm

Unit 73—Planning More Attractive School Grounds

The school garden provides almost unlimited educational opportunities for the imparting of useful information, the developing of valuable skills, and the cultivation of desirable pupil attitudes toward nature and manual labor. Too frequently the out-of-door work is limited to the planting of vegetables. This policy falls far short of satisfying the interests or the needs of either rural or urban pupils and is probably the cause of much unfavorable criticism of school gardens. The rural pupil probably obtains sufficient training in growing vegetables at home, but has not had his attention directed toward beautification of the home surroundings by the use of suitably arranged shrubs, perennials, and annual flowering plants to nearly as large an extent. The urban pupil's interests will center more largely in knowing how to improve the general appearance of his home surroundings than in growing vegetables in a comparatively small backyard. It is, therefore, suggested that emphasis be placed upon growing annual flowering plants in suitably arranged borders.

". . . a little garden brimming over with flowers should mark the days and weeks and months with bud and blossom. . . . A garden is a beautiful book, writ by the fingers of God; every flower and every leaf is a letter. You have only to learn them . . . and enjoy them, and then go on reading and reading, and you will find yourself carried away from the earth to the skies by the beautiful story."[1]

In Unit 13 we planned how we should like our school grounds to look. We decided upon the position of the lawn, where we should plant shrubs and perennial flowering plants, and where we would like the showy beds of annuals. We went further and prepared these areas as best we could in autumn so that our plants would get a good start this spring. But we did not decide what plants to put in each place. Let us do this now.

There is a tree, shrub, or flower to fill every need in making the grounds at home or at school attractive. If we were sufficiently familiar with all of these, we could make our own plans for beautification. But we are not. If, then, our planning is to result in the most effective landscape, we must depend upon those who know plants well to make suggestions for us. Among these are men who manage nurseries, and other horticulturists. In the absence of expert advice, we can combine with our knowledge gained from our own limited experience the information gained by the study of colored pictures and descriptive lists of trees, shrubs, and perennial flowering plants.

Trees and Shrubs

Too often this part of school-garden activity is considered merely as a part of an Arbor Day program without much previous planning or later care. Yet probably no part of the school's land-

---

1 *From The Flower Garden, by Douglas Jerrold.*

scaping provides more value by way of beauty, utility, and instruction than do the trees and shrubs. What a contrast there is between school grounds with the lawn, shrubbery, trees, and building harmonized into a pleasing whole, and a bare building standing alone in a bare and dreary setting! And what a different effect upon the development or the thwarting of the aesthetic tendencies of those who are compelled to live there most of their waking hours!

The informal or natural style of landscape gardening is more attractive and easier to maintain than a formal one. It follows nature's method of planting as we see it at the edge of a woodland. There the plants are grouped in masses, the edge usually following pleasing curves. In the background are trees, then shrubs and flowering plants intermingled, with a gradual gradation from tall to low.

Perhaps we should plan to have our school grounds resemble this style. See fig. 1. Trees will provide a setting for the buildings and give welcome shade. Evergreens will form shelters, screens, and windbreaks. The shrubs should blend with the trees, the lawn, the walks, and the building. They seldom look best when single. The foundation planting of shrubs around the building will break its harsh lines and blend it with the lawn. Those at the corners should be tallest; those between the windows, of medium height; those under the windows and in the outer edge of the shrubbery should be low. The shrubs selected should provide variety in color of foliage and of flowers throughout the summer, and should be hardy enough for the locality.

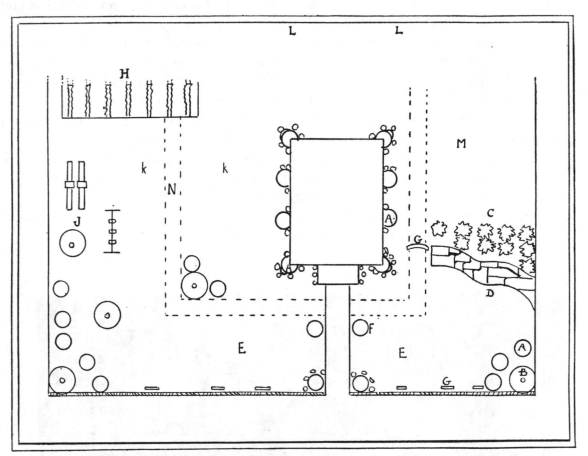

Figure 1—Landscape Plan for Rural School Grounds

A, shrubs of various heights, colors, and periods of bloom; B, shade trees; C, evergreen windbreak and flower background; D, annual or perennial border; E, well-kept lawn area; F, Japanese barberry, protecting grass on corners; G, arch and trellises with climbing roses; H, school garden continuing back into rear yard; J, play equipment for junior pupils; K, playground for junior pupils partially shaded; L, softball field, etc.; M, tennis, badminton, or volleyball area; N, cinder or gravel path.

No shrubs should be planted nearer than 2 feet from the building; all should be far enough apart to mature without overcrowding. Barberry shrubs will persuade pupils to keep to pathways instead of cutting corners.

Any reliable nursery manager will advise wisely on how to bank shrubs to break the harshness of the corners of the school building, form a bond of union between the foundation of the school and the lawn, form an attractive grouping in the corners of the grounds, or hide unsightly objects. The general effect before and after the summer holidays should be given first consideration. A few hardy shrubs are listed below, according to their particular merits.

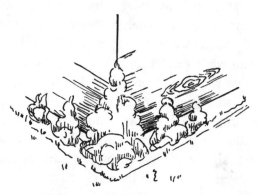

Figure 2—Foundation Planting at Corners of Building

For a succession of bloom throughout the growing season: *golden bell* (Forsythia), yellow flowers in April; *bridal wreath*, white flowers in abundance, May and June; *flowering almond*, double, pink flowers, in June; *honeysuckle varieties*, various colors, in June; *Hydrangea*, white, turning to rose, Sept.-Oct.

Shrubs with foliage brightly colored in summer: *golden mock orange*, low growing, foliage golden yellow; *silver-leaved dogwood*, low, with variegated silver foliage.

Shrubs with brightly colored foliage and with berries in autumn: *Japanese barberry*, good for hedges, foliage turning bright in autumn, clusters of red berries in autumn and winter; sumac, worthy of being transplanted from woods to schoolyard for the bright red foliage in autumn and for winter bird food; *panicled dogwood*, transplanted from the open fields to provide attractive foliage and creamy-white berries in autumn; *honeysuckle varieties*, red berries in autumn on both native and nursery varieties.

Shrubs with attractively colored bark in winter: *dogwood varieties*, bark yellow or scarlet; *Kerria*, low growing, much branched, with yellow flowers in June and July and green bark in winter.

Shrubs for a shady corner: *coralberry, elderberry, honeysuckle varieties*.

Climbing plants have their place, too, over arbours or upon trellises. Virginia creepers hide unsightly fences; Boston ivy clings to bricks and stone; climbing roses add grace and beauty.

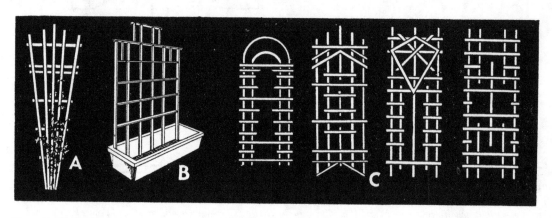

Figure 3—Trellis Designs

A, rose trellis; B, trellis box; C, other trellis designs.

Perennial Flowering Plants

Many school grounds can boast of a border of suitably chosen and well-arranged perennials. The autumn topics of the natural science course require their presence for recognition and appreciation studies. It is usually unwise, however, to start planting this type of plant without careful advance preparation of both the plant and the soil. In the meantime it would be advisable to select a suitable site for a fairly wide border, preferably about 5 feet wide, in a sunny place, easily viewed from the highway, and with a background of shrubs. Fertilize the area well; cultivate it thoroughly and grow a crop of annuals on it this year, to assist in getting it into good condition for the planting of perennials this coming autumn or next spring.

Seedling plants should be started in June or July in a well-protected but fertile nursery plot in the garden. Prepare the soil well and sow a variety of seeds of perennial plants for next year. Label each row or plot carefully. Keep the plot well moistened until growth starts, by shading it with evergreen twigs, lattice work, or coarse plant remains. Select only plants that are hardy, bloom heavily during the school months, and show a variety of heights.

Table I	
Perennial Flowering Plants for Various Heights and Seasons	
Low Growing Plants for the Front of the Border:	
May	Rock cress: 4-6 in. tall; white; gray foliage; sunny place. Various bulbs: crocus, single early tulips.
May-June	Forget-me-not: 6 in. tall; blue.
June	Snow-in-summer: 4 in. tall; white; silver foliage.
May-Oct	Viola: 6 in. tall; various colors; like small pansies.
Plants of Medium Height:	
May	Various bulbs such as tulips, daffodils, narcissi.
June	Sweet William: 1-1 ½ ft. tall; various colors; hardy; popular; free blooming. Iris: many colors; blooms from 3-6 weeks; plant very shallowly; avoid manure near them. Perennial flax: 1-1 ½ ft. tall; blue; flowers fall about noon; prefers loam to clay; very showy and hardy; self-sows.
June-Sept.	Carnation: 1 ft. tall; various colors; hardy; blooms freely; sweet perfume.
June-Aug.	Day lily: yellow, orange, or lemon; about 2 ft. tall; hardy and showy.
June to frost	Gaillardia (blanketflower): 2 ft. tall; yellow to red; very hardy and showy; excellent for cut flowers; withstands drought.
Plants of Tall Stature for Background:	
May	Darwin tulips and daffodils. Columbine: 3 ft. tall; various colors.
June	Pyrethrum: 2-3 ft. tall; various colors; showy; good for cut flowers. Canterbury bell: 2-3 ft. tall; blue, white, rose; biennial. Fox-glove: 3-4 ft. tall; various colors; biennial.
June-Aug	Lupine: 3 ft. tall; white, pink; pea-shaped flowers in long spikes. Coreopsis: 3 ft. tall; yellow; excellent with flax; keep flowers picked. Hollyhock: 5-8 ft. tall; splendid background; biennial.
June-Sept.	Delphinium (larkspur): 2-3 ft. tall; blue shades.
July-frost	Perennial aster: 2-6 ft. tall.
Sept.-frost	Shasta daisy: 4-7 ft. tall; white; blossoms freely.

Annual Flowering Plants

No part of the school's surroundings will be more colorful or useful educationally than the border, bed, or parts of the school garden which are planted with annual flowering plants. Some of their merits are: their display value the same year; their excellence for cut flowers and bouquets in school in September; an understudy to perennials and shrubs; their inexpensive nature; the ease of growing them; the varieties of colors, heights, growing habits, garden uses, and perfume. Educationally, they are adapted to teach lessons of persistence, orderliness, neatness, accuracy, and artistic taste in planning and planting. In autumn they provide materials for outdoor study: identification, appreciation of beauty of form and color and perfume, formation of seeds and seed dispersal, the work of bees, artwork and teaching of garden designing.

Some combinations of annuals are suggested from the standpoint of color, height, and hardiness: African marigolds in front of scarlet salvia; gaillardias and French marigolds; Orange King African marigolds bordered with blue ageratum; salpiglossis with California poppy; pink phlox edged with blue ageratum; pink verbena with yellow phlox; maroon snapdragon edged with sweet alyssum.

Table II				
Twenty-Five Common Annual Flowering Plants				
Name	**Height**	**Color**	**Time to Sow**	**Remarks**
Sweet alyssum	6 in.	white	I. March, O. April	E., F., S., S.S.
Ageratum	6 in.-1 ft.	blue	I. March. O. May	B., C.F., P.B.
Balsam	12-18 in.	various	O. May	S., hedge
China-aster	18 in.	various	I. March or April	B., C.F., S.
Cosmos	4-6 ft.	various	I. or O. April	B., C.F., S.S.
California poppy	6 in.	gold, pink	O. April or May	B., C.F., E., S.S.
Four-o'clock	3 ft.	various	O. April and May	low hedge
Morning glory	5 ft. or more	various	O. April or May	climbing
Nasturtium	dwarf to 4 ft.	scarlet to yellow	I. April, O. May	B., C.F., E., climbing
Nicotine	2-3 ft.	white, pink	I. March, O. May	B., C.F., F. S.
Marigold				
African	2-5 ft.	gold, lemon	I. March, O. April	B., C.F.
French	1 ft.	gold, lemon, crimson marks	I. March or April, O. May	B., C.F.
Mexican	6-8 in.	gold	I. March, O. May	E., lettering
Phlox	6-18 in.	various	I. March, O. May	B., F., P.B., C.F.
Petunia	1 ft.	various	I. March, O. April or May	B., F., P.B., S.
Portulaca	8 in.	various	O. May	B., E., S.S.
Snapdragon	1-3 ft.	various	I. March or April	B., C.F., F., P.B.
Sunflower	5-7 ft.	golden	O. May	bold background
Scarlet runner	6 ft.	scarlet	O. May	climbs fences, etc.
Salpiglossis	18 in.	various	I. April	B., C.F., P.B.
Salvia	18 in.	scarlet	I. March	B., showy
Verbena	1 ft.	various	I. March, O. May	B., C.F., E., F.
Zinnia	2-4 ft.	various	I. April	B., C.F., hardy

Note: Abbreviations used below: I.—sow indoors; O.—sow outdoors; B.— bedding plant; C.F.—good for cut flowers; Cl.—climbing plant; E.—edging plant; F.—fragrant; P.B.—pinch back young plants; S.—tolerates shade; S.S.— self-sows.

Table III	
Annuals for Special Purposes	
Annuals that self-sow (hardy):	calendula, clarkia, cornflower, pansy, poppy, portulaca, snapdragon, sweet alyssum.
Annuals that should be pinched back when transplanting, in order to produce branchy plants:	ageratum, petunia, phlox, salpiglossis, snapdragon, verbena, zinnia.
Annuals with fragrance:	alyssum, heliotrope, mignonette, nicotine, pansy, petunia, snapdragon, stock, sweet pea, verbena.
Annuals for a rockery:	alyssum, candytuft, California poppy, portulaca, pansy, sedum.
Annuals which are more fragrant at night:	nicotine, petunia, stock.

Activities

Primary Grades

- Make individual flower books. In them mount flower pictures from seed catalogues.
- Draw a simple garden plan, mount flower cutouts (colored) in correct positions.

Junior and Intermediate Grades

A group of eight boys, with very little teacher guidance, made a rock garden. One boy was chosen "head gardener." The group examined rock gardens in the district, and drew up plan for their own. The head gardener then divided his group, some to get earth, some to get rocks, etc. Interested parents donated seeds and plants. In two weeks the work was finished, and then the boys planned to care for the garden for the summer. In all, the rockery cost 15¢. You can do this, too.

Intermediate Grades

Make a drawing of the school grounds to scale. Show on it all buildings, paths, hedges, lawns, etc. Discuss in class what improvements can be made. Visits to other school grounds which have been beautified will suggest changes. Send a copy of the drawing to nursery firms and seed houses and ask for plans and for catalogues of seeds, shrubs, and other plants.

Read

Andrews, *Adventures in Science,* Book VI (grades 6-7), pp. 130-143. Moyer.
Comstock, *Handbook of Nature-Study,* pp. 560-590. Allen (Comstock).
Goldsmith, *Picture Primer of Dooryard Gardening.* Allen (Houghton Mifflin).
Zim & Martin, *Flowers.* Musson (Simon & Schuster).

New to this Edition

Soffer, Ruth. *Garden Flowers Coloring Book* (Dover, 2004).
Symonds, George W. *The Shrub Identification Book: The Visual Method for the Practical Identification of Shrubs, Including Woody Vines and Ground Covers* (William Morrow, 1973).
Ziller, Catie. *The Complete Garden Flower Book: Annuals, Perennials, Bulbs, Shrubs, Climbers* (Murdoch Books, 2001).

See also references for Unit 13 (page 53).

Unit 74—From Seeds To Plants

As wonderful things are hidden away
In the heart of a little brown seed,
As ever were found in the fairy net
Of which children sometimes read.
AUTHOR UNKNOWN

The age of miracles is not past. When children see a tiny, hard, brown radish seed break open and produce a growing, living, green radish plant, they have witnessed a miracle. Then when they learn that nature had stored away not only a living plant within the seed, but had also packed with it enough food to enable this tiny plant to get a start in life, they marvel all the more. To become a partner with nature by supplying the seed with the warmth, moisture, and air necessary for its germination is for them the climax in satisfaction.

The study of seeds and germination should be for children a study of developing life, not merely of form and structure. The development of a feeling of kinship toward the awakening seeds, of appreciation of their difficulties and successes, are of more value than their knowledge of parts or of successive changes in growth. Changes in pupil attitudes in these respects will do much to increase the joy which pupils get from nature and to lessen their destruction of flowering shrubs and wildflowers. But these results cannot be obtained unless the pupils plant the seeds, care for the seedlings, and make their observations from the living, growing material.

All seeds have three main parts: the tiny plant ready to grow, a food supply to feed this until it has green leaves which make their own food, and a protective cover which helps to keep the tiny shoot from becoming too moist or too dry, too hot or too cold.

Seeds require moisture, air, and warmth, but not light, to begin growth. The same conditions, and light, are needed to continue growth. When the tiny plant in the seed starts growth, it uses the food stored within as nourishment; as a result the seed shrinks in size, or shrivels. When green leaves have developed, the plant requires sunlight to make its own food from water and minerals taken in by the roots, and from carbon dioxide taken in by the leaves.

Primary pupils should learn that plants grow from seeds, that the seeds need warmth and moisture to start the tiny plant growing, that the young plant pushes its way up through the soil, that seeds will start growth without light, that the young plants soon have roots, stems, and leaves.

To learn these facts the pupils should plant seeds such as bean, corn, nasturtium, wheat, and radish in sand or in good garden soil, cover them very lightly, and keep the soil moist and in a warm place. They should watch for the first signs of growth, dig up a few young plants to see how they look before they come up, and watch the leaves and stems turn green when they reach the light. As these things are seen, the pupils should write simple stories and make simple drawings of what they see.

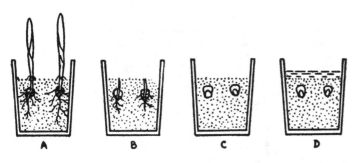

Figure 1—Finding the Conditions Favorable for Seed Germination

A, sufficient warmth, moisture, and air; B, sufficient moisture and air, but lacking warmth; C, sufficient warmth and air, but lacking mosture; D, sufficient warmth and moisture, but lacking air.

The children may wonder how the little plant can grow. Tell them that the tiny plant carried with it, in the coat of the seed, a lunch basket. By the time the lunch was all eaten, the little plant had green leaves—kitchens—in which it could make its own food and keep on growing.

Junior pupils should discover by experiments that warmth and moisture, but not light, are needed for germination. They should see the stages of growth of at least one kind of seedling and make drawn records.

Intermediate pupils should discover experimentally the need for air for germination and should observe that different kinds of plants start life in different ways. By examining soaked seeds they should discover the presence of the tiny plant within and the food supply which enables it to begin growth.

Germination Experiments

Two objectives are: first, to discover the conditions favorable for seed germination, in order that pupils may obtain an intelligent understanding of spring seeding operations; second, to realize the importance of sowing seed that will nearly all germinate, and to find a method of testing the seed for germination power. The experiments should be done in the classroom, preferably reinforced by individual pupil experiments at home. The observations will necessarily continue for some days. For convenience a blackboard space should be provided for class records, and pupils should keep individual records. Assign care of the experiments to certain pupils. Pupil participation and observation are far more valuable than their notes or examinations.

Problem 1. To discover what temperature is best for seed germination. Soak seeds of wheat, oats, radishes, etc. for half a day. Plant them in sawdust or soil in three glass tumblers, with the seeds about a half-inch deep close to the glass. Place one tumbler in the warm classroom, one in a very cold place, and one in a cool hall or cellar. Keep all moist, with no free water, for several days. Make sketches showing the amount of growth. The pupils will decide that room temperature seems best.

Problem 2. To discover what amount of moisture is best for germination. Arrange experiments as above, but with seeds in three tumblers of sawdust: one kept moist, but with no free water; another kept dry; and the third with the seeds covered with water. Keep all warm and exposed to air. Observations will show that moist soil or sawdust, without free water, gives best results.

Problem 3. To discover whether seeds require air to germinate. Discuss the above experiment to show that the water covering the seeds excluded air, thus preventing germination.

Problem 4. To find out what percentage of certain seeds will grow. Place 2 inches of well-moistened soil or sawdust in a shallow box. Cover it with cheesecloth marked off in 3-inch squares. On this, place groups of 20 each of several kinds of seeds for test. Cover them with another cloth and a thin layer of moist sawdust or soil. Keep this moist and warm. In a week, roll back the top cloth, count the number, and calculate the percentage of each kind of seed that grew. Discuss the advisability of

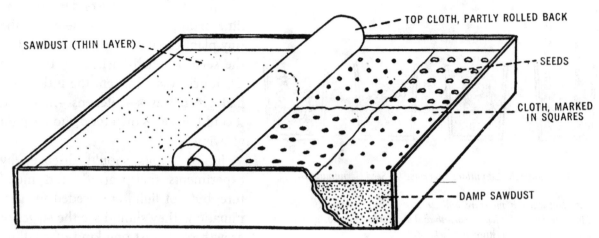

Figure 2—Finding What Percentage of Seeds Germinate

planting each kind or of buying new seed. Show that poor germination will lead to reduced crop yield, waste of land, wasteful labor, and a chance for weeds to grow.

Problem 5. To observe the changes that take place in seeds while they germinate. Line a glass jar with blotting-paper. Half fill the jar with sand or sawdust. Use a knife to push the blotting-paper away from the glass far enough to drop seeds behind it. Add enough water to thoroughly moisten the contents without leaving water around the seeds. Watch how the seeds start growth, send down the first roots, produce root branches, and send up leaves and a stem. Select two or three seedlings and draw them every second day.

Problem 6. To discover the rates of growth of several kinds of plants. Various methods may be used. Seeds may be germinated in boxes of sawdust or sand. One seedling should be dug up, drawn, and carefully replaced again every three days. The dated record may look like fig. 3. Each pupil may conduct a different experiment, and report his results to the class.

Seeds vary in the length of time it takes them to start growth. Some approximate periods in days required for germination follow: alyssum 5, California poppy 8, cosmos 5, marigold 5, morning glory 5, nasturtium 8, nicotine 20, pansy 8, petunia 20, phlox 20, portulaca 20, salvia 15, scarlet runner bean 8, verbena 8, snapdragon 20, zinnia 5. These periods will vary with temperature and moisture conditions. Pupils may test the accuracy of these figures.

Problem 7. To discover what there is in a seed which enables it to begin growth. After seeds have germinated and produced roots, stems, and leaves, we want to know from what these things grew. Soak some seeds of the same kind that you have watched germinate and grow. Beans are easily worked with. Remove the skin from the soaked seed—this protected it; split open the two halves. Find a little pointer-like or root-like object at the edge of one of the halves. This becomes a root. Find, attached to this, two small folded leaves. These are real leaves, ready to grow. As the seedling begins growth, the two halves of the bean become green for a while; then they shrivel and fall off. Place a drop of iodine on one of the halves. The blue color shows that they contain starch, the food which enables the tiny root and the two tiny leaves to begin growth.

Activities

All Grades

- Fill two tumblers with sand, soil, or sawdust. In one, plant seeds one-half inch deep close to the glass. In the other, plant the seeds one-half inch deep not close to the glass. Keep both moist and in a warm place. Is light needed for seeds to germinate? Does light prevent seeds from germinating?
- Plant different kinds of seeds and find out how each little plant comes out of the ground.
- See who can make seeds germinate and seedlings grow fastest. Each use the same kind of seed, but choose your own container, soil, place in the room, and other conditions which you think will be best for the seeds and seedlings. Since you all used the same kind of seeds, the pupil whose plant won the race must have provided the best growing conditions.

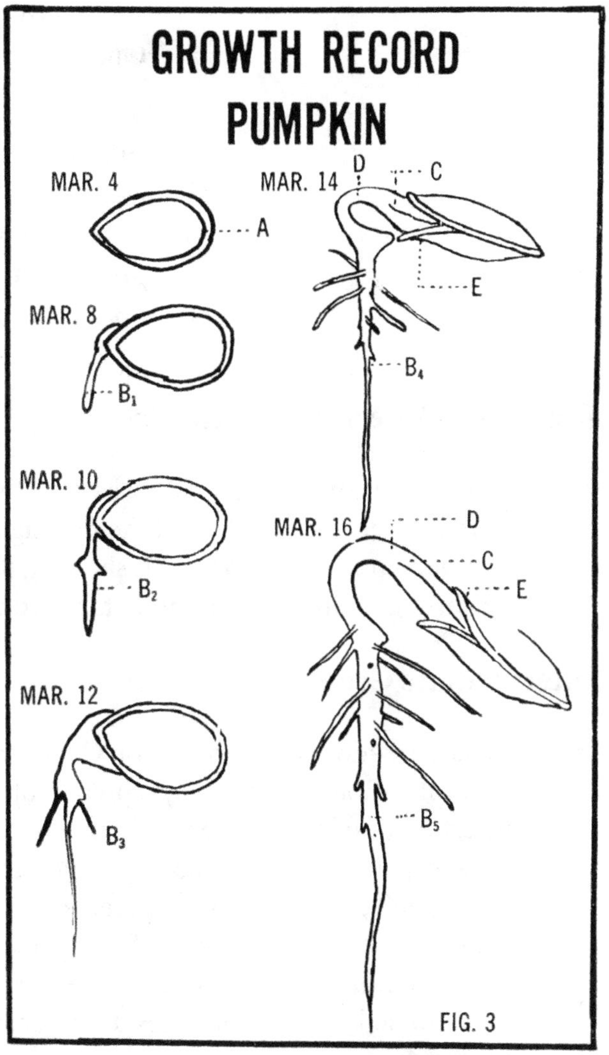

Primary and Junior Grades

Watch a seed hump up its back and then take its coat off. Plant some beans in sawdust or sand kept moist and in a warm place. Watch how the stem first loops out of the ground, then pulls up the seed, and then watch the seed take off its coat.

Now learn the memory gem:

In the heart of a seed
Buried deep, so deep,
A dear little plant
Lay fast asleep.

"Wake," said the sunshine,
"And creep to the light."
"Wake," said the voice
Of the raindrops bright.

The little plant heard,
And it rose to see

Figure 3—A, seed; B_1, B_2, B_3, B_4, B_5, stages in root development; C, young seed leaves emerging; D, arch forming and lifting seed leaves out; E, seed coat.

What the wonderful
Outside world might be.

From *Plant Baby and Its Friends,* by Kate L. Brown

O little seed so snug and tight,
Hidden away from morn till night,
I wonder what you'll grow to be
When spring's warm sun shall set you free!

A. R. Brown

Junior and Intermediate Grades

- Plant some corn. As it grows, observe: the first green tip to show above ground, how this unrolls to become the leaves, the first signs of a stem, how new leaves develop. Every third day, pull up a plant and draw it showing the development of both the root and the top.
- Perform germination experiments for yourself at home.

Intermediate Grades

- Make a rag-doll seed germinator. Cut a strip of cotton about a foot wide and 4 feet long. Lay it out flat. Roll it a little way; spread out 25 seeds from one sample. Roll it a little farther; insert seeds of another sample, etc. Roll the cloth tightly, tie it well, soak it, and leave it in a warm place. After about 5 days, open the roll and count the number of seeds which have made good growth. For your parents, test samples of grain, vegetable, and flower seeds.
- When disposing of the seeds from your rag-doll germinator, examine carefully the fuzzy growth on the roots. These are the delicate "root hairs" which on all plants gather moisture from the soil. You see them best here because they have not been destroyed by removing the plant from soil.
- Remove seedlings of corn or bean from the place where they are growing. Make India ink marks on their roots and stems. Replace the seedlings where they can continue growth. Examine them from time to time to see what part of the root and stem grows most.
- Bring several samples of oats and of other grains to school, then try to arrange them in order of quality after studying these characteristics of good seed: large and heavy, plump rather than shriveled; bright rather than dull in color; free from weed seeds and chaff, not mixed with other kinds of seeds; well matured rather than green or shrunken.

Read

Beauchamp el al., *Science Problems 2* (grades 7-8): "How Do Plants Grow from Seeds?" pp. 351-365. Gage (Scott Foresman)

Blough, *Plants Round the Year* (grades 2-3). The Basic Science Education Series. Copp Clark (Row, Peterson).

Craig & Hurley, *Discoveries with Science* (grades 5-6), pp. 129-135. Ginn.

Dowling et al., *Seeing Why* (junior), pp. 53-59. Winston.

Frasier et al., *Through the Year* (grades 1-2): "Let's Plant Seeds!" pp. 132-137; *Winter Comes and Goes* (grades 1-3): "How Doe Seeds Grow?" pp. 174-177, and "Some New Seeds," pp. 180-181. Dent (Singer).

Parker, *Flowers, Fruits, Seeds* (grades 5-6). Copp Clark (Row, Peterson).

Selsam, *Play with Plants* (grades 4-6), pp. 23-42. McLeod (Wm. Morrow).

Stephenson, *Nature at Work,* Book 1 (grades 4-5): "The Seed Becomes a Plant," pp. 70-76; *Nature at Work,* Book 2 (grades 4-6): "We Plant Some Flower Seeds," pp. 81-86. Macmillan (A. & C. Black).

New to this Edition

Carle, Eric. *The Tiny Seed* (Little Simon, 2009).
Cole, Joanna. *The Magic School Bus Plants Seeds: A Book About How Living Things Grow* (Scholastic, 1995).
Ehlert, Lois. *Planting a Rainbow* (Sandpiper, 1992).
Gardman. Gardman R687 4-Tier Mini Greenhouse.
Gibbons, Gail. *From Seed to Plant* (Holiday House, 1993).
Jordan, Helene. *How a Seed Grows (Let's-Read-and-Find-Out Science 1)* (Collins, 1992).
Sid the Science Kid. *Sid the Science Kid: How Do Plants Grow* (Kit for Primary students).

See also references in Units 75 and 81.

Unit 75—Starting Plants For The School Garden

Many flowering plants, and some vegetables, are too tender to be grown out of doors before all danger of frost is past. If the seeds are not sown until then, the plants will not reach maturity until late in the season. Market gardeners will then receive a lower price for their cabbages, tomatoes, and other vegetables, and in our gardens we will have to wait too long to enjoy the beauty of the flowers. To avoid these handicaps, we start the plants growing indoors or in a hotbed early enough to be several inches high by the time of the last frost. The time required will be from 10 to 12 weeks for petunias and snapdragons, and 7 or 8 weeks for tomatoes.

Getting Ready. Plan your garden and buy the seeds. Obtain large flowerpots, or shallow boxes about 12" × 15" and about 3" deep, with drainage holes in the bottom. First place a layer of broken pottery, cinders, or gravel to make sure that water can easily reach the drainage holes. For soil, sift a mixture of about equal parts of compost and sand, or of about equal parts of good garden loam, sand, and leaf-mold or peat moss. Place in the pot or box enough soil so that, when it has been leveled and pressed firmly with a flat leveling board, it will be about three-quarters of an inch from the top of the container. Now sow the seed.

Sowing the Seed. Mark shallow trenches about an inch apart. Sow the seed about half an inch apart in these, or broadcast the seed thinly but evenly over the surface. Tiny seeds, such as those of petunia and snapdragon, are more easily distributed if first mixed with some dry, fine sand. Cover the seeds to a depth of about twice that of their own diameter by sifting very sandy soil through a light sifter. Again press the soil firmly with the leveling board. Prepare and attach a label showing the name of the seed and the date.

Water the soil thoroughly by placing the flat or pot in a vessel of water until all surface soil appears wet, or by covering the soil with a cloth, then sprinkling on water until it drains through the holes in the bottom. Put the containers in a warm, sunny place. Shade them from direct sunlight by means of papers until the seedlings are well started. A glass will help to retain moisture.

Caring for the Seedlings. Water the soil as you did at first whenever signs of dryness are noticed. When green leaves appear, uncover them and put the pots where they will get plenty of light. Water only once in 2 or 3 days, as too much moisture will cause a disease called "damping off." A temperature of not more than 60° to 70° Fahrenheit is best. Turn the pots or box around every day or two so that the plants will not grow too much in one direction—toward the light.

In about 4 weeks, the seedlings will be large enough to be transplanted where each will have more room to grow. The right time has arrived when the little seedlings show two or more true leaves. Since the seedlings have used up all the food stored in the seed, we must plant them in a richer soil, containing a larger proportion of rotted manure or leaf-mold. Level the soil in shallow boxes with drainage holes, as before. Mark the places for plants about 2 inches apart each way. With a pencil, make deep holes. In these, place the seedlings, one in each place, deeper than they grew before. With the thumb and finger, press the soil firmly downward around the root, then level the soil around them. Water the soil thoroughly. Leave the plants in a warm, sunny place, free from frost, and at a temperature of not more than 65° to 70° Fahrenheit. For a week or so before transplanting them to the garden "harden them off" by exposing them to outside weather conditions most of each day. To make bushier plants, pinch off the top of snapdragons, verbenas, petunias, zinnias, phlox, and ageratum.

Activities

All Grades

Visit a local greenhouse or a market gardener's place and see how the soil is mixed and how flower seeds are sown and transplanted. Notice the whitewash on the glass to keep the place from becoming too warm. Ask the owner to show you how he pinches back seedlings to make them branch more.

Primary and Junior Grades

See activities in Unit 81 on page 336.

Intermediate Grades

Visit a gardener who starts seedlings in hotbeds and hardens them off in cold-frames. Find out how to make these; then make a hotbed at school. In it sow seeds of garden flowers and such vegetables as cabbage and tomatoes. Later use it as a cold-frame.

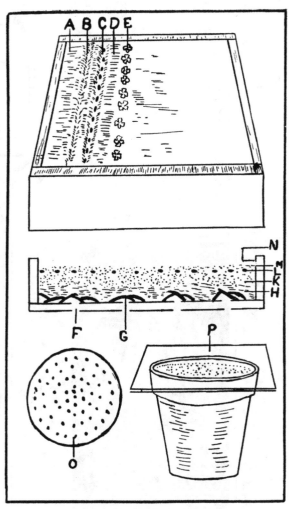

Figure 1—Starting Seedlings Indoors

A, soil levelled in seed flat; B, shallow trench for seeds; C, seeds evenly spaced; D, seeds covered; E, young seedlings; F, drainage holes in seed flat; G, drainage materials; H, coarse siftings; K, finely sifted soil; L, seeds sown; M, covering soil; N, water space; O, seeds sown in 6-inch pot; P, glass cover to retain moisture.

Read

Frasier et al., *We See* (grade 1), pp. 28-32; *Sunshine and Rain* (grades 1-2), pp. 44-47. Dent (Singer). Webber, *Bits That Grow Big.* Allen (Scott).

New to this Edition

Gardman. Gardman R687 4-Tier Mini Greenhouse.
Reilly, Ann. *Starting Seeds Indoors: Storey's Country Wisdom Bulletin A-104* (Storey, 1989).

http://www.humeseeds.com/indoor.htm
http://www.extension.umn.edu/distribution/horticulture/M1245.html

See also reading references for Unit 74 (page 310) and Unit 81 (page 336).

BEAUTIFY YOUR SURROUNDINGS – MARCH

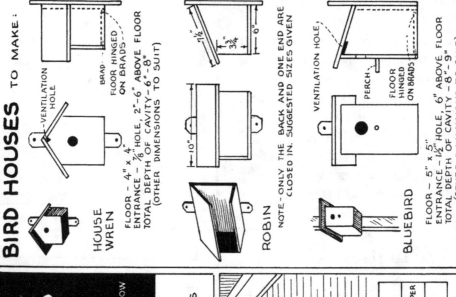

BIRD HOUSES TO MAKE:

VENTILATION HOLE
BRAD
FLOOR HINGED ON BRADS

HOUSE WREN
FLOOR – 4" x 4"
ENTRANCE – ⅞" HOLE, 2"-6" ABOVE FLOOR
TOTAL DEPTH OF CAVITY – 6"-8"
(OTHER DIMENSIONS TO SUIT)

9½"
7½"
3¾"
6"
10"

ROBIN
NOTE – ONLY THE BACK AND ONE END ARE CLOSED IN. SUGGESTED SIZES GIVEN.

VENTILATION HOLE
PERCH
FLOOR HINGED ON BRADS

BLUEBIRD
FLOOR – 5" x 5"
ENTRANCE – 1½" HOLE, 6" ABOVE FLOOR
TOTAL DEPTH OF CAVITY – 8"-9"
(OTHER DIMENSIONS TO SUIT)

WHITE
GREEN
YELLOW

ST. PATRICK'S DAY MEN –

CUT PARTS FROM COLOURED PAPER. PASTE ON CARTRIDGE PAPER. BLACK MAKES AN EFFECTIVE BACKGROUND

GUMMED PAPER
MAPS CAN BE FOLDED

FOR CURRENT EVENTS

A HELPFUL MAP OF THE WAR THEATRE CAN BE MADE BY USING POSTER COLOURS ON A LARGE SHEET OF PAPER.
BY ASSEMBLING 9"x12" ART PAPER AS SHOWN AT RIGHT, MAPS CAN BE MADE ANY SIZE DESIRED.

START SEEDS FOR THE GARDEN:

LEVEL THE SOIL
MAKE SHALLOW TRENCHES, ABOUT 1" APART, FOR SEEDS.
SPACE SEEDS ABOUT ½" APART.
SIFT SHALLOW COVERING OF SOIL OVER THEM.
KEEP MOIST.

FINE COVERING SOIL
SEEDS
FINE SOIL
COARSER SOIL
STONES OR BROKEN POTTERY FOR DRAINAGE

DRAINAGE HOLES

MAKE A HOTBED:

FRAME – SIZE TO SUIT YOUR SASH

FINISHED

FRAME
CLEAT
MANURE
SASH
SOIL
PIT

336

SEEDS:

SOAK SOME BEANS IN WATER OVERNIGHT. THEN REMOVE THE SKIN FROM ONE OF THEM. SEPARATE THE HALVES. CAN YOU FIND THE TINY ROOT AND THE TINY LEAVES?

TINY LEAVES — TINY ROOT

COVER A FEW SOAKED BEANS WITH MOIST BLOTTERS BETWEEN TWO PLATES. WHICH SPROUT FIRST — THE LEAVES OR THE ROOTS?

PLANT SOME BEANS IN MOIST SAWDUST. WHAT HAPPENS TO THE TWO HALVES OF THE SEED?

MOSSES:

FETCH SOME MOSSES FROM THE WOODS.

PUT SOME OF THIS MOSS ON A PLATE IN THE CLASSROOM. KEEP IT MOIST. WHAT CHANGES TAKE PLACE AFTER A FEW DAYS?

D. FARWELL

HARD AND SOFT WATER:

PARTLY FILL TWO SIMILAR TUMBLERS WITH "CITY" WATER. DISSOLVE A TEA-SPOONFUL OF WASHING SODA IN B. NOW ADD TEN DROPS OF STRONG SOAP SOLUTION TO EACH. SHAKE THOROUGHLY.

A   B

SUDS

CURDS

NOW, WHICH IS A AND WHICH IS B?

MAKE A CANDLE:

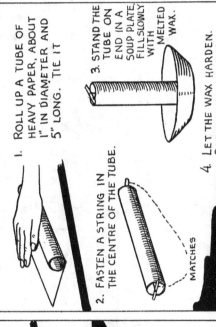

1. ROLL UP A TUBE OF HEAVY PAPER, ABOUT 1" IN DIAMETER AND 5" LONG. TIE IT

2. FASTEN A STRING IN THE CENTRE OF THE TUBE.

MATCHES

3. STAND THE TUBE ON END IN A SOUP PLATE. FILL SLOWLY WITH MELTED WAX.

4. LET THE WAX HARDEN. REMOVE THE PAPER.

MAKE A SIMPLE "TELEGRAPH"

DRY CELL

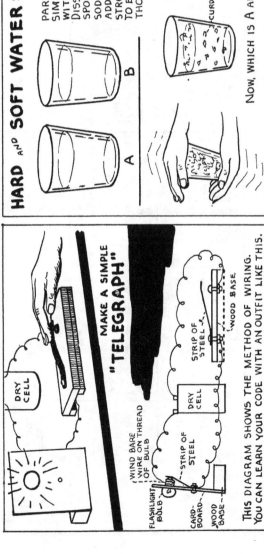

WIND BARE WIRE ON THREAD OF BULB

STRIP OF STEEL

WOOD BASE

FLASHLIGHT BULB

DRY CELL

STRIP OF STEEL

CARD-BOARD

WOOD BASE

THIS DIAGRAM SHOWS THE METHOD OF WIRING. YOU CAN LEARN YOUR CODE WITH AN OUTFIT LIKE THIS.

MAPLE SYRUP:

WHEN THE SAP BEGINS TO FLOW, TAP A HARD MAPLE TREE.

PUT A MEASURED AMOUNT OF SAP IN A SAUCEPAN AND BOIL THE SAP UNTIL IT BECOMES SYRUP. COOL. MEASURE AGAIN. ABOUT HOW MUCH SAP IS REQUIRED FOR EACH QUART OF SYRUP?

NATURAL SCIENCE — APRIL — DAY BY DAY

SUNDAY	MONDAY	TUESDAY	WEDNESDAY	THURSDAY	FRIDAY	SATURDAY
	1 Birds to look for this week or soon: Kingfisher; Flicker; Loon; Vesper Sparrow.	**2** Set up a rain gauge to measure April's rainfall.	**3** You may start new willow trees by placing cuttings in water.	**4** Make a toy windmill.	**5** Place more shrub branches in water in the classroom.	**6** Build a wren's home for your backyard.
7 Which way is the Big Dipper facing at 8 p.m.?	**8** Birds to look for this week or soon: Tree Swallow; Winter Wren; Sapsucker; Ruby-crowned Kinglet.	**9** Transplant indoor seedlings when the second leaves appear.	**10** Snakes will soon venture from their winter crevices.	**11** Watch for the first bees in search of nectar.	**12** Watch for new bright green growth on evergreens.	**13** Search for opening buds of hepaticas.
14 Visit your garden to discover which shrubs leaf out first.	**15** Start a seedling race by planting such seeds as beans, peas, wheat.	**16** Learn to write the music for a chickadee's song.	**17** Start a diary of a tree to show its rate of blossoming.	**18** What trees and shrubs have been in blossom already?	**19** Collect and plant seeds of maple, oak, and other trees.	**20** Visit a creek to look for yellow marsh marigolds. Pick them sparingly.
21 A stroll in the woods will show you what trees become active first.	**22** Why do bulbs on the southern slope of a bulb bed grow fastest?	**23** What lawn weeds have started growth?	**24** Plant a carrot from the cellar to the garden and observe its second year's growth.	**25** Collect poplar buds: you will enjoy their odour.	**26** Do bud scales of lilac, horse chestnut, and maple become leaves, or are they shed?	**27** Collect snails, dragon fly nymphs, and other water animals for a pond aquarium in your classroom.
28 Walk again in the woods. What changes since last week?	**29** Start a diary of a pair of birds from nest-building time.	**30** Make and set up a bird bath using a garbage pail cover.	NEW MOON - APR. 7	1ST QUARTER - APR. 15	FULL MOON - APR. 22	3RD QUARTER - APR. 29.

J.A. PARTRIDGE.
Drawn by D. Farwell.

Have your pupils build this calendar day by day on blackboard or chart. Use substitutions if desired.

APRIL

Unit 76—Traveling With The Birds

There is a power whose care
Teaches the way along that pathless coast,
The desert and illimitable air,
Lone wandering, but not lost.
BRYANT

These are the words of a bluebird: "Spring is here! Spring is here! I have brought it with me! Blackbirds and Robins may fool you into thinking that the thaws of February are announcing it, but believe them not. I am the real harbinger, and until I have arrived, know well that you may still have a foot of snow or zero temperature. We are not often misled into coming northward with the first rise in temperature. We usually wait until March anyway, and then if snows should come, we know they will not last long, and we can eke out an existence upon the dried berries of the cedar or barberry, or upon the sumac bobs, until the warm sun starts the canker-worm moths flying and the cut-worms to crawling. We do not mind a little cold weather if we can find plenty of food, but we prefer to wait until spring is really here before returning to the Northland . . ."
From *American Bird Biographies*, by A. A. Allen

Migration is one of the wonders of bird life, and will long remain a subject of careful study. In Unit 5 (page 17) we learned that scarcity of their natural food compels many birds to go south in winter, and in Unit 50 (page 212), that once there they have a sort of vacation with no homes to build and no young to rear. Now they make their way northward, doubtless full of hope as they plan to build new homes and rear new families.

The travels of birds vary widely in seasons, routes, and distances. Among the first to come north are the horned larks, robins, meadowlarks, blackbirds, and bluebirds. The dates of their arrival vary in different parts of the country and, to a certain extent, for different years according to weather conditions along the route. Weather in their winter homes, however, does not change appreciably, and probably has nothing to do with the decision of the birds to start northward in spring. Most of the later arrivals—some sparrows, the warblers, and scarlet tanagers—stick rather closely to schedule, affected very little by weather conditions. See fig. 1 and the table in Unit 87 (page 356).

Most birds, including the warblers, tanagers, and sparrows, travel by night. Though accidental deaths are probably greater then, they have the advantage of feeding by day. Ducks, geese, hawks,

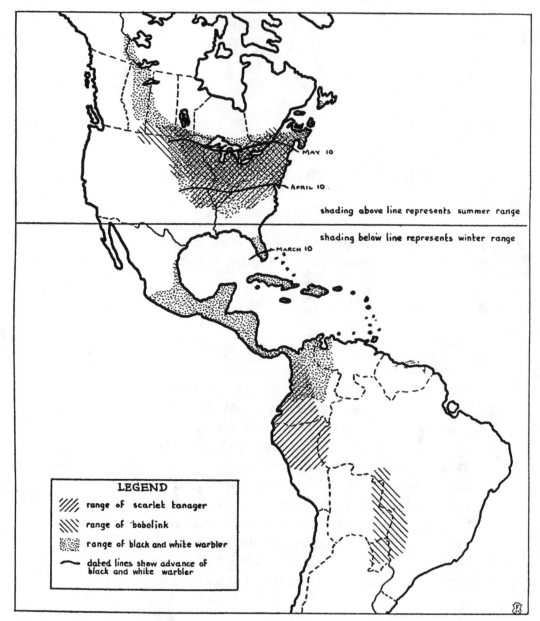

Figure 1—Summer and Winter Range of Birds

and flycatchers (such as the swallows, kingbirds, and chimney swifts) travel by day, the last-mentioned group catching their food as they fly. The speed of travel varies from about 20 to 50 miles per hour. However, the short flying hours and the alternating days of rest result in an average northward speed of only about 23 miles per day for all species. Some, like the bobolink, are thought to travel the full distance across the Gulf of Mexico, 500 to 700 miles, without a stop. Others follow the Mexican mainland. Food seems to determine the route followed by each kind of bird. Water birds migrate northward about as fast as the waters containing their food become open.

Some birds such as blue jays, and even robins, may migrate only a few miles; others travel great distances. The orioles, catbirds, yellow warblers, and hummingbirds must return from distant Panama; the chimney swifts, purple martins, nighthawks, scarlet tanagers, bobolinks, and barn swallows must make their way back from faraway parts of South America. See fig. 1, Unit 50. The warblers are largely birds of passage; they stay but a few days before going farther north to nest. But they will visit us again on their return southward in autumn.

Our winter residents—the brown creeper, junco, tree sparrow, and snow bunting—begin their northward journey here. They, too, go to their most northerly homes to rear their young.

Why do birds, so comfortable in the South, travel northward in spring? They cannot tell us, but there would seem to be three possible answers: by instinct they rear their young in the most northern part of their range; they suffer less overcrowding and find better feeding and nesting sites by spreading northward; they escape some of their enemies, though they may find new ones.

Activities

Teacher

Display pictures of birds soon to come back. Talk about them to arouse the pupils' interest in the birds' journeys northward.

Junior and Intermediate Grades

- Make a *Changeable Bird Migration Map*. On a piece of heavy card, wallboard, or similar stiff portable material, draw an accurate map of North and South America, including the main waterways and mountain ranges. As each returning bird leaves the south or arrives here place a colored picture of it on the outside margin of the mount. Attach colored ribbons with thumb tacks to show the winter home from which the bird comes, its course, and its destination. Place a piece of his color of ribbon along the edge of his picture. Do not include more than three or four birds at one time. Keep the ribbons and pictures changed at frequent intervals as spring advances. Include the date of each arrival.
- Make a mural or frieze entitled "We're on Our Way to Live with You."
- Start a bird calendar to be continued year after year as a school record of the first robin, bluebird, etc. to be seen each spring.
- Write the diary of a bird coming north.

Read

Boulton, *Traveling with the Birds*: richly illustrated by twelve full-page colored illustrations, 10 in. by 12 in. Book Society (Donohue).
Comstock, *Handbook of Nature-Study*. Allen (Comstock).
Eschmeyer, *Mac Mallard*. Book Society (Fisherman Press).
Flack, *The Restless Robin*. Allen (Houghton Mifflin).
Parker, *Animal Travels* (grades 4-6). Copp Clark (Row, Peterson).
Partridge, *Everyday Science*, Book Two: "Hawks and Owls on Trial," pp. 64-67. Dent.
Phillips and Wright, *Plants and Animals*: "Bird Travelers," pp. 154-163. Copp Clark (Row Peterson).

New to this Edition

Dunn, Jon L. *National Geographic Field Guide to the Birds of North America, Sixth Edition* (National Geographic, 2011).
Elphick and Lovejoy. *Atlas of Bird Migration: Tracing the Great Journeys of the World's Birds* (Firefly Books, 2011).
Gans, Roma. *How Do Birds Find Their Way? (Let's-Read-and-Find-Out Science 2)*, (Collins, 1996).
Lerner, Carol. *On the Wing: American Birds in Migration* (HarperCollins, 2001).
Nelson, Robin. *Migration (First Step Nonfiction: Discovering Nature's Cycles)*, (Lerner Classroom, 2010).
Sony Pictures: *Winged Migration* (DVD) directed by Jacques Perrin.
Weiddensaul, Scott. *Living on the Wind: Across the Hemisphere With Migratory Birds* (North Point Press, 2000).

Unit 77—Nature's Coming-Out Parties

Sweet and low the south wind blows.
And through the brown field calling goes,
"Come, Pussy! Pussy Willow!
Within your close brown wrapper stir,
Come out and show your silver fur,
Come, Pussy! Pussy Willow!"
ADAPTED

Spring is in the air: we feel it, pupils feel it, and nature shows it; the snow has melted, little freshets rush past, the wind and clouds tell us. Old life is awakening from its winter rest, and new life is coming forth. Now, if ever, is our opportunity to help pupils discover that the earth is brimful of living things of interest to us all.

As the sun gets higher and higher day by day, and therefore has a greater heating effect in our latitudes, all life responds. Buds of trees and shrubs, new growth of perennials and wildflowers, hibernating animals fresh from their winter sleep, moths and butterflies newly emerged from their protecting cradles—all these signs of awakening life show that spring is here.

New life, too, will soon be all around us. Chicks are hatching; birds are returning to raise new families; frogs, toads, and salamanders are gathering at streams ready to lay their eggs in a watery nest; clusters of tent-caterpillar eggs will soon hatch on shrubs and trees; gauzy moths and butterflies, free from their winter cases, will soon be laying their eggs; fish are ascending streams to spawn; bumblebee queens are about to start new generations; many mammals are giving birth to litters of young; little plants, dormant in seeds, will soon spring forth to produce new life.

At such times it is the teacher's task to quicken the imagination and thereby sharpen the eyes of pupils. To them each day should be a new adventure. Oral reports day by day, individual diaries and calendars, original drawing (with the teacher not too critical of the rules of English and the principles of art) will encourage pupils to make such discoveries that they will appreciate spring as the season of beginnings.

Pupils of intermediate grades are ready to discover that it takes both mother and father animals to produce young. Home and classroom experiences with butterfly eggs which do not hatch, observation of the courtship of birds, the discovery that some hen's eggs do not hatch because they were infertile, knowledge that pollen is needed for seeds to be produced—all these show that new life in the plant and animal kingdom requires both mothers and fathers.

Activities

Teacher

- Discuss the signs of spring under three headings: awakening life (opening buds, reviving perennials, emerging moths and butterflies, hibernating animals becoming active); new life (hatching eggs of tent caterpillars, of frogs and toads, of poultry and other birds; the birth of young to mammals); returning life (birds and monarch butterflies, fish ascending streams).
- Make a mural to illustrate these three phases. Let a third of the class be responsible for each one of the topics.
- Begin a blackboard calendar entitled "Signs of Spring."

All Grades

- Visit a marsh when the frogs are peeping or croaking. When one detects you and stops calling, do the others nearby stop also?
- Find Hepatica plants just wakening to the call of spring.
- Again bring some twigs of cherry, plum, forsythia, etc. into the classroom. What happens to the little scales as the buds open? What do buds form . . . leaves? Flowers? Both? Did these twigs take a longer or shorter time to bloom than the twigs used in Unit 57 (page 238)?
- Observe the fresh green of the new growth from the cluster of buds at the end of branches of pine and other evergreens.
- Find where grass and other plants in your schoolyard first begin to grow. Why?
- Try to find cocoons shown in fig. 3. Bring them to school and cage them. Watch for the moths to come out.
- Write stories using such titles as: "Spring's Handiwork," "Hurrah! It's Spring!"

Figure 1—A Sure Sign of Spring—The Frog Chorus

Figure 2—Hepaticas—in the Woods in Spring

The sun is very hot
And I have on my sweater;
If I could take it off
I'd feel a great deal better.
But then I mustn't mind—
Hepaticas don t care,
Because they still have on
Their fuzzy underwear.

Reprinted from
Better Homes and Gardens
Magazine

Primary Grades

- Rake away some leaves in the flowerbed. Are there any little plants coming up? How do they look? Find some which will later have flowers—daffodils, hyacinths, snowdrops, tulips.
- Gather willow twigs from several shrubs or trees. Place them in water. Watch the little protecting scale come off as the pussy grows. Feel the softness of the pussy. When the catkins are full grown, shake away some of the willow "gold dust." Watch where and how the roots form under water.
- Select one fruit tree or shrub. Look at it every day to find the first signs that the buds are getting bigger.
- Each pupil watch for pictures of things that happen in spring. Bring them to school. On another day all of you will work with the teacher in making a mural.
- Make Plasticine twigs, and to them attach—in proper arrangement—real willow pussies.

Primary and Junior Grades

- Make a sand-table scene to illustrate the coming of spring. Use good soil, not sand. Sow grass seed and care for the new growth. Plant some of the first woods plants that you see coming up—mosses, hepatica, violet. Have a little pond. Make and place swings, teeter-totters, and slides with Plasticine children playing on them.
- Make a poster entitled "Mr. Hoppy Steps Out" showing a toad leaving its winter quarters for the garden, and one of "Elfin Painters."

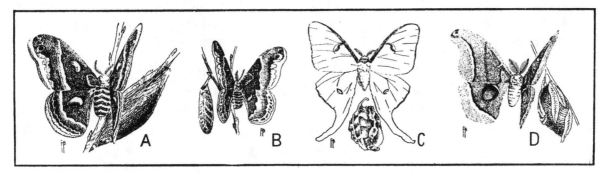

Figure 3—Well-Known Spring Moths and Their Cocoons

A, Cecropia: cocoon long, spindle-shaped, attached along twig; moth large, brownish-gray, a light crescent on the inner half of each wing. B, Promethea: cocoon small, hangs rolled in a leaf; moth with blue eye-spot near the tip of front wing, female buff and brown, male darker with light wing borders. C, Luna: cocoon oval, brown, papery; moth green, swallow-tailed. D, Polyphemus: cocoon oval, nearly white, often partly wrapped in fallen leaf; moth buff or fawn, with transparent "eyes" on all four wings.

Junior and Intermediate Grades

- Place some pussy-willow twigs in water and some others in a vase without water. Which make the more permanent ornament? Observe the yellow stamens on the "pussies" kept in water. Draw them as you see them; examine the pollen. You should learn that willow pussies are true flowers and that the pollen helps willow trees to produce seeds. Collect also "pussies" (catkins) of birch, alder, and poplar. Watch them develop in water in the classroom.
- Watch for these: groundhogs becoming active, frogs starting their chorus, toads traveling to water to lay their eggs, the first blossoms of red maple.
- Observe and identify some spring butterflies, such as the Swallowtail varieties, the Red Admiral, and the Painted Lady, as they flit from place to place.
- Begin a class diary with the same title as this chapter. All pupils will suggest entries. From these the best will be selected.
- Make a mural entitled "Good Morning, Nature."
- Draw staff lines for a common music selection. Attach willow pussies for notes.
- Have a poster contest, the basis of judgment to be originality, not talent in art. Here are some titles: Birds Are Coming, Trees Are Dressing, Nature's Waking Up, Children Welcome Spring.

Intermediate Grades

- Observe how birds use their songs, swell out their feathers, or proudly parade their attractive colors to please their mates.
- Look for snails' eggs surrounded by jelly on dead leaves in a stagnant pool, or on the glass in your aquarium. Watch the little snails hatching and coming out of the jelly—very much as do tadpoles.
- Find the eyes on a potato. Plant it in moist soil or saw-

BEN LIFTED UP AN OLD FLOWER CROCK IN THE GARDEN AND OUT STEPPED MR. HOPPY

Figure 4—Mr. Hoppy (American Nature Association

dust, and after two weeks examine it to see what has happened to the eyes. Yes, the eyes are buds ready to produce stems and leaves. All buds need food to grow. We have already found that potatoes contain a great amount of starch. This feeds the eye buds.

PANTOMIME. THE OPENING OF HORSE-CHESTNUT BUDS

Scene 1. A closed bud (pupils in circles—outer circle of pupils wearing brown dresses to represent bud scales).

Scene 2. Brown bud scales drop and green leaves dance about the pinkish flowers (inner groups of pupils).

Scene 3. The bud scales lie, green leaves stretch up, and the flowers open (by standing).

Scene 4. A butterfly visits the flower.

Figure 5—A Mural or a Window Transparency

Foliage, green; flowers, yellow; moon, silver; elfmen, black.

Read

Crew, *The More the Merrier.* Oxford.

Erickson, *The True Book of Animals of Small Pond:* "Baby mammals," pp. 27-38. Book Society (Children's Press).

Frasier et al., *Through the Year* (grades 1-2): "A Spring Walk," pp. 109-111; "Wake Up!" pp. 112-113; "Spring in the Garden," pp. 128-131; *Winter Come, and Goes* (grades 2-4): "Spring Is Here," pp. 139-141, and "The Apple Tree in Spring," pp. 144-145. Dent (Singer).

Hussey & Pessino, *Collecting Cocoons* (grades 4-7). Ambassador (Crowell).

Hylander, *Out of Doors in Spring* (grades 6-8): "The Trees Awaken," pp. 9-27. Macmillan.

Partridge, *Everyday Science,* Book One: "Awakening Life," pp. 259-272. Dent.

Selsam, *All About Eggs.* Allen (Wm. R. Scott).

Smith & Clarke, *Along the Way* (primary), pp. 103-125. Longmans, Green.

Stephenson, *Nature at Work,* Book 1 (grades 4-5): "Tree Budsand How They Open," pp. 60-64; *Nature at Work,* Book 3 (grades 5-6): "The Rise of Sap and Growth of Shoots," pp. 85-88. Macmillan (A. & C. Black).

Webb, *Song of the Seasons* (grades 4-6): "Spring," pp. 7-40. McLeod (Wm. Morrow).

New to this Edition

Catlin, Christine. *Raising Monarchs for Kids* (KidPub Press, 2010).

Frost, Helen, *Monarch and Milkweed* (Atheneum Books for Young Readers, 2008).

Leslie, Clare Walker. *The Nature Connection: An Outdoor Workbook for Kids, Families, and Classrooms* (Storey, 2010).

Swan, Susan. *It's Spring* (Millbrook Press, 2002).

Hussey. *Collecting Cocoons* (HarperCollins, 1962). [Find in used book search engines.]

Wright, Amy Bartlett. *Peterson First Guide to Caterpillars of North America* (Houghton Mifflin Harcourt, 1998).

Unit 78—Classroom Hatcheries

Spring is characterized by many forms of new life. Seeds are germinating, the young of mammals are being born, eggs are hatching. Of most interest to children, perhaps, is the hatching of eggs.

Primary children delight in seeing baby chicks, thrill to touch them, and long to have them as pets. But to see them hatch is the greatest thrill of all. Older children extend their curiosity into the fields of bird and insect life. Having found a nest containing birds' eggs, they impatiently await their hatching; they wonder whether caterpillars will come from the eggs laid by the newly emerged captive moths and butterflies. Then they discover to their great satisfaction that they can watch the eggs of tent caterpillar and mosquitoes—yes, of frogs and toads—producing active, living things before their own eyes. Surely there is no better way of developing attitudes which change the desire to shy a stone at the first frog's head in spring to a keen search for its first eggs!

The eggs of tent caterpillars, laid in autumn, are found in rings glued around a twig of such trees and shrubs as wild or cultivated fruit trees and Japanese quince. In water in the classroom place the cut ends of twigs bearing eggs. The little caterpillars will hatch about the time the leaf buds open, and will spin a tent-like web. If kept in a screened cage, they may be observed spinning, eating leaves by day, growing, perhaps molting.

Eggs of frogs and toads, along with some of the pond water and some plant life, may be brought from quiet pools and kept in a sunny window in large, open, glass containers. Frogs' eggs occur in jelly-like masses; toads' eggs in strings. The tadpoles of toads and of some frogs complete their development in the classroom in 2 months or more; those of green frogs will take a year or more to develop.

With primary and junior pupils the study should be limited to simple observations growing out of natural curiosity; intermediate pupils should come to understand the sequence of changes in habits and structure as the tadpoles develop into toads and frogs.

When the cocoons and pupae collected in autumn give forth moths and butterflies, a double interest comes to the pupils—first, the wonder of their getting out, drying and expanding their wings, and beginning, untaught, to fly; second, the laying of eggs, tiny, circular, often yellowish, glued to the walls of

Figure 1—An Interesting Classroom Hatchery

their cage. Will these hatch? After intermediate pupils have watched to see, and have been disappointed, the explanation that two parents are needed for even eggs to hatch will come from the teacher. If the teacher has been successful in caging both male and female moths and butterflies of the same species, the rest of the story may be provided by placing in the cage green plants, kept fresh in water, on which the eggs may be laid and the young may feed. After the hatching process has been seen, the growth and molting of the larvae may be observed and discussed.

Activities

All Grades

- Bring to school a box and some straw in which to set a hen. Place the box in a quiet place in the woodshed or in an unused basement room. A pupil may bring a broody hen to school and all watch how she is set. The owner take charge of feeding, watering, and exercising her each day. Keep a record of the date of setting and the date the chicks first appear. Mark eggs and see if the hen turns them when she gets on them. Listen to the voice of the mother hen when the chicks are hatched. Hold some eggs up to a strong light when they have been sat upon for 10 days. Notice that most are quite dark because the young chick is growing within, while the light may be seen through some because there is no chick in them to grow.
- From a cardboard carton or a wooden box, make a chick brooder for the classroom. For a brooder "stove" obtain a large tin ran which has a cover, or a honey pail. While holding the pail inverted over the end of a block of wood, use a chisel to cut a hole in the bottom of it large enough to take the base of an electric bulb. Screw the bulb through this into the socket of an extension cord. To ventilate the "stove," make nail holes in the base and lid. Hang the "stove" away from the sides and top of the box, 6 or 8 inches above the floor. Use netting or screen at the front of the brooder for ventilation, and glass over a part of the top.
- Keep the part of the brooder under the stove at a temperature of nearly 100° Fahrenheit. Do not feed the chicks for 48 hours. Then watch how the chicks first peck at sand, how they pick up the first feed, how they drink. Keep them at school for a week or two, constantly supplied with starting mash, fresh water, and clean, dry paper or sawdust. Observe how rapidly they grow.
- Search for frogs' eggs in still pools. Collect some along with pond water and plants and place them in a large glass vessel or an aquarium. Avoid overcrowding. Watch for tiny tadpoles moving about in the developing eggs, then sliding out and dashing about. Observe how they cling to plants, feed, and breathe by means of external gills when tiny. Keep a record of changes in their appearance as they grow. Observe the changes in their method of feeding and swimming.
- Play "Old Hen and Chickens." "One child representing the hen goes to the corner of the room and covers her eyes, or steps out of the room. A leader designates a number of children, usually from four to six, who are to be chickens. All of the children rest their heads on the desk and the mother hen returns to the room. As the hen comes near the children she calls 'Cluck, cluck,' and only those who were appointed to be chickens answer, 'Peep, peep.' If the hen can guess from which chickens the call comes, she touches them on the head and they sit up. The hen repeats her call often until she has found all of her chicks. Other groups of chicks are chosen until all of the children have had an opportunity to take part in the game."[1]

---

1   *Classroom Teacher, Vol. 5.*

Primary and Junior Grades

- Rear toads from eggs in the classroom. See what the little tadpoles look like (all head and tail); watch how they feed. See the first legs appear, then the other pair. Give the little toads a block of cork or bark to float upon in the water. See how both tadpoles and young toads swim.
- Make up and present little riddles such as "I am nearly black. I swim about in the water. The older I become, the shorter my tail becomes. Someday I shall learn to hop. Who am I?"

Junior and Intermediate Grades

- Make a frieze of three sections, one to illustrate returning life—birds and butterflies, fish going up streams; a second to show awakening life (Unit 77, page 324); another depicting various forms of new life—young mammals, birds, fish, insects.
- Rear and learn about mosquitoes. Place rainwater containing wrigglers in a glass jar in the classroom. Cover the jar with netting. Observe how they rest upside down at the surface of the water to breathe. Watch for some to change into pupae with their large "head and shoulders." Which way up are they when they breathe? You may see a mosquito work itself out of the pupa case and rest on the little empty boat while its wings dry.
- Try to find little rafts of mosquito eggs in stagnant water. Place the water and eggs in a screened glass jar indoors and see the wrigglers come out of the eggs. Place a few of the wrigglers in another vessel of water on which half a teaspoonful of kerosene has been poured. The wrigglers' breathing tubes cannot pierce this, and so they suffocate. Oil is often sprayed on stagnant pools to kill the young mosquitoes.

Intermediate Grades

Collect a pair of toads in early spring before they lay their eggs (the male does the piping, and the female's body is more extended by the eggs within). Place them in an aquarium or a similar vessel which has sand on the bottom and contains some water. Leave a stone projecting above the water. Keep the vessel in a light place. The mother toad may lay strings of eggs. Then watch how they hatch and the tadpoles grow.

Read

Frasier et al., *Through the Year* (grades 1-2): "The Story of a Toad," pp. 114-121, and "Betsy and Her Chicks," pp. 146-153; also *Winter Comes and Goes* (grades 2-3): "Frogs, Toads, and Salamanders," pp. 146-148. Dent (Singer).

Knight, *The Golden Nature Readers,* Book One (grades 4-6): "How the Tadpole Became a Frog." pp. 18-25. Clarke, Irwin (University of London Press). Logier, *From Egg to Tadpole to Frog.* Royal Ontario Museum of Zoology, 100 Queen's Park, Toronto 5.

Partridge, *Everyday Science,* Book One: "Classroom Discoveries," pp. 278-281. Dent.

New to this Edition

Blackaby, Susan. *Hatching Chicks (Read-It! Readers: Classroom Tales Yellow Level)* (Picture Window Books, 2004).

DK Readers: *Tale of a Tadpole* (DK Children, 2009).

Legg, Gerald. *From Egg to Chicken* (Chilren's Press, 1998).

Gibbons, Gail. *Chicks and Chickens* (Holiday House, 2005).

Pfeffer, Wendy. *From Tadpole to Frog (Let's-Read-And-Find-Out Science: Stage 1),* (Perfection Learning, 1994).

Heiligman, Deborah. *From Caterpillar to Butterfly (Let's-Read-and-Find-Out Science 1)* (Collins, 1996).

Wallace, Karen. *Born to be a Butterfly* (DK Children, 2010).

Unit 79—Spring Nature Diaries

As the title implies, the purpose of this unit is to encourage pupils to make intimate contacts with some one particular phase of nature as it changes through the spring season. Following the development of a tulip plant, a tree, a garden, a frog's egg or a tadpole gives the pupil not only a deepened interest in and appreciation of nature, but also a quickened consciousness of such ideas as life history, seasonal change, and the interdependence of living things.

From a large number of plants and animals suggested by the teacher, each pupil will select the one which interests him most, observe and investigate it from day to day, and keep a diary in graphic and written form. From time to time oral reports will be given in class so that all may know something about each phase. Blackboard records may even be made for some selected topics. However, no effort should be made to prescribe any uniform body of facts to be learned by all pupils.

Although the knowledge gained from this activity cannot be tested in the traditional way,

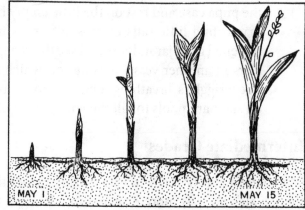

Figure 1—Four Weeks with a Lily of the Valley Plant

it is quite obvious from the following example that pupils will be gaining worthwhile nature knowledge: Molly made a diary of an elm tree from the time the buds were in the winter condition until its leaves were fully developed. She learned that the buds were formed in autumn and remained alive but inactive during the cold weather. Spring's warmth caused sap, containing stored food, to flow to them from the roots, trunk, and branches. Then they enlarged, their scales dropped, their leaves unfolded and grew. The little stems in the buds grew longer and produced new branches and side twigs. Meanwhile the flower buds produced their flowers and fruits. Near the end of her diary, Molly recorded the visits on which she discovered the orioles building their nest in the tree, what insects appeared, and what birds came to eat them.

Activities

Primary Grades

- Each pupil make a simple little diary book by folding the paper, tying it, and trimming the edges. Print simple titles such as "My Tulip." Each day, with the teacher's help, write a story

332

and make a drawing to show how much the tulip has grown.

- Each day look at a tree outside the window, and write a little story on the board to show its changes.
- Write the diary of a chicken, beginning with the day it pecked a hole through the shell.
- Write blackboard story diaries of the opening buds of a tree or shrub in the schoolyard. Omit dates, but from day to day add new stories to the diary. It may read like this: "The buds are getting bigger. Today they opened far enough for me to peek in. A leaf stuck its head out today."

Junior Grades

- If mother has a garden, ask her to help you keep a diary of it.
- Watch for the first swelling of the buds on a red maple tree. Draw it then and every third day until the flowers and leaves are out. On each drawing label the day, and whether the weather has been warm, cool, or cold.

Intermediate Grades

- Write and illustrate the diary of a tadpole from the time it first wriggled in the egg until it had legs.
- Make dated illustrations (preferably in color) of some of the following: a tulip from the time it becomes visible until the flower dies; a grapevine from the time the buds swell until the leaves are open; a fern from the time the little hairy curl appears until the leaves are fully developed.

Read

New to this Edition

Albert, Toni. *A Kid's Spring Ecojournal* (Tickle Creek Books, 1997).
Esbaum, Jill. *Everything Spring* (National Geographic Children's Books, 2010).
Fowler, Allan. *How Do You Know It's Spring? (Rookie Read About Science Series)* (Children's Press, 1991).

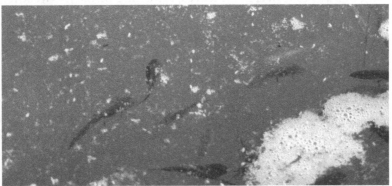

Figure 2—Larvae of newt and Marsh Frog.

Unit 80—Spring Nature Calendars

The making of nature calendars helps to keep the pupils conscious of nature round about them day by day—as they see it, rather than as the teacher sees it. Through firsthand contacts with their surroundings, rather than by mere facts taught by the teacher, pupils learn to appreciate and love nature. Daily records in calendar form demand careful observation and systematic organization. Instead of learning isolated facts or facts about isolated topics, pupils learn to see unity and interdependence in nature. They come to see that things of nature are not static, that they are constantly changing, but always according to some definite system or law.

The making of such calendars is not meant to replace the daily-discussion period in natural science, but to supplement it in an incidental manner. In addition to training in scientific ways of thinking, calendars provide wide scope for correlation, especially with art and English.

Blackboard calendars may express the combined observations of the class, or the specific observations of named pupils. Class calendars permit pupils to pool their resources. Individual calendars, like diaries, are personal things. In them the pupil expresses his own feelings in his own way. It therefore behooves the teacher to be very careful not to dampen the pupil's enthusiasm by overemphasis upon correct spelling and grammatical construction.

Figure 1

Calendar records should not be made out of school hours. They are a part of current events, and may well be discussed and reported in that period.

Spring nature calendars may apply to all phases of nature—the moon and stars by night, sunrise and sunset, the opening of buds of flowers and leaves, returning birds, the weather, etc.

Activities

All Grades

- Make a blackboard calendar entitled "I Spy." On it record such observations as the first robin seen, the first outdoor crocus in bloom, the first pussy willow brought in, the first hepatica flower seen, the first cherry blossom, the first frogs' eggs discovered. Use headings to show the date, the observation, and the observer's name.
- Rule a large sheet of mural paper in the form of a monthly calendar. For a few minutes each day discuss the new things seen in nature. Select the best and have the pupil or pupils who observed it draw it. Arrange to have every pupil take at least one turn.

Primary and Junior Grades

- For each week set apart a section of the bulletin board to show signs of spring. Display pictures to illustrate, as they are seen, such signs as these: melting snow, little streams, birds flying north, birds building nests, frogs, woodchucks out, buds opening, flowers of gardens and shrubs, wildflowers in bloom, green lawns, people carrying umbrellas, children playing marbles, farmers plowing.
- Rule a large weather calendar for a month. Observe and record the weather for each day, using such symbols as those suggested in Unit 27 (page 113).

Junior and Intermediate Grades

- Make a blackboard calendar entitled "Forest Trees Awaken," with columns headed: Name of Tree, Date of Swelling of Leaf Buds, Date of First Flat Leaves, Date of Opening of Flower Buds, Color of Blossoms, and Drawings. Complete it for such common trees is oak, elm, soft maple, sugar maple, willow, poplar, and basswood. (Pictures may be collected to take the place of drawings.) Select one of these trees and make a series of dated drawings to show the stages of swelling and opening of leaf and flower buds.
- Make a calendar, "Trees in Blossom," using the headings: Name of Tree, Date When Buds Begin to Open, Date When First Flower Opens, Date When Last Petals Fall. Fill in the names of shrubs, fruit trees, shade trees, etc.
- Make individual and blackboard calendars with such column headings as: Name of Tree or Shrub, Buds Begin to Swell, First Leaves Open, First Flowers Open, Leaves Full Size, Flowers Gone. Select a few shrubs and trees; observe the development of their buds; from day to day, record the correct dates in each column.

Intermediate grades

Make a calendar of blossoming fruit trees. Use these column headings: Name of Tree, First Buds Show New Colors, Flowers Wide Open, Petals Fallen, Little Fruits Seen. In the first column write the names of whatever fruit trees you can observe; in the others write the dates of the events. Make a similar calendar for garden shrubs.

Read

New to this Edition

Anderson, Maxine. *Explore Spring: 25 Great Ways to Learn About Spring* (Nomad Press, 2007).
Kutsch, Irmgard. *Spring Nature Activities for Children* (Floris Books, 2006).
Ross, Kathy. *Craft to Make in The Spring* (Millbrook Press, 1998).

Unit 81—Classroom Gardens

For children in urban schools where outdoor gardens are impossible at home or school, and for little tots in all schools, the activities in this unit are suggested. It is even more important that these pupils should have opportunities to prepare soil, sow seeds, tend seedlings, and appreciate the growth of plant life. The necessary indoor facilities will consist of the sand-table, some flowerpots and shallow wooden boxes with drainage holes in the bottom, an old table or other support near a window. Metal surfaces and waterproof bake tins or trays will keep water from injuring varnished surfaces. An old aquarium or vivarium will be useful.

No, you cannot have a spick-and-span classroom at the same time as you have indoor gardens under way! But you can have an educational workshop in which pupils learn to enjoy plant life, to understand some of its mysteries, and to develop habits and knowledge which will help them to make their own homes more interesting places in which to live.

To obtain full value from these activities, pupils must participate in all planning and working. They should help to mix the soil, sow the seed, water the plants, turn them round to prevent them from bending too much in one direction, etc. Each child should have his own little garden, even if only a flowerpot. This appeals to pride of ownership, and is the first step in training pupils to have respect for property of others. Blackboard calendars, individual notebooks, diaries, cooperative compositions, and blackboard readings are only a few of the worthwhile correlations with other subjects.

Activities

All Grades

In a large bowl or other suitable container place a layer of leaf-mold. In this, plant mosses, wild-flowers, little trees, and fern fronds, combined to represent a bit of woods. Keep it warm, moist, and in a sunny place. Observe the little pods forming on mosses, the opening of leaf and flower buds of trees and wildflowers, the uncoiling of fern fronds.

See Unit 74 (page 310) and Unit 75 (page 316) for other indoor activities.

Primary and Junior Grades

- Each child have a flowerpot garden. Put pebbles in the bottom; then good loamy soil. Sow seeds of quick-growing plants such as balsam, nasturtium, corn, beans, peas, radishes, tomatoes, and pumpkin. Have each pot labeled with the owner's name, and keep the pots

Figure 1—Children Like Making These Gardens

in or near a sunny window. Each pupil care for his own garden. By assignments and directions lead pupils to observe such things as: the way the plants come up, which plants show first, how some plants stand erect and others trail or climb, which grow fastest, the way the leaves unfold, the way they turn to light. When danger of frost is past, the plants may be transplanted into the school ground or taken home by each pupil for his own garden.

- Save some egg shells from which only a small part has been removed at one end. Arrange them in a shallow box containing sand or sawdust to keep them erect. Fill each with sandy garden loam. Plant two or three seeds in each; later remove all but one plant. Keep them moist, but not too wet. Watch how the little seedlings grow. Transplant your plant to the garden, shell and all, when there is no more danger of frost.

- Make a sand-table vegetable garden, with each pupil having his own plot. Replace the sand with good soil about 3 inches deep. Lay out paths and plots, and, in the moist soil, plant cuttings from shrubs for hedges. Each pupil choose his own seeds from those available and plant and care for his own garden. Use a bottle with a sprinkler top for watering.

- Make a community garden either in the sand-table or in a large box. If weather permits, this may be done out of doors. Store the sand and replace it with good garden soil. Construct a stucco home or school by plastering salt and flour on a model of stiff cardboard or of rough wood, then pushing little pebbles into it. Place the building as the center of interest. Around it make a lawn, paths, hedges, shrubbery, a flower garden, a vegetable garden, a little pool, birdhouses, birdbaths, etc.

- For this work, construct little spades by inserting pieces cut from vegetable tins in slits cut in wooden handles. Make rakes by driving inch nails through narrow strips of wood; use larger nails for handles. Use a tin can for a roller. For the lawn, cultivate the area planned, then sow and rake in grass seed. For paths, use sand, pebbles, or gray paper. Use evergreen twigs or leafy shoots of shrubs for hedges and shrubbery. Mark off the flower and vegetable gardens, and sow seeds of quick-growing plants as suggested above. Shallow vessels containing water and embedded in the soil will serve as a pool and birdbath. Make and erect birdhouses of paper or Plasticine.

- Make a mural of a garden. Use brown paper for earth, gray strips for pathways, little strips of red paper in rows for beets, of green paper for corn, etc. Represent trees and shrubs, homes and people, a robin pulling out an earthworm. etc.

Figure 2—Serious business, this study of new plants—even for juniors.

Read

Frasier et al., *Through the Year* (grades 1-2): "Let's Plant Seeds!" pp 132-137. Dent (Singer)

New to this Edition

Bearce, Stepahnie. *A Kid's Guide to Container Gardening* (Mitchell Lane Publishers, 2009).
Krezel, Cindy. *Kids' Container Gardening: Year-Round Projects for Inside and Out* (Ball Publishing, 2010).
Talmage, Ellen. *Container Gardening for Kids* (Sterling Publishing Co, 1997). [Find on used book search engines.]

See also reading references in Unit 74 (page 310) and Unit 75 (page 316).

Unit 82—Planting and Caring for Trees and Shrubs

Plant a tree in a spot that you love, my friend,
And know you have done a useful thing,
For you never can tell where good acts end—
A bird may rest that is weary of wing,
Or a traveler cool his burning brow
In the shade of the tree that you plant now.
And should you fall before your tree,
(And this may happen to you or me)
You have your living monument,
With its basic roots that are downward sent
And a lofty crest which will aspire,
E'en like a good deed, higher and higher.
HOMER HARPER

The idea of Arbor Day was first put forth in a resolution by the State of Nebraska Board of Agriculture, Jan. 4, 1872, naming April 10, 1872 as "especially set apart and consecrated to tree planting in the State of Nebraska and the State Board of Agriculture hereby name it Arbor Day." From that beginning the idea has spread throughout the United States, Canada, and other parts of the world.

But tree-planting and other school ground improvement activities should not be limited to Arbor Day. Local conditions may make some other date more suitable. Trees and shrubs should be planted as soon as soil conditions permit after the frost is out of the ground.

A few trees or shrubs may be added to the school grounds each year, but the planting should be according to a definite and permanent plan as described in Unit 73 (page 304). Small trees may be obtained from the Ontario Forestry Department, Toronto; larger ones may be purchased from commercial nurseries or selected from woods. The tree to be transplanted should be straight, shapely specimens of comparatively small size. They should be carefully dug around and lifted with as much of the root system and soil as possible. Unless they are to be planted at once, the roots should be wrapped in old sacks and kept moist. They should never be exposed to sunlight.

Planting the Tree or Shrub. Dig the hole several inches deeper and wider than the root system. Loosen the soil in the bottom and replace some of it with good topsoil. After pruning any injured roots, place the tree or shrub an inch or two lower than it was before, and spread the roots carefully and naturally. Sift fine topsoil among the roots while constantly moving the plant up and down so that the soil fills all spaces. Use only fertile soil. Tramp the soil firmly while filling. Leave a saucer-like depression at the top, and in this pour a pail of water.

When all the water has soaked away, fill the space with soil, but do not tramp it or water it.

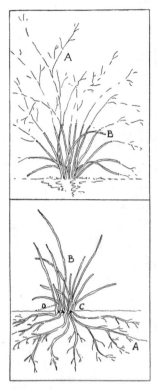

Figure 1— Pruning Shrubs When Planted, and Later

Upper: A, the original form of the Shrub; B, the wrong way to prune, leaving an un-natural form.

Lower: A, roots well spread out when planted; B, branches pruned to leave natural form; C, soil level around shrub; D, soil never heaped around roots.

Beside large trees, place a supporting stake and fasten the tree to it with raffia, rubber hose, or a strip of stout cloth. Prune the tree or shrub about one-third the way back to balance the setback to the root system.

Pruning Flowering Shrubs. Space permits only a brief reference, although this phase of school gardening requires much more attention than it has been given in the past. The need for pruning before and immediately after planting, the latter to prevent too great transpiration while the root system "is just becoming established, has been mentioned before. Regular pruning should follow, removing two or three older stalks, at the ground level, each year. This provides for constant renewal. Three other important points to remember are: (1) Prune *early flowering shrubs* only after the bloom has died. This avoids removal of buds formed the previous summer for early spring bloom; *e.g.,* forsythia, spirea, lilac. (2) *Late -flowering shrubs* grow new twigs in spring and later produce flowers on this wood. Prune these in late fall or early spring; *e.g.,* Hydrangea, Anthony Waterer spirea. (3) *Avoid late-summer pruning* of any shrubs, roses, or hedges as this encourages new growth which is too tender to survive winter.

New shrubs may be produced by making woody cuttings from old ones.

Activities

Teacher

When planting the trees and shrubs of the school grounds, see to it that all pupils, large and small, have a definite share in the work. This will appeal to their pride of ownership. Intermediate pupils will be capable of planting and caring for the larger shrubs and herbaceous plants in the background, junior pupils may be made responsible for those of medium height, and primary pupils would like to plant the smaller plants in the foreground.

All Grades

- Plant trees to celebrate birthdays—your own or someone else's.
- Plant acorns or hickory nuts in pots or boxes indoors. Have a race to see who can make his tree grow fastest. Make sketches of the little seedling as it starts growth.

Junior and Intermediate Grades

- Take a class excursion to explore places in your community where trees should be planted. Draw a map of the area, and on it mark these places.
- Search the woods for trees or shrubs which would look attractive in your school grounds. Carefully transplant a few of them.

- Trees do so much for us that we should help and not abuse them. Don't cut or carve into the bark; don't break branches when climbing trees. Any holes caused by decay should be cleaned out and filled by a "tree doctor." Cut off and burn branches containing the homes of tent caterpillars or other injurious insects.
- Interest those on your street in a street beautification campaign. Plant trees, shrubs, and flowers. Erect birdhouses and birdbaths.
- Write to the Provincial Forestry Department, Toronto, for bulletins or pamphlets concerning trees, and for seedling trees from government nurseries. Plant these in a little nursery plot in or near the school grounds, and see that they are kept cultivated and well cared for.

When planting a garden don't forget your allies, the birds. Plant especially those bird-attracting trees or shrubs which bear fruit in late winter and early spring. Those which bear fruit in summer will be useful in keeping birds from eating cultivated fruit. Some of the trees should be evergreens. Thorny trees protect birds from cats.

The following plants have fruit that attracts birds:[1]

*❦Dogwood—of several varieties, garden, thickets, roadsides.

❦Wintergreen—low, trailing, with red berries, in woods.

*❦Honeysuckle—wild and cultivated varieties, red berries.

*Cherry and plum—wild and cultivated varieties.

*Brambles—wild berry bushes.

*Elder—red and black berries.

Grapes, Shadbush, Virginia Creeper*, Barberry*, Snowberry❦, Blueberry, Mulberry.

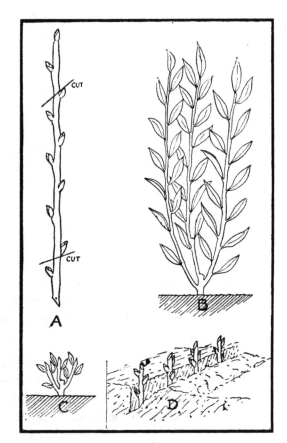

Figure 42—Growing Shrubs from Cuttings (Courtesy Better Homes and Gardens Magazine)

A, cutting made from new growth, but never from the tip of small twigs; B, a shrub after one season's growth in the nursery row; C, same shrub as in B cut back in the fall to produce a greater number of branches; D, calloused cuttings planted in a deep furrow in early spring, ready for the soil to be filled in and tramped firmly.

Read

Partridge, *General Science*, Intermediate, Book 1, pp. 290-302 and 407-409. Dent.

New to this Edition

Barrett, Patricia. *Flowering Shrubs: Storey's Country Wisdom Bulletin A-132* (Storey, 1992).
Rosenfeld, Richard. *Shrubs and Climbers* (DK Adult, 2004).

---

1   * *Provides nesting places*   ❦ *Retains fruit in winter*

Unit 83—Making and Caring for the Lawn

"A good lawn contributes the canvas on which the garden picture is painted."

Every school should have a lawn worthy of the name; it should be kept so. It is as important that pupils be trained to appreciate its beauty and its care as that they should be trained to appreciate literature. Lasting knowledge and appreciation will come to pupils only from firsthand experience as a part of the school activities, not from watching the janitor care for the lawn for them while the teacher and pupils talk indoors about the lawn.

Primary and junior pupils should distinguish good grass from weeds, observe level or even as compared with uneven places, see the need and methods of mowing, recognize common weeds by name, know how to remove them—*and do so*—see the homes of ants and the burrows of earthworms, watch birds getting these for food.

Intermediate pupils should be able to grade a lawn as poor, fair, or good; name and recognize common weeds and understand the harm they do—then remove them; observe the effect of shade upon the growth of grass; help to roll the lawn and cut the grass when needed, not neglecting the edges; dig, cultivate, level, and seed bare or undesirable places; observe and otherwise investigate the habits of ants and earthworms.

Preparing and Fertilizing the Soil. The area to be made into a lawn should have been plowed and graded to the desired level or slope the preceding autumn. It is advisable to see that 3 or 4 inches of topsoil covers the subsoil. All stones and refuse should be removed. If the site is low-lying, or wet and clayey, drain by tiles, and, if possible, mix in a couple of inches of sand or black earth. If necessary, fertilize the land by using 10 to 15 tons of well-rotted manure per acre, or some form of commercial fertilizer mixed especially for lawns or golf greens. The land should be thoroughly harrowed and rolled to break all lumps before sowing. Smaller areas may be leveled by driving in stakes and tying strings to these, parallel with and just above the ground, then raking to this grade.

An acid condition in the soil may be detected by inserting a clean knife blade an inch or so into the soil when wet, inserting a strip of blue litmus paper into the cut, and pressing the wet soil firmly against it. If, after being left there for 5 to 10 minutes, it is removed and seen to be red, the soil is acid. (Soil testing kits are widely available on the Internet or from your local county agricultural extension office.) Acidity may be corrected by applying 15 to 20 pounds of builders' lime to each square rod of soil.

Seeding the Lawn. Seed should be sown in early spring, late summer, or autumn. To obtain even distribution, mark off the area into strips 3 to 6 feet wide, and carefully broadcast the seed. Covering may be done by sifting good soil over the seed or by raking it in. Some is left uncovered and wasted by the latter method. Use half a pound to a pound of seed per square rod. Final rolling will give a smooth surface.

Caring for New Lawns. A newly sown area must be kept moist all the time until the lawn appears green. Hence the value of early sowing unless artificial watering is available. In the latter case, water daily until there is a dense growth, then every other day. Do not cut new grass until it is about 4 inches high, and then not too closely. Watch for weeds from the first, and pull or spud them out at once.

Caring for Established Lawns. Old lawns frequently require early-spring repairs on account of bare spots, weeds, or moss. Loosen the soil well before reseeding. Fertilizers will be helpful, and lime also, if moss is present. Lawns should be rolled each spring as soon as the soil is firm enough to walk on.

Keep constant watch for weeds; the lawn will never be entirely free from them. Remove dandelion and plantain plants by inserting the blade of a knife about an inch below the crown of the plant to cut off the root well below the surface. Pull crab grass and chickweed by hand, or remove them with a lawn rake. Place grass seed in holes from which weeds have been removed.

Watering should be done morning or evening, and done well. Light sprinklings are injurious since they encourage the roots to grow nearer the surface, where they suffer immediate injury in time of drought. Pupils should keep the school lawn cut frequently, leaving the cuttings to form humus. Leave the grass fairly long in the fall for winter protection.

Old lawns may be fertilized by applying ready-mixed commercial fertilizers, ammonium sulphate at the rate of about half a pound per square rod, or sodium nitrate, in the same amounts.

Read

Partridge, *General Science,* Intermediate, Book 1: "Caring for the Lawn," pp. 410-413, also *Everyday Science,* Book Two: "We Visit the Lawn," pp. 1-19, and "Caring for the Lawn," pp. 532-539. Dent.

New to this Edition

Martin, Alexander. *Weeds* (Golden Guide from St. Martin's Press, 2001).
Gift, Nancy. *Good Weed Bad Weed: Who's Who, What to Do, and Why Some Deserve a Second Chance (All You Need to Know About the Weeds in Your Yard)*, (St.Lynn's Press, 2011).

Figure 1—Weeds in the lawn.

Beautify Your Surroundings ~ April

PUSSY WILLOW

ROBIN

CHIPMUNK

TREE FROG

SNOWDROP

HEPATICA

MAKE A MURAL SHOWING · **SIGNS OF SPRING.** ADD TO IT FROM TIME TO TIME.

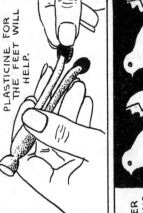

DON'T FORGET TO WATER YOUR SEEDLINGS FOR THE GARDEN!

D. FARWELL

HERE'S A **SPRING PARADE!**
CLOTHES-PEG FIGURES MEAN FUN FOR ALL.

USE: CLOTHES-PEGS
CLOTH
COLOURED PAPER
CREPE PAPER
THREAD
PLASTICINE
WIRE
PINS
OTHER ODDS AND
ENDS.

PLASTICINE FOR THE FEET WILL HELP.

FRESH MOSS FOR YOUR VIVARIUM! KEEP IT MOIST.

BIG DIPPER

NORTH STAR

LITTLE DIPPER

AN OUTDOOR SUGGESTION: MAKE CHARTS FROM WEEK TO WEEK SHOWING THE POSITION OF THE BIG DIPPER AT 8 P.M. NOTE CHANGES.

BORDER DESIGNS

SCIENCE IN ACTION -- APRIL

VIBRATING AIR PRODUCES SOUND:

SET UP EIGHT TEST TUBES IN A STAND. ADJUST THE AMOUNT OF WATER IN EACH SO THAT YOU CAN PRODUCE THE EIGHT NOTES IN AN OCTAVE BY BLOWING ACROSS THE MOUTHS OF THE TEST TUBES. TRY TO PLAY SIMPLE TUNES.

A HOME-MADE TWO-SOLUTION INK ERASER:

- GLASS TUBE THROUGH CORK
- CORK
- INK BOTTLE
- WATER
- BLEACHING SOLUTION (½ JAVELLE WATER + ½ WATER)

APPLY WATER TO WRITING. BLOT. APPLY BLEACHING SOLUTION. BLOT. APPLY WATER AGAIN. BLOT. ALLOW PAPER TO DRY BEFORE RE-WRITING.

D. FARWELL.

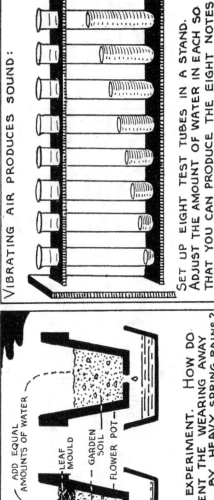

The TRILLIUM STORES FOOD IN ITS UNDER-GROUND PARTS. PICKING DESTROYS IT!

The ADDER'S TONGUE TAKES SEVEN YEARS TO FLOWER.

HEPATICA

MAKE A MURAL ABOUT WILD FLOWERS. INCLUDE SOME FACTS ABOUT THEIR GROWTH AND THE RESULTS OF PICKING THEM.

ADD EQUAL AMOUNTS OF WATER

- LEAF MOULD
- GARDEN SOIL
- FLOWER POT

TRY THE ILLUSTRATED EXPERIMENT. HOW DO TREES HELP PREVENT THE WEARING AWAY OF THE SOIL BY HEAVY SPRING RAINS? SUGGEST TWO WAYS.

PUT SOME BUDS OF THE HORSE CHESTNUT IN WATER AND WATCH THEM OPEN.

SPOTTED SALAMANDER

TOAD

FROG

VISIT NEARBY PONDS AND STREAMS. BRING BACK EGGS OF THE FROG, THE TOAD, AND THE SALAMANDER. PUT THEM IN JARS. WATCH THEM DEVELOP.

NATURAL SCIENCE – MAY – DAY BY DAY

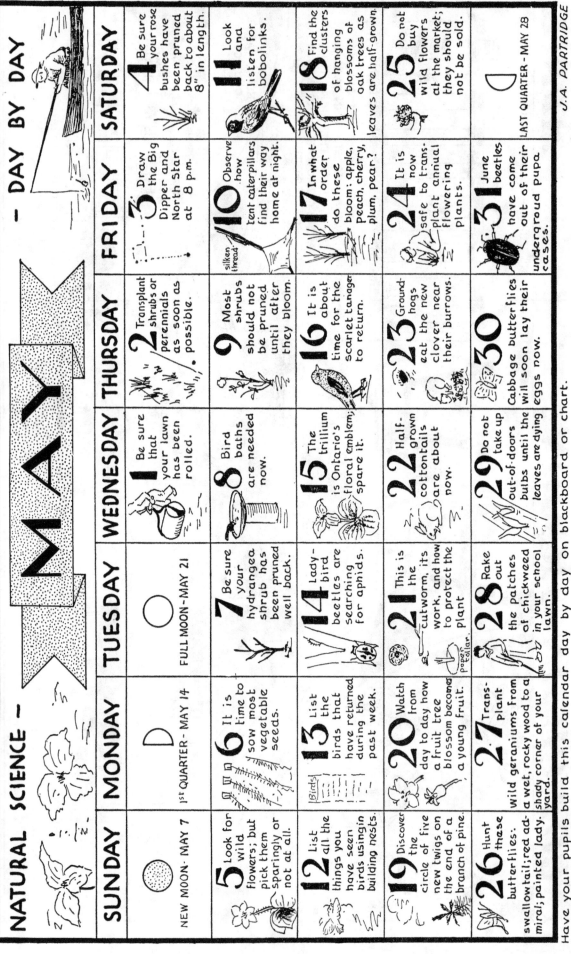

SUNDAY	MONDAY	TUESDAY	WEDNESDAY	THURSDAY	FRIDAY	SATURDAY
NEW MOON - MAY 7	1ST QUARTER - MAY 14	FULL MOON - MAY 21	**1** Be sure that your lawn has been rolled.	**2** Transplant shrubs or perennials as soon as possible.	**3** Draw the Big Dipper and North Star at 8 p.m.	**4** Be sure your rose bushes have been pruned back to about 8" in length.
5 Look for wild flowers; but pick them sparingly or not at all.	**6** It is time to sow most vegetable seeds.	**7** Be sure your hydrangea shrub has been pruned well back.	**8** Bird baths are needed now.	**9** Most shrubs should not be pruned until after they bloom.	**10** Observe how tent caterpillars find their way home at night. silken thread	**11** Look and listen for bobolinks.
12 List all the things you have seen birds using in building nests.	**13** List the birds that have returned during the past week.	**14** Lady-bird beetles are searching for aphids.	**15** The trillium is Ontario's floral emblem; spare it.	**16** It is about time for the scarlet tanager to return.	**17** In what order do these bloom: apple, peach, cherry, plum, pear?	**18** Find the clusters of hanging blossoms of oak trees as leaves are half-grown.
19 Discover the circle of five new twigs on the end of a branch of pine.	**20** Watch from day to day how a fruit tree blossom becomes a young fruit.	**21** This is the cutworm, its work, and how to protect the plant. paper collar	**22** Half-grown cottontails are about now.	**23** Ground-hogs eat the new clover near their burrows.	**24** It is now safe to trans-plant annual flowering plants.	**25** Do not buy wild flowers at the market; they should not be sold.
26 Hunt these butterflies. swallowtail; red ad-miral; painted lady.	**27** Trans-plant wild geraniums from a wet, rocky wood to a shady corner of your yard.	**28** Rake out the patches of chickweed in your school lawn.	**29** Do not take up out-of-doors bulbs until the leaves are dying.	**30** Cabbage butterflies will soon lay their eggs now.	**31** June beetles have come out of their underground pupa cases.	LAST QUARTER - MAY 28

Have your pupils build this calendar day by day on blackboard or chart.
Use substitutions if desired.

J.A. PARTRIDGE
Drawn by D. Farwell.

MAY

Unit 84—Let's Plant a Vegetable Garden

In the introduction to Unit 73 (page 304) mention was made of the need for greater emphasis upon training pupils concerning the beautification of home and school surroundings rather than upon having them grow mostly vegetables in the school garden. The vegetable garden has, however, a worthwhile contribution to make to pupils through the development of desirable attitudes and habits, the cultivation of practical skills, and the giving of useful knowledge. Conscientious attention to the natural sequence of activities in a vegetable garden helps to develop systematic methods and habits. Planning, planting, and caring for class plots will train pupils in cooperativeness. Trying out various fertilizers and varieties of vegetables develops correct attitudes and skills in experimentation. Manual dexterity grows with practice in cultivating, sowing seed, thinning, transplanting, and weeding. Knowledge useful throughout life will be gained with respect to the requirements of different plants in regard to soil, date and depth of planting, cultivation, protection from weeds and insects, and methods of harvesting and storing.

When vegetable gardening is carried out as a pupil cooperative enterprise, worthwhile business and social experiences come to pupils as they purchase seed and as they market the products, perhaps giving them to needy people or charitable organizations. Habits of industry cannot fail to be developed if the vegetable garden is given proper care throughout the summer—and this must be, if school vegetable gardens are to win back the public respect which they have lost in so many places.

School vegetable gardens have justified themselves in most schools where hot lunches are served throughout the winter. Not only do the products themselves contribute to the health of the pupils in this way, but the storing and preserving of vegetables and fruits teaches them scientific principles.

Choosing the Vegetables. Vegetables may be classified according to the nature and length of the season required for their growth. Some, such as carrots, lettuce, peas, potatoes, radish, parsley, and onion sets may be sown early since the young plants either can withstand frost or require a long enough period to germinate that all danger of frost will be past. Others, such as beans and tomatoes, must wait until later. Spinach is an early spring crop, since it is not tender if grown in summer weather. Cabbages and turnips may continue growing long after the first autumn frosts have killed corn and tomatoes. Radishes grow from seed to a usable size in as short a time as 3 weeks, while most kinds of potatoes and vine plants require 3 months or more. The following table gives a list of vegetables according to their period of growth.

Early spring until late fall—parsnips, parsley, salsify.
Early spring until midsummer or early fall—onion, pea, beet, early cabbage, carrot.
Late spring to early autumn—vegetables tender to frost such as corn, tomato, beans, vine plants.
Midsummer to late autumn—carrot, beet, turnip, late cabbage, cauliflower.

Late summer to autumn—lettuce, radish, spinach.

Some kinds of vegetables like radish and lettuce may be sown at intervals of 10 days or so until June. Some late vegetables may follow after early ones, e.g., celery after spinach; turnips, parsnips, or cabbage after lettuce or radish. The late vegetables may be sown in alternate rows with the early ones, and mature after the early ones are harvested, e.g., early lettuce and beets sown in rows 10" to 12" apart, alternating with parsnips, carrots, etc. Parsnips or carrots may be sown at the same time as and in the same row with lettuce or radish and complete their development after the latter are harvested.

Preparing the Soil. Do not attempt to prepare the garden soil until it is so dry that a handful crumbles readily. Rather permanent harm can be done by cultivating clay when wet. Where a plough is not used, be sure that pupils spade or fork the soil thoroughly to a depth of 5 or 6 inches, completely turning over each spadeful. Rotted or fresh manure should be covered while spading. Raking will serve the purpose of breaking all lumps and leveling the surface. Show pupils that every push or pull of the rake should be made with a definite purpose—either to fill a hollow or to level a high spot. Raking is both a mental and a physical activity.

A Planting Table for Vegetables						
Name	Seeds or Plants per 100 Foot Row	Time to Plant	Depth to Plant	Distance Between Rows	Distance Between Plants in Row	Crop Times
Beans	1 pt.	M. Jy.	1 ½-2"	2'	4-6"	W
Beets	2 oz.	M. Jy.	½"	1-1 ½'	3"	E, L
Cabbage, early	¼ oz.	A. M.	¼- ½"	1 ½-2 ½'	1-2"	
Carrot	½ oz.	A.-J.	¼- ½"	16"	2-3"	W, L
Corn, sweet	¼ pt.	M. J.	2"	2-2 ½'	2-3"	W, L
Lettuce	¼ oz.	A. M. J.	¼"	1-1 ½'	4-6"	E
Onion, sets	2 qt.	A. M.	1-1 ½"	1'	W	
Parsley	¼ oz.	A. M.	¼"	1-1 ½'	1"	W
Parsnip	1 oz.	A. M.	½-1"	1 ½-2'	3-4"	W
Peas	1 qt.	A.M.	2-3"	2'	½-1"	E
Potato	10 lbs.	A. M.	4"	2-2 1/2'	9-15"	W
Radish	1 oz.	A. S.	½"	6-12"	½-1"	E
Tomato (plants)	25-50	J.	3-4"	3-4' (staked 16")	3-4'	W, L

Note: (A.—April M.—May J.—June Jy.—July S.—September). (In the last column of the table, W indicates that the crop occupies the ground for the whole season, E that the crop is early enough to be followed by others, and L, that the crop is late, and may follow others.)

Sowing the Seed. Pupils should be given the task of planning the kinds of vegetables, the distance of the rows apart, and their arrangement with respect to each other. Let them plan for themselves methods of securing straight rows, using a stretched string or a straight-edged board. This should not be merely a lesson in obedience. Care must be taken to avoid sowing seed too thickly, a very common fault. Asking pupils to make the given amount of seed sow a certain length of row evenly should assist. The seed should be sown in a shallow trench so that it may be covered not more than the correct depth. Press the soil firmly over the seed with a foot, board, or hoe.

Tending the Vegetable Garden. Very shallow cultivation should begin as soon as the vegetables are up. While the seedlings are small, great care will be needed if the surface soil is to be loosened and all weeds destroyed without injuring or covering the tiny vegetables. As soon as they are large enough, all vegetables should be thinned according to directions in the table above. Frequent cultivation is needed to control weeds, to let air through the soil to the roots, to help to retain moisture in the soil, and to help keep the soil at a fairly uniform temperature. The garden should always be cultivated as soon as the soil is dry enough after a rain. This prevents the soil from forming a crust and drying out beneath. Every school that has a garden should have garden hoes with which to cultivate. Since children do most of the work, small hoes should be purchased.

Activities

All Grades

- Plan a vegetable garden in which you will have some vegetables that you can use at school. Study pictures in catalogues to decide what varieties you wish. Have a part of the garden on which all of you work, and a small section for each pupil as his own.
- Ask your mother or father to give you a small part of the vegetable garden at home. Care for it as well as your parents do the large garden.
- In early morning, look for tomato or cabbage plants cut off at the surface of the ground. Dig into the soil and find the greasy gray cutworm that did it. Kill it.

Junior and Intermediate Grades

- In a warm, sunny place at the school, as soon as the ground can be worked, sow seeds of radish and lettuce, and onion sets. Use these vegetables for lunches in late June.
- Divide the available space for a garden into two parts. Have two teams with a captain for each. From catalogues choose vegetables for their suitability for school lunches in the fall. Consult Agricultural magazines and Government bulletins. See which team can have the better garden.
- Plant perennial vegetables such as rhubarb and asparagus at one side of your garden where they may remain undisturbed for years.

Intermediate Grades

Send a sample of soil from your garden to the soil chemistry department of your state college's agricultural extension office and ask what commercial fertilizer you should use for vegetable growing.

Read

Bcauchamp et al., *Discovering Our World*, Book 2 (grades 5-6): "How Can You Make a Garden?" pp. 221-245. Gage (Scott, Forcsman).
Biles, *The Modern Family Garden Book* (teacher): "A Vegetable Garden," pp. 112-117. Longmans, Green (Ferguson & Associates).
Ferguson, *Vegetable Growing*. Publication 816. Department of Agriculture, Ottawa, Canada.
Foley, *Vegetable Gardening in Color*. Macmillan.
Frasier et al., *The How and Why Club* (grades 5-8): "A Vegetable Garden," pp. 294-305. Dent (Singer).

*Figure 2—A desirable habit—keeping garden tools clean **and organized**.*

Goldsmith, *Picture Primer of Dooryard Gardening.* Allen (Houghton Mifflin).
Gould, *Very First Garden* (grades 5 and up). Oxford.
Parker, *The Garden and Its Friends,* The Basic Science Education Series. Copp Clark (Row, Peterson).
Partridge, *General Science,* Intermediate, Book 1: "Let's Make a Vegetable Garden," pp. 383-398. Dent.
Smith & Henderson, *Across the Land* (grades 4-5): "Helping with the Garden," pp. 141-162. Longmans, Green.
The Gardener's Handbook. Publication 877. Department of Agriculture, Ottawa, Canada.

New to this Edition

Blass, Rosanne. *Beyond the Bean Seed: Gardening Activities for Grades 4-6* (Libraries Unlimited, annotated edition, 1996).
Bucklin-Sporer, Arden. *How to grow a school garden, a complete guide for parents and teachers* (Timber Press, 2010).
Hendy, Jenny. *Gardening Projects for Kids: Fantastic ideas for making things, growing plants and flowers, and attracting wildlife to the garden, with 60 practical projects and 500 photographs* (Anness, 2012).
Leavitt, Amie Jane. *A Backyard Vegetable Garden for Kids* (Mitchell Lane Publishers, 2008).
Lovejoy, Sharon. Roots, Shoots, Buckets & Boots: Gardening Together with Children (Workman, 1999).

Unit 85—Planting the School Flower Garden

Spring activities connected with beautifying home grounds and school grounds begin as soon as the snow disappears. At that time we plan the grounds as we would like to see them (Unit 73, page 304). We immediately sow indoors (Unit 75, page 316) the seeds of some of the plants to be transplanted to the garden later. When the frost is out, and the ground is dry enough, we transplant trees and shrubs (Unit 82, page 339), care for the lawn (Unit 83, page 342), and sow some of our vegetable seeds (Unit 84, page 347). Now that danger of frost is past, we can complete the planting of our garden. This unit aims at helping in this work.

Need and Time of Transplanting. Transplanting operations are of several kinds. Probably only three of these apply to school grounds. First, the small seedlings of annual flowering plants and of vegetables such as cabbage and tomato, which began growth in pots or flats (Unit 75, page 316), will need to be replanted. These should be placed about 2 inches apart in other boxes or flats as soon as they are large enough to handle. Second, in early May, we should transplant any perennial flowering plants, whether we obtain them from a cold-frame, another part of the garden, or a nursery. Third, as soon as all danger of frost is past, the annual flowering plants which we have grown, and others which we may buy, may be transplanted to the garden.

Preparation of the Soil. Thorough preparation of the soil is necessary for each of these activities. It should have been dug thoroughly in the fall and left in a rough state to obtain greater benefits from the action of frost. In spring the areas to be planted should again be spaded and then raked to break any lumps and to level it.

Transplanting Large Perennials. With the spade, cut vertically around all sides of the plant which is to be moved, to a depth of about 6 inches. Remove the soil from one side. Slide the spade carefully under the whole root system, and lift it with the mass of soil cut around. Do not jar it or let it off the spade. With another spade make a hole a little larger than the soil mass around the plant, and a little deeper. Loosen the soil in the bottom and see that it is good garden soil. Carefully slide the plant from the spade. Hold it in a natural position a little lower than it was growing before and fill around it with good soil. Tramp this soil around it securely. Leave a depression around the plant large enough to hold a volume of water approximately a third as large as the original hole. Fill the hollow with water. Let this soak away; then fill the depression with loose soil. Do not tramp this.

Transplanting Small Seedlings. Thoroughly soak the soil in which the seedlings are already growing before starting to remove any. This causes the soil to stick to the roots. Make the hole for the plant, following the above directions with respect to size, depth, and bottom soil. Carefully separate the plant from the others with the hands and trowel, retaining as much soil with the roots as possible. Handle the plant by grasping the soil around the root while placing it in the hole. Follow the directions above with respect to filling, pressing soil firmly with the thumbs, leaving the

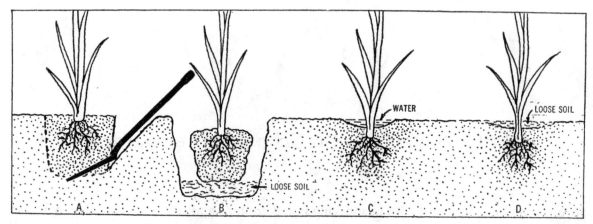

Figure 1—How to Transplant a Large Plant

depression for the water, watering at once, letting it soak away, and filling with ordinary soil. When all plants are in place, rake the soil lightly around the plants to leave a loose, dry layer with a level surface.

Sowing Flower Seeds in the Garden. The seeds of many hardy annuals, and of perennials, may be sown where the plants are to remain. Prepare the ground thoroughly until you have a seedbed of very fine, loose soil. Place strings to show where the rows are to be and to make sure they are straight. Follow the directions on the packets with respect to time and depth of sowing. Cover the seeds with a layer of fine soil, and firm it by means of a board, hoe, or rake.

Activities

All Grades

- Have window gardens at your school. The older pupils can make boxes to fit the outside of the window-ledge. Prepare the soil carefully (Unit 14, page 58). Plant geraniums, petunias, and a border of sweet alyssum and ivy or other trailing plants along the outer edge. Leave a one-inch water space above the soil. Water the soil thoroughly each day, for these plants growing so close together will need a great deal of moisture.
- Plan and plant a small flower garden at home. It, too, may be a window garden, or it may be a narrow border in front of the veranda or a large area in the backyard. Select the kinds of plants that you would like, according to color and height. If your garden is shady, get a gardener's advice as to what you should grow. Most plants should be at least a foot apart; and those that grow large about 18 inches apart.

Figure 2—An Outdoor Window Box

Read

Comstock, *Handbook of Nature-Study,* pp. 560-590. Allen (Comstock).
Parker, *The Garden and Its Friends,* The Basic Science Education Series. Copp Clark (Row, Peterson).

New to this Edition

Ehlert, Lois. *Planting a Rainbow* (Sandpiper, 1992).
Hanneman, Hulse, Johnson, Kurland, and Patterson. *Gardening with Children* (Brooklyn Botanic Garden, 2011).
Hendy, Jenny. *The Ultimate Step-by-Step Kids' First Gardening Book: Fantastic Gardening Ideas for 5--12 Year Olds, from Growing Fruit and Vegetables and Having Fun with Flowers to Indoor and Outdoor Nature Projects* (Anness, 2010).
Powell, Eileen. *The Gardener's A-Z Guide to Growing Flowers from Seed to Bloom: 576 annuals, perennials, and bulbs in full color* (Storey, 2004).
Schneller, Lee. *The Ever-Blooming Flower Garden: A Blueprint for Continuous Color* (Storey, 2009).

Unit 86—Have a Bird Hike

April and May are ideal months for outdoor studies of birds. The newly returned birds are full of song, and bright of color. They are happy, energetic, ready to get down to the summer's business of building nests, laying eggs, and rearing young. Early morning is the best time of day to watch them, for then the birds are hungry and actively searching for food whether or not they have just arrived from the South. The greatest variety of birds will be found in woods or thickets, or along the edges of fields or roadsides, especially near water.

The teacher will make the usual arrangements necessary for an excursion. She will, if possible, survey the territory in advance. Pupils will have been informed as to what birds are likely to be seen, and how to know them. The field marks given should be the bare essentials, e.g., meadowlark—yellow breast, bearing black V. Field glasses, identification helps, and small notebooks will be on hand. Further, the group must be small and enthusiastic.

More than half of birding is by ear; quietness therefore is a "must." Everyone must stop at the leader's signal. Slow motion, and standing with the sun behind you make it more probable for you

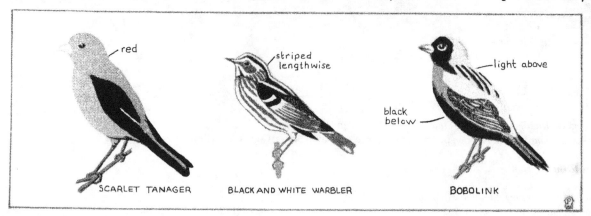

Figure 1—Welcome in May

to see the birds before they see you.

Records should be made of birds not identified. In these, tell whether the bird was seen in woods, thicket, or open field; whether near a stream or marsh; and whether alone or in flocks. Its size is compared to that of a robin or an English sparrow. Outstanding colors should be noted. Attention should be given to its habits—whether shy, tame, or quarrelsome; whether active or quiet; how it walks, hops, flies, climbs, and eats.

After the hike, in a class discussion, pupils' questions will be answered, new birds identified, and blackboard calendars brought up to date. Supplementary reading followed by oral reports will round out the educational values of your bird hike.

Activities

All Grades

- After your class hike, take two or three of your friends to the place visited, and try to show them the birds which you saw. Make a dated, permanent class record of the birds identified on each hike.
- In your class, take turns at broadcasting the description of a lost bird. The person who "finds" it (names it correctly) will make the next broadcast.
- Make a picture gallery of the birds seen on your hike.

Read

Candy, *Nature Notebook,* pp. 1-9 and 37-41. Allen (Houghton Mifflin).
Hausman, *Beginner's Guide to Attracting Birds,* pp. 104-118. Allen (Putnam's Sons).
Hickey, *A Guide to Bird Watching.* Oxford.
Hylander, *Out of Doors in Spring* (grades 6-8): "Our Songbirds Return from the South," pp. 117-143. Macmillan.
Kieran, *An Introduction to Birds.* Blue Ribbon (Garden City).
Peterson, *A Field Guide to the Birds (Eastern).* Allen (Houghton Mifflin).

New to this Edition

Guide Books:
Peterson Field Guides: Birds of North America; Birds of Western North America; Eastern and Central North America; Eastern Birds; First Guide to Birds of North America; Birding by Ear in Eastern and Central North America
Sibley Guide to Birds
Golden Guide to Birds of North America

Figure 2—American Robin

Unit 87—Welcoming the Birds

This is homecoming time for the birds. With the break of each new day we may expect to hear the call and see the flash of another bird that has just arrived. The procession that started in February will continue into the middle of May. Every swamp and marsh and stream, every tree and shrub and thicket, every orchard and dooryard may in turn become the choir place of some feathered songsters. Ground and grass, bush and tree, building and cliff may provide the nesting-site of some happy newlyweds. Garden and lawn, forest and field, earth and air will give a rich harvest of seeds and worms and insects to feed the returning birds and their families. And we, in turn, may expect to find life a little more worthwhile as we enjoy the sweet melodies, the happy chatter, and the beauty of form and flight and color of our newly arrived bird friends as they go about the daily routine of setting up new homes.

We should welcome birds because of their many values to us. Aesthetically we appreciate their beauty of song and color, their gracefulness of flight, and their cheery company. Economically they serve us well by controlling weeds, insects, mice, and other gnawing animals. As providers of food and sport, and as scavengers, we cannot overlook their value.

The greatest attraction to birds is a guarantee of safety. Protecting their nests from cats by placing cat-guards (Unit 72, page 301) on the trees, seeing that all people round about are friendly to them, and destroying birds which attack them and rob their nests—these things we can and should do to make the birds feel at home. They should be able to depend upon us to give them suitable food when their natural supply fails because of spring storms or other unfavorable conditions.

Figure 1— Bird sanctuary on Anacapa Island off the coast of California

Figure 2—Attracting and Protecting Birds (The American Humane Association)

The planting of trees, shrubs, or vines which produce berries or other fruits—elderberry, bittersweet, mulberry, barberries—forms a permanent attraction. Bird baths should be constantly supplied with fresh water in which the birds may bathe and quench their thirst. Nesting sites, bird homes, and nesting material are particularly necessary since man has cut the forests, replaced stump and rail fences with wire ones, removed the hollow trees and thickets, and drained the swamps. More than this, we can know and obey the laws protecting birds, set aside sanctuaries for their safety, and teach others to show their appreciation by befriending them in every way they can.

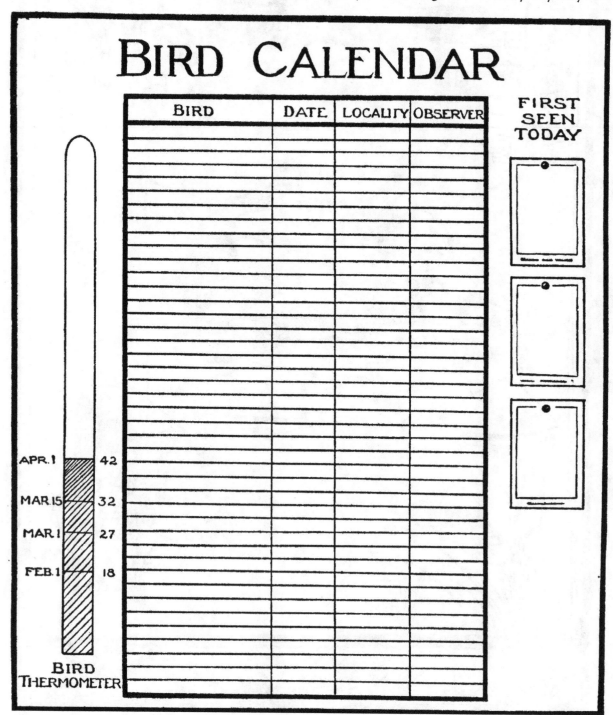

Figure 3—A Bird Calendar

In the table to follow, a number of our common summer resident birds are arranged in the order of their average dates of arrival in the Hamilton district, based upon observations made by Mr. George W. North over a period of several years. This arrangement should assist pupils and teachers in anticipating the arrival of birds and familiarizing themselves with their distinguishing markings. It will hardly follow that the list compiled by pupils of the class will be in the same order. The birds may not arrive according to exactly the same sequence this year, nor will they arrive in different localities at the same time.

	Some Common Summer Resident Birds		
	*Comparative sizes in brackets; special characteristics in italics; *nesting farther north as a rule)*		
Date	**Birds**	**Size**	**Description**
Feb. 12	prairie horned lark	(sparrow+)	open fields and country roads; sand-colored back, *black horns and tail; white line over eye*; throat whitish or yellow.
Mar. 7	robin	(10")	lawns and orchards; dark head, chestnut breast, *yellow bill*.
Mar. 8	*canada goose	(very large)	flying over in V-shaped formation; honking in flight; very long black neck, black head, and white throat.
Mar. 9	song sparrow	(sparrow)	thickets, hedges, bushes, along ditches; *striped breast*; tail jerked in flight; sweet song.
Mar. 10	marsh hawk	(crow+)	flies low over fields and marshes; long wings and tail, brown or gray, with *white rump*.
Mar. 12	red-winged blackbird	(robin−)	marshes; male with *red shoulders*.
Mar. 15	meadowlark	(robin)	fields, fence posts, trees; *black crescent on yellow breast*, white outer tail feathers show in flight.
Mar. 16	killdeer	(robin+)	fields and along water; double breast band, "killdeer" call.
Mar. 17	bluebird	(sparrow+)	fences and orchards; *bright blue bark, red breast*.
Mar. 20	crackle	(robin+)	towns, conifers; the *long-tailed blackbird*; yellow eye and metallic sheen (purple and bronze).
Mar. 24	cowbird	(robin−)	pastures and wood edges; small blackbird with *brown head*.
Mar. 25	red-tailed hawk	(crow+)	woods, overhead; broad wings; red fan tail.
Mar. 26	sparrow hawk	(robin+)	telephone poles; only small hawk with red tail; narrow, pointed wings.
Mar. 29	great blue heron	(very large)	ponds, rivers; blue-gray; long legs, noticeable in flight; long neck.
Mar. 29	*brown creeper	(small)	tree trunks; *creeps up tree trunks spirally* ; brown ; *stiff, propping tail*.
Mar. 29	phoebe	(sparrow)	small bridges; gray above, whitish below, black bill; *wags tail*; says "phoe-be"; no wing bars.
Mar. 30	*golden-crowned kinglet	(tiny)	woods; *orange or yellow crown, bordered by black*; white stripe over eye; chips.
Mar. 30	mourning; dove	(robin+)	orchards and telephone wires; small-headed pigeon with long, tapering tail.
Apr. 1	kingfisher	(robin+)	about streams, near fish; blue above, white below; *banded breast*; great head with ragged *crest*; rattling call
Apr. 2	flicker (woodpecker)	(robin+)	trees and ground; brown-backed woodpecker; white rump, *yellow wing linings*
Apr. 4	*loon	(goose)	lakes; *black above, white below, speckled back*; weird cries.
Apr. 5	vesper sparrow	(sparrow)	dusty roads and fields; chestnut patch on bend of wing; *outer tail feathers white*.
Apr. 6	savannah sparrow	(sparrow−)	grassy fields; small, short-tailed song sparrow with insect-like song; yellow in front of eye and at bend of wing.
Apr. 9	tree swallow	(sparrow+)	near water; *white underparts, bluish back; short, square tail*.
Apr. 10	*winter wren	(small)	woods and brush heaps; cinnamon; stubby, erect tail; chippery notes.
Apr. 11	*sapsucker	(robin−)	parks, woods; speckled woodpecker with white patch along wing; *red forehead patch*.
Apr. 13	*ruby-crowned kinglet	(small)	woods, orchards; short tail; *whitish eye-ring; scarlet crown patch*, often hidden.
Apr. 15	chipping sparrow	(small)	gardens, parks; *red crown*, gray breast, black line through eye.
Apr. 17	*white-throated sparrow	(sparrow)	brushy places; *striped, black and white crown; white throat patch*.

	Some Common Summer Resident Birds		
	*Comparative sizes in brackets; special characteristics in italics; *nesting farther north as a rule)*		
Date	**Birds**	**Size**	**Description**
Apr. 18	purple martin	(starling, sparrow+)	towns; large *blue-black* swallow; tail forked.
Apr. 20	barn swallow	(sparrow+)	barns and over water; dark blue back and *rusty below; very deeply forked tail.*
Apr. 21	*myrtle warbler	(small)	wood edges; gray and white, *yellow rump, crown, and shoulders.*
Apr. 22	brown thrasher	(robin+)	brushy woods; *red-brown,* striped below; *long tail.*
Apr. 24	bank swallow	(sparrow-)	sand banks near water; *brown breast band* and back, white below.
Apr. 27	spotted sandpiper	(robin)	near water; spotted breast; teeters on slim legs.
Apr. 30	house wren	(small)	gardens; *brown above,* long bill, up-turned tail; indignant actions.
May 2	chimney swift	(sparrow−)	high in air over towns; swallow-like; smoke colored; appears to beat wings alternately; hangs propped by *short, spiny, tail feathers.*
May 2	yellow warbler	(small)	garden or orchards; shrubs and trees; *all yellow;* faint red breast streaks. (Goldfinch has black wings and tail.)
May 3	black and white warbler	(small)	woods; black and white striped lengthwise; *creeps on branches.*
May 4	red-headed woodpecker	(robin)	fence posts, poles, etc.; *entire head red;* white wing patches.
May 4	bobolink	(sparrow+)	grassy fields; *black below, white above;* back of head buff.
May 6	catbird	(robin−)	swamps and thickets; *slate color;* dark cap, *mews.*
May 6	baltimore oriole	(sparrow+)	trees, around homes; *brilliant orange and black.*
May 7	redstart	(small)	woods; *black, with orange on tail and wings,* and white beneath.
May 7	ovenbird	(sparrow−)	on ground in woods; thrush-like; back greenish, *crown orange;* says "teacher."
May 8	blackburnian warbler	(small)	orchards; *flaming orange throat;* black and white wings.
May 8	veery	(sparrow+)	swamps and open woods; *tawny brown; dirty white breast.*
May 9	*magnolia warbler	(small)	wood edges; *yellow rump and below;* black on back and necklace, and end of tail.
May 9	kingbird	(robin−)	farmyards and orchards; black above, white below; *tail tipped with white.*
May 10	*rose-breasted grosbeak	(robin−)	woods, orchards; black and white; *rose breast.*
May 10	yellow-throat	(small)	brushy tangles; *black mask;* yellow under-parts.
May 14	scarlet tanacer	(sparrow+),	woods, parks; *scarlet; wings and tail black.*
May 15	indigo bunting	(small)	swamp edges; scrubby woods; *all indigo blue.*
May 16	nichthawk	(robin)	in the sky; *white bars on long, pointed wing.*
May 16	red-eyed vireo	(sparrow−)	trees; greenish above, white below; *white line above reddish eye.*
May 17	humming-bird	(very small)	about flowers in daylight; *ruby throat* (male only) ; insect-like flight.
May 19	wood pewee	(sparrow)	dry wood; olive brown above, whitish below; like phoebe; plaintive whistled note; *two white wing bars.*
May 20	black-billed cucko	(robin)	woods; tail long with outer tips white; *brown above, white below;* elusive.

Activities

Teacher

Let your class enjoy this entry in Jenny Wren's diary.

"May 3. Why, I have friends who have nested in the clothes-pin bag, the sleeve of a scare-crow, an old derby hat, and all sorts of freak places when bird-houses were scarce. Here on this place there are plenty of nesting-boxes, but everyone has got something in it that I don't like. There is that one on the side of the garage—chock-full of hornets—I'd have a lively time cleaning them out . . . Then there is that box on the side of the barn. I know from experience that it has been full of mites ever since those Phoebes nested on top of it. I planned to use it last year for my second brood, but no sooner had I landed on it than I felt crawly all over. I wish these good people would clean it out and paint it with creolin. It is a fine location, safe from cats and squirrels and snakes, and convenient to a lot of spiders, but I can't risk those mites being left over from last year. Then there is that rose-garden box where I almost lost my eye yesterday. Impudent little Chickadee, to treat her callers in such a fashion! I wonder if she knows it was I who pitched her eggs out of the box by the pond last year. It really was a shame to do it, but she had eight eggs, and I knew that when she began to feed her babies I couldn't stand the competition. So I took the easiest and most effective way of getting her to raise them somewhere else. I may have to do the same thing this year to the Bluebird's eggs in the box on the clothes-post if I decide to nest on the porch."

From *American Bird Biographies*, by A. A. Allen

All Grades

- On a large sheet of paper draw or paste a cutout of a large tree. As birds arrive from the South, mount their pictures on the tree.
- Each child write the name of any bird that he has been the first to see. Place the name in a birdhouse. Once a day the birdhouse will be cleared, and the name of both the bird and the observer written on the blackboard bird calendar.
- Prepare a birdbath in either of these ways. If there are no cats around, dig a hollow in the ground, line it with concrete, and paint it to make it waterproof. Otherwise attach a wash basin, garbage-pail cover, or dishpan to the top of a post; either place rubber under the heads of the screws or nails, or solder over them to make the birdbath waterproof. Keep the bath filled with fresh water.
- Listen to bird records such as "American Bird Songs." Thomas Alen, Limited, Toronto, or Comstock Publishing Company, Ithaca, N.Y.

Make a blackboard chart of "Expected Bird Guests." Display a picture bearing labeled recognition characteristics a week before each bird is expected.

Primary Grades

- Make a blackboard calendar with dates at the left, then such stories as "Robin Red-breast is back," "Jenny Wren came to live with us," and then the observer's name.
- Make little booklets—"We're Glad You're Coming, Birdies." Insert pictures, colored outlines, and little stories as the birds arrive.

- Place yarn, string, straw, or fine hay where birds may collect it for nest-making.
- Play the singing game, "Fly, Little Bluebird" (similar to "Here Comes a Bluebird").

Fly, little bluebird, through my window,
Through my window, through my window.
Fly, little bluebird, through my window.
Hey diddle-dee-dee.

Next stanza: "Take a little partner, skip, skip skyward." The new bluebird then flies in and out accompanied by the other bluebird—and so on until all are bluebirds.

Junior and Intermediate Grades

- Erect the birdhouses which you made earlier where birds will not be afraid to use them, and where cats cannot reach them. Keep a record of your bird "tenants."
- Watch the swallows darting about in the air catching flies, orioles seeking caterpillars on the branches of trees, robins pulling worms and other insects from the lawn, meadowlarks and bobolinks hunting about the meadows for insects, chickadees and warblers searching every nook and corner of a tree. Birds by their deeds convince us that we should welcome and protect them.
- Make a survey of your community to discover what trees have hollow centers suitable for woodpeckers and bluebirds to nest in.
- Establish a bird sanctuary among trees, shrubs, and vines in your schoolyard. Provide nesting-materials such as string, straw, and grass, and be sure to keep plenty of fresh water supplied. If you haven't the trees and shrubs, plant some which will protect and bear food for the birds: sumac, black elderberry, mountain ash, Virginia creeper.
- Make posters to illustrate birds catching insects in the air, woodpeckers taking grubs from under the bark of trees, goldfinches feeding upon thistle or sunflower plants, a nuthatch head down on a tree trunk searching for insects. Make bird posters, one for each of these: "Ceiling Cleaners" (swallows, swifts, night-hawks, fly-catchers, phoebe, pewee); "Furniture Cleaners"—trees, shrubs, low plants (chickadees, warblers, kinglets, nuthatches, woodpeckers); "Carpet Cleaners"—ground (sparrows, quails, pheasants, woodcocks); "Sink and Drain Cleaners"—waterways (sandpipers, ducks); "Destroyers of Vermin"—rats, mice (owls, hawks); "Garbage Cleaners" (gulls, crows, sparrows). Make a poster entitled "Save our birds, or lose our trees"—a slogan of the U. S. Bureau of Agriculture.
- Commence making a list of birds that you have recognized alone by sight or by hearing. Continue the list from year to year.
- Form an Audubon Junior Club (Unit 8, page 32). Another club reports as follows: "We held monthly meetings which were opened with a bird song. We saluted a flag we made of velvet showing a red-winged blackbird and the heading, 'Protect the Birds.' Our program included bird poems, songs, identification and other reports, games, feeding and protection activities."
- Sponsor a bird day in May. Invite parents and other interested citizens. Exhibit birdhouses, feeding devices, etc. Include suitable recitations, a small play or two, and songs. Present prizes to pupils who have contributed most to helping birds, and to interesting others in birds.
- Sing "la" to the music of the chickadee (Unit 37, page 149). Try to find the staffs and notes for the music of other birds.

- Draw bird outlines on plywood. Cut them out with a coping saw. Sketch the wings, eyes, and color areas; then mount the outlines on twigs, and paint them.
- Place feeding-trays where they will be cat-proof—on a post surrounded by a rose bush or wrapped with strips of tin or zinc 8-10 inches wide.
- Draw a map of the school grounds and mark places where birdhouses might be placed.
- Make charts telling the life story of individual birds. Each group of three or four pupils select one bird. Begin the story when the bird arrives; continue it until it leaves in autumn. Make a large, colored reproduction of the bird itself. Around this make smaller illustrations of nest-building, rearing the family, importance to man, and methods of attracting and protecting it. Display all charts at once or assemble them in a loose-leaf bird book.
- Build up a blackboard frieze of an ordinary rural scene or a park, including trees, shrubs, a stream, fences, telephone poles and wires, a home with its surroundings, and even a cliff. As birds are reported, show by pictures, drawing, or painting the proper place of each in the environment, along with the date and the name of the observer.
- Make a frieze illustrating the value of birds to farmers: eating insects from the ground (meadowlark, flicker), from tree branches (woodpecker), from tree leaves (chickadee, warblers), from the air (swallows, kingbird, swifts, night-hawks), eating weed seeds (sparrow, goldfinch).
- A bird calendar with a decorated top and a heading, "Look Who's Here," will be interesting.
- Solve this bird puzzle and make another like it. Rule a card into fifty to seventy-five adjoining squares. Insert a letter in each square so that several different birds' names may be spelled out by reading the letters from square to square, vertically, horizontally, diagonally.

R	L	B	T	E	N	C	A
E	O	I	H	R	U	T	H
D	R	B	W	S	H	B	L
S	E	G	I	M	M	U	B
L	O	N	P	N	D	E	I
G	F	I	C	E	L	R	W
L	D	H	R	A	Y	B	A
I	W	O	N	A	R	K	S

These letters spell the names of seventeen birds. To find the names use any letters in squares which touch. It is not fair to skip squares. Squares touch vertically, horizontally, and diagonally. One letter may be used twice for words containing that letter more than once or at a double, e.g., loon, oriole.

Bluebird	Oriole
Finch	Bobwhite
Crow	Wren
Warbler	Hummingbird
Wild Goose	Robin
Canary	Thrush
Lark	Nuthatch
Owl	Pigeon
Loon	

(Contributed by grade 7 pupil in a rural school, Halton County)

Intermediate Grades

- Assign for individual pupil investigation for report to class such topics as: Birds control insects, Birds as garbage collectors, Birds that eat weed seeds, The English sparrow—friend or foe?, Music made by birds.

- Write and act a play of four or five scenes to illustrate the poem "The Birds of Killingworth," by Longfellow. Suggestions:

  Scene 1:   People complaining that the birds are devouring their crops

  Scene 2:   A town meeting with the people voting to destroy the birds, despite the schoolmaster's fiery speech defending the birds

  Scene 3:   A plague of insects devouring crops

  Scene 4:   Another town meeting to reconsider their plight . . . the repeal of the law permitting birds to be killed, and the passing of another to protect birds

  Scene 5:   People and birds all happy, insects scarce, crops good

Read

Comstock, *Handbook of Nature-Study*. Allen (Comstock).
Doane, *A Book of Nature*, pp. 26-27, 66-71, and 98-99. Oxford.
Dowling et al., *Seeing Why* (junior), pp. 84-95. Winston.
Earle, *Robins in the Garden*. McLeod (Wm. Morrow).
Eschmeyer, *Bob White*. Book Society (Fisherman Press).
Hausman, *Beginner's Guide to Attracting Birds*, pp. 90-98 and 104-118. Allen (Putnam's Sons).
Kieran, *An Introduction to Birds*. Blue Ribbon (Garden City).
Mason, *Animal Sounds*, pp. 10-47. McLeod (Wm. Morrow).
Mason, *Picture Primer of Attracting Birds*. Allen (Houghton Mifflin).
Myers, *Pets and Friends*, pp. 84-98. Copp Clark (Heath).
Parker, *Birds* (grades 4-6), The Basic Science Education Series. Copp Clark (Row, Peterson).
Partridge, *General Science*, Intermediate, Book 2: "Birds in Relation to Man," pp. 107-130. Dent.
Peterson, *A Field Guide to the Birds (Eastern), How To Know the Birds,* and *Wildlife in Color*. Allen (Houghton Mifflin).
Phillips & Wright, *Plants and Animals:* "How Birds Help Us," and "Helping the Birds," pp. 163-185. Copp Clark (Row, Peterson).
Sears, *Downy Woodpecker*. Allen (Holiday).
Smith & Henderson, *Through the Seasons* (grades 5-6), pp. 149-176. Longmans, Green.
Williamson, *The First Book of Birds,* (grades 4-6). Copp Clark (Heath).
Zim, H. & G., *Birds* (a Golden Nature Guide). Musson (Simon A Shuster).
Lessons on Bird Protection, Attracting Birds with Food and Water, and *Bird Houses and Their Occupants*. National Parks Bureau, Ottawa. Longfellow, "The Birds of Killingworth."
Tennyson, "Little Birdie."

New to this Edition

Baicich, Paul. *A Guide to the Nests, Eggs, and Nestlings of North American Birds* (Princeton University Press, 2005).
Beals, Sharon. *Nests: Fifty Nests and the Birds that Built Them* (Chronicle Books, 2011).
Peterson, Harrison, and Smith. *Peterson Field Guide: Eastern Birds' Nests* (Houghton Mifflin Harcourt, 1998)
Boring, Mel. *Birds, Nests & Eggs (Take Along Guides)*, Cooper Square Publishing, 1998).

Unit 88—Nature Excursions in Spring

It is in May that spring reaches the crest of interest. Trees all about us are putting on their new verdure. Flowers of forest and garden alike decorate the landscape. Insect friends and foes have awakened from their winter sleep. At no other season may we stop so frequently to enjoy the sight and the song of returning bird neighbors. New life crowds upon the scene: the first nestlings bring joy to the earlier birds; ponds swarm with the young tadpoles of toads, frogs, and salamanders; myriads of tent caterpillars and other insects come into being; and many native mammals are busily engaged in training their young in successful and safe ways of living. Surely this is the time when both pupils and teachers should be enjoying and learning from the call of the out-of-doors.

Excursions should be adventures, voyages of discovery and exploration in which advantage is taken at every opportunity to see something new in nature. Primarily, they should be learning experiences, an integral part of the natural science program, and therefore taken in school time. To use them as a reward for good behavior, or to take them away as a penalty, is inadvisable because this attitude labels them as a special rather than a regular part of school activity. Only through field trips can what was said of Hiawatha be said of our pupils.

> Then the little Hiawatha
> Learned of every bird its language
> Learned their names and all their secrets,
> How they built their nests in summer,
> Where they hid themselves in winter,
> Talked with them whene'er he met them,
> Called them "Hiawatha's Chickens."
> LONGFELLOW

In Unit 1 we discussed the following features of excursions: their value; the teacher's organization for the hike—time, permissions, the preview of the place, the preparation of herself and of the class; problems connected with discipline and with getting pupils acquainted with this method of learning; and the use of directed observations.

As with other teaching, excursions with primary pupils must be in keeping with the pupils' interests, needs, and abilities. They serve not so much to have them learn facts as to give them first-hand contacts with nature, and impressions which they can express in various ways. Such excursions will be short and simple, and the activities connected with them spontaneous and childlike. To observe how flowers grow, or the kind of soil they need, or whether they can be transplanted safely to the school ground, is too advanced for primary children.

Here are some objectives for excursions with primary pupils: to see the difference between a garden or a good lawn and a weedy place; to see how mud is washed from a slope or bare hillside; to peek into a robin's nest; to collect pretty leaves or flowers; to learn the names of a few wildflowers, which ones can be picked safely, and how to do so.

After the excursions, it is essential for primary pupils to engage in some learning activities such as these: telling a story of the trip; simple blackboard readings; drawing things found; making a little home for salamanders and toads; building a nature sand-table of the place visited; composing a cooperative story about wildflowers; pantomiming how a farmer drives a tractor or plows a furrow; making booklets and friezes.

Junior and intermediate pupils will enjoy doing these: reporting the excursion in their nature diary—a personal report, not a "teacherish" note; reading for more information about things seen; setting up a vivarium or an aquarium; making posters or charts; discussing the ways of life of some things found; adding materials to the classroom museum; making a mural or frieze; constructing devices suggested by the trip—a vivarium, a birdhouse, an insect cage; making a booklet; compiling a class journal of the year's excursions; recording the trip in the monthly class paper.

With all grades, certain rules of safety and of hike etiquette should be developed during frequent excursions. A list follows. First of all, remember the first-aid kit. Then be sure to remember your rules of safety-first: do not climb through barbed-wire fences unless the teacher or owner is there to help; do not go near farm machinery while it is in motion; do not try to climb into cars unless they are standing perfectly still; walk to the left of the road when meeting cars. All pupils have two special duties to their teacher or leaders: obey all whistles or other signs; stick to business and carry out all instructions. And here are some simple rules of etiquette for the hiker: walk in paths, not across the corners of lovely grass plots or patches of wildflowers; don't mark rocks; pick up papers even if they have been dropped by others; put waste in rubbish receptacles or else take it home with you; ask permission before picking flowers belonging to someone else; don't spoil the beauty of a patch of flowers by picking too many; be quiet when nearing the homes of birds and other animals.

After your pleasant excursions remember to say "thank you" to those who made the trip possible. Letters of thanks take a comparatively short time to write: to parents who provided transportation or a lunch, to those who acted as guides through factories, to farmers who gave permission for the use of the fields or woods. This will ensure a welcome for other groups and for your own group another time.

Activities

Where to Go and What to See	Pupil Activities
A pasture field or a meadow: Kinds of weeds, shrubs, trees; presence or absence of gulleys; results of overgrazing—loose soil, washing.	Write to a farmer for permission to visit his farm. Learn to know the kinds of weeds; discover how pasture prevents erosion. Follow a gulley to its source to find its cause.
A cultivated field: Gulleys on hillsides; rich topsoil washed to low places; the direction in which the farmer cultivates to prevent washing.	Collect a sample of soil deposited by water. Discover methods of stopping erosion. Find out what crop was grown last and what one will be grown next.
A dirt road after a rain: Gulleys left by running water; puddles, and the soil deposited in them; pebbles carried by streams.	Which particles are carried farthest—coarse or fine? Collect some muddy water in a jar and let the soil particles settle.
The schoolyard during a rain: Soil worn away by water falling from the eave; where water runs most freely—on grassy plots or bare spots; that trees prevent washing of soil.	Measure the depth of rainfall in a flat pan. Discover why grass prevents erosion. Place stones in a gulley or on soil under an eave to prevent wearing away of the soil.

Where to Go and What to See	Pupil Activities
A creek after a heavy rain: The muddiness of the water; how running water cuts into bends in a stream; whether fast or slow streams carry coarser particles; debris on plants or fences showing how high the water rose; soil and rock worn away beneath falls.	Carefully observe the shape of the bank on each side of the stream at a curve. Make a list of things carried by the stream. Collect pebbles in the water and notice their shape. Make a map of the creek and the land along it. Build a toy water wheel and hold it beneath falling water. Discover whether or not people dump waste into the creek. If mosquitoes breed in a little bay beside the creek, place a little oil there to kill them.
A marsh: Listen to the songs of song sparrows and the noise of red-winged blackbirds; the first shoots of water iris; newts creeping about.	Try to imitate some bird calls. Compare land plants with water plants. Compare leaves under water with those above. Bring newts to the classroom for the vivarium.
The woods in May: Wildflowers: kinds, habits of growth, seed formation, soil and moisture conditions; ferns: how they uncoil, kinds, type of location; mosses: where found, kinds, formation of little "seed" cases, moisture-absorbing qualities.	Collect wildflowers and ferns and transplant them to the schoolyard. Bring back some mosses and arrange them in a vivarium. Erect signs in the woods encouraging people to protect wildflowers and ferns.
Flower patches visited by bees: Kinds of flowers preferred by the bees; the pollen, and the anthers which produce it; the value of pollen to flowers and to bees as food ; how bees gather and carry pollen.	Find out how bees make honey from nectar, and bee bread from pollen; how bees know their way to flowers.
A vacant lot or a deserted home: The different kinds of weeds; flowers, both wild and escaped from gardens; ground beetles and other insects under stones, boards, or rubbish.	Take a sample of each kind of weed. Learn which kinds of wildflowers may be picked. Make a home in the classroom for some of the insects found.
A moist field or rocky ledge: Garter snake, identified by three stripes, yellow, greenish, or reddish on a dark background; what it eats (flies, other insects, earthworms); how it catches prey; how it keeps prey from struggling out of the mouth; the wavy motion of the snake when traveling; the plates on the underside of the body, which catch the earth and help it move along; the way it sticks its tongue out to feel for things close by.	With a blunt object, pry open the mouth, and see and feel the fine teeth on the upper and lower jaws. Which way do they point? Follow a snake to its burrow. Take a snake to the classroom, and make a home for it (sod, stones, sand, dish of water, etc. in a glass-sided box); see if it can swim. Discuss how its feeding habits make it useful to man.

Read

Frasier et al., *Winter Comes and Goes* (grades 2-3). "Peter and Pan," pp. 186-191; *The How and Why Club* (grades 5-8): "A Trip to the Woods," pp. 239-249. Dent (Singer).

Gall & Crew, *All the Year Round,* pp. 3-13. Oxford.

Kieran, *An Introduction to Wild Flowers.* Blue Ribbon (Hanover House).

Parker, *Spring Is Here* (grades 2-3), The Basic Science Education Series. Copp Clark (Row, Peterson).

Peterson, *Wildlife in Color.* Allen (Houghton Mifflin).

Rutley, *Nature's Year,* Book III (grades 5-6), pp. 1-20. Macmillan.

Sterling, *Billy Goes Exploring.* Doubleday.

New to this Edition

http://flourishonline.org/2010/02/three-fun-ideas-for-a-nature-hike-with-kids-or-grownups/
http://listplanit.com/2011/05/list-of-games-to-play-when-hiking-with-children/
http://www.forsmallhands.com/newslettercustom/index/newslettercustomdetail?id=5&article=100914&type=newsletters

Unit 89—Six Weeks With Bird Families

All of us love small, helpless things. Children love them, too—so let's introduce them to birds in their homes. There is wonder and excitement in watching the parent birds build their nest, in seeing what the home is built of and how it is shaped so perfectly. Encourage the children to form a friendly acquaintance with one family in particular and notice the nest-building processes. Then they will want to watch the eggs to see when they hatch, to look at the tiny babies, to watch them grow, call for food, feather out, and become ready to fly. What excitement there will be when the baby birds learn to fly! They will have to learn how to protect themselves and find their own food. The children will want to go further and see what good the birds do. With this done, children will not need to be told that they should not harm the birds, the eggs, or the nest.

Pupils who have watched the robin gather grass, and then mud for mortar, cannot help but profit from this lesson of patience and skill. But the nests of other birds are even more wonderful masterpieces of architecture. The graceful, swinging nest of the oriole, cleverly woven and softly lined, fascinates all of us. Still more beautiful and wonderful is the tiny nest of the hummingbird, built of moss held together with spider webs and then so carefully covered with lichens and bark that one can scarcely distinguish it from a knot. Nor can they help but marvel at the ingenuity of the marsh wren when she gathers soft reeds and ties together a clump of cattail stems on which to build her nest.

> Among the dwellings framed by birds
> In field or forest with nice care
> Is none that with the little Wren's
> In snugness may compare.
> WORDSWORTH

Though birds cannot inscribe their names on signposts in front of their homes, we can easily tell who lives there by noticing the location and construction of the home. Nests are located in the ground, on the ground or in grass, or on or in some support above the ground.

Nests found grouped in sandbanks indicate bank swallows. The kingfisher's home is a burrow placed alone and without a nest. The rough-winged swallow's home is also in a burrow, but with a nest of feathers and straw.

The following common birds have nests on the ground or in grass: in moist places—marsh hawk, swamp sparrow, ducks; in woods—song sparrow, ruffed grouse, black and white warbler, brown thrasher, and ovenbird; in open fields—various sparrows, meadowlark, bobolink, and killdeer.

Hanging nests may be those of orioles, if over 2 inches deep, or of vireos, if under 2 inches deep. Those of the red-winged blackbird are found in marshes. Homes of the following birds are in holes in trees: woodpeckers (no nest), house wren (sticks and feathers), bluebird (grass), chickadee and nuthatch (moss, wool, feathers), house sparrow and tree swallow (straw and feathers).

Figure 1—Jenny Wren's Family Life

Mud is used in the nests of the robin, the bronzed grackle, the barn swallow, and the phoebe.

Sticks in a small nest probably indicate that it belongs to the blue jay or the catbird; in a large nest, to the hawk or the heron.

Warblers' nests are small, occur in low woods, and frequently contain small roots and bark. The warblers and some sparrows may use horse-hair also in making their nests.

BIRD TRADES

The swallow is a mason,
And underneath the eaves
He builds his house and plasters it
With mud and straw and leaves.
The woodpecker is hard at work.
A carpenter is he,
And you can hear him hammering
At his house up in the tree.
Of all the weavers that I know
The oriole is best,
High in the branches of the tree
He hangs his dainty nest.

ANONYMOUS

Not less wonderful than the building of the nests is the caring for the young. This is how Mrs. Rubythroat Hummingbird describes her experiences:

"Then comes the long quiet job of caring for the eggs, sitting on them, and knowing that life is gradually developing within. Most birds have a very definite period of incubation, and perhaps I would also if I had somebody to sit on the eggs while I went off to feed. But every time I leave them to feed they get chilled, in spite of my warm little nest, and the more they get chilled the longer it takes to hatch them. So if the weather is cold and wet, and food is scarce, it may take fifteen to sixteen days for them to hatch, while at other times they hatch in eleven. The same holds true for my babies as well. How rapidly they grow depends upon the amount of food they get, and this, in turn, depends on the abundance of flowers and tiny insects, which, of course, is controlled by favorable weather conditions. So you see we are creatures of circumstance. The weather is our greatest enemy from the time when we start life in the egg until, as grown birds, we may venture north too early in the spring and fly into storm and consequent food-shortage. Then it may snuff out the tiny spark that keeps the fire lit in our eyes. . . ."

From *American Bird Biographies,* by A. A. Allen

Activities

All Grades

- Watch a bird build its nest and rear its young. Begin a diary of its activities. Tell your class about it each day. Tell how long it took to build its nest, the materials used (string? mud? sticks? leaves?). Who did the work? When were the first eggs laid? When did you see the young birds first? How many were there? Notice how helpless they are, and how often the parents bring food to them. What do the parents feed them? How often? When do the young first perch on the edge of the nest? When do they fly first? When the young have flown, look for signs of the parents starting another brood.
- Find out what materials various birds use in building their nests. Place paper, string, moss, feathers, horse-hair, mud, etc. where birds can find them easily. Watch which birds take each.
- Watch birds drink, eat, sleep, oil their feathers, fluff out their feathers to keep warm. Notice how they fly, how the wings move, and how fast they fly.
- Watch a wren feeding her young. Count the number of times she brings food to her nest in an hour. (Someone has counted 30 trips.) She does this from daylight to dark. If she carries one insect on each trip, how many would she carry in one day?
- Have a "Current Events in Birdland" every morning, during which time pupils will tell any of the interesting observations that they have made.
- Make a mural showing a suitable environment for 20 or 30 common birds. Include farm buildings, an orchard, a forest, a pond and stream, open fields, hills, and any other places the children like. Some pupils will look up illustrations of birds. As the birds begin building their nests, paste in its right place the bird observed. When all the birds are in position, number them with numbers cut from a calendar. At the side of the mural place the numbers with the correct name of the bird beside each.

Primary Grades

- Find how baby robins and other baby birds differ from their parents.
- Observe how the mother and father robins feed and care for the young ones. Collect pictures of other birds feeding their young. Count how often the mother and father birds bring food to their babies in an hour. What food do they bring?

Junior and Intermediate Grades

Keep a diary of the family life of a pair of nesting birds from the starting of the nest until the young can fly. Fig. 1 gives some ideas.

Read

Comstock, *Handbook of Nature-Study.* Allen (Comstock).
Earle, *Birds and Their Nests* and *Robins in the Garden.* McLeod (Wm. Morrow).
Eschmeyer, *Mac Mallard.* Book Society (Fisherman Press).
Flack, *The Restless Robin.* Allen (Houghton Mifflin).
Frasier et al., *Winter Comes and Goes* (grades 2-3): "The Oriole Nest," pp. 201-205; *Through the Year* (grades 1-2): "Robins," pp. 138-

145; *The Seasons Pass* (grades 3-4): "The Cardinal's Family" and "Houses for Rent," pp. 226-241; *The How and Why Club* (grades 5-8): "A Pair of Flickers," pp. 258-265. Dent (Singer).

Friskey, *The True Book of Birds We Know*. Book Society (Children's Press).

Gates & McClenaghan, *Animals Work, Too* (grade 2): "Making a Bird Chart," pp. 5-9, "Mr. and Mrs. Swallow," pp. 15-36. Macmillan.
 Hethershaw & Baker, *Wonders to See:* "Home Life of Bird," pp. 229-270. Gage (World Book).

Kimball & Webb, *Birds in Their Homes*. Blue Ribbon (Garden City).

Parker, *Birds* (grades 4-6), The Basic Science Education Series. Copp Clark (Row, Peterson).

Rutley, *Nature's Year,* Book III (grades 5-6): "Baby Birds in the Garden" and "More Baby Birds," pp. 29-38. Macmillan.

Smith & Clarke, *Under the Sun* (primary), pp. 131-157. Longmans, Green.

Treat, *Bird Nests*. Audubon Nature Bulletin. National Audubon Society.

Williamson, *The First Book of Birds* (grades 4-6), pp. 40-52. Copp Clark (Heath).

New to this Edition

Boring, Mel. *Birds, Nests & Eggs (Take Along Guides)*, Cooper Square Publishing, 1998).

Frost, Helen. *Baby Birds* (Pebble Books, 1999).

_____. *Bird Eggs* (Capstone Press, 2006),

Kalman, Bobbie. *Baby Birds* (Crabtree Publishing Company, 2008).

Johnsgard, Paul. *Baby Bird Portraits by George Miksch Sutton: Watercolors in the Field Museum* (University of Oklahoma Press, 2006).

Figure 2—Killdeer on nest.

Unit 90—Knowing, Enjoying, and Conserving Wild Flowers

Down the road I heard childish voices, high-hearted gay young voices. They came nearer and soon three heads bobbed over the edge of the woods. "Good-bye, little flowers," I murmured. But I needn't have troubled. Not a bud did they touch. Just sat on the stones and oo-oo-ed.

"You musn't pick 'em," warned the oldest one as I showed myself. "You musn't pick 'em. They're to look at." The teacher did that. I think I shall name the woods in her honor. The little flowers will be her monument.[1]

Teach the children to look at the beauty of the flowers and keep their hands off. Show them the difference between the beautiful little flower growing in its mossy bed and the dead and dreary thing they hold in their hands. Teach them to love and preserve the beauty that gladdens their eyes and rests their souls in the fields and woods about them.[2]

After 25 years of continent-wide study Mr. P. L. Ricker, President of the Wild Flower Preservation Society, Inc., states that the three primary objectives of education concerning wildflower preservation are: first, nature education which instills into the minds of teachers and children a love of nature which should automatically interest them in conserving everything useful in nature; second, interesting the public in setting aside national parks and forests and, in every section of the country, one or more of the better wildflower areas where both the flowers and the nesting and feeding places of birds may be protected; third, the enforcement of such regulations as will preserve these preserves from vandalism and fire.

"Man's environment increases in value to him with the recognition and preservation of its natural beauty." This is the keynote struck by Dr. E. Lawrence Palmer of Cornell University in organizing a series of nature study experiences centering around the theme "Natural Beauty," for grades 1 to 6. All about us nature is filled with things of beauty, a priceless heritage for rich and poor alike, but available only to him who can see beyond mere names and descriptions and other forms of mere information. It is through developing the more intangible feelings that we as teachers may leave an indelible imprint upon memory and help to build up richer and more beautiful personalities. To accomplish this we must so arrange the school environment and organization that every pupil may have abundant

---

1   From *The Little Flowers*, by Angelo Patri, from literature of the Wild Flower Preservation Society, Inc., Washington.
2   From *The Vandals*, by Angelo Patri, from literature of the Wild Flower Preservation Society, Inc., Washington.

Figure 1—Trailing Hepatica

opportunities to experience the beauties of color in all flowers, the beauty of form in the columbine, the beauty of order in the trillium, the beauty of adaptation in all wildflowers, and the beauty of action in helping to conserve these same beauties of nature for the appreciation of others.

Adaptations for Early Bloom. The most common habitat of spring wildflowers is the woodland area. This makes it of real advantage to the plant to perform most of its year's work in a short time in the spring before the tree leaves above shut off most of the necessary light. By transplanting a hepatica plant in autumn and caring for it in the classroom, it may be brought into bloom in November. This is possible because the flower buds are already completely formed and a supply of stored food is present, ready to nourish the opening buds in spring. At about the time when the hepatica flowers are fully opened, a new crop of leaves appears. These immediately start manufacturing the plant food which is stored in the underground parts for the following spring. This work is probably nearly completed before the necessary light is cut off. Such is the mode of life of most of our early blooming wildflowers.

The Need of Wildflower Conservation. Many of us can recall with pleasing vividness the annual search for the first hepaticas to lift their dainty heads above the protecting layer of dead leaves on some sunny southern slope. Others of us have been privileged to enjoy a hidden patch of trailing arbutus (ground laurel or mayflower) whose flower clusters formerly carpeted the forest floor of many Ontario localities, but which has lured too many thoughtless searchers for beauty and sweetness of perfume. Soon will disappear the picture painted by Bryant in the words:

WITHIN THE WOODS

Tufts of ground-laurel, creeping underneath

The leaves of last summer, send their sweets

Upon the chilly air, and by the oak,

The squirrel cups[3], a graceful company,

Hide in their bells, a soft aerial blue.

And no longer could Whittier say:

"Yet, God be praised!" the Pilgrim said,

Who saw the blossoms peer

Above the brown leaves, dry and dead,

"Behold, our Mayflower here!"

The floral emblem of Ontario, the common white trillium is fast disappearing. Our beautiful native orchids are now to be found only in some secluded places. With these we shall soon lose many more species such as bloodroot, columbine, flowering dogwood, and maidenhair fern unless we are able through naturalist organizations and school influences to cultivate not only a love of beauty but also the application of the golden rule in respect to wild life. Surely here is a challenge to us to cultivate in our pupils an understanding desire to honor the motto, ENJOY, BUT DO NOT DESTROY, by making some practical efforts to conserve and increase this heritage of beauty for the benefit of generations yet unborn.

Life History Studies. A study of the life habits of three of our common species of wild flowers will help to explain why restraint in picking is more necessary with some than with others.

The *common white trillium* grows each spring from a fleshy, underground root stock, plentifully supplied with stored food. In producing the matured plant, including the leaves, flower, and fruit, this food supply becomes exhausted. It is therefore the work of the leaves to replenish the supply for the next year. But the leaves, the kitchen of the plant, are picked with the flower, preventing the possibility

Figure 2—White Trillium—Ontario's Floral Emblem

---

3   Squirrel cups are hepaticas.

of that plant making or storing any food for the next spring's growth. Death of the whole plant is almost certain to follow. That would prevent the plant from making the seeds necessary to replace itself.

The *dog's-tooth violet* or yellow adder's tongue (renamed fawn lily and trout lily by John Burroughs, from the fact that it is a true lily and from the resemblance of its spotted leaves to the "spotting" of young fawns and brook trout) has a unique life history. After the germination of the seed there is an annual recurrence of the following growth activities: the production of one or two leaves each spring from the deep-set bulb; the manufacture of food by these leaves and its storage in new, larger, and deeper bulbs for next year's growth. Not until about the sixth year does the plant bear the characteristic pair of leaves. The flower comes only after seven years of growth. These facts explain why we see only a few flowers in a dense mass of foliage, only a few paired leaves, and a wide range in leaf size—all dependent upon the age of the plants. The harm done by picking the flowers of this species comes from the picking of the leaves with the flowers, as well as from the prevention of seed formation after seven years of growth.

The *common yellow violet* has less need for protection. Near the ground special flowers are produced which are self-fertilized and produce seeds. Neither these nor the food-making leaves are disturbed by picking the flowers.

Suggestions for Teaching Wildflower Conservation. Primary children have no interest in a systematic description of wild flowers, but they do enjoy and profit from informal conversations concerning the names and colors of the "flowers," their perfume, the beauty of arrangement of the petals and the tiny yellow things (stamens) in the center, how to arrange them tastefully in a vase, and how to protect them so that others may enjoy them.

The common practice of always telling a story about the plants can hardly bear comparison with seeing, handling, talking about, and making simple drawings of them.

Activities

Teacher

- Make blackboard lists of wildflowers which should not be picked at all, those which should be picked only sparingly, and those which may be picked freely. Follow the advice of the

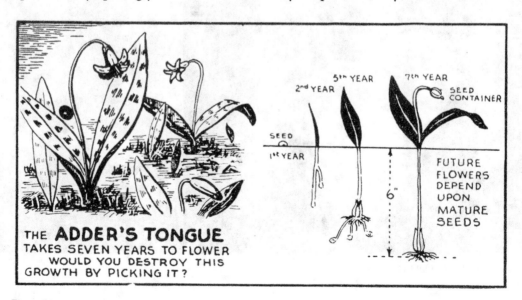

Figure 3

Wild Flower Preservation Society, Inc., the Pennsylvania Department of Agriculture, and more local naturalists by: (a) *refraining from picking* any of the following species, especially near large towns or cities: bellwort, birdfoot violet, bloodroot, columbine, Dutchman's breeches, false Solomon's seal, hepatica, Jack-in-the-pulpit, maidenhair fern, marsh-marigold, lady slipper, Solomon's seal, trillium, and flowering dogwood; (b) *picking sparingly,* and without disturbing the roots: mayapple, baneberry, blue flag, spring beauty, squirrel corn, yellow violet, toothwort, yellow adder's tongue; (c) *being content* to limit free picking to such wildflowers as blue violet, dandelion, wood sorrel, buttercup, chickweed, etc.

Figure 4—Red Columbine

Bumblebees and humming-birds are attracted by the nectar secreted and protected from rain in the spurs of the inverted flowers.

- Make pupils familiar with the need for conservation. Ask them to talk with elderly people to discover what varieties were once common in the locality, but are now either rare or extinct.
- Teach pupils to recognize all local species that should be protected, using such devices as: a bulletin-board display of pictures, posted as the time of bloom arrives; blackboard and individual charts or calendars, using such headings as "Wildflowers We Love" and showing dated observations of individual pupils; class or group excursions to nearby woods, roadsides, or parks: a sand-table model of a bit of local woods, using mosses, grasses, and paper cutouts for wildflowers.
- Cultivate a feeling that the flowers are more beautiful in their natural surroundings than in a vase. Refer to the rapid wilting of flowers while they are being brought home.
- Appeal to unselfishness in the pupils by showing that others have the same right as we to enjoy wildflowers in the woods.
- Develop an appreciation of the habits and the beauty of wildflowers, rather than a

knowledge of structure. Encourage pupils to observe insects visiting and pollinating local flowers, and discuss the value of the bees in enabling plants to produce seed and multiply.

- Encourage your Nature Club to carry out such activities as: locating, labeling, and protecting special patches of wildflowers; giving class talks on the life histories of a few species; excursions; a poster contest and parade; deciding upon a flower protection motto or pledge; presenting a conservation pageant; obtaining a lantern slide or moving picture lecture.
- Correlate wildflower study with: English, through the reading of appropriate poetry; art, by coloring outlines and making posters and signs; civics, by asking the editor of the local paper to publish information given him by you.
- Discourage pupils from bringing wildflowers to school except after discussion with you with respect to the variety, quantity, place, and method of picking.
- Practice conservation in class by using only a carefully potted specimen or a very few specimens with the stems wrapped in moist paper or placed in bottles of water. When finished, see that all specimens are tastefully arranged in a vase.

All Grades

- Take an excursion to a wildflower patch to observe the kinds of flowers, whether they grow in patches or singly, the conditions under which they grow, their color harmony, the correct way of picking them, and bees and butterflies visiting them. Pick only those kinds which can be spared, and, when doing so, use scissors or a knife. When collecting flowers from woody plants, take side branches, not the ends of main branches. Always cut, never break off the part you want. Avoid spoiling the beauty of the woods. Always pick trilliums above the green leaves; this will not injure the plant. Return later to observe the fruits or seeds of

Figure 5—Flowering Dogwood

A small tree or large shrub bearing white flowers with a greenish or purple center.

the wildflowers. Collect ripe seeds and plant them in the schoolyard.

- Plant a wildflower garden at school. *Bloodroot* should be transplanted in early spring to moist soil. *Wild columbine,* if moved, should be placed in a dry, sunny place. *Hepaticas* will do best under trees. Root stalks of *Trillium* are best planted in shade. *Ferns* should be planted where little sun reaches them—the northern side of building, where it is moist. *Jack-in-the-pulpit* needs deep, rich, shaded soil.

- Watch where people carelessly pick or destroy wildflowers and flowering shrubs. Then make posters encouraging protection of these. Display them nearby. Make and color outlines of the flowers; combine these into booklets with such titles as "Our Wildflower Friends."

Junior and Intermediate Grades

- Copy this. "The Outdoor Code," on your blackboard.

  > "Help save the Trees and Wildflowers,
  > Protect the Birds and Game,
  > Keep the Highways Beautiful,
  > Pick up the Picnic Rubbish,
  > Put out your Fire; then bury it."

- Visit a patch of dog's-tooth violets and find young plants with single small leaves, older ones with larger single leaves, and mature ones with two leaves and a flower.

- Find the underground parts of trillium, Jack-in-the-pulpit, and wild ginger, and discover the store of food as shown by taste (carefully), fleshiness, or starch test.

- Try to identify unknown varieties in the field, or take home notes rather than the plant. Do not pick newly discovered species unless you can leave five to ten times as many behind.

- Look for a place which is beautifully provided with wildflowers, other natural beauties, and wildlife. Make it into a wildflower preserve.

- By speaking with older citizens and by observing for yourself, find places nearby where wildflowers have been destroyed by selfish picking; by fires; by the building of roads, bridges, or buildings; by making gardens, golf links, lawns, pastures, or cultivated fields; by the disposal of junk or garbage; by removing trees, or by planting too many trees.

- Make a chart entitled "Who Finds Me First?" Decorate it with cutout pictures, correctly colored, of the wildflowers of the district. Rule it and name the headings: My Name, When I Was Found, Where I Was Found, Who Found Me.

Figure 6

- Make tables or calendars with such headings as: Red, Yellow, Blue, White, Pink; or By the Roadside, In Mr. Smith's Wood, In the Pasture, In Fields, By the Stream; fill in the names of wildflowers found to fit each heading. Make an illustrated blackboard calendar of wildflowers found, using such titles as, "In the Shady Wood," or "By the Stream," with columns headed: Pupil, Date, Flower, Why I Like It.
- Make a speech to the class, impersonating some wildflower, and making an appeal for protection.
- Prepare and act the play "Save the Wild Flowers." This may be had from "The Wild Flower Preservation Society, Inc.," 3740 Oliver St., Washington, D.C. The society also has much other inexpensive literature for distribution.
- Here are some other suggestions for the preservation of wildflowers. Albert A. Hansen of Purdue University has suggested that these rules be observed to protect wildflowers. Allow enough flowers to remain for seed; allow roots and other underground parts to remain undisturbed; never tear out creeping stems; substitute cultivated plants for rare wild plants for schoolwork whenever practicable; if you own woodland property, set part of it aside as a wildlife preserve; never pick more flowers than you really need; do not burn woodlands to get rid of dead leaves, but allow these to remain and protect wildflowers in winter; do not buy bunches of wildflowers from florists, children, or the market.

Read

Candy, *Nature Notebook,* pp. 10-11, 14-15, and 423. Allen (Comstock).

Comstock, *Handbook of Nature-Study,* pp. 460-511. Allen (Comstock).

Doane, *A Book of Nature,* pp. 20-23 and 54-57. Oxford.

Frasier et al., *Winter Comes and Goes* (grades 2-3): "Wild Flowers," pp. 182-185; *The Seasons Pass* (grades 3-5): "Spring Wild Flowers," pp. 254-257. Dent (Singer).

Friesner & Hill, *Wild Flowers of Spring:* a paper-covered text-activity book. Moyer (Kenworthy).

Hautman, *Beginner's Guide to Wild Flowers.* Allen (Putnam's Sons).

Hunt & Andrews, *Spring Wild Flowers.* Moyer.

Hylander, *Out of Doors in Spring* (grades 6-8): "The Flower Parade Begins," pp. 58-83. Macmillan.

Kieran, *An Introduction to Wild Flowers.* Blue Ribbon (Hanover House).

Morris, *Our Wild Flowers.* Federation of Ontario Naturalists, 187 Highbourne Road, Toronto.

Partridge, *General Science,* Intermediate, Book 2: "Protecting Wild Flowers," pp. 395-396; and *Everyday Science,* Book One: "Wild Flowers," pp. 264-268. Dent.

Wherry, *Wild Flower Guide.* Doubleday.

New to this Edition

Imes, Rick. *Wildflowers: How to Identify Flowers in the Wild and How to Grow Them in Your Garden* (Book Sales, 2001).

Niering, Olmstead, and Rayfield. *National Audubon Society Field Guide to North American Wildflowers (Eastern Region),* (Alfred A Knopf, 1979).

Lamar, Sharon. *Mountain Wildflowers for Young Explorers* (Mountain Press Publishing, 2011).

Niehaus, Peterson, and Ripper. *A Field Guide to Pacific States Wildflowers: Washington, Oregon, California and adjacent areas* (Houghton Mifflin Harcourt, 1998).

Whittle, Janet. *How to Draw Wildflowers in Simple Steps* (Search Press, 2011).

http://biologyjunction.com/how_to_make_a_wildflower_collect.htm
http://preservedgardens.com/how-to-press.htm
http://www.wildflower.org/action/

Orange Orchards in California

Unit 91—Getting Acquainted with Trees, Shrubs, and Other Perennials

May-time is blossom time in many ways. Fruit, forest, and shade trees bring forth the bloom which make their fruits possible. Garden shrubs provide a succession of blossoms which make May the most colorful month of the year. Many of our most common perennials reach their height of appeal in May.

This is the month, too, when it is most pleasant to go out with nature and enjoy it firsthand. And probably there is no month, unless it be September, when there are so many possibilities of becoming acquainted with the natural environment and so few excuses for not taking full advantage of these opportunities. Let all, teacher and pupils together, go forth and enjoy the wealth of beauty that Nature has spread.

Fruit Trees. In the first warm days of May, fruit trees begin their growth which will finally clothe them with their robes of delicate blossoms. The first to open are the pink flowers of peach trees growing close to the branches before the leaves come out. A little later, the long-stemmed, white blossoms of cherries decorate the trees. Then come the loose clusters of apple blossoms against a background of delicate green foliage.

Activities

All Grades

Examine wild fruit trees for newly made tents of the tent caterpillar; watch how the caterpillars enlarge the tent from day to day, and how they cover up the castings within.

Intermediate Grades

- Visit an apple tree. Find the pink buds and open flowers. The colored parts are called petals. See how they unfold. Watch for bees visiting the blossoms. What can you see them doing? Is there any yellow dust on them? Find and touch the yellow center of a flower. This yellow powder is pollen. When carried to other apple blossoms, it helps the flowers to form apples. The bees help to carry it, but they take some of it to feed their young, too. Use a paint brush to transfer pollen from the stamens of some mature blossoms to the sticky centers of others. Mark the pollinated blossoms by means of colored strings. Observe how the fruits form and enlarge.
- Tie a string to one blossom and visit it each day. How long is it before the petals fall? When can you first see a little apple? Where? Does the stem hold it up or down? Watch it from day to day as it grows. Examine small apple fruits to discover the opening, at the blossom end, through which apple worms may enter at this stage of fruit development.
- Notice how the blossoms of cherry, plum, peach, and apple differ in color, perfume, size, nature of clusters, and placement on twigs.

Forest and Shade Trees. Even after we know that such trees as maple, elm, oak, and pine have fruits, and that all fruits are formed from flowers, it seems strange to think of such trees as bearing flowers. This is because we are so accustomed to associating the word flowers only with those showy blossoms which have brightly colored petals. It is all the more difficult for pupils to think of forest and shade trees as bearing flowers. We must see to it that as a result of many carefully directed assignments and observations pupils see these flowers for themselves, and learn by experience how some of the flowers produce seeds.

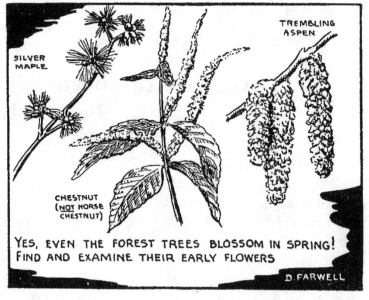

Figure 1

Activities

All Grades

Find the little, red, cup-shaped flowers on the red or swamp maple, the greenish-yellow flowers hanging like tassels from the sugar maple, the long catkins hanging from poplars and alders, and the "pussies" on willows. These are all flowers. Watch for pollen drifting from pine trees; then find the little cones (flowers) from which it comes.

Junior and Intermediate Grades

- Make a whistle of willow or basswood. Select a twig about as large as a piece of chalk. Shape the end, cut the notch, and cut through the bark around the twig about 2 inches back. Pound the bark with your knife handle until it slips off. Cut the groove to blow through, and make an air cavity beneath the notch. Replace the bark, and blow.
- Play the game "How do you do, Mr. Maple? I know you." One pupil describes the tree as he saw it while on a hike. The others listen or take notes as he speaks. The first to recognize the tree says, "How do you do, Mr. _____? I know you."

Intermediate Grades

- Watch the stamens of poplar and willow catkins develop. When the poplar catkins are ready, shake a cloud of dusty pollen from them. This is carried by wind to other poplar flowers. Notice how different the willow catkins are. Their pollen is carried by bees. On older trees find two kinds of catkins—those which produce pollen, and those which produce seeds.
- Examine and draw a particular flower of horse-chestnut three times a week from the time the bud scales open until the flower is fully developed. Date each drawing. Repeat this assignment for other trees.
- Find two kinds of young cones on pine or other evergreen trees: those that produce pollen, and those that produce seeds at a later date. Examine them from time to time throughout early summer. Find cones a year old, and see how the scales hold the seeds.
- Label a glass jar "For Flowers of Forest and Shade Trees." Keep it handy in the classroom. Keep twigs of some of the following in it as they blossom: maple, willow, elm, poplar, oak.

Flowering Shrubs. How bare our homes and lawns would look without flowering shrubs to blend the buildings with the grass, and to form hedges and borders about our lawns. These are about as important outdoors as curtains are indoors. How easy it is to lead pupils to appreciate the beauty of these shrubs if we take little trips to see and talk about them when their buds are producing their showy flowers. Fortunately there are different shrubs to give bloom for every month except those of winter. If our grounds have been planted with a suitable variety of shrubs, opportunities for developing pupil appreciation are always present. See Unit 73 (page 304) for a list of common shrubs from home grounds or school grounds.

Most shrubs may be distinguished from trees by their smaller size, and by their habit of branching freely from near the ground, whereas trees have one main stem or trunk.

Activities

Teacher

- To identify shrubs as they come into bloom in spring, take the class for frequent short hikes around the school ground, to a nearby home garden, or to clumps of shrubs in a park.

- Make an effort to have one new kind of shrub added to your school ground each year until you have enough kinds to provide for continual bloom.

All Grades

- Keep the classroom supplied with carefully assembled bouquets of flowering shrubs, in single varieties and mixed. Identify all kinds used and attach printed labels.
- Make blackboard and individual calendars entitled "Flowering Shrubs on Parade." Use the headings: Name, Color of Flowers, Date in Full Dress, Best Place for the Shrub. Continue the table from the time the yellow Forsythia blossoms appear in early spring until Hydrangea blossoms are largest in autumn. In the last column tell whether the shrub is suitable for a tall background or a low border.

Perennial Flowering Plants. A well-planned perennial border will have bloom in all months of the year. As with people, so with birds, trees, and shrubs, pupils will become familiar with these most easily by associating with them often and learning about them a few at a time. This, again, requires frequent excursions to gardens at school, in parks, or at home. See Unit 73 (page 304).

Activities

All Grades

- Collect pictures of as many kinds of common perennial flowering plants as can be obtained from seed and other garden catalogues. Place these on the bulletin board and use them to identify perennials as they come into bloom in the school gardens or in home gardens.
- Plant a few perennials in the school grounds, making a selection on the basis of height, color, season of bloom, and use.
- Make a calendar which will show the dates of bloom, the color, and the height of common perennial flowering plants observed by pupils.

Read

Comstock, *Handbook of Nature-Study*, pp. 618-692. Allen (Comstock).

Doane, *A Book of Nature*, pp. 24-25, 60-63, and 96-97. Oxford.

Foley, *Garden Flowers in Color*, Macmillan.

Kieran, *An Introduction to Trees*. Blue Ribbon (Hanover House).

Oliver, *Ornamental Shrubs and Woody Climbers for Canadian Gardens*. Publication 713. Department of Agriculture, Ottawa, Canada.

Parker, *Flowers, Fruits, Seeds*. Copp Clark (Row, Peterson).

Partridge, *Everyday Science*, Book One: "Blossom Time," pp. 305-314. Dent.

Selsam, *Play with Trees* (grades 4-6), pp. 5-l8. McLeod (Wm. Morrow).

Sterling, *Tries and Their Story*. Blue Ribbon (Hanover House).

Swenson, *A Child's Book of Trees*. Ryerson (Maxton).

Van Camp & Shaw, *Fifty Trees of Canada*. Book Society.

New to this Edition

Bluemel, Kurt, Editor. *Encyclopedia of Perennials* (American Horticultural Society), (DK Adult, 2006).

Unit 92—Insect Friends and Foes In Spring

And there's never a leaf nor a blade too mean
To be some happy creature's palace.
JAMES RUSSELL LOWELL

The phases of insect study taken in spring should be seasonal, and, with intermediate grades, should lead from the study of particular insects to some general concepts. Three of these are suggested below.

Insects render an enormous service to man by pollinating flowers. Without them we would have few vegetables, fruits, or flowers, and no clover, linen, or coffee, for these plants are pollinated mostly by bees, and partly by other insects. In spring, pupils have many opportunities to watch bees busily gathering nectar and pollen from flowers for food. It is then that pupils should learn that the carrying of pollen from flower to flower by bees is merely accidental, but nevertheless of great economic value.

The method of controlling insects depends upon the way in which they feed. Some have *biting mouth parts,* and nibble away the leaves bit by bit (cutworm, tomato worm, white grub, and larvae of tent caterpillar and potato beetle). To control these we spray poisons on the foliage which they will eat. Many other insects pierce the skin of plants or animals and suck the juices from within; they have *sucking mouth parts.* Among these are mosquitoes, plant lice (aphids), and scale insects common on ferns and fruit trees. To control these, we use a spray which will suffocate them or, by contact with the skin, will kill them.

Insect study may be closely correlated with the teaching of health. While learning about the housefly, pupils of all grades should be thinking chiefly of how its habits contribute to the spread of disease. All the following facts point in this direction: it feeds almost everywhere, in filthy places and on our food; its hairy feet are constantly picking up and letting go the material on which it feeds, thus carrying germs from filth to food; it is most active in warm weather when germs multiply most rapidly; then, too, its numbers multiply quickly wherever manure or refuse provide suitable breeding places. This menace to health can be abolished only when we all cooperate to prevent it from finding suitable breeding-places and to keep it from our food. The past experiences of pupils, reinforced by teacher-directed activities, will of course enlarge each of the concepts mentioned while maintaining the health point of view.

The insects described below are illustrated in fig. 1, Unit 25 (page 103).

Insects Injurious To Garden Plants

Cutworm. *Recognition:* caterpillars around base of newly planted vegetables and flowering plants, stout, curled up when at rest, hairless; dull-colored moths in July. *Habits:* caterpillars cut plants at ground or slightly beneath it at night, become full grown by end of June and pupate in soil; moths appear in July, active at night; eggs laid on weeds or grass in Aug. and Sept.; caterpillars become partly grown in fall and pass winter in soil; usually two broods a year. *Harm:* greatest in May and early June, destroying young plants. *Control:* poison baits—bran, 50 pounds, Paris green, 1 pound, water to moisten; ½ teaspoonful near, but not touching, each plant; keep cutworms from plants by a collar of paper. *Seasonal Activities:* May, find cutworms just under soil of cut plants; practice control measures.

Potato Beetle. *Recognition:* adults emerge in May, with hard, striped backs, black and yellow; eggs, yellow to orange, in clusters under leaves; larvae soft, red, spotted. *Habits:* adults winter beneath frost and come out in May; eggs hatch in about a week; larvae feed on potato leaves 2 to 3 weeks, crawl into ground and pupate; adults emerge in about 2 weeks. *Harm:* reduce leaf surface, lessen making of plant food, giving smaller potatoes. *Control:* spraying or dusting—Paris green or arsenate of lead mixture. *Seasonal Activities:* May, handpick first ones to appear, observe stages in development; June, note feeding activities and practice control.

White Grub. *Recognition:* stout brown beetles at night in May and June; large, white, curved larvae with brown heads, underground in sod, strawberry patches, etc. *Habits:* adults emerge from underground pupa cases in May, feeding at night on tree foliage; white eggs laid singly in small balls of earth just below surface of soil where there is vegetation; eggs hatch in 2 or 3 weeks; grubs eat decaying vegetable matter first year, doing little harm, wintering deep in soil; grubs, second year, feed on roots near surface and go deeper in winter; grubs, third year, full grown by June, pupate in earthen cases in July and August; adults spend third winter in pupa cases in soil. *Harm:* injury to roots of strawberry plants and tubers of potatoes. *Control:* fall plowing, rotation of crops, spraying of trees. *Activities:* May, observe adaptations of adults for flight and feeding; find grub in old pastures; practice control.

Insects Injurious To Shade Or Fruit Trees

Tent Caterpillar. *Recognition:* dark gray girdles of egg masses on shrub and fruit tree twigs; web-like nests in crotches of trees; bluish-gray caterpillars with white line or spots on back, in or near nests. *Habits:* eggs hatch in early May; caterpillars make a web or tent for their family home; caterpillars spend nights in the tent and days out feeding on foliage, maturing in June; pupate in whitish cocoons under bark or rubbish, adults emerging in 3 weeks; eggs laid in midsummer and remain until spring. *Harm:* caterpillars devour foliage from trees, reducing food-making and fruit growth, and weakening tree for the next year. *Control:* burn out tents on rainy days or at night; spray at budding time— 3 pounds arsenate of lead to 40 gallons water. *Activities:* May, note youngest caterpillars when first hatched, observe their tent-building, watch the enlarging of the tent as the caterpillars get bigger; observe caterpillars returning home in evening.

Oyster-shell Scale. *Recognition:* small, elongated scales like miniature oyster shells, on fruit and shrub twigs (San Jose scale is smaller and round). *Habits:* numerous eggs, having wintered under dead scale, hatch in May; larvae move about for about a day, then work mouth parts through bark and build wax scale over body; females lay eggs in August and die shortly. *Harm:* suck sap from twigs, reducing tree's food supply, weakening tree. *Control:* spraying—1 gallon commercial lime-sulphur with 8 or 9 gallons water during budding time. *Activities:* May, find scales on apple or other fruit trees; remove cover and observe eggs or young insects; practice control.

Insects Injurious or Annoying to Man

Housefly. *Recognition:* adult too commonly known; tiny white legless maggots in manure or other refuse throughout summer; pupae like kernels of wheat. *Habits:* adults crawl from hiding-places and become active in May, eating anything from filth to delicate foods; live everywhere; oval white eggs laid in manure or other decaying matter, hatch in one day; legless maggots absorb juices from refuse, grow rapidly, molt twice, and mature in 5 days: pupae exist 5 days in manure; young adults lay eggs in few days; winter as larvae or pupae in manure piles or as adults in warm hiding-places. *Harm:* carry filth and disease germs. *Control:* cleanliness, screens, traps, fly paper. *Activities:* a "war on flies" campaign in May, stressing cleanliness; observe their germ-carrying feet; find larvae and pupae; investigate relation of flies to typhoid fever.

Mosquito. *Recognition:* larvae found in stagnant water (wrigglers); adult well known. *Habits:* become active in May; males feed on plant juices, females also on blood; frequent marshy places; eggs laid in rafts on stagnant water, hatch in 1 to 7 days; larvae fully developed in 1 to 3 weeks; pupae similar to larvae, but with larger heads; larvae and pupae breathe through tubes stuck out of water. *Harm:* annoyance. *Control:* drain or fill swamps or pools of standing water; put oil over surface of water; cover rain barrels; avoid water standing in eaves-troughs. *Activities:* May, collect larvae in pond water; keep in screen-covered aquarium or jar; observe changes.

Insect Friends

Dragonfly. *Recognition:* adult with long body, slender abdomen, two pairs long, membranous wings; nymph found in mud at bottom of ponds in spring, has no wings. *Habits:* nymph crawls out of water on plant stem and adult emerges; adult feeds on smaller insects caught while flying; eggs laid in water; nymph eats tiny water insects, including mosquito larvae, and lives over winter. *Benefit to Man:* eats harmful insects in air and water. *Activities:* May, dip mud from bottom of stagnant stream and search mud for nymphs; place in jar of pond water, or aquarium (without fish), for class observation; feed them insects, watch their method of travel; June to September, observe flying, egg-laying, and feeding habits of dragonflies on sunny days about ponds.

Honeybee. *Recognition:* commonly known. *Habits:* lives in colonies; three kinds in the family—queen, workers, and drones; the queen lays the eggs in wax cells; the workers keep house, act as nurses, make wax, build comb, guard the hive, gather nectar and pollen from flowers which they accidently pollinate at the same time, make honey and bee-bread; the drones are males; surviving queens and workers remain inactive in winter, but frequently feed; new colonies are formed by a queen and a large number of worker bees setting forth from the old colony (swarming). *Benefit to Man:* workers make wax and honey, and pollinate flowers of fruit trees and gardens. *Activities:* visit a beehive and observe workers coming and going, sentinels guarding the entrance, returning bees with legs laden with pollen; visit flowers and observe how the bees reach for nectar, how they store pollen in the pollen baskets on their legs, and how their backs become accidently covered with pollen; have an observation hive in the classroom; catch bees and watch them suck up honey or sweetened water; ask a bee keeper to let you see inside a hive.

Activities

All Grades

- In the morning visit young cabbages and flowering plants in the garden. Look for plants cut off at the surface of the ground. Dig around the roots of these and look for the greasy gray cutworms. Place a roll of paper reaching just under the soil around the remaining plants.

Are any of these plants cut off the next night? Find out how to mix poisoned bran mash to place around plants where cutworms may eat it.

- Find a potato beetle on a young plant. Don't kill it, but watch for its eggs on the underside of a leaf. Then kill the beetle. How long do the eggs take to hatch? What do the larvae eat? How long do they take to grow up and dig into the soil? Keep a diary of your observations from day to day.
- Look for little rafts of mosquito eggs floating on stagnant water (rain barrels, stagnant pools, ditches, eaves-troughs), and for "wiggletails."

Junior and Intermediate Grades

- Declare war on houseflies, but first find out all about the enemy—where he camps, where he eats, how he fights, how rapidly his army increases. Then plan your attack.
- Build two cardboard houses, one with screens, covered garbage pails, etc., and labeled "Housefly Peddlers Not Wanted," and the other house open, a standing invitation to flies to enter.
- Make a motion picture entitled "Why and How We War Against Insects." Include such scenes as houseflies spreading disease, and people spreading poison bait for grasshoppers.

Read

Barlowe, *A Child's Book of Insects*. Ryerson (Maxton).

Biles, *The Modern Family Garden Book* (teacher): "Pest Control," pp. 122-126, Longmans, Green (Ferguson & Associates).

Blough & Parker, *The Insect Parade* (grades 4-6), The Basic Science Education Series. Copp Clark (Row, Peterson).

Frasier et al., *Winter Comes and Goes* (grades 3-4): "The Insects in Spring," pp. 158-171. Dent (Singer).

Parker, *Six-legged Neighbors* (grades 2-3), The Basic Science Education Series. Copp Clark (Row, Peterson).

Partridge, *General Science*, Intermediate, Book 2 "Insect Friends and Foes," pp. 83-106; and *Everyday Science*, Book One: "Insect Pests in the Home," pp. 335-345. Dent.

Peterson, *Wildlife in Color*. Allen (Houghton Mifflin).

Phillips & Wright, *Some Animal Neighbors* (grades 4-6): "The May Beetle and Some of His Relatives," pp. 67-70; "Some Two-winged Insect Neighbors," pp. 39-57. Copp Clark (Row, Peterson).

Rutley, *Nature's Year*, Book III (grades 5-6): "A Swarm of Bees" and "Wasps," pp. 21-28 Macmillan.

Sherman, *The Real Book about Bugs, Insects and Such*. Blue Ribbon (Garden City).

Sterling, *Insects and the Homes They Build*. Doubleday.

New to this Edition

Cottam, Clarence. *Insects: Revised and Updated* (Golden Guides from St. Martin's Press, 2001).

Crenshaw, Whitney. *Garden Insects of North America: The Ultimate Guide to Backyard Bugs* (Princeton University Press, 2004).

Frederick, Anthony. *Under One Rock: Bugs, Slugs, and Other Ughs* (Dawn Publishers, 2001).

Insect Lore. *Insect Lore Ladybug Land* (Kit: Watch life cycle of ladybugs).

Leahy, Christopher. *Peterson First Guide to insects of North America* (Houghton Mifflin Harcourt, 1998).

Pleasant, Barbara. *Garden Insects of North America: The Ultimate Guide to Backyard Bugs* (Storey, 1997).

Walliser, Jennifer. *Good Bug Bad Bug: Who's Who, What They Do, and How to Manage Them Organically (All You Need to Know about the Insects in Your Garden)*, (St. Lynn's Press, Second Edition, 2011).

Winner, Cherie. *Everything Bug: What Kids Really Want to Know about Bugs* (Northword Press, 2004).

See also reading references in Unit 25 (page 103).

Nature Journal Excerpts

Praying Mantis catching a Beetle.

Mark 8-4-09

Rufous-sided Towhee

We saw this bird at our bird-feeder. It's unusual to see this bird here in summer. He is not common here.

coopers hawk (Gary)

Beautify Your Surroundings --- May

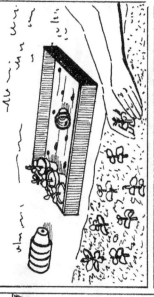

WHEN DANGER FROM LOCAL FROST IS OVER, TRANSPLANT YOUR ANNUAL FLOWERING PLANTS TO THE PLACES YOU HAVE PLANNED FOR THEM.

BIRD CALENDARS:

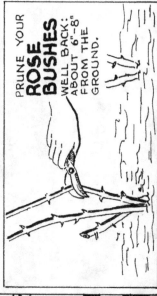

RED-HEADED WOODPECKER

KEEP THEM GOING. MAY IS AN IMPORTANT MONTH FOR BIRD MIGRATIONS.

PRUNE YOUR **ROSE BUSHES** WELL BACK: ABOUT 6"-8" FROM THE GROUND.

TENT CATERPILLAR — LARVAE AND "TENT" — PUPAE — ADULT — EGG MASSES

CODLING MOTH — EGGS ARE LAID IN APPLE BLOSSOM — LARVA IN APPLE — PUPA — ADULT

COLORADO POTATO BEETLE — EGGS — YOUNG LARVA — FULL-GROWN LARVA — ADULT

HOUSE FLY — EGGS ARE LAID IN MANURE AND DECAYING REFUSE — LARVA — PUPA — ADULT

MAKE A CHART ILLUSTRATING THE LIFE HISTORIES OF HARMFUL INSECTS. STUDY AND PRACTISE MEANS OF CONTROL.

HAVE YOU YET BEEN OUT TO GET NEW POND LIFE FOR YOUR AQUARIUM AND VIVARIUM?

NOW IS A GOOD TIME TO CLEAR YOUR LAWN OF SUCH WEEDS AS DANDELION, PLANTAIN, AND CHICKWEED.

DON'T FORGET TO ROLL YOUR LAWN, TOO.

BORDER DESIGNS

FARWELL

SCIENCE IN ACTION — MAY.

BIRDS:

YELLOW

MEADOWLARK

GO ON A BIRD HIKE. HOW MANY DIFFERENT BIRDS CAN YOU SEE? IF THERE ARE SOME YOU DO NOT RECOGNIZE, MAKE NOTES OF THEIR SIZE, COLOURINGS, MARKINGS, AND WHERE YOU SAW THEM. THEN LOOK THEM UP IN BIRD BOOKS AT SCHOOL OR IN THE LIBRARY.

TENT CATERPILLARS:

RAG SOAKED IN COAL OIL

BURN OUT THE "TENTS" OF THESE TROUBLE-MAKERS AT NIGHT. WHY AT NIGHT RATHER THAN DURING THE DAY?

D. FARWELL

WILD FLOWERS:

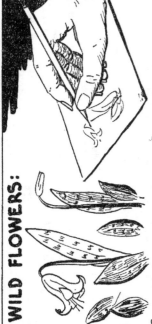

SKETCH THE WILD FLOWERS INSTEAD OF PICKING THEM. SEE HOW MUCH YOU WILL LEARN ABOUT THEM BY THIS METHOD OF GATHERING!

 THIS?
 THIS?
 OR THIS?

GO FISHING!

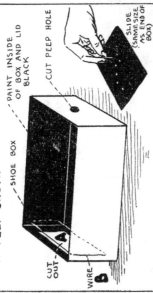

FRESH AIR, SUN, QUIETNESS, REST, EXERCISE, FUN, KNOWLEDGE, HEALTH, — AND FOOD! TRY IT!

STAR GROUPS:

LEARN THE CONSTELLATIONS WITH A PEEP SHOW.

SHOE BOX

PAINT INSIDE OF BOX AND LID BLACK

CUT PEEP HOLE

SLIDE (SAME SIZE AS END OF BOX)

CUT OUT A

WIRE B

CUT OUT MOST OF ONE END OF BOX AS AT A. WIRE B IS TO HOLD SLIDES IN PLACE. ON BLACK PAPER, PRICK OUT STAR MAPS WITH NEEDLE. INSERT STAR MAP BETWEEN END A AND WIRE B. COVER.

TREES:

LEAF GROWTH 1942

MAY 1   MAY 4   MAY 8   MAY 11   MAY 15

MAKE A BLUEPRINT BOOKLET SHOWING LEAF GROWTH. KEEP THE RECORD FOR COMPARISON IN FUTURE YEARS.

(FOR BLUEPRINTING INSTRUCTIONS, SEE "THE SCHOOL", JUNE, 1941, PAGE 901)

NATURAL SCIENCE — JUNE — DAY BY DAY

SUNDAY	MONDAY	TUESDAY	WEDNESDAY	THURSDAY	FRIDAY	SATURDAY
NEW MOON — JUNE 5.	1st QUARTER — JUNE 13.	FULL MOON — JUNE 19.	LAST QUARTER — JUNE 27.			**1** Read "What is so rare as a day in June?"
2 What constellations can you name to-night? BOÖTES	**3** Visit a local stream and collect water life for a school aquarium.	**4** Set up an aquarium with sand, pond water, water plants and animals.	**5** List the names of birds nesting nearby — but do not disturb the nests!	**6** What birds nest under bridges, in cliffs, or near water?	**7** Visit the school lawn and list all the weeds you can find.	**8** Have maple leaves reached their full size yet?
9 In what direction does the moon move between 8 and 9 p.m. to-night?	**10** Make a sketch of young apples, peaches, pears, or cherries on a small twig.	**11** Listen for the call of the ovenbird: "Teacher! Teacher! Teacher!"	**12** Where, and at what time, does the moon set to-night?	**13** Why is to-night's shape of the moon called "First Quarter"?	**14** Record time of sunrise and sunset, and the length of day.	**15** Compare the shape of the moon to-night with that of June 13.
16 Look for wild geranium plants in a damp woods.	**17** Find all the kinds of clover that you can.	**18** Collect about moths an outdoor flame at night. Some are likely may-flies and some caddis-flies.	**19** Bring five roadside weeds to school and look up their names.	**20** Blossoms of evening primrose open at night. Find them by the roadside.	**21** Record time of sunrise and sunset, and the length of day. Compare with June 14.	**22** Pond lilies are rooted in the mud at the bottom of the pond.
23 You will enjoy a bouquet of buttercups from the roadside now. Side may **30** be beautiful.	**24** Using a flash-light, find out what you can about the habits of dew-worms in your lawn at night.	**25** Find the small rose-pink sphinx moth visiting the flowers at night.	**26** Mother bats fly about now with their young clinging to them.	**27** Make a list of ways in which Nature has appealed to you in June.	**28** Record time of sunrise and sun-set, and the length of day. Compare with June 14 and June 21.	**29** The population of birds and mammals is at about its highest now.

J. A. PARTRIDGE.
Drawn by D. Farwell

Have your pupils build this calendar day by day on blackboard or chart.
Use substitutions if desired.

JUNE

Unit 93—Plants in the Wrong Places—Weeds

I will go root away
The noisome weeds, that without profit suck
The soil's fertility from wholesome flowers.
SHAKESPEARE

The amount of knowledge concerning weeds which will be of interest and use to pupils naturally varies with their home surroundings and experiences as well as with their ages. Pupils of primary grades in city or town have observed that some lawns look less attractive than others because of the weeds in them. They are capable of observing and learning the names of such common lawn weeds as dandelion, plantain, and chickweed, and of seeing for themselves how they kill the grass by crowding it out or growing over it. They can learn to dig out such weeds and sow some grass seed in the bare places. Primary pupils in rural schools have broader experiences and may profitably learn a little about the weeds of the garden, the hoed crop, and the grain fields.

In junior and intermediate grades the subject matter for urban pupils should still be limited largely to those weeds which they can find in lawns, small gardens, vacant lots, or nearby roadsides. With rural pupils the knowledge to be gained has more direct economic value since it concerns their livelihood. In these grades the average pupil should understand the following facts: that all green plants need light, moisture, and foods from the soil to grow; that weeds usually grow faster than grass, grain, or hoed crops, and therefore both shade and crowd them out, and use up the moisture and food which the cultivated plants should have; that any plants, however attractive, growing where we do not want them, are weeds; that weeds may spread widely and rapidly because of the large numbers of their seeds, or the way the seeds are carried by water, wind, and animals, or, as in the case of the Canada thistle, sow thistle, and twitch grass, by sending up new plants from every joint of the underground stems (Unit 22, page 91); the harm done by weeds in the community, and the methods used to kill them and to prevent them from going to seed.

Weeds are harmful in many ways. In addition to robbing desirable plants of the space, moisture, and other foods in the soil which they require to grow, the taller ones keep the surrounding plants from receiving the light needed to make plant foods. Both the hay crop and the seed of grains, clovers, and grasses harbor weed seeds which lower their sales value. The consequent decrease in both quantity and quality of farm products brings serious financial loss to the farmer. Some weeds harbor harmful insects and plant diseases; others are poisonous to livestock (water hemlock) and to man (poison ivy). Weeds always reduce the sales value of the farm itself.

To prevent weeds from going to seed is better than to kill them after they begin growth. In open fields and in hoed crops, frequent cultivation keeps weeds from maturing. In grain crops, wild mustard is usually pulled by hand, but may be killed by weed sprays. Canada thistle and quack grass in pastures are eaten by sheep; weeds on roadsides, in vacant lots, and in meadows must, according to law, be mowed. When ripe seeds or living underground stems of weeds are in the ground, frequent cultivation is the best means of destroying them. When the soil is stirred up, new growth begins; the next cultivation kills this, especially in sunny, dry weather. For this reason, summer fallowing and growing hoed crops help to clean soil of weeds and weed seeds. Weeds in lawns can be destroyed only by pulling, spudding, or killing them with chemicals sold for this purpose.

Activities

Teacher

Take the primary pupils to the lawn to identify dandelion, duckweed, and plantain. Notice the space each takes, and therefore the amount of grass killed by each. Show that they are low enough not to be cut by the lawnmower. Remove a few, and see their deep or spreading roots. Sprinkle some grass seed in the holes and cover it with soil.

Junior and Intermediate Grades

- Visit vacant lots, roadsides, fields, and cultivated places. Learn to know two or three common weeds in each place. Make a classroom collection of living weeds, each carefully dug from the soil, its root wrapped in moist paper while it is being brought to school, then placed in a jar of water changed daily. Label each to show its name and the kind of place in which it is found. Give sight recognition tests, but avoid detailed descriptions.
- Collect habitat groupings of weeds, and display them in the classroom. Suggested groupings are: weeds of lawns, such as common chickweed, common plantain, dandelion, knotweed, and crab grass; weeds of gardens, such as purslane, red-root pigweed, foxtail, peppergrass,

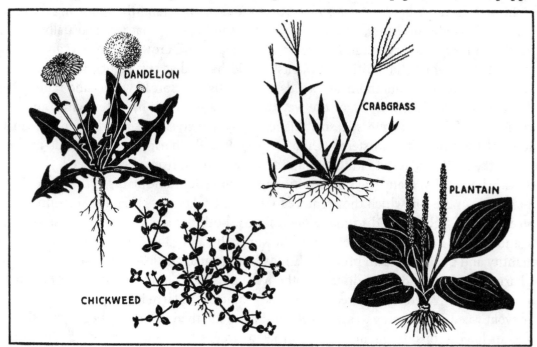

Figure 1

etc.; weeds of meadows, of grain fields, of roadsides, and of waste places. Class collections of such groups may profitably be mounted in old picture frames, each with a protecting glass front, for temporary placement in your museum.

- Dig and bring to school the underground parts of Canada thistle, twitch (quack) grass, and perennial sow thistle. Find the joints and, at these, the buds from which new plants grow.
- Make a survey of weeds in your community. Ask farmers or gardeners which ones are most injurious, and why, also how they control them. Ask a seed merchant how he gets grain, clover, and timothy seed free from weed seeds.
- Find out: whose lawn on your street contains fewest weeds; how the owner keeps his lawn so well; who is responsible for controlling weeds on roadsides and in vacant lots.

Read

Comstock, *Handbook of Nature-Study*, pp. 512-545. Allen (Comstock).

Partridge, *Everyday Science*, Book Two: "Plants To Be Rooted Out," pp. 13-16, and "Weeds," pp. 35-42. Dent. *Farm Weeds*. $1.00 per copy, from the Queen's Printer, Ottawa.

New to this Edition

Gift, Nancy. *Good Weed Bad Weed: Who's Who, What to Do, and Why Some Deserve a Second Chance (All You Need to Know About the Weeds in Your Yard)*, (St.Lynn's Press, 2011).

Pleasant, Barbara. *Controlling Garden Weeds: Storey's Country Wisdom Bulletin A-171* (Storey, 1997).

Figure 2—Weed: Chenopodium album.

Unit 94—The Earth—Our Home

Our Earth is like a transport plane,
That carries wealth surpassing gold.
It traffics not for paltry gain:
Its cargoes are not bought nor sold.
It holds its course around the sun:
Nor rolls, nor banks, nor stalls, nor spins.
Its yearly flight is never done;
When winter ends, the spring begins.
At eighteen-miles-per-second speed
Without an instrument in sight,
No stick to hold, no maps to read,
It travels on by day and night.
It bears a load of human freight;
From birth to death, men come and go.
They live and love, they toil and hate
For good or ill, for weal or woe.
A billion walk its crowded ways;
And billions sleep beneath its sod.
But souls are safe through stormy days:
The unseen Pilot's name is God.
CARL RUFUS

Modern methods of communication and travel make the earth appear very small to us. As a whole it becomes more and more our home. Pupils in intermediate grades learn of its peoples through social studies. But to understand how the various peoples of the earth live, pupils should have some scientific understanding of the earth itself.

Some of the essential facts to be taught concerning the earth as a whole are: its shape, the distance around it in terms of travel time, its position out in space, its traveling around the sun every year, the middle line called the equator, the northern and the southern hemispheres, its rotation on an imaginary line called the axis (which extends from the North Pole to the South Pole), the cause of day and night, the speed of travel of a point on its circumference at the equator.

Some understanding of the physical make-up of the earth—its rock, soil, water, and atmosphere—should be gained. At first the earth was very hot; then it cooled. In doing so, it wrinkled, causing mountains and valleys to be formed. Then a blanket of air gathered over it. Later some

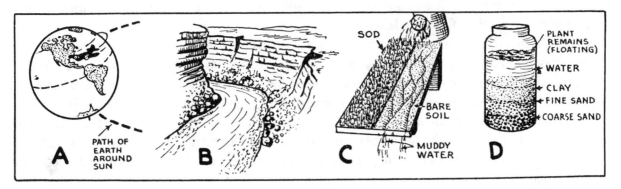

Figure 1— Learning About the Earth

A, a plane traveling around the rotating earth while the earth travels around the sun; B, weather and stream remove rocks; C, sod prevents erosion; D, the constituents of loam soil shown by experiment.

steam puffed forth from crevices in the rock. As this cooled, it changed to water, which trickled down mountainsides, forming first little streams, then larger ones. Finally oceans and lakes, covering about three-quarters of the earth's surface, were formed in the low places.

As yet there was no soil, but the air and the moisture on the earth gradually changed some of its rock to particles of sand. It happened this way. Just as water falling from an eaves-trough gradually makes a hollow in a rock, so water running over rocks can wear away rock particles and form soil. When some pebbles and sand flow with this water, the wearing effect is all the greater. Some of the water may lodge in crevices and may freeze there. The pressure thus formed breaks away some pieces. In a similar manner the roots of trees growing in crevices break the rocks. As pieces of rocks are jostled together by running water, sliding ice, and falling stones, they are broken still finer. Even the wind, carrying sand with it, grinds some particles from solid rock.

As all such rock particles were carried by streams into low places, little patches of soil were formed. Then some little plants took root, grew to maturity, and died. Their remains, when decayed, added some humus to the soil. Then larger plants could grow. Gradually enough soil gathered on the earth's surface to support a wide range of vegetation, and therefore of animal life. Since then, burrowing animals such as earthworms, ants, mice, and woodchucks helped to improve the soil as they mixed its particles more thoroughly and let air and water enter it more freely, ready to act on the rock particles of the soil and make them even finer.

Then came man. At first he was content to gather wild plants and to hunt wild animals for food, clothing, and shelter. Later he discovered how to tame the wild animals—the cow, horse, camel, dog, goat, and others—in order to use them more conveniently as food and as servants. He stopped his wandering ways and settled down to live a civilized life, soon to discover that even plants when tamed could, by cultivation, be made to yield a more bounteous and useful harvest.

Activities

Teacher

Primary pupils should learn by firsthand experience that the earth, our home, is made up of land and water. Water may be in rain, in little streams, or in larger bodies of water. Water always flows downhill; it carries bits of leaves and twigs, even soil, with it. Little creeks join together to make larger rivers. Rivers then flow into lakes.

Correlate this work with social studies. Take field trips for the identification of land and water forms—mountains, hills, plains, valleys, islands, creeks, rivers, lakes, etc.; then make a sand-table scene showing land and water forms. Use boxes over which to build hills and valleys. Mirrors, or blue paper under glass, will look like water. For vegetation, some seeds of grain may be sown. Place the sand-table so that the side farthest from the class is to the north. Then draw a large map of the same area or of the neighborhood and place it in the same direction. From it, teach the conventional method of showing directions on a map. Be sure that the pupils actually face north in all these early stages of map teaching.

Use little stories about all these things, and about rocks, for blackboard reading.

In junior and intermediate grades pupils should begin to see that the land of the earth helps us in many ways. It gives us garden and field crops, lawns and pastures, parks and forests. Beneath its surface we obtain coal and minerals. The water on the earth's surface enables us to travel about. It provides fish and other water animals.

All Grades

- After a rain, go into the schoolyard to see what happens to the water. Does it soak in, or does most of it run off? If it runs off, decide what should be done to prevent this; then do it.
- Get two baking-tins or other deep, flat pans, and some soil. In each tin, model sloping fields. Sow grass seed or place sod in one, leaving the other bare. Now sprinkle water on both, trying to keep it as much like rain as possible. Where is the greater loss of topsoil? Why?
- On a trip watch for gullies cut by running water. Make records of your observations, and visit the place after a heavy rain. How deep are the gullies now?
- Scout around to find a place where a cellar is being dug or a roadway is being cut. Take a sample of soil from the top and from farther down. Compare these soils. What differences are there?
- Collect some muddy water in a tumbler. Watch how the water becomes clear as the mud settles.
- Watch the current flow in a stream. Where does it flow fastest, in the middle or at the sides? On the outside or on the inside of a curve? Where are the banks worn most? Where do plants grow in the water? Where are little sandbars formed?
- Find out how leaves become soil. Dig under forest trees. Observe the top layer of dry leaves, layers of partly decayed leaves, earthworms working, layers of black leaf-mold so fine that you cannot find leaves or their parts. This soil is good for house plants.

Primary Grades

- Each pupil collect the prettiest stones he can find. Get smooth round ones from the beach, or from a gravel pit, rough broken ones from the roadside, flat ones from a cliff. See how many colors you can find in stones. Drop pebbles into the aquarium and notice how they sink. See that sand is made up of tiny little stones of different colors. Find what kinds of stones are in people's rings.
- Watch water wearing away little tracks on the hillsides, and carrying away mud. See where it leaves the mud.

Junior and Intermediate Grades

- When it rains, watch what happens to the soil on an incline. (This may be imitated by pouring water from a watering-can.) Where the water forms a pool and then dries up, what kind of soil is left on the ground? Visit a rocky cliff or an old stone wall; notice cracks, holes, and crumbling rock. Find roots in rock crevices. When water enters these cracks, it freezes and breaks the rocks some more.
- Plant peas in a shallow layer of soil on a slab of limestone. Keep the stone in an inclined position until good roots are developed in contact with the limestone. Remove the plants and soil. What caused the markings on the stone? How does this show that growing plants help to form soil?
- During a field trip, collect rocks and minerals, see how the rocks are arranged on a mountainside, notice the course of a gulley or small valley from the top of the hill to the lowest point visible.
- Make a collection of rocks and minerals found in your locality. Include some made smooth by water. Display them in a shallow box, divided into compartments of thin partitions. Look in rocks for fossils which show different kinds of animals that lived long ago. Collect pictures of quarries. Label each to tell what kind of rock is quarried there. If possible, visit a quarry. Collect and label for the classroom museum different kinds of building stone.
- Act a tableau, "The Story of the Earth," as described in Dickie, *The Book of the Rocks* (Dent), pp. 155-158.

Intermediate Grades

- Collect various stones. Use charts, books, and pictures to help name them. Break some with a hammer to see the inside. Examine a new surface with a magnifying glass. Some of the rocks may contain minerals.
- Spread a little soil thinly on paper. Feel its grittiness (rock particles). Examine it with a lens to find grains of sand of various sizes and colors, also bits of decaying plant material.
- Place about 2 inches of garden soil in a tall jar nearly filled with water. Shake the mixture well and permit the soil to settle. Notice the sand particles at the bottom and the finer particles farther up; notice also the bits of vegetation. Draw what you see. Place some pebbles on a piece of iron or on a large stone. Hammer them to fine particles. Then mix some finely pulverized decayed plant matter with the broken particles. Place the mixture in a bottle and shake it thoroughly with water. Notice the nature of the particles when the mixture has settled. Compare these particles with those seen when garden soil was so shaken with water. Of what is soil made?
- Make a model of the earth round a knitting-needle as the axis. Mark and label the north and the south poles and the equator. Turn the earth round the needle. Make small paper cutouts of the continents and attach them in correct positions on the model of the earth.

Read

Andrewa, *All About Dinosaurs* (grades 5-8). Random Home.

Beauchamp et al., *Discovering Our World.* Book 3 (grades 6-7): "How Is the Earth's Surface Changed?" pp. 61-93; and *Science Problems 2* (grades 6-8): "How Does the Earth's Surface Change?" pp. 132-179. Gage (Scott, Foresman).

Blough & Huggett, *Methods and Activities in Elementary-School Science:* "The Earth and Its Surface," pp. 99-103. Ryerson (Dryden).

Carpenter et al., *Mountains and Valleys*. Blue Ribbon (Hanover House).

Comstock, *Handbook of Nature-Study*, pp 736-775. Allen (Comstock).

Cormack, *The First Book of Stones* (grades 6-8). Ambassador (Watts).

Craig et al., *Science Near You* (primary), pp. 56-95; *Science Around You* (junior), pp. 40-51; *Science Everywhere* (grades 4-5), pp. 98-115; *Discovering with Science* (grades 5-6): "Where Plants Grow," pp. 50-63; "The Earth," pp. 64-85; "The Waters of the Earth," pp. 184-209; and "Studying Rocks and Minerals," pp. 210-235; *Adventuring in Science* (grades 6-7): "Wind and Water Change the Earth," pp. 180-201. Ginn.

Dowling et al., *Explaining Why* (grades 4-5), pp. 187-216; *Discovering Why* (grades 5-7), pp. 285-306; and *Understanding Why* (grades 6-8), pp. 77-120 and 217-242. Winston.

Fenton & Fenton, *The Land We Live On; Our Changing Weather;* and *Rocks and Their Stories*. Doubleday.

Fisher, *The Wonderful World—the Adventure of the Earth We Live On*: "How the World Began," "The World in the Making," "Ages of Life," "The Face of the World," "The Work of Wind and Water," "The Work of Sea and Ice," "Man and Minerals," "Man and Power," etc. Blue Ribbon (Hanover House).

Frasier et al., *Winter Comes and Goes* (grades 2-3): "Finding Rocks Is Fun," pp. 104-109; *The Season, Pass* (grades 3-5): "Pictures in Rocks," "How Soil Is Made," "We Need Soil," pp. 200-223; *The How and Why Club* (grades 5-6) : "Jack Finds Some Fossils," pp. 128-147, and "Weather Changes Rocks and Soil," pp. 193-203. Dent (Singer).

Hood, *How the Earth Is Made* (senior grades): a simple presentation of the geology and history of the earth—rocks and mountains, rivers and seas; plants, animals and man; appropriately illustrated. Oxford.

Lane, *All About the Sea* (grades 4-7). Random House.

Melrose et al., *Nature's Bank, the Soil* (grades 6-8)—one of a set of four conservation booklets, listed in Unit 99. National Wildlife Federation, Washington, D.C.

Parker, *The Earth's Changing Surface; Stories Read from the Rocks;* and *Water* (grades 4-6). The Basic Science Education Series. Copp Clark (Row, Peterson).

Partridge, *Everyday Science*, Book Two: "Rocks through the Ages," pp. 100-119, and "Stories in the Rocks," pp. 137-146. Dent.

Pease, *This Is the World*. Allen (Rand McNally).

Pough, *All About Volcanoes and Earthquakes* (grades 5-8). Random House.

Pough, *Field Guide to the Rocks and Minerals*. Allen (Houghton Mifflin).

Schneider, *Rocks, Rivers, the Changing Earth* and *Science Far and Near* (grade 3): "The Earth's Cover," pp. 2-22, and "The Ocean," pp. 100-114. Copp Clark (Heath).

Smith & Clarke, *Around the Clock* (grades 3-4), pp. 65-74; and *Under the Sun* (primary), pp. 91-114. Longmans, Green.

Stephenson, *Nature at Work*, Book 3 (grades 5-6): "Earth, What Is It?" "Earth, What It Does with Rain," "Earth and Ground Water," "Earth, a Hidden Workshop," pp. 48-63. Macmillan (A. & C. Black).

Treat, *Rock Stories and How to Read Them*, Audubon Nature Bulletin, National Audubon Society.

New to this Edition

Bailey, Jacqui. *Cracking Up: A Story About Erosion* (Picture Window Books, 2006).

Gibbons, Gail. *Planet Earth/Inside Out* (HarperCollins, 1998).

Knowlton, Jack. *Geography from A to Z: A Picture Glossary* (HarperCollins, 1997).

_____. *Maps and Globes* (HarperCollins, 1986).

Levy, Matthys. *Earthquakes, Volcanoes, and Tsunamis: Projects and Principles for Beginning Geologists* (Chicago Press Review, 2009).

Tomecek, Steve. *Jump Into Science: Dirt* (National Geographic Books, 2007).

Rissman, Rebecca. *What is a Landform?* (Heinemann-Raintree, 2009).

Rosinsky, Natalie. *Rocks: Hard, Soft, Smooth, and Rough* (Picture Window Books, 2006).

Van Cleave, Janice. *Jancie VanCleave's Earth Science for Every Kid: 101 Easy Experiments that Really Work* (Wiley, 1991).

Unit 95—A Hike to a Marsh, Pond, or Stream

Figure 1—Field trip along a creek.

What is so natural to a normal child as to tramp along the shore of a local stream or pond, listen to the splash of startled frogs, watch the turtles slowly crawl from a projecting stone or log into the water, chase the flitting forms of dragonflies, listen to the "kong queeree" of the red-winged blackbirds swaying on slender cattails, stare at the unique antics of water-striders or whirligig beetles, or wade about on slippery, slimy stones, turning them over to watch or catch the backward-darting crayfish?

An excursion to a marsh, pond, or stream brings many vital nature experiences to pupils—mosquito bites, queer noises, smells they like and smells they don't like, wet feet and muddy clothes laden with seeds and fruits stealing a ride. There they will gain firsthand knowledge of breeding frogs and toads, of busy muskrats, of creeping reptiles, and of birds fighting to protect their nesting-grounds. And then the trip home with minnows, snails, tadpoles, even an adult frog in a rusty old tin can! Each will be anxious to

set up a pond of his own even if it be in an old washtub or pail. This is real life for lively boys and girls—and for teachers.

Before taking the trip to the pond, make and collect the necessary equipment. One essential is a net which can be easily made by fastening cheesecloth or cotton onto a wire clothes hanger bent to form a circle and wired onto a wooden pole. With this, pupils can catch pond life. Take along also some old jars or pails to bring home the finds.

After the hike we may have in our classroom opportunities for continued observations and discoveries. Set up an aquarium, using sand and mud, a variety of water plants which thrive in real pond water, snails and crayfish, water insects and fish.

> Blue dragonflies knitting
> To and fro in the sun,
> With sidelong jerk flitting,
> Sink down on the rushes,
> And, motionless sitting . . .
> On green tasseled rushes,
> To dream in the sun.
> JAMES RUSSELL LOWELL

Activities

Teacher

When you find water animals, emphasize their habits rather than their structure. For example, when you find a dragonfly nymph, talk about dragonflies as follows. This young dragonfly was hatched from an egg laid on the surface of the water last summer. It has fed well on water insects, snails, and tadpoles, using its long, fierce-looking jaws to catch them. Of course this nymph had to shed its skin several times as it grew. Here is another on this cattail. It has just crawled out of the water. Notice its skin is splitting down the center of its back. The full-grown dragonfly will soon crawl out, dry its wings, and gracefully dart about over sunny ponds. We shall see later how skillful it is at catching mosquitoes and other insects.

All Grades

- Armed with a kitchen strainer and old tin cans, visit and explore a local pond or stream. Look for marsh marigolds, swamp grasses, and sedges with their three-angled stems, along the shore. Wade into the shallow water to discover cattails, arrow-heads (recognized by leaf shape), and pickerel weeds. Look across the deeper water for the floating leaves of water-lilies with their long delicate stems connecting with the mud-embedded roots. Gather specimens of smaller rooted water plants or of the tiny floating duckweed plants for the school aquarium. Skim off a few of the water-striders as they skim about on the surface film of the water and cast their dimple-like shadows on the sunny stream bed, or a group of whirligig beetles as they circle about. Dig into the muddy bottom or pull out some of the decaying submerged leaves to find snails, dragonfly nymphs, water fleas, and even bloodsuckers. From streams collect catfish, minnows, and sticklebacks. Bring some of these water animals back for classroom observations in an aquarium. Observe how snails crawl on the inside of the glass, go up and down in water, and reap food from the surface of plants and glass.
- Find the little brown newts with red spots. They live part of their lives in the water, and then

crawl about on wet land. Turn over decaying logs and stones and look for spotted salamanders. These, too, lay their eggs in water; these hatch into tadpoles. Now look for painted turtles, commonly found in marshes, or sunning themselves on logs or stones above the water in ponds. You may find snapping turtles—larger, rougher, and more plainly colored—travelling through marshy places to find loose, damp soil in which to lay their eggs.

- Look for discarded winter houses of muskrats. Near them you may see the muskrats fighting for a mate, or warning each other of the approach of danger by slapping the water with their tails.

- Tramp through the drier places in the marsh. You may find the grassy runways of mice, or ants' nests built rather high. About you will be mosquitoes, mayflies, dragonflies, stoneflies, damselflies. Better still, you may spy a dragonfly crawling out of its old skin on a marsh plant, and, between the plants, you may see the webs of many different kinds of spiders.

- Among the dry tops of cattails, find the nests of red-winged blackbirds— but do not disturb them.

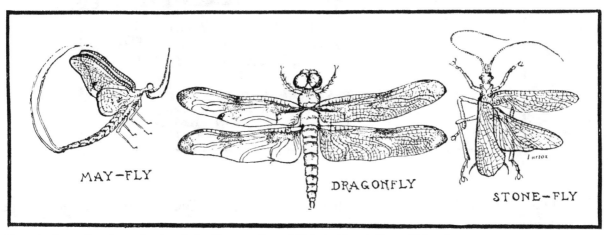

Figure 2—Insects Found near Ponds or Lakes (Courtesy General Biological Supply House, Chicago)

- Pull up a few marsh plants. Notice how soft is the mud in which they are anchored. Trees could not grow here: their roots could not anchor them in such soft places when the wind blows.

- Watch turtles thrusting their heads out of the water for new supplies of air. Notice how some water beetles come to the surface for air which they carry down again as shiny bubbles among the hairs on the body.

- Collect eggs or other life stages of the mosquito and rear them in the classroom.

Junior and Intermediate Grades

- Find out how animals travel in water in the stream and in the aquarium. Watch how a frog takes off when disturbed while floating with its nostrils out of the water. See how some water beetles paddle with their oar-like legs. Find out how rapidly snails can glide along on the glass of the aquarium or on plants or sticks. Conduct a snail race. Observe the trenched paths of clams which have slowly pulled themselves along in the mud or sand of the aquarium or stream bed. Disturb a crayfish and see how gracefully it can dart backward by a downward flip of its tail, watching by means of its stalked eyes where it is going, and at the same time

Figure 3

stirring up a mud screen to obscure the view of its enemies. You may find a year-old tadpole of the green frog.

- Try to find and catch a spring peeper. Watch how he clings to your hands or to the sides of a glass vessel. Find, on his fingers and toes, the little pads with which he does this. Take him from a dark to a light surface. Watch his color change. Place peepers on wet moss in a dark box. If any of them are males, you will hear their chorus when you bring them into a warm room.

Intermediate Grades

- Discover how water plants can live where they do. Notice how the buoyancy of the water supports such delicate-stemmed plant as the water-lilies. Cut across stems to see their air channels. Notice how easily water plants may be bent or pushed about by running water or waves without harm, and how they always lift their flowers above the surface of the water. Scrape off some of the slimy green scum that covers submerged stones. Watch submerged plants give off bubbles of oxygen so necessary for fish. Bring home some other plants for the school aquarium.
- Trace the story of the valley through which a stream flows. Estimate the speed of the water by timing a floating stick for a measured distance. Measure the width and depth of the stream. Notice where and how the water has cut back the banks. Where is the sediment finally deposited most? Why? Why do water plants grow well where the soil is thus

dropped? Ask older residents how the stream of several years ago compares with that today. Try to discover reasons for the change. Have forests been cut down? Make a map showing the course of the stream for a mile or so. Find out why it has taken the particular path it has. Examine adjoining fields and gullies. What effect have grass and trees upon their formation? Examine the stones in the bottom of the stream or along the shore. How do they compare with crushed stone? Why are they rounded? Why are stones in gravel pits similarly rounded?

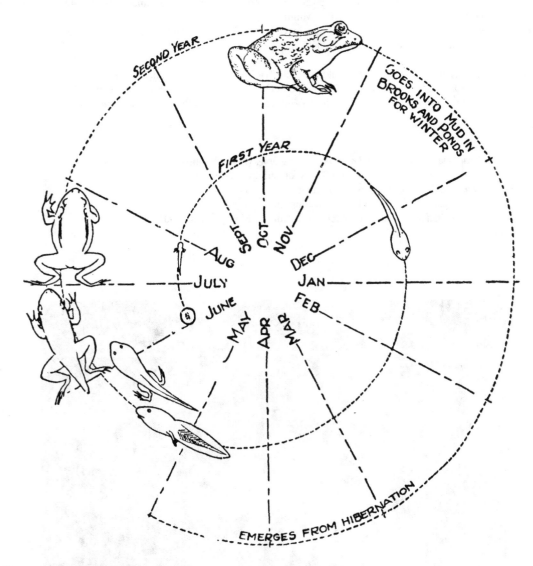

Figure 4—Life History of the Green Frog

Read

Andirews, *Adventures in Science.* Book VI (grades 6-7), pp. 111-121. Moyer.
Beauchamp et al., *How Do We Know?* (primary and junior): "Land and Water," pp. 37-52. Gage (Scott, Foresman).
Candy, *Nature Notebook,* pp. 46-55 and 86-93. Allen (Houghton Mifflin).
Crew, *The More the Merrier.* Oxford.
Erickson, *The True Book of Animals of Small Pond.* Book Society (Children's Press).
Eschmeyer, *Tommy Trout.* Book Society (Fisherman Press).

Frasier et al, *Sunshine and Rsin* (grades 1-2), pp. 56-57; *Through the Year* (grades 2-3): "The Story of a Toad," pp. 114-121; *Winter Comes and Goes* (grades 3-4): "The Crayfish," pp. 150-153, and "Wigglers," pp. 154-157. Dent (Singer).

Graham &Dersal, *Wildlife for America,* pp. 75-92. Oxford.

Hausman, *Beginner's Guide to Fresh-Water Life.* Allen (Putnam's Sons).

Hunt & Andrews, *Amphibians and Reptiles,* Moyer.

Huntingtun, *Let's Go to the Brook.* Doubleday.

Hylander, *Out of Doors in Spring* (grades 6-8): "Amphibians," pp. 40-57. Macmillan.

Mason, *Animal Sounds:* "Spring Peepers," pp. 54-58. McLeod (Wm. Morrow).

Partridge, *Everyday Science,* Book One: "Creek Dwellers," pp. 346-355, and "The Work and Play of a Creek," pp. 356-362; *Everyday Science,* Book Two: "The Frog and His Neighbors," pp. 572-593, and "How Plants and Animals Live in Water," pp. 594-605. Dent

Peterson, *Wildlife in Color,* pp. 74-117. Allen (Houghton Mifflin).

Phillips & Wright, *Some Animal Neighbors:* "Some Filmy-winged Insect Neighbors," pp 97-117. Copp Clark (Row, Peterson).

Porter & Hansen, *The Pond Book.* Gage (American Book Co.).

Sears, *Tree Frog.* Allen (Holiday).

Smith & Henderson, *Beneath the Skies* (grade 6): "Taking a Field Trip," pp. 167-188. Longmans, Green.

Stephenson, *Nature at Work,* Book 1 (grades 4-5): "The Tadpoles Grow Up," pp. 77-80. Macmillan (A. & C. Black).

Williams & Campbell, *Easy Lessons in Nature Study,* Book IV (grades 4-6): "Life in the Pond," pp. 85-94. Oxford.

New to this Edition

Fredericks, Athony. *Near One Cattail: Turtles, Logs And Leaping Frogs* (Dawn Publishers, 2005).

Hunter, Anne. *What's in the Pond* (Houghton Mifflin Books for Children, 1999).

Kalman, Bobbie. *Wetland Food Chains* (Crabtree Publishing, 2006).

Kurtz, Kevin. *A Day in the Salt Marsh* (Sylvan Dell Publishing, 2007).

Reid, George. *Pond Life: Revised and Updated* (Golden Guide from St. Martin's Press, 2001).

Silver, Donald. *Pond* (McGraw-Hill, 1997).

Figure 5—White water lily.

Unit 96—Safety and First Aid

The old saying, "Accidents will happen," has truth only when the accidents result from carelessness, ignorance, or lack of skill—carelessness in not removing hazards from streets, factories, and homes, in not being alert in the presence of possible danger, and in taking unnecessary and foolish risks; ignorance of traffic rules, of safety regulations, of the potential danger in gasoline, coal gas, etc.; lack of skill in driving cars and in operating machines.

But accidents do happen in alarming numbers in the home, on the street, at school, and in the factory, and will continue to happen until the school undertakes the responsibility of training pupils, the citizens of tomorrow, in safety consciousness, safety habits, and safety knowledge.

Safety First

Safety about the School. *In the Classroom.* Keep all equipment in its proper place. Keep small objects (crayons, erasers, etc.) away from the eyes, the ears, and the mouth. Keep your feet under the desk to avoid tripping others. Be careful with scissors and other sharp-pointed articles. Be silent and give immediate obedience as soon as the fire bell sounds. Do not stand on seats. Learn to carry chairs correctly.

In the Schoolyard. Keep the playground free from glass, nails, rocks, etc. Avoid collisions, rough play, tripping, and practical jokes. Take your turn and play fair.

On the Way to and from School. Obey all traffic signs and rules. Obey traffic officers at street crossings. Go directly to and from school; avoid dangerous places—railroad yards, sewer excavations, etc. Keep on the sidewalk, and cross only at corners. Don't run into the street after balls or each other, or play on the street with scooters and sleighs. Remember all safety and courtesy rules when riding a bicycle. Do not hitch on vehicles. Don't touch fallen wires or other electrical installations. Help younger children to be careful by being careful yourself.

Activities

- List as many accidents as you can that have happened at school. How could they have been avoided?
- Male up jingles to fit familiar little singing games such as "Mulberry Bush," e.g., "We'll show you how we cross the street,—" Make up other jingles such as:
  > The world is so full of good places to play,
  > I'm sure we should stay off the street every day.
- Dramatize crossing the street safely. Learn safety rhymes. Draw scenes showing dangers in various places. Draw up safety rules or "Do's and Don'ts" for the class.
- Form a safety club in your school.

Safety at Home. Most accidents in the home are caused by carelessness (leaving unsafe steps, holes in carpets, bad wiring) and by defective home-planning or building (sharp corners on posts, winding stairs, low cellar ceilings). These are not within the control of children.

Be careful with waxed floors, small rugs, and holes in carpets. Do not leave drawers open where people may walk against them. Never leave toys on steps or walks. Don't climb on chairs or boxes to reach things. Stack all things on shelves carefully so that they won't fall. Never leave objects lying on stairways or in dark corners. Do not run while holding pencils or other sharp objects in the hand or mouth.

Place the teakettle so that steam from the spout cannot reach a passerby. Do not place glass, jagged-edged cans, or poison in a wastepaper basket.

Under no conditions use gasoline for dry-cleaning or for lighting a fire. Build bonfires and burn rubbish in safe places, and when there is no wind.

See that children do not play with objects that they may swallow, or with other dangerous objects.

Sprinkle icy steps and walks with cinders, sand, or salt. See that oil and grease do not make the garage floor slippery—use sand to catch the oil. Never start a car with the garage doors closed. Never leave a hoe or rake facing upward. Keep the well safely covered.

Avoid using an electric appliance where you may touch it and a water pipe at the same time. Use only porcelain fixtures in cellars or bathrooms, and only rubber-coated electric cords near water.

Activities

- Look for dangerous things around your home—matches, iodine, small rugs on waxed floors, etc. Make safe as many of these as you can.
- Play hopscotch on the sidewalk; not on the street.
- Make posters advocating care with poisons.
- Make a complete survey of your home to find out what substances are labeled "poison." Paint a red danger sign on all such containers.

Safety on the Farm. Keep your hands away from all moving parts of threshing, sawing, or chopping machines, of binders and mowers. Keep all hallways in barns clear of pails, rakes, forks. Never leave boards containing exposed nails lying around. If injured by a nail, be sure to wash, disinfect, and bandage the wound at once. See that kerosene and gasoline are not stored near the barn. Do not light matches near hay or straw. Do not carry matches in your pockets. Never throw greasy or oily rags in a corner—they may start a fire. Avoid frightening horses—even the tamest horse may cause an accident. Keep away from strange bulls, cows with newborn calves, a mother hog and her litter. Put away all hoes, rakes, saws, etc., where they cannot injure anyone. During a thunderstorm keep away from tall trees standing alone in a field, from wire fences, telephone and radio connections, and stoves. Use safe places for sliding, tobogganing, etc.

Activities

Name six farm machines and state one safety precaution connected with each. Survey the yards around the house and barn for dangerous things—nails in boards, broken glass, wire in grass, etc. Make such places safe.

Safety with Tools. When driving a nail, hold it only long enough to start it with a few light taps of the hammer.

Never leave tools on top of a ladder: you are likely to forget and move the ladder. A serious accident may result.

Cutting-tools should be handled with care. Keep both hands behind the cutting edge. Never cut toward any part of body. Never try to catch a falling tool that has a sharp edge.

Safety concerning Fires.

Little sparks from bonfires,
Left by careless hands,
Make our mighty forest,
Into desert lands.

Preventing Fires in the Home. Keep matches out of the reach of children, and in containers that will not burn. Carry safety matches only. Have electrical appliances installed by a qualified electrician. See that furnaces, furnace pipes, and chimneys are safe, or are made safe. Keep no gasoline in the house. Do not store papers or kindling near a furnace or stove. Keep the attic tidy so that it will not be a fire hazard.

When There Is a Fire. Water puts out fire because it cools the burning object, creates steam, and drives away the air. A fire extinguisher supplies a chemical which prevents the fire from burning. The teacher should burn a small object on a safe surface and show that the fire can be "smothered" with sand or a rug. Then dramatize how to put out the fire of burning clothes: by wrapping the supposed victim in a rug, rolling him on the ground, or laying him down and rolling him in a rug. Never run when clothing is burning; the motion causes the air to fan the flame.

Activities

- See that the fireplace is screened to retain sparks.
- Learn the causes of all fires in your community in the past year.
- Write a list of safety rules about matches.
- Write a poem about matches with successive lines beginning with the letters M-A-T-C-H-E-S.

General Activities

Teacher

- Let children supply rules and illustrations. Make truths clear by demonstrations, when possible. Use memory gems, stories, pictures, posters.
- Use the problem method of teaching: Why keep to the right? Why not dash from behind a parked car? Why look first to the left and then to the right? Why should each child know his name, address, and telephone number?

All Grades

- Make up rhymes, songs, and slogans on safety. Write safety stories and compositions; act original plays and dramatizations.
- Make up songs to popular tunes such as: "Take a long look at every crossing, Take a long look around . . . to the tune of "Tipperary."
- On the safety bulletin board, post clippings, pictures, reports of accidents.
- Give each pupil a sheet of paper, each bearing a different safety heading such as: Things I Keep Away from, Things I Do Not Put in My Mouth, Places Where I Do Not Play, etc. Each pupil will fill in one answer and then pass the sheet to the next pupil, who will read it and add another.

- Repeat some safety reminder just before each dismissal.

Junior and Intermediate Grades

- List all the safe and the unsafe places in your neighborhood where you play. Why are they safe or unsafe? Draw a map of your district. Mark on it the safest route to school, also all dangerous places. Think of how your safety is protected at these spots.
- Older children act as safety patrols to guide younger ones across the street.
- Make posters such as "Icy Walks Are Dangerous," "Safety First While Playing," "Beware of Carelessness," "Fire is a Good Servant but a Bad Master."
- Find out the causes of accidents in various places.

First Aid

Accidents are as likely to happen in the school or schoolyard as elsewhere. Then it becomes the teacher's responsibility either to treat the injury or to render first aid and seek medical aid.

Every school should be supplied with a first-aid kit containing at least: rolls of one-inch and two-inch gauze bandage, absorbent cotton, adhesive tape, an antiseptic solution such as iodine, white vaseline, baking-soda, a pair of scissors and forceps, safety pins, and a strong triangular bandage such as a large handkerchief. These materials should be kept in a clean box marked with a red cross and used only when needed.

Cuts and Wounds. Wash the injured spot thoroughly with soap and water until no dirt particles are visible. Cleanse the wound with an antiseptic solution of iodine or mercurochrome. When bleeding has stopped, dress it with a clean sterile bandage. Attach this with adhesive rather than by tying. Do not put oily or greasy salves on fresh wounds—they prevent healing. Never remove a scab or a dressing in such a way as to leave a raw surface.

Something in the Eye. To remove specks from the eye: wash it with clean water by tipping a glass of water so that the eye can be blinked in it, or by using an eye cup.

Pull the upper lid over the lower, turn the upper lid upward and remove the object with the tip of a clean handkerchief—but do not touch the black spot in the eye (pupil) with it.

Frost Bites. *Do not* apply snow to the frozen part or rub it vigorously. Leave it to thaw out gradually, or apply cold water or *melting* snow.

Black and Blue Spots from Bruises. Apply cold water or an ice pack immediately.

Shock. There is nearly always shock after an accident. Lay the patient flat; keep him quiet. Apply blankets and, if necessary, hot-water bottles to keep him warm. If there is no internal injury, stimulate him with hot cocoa.

Fainting. Place the patient with his head lower than the rest of his body, and apply cold water to the face. Loosen his clothing. Keep people away.

Burns and Scalds. Give first aid only until the doctor arrives. Relief is given by covering the wound with a white cloth wet with clean water.

Sprains. Raise the sprained part in a restful position. Apply heat or cold compresses without rubbing; then bandage it. Consult a doctor.

Broken Bones and Fractures. Do not move or otherwise disturb the patient. Keep him comfortable. If necessary, cover him with a blanket, and put a hot-water bottle beside him. If the weather is warm, shade him. Send for a doctor at once.

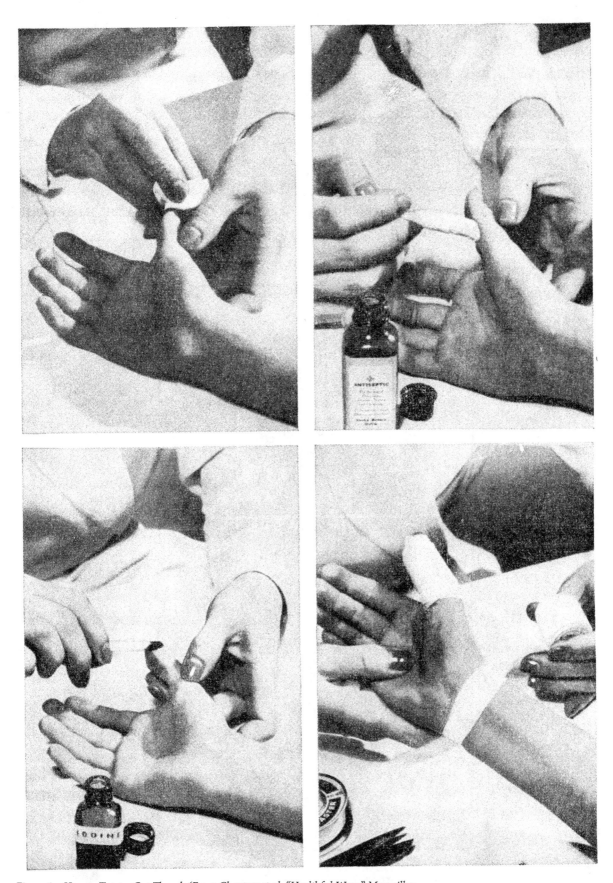

Figure 1—How to Treat a Cut Thumb (From Charters et al, "Healthful Ways," Macmillan.

Insect Stings. Remove the sting; then apply ammonia or a paste of baking-soda. Apply cold-water packs to reduce swelling.

Bites. *By Mosquitoes.* Relieve the itching by applying moist baking soda. *By Dogs.* Immediately wash the wound, and apply iodine or some other strong antiseptic solution. Call the doctor. *By Snakes.* The rattlesnake will only bite when bothered. Keep a bitten person warm and quiet until the doctor comes.

Poisons. *Poison Ivy.* Wash the affected surfaces with a strong solution of soap in hot water, or bathe them with alcohol or gasoline. Get medical advice. *Internal.* Give the patient an emetic, either mustard in water, or salt in warm water, to cause vomiting. If you know the antidote for the particular poison, give it; if not, give milk or white of egg—but call the doctor at once and, if possible, tell him what poison has been taken.

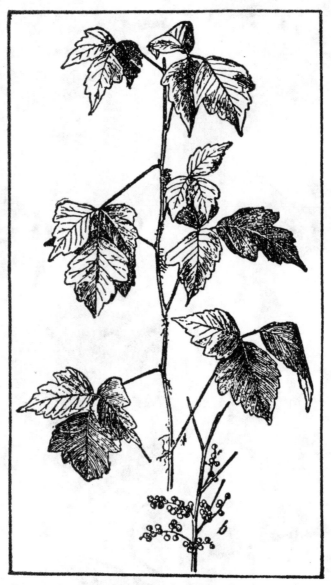

Figure 2—Poisong Ivy. Every pupil should know this plant by sight.
(From Sargent's "Plants and Their Uses," and Peabody and Hunt, "Biology and Human Welfare." Macmillan.)

General activities

Teacher

- Be sure each pupil can give his name and address, his father's first name, and perhaps the home telephone number, as safety precautions if lost.
- Treat all scratches, cuts, or injuries—no matter how small—immediately. Otherwise infection may result.
- Train pupils to feel that it is foolish, not heroic, to conceal an injury and not give others a chance to treat it.
- Insist that pupils do not play around washroooms, shower rooms, lockers, or cloakrooms. Floors which are wet or otherwise slippery are dangerous.
- Keep a motto, "Safety First," at the front of the classroom.

Read

Bibby, Healthy and Happy (grades 4-6): "Safe and Sound," pp. 109-134. Macmillan.

Bowman & Boston, Living Safely (workbook; grades 5-8): "First Aid," pp. 30-39. M acmillan.

Brownell & Williams, Hale and Hearty: "Safety First," pp. 251-286. Gage (American Book Co.).

Buckley et al., "The Road to Safety," a series of eight graded readers—Book E, *Here and There* (grades 5-6): "On the Way to School," "In Time of Fire," "When Winter Comer," "On Spring Days," "Summer Fun"; Book G, *On Land and Water* (grade 7): "On Street and Highway," "Safety at Home," "Safety on the Water"; Book H, *Who Travels There* (grade 8): "Safety in Travel," "Adventures in Summer." Gage (American Book Co.).

Charters et al., *All through the Day* (primary); short stories dealing with safe playing, safe places, and safety in school; *Health and Fun* (workbook; grade 1): "Getting to and from School Safely," pp. 17-22; "Safety and Fun," pp. 37-40; and "After School Safety and Health," pp. 73-92; *Health through the Year*, Revised (grades II-Il1): several short stories organized seasonally, encouraging care and safe play; *Health Secrets*, Revised (grades 3-4): "Safe and Sane," pp. 175-202; *Healthful Ways*, Revised (grades 4-5): "Accidents Need Not Happen," pp. 187-220; *Let's Be Healthy*, Revised (grades 5-6): "Let's Be Safe!" pp. 1-40; and *Habits Healthful and Safe*, Revised (grades 6-7): "Safety as a Game," pp. 197-232. Macmillan.

Haynes, *The True Book of Health* (primary), pp. 38-43. Book Society (Children's Press).

Hippler & Durfee, *Safe Living*. Longmans, Green (Benj. Sanborn).

Hollock & Allen, *Health and Safety for You*. Ginn.

Artificial Respiration, First Aid Manual, First Aid Illustrated, and *Fundamentals of First Aid*. Canadian Red Cross Society.

A Preliminary Course of First Aid to the Injured. St. John Ambulance, 46 Wellesley St. East, Toronto.

First Aid and *Safety Begins at Home*. Metropolitan Life Insurance Company.

New to this Edition

Boelts, Maribeth and Darwin. *Kids to the Rescue: First Aid Techniques for Kids* (Parenting Press, 2003).

Gale and Buhler. *The Kids' Guide to First Aid: All about Bruises, Burns, Stings, Sprains & Other Ouches* (Williamson Publishing Company, 2001).

Llewellyn, Claire. *Watch Out! At Home* (Barron Educational Series, 2006).

Pendziwol, Jean E. *No Dragons for Tea: Fire Safety for Kids* (Kids Can Press, 1999).

Rothenberg, Nancy. *Fun to Know First Aid for Kids* DVD (Millennium).

Saubers, Nadine. *Everything First Aid Book: How to Handle Falls and Breaks, Choking, Cuts and Scrapes, Insect Bites and Rashes, Burns, Poisoning, and When to Call 911* (Adams Media, 2008).

See also reading references for Unit 97.

Unit 97—Safety While on a Holiday

Holiday time not only brings pupils into new and more dangerous places, but seems to bring about greater thoughtlessness and carelessness in actions and habits. Children come into contact with the hazards of camping-places and campfires, dangers near water, and strange, perhaps poisonous, plants. To meet these hazards, certain knowledge and habits need to be impressed upon pupils.

Safety at Camp. Choose a safe and healthful camping-place, one with sunlight part of the day, with good drainage, away from swamps and stagnant water.

Remember to get your suntan gradually by doing most of your playing when the sun is low or by playing in the shade at other times—especially the first few hot days. Apply aloe vera and cold compresses to a sunburn.

Don't get lost if you can help it, but if you do, try these. With a compass locate the four main directions. Follow toward the direction from which you came. Use your watch as a compass as follows: hold a match or a similar stick upright at the center of the watch. Turn the watch until the shadow falls along the hour hand. North is halfway between the shadow and the figure 12 (S.T.) on the watch (fig. 1). Or hold the watch so that the hour hand points directly to the sun. A line from the center of the watch toward the south is halfway between the hour hand and the figure 12. At night find the North Star and locate the other directions accordingly.

Build fires only on surfaces which will not burn, preferably bare soil. Everything that will burn should be cleared away from the fire. Use as small a fire as will serve. Be sure your campfire is out before leaving it; smother it with water or subsoil.

Figure 1—Telling Direction by Means of Watch
(Drawing from New York State College of Agriculture)

Pupils should understand that pure water is as important as pure food and that appearance will not tell whether water is fit to drink or not. Disease-producing germs may be present in water that looks the clearest and smells the freshest. Have the water tested by your local health department. In the meantime add chlorine tablets to it, or use purifying methods shown in fig. 2.

Dispose of all refuse safely. Burn all garbage and bury, or treat with chemicals, all wastes which cannot be burned, thus avoiding flies and other pests. Leave tin cans in the fire until the paint covering is destroyed; then remove, flatten, and bury them where they will rust. Keep the camp clear of glass, nails, and scrap metal.

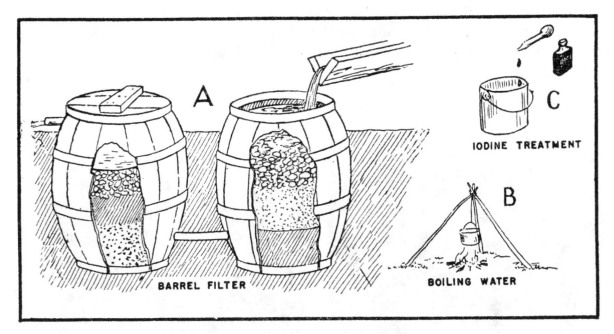

Figure 2—Making Water Safe to Drink (Drawings from New York State College of Agriculture)

Here are three ways of making water safer to drink. A. Arrange two barrels as shown with a pipe connecting them at the base. When the water enters the one at the right, it is filtered through the layers of gravel, sand, and charcoal in the first barrel, then through layers of sand, charcoal, and gravel as it rises in the second barrel. Many impurities are removed as it goes, leaving the water relatively pure. To clean the filtering layers, reverse the flow of water for a while. B. Boil water for a half-hour, cool it, and boil it again. C. Add a drop of tincture of iodine to each quart of doubtful water.

Safety around Water. Most drowning accidents could be prevented by following reasonable safety rules. All people should obey these precautions: Do not try to swim too far or in very cold water—cramps may cause even the best of swimmers to drown. Do not swim for at least an hour after meals, or immediately after heavy exercises. Dive only where you are sure that the water is deep enough and clear enough to be safe; avoid slippery diving-boards. When boating long distances, take a life belt. Don't try to swim to shore from an overturned boat unless you are sure you can make it. If someone is with you, grasp wrists across the middle of the overturned boat. Don't try to climb into an overturned boat.

If you cannot swim, adhere to the following rules, too: Do not try to wade where the bottom is slippery, near deep water in a swift current, or when waves are strong. When learning, swim from the deeper toward the shallower water. Do not take out a canoe unless you can paddle it—and then only when comparatively close to shallow water or shore. Never change seats in a canoe, and be very careful when changing seats in a rowboat.

Learn how to rescue the drowning (fig. 3).

When someone appears to have been drowned, always call a doctor or another person capable of administering

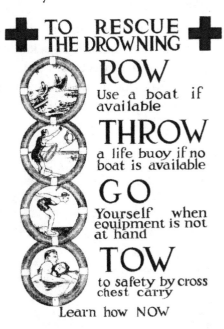

Figure 3—American Red Cross

415

artificial respiration. There may still be time to restore breathing and save a life.

Safety from Undesirable Plants and Animals. All campers should know how to recognize poison ivy by its trailing habit, the three downward-hanging leaflets, and the white.

> Berries red, have no dread!
> Berries white, poisonous sight!
> Leaflets three, quickly flee!

Figure 4—Poison ivy

Figure 5—Poison oak.

The plants may be killed if waste oil mixed with kerosene or a strong salt solution (3 pounds of salt to a gallon of water) is applied to the roots. See also Unit 96 (page 407).

The stinging nettle will irritate the skin for several minutes, even hours. A paste of baking-soda will give relief.

Eat no mushrooms unless someone knows from experience that they are edible.

Bumblebees and yellow-jacket wasps will sting viciously if you disturb their nests. When stung by these or other insects, put mud or spirits of ammonia on the injured spot.

Learn to recognize the rattlesnake by the sight or sound of the rattles on its tail. If by the rarest chance you are near where they live, avoid them. If bitten, call a doctor at once.

Read

Beauchamp et al., *Discovering Our World,* Book 1 (grades 4-5), pp. 174-181. Gage (Scott, Foresman).
Bowman & Boston, *Living Safely* (workbook; grades 5-8): "Safety While We Play," pp. 58-81. Macmillan.
Charters et al., *Healthful Ways,* Revised (grades 4-5): "A Happy Vacation," pp. 221-231. Macmillan.
Swimming and Water Safety Manual. Canadian Red Cross Society.

New to this Edition

Amdahl, Paul. *The Barefoot Fisherman: A Fishing Book for Kids* (Clearwater Publishing, 2000).
Autswim Inc. *Teaching Swimming and Water Safety* (Human Kinetics, 2000).
Boelts, Maribeth. *A Kid's Guide to Staying Safe Around Water* (PowerKids Press, 1997).
Llewellyn, Claire. *Watch Out Book Series: On the Road and Near Water* (Barron Educational Series, 2006).

Unit 98—Wandering among the Stars in June

Note: This unit continues the study of the stars, begun in Unit 36 (page 145).

Find the Big Dipper and the North Star on the map. Notice that the two stars on the bowl of the Dipper, farthest from the handle, point to the North Star. Find these also in the north sky. Now you are ready to use the map to locate other constellations. Face to the south at 8 p.m., E.S.T., and hold the map over your head, with its directions pointing correctly. The map now gives you a chart of the sky as you will see it when you lower the map. A flashlight will help. Again locate the Big Dipper, now almost overhead, and the North Star. Find Queen Cassiopeia, a group of five stars forming a "W," low in the north sky. Just ahead of Cassiopeia is Cepheus, somewhat like a church spire pointing up to the North Star. Ahead of Cepheus is Draco, the Dragon, extending around the Little Dipper. The handle of the latter ends in the North Star.

Let us follow along the handle of the Big Dipper and beyond it to double its length, keeping to the same curve. We arrive at the bright, orange star, Arcturus, which forms the tip of the kite-shaped constellation, Bootes, the Hunter. As a hunter he is looked upon as driving the big bear and the little bear around the pole star. If we continue past Arcturus in the same curve and to double the length of the dipper handle again, we arrive at a brilliant, bluish-white star, Spica, in the constellation Virgo, the Virgin. The light that we now see from Spica has taken 200 years to reach us at 186,000 miles per second.

East of Bootes is Corona, the Northern Crown, a semicircle of stars open toward the north. Look farther east and find the beautiful summer constellation, Hercules, the Giant, and northeast of that, a bright, blue star, Vega, with a train of five paler stars forming Lyra, the Harp. Still farther north we find the Northern Cross, with its long axis in the Milky Way directed toward Cassiopeia, and having a bright star, Deneb, at its head.

Now turn to the southeast for the most brilliant constellation visible in summer, namely, Scorpio, the Scorpion, with the fiery red star, Antares, appearing above the horizon about midsummer.

Turn to the west for a bright star, Regulus, at the end of the handle of the Sickle, and forming a part of the constellation, Leo, the Lion.

The Big Dipper serves as a clock in the sky. As the earth rotates on its axis, which is in line with the North Star, and carries us along with it, the stars are, of course, seemingly left behind. As we move from west to east, the stars seem to move from east to west. And so the Big Dipper seems to revolve about the North Star. The circle at the right of fig. 1 shows the various positions of the Dipper during 24 hours, in June. The lower circle shows its position at 8 p.m., standard time, about June 15, along with those of other constellations. The whole group, of course, rotates, and provides a natural clock. But our watches and clocks register only 23 hours, 56 minutes for each apparent rotation of the heavens. The star clock gains 4 minutes a day, that is, 2 hours a month, or 24 hours

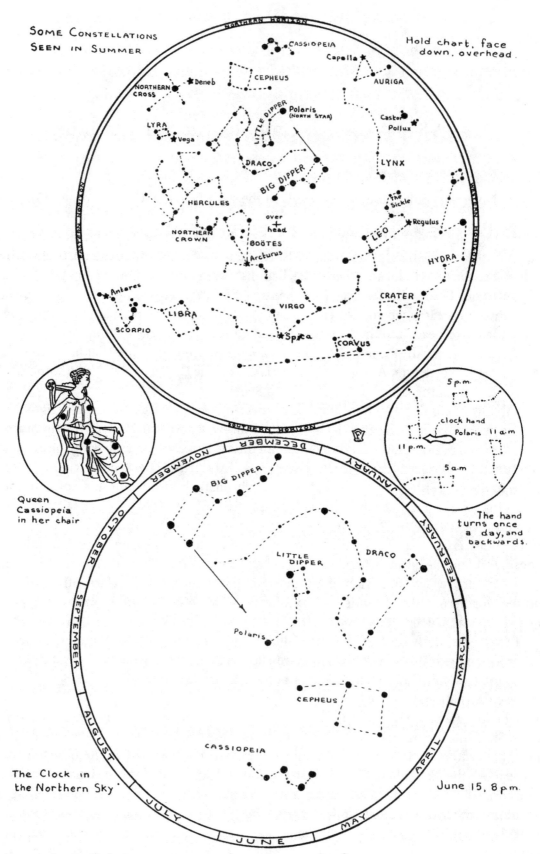

Figure 1—Star Studies for June

in a year. Thus our star clock registers differently for each month.

To use the lower drawing in fig. 1 as a star clock and calendar, make a very accurate copy of it the same or a larger size, and cut out the outer circle. Face north and hold the map with the name of the month of the year vertically downward. The position should be then correct for 8 p.m. Turn the chart slowly to successive months and note how the Big Dipper changes positions during the year. To find what the position of the Big Dipper will be 2 hours later, that is, at 10 p.m., rotate the chart through one month's space, until July is downward, and note the direction of those

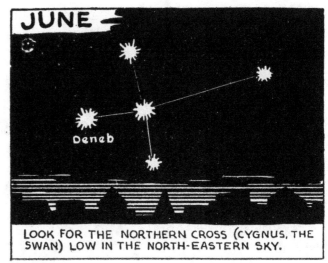

LOOK FOR THE NORTHERN CROSS (CYGNUS, THE SWAN) LOW IN THE NORTH-EASTERN SKY.

Figure 2

stars of the Dipper which point to the North Star. For 12 p.m., turn the chart until August is down. Go out and test it by comparing it with the position of the stars in the north sky at various hours. A little practice will enable you and your pupils to tell either the month of the year or the hour of the night when you know the alternative fact.

Activities

All Grades

Use a mailing-tube, or make a similar cardboard tube, for a toy telescope. Construct one end so that it will hold removable circular cards. In several of these prick holes to represent the stars of constellations. When the telescope is held up to the light, the constellation is clearly seen at the other end.

Primary Grades

- Look for stars on a clear night. Watch them twinkle. Learn the memory gem, "Twinkle, etc." See that some stars are larger and brighter than others. When there are clouds we cannot see the stars. Some stars make pictures in the sky (the Dippers).
- Learn this memory gem:

> Does the old man in the moon
> Use the dipper, do you think
> For all the thirsty stars
> That chance to want a drink?

Junior and Intermediate Grades

- Find pictures of stars which, as was once thought, represent a bear, a fish, a queen, a hunter, a serpent.
- Use the map to find these two most brilliant and beautiful of the summer stars, Vega in Lyra,

and the orange-colored star, Arcturus, in Bootes.

- Near the eastern horizon, find the constellation Scorpio, the most brilliant of summer constellations, and in it the giant red star, Antares, more than seventy-five times as large as the sun.
- What star would you use to tell time at night? At noon? How does the North Star form a connecting link between the Big Dipper and the Little Dipper?
- Find out what Nokomis taught Hiawatha about the Milky Way (*Song of Hiawatha,* Longfellow).
- Learn how to tell direction by the North Star, and how to use the Dipper as a clock.
- Make a star map showing five constellations that you know.
- Sketch a newly discovered constellation as accurately as possible, then identify it from a sky map at school.

Read

Barlowe, *A Child's Book of Stars.* Ryerson (Maxton).
Proctor, *Wonders of the Sky.* Allen (Warne).
Rey *Find the Constellations* and *The Stars.* Allen (Houghton Mifflin).
Schneider, *You among the Stars.* Allen (Wm. R. Scott).

New to this Edition

Chandler, David S. *The Night Sky 30°-40° (Large; North Latitude)* [Star finder map] (David Chandler Co, 1998).
Dickinson, Terence. *Exploring the Night Sky: The Equinox Astronomy Guide for Beginners* (Firefly, 1987).
_____. *NightWatch: A Practical Guide to Viewing the Universe* (Firefly, 2006)
_____. *Summer Stargazing: A Practical Guide for Recreational Astronomers* (Firefly Books, 2005).
Sinnott, Roger W. *Sky & Telescope's Pocket Sky Atlas* (Sky Publishing, 2006).

See also reading references in Unit 36 .

Figure 3—The Constellations for Each Month of the Year: This rare hand colored map of the stars of the northern hemisphere was engraved W. G. Evans of New York for Burritt's 1856 edition of the Atlas to Illustrate the Geography of the Heavens. It represents the night sky and constellations of the Northern Hemisphere. Constellations are drawn in detail and include depictions of the Zodiacal figures the stars are said to represent. (http://www.geographicus.com/)

Unit 99—Let's Help to Conserve Our Natural Resources

Conservation of our natural resources is a national necessity. The problem concerns everyone, for all people depend directly or indirectly upon soil, water, forests, minerals, and wildlife.

Conservation is the wise use of our natural resources. It means using them today in such ways that they will serve well the present generation, but will continue to serve future generations equally well. To conserve well is to follow the "Golden Rule"; it means "the greatest good to the greatest number and that for the longest time." Conservation is an attitude of the mind, a way of thinking and feeling that leads to right action in the best interests of everyone, present and future. Therefore, conservation is of vital concern to all teachers, for they, through every phase of teaching, can play the dominant role in making pupils conservation-conscious, and in imparting the knowledge upon which both the desire and the methods of conserving our natural resources may best be founded.

Good teachers at all grade levels will day by day find ways and means of teaching conservation, that is, of developing in pupils desirable attitudes of conservation. When courses of study fail to define ways and means of integrating conservation-thinking with the subject matter of science, social studies, literature, reading, and other subjects of the elementary school, such teachers will find ways of doing so. The subject matter and discussions of regular lessons, the directed pupil investigations and reading, and the daily expression activities, whether they be oral, written, or manual, will provide many opportunities to direct the knowledge and the attitudes of pupils into channels that will contribute to the conservation of our natural resources.

The teaching of conservation should begin in the primary grades and should continue through school life. Because conservation depends upon attitudes of mind and feelings of appreciation, it can be taught successfully only when it becomes an integral part of all teaching of nature and science and related subjects. Whether grade 1 pupils are being led to like garden flowers, grade 3 pupils to appreciate colors in the autumn wood, grade 5 pupils to make nesting devices and feeding boxes for birds, or grade 8 pupils to understand the harm done by erosion—all such teaching activities may be so conducted as to cultivate an ever-deepening appreciation of the need for and the methods of conserving our heritage of natural wealth.

Note: See "Some Suggestions for a Program of Conservation Teaching," given after the reading references (page 423).

Read

Andrews, *Adventures in Science.* Book VI (grades 6-7), pp. 173-187. Moyer.
Beauchamp et al., *Discovering Our World,* Book 2 (grades 5-6): "How Do We Control Fire?" pp. 149-175. Gage (Scott, Foresman).
Blough & Huggett, *Methods and Activities in Elementary-School Science:* "Conservation of Our Resources," pp. 189-199. Ryerson (Dryden).

Bowers & Bissonnette, *General Science,* Intermediate, Book 3: "The Water We Drink," pp. 1-35. Dent.

Comstock, *Handbook of Nature-Study,* pp. 766-775. Allen (Comstock).

Craig & Hurley, *Discovering with Science* (grades 5-6): "Using Materials Wisely," pp. 236-254. Ginn.

Craig & Lembach, *Science Everywhere* (grades 4-5): "Using Writer Wisely," pp. 134-157. Ginn.

Curtis, *Conservation in America* (grades 5-8): conservation of water, forests, soil, and wildlife. Lyons & Carnahan.

Dersal & Graham, *The Land Renewed* (senior grades and teachers): a complete guide to soil conservation; profusely illustrated by photographs. Oxford.

Deusing, *Soil, Water, and Man,* The Basic Science Education Series. Copp Clark (Row, Peterson).

Erickson, *Cattail House* (grades 3-5) and *The True Book of Animals of Small Pond.* Book Society (Children's Press).

Eschmeyer, *Billy Bass; Freddy Fox Squirrel; Mac Mallard; Tommy Trout;* and *Willie White-tail.* Book Society (Fisherman Press).

Parker, *Saving Our Wildlife* (grades 4-6); and *Water* (grades 4-6), The Basic Science Education Series. Copp Clark (Row, Peterson).

Partridge, *General Science,* Intermediate, Book 1 : an integrated conservation program throughout much of the book, but especially in chapters 7, 14, 15, 16, 20, and 21; *General Science,* Intermediate, Book 2: conservation integrated with much of the text matter, but especially in chapters 3, 5, 6, 12, 21, and 22; *Everyday Science,* Book One: chapters v, vi, xxi, xxiii, xxiv; and *Everyday Science,* Book Two: chapters 3, 6, 7, 12, 26, and 28.

Rounds, *Lone Muskrat.* Allen (Holiday).

Schneider, *Science Far and Near* (grade 3): "Water for Farms and Homes," pp. 58-74. Copp Clark (Heath & Co.).

Smith, *The First Book of Conservation* (grades 4-8). Ambassador (Watts).

Smith & Henderson, *Across the Land* (grades 4-5), pp. 163-180. Longmans, Green,

Wanklyn, *Flip: The Story of an Otter.* Allen (Warne).

Conservation, A Handbook for Teachers. Cornell Rural School Leaflet, Volume 45, Number 1. September 1951. New York State College of Agriculture, Cornell University, Ithaca, N.Y.

Guide to Conservation Education in Wisconsin Schools and *Helps in Planning Conservation*

Learning Experiences. Department of Public Instruction, State Capitol, Madison 2. Wisconsin.

Guidebook for Conservation Education. State Department of Education, Sacramento, California.

Instructional Units in Conservation in Elementary Schools. College of Education, University of Wyoming, Laramie, Wyoming.

From National Wildlife Federation, 232 Cornell St. N.W., Washington 12, D.C.: *The Save America! series of Thirteen Approaches to Conservation*—13 short, concise pamphlets.

"My Land and Your Land" Conservation Series—4 booklets, profusely illustrated in color:

Would You Like to Have Lived When--? (grades 3-4);

Raindrops and Muddy Rivers (grades 4-6);

Plants and Animals Live Together (grades 5-7); and

Nature's Bank—The Soil (grades 6-8).

Reports of Select Committee on Conservation—1950, and *Don Valley Conservation Reports—1950,* by the Ontario Department of Planning and Development. Queen's Printer, Toronto.

New to this Edition

Amsel, Sheri. *365 Ways to Live Green for Kids: Saving the Environment at Home, School, or at Play—Every Day!* (Adams Media, 2009).

_____. *The Everything Kids' Environment Book: Learn how you can help the environment-by getting involved at school, at home, or at play* (Adams Media, 2007).

Inches Alison. *The Adventures of an Aluminum Can: A Story About Recycling* (Little Simon, 2009).

_____. *The Adventures of a Plastic Bottle: A Story About Recycling* (Little Simon, 2009).

Javna, Sophie. *The New 50 Simple Things Kids Can Do to Save the Earth* (Andrews McMeel Publishing, 2009).

Some Suggestions for a Program of Conservation Teaching

I. Conservation of Soil

Understandings to Be Developed

- Because man depends upon plants and animals and their products, he depends upon fertile soil.
- Soil erosion today robs future generations of food, clothing, and wealth.
- Erosion of soil by water removes fertile topsoil, reduces the water-holding capacity of the remaining soil, forms ditches and gullies, and makes the land less favorable for wildlife.
- Soil erosion may be prevented or reduced by forests, vegetative cover, contour farming, strip cropping, terracing, stubble-mulch farming.

Learning Activities

- Observe erosion in the schoolyard, a park, or a field.
- Find deposits of soil washed by running water from sloping land. Notice that they usually contain fertile soil.
- In a sloping garden discover how erosion may be prevented or reduced by sodding, covering the soil with leaves and garden litter, cultivating across the slope, etc.
- Keep a record of the progress made on different farms in controlling erosion.

Attitudes and Continuing Interest

Fertile topsoil is the nation's most valuable natural resource. It is the moral responsibility of whoever owns and farms it to maintain fertility to such an extent that those who come after him may profit from it as much as he. To prevent loss of topsoil by erosion is his first responsibility.

II. Conservation of Water

Understandings to Be Developed

- All life depends upon water.
- Water is our daily servant for washing and cleaning, for cooking, as drink, etc.
- Underground water fills wells, feeds plants, supplies streams, etc.

- The nature of the water cycle: rain, streams, evaporation, water vapor, condensation, clouds, rain.
- Grass and forests help to prevent water from running off the land, thereby conserving it and preventing floods.

Learning Activities

- Perform experiments to illustrate evaporation and condensation.
- Find out why rain falls and what becomes of it afterward.
- When it rains, observe where water sinks into the soil best—in woods, in grass, or in cultivated fields.
- Find out how water may be conserved by proper methods of cultivation, leaving hillsides grass-covered, and planting forests.
- Investigate ways in which river water is polluted.

Attitudes and Continuing Interest

- An appreciation of the beauty of water in the form of dew, clouds, snow, frost, etc.
- An appreciation of the importance of water in everyday living—ways in which it serves us, and ways in which it may, when not controlled, bring harm to us.

III. Conservation of Forests

Understandings to Be Developed

- Forests satisfy many of our daily needs. Forests reduce the speed of the wind and help to prevent wind erosion.
- A forest, like grain, is a crop; it requires good management.
- Fire, disease, insects, and wasteful methods of lumbering are destroying forests more rapidly than growth can replace them. Forests can be protected and improved by preventing forest fires, by controlling injurious insects and diseases, and by wise forest management.
- Trees by the side of streams prevent erosion, keep the water cool and clear, and make it more favorable for fish and other life.

Learning Activities

- List all the things you can think of that are made of wood or of substances manufactured from wood.
- Learn to recognize trees of your community.
- Organize excursions to study trees and forest plants.
- Find pictures of insects that destroy forests.
- Investigate the depth of the rich, dark soil and decaying materials in the forest floor.
- Make forestry scrapbooks containing pictures of trees and forests, interesting poems, etc.
- Collect literature describing national, provincial, and state parks.
- Plant trees and shrubs at school and at home.

Attitudes and Continuing Interest

- An appreciation of autumn colors of foliage.
- An appreciation of the close relationship between forests and such other natural resources as water, soil, and wildlife.
- An appreciation of laws and regulations designed to conserve forests.
- Showing one's appreciation of trees by drawing and painting.
- Reading or writing poems about trees.
- "To leave the woods and parks as beautiful as you find them—this is outdoor good manners."

IV. Conservation of Minerals

Understandings to Be Developed

- Coal, oil, iron, and other minerals are foundations of our present civilization. The meanings of the terms: mineral, ore, metal.
- Mineral deposits, slowly formed by nature, are the heritage of all mankind. Each new oil field found leaves one less to be discovered.
- New machinery and new inventions reduce waste in mining.

Learning Activities

- Collect attractive pebbles and stones.
- List ways of conserving coal. Consider home insulation, proper care of fires, etc.
- List ways in which oil may be conserved.
- Consider fire prevention, adjusting carburetors, etc.
- Investigate methods of preventing rust and wear of iron and steel products.

Attitudes and Continuing Interest

- An appreciation of coal and other minerals daily living.
- Minerals that have been mined can never be replaced.

V. Conservation of Wildlife

Understandings to Be Developed

- "A bird's life can make man's life richer and better."
- Birds are man's best protectors by controlling insects.Wildlife provides food, clothing, employment, recreation, and enjoyment. Every kind of wildlife needs an environment that will provide shelter, food, and safety. Some varieties of wildflowers have disappeared; others are becoming scarce. Many people destroy wildflowers by careless picking.
- Fires in field and forest destroy wildflowers, and even their roots.

Learning Activities

- Have excursions to discover how birds depend upon trees, shrubs, and long grass, etc. for nesting places.
- Make feeding-stations for birds. Construct birdbaths and notice what birds use them. Build and erect bird houses after investigating the requirements of individual kinds of birds. Learn to recognize birdcalls and songs. Make a list of some birds that farmers accuse of doing harm, then investigate the truth of their accusations. Consider hawks, owls, crows, sparrows.
- Find out how your local province or state is helping to conserve fish, game birds, fur-bearing animals, and other forms of wildlife. List enemies of wild animals in your community.
- For pupil activities in conservation of wildflowers and birds see Unit 37 (page 149), Unit 39 (page 159), Unit 87 (page 356), Unit 89 (page 368) and Unit 90 (page 373).

Attitudes and Continuing Interest

- Appreciation of delicateness of color, melody of song, and grace of flight, also the "Beauty of strength."
- It is better to leave wildflowers for all to enjoy than to pick them for personal pleasure.
- Fostering a deeper appreciation of wildlife reading.
- Hunting and fishing are good sport for good sportsmen.

Figure 1—Wildflowers in a National Park in Idaho.

Unit 100—What Of Next Year?

How often have we failed in our efforts to enrich pupil experience through the absence of some minor item of equipment or some particular material that could not be obtained on short notice! Even the most resourcefully prepared substitute cannot make up for our lack of foresight when the opportunity was ripe. From this point of view the purpose of this unit is merely to offer a few suggestions which may assist in making more efficient preparations for next year's science teaching.

Making the Most of Present Science Facilities

In the clean-up of the classroom in which a general nature atmosphere has been created through various facilities for the care of living plants and animals, and through a generous use of pupil activities connected with them, some of the following ideas may be applicable.

Summer Care of the Aquarium. This need not cause any worries. Place the aquarium away from too direct sunlight in the classroom, or near a window in the cooler basement. Fill it full of water. The plants will thrive throughout the summer and provide a good supply for September use. Snails will increase and feed upon the algae on the glass. Clams should be returned to a stream. Fish may be left in the aquarium and fed weekly or half-weekly. Some pupil may strongly desire to take care of the complete aquarium at home.

The vivarium should be dismantled, and all living animals returned to their natural environment. Ferns may be planted in a shady corner of the grounds. Save the stones and soil foundation for use next fall.

Pupil collections may serve a valuable purpose next autumn in leading the new class to make similar or better contacts with nature. Cocoons that have failed to produce moths, or empty ones, may serve well to illustrate the protective nature of this phase of insect life when cocoons are being spun next September and October. The strength of the silken case is well shown by trying to break a few strands. Identification work is made easier by showing a few named varieties as the search begins. Mounted weed and leaf collections, individual and class charts or calendars of birds, flowering plants, trees, etc. may be useful next year.

Displays prepared during natural science enterprises this year may serve as a starting-place from which greater results will grow with next year's class. Pupils gladly lend their work for such a use.

Summer Care of Indoor School Plants. Potted plants may be left in the pots when school closes in June if they are sunk in soil to the level of the top of the pots. A layer of coal ashes beneath the pot will keep out worms. Shady places will provide more uniform moisture conditions. Plants grown in window boxes should be removed and carefully transplanted in a suitable place. Bloom may be increased during the next winter by preventing plants from flowering during the summer.

Preparing for Better Facilities for Next Year

Now is the time to plan for next year rather than to wait until school open in September. When money expenditures are desired of the school board, fair notice should be given by planning in advance. Other requirements must be met by personal efforts made now. Start a special list of such needs, and add to it as the ideas come. It will surprise one how fast such a list grows and how easily many needs or desires may be fulfilled.

The Indoor Equipment. If you haven't an aquarium now, plan to have one ready for school opening. The materials may be easily obtained for the construction of your own vivarium (Unit 7, page 24). September provides the richest opportunities for stocking the aquarium and the vivarium with locally collected materials.

If you have not had a nature museum or a nature corner in your classroom, plan for it now. Unit 33 (page 131) gives you valuable suggestions. Let us remind ourselves that very frequently pupils are better teachers of each other than we are of them, that quiet discussions by two or three pupils around a nature table are effective not only in increasing pupils' interests in nature, but also in developing resourcefulness and a sense of responsibility to other pupils of the class.

Storage and display cases are quite necessary for the many types of illustrative material in natural science and for equipment for experimental work. The summer months are the more likely ones in which to get such school improvements from trustees.

Bulletin boards, both permanent and portable, serve many useful purposes for all subjects. Ten-test, insul-board, and such products cost only a few cents per square foot. Small display boards about 2 feet by 3 feet are particularly convenient for temporary display and for passing around the room. Practically all lumber supply firms sell the material in 4-foot width and various lengths.

Free floor space for group activities, sand-table work, etc. may be obtained in most classrooms by judicious rearrangement of pupil seats. This space is best near the back of the room. Have such changes made during the summer months.

Incidental supplies that we ordinarily do not think of until the need for them arises may be prepared for in advance by posting a memo sheet on which one may list them as the ideas occur. On such a list we may soon read items like these: one or more hand lenses, a few small vials for seed samples, gummed labels, a selection of flowerpots of various sizes with saucers to match, an alcohol lamp and a quart of wood alcohol, a pair of pruning shears, various garden tools, a hand sprayer for indoor and outdoor plants, thumbtacks, beakers, tumblers, a glass funnel, test tubes and rack, vases or sealers for bouquets, a graduate, a thermometer, catalogues of various seed houses for pictures for identification of shrubs and flowering plants, government pamphlets and bulletins, lumber for bird boxes and window boxes, cages for classroom pets, six-ply cardboard, 22" × 28", for charts and calendars, construction paper for correlation work, etc. A small expenditure will meet many future needs for such articles.

Books of the type readily available now for science reading always make a strong appeal to the natural curiosity of pupils. Probably the summer months will provide opportunities to see and buy a broader selection of these.

The School Surroundings. It is not an unusual thing in July or August to observe a school garden which shows evidence of neglect after the closing of school. Such a condition discounts seriously the value of the time devoted to planning and planting, the possible use of vegetable products for hot lunches the next winter, the opportunities for out-of-door study of various phases of plant life in the autumn months, and the respect that the public has for school garden work. In the absence of the teacher, the interest that she has built up in pupils and citizens of the community will be most evident in the manner in which they carry out plans initiated by her for the proper care of all parts of the school grounds. Some scheme of weekly pupil responsibility, with the cooperation of one or more interested parents, will usually prove quite effective. The future of the campaign for more attractive school grounds in any locality will be quite dependent upon the efficiency with which summer care is arranged.

One of the important autumn activities will be the planting of bulbs and potted plants for the classroom. For this purpose a supply of fertile and well-mixed soil is imperative. No better provision for this necessity can be made than to have a mixture of good soil and well-rotted manure prepared in a screened part of the school grounds. (See also Unit 14 on page 58.)

Cuttings for indoor plants for next winter should be started in the summer months. Choose a shaded area and start them directly in the garden soil, preferably sandy soil. Watering may be necessary unless they are grown in a damp, shady place.

At the same time it is well to sow the seed of a few common perennials, in order that large enough plants may be ready for transplanting in September or early the next spring.

Taking an Inventory of Our Personal Interests in Nature

It is in June that we should take stock of the year's successes and failures, its satisfactions and its unfulfilled hopes, while they are still fresh in mind, in an effort to profit next year from the experiences of the year just past. More than to our other teaching duties, this applies to our efforts to lead our pupils into ever-increasing contacts with their natural surroundings, and a constantly deepening appreciation of and love for nature in general. To succeed in these efforts, we must not only take stock of our own appreciation of nature, but also take measures to deepen that appreciation.

Most of us must confess that our past training in natural science has been too largely from books and too little from personal contact with real nature. The summer months always provide many opportunities for us to partially remedy this handicap by consciously cultivating a closer acquaintance with all phases of nature: the common trees and shrubs and flowers of field and garden; the wealth of animal life, from the lowly insects and soil-inhabiting worms to the feathered songsters of the air; the shy wild animals about the summer homes of the north woods; the life of stream and hillside alike; and the evening lights that shine from skies afar. The thrill of watching a spider tear down and rebuild its web or of watching a colony of young spiders sport about on their almost invisible network of delicate silk, as they enjoy the warmth of an afternoon sun; the joy of seeing for the first time the wonders of the heavens through a telescope; the feeling of awe when we marvel at the instinct that prompts the young robin nestlings to confidently open their mouths for the food supplied by the mother, or that leads the mother grouse to place her eggs where she and they may be protected by the harmony of color of her surroundings and herself; the beauty that nature provides when the pure white pond lily flowers are raised above the olive green pads floating in a lazy stream—these are our heritage to enjoy. And by enjoying them to the full ourselves we may hope to excite a spark of inspiration in the minds and hearts of the children who will be our pupils next year, and thus help them to make that same heritage a part of themselves.

Read

New to this Edition

Albert, Toni. *A Kid's Summer EcoJournal: With Nature Activities for Exploring the Season* (Trickle Creek Books, 1998).
Carlton and Dammel. *Kids Camp!: Activities for the Backyard or Wilderness* (Chicago Review Press, 1995).
Drake, Love, and Collins. *The Kids Campfire Book: Official Book of Campfire Fun* (Kids Can Press. 1998).
_____. *The Kids' Summer Handbook* (Sandpiper, 1994).

BEAUTIFY YOUR SURROUNDINGS ~~~ JUNE

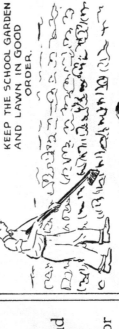

↖ OUTDOOR SKETCHING IS INTERESTING.

SUMMER SUGGESTIONS:

KEEP THE SCHOOL GARDEN AND LAWN IN GOOD ORDER.

MAKE COLLECTIONS OF SUCH THINGS AS LEAVES, WEEDS, AND SEEDS FOR STUDY IN THE FALL.

D. FARWELL

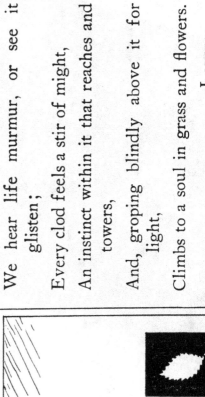

And what is so rare as a day in June?
Then, if ever, come perfect days;
Then Heaven tries earth if it be in tune,
And over it softly her warm ear lays;
Whether we look, or whether we listen,
We hear life murmur, or see it glisten;
Every clod feels a stir of might,
An instinct within it that reaches and towers,
And, groping blindly above it for light,
Climbs to a soul in grass and flowers.

LOWELL

PREPARE A BOOKLET OF ILLUSTRATIONS BASED UPON THE TOPIC: "WHAT IS SO RARE AS A DAY IN JUNE?"

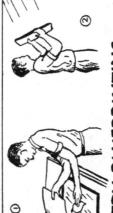

① ②

TRY BLUEPRINTING:

① CLAMP LEAF BLUEPRINT PAPER, PAD, AND STIFF BACKING AGAINST GLASS IN PICTURE FRAME.
② EXPOSE TO SUN UNTIL PAPER IS WELL FADED OUT.
③ WASH IN WATER TO WHICH A FEW CRYSTALS OF POTASSIUM BICHROMATE HAVE BEEN ADDED.
④ DRY.

BORDER DESIGNS

SCIENCE IN ACTION

-- JUNE

SEARCH ALONG THE SHORES OF CREEKS AND PONDS FOR THESE COMMON VARIETIES OF FROGS:

"GREEN" FROG (SMALL, NOT SPOTTED, GREENISH-BROWN).

BULL FROG (LARGE, BROWN)

LEOPARD FROG (SMALL, SPOTTED (USUALLY GREEN).

GOING CAMPING THIS SUMMER? HERE'S HOW TO MAKE A SIMPLE "REFRIGERATOR" TO HELP KEEP YOUR FOOD COOL.

GET OR MAKE A BOX 3" DEEPER THAN A MILK BOTTLE. MAKE A LID LIKE THIS FOR IT:

INSIDE LENGTH OF BOX

INSIDE WIDTH OF BOX

FILL WITH LOOSELY-PACKED SAWDUST. NAIL ON AN EXACT-SIZED COVER.

(LID IS SHOWN UPSIDE DOWN)

HANDLE

LID

GROUND LEVEL

MILK

BURY BOX IN COOL GROUND, IN SHADE. IF ICE IS OBTAINABLE, A SMALL PIECE BESIDE THE FOOD WILL LAST WELL. PROVIDE DRAINAGE HOLE.

D.FARWELL

FIND THESE CONSTELLATIONS IN THE SOUTHERN SKY. TIME — JUNE 15— ABOUT 9 P.M.

+ overhead

BOÖTES

ARCTURUS

NORTHERN CROWN

THE SERPENT

VIRGO

SPICA

CORVUS

LIBRA

SOUTH

LIFE HISTORY of the MOSQUITO

EGGS

PUPA

LARVA

ADULT

LIFE HISTORY of the HOUSE FLY

PUPAE

LARVAE

ADULT

LIFE HISTORY OF the CLOTHES MOTH

EGGS

LARVA

ADULT

FOR REFERENCE, MAKE CHARTS SHOWING THE LIFE HISTORIES OF HOUSEHOLD INSECT PESTS. DO WHAT YOU CAN TO CONTROL THEM.

PROTECT YOUR GARDEN AGAINST INSECTS:

FOR POTATO BEETLES: DUST OR SPRAY, PARIS GREEN OR ARSENATE OF LEAD.

FOR CABBAGE BUTTERFLIES: SPRAY, 1 LB. ARSENATE OF LEAD TO 20 GALLONS OF WATER.

CAN YOU REPLACE THE WASHER OF A LEAKY TAP?

① TURN OFF WATER AT THE MAIN VALVE.

② REMOVE CAP NUT WITH WRENCH.

PAPER TO PREVENT MARKING CAP NUT

③ REMOVE HANDLE ASSEMBLY FROM TAP.

WORN-OUT WASHER

④ REPLACE WORN-OUT WASHER WITH A NEW ONE.

⑤ REPLACE HANDLE ASSEMBLY AND CAP NUT. TIGHTEN WITH WRENCH.

⑥ TURN ON WATER AT MAIN VALVE.

VACATION

I have shut *my* books and hidden my slate
And tossed my satchel across the gate.
My school is out for a summer of rest,
And now for the schoolroom I love the best!
My schoolroom lies on the meadow wide,
Where under the clover the sunbeams hide,
Where the long vines cling to the mossy bars
And the daisies twinkle like fallen stars.
My lessons are written in clouds and trees,
And no one whispers except the breeze,
That something blows—from a secret place—
A stray, sweet blossom against my face.
My teacher is patient and never yet
A lesson of hers did I once forget,
For wonderful lore do her lips impart,
And all her lessons are learned by heart.
Oh come! Oh come! Or we shall be late,
And Autumn will fasten the golden gate.
Of all the schoolrooms east or west,
The school of Nature I love the best.

KATHARINE LEE BATES

General Reading References

Adventures in Science, Grades II, III, IV, V, VI. Moyer. Audubon Nature Bulletins. National Audubon Society.
> More than fifty excellent guides for teachers and naturalists presenting teaching aids and information about plants and animals of all kinds, also conservation. Each 15c.

The Basic Science Education Series. Copp dark (Row, Peterson).
> A series of unit readers graded from the second year to the end of the elementary school, each volume thoroughly illustrated, usually in full colour; complete list of titles available from publishers.

Beauchamp et al, *Discovering Our World*, Books 1, 2, and 3. Gage (Scott, Foresman).
> A carefully edited and excellently illustrated graded series written for Grades 4-6.

Blough & Campbell, *Making and Using Classroom Science Materials in the Elementary School*. Ryerson (Dryden).
> For teachers and prospective teachers, a helpful guide in making science teaching practical and effective. 1954. 229 pp.

Blough & Huggett, *Methods and Activities in Elementary-School Science*. Ryerson (Dryden).
> A practical book on how to help children study science in the elementary school.

Brown, *The Amateur Naturalist's Handbook*. Little, Brown.
> An inspiring and instructional guide for teachers who are endeavouring to become better naturalists—and a source book for every phase of natural science.

Candy, *Nature Notebook*. Allen (Houghton Mifflin).
> The story of a day's field trip, enriched by detailed scientific information on the life of woods and streams, beautifully illustrated in colour and black and white.

Charters et al, *Today's Health and Growth Series*, Revised. Macmillan.
> An excellently organized and illustrated graded series, presenting basic information on healthful living and healthful environment.

Compton's pictured encyclopedia.
> Fifteen well-illustrated volumes with material compiled in an extremely interesting and well-organized manner; an ideal set for research work.

Comstock, Handbook of Nature-Study. Alien (Comstock).
> A teacher's source book in all phases of nature study; a wealth of suggestions for science activities.

Cory, *Wild Life Ways*. Clarke, Irwin (University of London Press).
> A series of four books: *The Beaver People*; *Teddy Bear's Family*; *Queenie, the Broncho*; and *Rover, a Collie-coyote*.

Crag et al, *Science Today and Tomorrow Series*. Ginn.
> An up-to-date series of science readers for all grades of the elementary school.

Dahlberg: *Conservation of Renewable Resources*. Clarke, Irwin (C. C. Nelson).

Devoe, *This Fascinating Animal World*. McGraw-Hill.
> A stimulating book for teachers, combining philosophical insight with scientific answers to many frequently-asked questions about animals of all kinds.

Fenton, *Our Living World*. Doubleday.
> A readable and dramatic story of life—human, animal, and plant; for teachers.

Fenton & fenton, *Rocks and Their Stories*. Doubleday.
> Fifty pages of photographs.

Frasier et al, *Scientific Living Series*. Dent (Singer).
> An attractive, well-illustrated set of science readers graded from pre-primer to Grade 8—each volume challenging immediate pupil interest.

Freeman et al, *Helping Children Understand Science*. Winston.
> Prepared to help teachers and teachers-in-training to apply the best principles of pedagogy in their teaching of science; guidance for curriculum making, equipment, and audio-visual aids.

Hillcourt, *Field Book of Nature Activities*. Alien (Putnam's Sons).
Bringing nature into the home, camp, garden, and classroom.

Huntington, *"Let's Go –" Series*. Doubleday.
Four easy-to-read science-picture books: Let's Go to the Brook; Let's Go Outdoors; Let's go to the Desert, Let's Go to the Seashore.

Hylander, Out of Doors (in Autumn, in Winter, in Spring, in Summer). Macmillan.
A set of four books aimed at helping- young people make, or renew, acquaintance with nature.

Knox et al, *The Canadian Wonderworld of Science*. Book Society. The Wonderworld of Science. Scribner.
A well-balanced series of graded science readers.

Logier, *The Frogs, Toads, and Salamanders of Eastern Canada*. Clarke, Irwin.
A guide to the natural history, economic importance, etc. of amphibians.

Macdonald, *The Birds of Brewery Creek*. Oxford.
A book of rare narrative style, precise observation, and fine description; presenting" the triumphs and tragedies of many birds in Eastern Canada, including their migration, daily routine, and the rearing of young"; superb photographs.

Palmer, *The Mammal Guide*. Doubleday.
For each mammal—description, habitat, reproduction, habits, and economic status; colour plates and line drawing's.

Partridge, *Everyday Science*, Book One; *Everyday Science*, Book Two; *General Science*, Intermediate, Book 1; and *General Science*, Intermediate, Book 2. Dent.
These four books carry the work of science in the elementary schools into and through Grade 7 and 8.

Peterson, A Field Guide to the Birds (Eastern). Alien (Houghton Mifflin).
Used by leading bird enthusiasts; 1000 illustrations, 500 in colour; 60 full-page plates and accompanying tables.

Peterson, *A Field Guide to the Mammals, A field Guide to the Butterflies, and A Field to Animal Tracks*. All similar to above. Alien (Houghton Mifflin).

Peterson, *Wildlife in Color*. Alien (Houghton Mifflin).
Descriptive text and colour plates for birds, butterflies, mammals, flowers, trees, etc.; 200 pages.

Shulttlesworth, *Exploring Nature with Your Child*. Nelson (Greystone).
For teachers, and pupils of ages 4 to 11, a very readable and fascinating guide to the enjoyment and understanding of nature.

Snyder, *Ontario Birds*. Clarke, Irwin.
A source book for teachers, pupils, and naturalists; the natural history of Ontario birds—food, songs, nesting habits, migration, etc.

Stephenson, *Nature Study and Rural Science*. Macmillan (A. & C. Black).
A teacher's book to accompany the series of three books for Juniors, Nature at Work—128 pages of notes arranged by seasons for the first three grades.

Understanding Science series: I Wonder Why, Seeing Why, Learning Why, Explaining Why, Discovering Why, Understanding Why, Investigating Why, and Answering Why, Winston.

Urquhart, *Introducing the Insect*. Clarke, Irwin.
Teacher Reference; classification, life histories and habits, descriptions, and instructions for collection.

Wherry, *Wild Flower Guide*. Doubleday.
For Eastern United States and Canada; sponsored by the Wild Flower Preservation Society; line drawings and color plates.

The Oxford Junior Encyclopaedia, Volume II: Natural History, Oxford.
Alphabetically arranged and well illustrated; detailed information covering the whole field of natural history.

From Metropolitan Life Insurance Company, Ottawa (and New York, N.Y.).
Free booklets: *Common Childhood Diseases and First Steps on Health Education.*

From National Audubon Society, 1130 Fifth Avenue, New York 28, or Audubon Society of Canada, 181 Jarvis St., Toronto 2:
A sample kit explaining Audubon Junior Clubs, also a teachers' guide book entitled *Nature Program Guide*—both free.

From National Wildlife Federation, 232 Carroll St. N.W., Takoma Park, Washington 12:
A set of four conservation booklets ($1.00 per set) as follows: *Would You Like To Have Lived When . . . ?* (Grades 3-4; *Raindrops and. Muddy Rivers* (Grades 4-6) ; *Plants and Animals Live Together* (Grades 6-7) ; Nature's Bank—the Soil (Grades 6-8).

Large Nature Books, Beautifully Illustrated, with Many Full-Page Illustrations

Bauer, *Animal Sables. Book Society* (Donohue).
  Twelve excellent, full-color illustrations that children will enjoy looking at.
Boulton, *Traveling with the Birds*. Book Society (Donohue).
D'aulaire, *Animals Everywhere*. Doubleday.
Fisher, *The Wonderful World—the Adventure of the Earth We Live On. Blue Ribbon* (Hanover House).
  Describes the earth's history, surface and weathering agencies, and living thing!.
Henry, *Birds at Home.* Book Society (Donohue).
Jordan, *Hammond's Nature Atlas of America*. Book Society (Hammond).
  A pictorial guide to all kinds of plant and animal life; 320 coloured paintings and 34 pages of colored maps.
Jordan, *Hammond's Guide to Nature Hobbies*. Book Society (Hammond).
Kieran, "Introduction to ———" Series: *An Introduction to Birds, An Introduction to Wild Flowers, An Introduction to Trees*. Blue Ribbon (Garden City).
  Each book describing 100 species and illustrating them in color.
Kimball & Webb, *Birds in Their Homes*. Blue Ribbon (Garden City).
  Describes 54 birds of city, country, and garden—habits, nests, young.
Parker, *The Golden Treasury of Natural History*. Musson (Simon & Schuster).
Schmidt, *Friendly Animals and Homes and Habits of Wild Animals*. Book Society (Donohue).
  Informal text and large full-color drawings of North American mammals.
H. & G., Birds (a Golden Nature Guide). Musson (Simon & Schuster).
  118 paintings in color; an excellent teacher reference.

Addresses of Publishing Firms and Other Sources Referred To

Thomas Alien, Ltd., 266 King Street West, Toronto
Ambassador Books Limited, 1149 King St. W., Toronto
The American Humane Association, 896 Pennsylvania St., Denver 3, Colo.
Blue Ribbon Books, 105 Bond Street, Toronto
The Book Society of Canada Limited, Sheppard Avenue East, Agincourt, Ont.
Canadian Red Cross Society, 95 Wellesley Street East, Toronto
Clarke, Irwin & Co., Ltd., 103 St. Clair Avenue West, Toronto
The Copp Clark Co., Ltd., 517 Wellington Street West, Toronto
J. M. Dent & Sons (Canada) Ltd., 224 Bloor Street West, Toronto
Doubleday Publishers, 105 Bond Street, Toronto
W. J. Gage & Co., Ltd., 82 Spadina Avenue, Toronto
Ginn & Co., 1331 Yonge Street. Toronto
Little, Brown & Co., 25 Hollinger Road, Toronto
Longmans, Green & Co., 20 Cranfield Road, Toronto 16
The Macmillan Company of Canada Limited, 70 Bond Street, Toronto
McClelland & Stewart, Ltd., 25 Hollinger Road, Toronto 16
McGraw-Hill Co. of Canada, Ltd., 253 Spadina Road, Toronto
George J. McLeod, Ltd., 73 Bathurst Street, Toronto
Moyer School Supplies, Ltd., 108 York Street, Toronto
Musson Book Co., Ltd., 103-107 Vanderhoof Avenue, Toronto
National Audubon Society, 1130 Fifth Avenue, New York 28
Thos. Nelson & Sons (Canada) Ltd., 91 Wellington Street West, Toronto
Oxford University Press, 480 University Avenue, Toronto
Random House of Canada Limited, 1149 King St. W., Toronto
Sir Isaac Pitman & Sons, Ltd., 383 Church Street, Toronto
The Ryerson Press, 299 Queen Street West, Toronto
Smithers and Bonellie, 266 King Street West, Toronto
G. R. Welch Co., Ltd., 1149 King Street West, Toronto
The John C. Winston Co., Ltd., 292 Parliament Street, Toronto

Index